Public Administration and Information Technology

Volume 10

Series Editor
Christopher G. Reddick
San Antonio, Texas, USA

More information about this series at http://www.springer.com/series/10796

Marijn Janssen • Maria A. Wimmer
Ameneh Deljoo
Editors

Policy Practice and Digital Science

Integrating Complex Systems, Social Simulation and Public Administration in Policy Research

 Springer

Editors

Marijn Janssen
Faculty of Technology, Policy, and
Management
Delft University of Technology
Delft
The Netherlands

Ameneh Deljoo
Faculty of Technology, Policy, and
Management
Delft University of Technology
Delft
The Netherlands

Maria A. Wimmer
Institute for Information Systems Research
University of Koblenz-Landau
Koblenz
Germany

ISBN 978-3-319-12783-5   ISBN 978-3-319-12784-2 (eBook)
Public Administration and Information Technology
DOI 10.1007/978-3-319-12784-2

Library of Congress Control Number: 2014956771

Springer Cham Heidelberg New York London

Printed on acid-free paper

Springer is part of Springer Science+Business Media (www.springer.com)

Preface

The last economic and financial crisis has heavily threatened European and other economies around the globe. Also, the Eurozone crisis, the energy and climate change crises, challenges of demographic change with high unemployment rates, and the most recent conflicts in the Ukraine and the near East or the Ebola virus disease in Africa threaten the wealth of our societies in different ways. The inability to predict or rapidly deal with dramatic changes and negative trends in our economies and societies can seriously hamper the wealth and prosperity of the European Union and its Member States as well as the global networks. These societal and economic challenges demonstrate an urgent need for more effective and efficient processes of governance and policymaking, therewith specifically addressing crisis management and economic/welfare impact reduction.

Therefore, investing in the exploitation of innovative information and communication technology (ICT) in the support of good governance and policy modeling has become a major effort of the European Union to position itself and its Member States well in the global digital economy. In this realm, the European Union has laid out clear strategic policy objectives for 2020 in the **Europe 2020 strategy**[1]: *In a changing world, we want the EU to become a smart, sustainable, and inclusive economy. These three mutually reinforcing priorities should help the EU and the Member States deliver high levels of employment, productivity, and social cohesion. Concretely, the Union has set five ambitious objectives—on employment, innovation, education, social inclusion, and climate/energy—to be reached by 2020.* Along with this, Europe 2020 has established four priority areas—smart growth, sustainable growth, inclusive growth, and later added: A strong and effective system of economic governance—designed to help Europe *emerge from the crisis stronger* and to coordinate policy actions between the EU and national levels.

To specifically support European research in strengthening capacities, in overcoming fragmented research in the field of policymaking, and in advancing solutions for

---

[1] Europe 2020 http://ec.europa.eu/europe2020/index_en.htm

ICT supported governance and policy modeling, the European Commission has co-funded an international support action called eGovPoliNet[2]. The overall objective of eGovPoliNet was to create an international, cross-disciplinary community of researchers working on ICT solutions for governance and policy modeling. In turn, the aim of this community was to advance and sustain research and to share the insights gleaned from experiences in Europe and globally. To achieve this, eGovPoliNet established a dialogue, brought together experts from distinct disciplines, and collected and analyzed knowledge assets (i.e., theories, concepts, solutions, findings, and lessons on ICT solutions in the field) from different research disciplines. It built on case material accumulated by leading actors coming from distinct disciplinary backgrounds and brought together the innovative knowledge in the field. Tools, methods, and cases were drawn from the academic community, the ICT sector, specialized policy consulting firms as well as from policymakers and governance experts. These results were assembled in a knowledge base and analyzed in order to produce comparative analyses and descriptions of cases, tools, and scientific approaches to enrich a common knowledge base accessible via www.policy-community.eu.

This book, entitled "Policy Practice and Digital Science—Integrating Complex Systems, Social Simulation, and Public Administration in Policy Research," is one of the exciting results of the activities of eGovPoliNet—fusing community building activities and activities of knowledge analysis. It documents findings of comparative analyses and brings in experiences of experts from academia and from case descriptions from all over the globe. Specifically, it demonstrates how the explosive growth in data, computational power, and social media creates new opportunities for policymaking and research. The book provides a first comprehensive look on how to take advantage of the development in the digital world with new approaches, concepts, instruments, and methods to deal with societal and computational complexity. This requires the knowledge traditionally found in different disciplines including public administration, policy analyses, information systems, complex systems, and computer science to work together in a multidisciplinary fashion and to share approaches. This book provides the foundation for strongly multidisciplinary research, in which the various developments and disciplines work together from a comprehensive and holistic policymaking perspective. A wide range of aspects for social and professional networking and multidisciplinary constituency building along the axes of technology, participative processes, governance, policy modeling, social simulation, and visualization are tackled in the 19 papers.

With this book, the project makes an effective contribution to the overall objectives of the Europe 2020 strategy by providing a better understanding of different approaches to ICT enabled governance and policy modeling, and by overcoming the fragmented research of the past. This book provides impressive insights into various theories, concepts, and solutions of ICT supported policy modeling and how stakeholders can be more actively engaged in public policymaking. It draws conclusions

---

[2] eGovPoliNet is cofunded under FP 7, Call identifier FP7-ICT-2011-7, URL: www.policy-community.eu

of how joint multidisciplinary research can bring more effective and resilient findings for better predicting dramatic changes and negative trends in our economies and societies.

It is my great pleasure to provide the preface to the book resulting from the eGovPoliNet project. This book presents stimulating research by researchers coming from all over Europe and beyond. Congratulations to the project partners and to the authors!—Enjoy reading!

Thanassis Chrissafis
Project officer of eGovPoliNet
European Commission
DG CNECT, Excellence in Science, Digital Science

Contents

Contributors

Tanko Ahmed National Institute for Policy and Strategic Studies (NIPSS), Jos, Nigeria

Petra Ahrweiler EA European Academy of Technology and Innovation Assessment GmbH, Bad Neuenahr-Ahrweiler, Germany

Tjeerd C. Andringa University College Groningen, Institute of Artificial Intelligence and Cognitive Engineering (ALICE), University of Groningen, AB, Groningen, the Netherlands

Tina Balke University of Surrey, Surrey, UK

Dominik Bär University of Koblenz-Landau, Koblenz, Germany

Cees van Beers Faculty of Technology, Policy, and Management, Delft University of Technology, Delft, The Netherlands

Stefano Bragaglia University of Bologna, Bologna, Italy

Laurence Brooks Brunel University, Uxbridge, UK

Yannis Charalabidis University of the Aegean, Samos, Greece

Federico Chesani University of Bologna, Bologna, Italy

Andrei Chugunov ITMO University, St. Petersburg, Russia

Gerry Cotterell Centre of Methods and Policy Application in the Social Sciences (COMPASS Research Centre), University of Auckland, Auckland, New Zealand

Jens Dambruch Fraunhofer Institute for Computer Graphics Research, Darmstadt, Germany

Peter Davis Centre of Methods and Policy Application in the Social Sciences (COMPASS Research Centre), University of Auckland, Auckland, New Zealand

Sharon Dawes Center for Technology in Government, University at Albany, Albany, New York, USA

Zamira Dzhusupova Department of Public Administration and Development Management, United Nations Department of Economic and Social Affairs (UNDESA), New York, USA

Bruce Edmonds Manchester Metropolitan University, Manchester, UK

Theo Fens Faculty of Technology, Policy, and Management, Delft University of Technology, Delft, The Netherlands

Marco Gavanelli University of Ferrara, Ferrara, Italy

Lasse Gerrits Department of Public Administration, Erasmus University Rotterdam, Rotterdam, The Netherlands

Nigel Gilbert University of Surrey, Guildford, UK

Jozef Glova Technical University Kosice, Kosice, Slovakia

Natalie Helbig Center for Technology in Government, University at Albany, Albany, New York, USA

Paulier Herder Faculty of Technology, Policy, and Management, Delft University of Technology, Delft, The Netherlands

Jeroen van den Hoven Faculty of Technology, Policy, and Management, Delft University of Technology, Delft, The Netherlands

Wander Jager Groningen Center of Social Complexity Studies, University of Groningen, Groningen, The Netherlands

Marijn Janssen Faculty of Technology, Policy, and Management, Delft University of Technology, Delft, The Netherlands

Geerten van de Kaa Faculty of Technology, Policy, and Management, Delft University of Technology, Delft, The Netherlands

Eleni Kamateri Information Technologies Institute, Centre for Research & Technology—Hellas, Thessaloniki, Greece

Bram Klievink Faculty of Technology, Policy and Management, Delft University of Technology, Delft, The Netherlands

Jörn Kohlhammer GRIS, TU Darmstadt & Fraunhofer IGD, Darmstadt, Germany

Christopher Koliba University of Vermont, Burlington, VT, USA

Michel Krämer Fraunhofer Institute for Computer Graphics Research, Darmstadt, Germany

Roy Lay-Yee Centre of Methods and Policy Application in the Social Sciences (COMPASS Research Centre), University of Auckland, Auckland, New Zealand

Deirdre Lee INSIGHT Centre for Data Analytics, NUIG, Galway, Ireland

Andreas Ligtvoet Faculty of Technology, Policy, and Management, Delft University of Technology, Delft, The Netherlands

Euripidis Loukis University of the Aegean, Samos, Greece

Dragana Majstorovic University of Koblenz-Landau, Koblenz, Germany

Michela Milano University of Bologna, Bologna, Italy

Simona Milio London School of Economics, Houghton Street, London, UK

Catherine Gerald Mkude Institute for IS Research, University of Koblenz-Landau, Koblenz, Germany

Rebecca Moody Department of Public Administration, Erasmus University Rotterdam, Rotterdam, The Netherlands

Diego Navarra Studio Navarra, London, UK

Adegboyega Ojo INSIGHT Centre for Data Analytics, NUIG, Galway, Ireland

Eleni Panopoulou Information Technologies Institute, Centre for Research & Technology—Hellas, Thessaloniki, Greece

Anastasia Papazafeiropoulou Brunel University, Uxbridge, UK

David Price Thoughtgraph Ltd, Somerset, UK

Erik Pruyt Faculty of Technology, Policy, and Management, Delft University of Technology, Delft, The Netherlands; Netherlands Institute for Advanced Study, Wassenaar, The Netherlands

Tobias Ruppert Fraunhofer Institute for Computer Graphics Research, Darmstadt, Germany

Efthimios Tambouris Information Technologies Institute, Centre for Research & Technology—Hellas, Thessaloniki, Greece; University of Macedonia, Thessaloniki, Greece

Konstantinos Tarabanis Information Technologies Institute, Centre for Research & Technology—Hellas, Thessaloniki, Greece; University of Macedonia, Thessaloniki, Greece

Dmitrii Trutnev ITMO University, St. Petersburg, Russia

Gerben van der Vegt Faculty of Economics and Business, University of Groningen, Groningen, The Netherlands

Lyudmila Vidyasova ITMO University, St. Petersburg, Russia

Maria A. Wimmer University of Koblenz-Landau, Koblenz, Germany

Asim Zia University of Vermont, Burlington, VT, USA

Chapter 1
Introduction to Policy-Making in the Digital Age

Marijn Janssen and Maria A. Wimmer

*We are running the 21st century using 20th century systems on
top of 19th century political structures. . . .*
John Pollock, contributing editor MIT technology review

Abstract The explosive growth in data, computational power, and social media
creates new opportunities for innovating governance and policy-making. These information and communications technology (ICT) developments affect all parts of
the policy-making cycle and result in drastic changes in the way policies are developed. To take advantage of these developments in the digital world, new approaches,
concepts, instruments, and methods are needed, which are able to deal with societal complexity and uncertainty. This field of research is sometimes depicted
as e-government policy, e-policy, policy informatics, or data science. Advancing
our knowledge demands that different scientific communities collaborate to create
practice-driven knowledge. For policy-making in the digital age disciplines such as
complex systems, social simulation, and public administration need to be combined.

1.1 Introduction

Policy-making and its subsequent implementation is necessary to deal with societal
problems. Policy interventions can be costly, have long-term implications, affect
groups of citizens or even the whole country and cannot be easily undone or are even
irreversible. New information and communications technology (ICT) and models
can help to improve the quality of policy-makers. In particular, the explosive growth
in data, computational power, and social media creates new opportunities for innovating the processes and solutions of ICT-based policy-making and research. To

M. Janssen (✉)
Faculty of Technology, Policy, and Management, Delft University of Technology,
Delft, The Netherlands
e-mail: m.f.w.h.a.janssen@tudelft.nl

M. A. Wimmer
University of Koblenz-Landau, Koblenz, Germany

© Springer International Publishing Switzerland 2015   1
M. Janssen et al. (eds.), *Policy Practice and Digital Science,*
Public Administration and Information Technology 10, DOI 10.1007/978-3-319-12784-2_1

take advantage of these developments in the digital world, new approaches, concepts, instruments, and methods are needed, which are able to deal with societal and computational complexity. This requires the use of knowledge which is traditionally found in different disciplines, including (but not limited to) public administration, policy analyses, information systems, complex systems, and computer science. All these knowledge areas are needed for policy-making in the digital age. The aim of this book is to provide a foundation for this new interdisciplinary field in which various traditional disciplines are blended.

Both policy-makers and those in charge of policy implementations acknowledge that ICT is becoming more and more important and is changing the policy-making process, resulting in a next generation policy-making based on ICT support. The field of policy-making is changing driven by developments such as open data, computational methods for processing data, opinion mining, simulation, and visualization of rich data sets, all combined with public engagement, social media, and participatory tools. In this respect Web 2.0 and even Web 3.0 point to the specific applications of social networks and semantically enriched and linked data which are important for policy-making. In policy-making vast amount of data are used for making predictions and forecasts. This should result in improving the outcomes of policy-making.

Policy-making is confronted with an increasing complexity and uncertainty of the outcomes which results in a need for developing policy models that are able to deal with this. To improve the validity of the models policy-makers are harvesting data to generate evidence. Furthermore, they are improving their models to capture complex phenomena and dealing with uncertainty and limited and incomplete information. Despite all these efforts, there remains often uncertainty concerning the outcomes of policy interventions. Given the uncertainty, often multiple scenarios are developed to show alternative outcomes and impact. A condition for this is the visualization of policy alternatives and its impact. Visualization can ensure involvement of nonexpert and to communicate alternatives. Furthermore, games can be used to let people gain insight in what can happen, given a certain scenario. Games allow persons to interact and to experience what happens in the future based on their interventions.

Policy-makers are often faced with conflicting solutions to complex problems, thus making it necessary for them to test out their assumptions, interventions, and resolutions. For this reason policy-making organizations introduce platforms facilitating policy-making and citizens engagements and enabling the processing of large volumes of data. There are various participative platforms developed by government agencies (e.g., De Reuver et al. 2013; Slaviero et al. 2010; Welch 2012). Platforms can be viewed as a kind of regulated environment that enable developers, users, and others to interact with each other, share data, services, and applications, enable governments to more easily monitor what is happening and facilitate the development of innovative solutions (Janssen and Estevez 2013). Platforms should provide not only support for complex policy deliberations with citizens but should also bring together policy-modelers, developers, policy-makers, and other stakeholders involved in policy-making. In this way platforms provide an information-rich, interactive environment that brings together relevant stakeholders and in which complex phenomena can be modeled, simulated, visualized, discussed, and even the playing of games can be facilitated.

1.2   Complexity and Uncertainty in Policy-Making

Policy-making is driven by the need to solve societal problems and should result in interventions to solve these societal problems. Examples of societal problems are unemployment, pollution, water quality, safety, criminality, well-being, health, and immigration. Policy-making is an ongoing process in which issues are recognized as a problem, alternative courses of actions are formulated, policies are affected, implemented, executed, and evaluated (Stewart et al. 2007). Figure 1.1 shows the typical stages of policy formulation, implementation, execution, enforcement, and evaluation. This process should not be viewed as linear as many interactions are necessary as well as interactions with all kind of stakeholders. In policy-making processes a vast amount of stakeholders are always involved, which makes policy-making complex.

Once a societal need is identified, a policy has to be formulated. Politicians, members of parliament, executive branches, courts, and interest groups may be involved in these formulations. Often contradictory proposals are made, and the impact of a proposal is difficult to determine as data is missing, models cannot

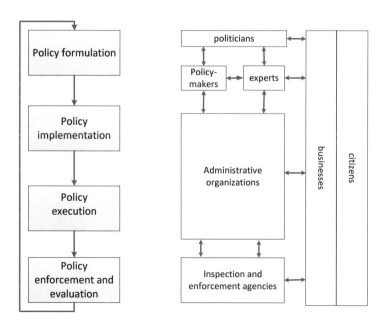

Fig. 1.1 Overview of policy cycle and stakeholders

capture the complexity, and the results of policy models are difficult to interpret and even might be interpreted in an opposing way. This is further complicated as some proposals might be good but cannot be implemented or are too costly to implement. There is a large uncertainty concerning the outcomes.

Policy implementation is done by organizations other than those that formulated the policy. They often have to interpret the policy and have to make implementation decisions. Sometimes IT can block quick implementation as systems have to be changed. Although policy-making is the domain of the government, private organizations can be involved to some extent, in particular in the execution of policies.

Once all things are ready and decisions are made, policies need to be executed. During the execution small changes are typically made to fine tune the policy formulation, implementation decisions might be more difficult to realize, policies might bring other benefits than intended, execution costs might be higher and so on. Typically, execution is continually changing. Evaluation is part of the policy-making process as it is necessary to ensure that the policy-execution solved the initial societal problem. Policies might become obsolete, might not work, have unintended affects (like creating bureaucracy) or might lose its support among elected officials, or other alternatives might pop up that are better.

Policy-making is a complex process in which many stakeholders play a role. In the various phases of policy-making different actors are dominant and play a role. Figure 1.1 shows only some actors that might be involved, and many of them are not included in this figure. The involvement of so many actors results in fragmentation and often actors are even not aware of the decisions made by other actors. This makes it difficult to manage a policy-making process as each actor has other goals and might be self-interested.

Public values (PVs) are a way to try to manage complexity and give some guidance. Most policies are made to adhere to certain values. Public value management (PVM) represents the paradigm of achieving PVs as being the primary objective (Stoker 2006). PVM refers to the continuous assessment of the actions performed by public officials to ensure that these actions result in the creation of PV (Moore 1995). Public servants are not only responsible for following the right procedure, but they also have to ensure that PVs are realized. For example, civil servants should ensure that garbage is collected. The procedure that one a week garbage is collected is secondary. If it is necessary to collect garbage more (or less) frequently to ensure a healthy environment then this should be done. The role of managers is not only to ensure that procedures are followed but they should be custodians of public assets and maximize a PV.

There exist a wide variety of PVs (Jørgensen and Bozeman 2007). PVs can be long-lasting or might be driven by contemporary politics. For example, equal access is a typical long-lasting value, whereas providing support for students at universities is contemporary, as politicians might give more, less, or no support to students. PVs differ over times, but also the emphasis on values is different in the policy-making cycle as shown in Fig. 1.2. In this figure some of the values presented by Jørgensen and Bozeman (2007) are mapped onto the four policy-making stages. Dependent on the problem at hand other values might play a role that is not included in this figure.

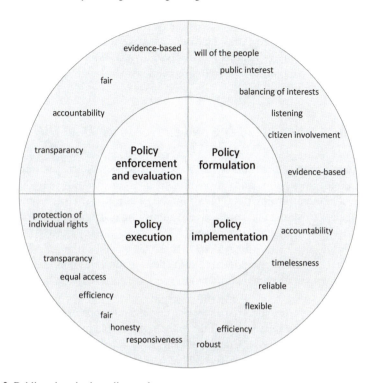

Fig. 1.2 Public values in the policy cycle

Policy is often formulated by politicians in consultation with experts. In the PVM paradigm, public administrations aim at creating PVs for society and citizens. This suggests a shift from talking about what citizens expect in creating a PV. In this view public officials should focus on collaborating and creating a dialogue with citizens in order to determine what constitutes a PV.

1.3 Developments

There is an infusion of technology that changes policy processes at both the individual and group level. There are a number of developments that influence the traditional way of policy-making, including social media as a means to interact with the public (Bertot et al. 2012), blogs (Coleman and Moss 2008), open data (Janssen et al. 2012; Zuiderwijk and Janssen 2013), freedom of information (Burt 2011), the wisdom of the crowds (Surowiecki 2004), open collaboration and transparency in policy simulation (Wimmer et al. 2012a, b), agent-based simulation and hybrid modeling techniques (Koliba and Zia 2012) which open new ways of innovative policy-making. Whereas traditional policy-making is executed by experts, now the public is involved to fulfill requirements of good governance according to open government principles.

Also, the skills and capabilities of crowds can be explored and can lead to better and more transparent democratic policy decisions. All these developments can be used for enhancing citizen's engagement and to involve citizens better in the policy-making process. We want to emphasize three important developments.

1.3.1 The Availability of Big and Open Linked Data (BOLD)

Policy-making heavily depends on data about existing policies and situations to make decisions. Both public and private organizations are opening their data for use by others. Although information could be requested for in the past, governments have changed their strategy toward actively publishing open data in formats that are readily and easily accessible (for example, European_Commission 2003; Obama 2009). Multiple perspectives are needed to make use of and stimulate new practices based on open data (Zuiderwijk et al. 2014). New applications and innovations can be based solely on open data, but often open data are enriched with data from other sources. As data can be generated and provided in huge amounts, specific needs for processing, curation, linking, visualization, and maintenance appear. The latter is often denoted with big data in which the value is generated by combining different datasets (Janssen et al. 2014). Current advances in processing power and memory allows for the processing of a huge amount of data. BOLD allows for analyzing policies and the use of these data in models to better predict the effect of new policies.

1.3.2 Rise of Hybrid Simulation Approaches

In policy implementation and execution, many actors are involved and there are a huge number of factors influencing the outcomes; this complicates the prediction of the policy outcomes. *Simulation models* are capable of capturing the interdependencies between the many factors and can include stochastic elements to deal with the variations and uncertainties. Simulation is often used in policy-making as an instrument to gain insight in the impact of possible policies which often result in new ideas for policies. Simulation allows decision-makers to understand the essence of a policy, to identify opportunities for change, and to evaluate the effect of proposed changes in key performance indicators (Banks 1998; Law and Kelton 1991). Simulation heavily depends on data and as such can benefit from big and open data.

Simulation models should capture the essential aspects of reality. Simulation models do not rely heavily on mathematical abstraction and are therefore suitable for modeling complex systems (Pidd 1992). Already the development of a model can raise discussions about what to include and what factors are of influence, in this way contributing to a better understanding of the situation at hand. Furthermore, experimentation using models allows one to investigate different settings and the influence of different scenarios in time on the policy outcomes.

The effects of policies are hard to predict and dealing with uncertainty is a key aspect in policy modeling. Statistical representation of real-world uncertainties is an integral part of simulation models (Law and Kelton 1991). The dynamics associated with many factors affecting policy-making, the complexity associated with the interdependencies between individual parts, and the stochastic elements associated with the randomness and unpredictable behavior of transactions complicates the simulations. Computer simulations for examining, explaining, and predicting social processes and relationships as well as measuring the possible impact of policies has become an important part of policy-making. Traditional models are not able to address all aspects of complex policy interactions, which indicates the need for the development of hybrid simulation models consisting of a combinatory set of models built on different modeling theories (Koliba and Zia 2012). In policy-making it can be that multiple models are developed, but it is also possible to combine various types of simulation in a single model. For this purpose agent-based modeling and simulation approaches can be used as these allow for combining different type of models in a single simulation.

1.3.3 Ubiquitous User Engagement

Efforts to design public policies are confronted with considerable complexity, in which (1) a large number of potentially relevant factors needs to be considered, (2) a vast amount of data needs to be processed, (3) a large degree of uncertainty may exist, and (4) rapidly changing circumstances need to be dealt with. Utilizing computational methods and various types of simulation and modeling methods is often key to solving these kinds of problems (Koliba and Zia 2012). The open data and social media movements are making large quantities of new data available. At the same time enhancements in computational power have expanded the repertoire of instruments and tools available for studying dynamic systems and their interdependencies. In addition, sophisticated techniques for data gathering, visualization, and analysis have expanded our ability to understand, display, and disseminate complex, temporal, and spatial information to diverse audiences. These problems can only be addressed from a complexity science perspective and with a multitude of views and contributions from different disciplines. Insights and methods of complexity science should be applied to assist policy-makers as they tackle societal problems in policy areas such as environmental protection, economics, energy, security, or public safety and health. This demands user involvement which is supported by visualization techniques and which can be actively involved by employing (serious) games. These methods can show what hypothetically will happen when certain policies are implemented.

1.4   Combining Disciplines in E-government Policy-Making

This new field has been shaped using various names, including e-policy-making, digital policy science, computational intelligence, digital sciences, data sciences, and policy informatics (Dawes and Janssen 2013). The essence of this field it that it is

1. Practice-driven
2. Employs modeling techniques
3. Needs the knowledge coming from various disciplines
4. It focused on governance and policy-making

This field is practice-driven by taking as a starting point the public policy problem and defining what information is relevant for addressing the problem under study. This requires understanding of public administration and policy-making processes. Next, it is a key to determine how to obtain, store, retrieve, process, model, and interpret the results. This is the field of e-participation, policy-modeling, social simulation, and complex systems. Finally, it should be agreed upon how to present and disseminate the results so that other researchers, decision-makers, and practitioners can use it. This requires in-depth knowledge of practice, of structures of public administration and constitutions, political cultures, processes and culture and policy-making.

Based on the ideas, the FP7 project EgovPoliNet project has created an international community in ICT solutions for governance and policy-modeling. The "policy-making 2.0" LinkedIn community has a large number of members from different disciplines and backgrounds representing practice and academia. This book is the product of this project in which a large number of persons from various disciplines and representing a variety of communities were involved. The book shows experiences and advances in various areas of policy-making. Furthermore, it contains comparative analyses and descriptions of cases, tools, and scientific approaches from the knowledge base created in this project. Using this book, practices and knowledge in this field is shared among researchers. Furthermore, this book provides the foundations in this area. The covered expertise include a wide range of aspects for social and professional networking and multidisciplinary constituency building along the axes of technology, participative processes, governance, policy-modeling, social simulation, and visualization. In this way eGovPoliNet has advanced the way research, development, and practice is performed worldwide in using ICT solutions for governance and policy-modeling.

Although in Europe the term "e-government policy" or "e-policy," for short, is often used to refer to these types of phenomena, whereas in the USA often the term "policy informatics" is used. This is similar to that in the USA the term digital government is often used, whereas in Europe the term e-government is preferred. Policy informatics is defined as "the study of how information is leveraged and efforts are coordinated towards solving complex public policy problems" (Krishnamurthy et al. 2013, p. 367). These authors view policy informatics as an emerging research space to navigate through the challenges of complex layers of uncertainty within governance processes. Policy informatics community has created Listserv called Policy Informatics Network (PIN-L).

E-government policy-making is closely connected to "data science." Data science is the ability to find answers from larger volumes of (un)structured data (Davenport and Patil 2012). Data scientists find and interpret rich data sources, manage large amounts of data, create visualizations to aid in understanding data, build mathematical models using the data, present and communicate the data insights/findings to specialists and scientists in their team, and if required to a nonexpert audience. These are activities which are at the heart of policy-making.

1.5 Overview of Chapters

In total 54 different authors were involved in the creation of this book. Some chapters have a single author, but most of the chapters have multiple authors. The authors represent a wide range of disciplines as shown in Fig. 1.2. The focus has been on targeting five communities that make up the core field for ICT-enabled policy-making. These communities include e-government/e-participation, information systems, complex systems, public administration, and policy research and social simulation. The combination of these disciplines and communities are necessary to tackle policy problems in new ways. A sixth category was added for authors not belonging to any of these communities, such as philosophy and economics. Figure 1.3 shows that the authors are evenly distributed among the communities, although this is less with the chapter. Most of the authors can be classified as belonging to the e-government/e-participation community, which is by nature interdisciplinary.

Foundation The first part deals with the *foundations* of the book. In their Chap. 2 Chris Koliba and Asim Zia start with a best practice to be incorporated in public administration educational programs to embrace the new developments sketched in

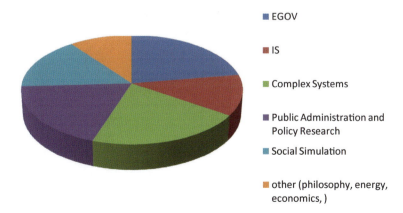

Fig. 1.3 Overview of the disciplinary background of the authors

this chapter. They identify two types of public servants that need to be educated. The policy informatics include the savvy public manager and the policy informatics analyst. This chapter can be used as a basis to adopt interdisciplinary approaches and include policy informatics in the public administration curriculum.

Petra Ahrweiler and Nigel Gilbert discuss the need for the quality of simulation modeling in their Chap. 3. Developing simulation is always based on certain assumptions and a model is as good as the developer makes it. The user community is proposed to assess the quality of a policy-modeling exercise. Communicative skills, patience, willingness to compromise on both sides, and motivation to bridge the formal world of modelers and the narrative world of policy-makers are suggested as key competences. The authors argue that user involvement is necessary in all stages of model development.

Wander Jager and Bruce Edmonds argue that due to the complexity that many social systems are unpredictable by nature in their Chap. 4. They discuss how some insights and tools from complexity science can be used in policy-making. In particular they discuss the strengths and weaknesses of agent-based modeling as a way to gain insight in the complexity and uncertainty of policy-making.

In the Chap. 5, Erik Pruyt sketches the future in which different systems modeling schools and modeling methods are integrated. He shows that elements from policy analysis, data science, machine learning, and computer science need to be combined to deal with the uncertainty in policy-making. He demonstrates the integration of various modeling and simulation approaches and related disciplines using three cases.

Modeling approaches are compared in the Chap. 6 authored by Dragana Majstorovic, Maria A. Wimmer, Roy Lay-Yee, Peter Davis,and Petra Ahrweiler. Like in the previous chapter they argue that none of the theories on its own is able to address all aspects of complex policy interactions, and the need for hybrid simulation models is advocated.

The next chapter is complimentary to the previous chapter and includes a comparison of ICT tools and technologies. The Chap. 7 is authored by Eleni Kamateri, Eleni Panopoulou, Efthimios Tambouris, Konstantinos Tarabanis, Adegboyega Ojo, Deirdre Lee, and David Price. This chapter can be used as a basis for tool selecting and includes visualization, argumentation, e-participation, opinion mining, simulation, persuasive, social network analysis, big data analytics, semantics, linked data tools, and serious games.

Social Aspects, Stakeholders and Values Although much emphasis is put on modeling efforts, the social aspects are key to effective policy-making. The role of values is discussed in the Chap. 8 authored by Andreas Ligtvoet, Geerten van de Kaa, Theo Fens, Cees van Beers, Paulien Herder, and Jeroen van den Hoven. Using the case of the design of smart meters in energy networks they argue that policy-makers would do well by not only addressing functional requirements but also by taking individual stakeholder and PVs into consideration.

In policy-making a wide range of stakeholders are involved in various stages of the policy-making process. Natalie Helbig, Sharon Dawes, Zamira Dzhusupova, Bram Klievink, and Catherine Gerald Mkude analyze five case studies of stakeholder engagement in policy-making in their Chap. 9. Various engagement tools are discussed and factors identified which support the effective use of particular tools and technologies.

The Chap. 10 investigates the role of values and trust in computational models in the policy process. This chapter is authored by Rebecca Moody and Lasse Gerrits. The authors found that a large diversity exists in values within the cases. By the authors important explanatory factors were found including (1) the role of the designer of the model, (2) the number of different actors (3) the level of trust already present, and (4) and the limited control of decision-makers over the models.

Bureaucratic organizations are often considered to be inefficient and not customer friendly. Tjeerd Andringa presents and discusses a multidisciplinary framework containing the drivers and causes of bureaucracy in the Chap. 11. He concludes that the reduction of the number of rules and regulations is important, but that motivating workers to understand their professional roles and to learn to oversee the impact of their activities is even more important.

Crowdsourcing has become an important policy instrument to gain access to expertise ("wisdom") outside own boundaries. In the Chap. 12, Euripids Loukis and Yannis Charalabidis discuss Web 2.0 social media for crowdsourcing. Passive crowdsourcing exploits the content generated by users, whereas active crowdsourcing stimulates content postings and idea generation by users. Synergy can be created by combining both approaches. The results of passive crowdsourcing can be used for guiding active crowdsourcing to avoid asking users for similar types of input.

Policy, Collaboration and Games Agent-based gaming (ABG) is used as a tool to explore the possibilities to manage complex systems in the Chap. 13 by Wander Jager and Gerben van der Vegt. ABG allows for modeling a virtual and autonomous population in a computer game setting to exploit various management and leadership styles. In this way ABG contribute to the development of the required knowledge on how to manage social complex behaving systems.

Micro simulation focuses on modeling individual units and the micro-level processes that affect their development. The concepts of micro simulation are explained by Roy Lay-Yee and Gerry Cotterell in the Chap. 14. Micro simulation for policy development is useful to combine multiple sources of information in a single contextualized model to answer "what if" questions on complex social phenomena.

Visualization is essential to communicate the model and the results to a variety of stakeholders. These aspects are discussed in the Chap. 15 by Tobias Ruppert, Jens Dambruch, Michel Krämer, Tina Balke, Marco Gavanelli, Stefano Bragaglia, Federico Chesani, Michela Milano, and Jörn Kohlhammer. They argue that despite the significance to use evidence in policy-making, this is seldom realized. Three case studies that have been conducted in two European research projects for policy-modeling are presented. In all the cases access for nonexperts to the computational models by information visualization technologies was realized.

Applications and Practices Different projects have been initiated to study the best suitable transition process towards renewable energy. In the Chap. 16 by Dominik Bär, Maria A. Wimmer, Jozef Glova, Anastasia Papazafeiropoulou,and Laurence Brooks five of these projects are analyzed and compared. They please for transferring models from one country to other countries to facilitate learning.

Lyudmila Vidyasova, Andrei Chugunov, and Dmitrii Trutnev present experiences from Russia in their Chap. 17. They argue that informational, analytical, and fore-casting activities for the processes of socioeconomic development are an important element in policy-making. The authors provide a brief overview of the history, the current state of the implementation of information processing techniques, and prac-tices for the purpose of public administration in the Russian Federation. Finally, they provide a range of recommendations to proceed.

Urban policy for sustainability is another important area which is directly linked to the first chapter in this section. In the Chap. 18, Diego Navarra and Simona Milio demonstrate a system dynamics model to show how urban policy and governance in the future can support ICT projects in order to reduce energy usage, rehabilitate the housing stock, and promote sustainability in the urban environment. This chapter contains examples of sustainable urban development policies as well as case studies.

In the Chap. 19, Tanko Ahmed discusses the digital divide which is blocking online participation in policy-making processes. Structuration, institutional and actor-network theories are used to analyze a case study of political zoning. The author recommends stronger institutionalization of ICT support and legislation for enhancing participation in policy-making and bridging the digital divide.

1.6 Conclusions

This book is the first comprehensive book in which the various development and disci-plines are covered from the policy-making perspective driven by ICT developments. A wide range of aspects for social and professional networking and multidisciplinary constituency building along the axes of technology, participative processes, gover-nance, policy-modeling, social simulation, and visualization are investigated. Policy-making is a complex process in which many stakeholders are involved. PVs can be used to guide policy-making efforts and to ensure that the many stakeholders have an understanding of the societal value that needs to be created. There is an infusion of technology resulting in changing policy processes and stakeholder involvement. Technologies like social media provides a means to interact with the public, blogs can be used to express opinions, big and open data provide input for evidence-based policy-making, the integration of various types of modeling and simulation tech-niques (hybrid models) can provide much more insight and reliable outcomes, gam-ing in which all kind of stakeholders are involved open new ways of innovative policy-making. In addition trends like the freedom of information, the wisdom of the crowds, and open collaboration changes the landscape further. The policy-making landscape is clearly changing and this demands a strong need for interdisciplinary research.

References

Banks J (1998) Handbook of simulation: principles, methodology, advances, applications, and practice. Wiley, New York

Bertot JC, Jaeger PT, Hansen D (2012) The impact of polices on government social media usage: Issues, challenges, and recommendations. Gov Inform Q 29:30–40

Burt E (2011) Introduction to the freedom of information special edition: emerging perspectives, critical reflections, and the need for further research. Inform Polit 16(2):91–92.

Coleman S, Moss G (2008) Governing at a distance—politicians in the blogosphere. Inform Polit 12(1–2):7–20.

Davenport TH, Patil DJ (2012) Data scientist: the sexiest job of the 21st century. Harv Bus Rev 90(10):70–76

Dawes SS, Janssen M (2013) Policy informatics: addressing complex problems with rich data, computational tools, and stakeholder engagement. Paper presented at the 14th annual international conference on digital government research, Quebec City, Canada

De Reuver M, Stein S, Hampe F (2013) From eparticipation to mobile participation: designing a service platform and business model for mobile participation. Inform Polit 18(1):57–73

European_Commission (2003) Directive 2003/98/EC of the European Parliament and of the council of 17 November 2003 on the re-use of public sector information. http://ec.europa.eu/information_society/policy/psi/rules/eu/index_en.htm. Accessed 12 Dec 2012

Janssen M, Estevez E (2013) Lean government and platform-based governance—doing more with less. Gov Inform Quert 30(suppl 1):S1–S8

Janssen M, Charalabidis Y, Zuiderwijk A (2012) Benefits, adoption barriers and myths of open data and open government. Inform Syst Manage 29(4):258–268

Janssen M, Estevez E, Janowski T (2014) Interoperability in big, open, and linked data—organizational maturity, capabilities, and data portfolios. Computer 47(10):26–31

Jørgensen TB, Bozeman B (2007) Public values: an inventory. Adm Soc 39(3):354–381

Koliba C, Zia A (2012) Governance Informatics: using computer simulation models to deepen situational awareness and governance design considerations policy informatics. MIT Press, Cambridge.

Krishnamurthy R, Bhagwatwar A, Johnston EW, Desouza KC (2013) A glimpse into policy informatics: the case of participatory platforms that generate synthetic empathy. Commun Assoc Inform Syst 33(Article 21):365–380.

Law AM, Kelton WD (1991) Simulation modeling and analysis 2nd ed. McGraw-Hill, New York

Moore MH (1995) Creating public value: strategic management in government. Harvard University Press, Cambridge

Obama B (2009) Memorandum for the Heads of executive Departments and Agencies: transparency and open government. Retrieved February 21, 2013, from http://www.whitehouse.gov/the_press_office/Transparency_and_Open_Government

Pidd M (1992) Computer simulation in management science, 3rd ed. John Wiley, Chichester

Slaviero C, Maciel C, Alencar F, Santana E, Souza P (2010) Designing a platform to facilitate the development of virtual e-participation environments. Paper presented at the ICEGOV '10 proceedings of the 4th international conference on theory and practice of electronic governance, Beijing

Stewart JJ, Hedge DM, Lester JP (2007) Public policy: an evolutionary approach 3rd edn. Cengage Learning, Wadsworth

Stoker G (2006) Public value management: a new narrative for networked governance? Am Rev Public Adm 3(1):41–57

Surowiecki J (2004) The wisdom of crowds: why the many are smarter than the few and how collective wisdom shapes business economies, societies and nations. Doubleday

Welch EW (2012) The rise of participative technologies in government. In: Shareef MA, Archer N, Dwivedi YK, Mishra A, Pandey SK (eds) Transformational government through eGov practice: socioeconomic, cultural, and technological issues. Emerald Group Publishing Limited

Wimmer MA, Furdik K, Bicking M, Mach M, Sabol T, Butka P (2012a) Open collaboration in policy development: concept and architecture to integrate scenario development and formal policy modelling. In: Charalabidis Y, Koussouris S (eds) Empowering open and collaborative governance. Technologies and methods for online citizen engagement in public policy making. Springer, Berlin, pp 199–219

Wimmer MA, Scherer S, Moss S, Bicking M (2012b) Method and tools to support stakeholder engagement in policy development the OCOPOMO project. Int J Electron Gov Res (IJEGR) 8(3):98–119

Zuiderwijk A, Janssen M (2013) A coordination theory perspective to improve the use of open data in policy-making. Paper presented at the 12th conference on Electronic Government (EGOV), Koblenz

Zuiderwijk A, Helbig N, Gil-García JR, Janssen M (2014) Innovation through open data—a review of the state-of-the-art and an emerging research agenda. J Theor Appl Electron Commer Res 9(2):I–XIII.

Chapter 2
Educating Public Managers and Policy Analysts in an Era of Informatics

Christopher Koliba and Asim Zia

Abstract In this chapter, two ideal types of practitioners who may use or create policy informatics projects, programs, or platforms are introduced: the policy informatics-savvy public manager and the policy informatics analyst. Drawing from our experiences in teaching an informatics-friendly graduate curriculum, we discuss the range of learning competencies needed for traditional public managers and policy informatics-oriented analysts to thrive in an era of informatics. The chapter begins by describing the two different types of students who are, or can be touched by, policy informatics-friendly competencies, skills, and attitudes. Competencies ranging from those who may be users of policy informatics and sponsors of policy informatics projects and programs to those analysts designing and executing policy informatics projects and programs will be addressed. The chapter concludes with an illustration of how one Master of Public Administration (MPA) program with a policy informatics-friendly mission, a core curriculum that touches on policy informatics applications, and a series of program electives that allows students to develop analysis and modeling skills, designates its informatics-oriented competencies.

2.1 Introduction

The range of policy informatics opportunities highlighted in this volume will require future generations of public managers and policy analysts to adapt to the opportunities and challenges posed by big data and increasing computational modeling capacities afforded by the rapid growth in information technologies. It will be up to the field's Master of Public Administration (MPA) and Master of Public Policy (MPP) programs to provide this next generation with the tools needed to harness the wealth of data, information, and knowledge increasingly at the disposal of public

C. Koliba (✉)
University of Vermont, 103 Morrill Hall, 05405 Burlington, VT, USA
e-mail: ckoliba@uvm.edu

A. Zia
University of Vermont, 205 Morrill Hall, 05405 Burlington, VT, USA
e-mail: azia@uvm.edu

© Springer International Publishing Switzerland 2015   15
M. Janssen et al. (eds.), *Policy Practice and Digital Science,*
Public Administration and Information Technology 10, DOI 10.1007/978-3-319-12784-2_2

administrators and policy analysts. In this chapter, we discuss the role of policy informatics in the development of present and future public managers and policy analysts. Drawing from our experiences in teaching an informatics-friendly graduate curriculum, we discuss the range of learning competencies needed for traditional public managers and policy informatics-oriented analysts to thrive in an era of informatics. The chapter begins by describing the two different types of students who are, or can be touched by, policy informatics-friendly competencies, skills, and attitudes. Competencies ranging from those who may be users of policy informatics and sponsors of policy informatics projects and programs to those analysts designing and executing policy informatics projects and programs will be addressed. The chapter concludes with an illustration of how one MPA program with a policy informatics-friendly mission, a core curriculum that touches on policy informatics applications, and a series of program electives that allows students to develop analysis and modeling skills, designates its informatics-oriented competencies.

2.2 Two Types of Practitioner Orientations to Policy Informatics

Drawn from our experience, we find that there are two "ideal types" of policy informatics practitioner, each requiring greater and greater levels of technical mastery of analytics techniques and approaches. These ideal types are: policy informatics-savvy public managers and policy informatics analysts.

A policy informatics-savvy public manager may take on one of two possible roles relative to policy informatics projects, programs, or platforms. They may play instrumental roles in catalyzing and implementing informatics initiatives on behalf of their organizations, agencies, or institutions. In the manner, they may work with technical experts (analysts) to envision possible uses for data, visualizations, simulations, and the like. Public managers may also be in the role of using policy informatics projects, programs, or platforms. They may be in positions to use these initiatives to ground decision making, allocate resources, and otherwise guide the performance of their organizations.

A policy informatics analyst is a person who is positioned to actually execute a policy informatics initiative. They may be referred to as analysts, researchers, modelers, or programmers and provide the technical assistance needed to analyze databases, build and run models, simulations, and otherwise construct useful and effective policy informatics projects, programs, or platforms.

To succeed in either and both roles, managers and analysts will require a certain set of skills, knowledge, or competencies. Drawing on some of the prevailing literature and our own experiences, we lay out an initial list of potential competencies for consideration.

2.2.1 Policy Informatics-Savvy Public Managers

To successfully harness policy informatics, public managers will likely *not* need to know how to explicitly build models or manipulate big data. Instead, they will need to know what kinds of questions that policy informatics projects or programs can answer or not answer. They will need to know how to contract with and/or manage data managers, policy analysts, and modelers. They will need to be savvy consumers of data analysis and computational models, but not necessarily need to know how to technically execute them. Policy informatics projects, programs, and platforms are designed and executed in some ways, as any large-scale, complex project.

In writing about the stages of informatics project development using "big data," DeSouza lays out project development along three stages: planning, execution, and postimplementation. Throughout the project life cycle, he emphasizes the role of understanding the prevailing policy and legal environment, the need to venture into coalition building, the importance of communicating the broader opportunities afforded by the project, the need to develop performance indicators, and the importance of lining up adequate financial and human resources (2014).

Framing what traditional public managers need to know and do to effectively interface with policy informatics projects and programs requires an ability to be a "systems thinker," an effective evaluator, a capacity to integrate informatics into performance and financial management systems, effective communication skills, and a capacity to draw on social media, information technology, and e-governance approaches to achieve common objectives. We briefly review each of these capacities below.

Systems Thinking Knowing the right kinds of questions that may be asked through policy informatics projects and programs requires public managers to possess a "systems" view. Much has been written about the importance of "systems thinking" for public managers (Katz and Kahn 1978; Stacey 2001; Senge 1990; Korton 2001). Taking a systems perspective allows public managers to understand the relationship between the "whole" and the "parts." Systems-oriented public managers will possess a level of situational awareness (Endsley 1995) that allows them to see and understand patterns of interaction and anticipate future events and orientations. Situational awareness allows public mangers to understand and evaluate where data are coming from, how best data are interpreted, and the kinds of assumptions being used in specific interpretations (Koliba et al. 2011). The concept of system thinking laid out here can be associated with the notion of transition management (Loorbach 2007).

Process Orientations to Public Policy The capacity to view the policy making and implementation process as a *process* that involves certain levels of coordination and conflict between policy actors is of critical importance for policy informatics-savvy public managers and analysts. Understanding how data are used to frame problems and policy solutions, how complex governance arrangements impact policy implementation (Koliba et al. 2010), and how data visualization can be used to facilitate the setting of policy agendas and open policy windows (Kingdon 1984) is of critical importance for public management and policy analysts alike.

Research Methodologies Another basic competency needed for any public manager using policy informatics is a foundational understanding of research methods, particularly quantitative reasoning and methodologies. A foundational understanding of data validity, analytical rigor and relevance, statistical significance, and the like are needed to be effective consumers of informatics. That said, traditional public managers should also be exposed to qualitative methods as well, refining their powers of observation, understanding how symbols, stories, and numbers are used to govern, and how data and data visualization and computer simulations play into these mental models.

Performance Management A key feature of systems thinking as applied to policy informatics is the importance of understanding how data and analysis are to be used and who the intended users of the data are (Patton 2008). The integration of policy informatics into strategic planning (Bryson 2011), performance management systems (Moynihan 2008), and ultimately woven into an organization's capacity to learn, adapt, and evolve (Argyis and Schön 1996) are critically important in this vein. As policy informatics trends evolve, public managers will likely need to be exposed to uses of decision support tools, dashboards, and other computationally driven models and visualizations to support organizational performance.

Financial Management Since the first systemic budgeting systems were put in place, public managers have been urged to use the budgeting process as a planning and evaluation tool (Willoughby 1918). This approach was formally codified in the 1960s with the planning–programming–budgeting (PPB) system with its focus on planning, managerial, and operational control (Schick 1966) and later adopted into more contemporary approaches to budgeting (Caiden 1981). Using informative projects, programs, or platforms to make strategic resource allocation decisions is a necessary given and a capacity that effective public managers must master. Likewise, the policy analyst will likely need to integrate financial resource flows and costs into their projects.

Collaborative and Cooperative Capacity Building The development and use of policy informatics projects, programs, or platforms is rarely, if ever, undertaken as an individual, isolated endeavor. It is more likely that such initiatives will require interagency, interorganizational, or intergroup coordination. It is also likely that content experts will need to be partnered with analysts and programmers to complete tasks and execute designs. The public manager and policy analyst must both possess the capacity to facilitate collaborative management functions (O'Leary and Bingham 2009).

Basic Communication Skills This perhaps goes without saying, but the heart of any informatics project lies in the ability to effectively communicate findings and ideas through the analysis of data.

Social Media, Information Technology, and e-Governance Awareness A final competency concerns public managers' capacity to deepen their understanding of how social media, Web-based tools, and related information technologies are being employed to foster various e-government, e-governance, and related initiatives (Mergel 2013). Placing policy informatics projects and programs within the context of these larger trends and uses is something that public managers must be exposed to.

Within our MPA program, we have operationalized these capacities within a four-point rubric that outlines what a student needs to do to demonstrate meeting these standards. The rubric below highlights 8 of our program's 18 capacities. All 18 of these capacities are situated under 1 of the 5 core competencies tied to the accreditation standards of the Network of Schools of Public Affairs and Administration (NASPAA), the professional accrediting association in the USA, and increasingly in other countries as well, for MPA and MPP programs. A complete list of these core competencies and the 18 capacities nested under them are provided in Appendix of this chapter.

The eight capacities that we have singled out as being the most salient to the role of policy informatics in public administration are provided in Table 2.1. The rubric follows a four-point scale, ranging from "does not meet standard," "approaches standard," "meets standard," and "exceeds standard."

2.2.2 Policy Informatics Analysts

A second type of practitioner to be considered is what we are referring to as a "policy informatics analyst." When considering the kinds of competencies that policy informatics analysts need to be successful, we first assume that the basic competencies outlined in the prior section apply here as well. In other words, effective policy informatics analysts must be systems thinkers in order to place data and their analysis into context, be cognizant of current uses of decision support systems (and related platforms) to enable organizational learning, performance, and strategic planning, and possess an awareness of e-governance and e-government initiatives and how they are transforming contemporary public management and policy planning practices. In addition, policy analysts must possess a capacity to understand policy systems: How policies are made and implemented? This baseline understanding can then be used to consider the placement, purpose, and design of policy informatics projects or programs. We lay out more specific analyst capacities below.

Advanced Research Methods of Information Technology Applications In many instances, policy informatics analysts will need to move beyond meeting the standard. This is particularly true in the area of exceeding the public manager standards for research methods and utilization of information technology. It is assumed that effective policy informatics analysts will have a strong foundation in quantitative methodologies and applications. To obtain these skills, policy analysts will need to move beyond basic surveys of research methods into more advanced research methods curriculum.

Table 2.1 Public manager policy informatics capacities

Capacity	Does not meet standard	Approaches standard	Meets standard	Exceeds standard
Capacity to apply knowledge of system dynamics and network structures in public administration practices	Does not understand the basic operations of systems and networks; cannot explain why understanding cases and contexts in terms of systems and networks is important	Can provide a basic overview of what system dynamics and network structures are and illustrate how they are evident in particular cases and contexts	Is able to undertake an analysis of a complex public administration issue, problem, or context using basic system dynamics and network frameworks	Can apply system dynamics and network frameworks to existing cases and contexts to derive working solutions or feasible alternatives to pressing administrative and policy problems
Capacity to apply policy streams, cycles, systems foci upon past, present, and future policy issues, and to understand how problem identification impacts public administration	Possesses limited capacity to utilize policy streams and policy stage heuristics model to describe observed phenomena. Can isolate simple problems from solutions, but has difficulty separating ill-structured problems from solutions	Possesses some capacity to utilize policy streams and to describe policy stage heuristics model observed phenomena. Possesses some capacity to define how problems are framed by different policy actors	Employs a policy streams or policy stage heuristics model approach to the study of observed phenomena. Can demonstrate how problem definition is defined within specific policy contexts and deconstruct the relationship between problem definitions and solutions	Employs a policy streams or policy stage heuristics model approach to the diagnosis of a problem raised in real-life policy dilemmas. Can articulate how conflicts over problem definition contribute to wicked policy problems
Capacity to employ quantitative and qualitative research methods for program evaluation and action research	Possesses a limited capacity to employ survey, interview, or other social research methods to a focus area. Can explain why it is important to undertake program or project evaluation, but possesses limited capacity to actually carrying it out	Demonstrates a capacity to employ survey, interview, or other social research methods to a focus area and an understanding of how such data and analysis are useful in administrative practice. Can provide a rationale for undertaking program/project	Can provide a piece of original analysis of an observed phenomenon employing one qualitative or quantitative methodology effectively. Possesses capacity to commission a piece of original research. Can provide a detailed account for how a	Demonstrates the capacity to undertake an independent research agenda through employing one or more social research methods around a topic of study of importance to public administration. Can demonstrate the successful execution of a program or

Table 2.1 (continued)

Capacity	Does not meet standard	Approaches standard	Meets standard	Exceeds standard
		evaluation and explain what the possible goals and outcomes of such an evaluation might be	program or project evaluation project should be structured within the context of a specific program or project	project evaluation or the successful utilization of a program or project evaluation to improve administrative practice
Capacity to apply sound performance measurement and management practices	Can provide an explanation of why performance goals and measures are important in public administration, but cannot apply this reasoning to specific contexts	Can identify the performance management considerations for a particular situation or context, but has limited capacity to evaluate the effectiveness of performance management systems	Can identify and analyze performance management systems, needs, and emerging opportunities within a specific organization or network	Can provide new insights into the performance management challenges facing an organization or network, and suggest alternative design and measurement scenarios
Capacity to apply sound financial planning and fiscal responsibility	Can identify why budgeting and sound fiscal management practices are important, but cannot analyze how and/or if such practices are being used within specific contexts	Can identify fiscal planning and budgeting practices for a particular situation or context, but has limited capacity to evaluate the effectiveness of a financial management system	Can identify and analyze financial management systems, needs, and emerging opportunities within a specific organization or network	Can provide new insights into the financial management challenges facing an organization or network, and suggest alternative design and budgeting scenarios
Capacity to achieve cooperation through participatory practices	Can explain why it is important for public administrators to be open and responsive practitioners in a vague or abstract way, but cannot provide specific explanations or justifications applied to particular contexts	Can identify instances in specific cases or contexts where a public administrator demonstrated or failed to demonstrate inclusive practices	Can demonstrate how inclusive practices and conflict management leads to cooperation for forming coalitions and collaborative practices	Can orchestrate any of the following: coalition building across units, organizations, or institutions, effective teamwork, and/or conflict management

Table 2.1 (continued)

Capacity	Does not meet standard	Approaches standard	Meets standard	Exceeds standard
Capacity to undertake high quality oral, written communication	Demonstrates some ability to express ideas verbally and in writing. Lacks consistent capacity to present and write	Possesses the capacity to write documents that are free of grammatical errors and are organized in a clear and efficient manner. Possesses the capacity to present ideas in a professional manner. Suffers from a lack of consistency in the presentation of material and expression or original ideas and concepts	Is capable of consistently expressing ideas verbally and in writing in a professional manner that communicates messages to intended audiences	Can demonstrate some instances in which verbal and written communication has persuaded others to take action
Capacity to undertake high quality electronically mediated communication and utilize information systems and media to advance objectives	Can explain why information technology is important to contemporary workplaces and public administration environments. Possesses direct experience with information technology, but little understanding for how IT informs professional practice	Can identify instances in specific cases or context where a public administrator successfully or unsuccessfully demonstrated a capacity to use IT to foster innovation, improve services, or deepen accountability. Analysis at this level is relegated to descriptions and thin analysis	Can identify how IT impacts workplaces and public policy. Can diagnose problems associated with IT tools, procedures, and uses	Demonstrates a capacity to view IT in terms of systems design. Is capable of working with IT professionals in identifying areas of need for IT upgrades, IT procedures, and IT uses in real setting

IT information technology

Competencies in advanced quantitative methods in which students learn to clean and manage large databases, perform advanced statistical tests, develop linear regression models to describe causal relationship, and the like are needed. Capacity to work across software platforms such as Excel, Statistical Package for the Social Sciences (SPSS), Analytica, and the like are important. Increasingly, the capacity to triangulate different methods, including qualitative approaches such as interviews, focus groups, participant observations is needed.

Data Visualization and Design Not only must analysts be aware of how these methods and decision support platforms may be used by practitioners but also they must know how to design and implement them. Therefore, we suggest that policy informatics analysts be exposed to design principles and how they may be applied to decision support systems, big data projects, and the like. Policy informatics analysts will need to understand and appreciate how data visualization techniques are being employed to "tell a story" through data.

Figure 2.1 provides an illustration of one student's effort to visualize campaign donations to state legislatures from the gas-extraction (fracking) industry undertaken by a masters student, Jeffery Castle for a *system analysis and strategic management* class taught by Koliba.

Castle's project demonstrates the power of data visualization to convey a central message drawing from existing databases. With a solid research methods background and exposure to visualization and design principles in class, he was able to develop an insightful policy informatics project.

Basic to Advanced Programming Language Skills Arguably, policy informatics analysts will possess a capacity to visualize and present data in a manner that is accessible. Increasingly, web-based tools are being used to design user interfaces. Knowledge of JAVA and HTML are likely most helpful in these regards. In some instances, original programs and models will need to be written through the use of programming languages such as Python, R, C++, etc. The extent to which existing software programs, be they open source or proprietary, provide enough utility to execute policy informatics projects, programs, or platforms is a continuing subject of debate within the policy informatics community. Exactly how much and to what extent specific programming languages and software programs are needing to be mastered is a standing question. For the purposes of writing this chapter, we rely on our current baseline observations and encourage more discussion and debate about the range of competencies needed by successful policy analysts.

Basic to More Advanced Modeling Skills More advanced policy informatics analysts will employ computational modeling approaches that allow for the incorporation of more complex interactions between variables. These models may be used to capture systems as dynamic, emergent, and path dependent. The outputs of these models may allow for scenario testing through simulation (Koliba et al. 2011). With the advancement of modeling software, it is becoming easier for analysts to develop system dynamics models, agent-based models, and dynamic networks designed to simulate the features of complex adaptive systems. In addition, the ability to manage and store data and link or wrap databases is often necessary.

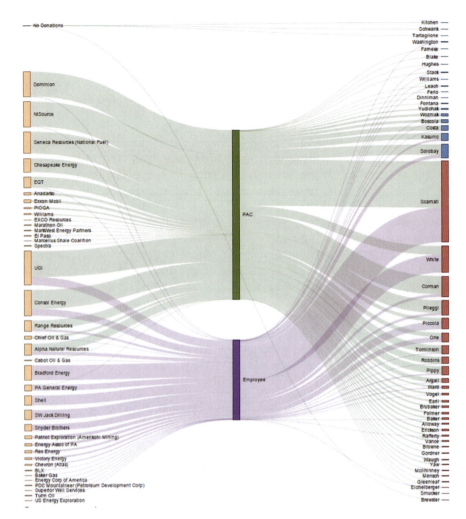

Fig. 2.1 Campaign contributions to the Pennsylvania State Senate and party membership. The goal of this analysis is to develop a visualization tool to translate publically available campaign contribution information into an easily accessible, visually appealing, and interactive format. While campaign contribution data are filed and available to the public through the Pennsylvania Department of State, it is not easily synthesized. This analysis uses a publically available database that has been published on marcellusmoney.org. In order to visualize the data, a tool was used that allows for the creation of a Sankey diagram that is able to be manipulated and interacted within an Internet browser. A Sankey diagram visualizes the magnitude of flow between the nodes of a network (Castle 2014)

The ability of analysts to draw on a diverse array of methods and theoretical frameworks to envision and create models is of critical importance. Any potential policy informatics project, program, or platform will be enabled or constrained by the modeling logic in place. With a plurality of tools at one's disposal, policy informatics analysts will be better positioned to design relevant and legitimate models.

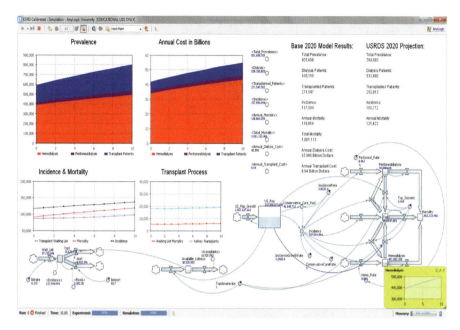

Fig. 2.2 End-stage renal disease (ESRD) system dynamics population model. To provide clinicians and health care administrators with a greater understanding of the combined costs associated with the many critical care pathways associated with ESRD, a system dynamics model was designed to simulate the total expenses of ESRD treatment for the USA, as well as incidence and mortality rates associated with different critical care pathways: kidney transplant, hemodialysis, peritoneal dialysis, and conservative care. Calibrated to US Renal Data System (USRDS) 2013 Annual and Historical Data Report and the US Census Bureau for the years 2005–2010, encompassing all ESRD patients under treatment in the USA from 2005 to 2010, the ESRD population model predicts the growth and costs of ESRD treatment type populations using historical patterns. The model has been calibrated against the output of the USRDS's own prediction for the year 2020 and also tested by running historic scenarios and comparing the output to existing data. Using a web interface designed to allow users to alter certain combinations of parameters, several scenarios are run to project future spending, incidence, and mortalities if certain combinations of critical care pathways are pursued. These scenarios include: a doubling of kidney donations and transplant rates, a marked increase in the offering of peritoneal dialysis, and an increase in conservative care routes for patients over 65. The results of these scenario runs are shared, demonstrating sizable cost savings and increased survival rates. Implications of clinical practice, public policy, and further research are drawn (Fernandez 2013)

Figure 2.2 provides an illustration of Luca Fernandez's system dynamics model of critical care pathways for end-stage renal disease (ESRD). Fernandez took Koliba's *system analysis and strategic management* course and Zia's *decision-making modeling* course. This model, constructed using the proprietary software, AnyLogic, was initially constructed as a project in Zia's course.

Castle and Fernandez's projects illustrate how master's-level students with an eye toward becoming policy informatics analysts can build skills and capacities to develop useful informatics projects that can guide policy and public management. They were guided to this point by taking advanced courses designed explicitly with policy informatics outcomes in mind.

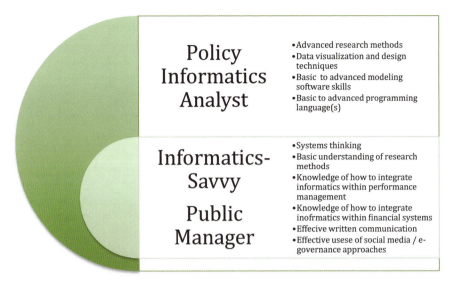

Policy Informatics Analyst
- Advanced research methods
- Data visualization and design techniques
- Basic to advanced modeling software skills
- Basic to advanced programming language(s)

Informatics-Savvy Public Manager
- Systems thinking
- Basic understanding of research methods
- Knowledge of how to integrate informatics within performance management
- Knowledge of how to integrate inofrmatics within financial systems
- Effecive written communication
- Effective usese of social media / e-governance approaches

Fig. 2.3 The nested capacities of informatics-savvy public managers and policy informatics analysts

Figure 2.3 illustrates how the competencies of the two different ideal types of policy informatics practitioners are nested inside of one another. A more complete list of competencies that are needed for the more advanced forms of policy analysis will need to emerge through robust exchanges between the computer sciences, organizational sciences, and policy sciences. These views will likely hinge on assumptions about the sophistication of the models to be developed. A key question here concerning the types of models to be built is: Can adequate models be built using existing software or is original programming needed or desired? Ideally, advanced policy analysts undertaking policy informatics projects are "programmers with a public service motivation."

2.3 Applications to Professional Masters Programs

Professional graduate degree programs have steadily moved toward emphasizing the importance of the mission of particular graduate programs in determining the optimal curriculum to suit the learning needs of it students. As a result, clear definitions of the learning outcomes and the learning needs of particular student communities are defined. Some programs may seek to serve regional or local needs of the government and nonprofit sector, while others may have a broader reach, preparing students to work within federal or international level governments and nonprofits.

In addition to geographic scope, accredited MPA and MPP programs may have specific areas of concentration. Some programs may focus on preparing public managers who are charged with managing resources, making operational, tactical, and strategic decisions and, overall, administering to the day-to-day needs of a government or nonprofit organization. Programs may also focus on training policy analysts who are responsible for analyzing policies, policy alternatives, problem definition, and the like. Historically, the differences between public management and policy analysis have distinguished the MPA degree from the MPP degree. However, recent studies of NASPAA-accredited programs have found that the lines between MPA and MPP programs are increasingly blurred (Hur and Hackbart 2009). The relationship between public management and policy analysis matters to those interested in policy informatics because these distinctions drive what policy informatics competencies and capacities are covered within a core curriculum, and what competencies and capacities are covered within a suite of electives or concentrations.

Competency-based assessments are increasingly being used to evaluate and design curriculum. Drawing on the core tenants of adult learning theory and practice, competency-based assessment involves the derivation of specific skills, knowledge, or attitudes that an adult learner must obtain in order to successfully complete a course of study or degree requirement. Effective competency-based graduate programs call on students to demonstrate a mastery of competencies through a variety of means. Portfolio development, test taking, and project completion are common applications. Best practices in competency-based education assert that curriculum be aligned with specific competencies as much as possible.

By way of example, the University of Vermont's MPA Program has had a "systems thinking" focus since it was first conceived in the middle 1980s. Within the last 10 years, the two chapter coauthors, along with several core faculty who have been associated with the program since its inception, have undertaken an effort to refine its mission based on its original systems-focused orientation.

As of 2010, the program mission was refined to read:

> Our MPA program is a professional interdisciplinary degree that prepares pre and in-service leaders, managers and policy analysts by combining the theoretical and practical foundations of public administration focusing on the complexity of governance systems and the democratic, collaborative traditions that are a hallmark of Vermont communities.

The mission was revised to include leaders and managers, as well as policy analysts. A theory-practice link was made explicit. The phrase, "complexity of governance systems" was selected to align with a commonly shared view of contemporary governance as a multisectoral and multijurisdictional context. Concepts such as bounded rationality, social complexity, the importance of systems feedback, and path dependency are stressed throughout the curriculum. The sense of place found within the State of Vermont was also recognized and used to highlight the high levels of engagement found within the program.

The capacities laid out in Table 2.1 have been mapped to the program's core curriculum. The program's current core is a set of five courses: *PA 301: Foundations of Public Administration*; *PA 302: Organizational Behavior and Change*; *PA 303: Research Methods*; *PA 305: Public and Nonprofit Budgeting and Finance and PA 306: Policy Systems*. In addition, all students are required to undertake a three-credit internship and a three-credit Capstone experience in which they construct a final learning portfolio. It is within this final portfolio that students are expected to provide evidence of meeting or exceeding the standard. An expanded rubric of all 18 capacities is used by the students to undertake their own self-assessment. These assessments are judged against the Capstone instructor's evaluation.

In 2009, the MPA faculty revised the core curriculum to align with the core competencies. Several course titles and content were revised to align with these competencies and the overall systems' focus of our mission. The two core courses taught by the two coauthors, PA 301 and PA 306, are highlighted here.

2.4 PA 301: Foundations of Public Administration

Designed as a survey of the prevailing public administration literature during the past 200 plus years, *Foundations of Public Administration* is arranged across a continuum of interconnected themes and topics that are to be addressed in more in-depth in other courses and is described in the syllabus in the following way:

> This class is designed to provide you with an overview of the field of public administration. You will explore the historical foundations, the major theoretical, organizational, and political breakthroughs, and the dynamic tensions inherent to public and nonprofit sector administration. Special attention will be given to problems arising from political imperatives generated within a democratic society.

Each week a series of classic and contemporary texts are read and reviewed by the students. In part, to fill a noticeable void in the literature, the authors co-wrote, along with Jack Meek, a book on governance networks called: *Governance Networks in Public Administration and Public Policy* (Koliba et al. 2010). This book is required reading. Students are also asked to purchase Shafritz and Hyde's edited volume, *Classics of Public Administration*.

Current events assignments offered through blog posts are undertaken. Weekly themes include: the science and art of administration; citizens and the administrative state; nonprofit, private, and public sector differences; governance networks; accountability; and performance management.

During the 2009 reforms of the core curriculum, discrete units on governance networks and performance management were added to this course. Throughout the entire course, a complex systems lens is employed to describe and analyze governance networks and the particular role that performance management systems play in providing feedback to governance actors. Students are exposed to social network and system dynamics theory, and asked to apply these lenses to several written cases taken from the Electronic Hallway. A unit on performance management systems and their role within fostering organizational learning are provided along with readings and examples of decision support tools and dashboard platforms currently in use by government agencies.

Across many units, including units on trends and reforms, ethical and reflective leadership, citizens and the administrative state, and accountability, the increasing use of social media and other forms of information technology are discussed. Trends shaping the "e-governance" and "e-government" movements serve as a major focus on current trends. In addition, students are exposed to current examples of data visualizations and open data platforms and asked to consider their uses.

2.5 PA 306: Policy Systems

Policy Systems is an entry-level graduate policy course designed to give the MPA student an overview of the policy process. In 2009, the course was revised to reflect a more integrated systems focus. The following text provides an overview of the course:

> In particular, the emphasis is placed upon meso-, and macro-scale policy system frameworks and theories, such as Institutional Analysis and Development Framework, the Multiple Streams Framework; Social Construction and Policy Design; the Network Approach; Punctuated Equilibrium Theory; the Advocacy Coalition Framework; Innovation and Diffusion Models and Large-N Comparative Models. Further, students will apply these micro-, meso- and macro-scale theories to a substantive policy problem that is of interest to a community partner, which could be a government agency or a non-profit organization. These policy problems may span, or even cut across, a broad range of policy domains such as (included but not limited to) economic policy, food policy, environmental policy, defense and foreign policy, space policy, homeland security, disaster and emergency management, social policy, transportation policy, land-use policy and health policy.

The core texts for this class are Elinor Ostrom's, *Understanding Institutional Diversity,* Paul Sabatier's edited volume, *Theories of the Policy Process,* and Deborah Stone's *Policy Paradox: The Art of Political Decision-Making.* The course itself is staged following a micro, to meso, to macro level scale of policy systems framework. A service-learning element is incorporated. Students are taught to view the policy process through a systems lens. Zia employs examples of policy systems models using system dynamics (SD), agent-based modeling (ABM), social network analysis (SNA), and hybrid approaches throughout the class. By drawing on Ostrom, Sabatier, and other meso level policy processes as a basis, students are exposed to a number of "complexity-friendly" theoretical policy frameworks (Koliba and Zia 2013). Appreciating the value of these policy frameworks, students are provided with heuristics for understanding the flow of information across a system. In addition, students are shown examples of simulation models of different policy processes, streams, and systems.

In addition to PA 301 and PA 306, students are also provided an in-depth exploration of organization theory in *PA 302 Organizational Behavior and Change* that is taught through an organizational psychology lens that emphasizes the role of organizational culture and learning. "Soft systems" approaches are applied. *PA 303 Research Methods for Policy Analysis and Program Evaluation* exposes students to a variety of research and program evaluation methodologies with a particular focus on quantitative analysis techniques. Within *PA 305 Public and Nonprofit Budgeting and Finance,* students are taught about evidence-based decision-making and data management.

By completing the core curriculum, students are exposed to some of the foundational competencies needed to use and shape policy informatics projects. However, it is not until students enroll in one of the several electives, that more explicit policy informatics concepts and applications are taught. Two of these elective courses are highlighted here. A third, PA 311 Policy Analysis, also exposes students to policy analyst capacities, but is not highlighted here.

2.6   PA 308: Decision-Making Models

A course designated during the original founding of the University of Vermont (UVM)-MPA Program, *PA 308: Decision-Making Models* offers students with a more advanced look at decision-making theory and modeling. The course is described by Zia in the following manner:

> In this advanced graduate level seminar, we will explore and analyze a wide range of normative, descriptive and prescriptive decision making models. This course focuses on systems level thinking to impart problem-solving skills in complex decision-making contexts. Decision making problems in the real-world public policy, business and management arenas will be analyzed and modeled with different tools developed in the fields of Decision Analysis, Behavioral Sciences, Policy Sciences and Complex Systems. The emphasis will be placed on imparting cutting edge skills to enable students to design and implement multiple criteria decision analysis models, decision making models under risk and uncertainty and computer simulation models such as Monte Carlo simulation, system dynamic models, agent based models, Bayesian decision making models, participatory and deliberative decision making models, and interactive scenario planning approaches. AnyLogic version 6.6 will be made available to the students for working with some of these computer simulation models.

2.7   PA 317: Systems Analysis and Strategic Management

Another course designate during the early inception of the program, systems analysis and strategic management is described by Koliba in the course syllabus as follows:

> This course combines systems and network analysis with organizational learning theory and practices to provide students with a heightened capacity to analyze and effectively operate in complex organizations and networks. The architecture for the course is grounded in many of the fundamental conceptual frameworks found in network, systems and complexity analysis, as well as some of the fundamental frameworks employed within the public administration and policy studies fields. In this course, strategic management and systems analysis are linked together through the concept of situational awareness and design principles. Several units focusing on teaching network analysis tools using UCINet have been incorporated.

One of the key challenges to offering these informatics-oriented electives lies in the capacities that the traditional MPA students possess to thrive within them. Increasingly, these elective courses are being populated by doctoral and master of science students looking to apply what they are learning to their dissertations or thesis. Our MPA program offers a thesis option and we have had some success with these more professionally oriented students undertaking high quality informatics focused thesis. Our experience begs a larger question pertaining to the degree to which the baseline informatics-savvy public manager capacities lead into more complex policy analysts competencies associated with the actual design and construction of policy informatics projects, programs, and platforms.

Table 2.2 provides an overview of where within the curriculum certain policy informatics capacities are covered. When associated with the class, students are exposed to the uses of informatics projects, programs, or platforms or provided opportunities for concrete skill development.

The University of Vermont context is one that can be replicated in other programs. The capacity of the MPA program to offer these courses hinges on the expertise of two faculties who teach in the core and these two electives. With additional resources, a more advanced curriculum may be pursued, one that pursues closer ties with the computer science department (Zia has a secondary appointment) around curricular alignment. Examples of more advanced curriculum to support the development of policy informatics analysts may be found at such institutions as Carnegie Mellon University, Arizona State University, George Mason University, University at Albany, Delft University of Technology, Massachusetts Institute of Technology, among many others. The University of Vermont case suggests, however, that policy informatics education can be integrated into the main stream with relatively low resource investments leveraged by strategic relationships with other disciplines and core faculty with the right skills, training, and vision.

2.8 Conclusion

It is difficult to argue that with the advancement of high speed computing, the digitization of data and the increasing collaboration occurring around the development of informatics projects, programs, and platforms, that the educational establishment, particularly at the professional master degree levels, will need to evolve. This chapter lays out a preliminary look at some of the core competencies and capacities that public managers and policy analysts will need to lead the next generation of policy informatics integration.

Table 2.2 Policy informatics capacities covered within the UVM-MPA program curriculum

Course title	Policy informatics-savvy public management capacities covered	Policy informatics analysis capacities covered
PA 301: Foundations of public administration	Systems thinking Policy as process Performance management Financial management Basic communication Social media/IT/e-governance Collaborative–cooperative capacity building	Data visualization and design
PA 306: Policy systems	Systems thinking Policy as process Basic communication	Basic modeling skills
PA 302: Organizational behavior and change	Systems thinking Basic communication Collaborative–cooperative capacity building	
PA 303: Research methods for policy analysis and program evaluation	Research methods Basic communication	Data visualization and design
PA 305: Public and nonprofit budgeting and finance	Financial management Performance management Basic communication	
PA 308: Decision-making modeling	Systems thinking Policy as process Research methods Performance management Social media/IT/e-governance	Advanced research methods Data visualization and design techniques Basic modeling skills
PA 311: Policy analysis	Systems thinking Policy as process Research methods Performance management Basic communication	Advanced research methods Data visualization and design Basic modeling skills
PA 317: Systems analysis and strategic analysis	Systems thinking Policy as process Research methods Performance management Collaborative–cooperative capacity building Basic communication Social media/IT/e-governance	Data visualization and design Basic modeling skills

2.9   Appendix A: University of Vermont's MPA Program Learning Competencies and Capacities

NASPAA core standard	UVM-MPA learning capacity
To lead and manage in public governance	Capacity to understand accountability and democratic theory
	Capacity to manage the lines of authority for public, private, and nonprofit collaboration, and to address sectorial differences to overcome obstacles
	Capacity to apply knowledge of system dynamics and network structures in PA practice
	Capacity to carry out effective policy implementation
To participate in and contribute to the policy process	Capacity to apply policy streams, cycles, systems foci upon past, present, and future policy issues, and to understand how problem identification impacts public administration
	Capacity to conduct policy analysis/evaluation
	Capacity to employ quantitative and qualitative research methods for program evaluation and action research
To analyze, synthesize, think critically, solve problems, and make decisions	Capacity to initiate strategic planning, and apply organizational learning and development principles
	Capacity to apply sound performance measurement and management practices
	Capacity to apply sound financial planning and fiscal responsibility
	Capacity to employ quantitative and qualitative research methods for program evaluation and action research
To articulate and apply a public service perspective	Capacity to understand the value of authentic citizen participation in PA practice
	Capacity to understand the value of social and economic equity in PA practices
	Capacity to lead in an ethical and reflective manner
	Capacity to achieve cooperation through participatory practices
To communicate and interact productively with a diverse and changing workforce and citizenry	Capacity to undertake high quality oral, written, and electronically mediated communication and utilize information systems and media to advance objectives
	Capacity to appreciate the value of pluralism, multiculturalism, and cultural diversity
	Capacity to carry out effective human resource management
	Capacity to undertake high quality oral, written, and electronically mediated communication and utilize information systems and media to advance objectives

NASPAA Network of Schools of Public Affairs and Administration, *UVM* University of Vermont, *MPA* Master of Public Administration, *PA* Public administration

References

Argyis C, Schön DA (1996) Organizational learning II: theory, method, and practice. Addison-Wesley, Reading

Bryson J (2011) Strategic planning for public and nonprofit organizations: a guide to strengthening and sustaining organizational achievement. Jossey-Bass, San Francisco

Caiden N (1981) Public budgeting and finance. Blackwell, New York

Castle J (2014) Visualizing natural gas industry contributions in Pennsylvania Government, PA 317 final class project

Desouza KC (2014) Realizing the promise of big data: implementing big data projects. IBM Center for the Business of Government, Washington, DC

Endsley MR (1995) Toward a theory of situation awareness in dynamic systems. Hum Fact 37(1):32–64

Fernandez L (2013) An ESRD system dynamics population model for the United States. Final project for PA 308

Hur Y, Hackbart M (2009) MPA vs. MPP: a distinction without a difference? J Public Aff Educ 15(4):397–424

Katz D, Khan R (1978) The social psychology of organizations. Wiley, New York

Kingdon J (1984) Agendas, alternatives, and public policies. Harper Collins, New York

Koliba C, Zia A (2013) Complex systems modeling in public administration and policy studies: challenges and opportunities for a meta-theoretical research program. In: Gerrits L, Marks PK (eds) COMPACT I: public administration in complexity. Emergent, Litchfield Park

Koliba C, Meek J, Zia A (2010) Governance networks in public administration and public policy. CRC, Boca Raton

Koliba C, Zia A, Lee B (2011) Governance informatics: utilizing computer simulation models to manage complex governance networks. Innov J Innov Publ Sect 16(1):1–26 (Article 3). (http://www.innovation.cc/scholarly-style/koliba_governance_informaticsv16i1a3.pdf)

Korton DC (2001) The management of social transformation. In: Stivers C (ed) Democracy, bureaucracy, and the study of administration. Westview, Boulder, pp 476–497

Loorbach D (2007) Transition management: new modes of governance for sustainable development. International Books, Ultrecht

Mergel I (2013) Social media adoption and resulting tactics in the U.S. federal government. Gov Inf Quart 30(2):123–130

Moynihan DP (2008) The dynamics of performance management: constructing information and reform. Georgetown University Press, Washington, DC

O'Leary R, Bingham L (eds) (2009) The collaborative public manager: new ideas for the twenty-first century. Georgetown University Press, Washington, DC

Patton M (2008) Utilization-focused evaluation. Sage, New York

Schick A (1966) The road to PPB: the stages of budget reform. Public Admin Rev 26(4):243–259

Senge PM (1990) The fifth discipline: the art and practice of the learning organization. Doubleday Currency, New York

Stacey RD (2001) Complex responsive processes in organizations: learning and knowledge creation. Routledge, London

Willoughby WF (1918) The movement of budgetary reform in the states. D. Appleton, New York

Chapter 3
The Quality of Social Simulation: An Example from Research Policy Modelling

Petra Ahrweiler and Nigel Gilbert

Abstract This chapter deals with the assessment of the quality of a simulation. The first section points out the problems of the *standard view* and the *constructivist view* in evaluating social simulations. A simulation is good when we get from it what we originally would have liked to get from the target; in this, the evaluation of the simulation is guided by the expectations, anticipations, and experience of the community that uses it. This makes the user community view the most promising mechanism to assess the quality of a policy-modelling exercise. The second section looks at a concrete policy-modelling example to test this idea. It shows that the very first negotiation and discussion with the user community to identify their questions is highly user-driven, interactive, and iterative. It requires communicative skills, patience, willingness to compromise on both sides, and motivation to make the formal world of modellers and the narrative world of practical policy making meet. Often, the user community is involved in providing data for calibrating the model. It is not an easy issue to confirm the existence, quality, and availability of data and check for formats and database requirements. As the quality of the simulation in the eyes of the user will very much depend on the quality of the informing data and the quality of the model calibration, much time and effort need to be spent in coordinating this issue with the user community. Last but not least, the user community has to check the validity of simulation results and has to believe in their quality. Users have to be enabled to understand the model, to agree with its processes and ways to produce results, to judge similarity between empirical and simulated data, etc. Although the *user community* view might be the most promising, it is the most work-intensive mechanism to assess the quality of a simulation. Summarising, to trust the quality of a simulation means to trust the process that produced its results. This process includes not only the design and construction of the simulation model itself but also the whole interaction between stakeholders, study team, model, and findings.

P. Ahrweiler (✉)
EA European Academy of Technology and Innovation Assessment GmbH,
Bad Neuenahr-Ahrweiler, Germany
e-mail: Petra.Ahrweiler@ea-aw.de

N. Gilbert
University of Surrey, Guildford, UK

© Springer International Publishing Switzerland 2015   35
M. Janssen et al. (eds.), *Policy Practice and Digital Science,*
Public Administration and Information Technology 10, DOI 10.1007/978-3-319-12784-2_3

Table 3.1 Comparing simulations

	Caffè Nero simulation	Science simulation
Target	Venetian Café	"Real system"
Goal	Getting "the feeling" (customers) and profit (owners) from it	Getting understanding and/or predictions from it
Model	By reducing the many features of a Venetian Café to a few parameters	By reducing the many features of the target to a few parameters
Question	Is it a good simulation, i.e. do we get from it what we want?	Is it a good simulation, i.e. do we get from it what we want?

This chapter deals with the assessment of the quality of a simulation. After discussing this issue on a general level, we apply and test the assessment mechanisms using an example from policy modelling.

3.1 Quality in Social Simulation

The construction of a scientific social simulation implies the following process: "We wish to acquire something from a target entity *T*. We cannot get what we want from *T* directly. So, we proceed indirectly. Instead of *T* we construct another entity *M*, the 'model', which is sufficiently similar to *T* that we are confident that *M* will deliver (or reveal) the acquired something which we want to get from *T*. [...] At a moment in time, the model has structure. With the passage of time the structure changes and that is behaviour. [...] Clearly we wish to know the behaviour of the model. How? We may set the model running (possibly in special sets of circumstances of our choice) and watch what it does. It is this that we refer to as 'simulation' of the target" (quoted with slight modifications from Doran and Gilbert 1994).

We also habitually refer to "simulations" in everyday life, mostly in the sense that a simulation is "an illusory appearance that manages a reality effect" (cf. Norris 1992), or as Baudrillard put it, "to simulate is to feign to have what one hasn't" while "substituting signs for the real" (Baudrillard 1988). In a previous publication (Ahrweiler and Gilbert 2005), we used the example of the Caffè Nero in Guildford, 50 km southwest of London, as a simulation of a Venetian café—which will serve as the "real" to illustrate this view. The purpose of the café is to "serve the best coffee north of Milan". It tries to give the impression that you are in a real Italian café—although, most of the time, the weather outside can make the illusion difficult to maintain.

The construction of everyday simulations like Caffè Nero has some resemblance to the construction of scientific social simulations (see Table 3.1):

In both cases, we build models from a target by reducing the characteristics of the latter sufficiently for the purpose at hand; in each case, we want something from the model we cannot achieve easily from the target. In the case of Caffè Nero, we cannot simply go to Venice, drink our coffee, be happy, and return. It is too expensive and time-consuming. We have to use the simulation. In the case of a science simulation, we cannot get data from the real system to learn about its behaviour. We have to use the simulation.

The question, whether one or the other is a good simulation, can therefore be reformulated as: Do we get from the simulation what we constructed it for?

Heeding these similarities, we shall now try to apply evaluation methods typically used for everyday simulations to scientific simulation and vice versa. Before doing so, we shall briefly discuss the "ordinary" method of evaluating simulations called the "standard view" and its adversary, a constructivist approach asserting, "anything goes".

3.1.1   The Standard View

The standard view refers to the well-known questions and methods of *verification,* namely whether the code does what it is supposed to do and whether there are any bugs, and *validation,* namely whether the outputs (for given inputs/parameters) resemble observations of the target, although (because the processes being modelled are stochastic and because of unmeasured factors) identical outputs are not to be expected, as discussed in detail in Gilbert and Troitzsch (1997). This standard view relies on a realist perspective because it refers to the observability of reality in order to compare the "real" with artificial data produced by the simulation.

Applying the standard view to the Caffè Nero example, we can find quantitative and sometimes qualitative measures for evaluating the simulation. Using quantitative measures of similarity between it and a "real" Venetian café, we can ask, for example,

- Whether the coffee tastes the same (by measuring, for example, a quality score at blind tasting),
- Whether the Caffè is a cool place (e.g. measuring the relative temperatures inside and outside),
- Whether the noise level is the same (using a dB meter for measuring purposes),whether the lighting level is the same (using a light meter), and
- Whether there are the same number of tables and chairs per square metre for the customers (counting them), and so on.

In applying qualitative measures of similarity, we can again ask:

- Whether the coffee tastes the same (while documenting what comes to mind when customers drink the coffee),
- Whether the Caffè is a "cool" place (this time meaning whether it is a fashionable place to hang out),
- Whether it is a vivid, buzzing place, full of life (observing the liveliness of groups of customers),
- Whether there is the same pattern of social relationships (difficult to operationalise: perhaps by observing whether the waiters spend their time talking to the customers or to the other staff), and

- Whether there is a ritual for serving coffee and whether it is felt to be the same as in a Venetian café.

The assumption lying behind these measures is that there is a "real" café and a "simulation" café and that in both of these, we can make observations. Similarly, we generally assume that the theories and models that lie at the base of science simulations are well grounded and can be validated by observation of empirical facts. However, the philosophy of science forces us to be more modest.

3.1.1.1   The Problem of Under-determination

Some philosophers of science argue that theories are under-determined by observational data or experience, that is, the same empirical data may be in accord with many alternative theories. An adherent of the standard view would respond in that one important role of simulations (and of any form of model building) is to derive from theories as many testable implications as possible so that eventually validity can be assessed in a cumulative process[1]. Simulation is indeed a powerful tool for testing theories in that way if we are followers of the standard view.

However, the problem that theories are under-determined by empirical data cannot be solved by cumulative data gathering: it is more general and therefore more serious. The under-determination problem is not about a missing quantity of data but about the relation between data and theory. As Quine (1977) presents it: If it is possible to construct two or more incompatible theories by relying on the same set of experimental data, the choice between these theories cannot depend on "empirical facts". Quine showed that there is no procedure to establish a relation of uniqueness between theory and data in a logically exclusive way. This leaves us with an annoying freedom: "sometimes, the same datum is interpreted by such different assumptions and theoretical orientations using different terminologies that one wonders whether the theorists are really thinking of the same datum" (Harbodt 1974, p. 258 f., own translation).

The proposal mentioned above to solve the under-determination problem by simulation does not touch the underlying reference problem at all. It just extends the theory, adding to it its "implications", hoping them to be more easily testable than the theory's core theorems. The general reference between theoretical statement— be it implication or core theorem—and observed data has not changed by applying this extension: The point here is that we cannot establish a relation of uniqueness between the observed data and the theoretical statement. This applies to any segment of theorising at the centre or at the periphery of the theory on any level—a matter that cannot be improved by a cumulative strategy.

---

[1] We owe the suggestion that simulation could be a tool to make theories more determined by data to one of the referees of Ahrweiler and Gilbert (2005).

3.1.1.2   The Theory-Ladenness of Observations

Observations are supposed to validate theories, but in fact theories guide our observations, decide on our set of observables, and prepare our interpretation of the data. Take, for example, the different concepts of two authors concerning Venetian cafés: For one, a Venetian café is a quiet place to read newspapers and relax with a good cup of coffee; for the other, a Venetian café is a lively place to meet and talk to people with a good cup of coffee. The first attribute of these different conceptions of a Venetian café is supported by one and the same observable, namely the noise level, although one author expects a low level, the other a high one. The second attribute is completely different: the first conception is supported by a high number of newspaper readers, the second by a high number of people talking. Accordingly, a "good" simulation would mean a different thing for each of the authors. A good simulation for one would be a poor simulation for the other and vice versa. Here, you can easily see the influence of theory on the observables. This example could just lead to an extensive discussion about the "nature" of a Venetian café between two authors, but the theory-ladenness of observations again leads to more serious difficulties. Our access to data is compromised by involving theory, with the consequence that observations are not the "bed rock elements" (Balzer et al. 1987) our theories can safely rely on. At the very base of theory is again theory. The attempt to validate our theories by "pure" theory-neutral observational concepts is mistaken from the beginning.

Balzer et al. summarise the long debate about the standard view on this issue as follows: "First, all criteria of observability proposed up to now are vulnerable to serious objections. Second, these criteria would not contribute to our task because in all advanced theories there will be no observational concepts at all—at least if we take 'observational' in the more philosophical sense of not involving any theory. Third, it can be shown that none of the concepts of an advanced theory can be defined in terms of observational concepts" (Balzer et al. 1987, p. 48). Not only can you not verify a theory by empirical observation, but you cannot even be certain about falsifying a theory. A theory is not validated by "observations" but by other theories (observational theories). Because of this reference to other theories, in fact a nested structure, the theory-ladenness of each observation has negative consequences for the completeness and self-sufficiency of scientific theories (cf. Carrier 1994, pp. 1–19). These problems apply equally to simulations that are just theories in process.

We can give examples of these difficulties in the area of social simulation. To compare Axelrod's *The Evolution of Cooperation* (Axelrod 1984) and all the subsequent work on iterated prisoners' dilemmas with the "real world", we would need to observe "real" IPDs, but this cannot be done in a theory-neutral way. The same problems arise with the growing body of work on opinion dynamics (e.g. Deffuant et al. 2000; Ben-Naim et al. 2003; Weisbuch 2004). The latter starts with some simple assumptions about how agents' opinions affect the opinions of other agents, and shows under which circumstances the result is a consensus, polarisation, or fragmentation. However, how could these results be validated against observations without involving again a considerable amount of theory?

Important features of the target might not be observable at all. We cannot, for example, observe learning. We can just use some indicators to measure the consequences of learning and assume that learning has taken place. In science simulations, the lack of observability of significant features is one of the prime motivations for carrying out a simulation in the first place.

There are also more technical problems. Validity tests should be "exercised over a full range of inputs and the outputs are observed for correctness" (Cole 2000, p. 23). However, the possibility of such testing is rejected: "real life systems have too many inputs, resulting in a combinatorial explosion of test cases". Therefore, simulations have "too many inputs/outputs to be able to test strictly" (Cole 2000, p. 23).

While this point does not refute the standard view in principle but only emphasises difficulties in execution, the former arguments reveal problems arising from the logic of validity assessment. We can try to marginalise, neglect, or even deny these problems, but this will disclose our position as mere "believers" of the standard view.

3.1.2   The Constructivist View

Validating a simulation against empirical data is not about comparing "the real world" and the simulation output; it is comparing *what you observe as the real world* with what you observe as the output. Both are constructions of an observer and his/her views concerning relevant agents and their attributes. Constructing reality and simulation are just two ways of an observer seeing the world. The issue of object formation is not normally considered by computer scientists relying on the standard view: data is "organized by a human programmer who appropriately fits them into the chosen representational structure. Usually, researchers use their prior knowledge of the nature of the problem to hand-code a representation of the data into a near-optimal form. Only after all this hand-coding is completed is the representation allowed to be manipulated by the machine. The problem of representation-formation [...] is ignored" (Chalmers et al. 1995, p. 173).

However, what happens if we question the possibility of validating a simulation by comparing it with empirical data from the "real world"? We need to refer to the modellers/observers in order to get at their different constructions. The constructivists reject the possibility of evaluation because there is no common "reality" we might refer to. This observer-oriented opponent of the realist view is a nightmare to most scientists: "Where anything goes, freedom of thought begins. And this freedom of thought consists of all people blabbering around and everybody is right as long as he does not refer to truth. Because truth is divisible like the coat of Saint Martin; everybody gets a piece of it and everybody has a nice feeling" (Droste 1994, p. 50).

Clearly, we can put some central thoughts from this view much more carefully: "In dealing with experience, in trying to explain and control it, we accept as legitimate and appropriate to experiment with different conceptual settings, to combine the flow of experience to different 'objects'" (Gellner 1990, p. 75).

However, this still leads to highly questionable consequences: There seems to be no way to distinguish between different constructions/simulations in terms of "truth", "objectivity", "validity", etc. Science is going coffeehouse: Everything is just construction, rhetoric, and arbitrary talk. Can we so easily dismiss the possibility of evaluation?

3.1.3   The User Community View

We take refuge at the place we started from: What happens if we go back to the Venetian café simulation and ask for an evaluation of its performance? It is probably the case that most customers in the Guildford Caffè Nero have never been to an Italian café. Nevertheless, they manage to "evaluate" its performance—against their concept of an Italian café that is not inspired by any "real" data. However, there is something "real" in this evaluation, namely the customers, their constructions, and a "something" out there, which everybody refers to, relying on some sort of shared meaning and having a "real" discussion about it. The philosopher Searle shows in his work on the *Construction of Social Reality* (Searle 1997) how conventions are "real": They are not deficient for the support of a relativistic approach because they are constructed.

Consensus about the "reality observed by us" is generated by an interaction process that must itself be considered real. At the base of the constructivist view is a strong reference to reality, that is, conventions and expectations that are socially created and enforced. When evaluating the Caffè Nero simulation, we can refer to the expert community (customers, owners) who use the simulation to get from it what they would expect to get from the target. A good simulation for them would satisfy the customers who want to have the "Venetian feeling" and would satisfy the owners who want to get the "Venetian profit".

For science, equally, the foundation of every validity discussion is the ordinary everyday interaction that creates an area of shared meanings and expectations. This area takes the place left open by the under-determination of theories and the theoreticity problem of the standard view.[2] Our view comes close to that of empirical epistemology, which points out that the criteria for quality assessment "do not come from some a priori standard but rest on the description of the way research is actually conducted" (Kértesz 1993, p. 32).

---

[2] Thomas Nickles claims new work opportunities for sociology at this point: "the job of philosophy is simply to lay out the necessary logico-methodological connections against which the under-determination of scientific claims may be seen; in other words, to reveal the necessity of sociological analysis. Philosophy reveals the depths of the under-determination problem, which has always been the central problem of methodology, but is powerless to do anything about it. Under-determination now becomes the province of sociologists, who see the limits of under-determination as the bounds of sociology. Sociology will furnish the contingent connections, the relations, which a priori philosophy cannot" (Nickles 1989, p. 234 f.).

If the target for a social science simulation is itself a construction, then the simulation is a *second-order* construction. In order to evaluate the simulation, we can rely on the ordinary (but sophisticated) institutions of (social) science and their practice. The actual evaluation of science comes from answers to questions such as: Do others accept the results as being coherent with existing knowledge? Do other scientists use it to support their work? Do other scientists use it to inspire their own investigations?

An example of such validity discourse in the area of social simulation is the history of the tipping model first proposed by Schelling, and now rather well known in the social simulation community. The Schelling model purports to demonstrate the reasons for the persistence of urban residential segregation in the USA and elsewhere. It consists of a grid of square cells, on which are placed agents, each either black or white. The agents have a "tolerance" for the number of agents of the other colour in the surrounding eight cells that they are content to have around them. If there are "too many" agents of the other colour, the unhappy agents move to other cells until they find a context in which there are a tolerable number of other-coloured agents. Starting with a random distribution, even with high levels of tolerance, the agents will still congregate into clusters of agents of the same colour. The point Schelling and others have taken from this model is that residential segregation will form and persist even when agents are rather tolerant.

The obvious place to undertake a realist validation of this model is a US city. One could collect data about residential mobility and, perhaps, on "tolerance". However, the exercise is harder than it looks. Even US city blocks are not all regular and square, so the real city does not look anything like the usual model grid. Residents move into the city from outside, migrate to other cities, are born and die, so the tidy picture of mobility in the model is far from the messy reality. Asking residents how many people of the other colour they would be tolerant of is also an exercise fraught with difficulty: the question is hypothetical and abstract, and answers are likely to be biased by social desirability considerations. Notwithstanding these practical methodological difficulties, some attempts have been made to verify the model. The results have not provided much support. For instance, Benenson (2005) analysed residential distribution for nine Israeli cities using census data and demonstrated that whatever the variable tested—family income, number of children, education level— there was a great deal of ethnic and economic heterogeneity within neighbourhoods, contrary to the model's predictions.

This apparent lack of empirical support has not, however, dimmed the fame of the model. The difficulty of obtaining reliable data provides a ready answer to doubts about whether the model is "really" a good representation of urban segregation dynamics. Another response has been to elaborate the model at the theoretical level. For instance, Bruch (2005) demonstrates that clustering only emerges in Schelling's model for discontinuous functional forms for residents' opinions, while data from surveys suggest that people's actual decision functions for race are continuous. She shows that using income instead of race as the sorting factor also does not lead to clustering, but if it is assumed that both race and income are significant, segregation appears. Thus, the model continues to be influential, although it has little or no empirical support, because it remains a fruitful source for theorising and for developing new models. In short, it satisfies the criterion that it is "valid" because it generates further scientific work.

Summarising the first part of this chapter, we have argued that a simulation is good when we get from it what we originally would have liked to get from the target. It is good if it works. As Glasersfeld (1987, p. 429) puts it: "Anything goes if it works". The evaluation of the simulation is guided by the expectations, anticipations and experience of the community that uses it—for practical purposes (Caffè Nero), or for intellectual understanding and for building new knowledge (science simulation).

3.2   An Example of Assessing Quality

In this part, we will apply and test the assessment mechanisms outlined using as an example our work with the simulating knowledge dynamics in innovation networks (SKIN) model in its application to research policy modelling.

There are now a number of policy-modelling studies using SKIN (Gilbert et al. 2014). We will here refer to just one recent example, on the impact, assessment and ex-ante evaluation of European funding policies in the Information and Communication Technologies (ICT) research domain (Ahrweiler et al. 2014b).

3.2.1   A Policy-Modelling Application of SKIN

The basic SKIN model has been described and discussed in detail elsewhere (e.g. Pyka et al. 2007; Gilbert et al. 2007; Ahrweiler et al. 2011). On its most general level, SKIN is an agent-based model where agents are knowledge-intensive organisations, which try to generate new knowledge by research, be it basic or applied, or creating new products and processes by innovation processes. Agents are located in a changing and complex social environment, which evaluates their performance; e.g. the market if the agents target innovation or the scientific community if the agents target publications through their research activities. Agents have various options to act: each agent has an individual knowledge base called its "kene" (cf. Gilbert 1997), which it takes as the source and basis for its research and innovation activities. The agent kene is not static: the agent can learn, either alone by doing incremental or radical research, or from others, by exchanging and improving knowledge in partnerships and networks. The latter feature is important, because research and innovation happens in networks, both in science and in knowledge-intensive industries. This is why SKIN agents have a variety of strategies and mechanisms for collaborative arrangements, i.e. for choosing partners, forming partnerships, starting knowledge collaborations, creating collaborative outputs, and distributing rewards. Summarising, usually a SKIN application has agents interacting on the knowledge level and on the social level while both levels are interconnected. It is all about knowledge and networks.

This general architecture is quite flexible, which is why the SKIN model has been called a "platform" (cf. Ahrweiler et al. 2014a), and has been used for a variety of applications ranging from the small such as simulating the Vienna biotech cluster (Korber and Paier 2014) to intermediate such as simulating the Norwegian defence industry (Castelacci et al. 2014), to large-scale applications such as the EU-funded ICT research landscape in Europe (Ahrweiler et al. 2014b). We will use the latter study as an example after explaining why the SKIN model is appropriate for realistic policy modelling in particular.

The birth of the SKIN model was inspired by the idea of bringing a theory on innovation networks, stemming mainly from innovation economics and economic sociology, onto the computer—a computer theory, which can be instantiated, calibrated, tested, and validated by empirical data. In 1998, the first EU project developing the model "Simulating Self-Organizing Innovation Networks" (SEIN) consisted of a three-step procedure: theory formation, empirical research collecting data both on the quantitative and on the case study level, and agent-based modelling implementing the theory and using the data to inform the model (Pyka et al. 2003).

This is why the SKIN model applications use empirical data and claim to be "realistic simulations" insofar as the aim is to derive conclusions by "inductive theorising". The quality of the SKIN simulation derives from an interaction between the theory underlying the simulation and the empirical data used for calibration and validation.

In what way does the SKIN model handle empirical data? We will now turn to our policy-modelling example to explain the data-to-model workflow, which is introduced in greater detail in Schilperoord and Ahrweiler (2014).

3.2.1.1 Policy Modelling for Ex-ante Evaluation of EU Funding Programmes

The INFSO-SKIN application, developed for the Directorate General Information Society and Media of the European Commission (DG INFSO), was intended to help to understand and manage the relationship between research funding and the goals of EU policy. The agents of the INFSO-SKIN application are research institutions such as universities, large diversified firms or small and medium-sized enterprises (SMEs). The model (see Fig. 3.1) simulated real-world activity in which the calls of the commission specify the composition of consortia, the minimum number of partners, and the length of the project; the deadline for submission; a range of capabilities, a sufficient number of which must appear in an eligible proposal; and the number of projects that will be funded. The rules of interaction and decision implemented in the model corresponded to Framework Programme (FP) rules; to increase the usefulness for policy designers, the names of the rules corresponded closely to FP terminology. For the Calls 1–6 that had occurred in FP7, the model used empirical information on the number of participants and the number of funded projects, together with data on project size (as measured by participant numbers), duration and average funding. Analysis of this information produced data on the functioning of, and relationships within, actual collaborative networks within the

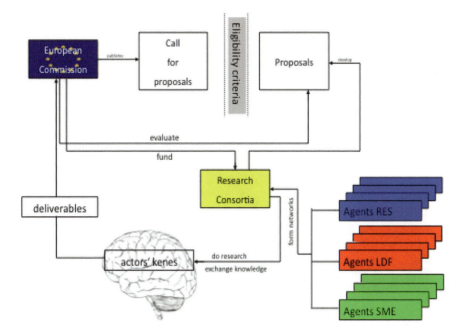

Fig. 3.1 Flowchart of INFSO-SKIN

context of the FP. Using this data in the model provided a good match with the empirical data from EU-funded ICT networks in FP7: the model accurately reflected what actually happened and could be used as a test bed for potential policy choices (cf. Ahrweiler et al. 2014b).

Altering elements of the model that equate to policy interventions, such as the amount of funding, the size of consortia, or encouraging specific sections of the research community, enabled the use of INFSO-SKIN as a tool for modelling and evaluating the results of specific interactions between policies, funding strategies and agents. Because changing parameters within the model is analogous to applying different policy options in the real world, the model could be used to examine the likely real-world effects of different policy options before they were implemented.

3.2.1.2   The Data-to-Model Workflow

The first contact with "the real world" occurred in the definition phase of the project. What do the stakeholders want to know in terms of policies for a certain research or innovation network? Identifying relevant issues, discussing interesting aspects about them, forming questions and suggesting hypotheses for potential answers formed a first important step. This step was intended to conclude with a set of questions and a corresponding set of designs for experiments using the model that could answer those questions. This was an interactive and participative process between the study team, which knew about the possibilities and limitations of the model, and the stakeholders, who could be assumed to know what are the relevant issues in their day-to-day practice of policy making.

After discussing the evaluative questions for the ex-ante evaluation part of this study with the stakeholders from DG INFSO, the following questions were singled out for experiments:

1. What if there are no changes, and funding policies of DG INFSO continued in Horizon 2020 as they were in FP7?
2. What if there are changes to the currently eight thematic areas funded in the ICT domain prioritising certain areas in Horizon 2020?
3. What if there are changes to the instruments of funding and fund larger/smaller consortia in Horizon 2020 than in FP7?
4. What if there are interventions concerning the scope or outreach of funding providing much more/much less resource to more/fewer actors?
5. What if there are interventions concerning the participation of certain actors in the network (e.g. SMEs)?

The next step (see Fig. 3.2) was to collect relevant data to address these questions and hypotheses. The issues were not different from the ones every empirical researcher is confronted with. To identify relevant variables for operationalising hypotheses, to be as simple as possible but as detailed as necessary for description and explanation, is in line with the requirements of all empirical social research. For SKIN, the most important data are about knowledge dynamics (e.g. knowledge flows, amount of knowledge, and diversity of knowledge) and their indicators (e.g. publications, patents, and innovative ideas), and about dynamics concerning actors, networks, their measures, and their performance (e.g. descriptive statistics about actors, network analysis measures, and aggregate performance data).

These data were used to calibrate the initial knowledge bases of the agents, the social configurations of agents ("starting networks"), and the configuration of an environment at a given point in time. DG INFSO provided the data needed to calibrate the knowledge bases of the agents (in this case the research organisations in the European research area), the descriptive statistics on agents and networks and their interactions (in this case data on funded organisations and projects in ICT under FP7).

The time series data were used to validate the simulations by comparing the empirical data with the simulation outputs. Once we were satisfied with the model performance in that respect, experiments were conducted and the artificially produced data analysed and interpreted. The stakeholders were again invited to provide their feedback and suggestions about how to finetune and adapt the study to their changing user requirements as the study proceeded.

The last step was again stakeholder-centred as it involved visualisation and communication of data and results. We had to prove the credibility of the work and the commitment of the stakeholders to the policy-modelling activity.

We worked from an already existing application of the SKIN model adapted to the European research area (Scholz et al. 2010), implemented the scenarios according

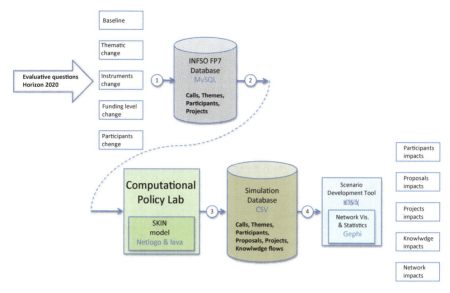

Fig. 3.2 Horizon 2020 study workflow (Schilperoord and Ahrweiler 2014). First (on the *left*), a set of issues was isolated, in discussion with stakeholders. Data describing the network of FP7 projects and participants, by theme and Call, obtained from DG INFSO were entered into a database. These data were used to calibrate the INFSO-SKIN model. This model was then used to generate simulated data under various policy options. The simulated data were fed into a second database and visualised using additional network visualisation and statistical software in order to assess the expected impacts of those policy options

to the evaluative questions, and produced artificial data as output of the simulations. The results are reported in the final report presented to the European Cabinet, and were communicated to the stakeholders at DG INFSO.

3.2.2   The INFSO-SKIN Example as Seen by the Standard View

The standard view refers to *verification*, namely whether the code does what it is supposed to do, and *validation*, namely whether the outputs (for given inputs/parameters) sufficiently resemble observations of the target. To aid in verifying the model, it was completely recoded in another programming language and the two implementations cross-checked to ensure that they generated the same outputs given the same inputs.

To enable validation of the model, we needed to create a simulation resembling the stakeholders' own world as they perceived it. The simulation needed to create the effect of similar complexity, similar structures and processes, and similar objects and options for interventions. To be under this *similarity threshold* would have led to the rejection of the model as a "toy model" that is not realistic and is under-determined by empirical data.

In the eyes of these stakeholders, the more features of the model that can be validated against empirical data points, the better. Of course, there will always be an empirical "under-determination" of the model due to the necessary selection and abstraction process of model construction, empirical unobservables, missing data for observables, random features of the model, and so on. However, to find the "right" trade-off between empirical under-determination and model credibility was a crucial issue in the discussions between the study team and the stakeholders.

3.2.3   The INFSO-SKIN Example as Seen by the Constructivist View

The strength of a modelling methodology lies in the opportunity to ask what-if questions (ex-ante evaluation), an option that is normally not easily available in the policy-making world. INFSO-SKIN uses scenario modelling as a worksite for "reality constructions", in line with Gellner's statement quoted above about the constructivist approach: "In dealing with experience, in trying to explain and control it, we accept as legitimate and appropriate to experiment with different conceptual settings, to combine the flow of experience to different 'objects'" (Gellner 1990, p. 75). Scenario modelling was employed in the study both for the impact assessment of existing funding policies, where we measured the impact of policy measures by experimenting with different scenarios where these policies are absent, changed or meet different conditions, and for ex-ante evaluation, where we developed a range of potential futures for the European Research Area in ICT by asking what-if questions.

These are in-silico experiments that construct potential futures. Is this then a relativist approach where "anything goes", because everything is just a construction? For the general aspects of this question, we refer to Part I of this article. There we talk about the "reality requirements" of the constructivist approach, which mediates its claims. For the limits of constructivist ideas applied to SKIN, we refer to Sect. 2.1.

3.2.4   The INFSO-SKIN Example as Seen by the User Community View

The user community view is the most promising, although the most work-intensive mechanism to assess the quality of this policy-modelling exercise.

3.2.4.1   Identifying User Questions

In our example, SKIN was applied to a tender study with a clear client demand behind it, where the questions the simulation needs to answer were more or less predefined from the onset of the project. Enough time should, however, be dedicated to identifying and discussing the exact set of questions the stakeholders of the work want to see addressed. We found that the best way to do this is applying an iterative process of communication between study team and clients, where stakeholders learn about the scope and applicability of the methods, and where researchers get acquainted with the problems policy makers have to solve and with the kind of decisions for which sound background information is needed. This iterative process should result in an agreed set of questions for the simulation, which will very often decisively differ from the set proposed at the start of the study. In our example, the so-called "steering committee" was assigned to us by the European Commission consisting of policy makers and evaluation experts of DG INFSO.

There are various difficulties and limitations to overcome in identifying user questions. In the case of the DG INFSO study, although the questions under study were outlined in the Tender Specifications in great detail, this was a complicated negotiation process where the stakeholder group:

- Had to find out about the exact nature and direction of their questions while they talked to the study team;
- Had questioned the original set of the Tender Specifications in the meantime and negotiated among each other for an alternative set;
- Did not share the same opinion about what questions should be in the final sample, and how potential questions should be ranked in importance;
- Did not share the same hypotheses about questions in the final sample.

The specification of evaluative questions might be the first time stakeholders talk to each other and discuss their viewpoints.

What is the process for identifying user questions for policy modelling? In the INFSO-SKIN application, the following mechanism was used by the study team and proved to be valuable:

- Scan written project specification by client (in this case the Tender Specifications of DG INFSO) and identify the original set of questions;
- Do a literature review and context analysis for each question (policy background, scope, meaning, etc.) to inform the study team;
- Meet stakeholders to get their views on written project specifications and their view on the context of questions; inform the stakeholders about what the model is about, what it can and cannot do; discuss until stakeholder group and study team is "on the same page";
- Evaluate the meeting and revise original set of questions if necessary (probably an iterative process between study team and different stakeholders individually where study team acts as coordinator and mediator of the process);
- Meet stakeholders to discuss the final set of questions, get their written consent on this, and get their hypotheses concerning potential answers and potential ways to address the questions;
- Evaluate the meeting and develop experiments that are able to operationalise the hypotheses and address the questions;

- Meet stakeholders and get their feedback and consent that the experiments meet questions/hypotheses;
- Evaluate the meeting and refine the experimental setup concerning the final set of questions.

This negotiation and discussion process is highly user-driven, interactive, and iterative. It requires communicative skills, patience, willingness to compromise on both sides, and motivation to make both ends meet—the formal world of modellers and the narrative world of policy making in practice. The process is highly time-consuming. In our example, we needed about 6 months of a 12-month-contract research study to get to satisfactory results on this first step.

3.2.4.2   Getting Their Best: Users Need to Provide Data

The study team will know best what types of empirical data are needed to inform the policy modelling. In SKIN, data availability is an important issue, because the findings need to be evidence-based and realistic. This is in the best interest of the stakeholders, who need to trust the findings. This will be the more likely to the extent that the simulated data resembles the empirical data known to the user (see Sect. 2.1). However, the study team might discover that the desired data is not available, either because it does not exist or because it is not willingly released by the stakeholders or whoever holds it.

In our example, the stakeholders were data collectors on a big scale themselves. The evaluation unit of DG INFSO employs a data collection group, which provides information about funded projects and organisations at a detailed level. Furthermore, the DG is used to provide data to the study teams of the projects they contract for their evaluation projects. Consequently we benefitted from having a large and clean database concerning all issues the study team was interested in. However, it was still an issue to confirm the existence, quality and availability of the data and check for formats and database requirements. Even if the data is there in principal, enough time should be reserved for data management issues. The quality of the simulation in the eyes of the user will very much depend on the quality of the informing data and the quality of the model calibration.

What would have been the more common process if the study team had not struck lucky as in our example? In other SKIN applications, the following mechanism was used by the study team and proved to be valuable (the ones with asterisks apply to our INFSO-SKIN example as well):

- Identify the rough type of data required for the study from the project specifications
- Estimate financial resources for data access in the proposal of project to stakeholders (this can sometimes happen in interaction with the funding body);
- After the second meeting with stakeholders (see Sect. 2.3.1), identify relevant data concerning variables to answer study questions and address/test hypotheses of Sect. 2.3.1*;

- Communicate exact data requirements to those stakeholders who are experts on their own empirical data environment*;
- Review existing data bases including the ones stakeholders might hold or can get access to*;
- Meet stakeholders to discuss data issues; help them understand and agree on the scope and limitations of data access*;
- If needed and required by stakeholders, collect data;
- Meet stakeholders to discuss the final database;
- Evaluate the meeting and develop data-to-model procedures*.

3.2.4.3 Interacting with Users to Check the Validity of Simulation Results

The stakeholders put heavy demands on the study team concerning understanding and trusting the simulation findings. The first and most important is that the clients want to understand the model. To trust results means to trust the process that produced them. Here, the advantage of the adapted SKIN model is that it relies on a narrative that tells the story of the users' every-day world of decision-making (see Sect. 2.1.1). In the SKIN model, a good example for "reality" requirements is the necessity to model the knowledge and behaviour of agents. Blackboxing knowledge of agents or creating merely reactive simple agents would not have been an option, because stakeholders do not think the world works that way.

The SKIN model is based on empirical quantitative and qualitative research in innovation economics, sociology, science and technology studies, and business studies. Agents and behaviours are informed by what we know about them; the model is calibrated by data from this research. We found that there is a big advantage in having a model where stakeholders can recognise the relevant features they see at work in their social contexts. In setting up and adapting the model to study needs, stakeholders can actively intervene and ask for additional agent characteristics or behavioural rules; they can refine the model and inform blackbox areas where they have information on the underlying processes.

However, here again, we encountered the diversity of stakeholder preferences. Different members of the DG INFSO Steering Committee opted for different changes and modifications of the model. Some were manageable with given time constraints and financial resources; some would have outlived the duration of the project if realised. The final course of action for adapting the model to study needs was the result of discussions between stakeholders about model credibility and increasing complexity and of discussions between stakeholders and the study team concerning feasibility and reducing complexity.

Once the stakeholders were familiar with the features of the model and had contributed to its adaptation to study requirements, there was an initial willingness to trust model findings. This was strengthened by letting the model reproduce FP7 data as the baseline scenario that all policy experiments would be benchmarked against. If the networks created by real life and those created by the agent-based model correspond closely, the simulation experiments can be characterized as history-friendly experiments, which reproduce the empirical data and cover the decisive mechanisms and resulting dynamics of the real networks (see standard view).

In presenting the results of the INFSO-SKIN study, however, it became clear that there were, again, certain caveats coming from the user community. The policy analysts did not want to look at a multitude of tables and scan through endless numbers of simulation results for interesting parameters; nor did they expect to watch the running model producing its results, because a typical run lasted 48 hours. Presenting results in an appealing and convincing way required visualisations and interactive methods where users could intuitively understand what they see, had access to more detailed information if wanted, e.g. in a hyperlink structure, and could decide themselves in which format, in which order and in which detail they want to go through findings. This part of the process still needs further work: new visualisation and interactive technologies can help to make simulation results more accessible to stakeholders.

This leads to the last issue to be discussed in this section. What happens after the credibility of simulation results is established? In the INFSO-SKIN study, the objective was policy advice for Horizon 2020. The stakeholders wanted the study team to communicate the results as "recommendations" rather than as "findings". They required a so-called "utility summary" that included statements about what they should do in their policy domain justified according to the results of the study. Here the study team proved to be hesitant—not due to a lack of confidence in their model, but due to the recognition of its predictive limitations and a reluctance to formulate normative statements, which were seen as a matter of political opinion and not a responsibility of a scientific advisor. The negotiation of the wording in the Utility Summary was another instance of an intense dialogue between stakeholders and study team. Nevertheless, the extent to which the results influenced or were somehow useful in the actual political process of finalising Horizon 2020 policies was not part of the stakeholder feedback after the study ended and is still not known to us. The feedback consisted merely of a formal approval that we had fulfilled the project contract.

3.3 Conclusions

To trust the quality of a simulation means to trust the process that produced its results. This process is not only the one incorporated in the simulation model itself. It is the whole interaction between stakeholders, study team, model, and findings.

The first section of this contribution pointed out the problems of the Standard View and the *constructivist view* in evaluating social simulations. We argued that a simulation is good when we get from it what we originally would have liked to get from the target; in this, the evaluation of the simulation would be guided by the expectations, anticipations, and experience of the community that uses it. This makes the user community view the most promising mechanism to assess the quality of a policy-modelling exercise.

The second section looked at a concrete policy-modelling example to test this idea. It showed that the very first negotiation and discussion with the user community to identify their questions were highly user-driven, interactive, and iterative. It required communicative skills, patience, willingness to compromise on both sides, and motivation to link the formal world of modellers and the narrative world of policy making in practice.

Often, the user community is involved in providing data for calibrating the model. It is not an easy issue to confirm the existence, quality, and availability of the data and check for formats and database requirements. Because the quality of the simulation in the eyes of the user will depend on the quality of the informing data and the quality of the model calibration, much time and effort need to be spent in coordinating this issue with the user community.

Last but not least, the user community has to check the validity of simulation results and has to believe in their quality. Users have to be helped to understand the model, to agree with its processes and ways to produce results, to judge similarity between empirical and simulated data, etc.

The standard view is epistemologically questionable due to the two problems of under-determination of theory and of theory-ladenness of observations; the constructivist view is difficult due to its inherent relativism, which annihilates its own validity claims. The user community view relies on social model building and model assessment practices and, in a way, bridges the two other views, because it rests on the realism of these practices. This is why we advocate its quality assessment mechanisms.

Summarising, in our eyes, the user community view might be the most promising, but is definitely the most work-intensive mechanism to assess the quality of a simulation. It all depends on who the user community is and whom it consists of: if there is more than one member, the user community will never be homogenous. It is difficult to refer to a "community", if people have radically different opinions.

Furthermore, there are all sorts of practical contingencies to deal with. People might not be interested, or they might not be willing or able to dedicate as much of their time and attention to the study as needed. There is also the time dimension: the users at the end of a simulation project might not be the same as those who initiated it, as a result of job changes, resignations, promotions, and organisational restructuring. Moreover, the user community and the simulation modellers may affect each other, with the modellers helping in some ways to construct a user community in order to solve the practical contingencies that get in the way of assessing the quality of the simulation, while the user community may in turn have an effect on the modellers (not least in terms of influencing the financial and recognition rewards the modellers receive).

If trusting the quality of a simulation indeed means trusting the process that produced its results, then we need to address the entire interaction process between user community, researchers, data, model, and findings as the relevant assessment mechanism. Researchers have to be aware that they are codesigners of the mechanisms they need to participate in with the user community for assessing the quality of a social simulation.

References

Ahrweiler P, Gilbert N (2005) Caffe Nero: the evaluation of social simulation. J Artif Soc Soc Simul 8(4):14

Ahrweiler P, Pyka A, Gilbert N (2011) A New model for university-industry links in knowledge-based economies. J Prod Innov Manag 28:218–235

Ahrweiler P, Schilperoord M, Pyka A, Gilbert N (2014a, forthcoming): Testing policy options for horizon 2020 with SKIN. In: Gilbert N, Ahrweiler P, Pyka A (eds) Simulating knowledge dynamics in innovation networks. Springer, Heidelberg

Ahrweiler P, Pyka A, Gilbert N (2014b, forthcoming): Simulating knowledge dynamics in innovation networks: an introduction. In: Gilbert N, Ahrweiler P, Pyka A (eds) Simulating knowledge dynamics in innovation networks. Springer, Heidelberg

Axelrod R (1984) The evolution of cooperation. Basic Books, New York

Balzer W, Moulines CU, Sneed JD (1987) An architectonic for science. The structuralist program. Reidel, Dordrecht

Baudrillard J (1988) Jean Baudrillard selected writings. Polity Press, Cambridge

Ben-Naim E, Krapivsky P, Redner S (2003) Bifurcations and patterns in compromise processes. Phys D 183:190–204

Benenson I (2005) The city as a human-driven system. Paper presented at the workshop on modelling urban social dynamics. University of Surrey, Guildford, April 2005.

Bruch E (2005) Dynamic models of neighbourhood change. Paper presented at the workshop on modelling urban social dynamics. University of Surrey, Guildford, April 2005.

Carrier M (1994) The completeness of scientific theories. On the derivation of empirical indicators within a theoretical framework: the case of physical geometry. Kluwer, Dordrecht

Castelacci F, Fevolden A, Blom M (2014) R & D policy support and industry concentration: a SKIN model analysis of the European defence industry. In: Gilbert N, Ahrweiler P, Pyka A (eds) Simulating knowledge dynamics in innovation networks. Heidelberg, Springer

Chalmers D, French R, Hofstadter D (1995) High-level perception, representation, and analogy. In: Hofstadter D (ed) Fluid concepts and creative analogies. Basic Books, New York, pp 165–191

Cole O (2000) White-box testing. Dr. Dobb's Journal, March 2000, pp 23–28

Deffuant G, Neau D, Amblard F, Weisbuch G (2000) Mixing beliefs among interacting agents. Advances in complex systems. Adv Complex Syst 3:87–98

Doran J, Gilbert N (1994) Simulating Societies: an Introduction. In: Doran J, Gilbert N (eds) Simulating societies: the computer simulation of social phenomena. UCL Press, London, pp 1–18

Droste W (1994) Sieger sehen anders aus (Winners look different). Schulenburg, Hamburg

Gellner E (1990) Pflug, Schwert und Buch. Grundlinie der Menschheitsgeschichte (Plough, Sword and Book. Foundations of human history). Klett-Cotta, Stuttgart

Gilbert N (1997) A simulation of the structure of academic science, Sociological Research Online 2(1997). http://www.socresonline.org.uk/socresonline/2/2/3.html

Gilbert N, Troitzsch K (1997) Simulation for the social scientist. Open University Press, Buckingham

Gilbert N, Ahrweiler P, Pyka A (2007) Learning in innovation networks: some simulation experiments. Phys A: Stat Mech Appl 378(1):667–693

Gilbert N, Ahrweiler P, Pyka A (eds) (2014, forthcoming) Simulating knowledge dynamics in innovation networks. Springer, Heidelberg

Glasersfeld E von (1987) Siegener Gespräche über Radikalen Konstruktivismus (Siegen Discussions on Radical Constructivism). In: Schmidt SJ (ed) Der Diskurs des Radikalen Konstruktivismus. Suhrkamp, Frankfurt a. M., pp 401–440

Harbodt S (1974) Computer simulationen in den Sozialwissenschaften (Computer simulations in the social sciences). Rowohlt, Reinbek

Kértesz A (1993) Artificial intelligence and the sociology of scientific knowledge. Lang, Frankfurt, a. M.

Korber M, Paier M (2014) Simulating the effects of public funding on research in life sciences: direct research funds versus tax incentives. In: Gilbert N, Ahrweiler P, Pyka A (eds) Simulating knowledge dynamics in innovation networks. Springer, Heidelberg

Nickles T (1989) entegrating the science studies disciplines. In: Fuller S, de Mey M, Shinn T, Woolgar S (eds) The cognitive turn. Sociological and psychological perspectives on science. Kluwer, Dordrecht, pp 225–256

Norris C (1992) Uncritical theory. Lawrence and Wishart, London

Pyka A, Gilbert N, Ahrweiler P (2003) Simulating Innovation networks. In: Pyka A, Küppers G (eds) Innovation networks—theory and practice. Edward Elgar, Cheltenham, pp 169–198

Pyka A, Gilbert N, Ahrweiler P (2007) Simulating knowledge generation and distribution processes in innovation collaborations and networks. Cybern Syst 38(7):667–693

Quine W (1977) Ontological relativity. Columbia University Press, Columbia

Schilperoord M, Ahrweiler P (2014, forthcoming) Towards a prototype policy laboratory for simulating innovation networks. In: Gilbert N, Ahrweiler P, Pyka A (eds) Simulating knowledge dynamics in innovation networks. Springer, Heidelberg

Scholz R, Nokkala T, Ahrweiler P, Pyka A, Gilbert N (2010) The agent-based NEMO model (SKEIN): simulating European Framework programmes. In: Ahrweiler P (ed) Innovation in complex social systems, Routledge studies in global competition. Routledge, London, pp 300–314

Searle J (1997) The construction of social reality. Free Press, New York

Weisbuch G (2004) Bounded confidence and social networks. Special Issue: application of complex networks in biological information and physical systems. Eur Phys JB 38:339–343

Chapter 4
Policy Making and Modelling in a Complex World

Wander Jager and Bruce Edmonds

Abstract In this chapter, we discuss the consequences of complexity in the real world together with some meaningful ways of understanding and managing such situations. The implications of such complexity are that many social systems are unpredictable by nature, especially when in the presence of structural change (transitions). We shortly discuss the problems arising from a too-narrow focus on quantification in managing complex systems. We criticise some of the approaches that ignore these difficulties and pretend to predict using simplistic models. However, lack of predictability does not automatically imply a lack of managerial possibilities. We will discuss how some insights and tools from "complexity science" can help with such management. Managing a complex system requires a good understanding of the dynamics of the system in question—to know, before they occur, some of the real possibilities that might occur and be ready so they can be reacted to as responsively as possible. Agent-based simulation will be discussed as a tool that is suitable for this task, and its particular strengths and weaknesses for this are discussed.

4.1 Introduction

Some time ago, one of us (WJ) attended a meeting of specialists in the energy sector. A former minister was talking about the energy transition, advocating for directing this transition; I sighed, because I realized that the energy transition, involving a multitude of interdependent actors and many unforeseen developments, would make a planned direction of such a process a fundamental impossibility. Yet I decided not to interfere, since my comment would have required a mini lecture on the management of complex systems, and in the setting of this meeting this would have required too much time. So the speaker went on, and one of the listeners stood up and asked, "But

W. Jager (✉)
Groningen Center of Social Complexity Studies, University Groningen, Groningen,
The Netherlands
e-mail: w.jager@rug.nl

B. Edmonds
Manchester Metropolitan University, Manchester, UK

© Springer International Publishing Switzerland 2015   57
M. Janssen et al. (eds.), *Policy Practice and Digital Science,*
Public Administration and Information Technology 10, DOI 10.1007/978-3-319-12784-2_4

Fig. 4.1 Double pendulum.
(Source: Wikipedia)

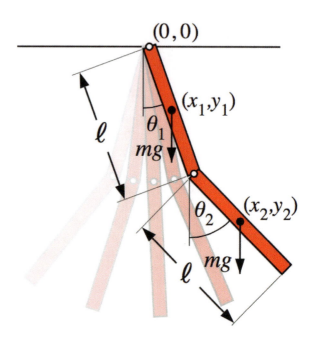

sir, what if the storage capacity of batteries will drastically improve?" The speakers
answered, "this is an uncertainty we cannot include in our models, so in our transition
scenarios we don't include such events". This remark made clear that, in many cases,
policymakers are not aware of the complexities in the systems they operate in, and are
not prepared to deal with surprises in systems. Because the transitional idea is being
used very frequently to explain wide-ranging changes related to the transformation
of our energy system, and the change towards a sustainable society, it seems relevant
to address the issue of complexity in this chapter, and discuss the implications for
policy making in complex behaving system. After explaining what complexity is,
we will discuss the common mistakes being made in managing complex systems.
Following that, we will discuss the use of models in policy making, specifically
addressing agent-based models because of their capacity to model social complex
systems that are often being addressed by policy.

4.2   What is Complexity?

The word "complexity" can be used to indicate a variety of kinds of difficulties.
However, the kind of complexity we are specifically dealing with in this chapter
is where a system is composed of multiple interacting elements whose possible
behavioural states can combine in ways that are hard to predict or characterise. One
of the simplest examples is that of a double pendulum (Fig 4.1).

Although only consisting of a few parts connected by joints, it has complex and unpredictable behaviour when set swinging under gravity. If this pendulum is released,
it will move chaotically due to the interactions between the upper (θ_1) and lower (θ_2)
joint. Whereas it is possible to formally represent this simple system in detail, e.g.
including aspects such as air pressure, friction in the hinge, the exact behaviour of
the double pendulum is unpredictable.[1] This is due to the fundamental uncertainty
of the precise position of its parts[2] and the unsolvability of the three-body problem as
proven by Bruns and Poincaré in 1887. Just after release, its motion is predictable to
a considerable degree of accuracy, but then starts to deviate from any prediction until
it is moving in a different manner. Whereas the precise motion at these stages is not
predictable, we know that after a while, the swinging motion will become less erratic,
and ultimately it will hang still (due to friction). This demonstrates that even in very
simple physical systems, interactions may give rise to complex behaviour, expressed
in different types of behaviour, ranging from very stable to chaotic. Obviously, many
physical systems are much more complicated, such as our atmospheric system. As
can be expected, biological or social systems also display complex behaviour because they are composed of large numbers of interacting agents. Also, when such
systems are described by a simple set of equations, complex behaviour may arise.
This is nicely illustrated by the "logistic equation", which was originally introduced
as a simple model of biological populations in a situation of limited resources (May
1976). Here the population, x, in the next year (expressed as a proportion of its maximum possible) is determined based on the corresponding value in the last year as
$rx(1-x)$, where r is a parameter (the rate of unrestrained population increase). Again,
this apparently simple model leads to some complex behaviour. Figure 4.2 shows
the possible long-term values of x for different values of r, showing that increasing
r creates more possible long-term states for x. Where on the left hand side ($r < 3.0$)
the state of x is fixed, at higher levels the number of possible states increases with
the number of states increasing rapidly until, for levels of r above 3.6, almost any
state can occur, indicating a chaotic situation. In this case, although the system may
be predictable under some circumstances (low r), in others it will not be (higher r).

What is remarkable is that, despite the inherent unpredictability of their environment, organisms have survived and developed intricate webs of interdependence in
terms of their ecologies. This is due to the adaptive capacity of organisms, allowing
them to self-organise. It is exactly this capacity of organisms to adapt to changing circumstances (learning) that differentiates 'regular' complex systems from 'complex
adaptive systems' (CAS). Hence complex adaptive systems have a strong capacity
to self-organise, which can be seen in, i.e. plant growth, the structure of ant nests
and the organisation of human society. Yet these very systems have been observed
to exist in both stable and unstable stages, with notable transitions between these

---

[1] Obviously predictions can always be made, but it has been proved analytically that the predictive
value of models is zero in these cases.
[2] Even if one could measure them with extreme accuracy, there would never be complete accuracy
due to the uncertainty theorem of Heisenberg (1927).

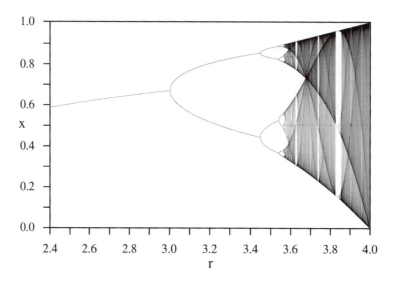

Fig. 4.2 Bifurcation diagram. (Source: Wikipedia)

stages. Ecological science has observed that major transitions in ecological systems towards a different regime (transition) are often preceded by increased variances, slower recovery from small perturbations (critical slowing down) and increased return times (Boettiger and Hastings 2012; Dai and Vorselen et al. 2012; Dakos and Carpenter et al. 2012). A classic example here is that of the transition from a clear lake to a turbid state due to eutrophication. Here an increase in mineral and organic nutrients in the water gives rise to the growth of plants, in particular algae. In the stage preceding to a transition, short periods of increased algal blooms may occur, decreasing visibility and oxygen levels, causing the population of top predating fish hunting on eyesight to decrease, causing a growth in populations of other species, etc. The increased variance (e.g. in population levels of different species in the lake) indicates that a regime shift is near, and that the lake may radically shift from a clear state to a turbid state with a complete different ecosystem, with an attendant loss of local species.

The hope is that for other complex systems, such indicators may also identify the approach of a tipping point and a regime shift or transition (Scheffer et al. 2009). For policy making, this is a relevant perspective, as it helps in understanding what a transition or regime shift is, and has implications for policy development. A transition implies a large-scale restructuring of a system that is composed of many interacting parts. As such, the energy system and our economy at large are examples of complex systems where billions of actors are involved, and a large number of stakeholders such as companies and countries are influencing each other. The transformation from, for example, a fossil fuel-based economy towards a sustainable energy system requires that many actors that depend on each other have to simultaneously change their behaviour. An analogy with the logistic process illustrated in Fig. 4.2 can be made.

Imagine a move from the lower stable situation $x = 0.5$ at $r = 3.3$ to the upper stable situation $x = 0.8$. This could be achieved by increasing the value of r, moving towards the more turbulent regime of the system and then reducing r again, allowing the new state to be settled into. This implies that moving from one stable regime towards another stable regime may require a period of turbulence where the transition can happen. Something like a period of turbulence demarcating regime shifts is what seems to have occurred during many transitions in the history of the world.

4.3 Two Common Mistakes in Managing Complex Systems

Turbulent stages in social systems are usually experienced as gruesome by policy-makers and managers. Most of them prefer to have grip on a situation, and try to develop and communicate a clear perspective on how their actions will affect future outcomes. Especially in communicating the rationale of their decisions to the outside world, the complex nature of social systems is often lost. It is neither possible nor particularly useful to try and list all of the "mistakes" that policymakers might make in the face of complex systems, but two of the ways in which systems are oversimplified are *quantification* and *compartmentalisation*.

Quantification implies that policy is biased towards those attributes of a system that are easy to quantify. Hence, it comes as no surprise that economic outcomes, in terms of money, are often the dominating criteria in evaluating policy. Often, this results in choosing a solution that will result in the best financial economic outcome. Whereas non-quantifiable outcomes are often acknowledged, usually the bottom line is that "we obviously have to select the most economical viable option" because "money can be spent only once". In such a case, many other complex and qualitative outcomes might be undervalued or even ignored since the complex system has been reduced to easily measurable quantities. In many situations, this causes resistance to policies, because the non-quantifiable outcomes often have an important impact on the quality of life of people. An example would be the recent earthquakes in the north of the Netherlands due to the extraction of natural gas, where the policy perspective was mainly focussing on compensating the costs of damage to housing, whereas the population experienced a loss of quality of life due to fear and feelings of unfair treatment by the government, qualities that are hard to quantify and were undervalued in the discussion. The more complex a system is, the more appealing it seems to be to get a grip on the decision context by quantifying the problem, often in economical terms. Hence, in many complex problems, e.g. related to investments in sustainable energy, the discussion revolves around returns on investment, whereas other relevant qualities, whereas being acknowledged, lose importance because they cannot be included in the complicated calculations. Further, the ability to encapsulate and manipulate number-based representations in mathematics may give such exercises an appearance of being scientific and hence reinforce the impression that the situation is under control. However, what has happened here is a conflation of indicators with the overall quality of the goals and outcomes themselves. Indicators may well be useful to help judge goals and outcomes; but in complex situations, it is rare that such a judgement can be reduced to such simple dimensions.

Compartimentalization is a second response of many policymakers in trying to simplify complex social systems. This is a strategy whereby a system or organisation is split into different parts that act (to a large extent) independently of each other as separated entities, with their own goals and internal structures. As a consequence, the policy/management organization will follow the structure of its division into parts. Being responsible for one part of the system implies that a bias emerges towards optimizing the performance of the own part. This is further stimulated by rewarding managers for the performance of the subsystem they are responsible for, independently of the others. However, this approach makes it difficult to account for *spillover effects* towards other parts of the system, particularly when the outcomes in related parts of the system are more difficult to quantify. An example would be the savings on health care concerning psychiatric care. Reducing the number of maximum number of consults being covered by health insurance resulted in a significant financial savings in health care nationally. However, as a result, more people in need of psychiatric help could not afford this help, and, as a consequence, may have contributed to an increase in problems such as street crime, annoyance, and deviant behaviour. Because these developments are often qualitative in nature, hard numbers are not available, and hence these effects are more being debated than actually being included in policy development. Interestingly, due to this compartmentalisation, the direct financial savings due to the reduction of the insurance conditions may be surpassed by the additional costs made in various other parts as the system such as policing, costs of crime, and increased need for crisis intervention. Thus, the problems of quantification and compartmentalisation can exacerbate each other: A quantitative approach may facilitate compartmentalisation since it makes measurement of each compartment easier and if one takes simple indicates *as* one's goals, then it is tempting to reduce institutional structures to separate compartments that can concentrate on these narrow targets. We coin the term "Excellification"—after Microsoft Excel—to express the tendency to use quantitative measurements and compartmentalise systems in getting a grip on systems.

Whereas we are absolutely convinced of the value of using measurements in developing and evaluating policy/management, it is our stance that policy making in complex systems is requiring a deeper level of understanding the processes that guide the developments in the system at hand. When trying to steer policy in the face of a complex and dynamic situation, there are essentially two kinds of strategies being used in developing this understanding: *instrumental* and *representational*. We look at these next, before we discuss how agent-based modelling may contribute to understanding and policy making in complex systems.

4.4 Complexity and Policy Making

An instrumental approach is where one chooses between a set of possible policies and then evaluates them according to some assessment of their past effectiveness.

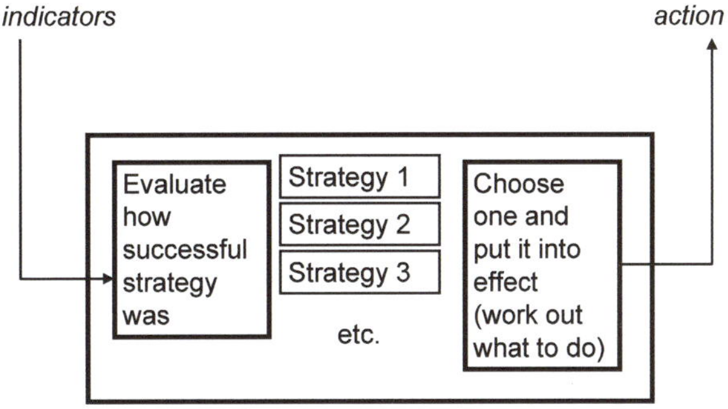

Fig. 4.3 An illustration of the instrumental approach

indicators   *action*

Evaluate how successful strategy was	Strategy 1 Strategy 2 Strategy 3 etc.	Choose one and put it into effect (work out what to do)

In future iterations, one then adapts and/or changes the chosen policy in the light of its track record. The idea is illustrated in Fig. 4.3. This can be a highly adaptive approach, reacting rapidly in the light of the current effectiveness of different strategies. No initial knowledge is needed for this approach, but rather the better strategies develop over time, given feedback from the environment. Maybe, the purest form of this is the "blind variation and selective retention" of Campbell (1960), where new variants of strategies are produced (essentially) at random, and those that work badly are eliminated, as in biological evolution. The instrumental approach works better when: there is a sufficient range of strategies to choose between, there is an effective assessment of their efficacy, and the iterative cycle of trial and assessment is rapid and repeated over a substantial period of time. The instrumental approach is often used by practitioners who might develop a sophisticated "menu" of what strategies seem to work under different sets of circumstances.

An example of this might be adjusting the level of some policy instrument such as the level of tolls that are designed to reduce congestion on certain roads. If there is still too much congestion, the toll might be raised; if there is too little usage, the toll might be progressively lowered.

The representational approach is a little more complicated. One has a series of "models" of the environment. The models are assessed by their ability to predict/mirror observed aspects of the environment. The best model is then used to evaluate possible actions in terms of an evaluation of the predicted outcomes from those actions and the one with the best outcome chosen to enact. Thus, there are two "loops" involved: One in terms of working out predictions of the models and seeing which best predicts what is observed, and the second is a loop of evaluating possible actions using the best model to determine which action to deploy. Figure 4.4 illustrates this approach. The task of developing, evaluating, and changing the models is an expensive one, so the predictive power of these models needs to be weighed against this cost. Also, the time taken to develop the models means that this approach is often slower to adapt to changes in the environment than a corresponding instrumental approach. However, one significant advantage of this approach is that, as a result of the models, one might have a good idea of *why* certain things were happening in the environment, and hence know which models might be more helpful,

Fig. 4.4 An illustration of the representational approach

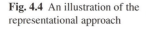

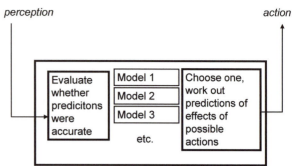

as well as allowing for the development of longer term strategies addressing the root causes of such change. The representational approach is the one generally followed by scientists because they are interested in understanding what is happening.

An example of the representational approach might be the use of epidemiological models to predict the spread of an animal disease, given different containment/mitigation strategies to deal with the crisis. The models are used to predict the outcomes of various strategies, which can inform the choice of strategy. This prediction can be useful even if the models are being improved, at the same time, due to the new data coming in because of the events.

Of course, these two approaches are frequently mixed. For example, representational models might be used to constrain which strategies are considered within an otherwise instrumental approach (even if the representational models themselves are not very good at prediction). If a central bank is considering what interest rate to set, there is a certain amount of trial and error: thus, exactly how low one has to drop the interest rates to get an economy going might be impossible to predict, and one just has to progressively lower them until the desired effect achieved. However, some theory will also be useful: thus, one would know that dropping interest rates would not be the way to cool an over-heating economy. Thus, even very rough models with relatively poor predictive ability (such as "raising interest rates tends to reduce the volume of economic activity and lowering them increases it") can be useful.

Complexity theory is useful for the consideration of policy in two different ways. *First*, it can help provide representational models that might be used to constrain the range of strategies under consideration and, *second,* can help inform second-order considerations concerning the ways in which policy might be developed and/or adopted—the policy adaption process itself. In the following section, we first look at the nature and kinds of models so as to inform their best use within the policy modelling, and later look at how second-order considerations may inform *how* we might use such models.

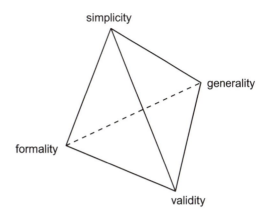

Fig. 4.5 An illustration in some of the opposing desiderata of models

4.4.1   Using Formal Models in Policy Making

The use of models in policy making starts with the question—what the appropriate policy models are? Many models are often available because (1) improving models following the representational approach will yield series of models that further improve the representation of the process in terms of cause–effect relations, and (2) sometimes more extended models are required for explaining a process, whereas often simpler models are used to represent a particular behaviour.

Realising that many models are often available, we still have to keep in mind that any *model* is an abstraction. A *useful model* is necessarily simpler than what it represents, so that much is left out—abstracted away. However, the decision as to what needs to be represented in a model and what can be safely left out is a difficult one. Some models will be useful in some circumstances and useless in others. Also, a model that is useful for one purpose may well be useless for another. Many of the problems associated with the use of models to aid the formulation and steering of policy derive from an assumption that a model will have value per se, independent of context and purpose.

One of the things that affect the uses to which models can be put is the compromise that went into the formulation of the models. Figure 4.5 illustrates some of these tensions in a simple way.

These illustrated desiderata refer to a model that is being used. *Simplicity* is how simple the model is, the extent to which the model itself can be completely understood. Analytically solvable mathematical models, most statistical models, and abstract simulation models are at the relatively simple end of the spectrum. Clearly, a simple model has many advantages in terms of using the model, checking it for bugs and mistakes (Galán et al. 2009), and communicating it. However, when modelling complex systems, such as what policymakers face, such simplicity may not be worth it if gaining it means a loss of other desirable properties. *Generality* is the extent of the model scope: How many different kinds of situations could the model be usefully applied. Clearly, *some* level of generality is desirable; otherwise one could only apply the model in a single situation. However, all policy models will not be completely general—there will always be assumptions used in their construction, which limit their generality. Authors are often rather lax about making the scope of their models clear—often implying a greater level of generality that can be substantiated. Finally, *validity* means the extent to which the model outcomes match what is observed to occur—it is what is established in the process of model validation. This might be as close a match as a point forecast, or as loose as projecting qualitative aspects of possible outcomes.

What policymakers want, above all, is validity, with generality (so they do not have to keep going back to the modellers) and simplicity (so there is an accessible narrative to build support for any associated policy) coming after this. Simplicity and generality are nice if you can get them, but one cannot assume that these are achievable (Edmonds 2013). Validity *should* be an overwhelming priority for modellers; otherwise, they are not doing any sort of empirical science. However, they often put this off into the future, preferring the attractions of the apparent generality offered by analogical models (Edmonds 2001, 2010).

Formality is the degree to which a model is built in a precise language or system. A system of equations or a computer simulation is formal, vague, but intuitive ideas expressed in natural language are informal. It must be remembered that formality for those in the policy world is not a virtue but more of a problem. They may be convinced it is necessary (to provide the backing of "science"), but it means that the model is inevitably somewhat opaque and not entirely under their control. This is the nub of the relationship between modellers and the policy world—if the policy side did not feel any need for the formality, then they would have no need of modellers—they are already skilled at making decisions using informal methods. For the modellers, the situation is reverse. Formality is at the root of modelling, so that they can replicate their results and so that the model can be unambiguously passed to other researchers for examination, critique, and further development (Edmonds 2000). For this reason, we will discuss formality a bit and analyse its nature and consequences.

Two dimensions of formality can be usefully distinguished here, these are:

a. The extent to which the referents of the representation are constrained ("specificity of reference").
b. The extent to which the ways in which instantiations of the representation can be manipulated are constrained ("specificity of manipulation").

For example, an analogy expressed in natural language has a low specificity of reference since, what its parts refer to are reconstructed by each hearer in each situation. For example, the phrase "a tidal wave of crime" implies that concerted and highly coordinated action is needed in order to prevent people being engulfed, but the level of danger and what (if anything) is necessary to do must be determined by each listener. In contrast to this is a detailed description where what it refers to is severely limited by its content, e.g. "Recorded burglaries in London rose by 15 % compared to the previous year". Data are characterised by a high specificity of reference, since what it refers to is very precise, but has a low specificity of manipulation because there are few constraints in what one can do with it.

A system of mathematics or computer code has a high specificity of manipulation since the ways these can be manipulated are determined by precise rules—what one person infers from them can be exactly replicated by another. Thus, all formal models (the ones we are mostly concentrating on here) have a high specificity of manipulation, but not necessarily a high specificity of representation. A piece of natural language that can be used to draw inferences in many different ways, only limited by the manipulators' imagination and linguistic ability, has a low specificity of manipulation. One might get the impression that any "scientific" model expressed in mathematics must be formal in both ways. However, just because a representation has high specificity of manipulation, it does not mean that the meaning of its parts in terms of what it represents is well determined.

Many simulations, for example, do not represent anything we observe directly, but are rather explorations of ideas. We, as intelligent interpreters, may mentally fill in what it might refer to in any particular context but these "mappings" to reality are not well defined. Such models are more in the nature of an analogy, albeit one in formal form—they are not testable in a scientific manner since it is not clear as to precisely what they represent. Whilst it may be obvious when a system of mathematics is very abstract and not directly connected with what is observed, simulations (especially agent-based simulations) can give a false impression of their applicability because they are readily interpretable (but informally). This does not mean they are useless for all purposes. For example, Schelling's abstract simulation of racial segregation did not have any direct referents in terms of anything measurable,[3] but it was an effective counterexample that can show that an assumption that segregation must be caused by strong racial prejudice was unsound. Thus, such "analogical models" (those with low specificity of reference) can give useful insights—they can inform thought, but cannot give reliable forecasts or explanations as to what is observed.

In practice, a variety of models are used by modellers in the consideration of any issue, including: informal analogies or stories that summarise understanding and are used as a rough guide to formal manipulation, data models that abstract and represent the situation being modelled via observation and measurement, the simulation or mathematical model that is used to infer something about outcomes from initial situations, representations of the outcomes in terms of summary measures and graphs, and the interpretations of the results in terms of the target situation. When considering very complex situations, it is inevitable that more models will become involved, abstracting different aspects of the target situation in different ways and "staging" abstraction so that the meaning and reference can be maintained. However, good practice in terms of maintaining "clusters" of highly related models has yet to be established in the modelling community, so that a policymaker might well be bewildered by different models (using different assumptions) giving apparently conflicting results. However, the response to this should not be to reject this variety, and enforce comforting (but ultimately illusory) consistency of outcomes, but accept

---

[3] Subsequent elaborations of this model have tried to make the relationship to what is observed more direct, but the original model, however visually suggestive, was not related to any data.

that it is useful to have different viewpoints from models as much as it is to have different viewpoints from experts. It is the job of policymakers to use their experience and judgement in assessing and combining these views of reality. Of course, equally it is the job of the modellers to understand and explain why models appear to contradict each other and the significance of this as much as they can.

A model that *looks* scientific (e.g. is composed of equations, hence quantified) might well inspire more confidence than one that does not. In fact, the formality of models is very much a two-edged sword, giving advantages and disadvantages in ways that are not immediately obvious to a nonmodeller. We will start with the disadvantages and then consider the advantages.

Most formal models will be able to output series of numbers composed of measures on the outcomes of the model. However, just because numbers are by their nature precise,[4] does not mean that this precision is representative of the certainty to which these outcomes will map to observed outcomes. Thus, numerical outcomes can give a very false sense of security, and lead those involved in policy to falsely think that prediction of such values is possible. Although many forecasters now will add indications of uncertainty "around" forecasts, this can still be deeply misleading as it still implies that there is a central tendency about which future outcomes will gravitate.[5]

Many modellers are now reluctant to make such predictions because they know how misleading these can be. This is, understandably, frustrating for those involved in policy, whose response might be, "I know its complex, but we do not have the time/money to develop a more sophisticated model so just give me your 'best guess'". This attitude implies that some prediction is better than none, and that the reliability of a prediction is monotonic to the amount of effort one puts in. It seems that many imagine that the reliability of a prediction increases with effort, albeit unevenly—so a prediction with a small amount of effort will be better than none at all. Unfortunately, this is far from the case, and a prediction based on a "quick and dirty" method may be more misleading than helpful and merely give a false sense of security.

One of the consequences of the complexity of social phenomena is that the prediction of policy matters is hard, rare, and only obtained as a result of the most specific and pragmatic kind of modelling developed over relatively long periods of time.[6] It is more likely that a model is appropriate for establishing and understanding candidate explanations of what is happening, which will inform policy making in a less exact manner than prediction, being part of the mix of factors that a policymaker will take into account when deciding action. It is common for policy people to want a prediction of the impact of possible interventions "however rough", rather than settle for some level of understanding of what is happening. However, this can be

---

[4] Even if, as in statistics, they are being precise about variation and levels of uncertainty of other numbers.

[5] This apparent central tendency might be merely the result of the way data are extracted from the model and the assumptions built into the model rather than anything that represents the fundamental behaviour being modelled.

[6] For an account of actual forecasting and its reality, see Silver (2012).

illusory—if one really wanted a prediction "however rough", one would settle for a random prediction[7] dressed up as a complicated "black box" model. If we are wiser, we should accept the complexity of what we are dealing and reject models that give us ill-founded predictions.

Maybe a better approach is to use the modelling to inform the researchers about the kinds of process that might emerge from a situation—showing them possible "trajectories" that they would not otherwise have imagined. Using visualisations of these trajectories and the critical indicators clarifies the complex decision context for policymakers. In this way, the burden of uncertainty and decision making remains with the policymakers and not the researchers, but they will be more intelligently informed about the complexity of what is currently happening, allowing them to "drive" decision making better.

As we have discussed above, one feature of complex systems is that they can result in completely unexpected outcomes, where due to the relevant interactions in the system, a new *kind* of process has developed resulting in qualitatively different results. It is for this reason that complex models of these systems do not give probabilities (since these may be meaningless, or worse be downright misleading) but rather trace some (but not all) of the possible outcomes. This is useful as one can then be as prepared as possible for such outcomes, which otherwise would not have been thought of.

On the positive side, the use of formal modelling techniques can be very helpful for *integrating* different kinds of understanding and evidence into a more "well-rounded" assessment of options. The formality of the models means that it can be shared without ambiguity or misunderstanding between experts in different domains. This contrasts with communication using natural language where, inevitably, people have different assumptions, different meanings, and different inferences for key terms and systems. This ability to integrate different kinds of expertise turns out to be especially useful in the technique we will discuss next—agent-based simulation.

4.4.2   The Use of Agent-Based Models to Aid Policy Formation

In recent years, agent-based simulation has gained momentum as a tool allowing the computer to simulate the interactions between a great number of agents. An agent-based simulation implies that individuals can be represented as separate computer models that capture their motives and behaviour. Letting these so-called agents interact though a network, and confront them with changing circumstances, creates an artificial environment where complex and highly dynamic processes can be studied. Because agent-based models address the interactions between many different agents, they offer a very suitable tool to represent and recreate the complexities in social systems. Hence, agent-based modeling has become an influential methodology

---

[7] Or other null model, such as "what happened last time" or "no change".

to study a variety of social systems, ranging from ant colonies to aspects of human society. In the context of agent-based simulation of human behaviour, one of the challenges is connecting the knowledge from behavioural sciences in agent-based models that can be used to model behaviour in some kind of environment. These modelled environments may differ largely, and may reflect different (inter)disciplinary fields. Examples of environments where agents can operate in are, e.g. financial markets, agricultural settings, the introduction of new technologies in markets, and transportation systems, just to name a few. A key advantage here is that a model creates a common formal language for different disciplines to communicate. This is important, as it allows for speaking the same language in targeting issues that are interdisciplinary by nature. Rather than taking information from social scientists as an interesting qualitative advice, it becomes possible to actually simulate what the behaviour dynamical effects of policies are. This is, in our view, an important step in addressing interdisciplinary policy issues in an effective way. An additional advantage of social simulation is that formalizing theory and empirical data in models requires researchers to be exact in the assumptions, which, in turn, may result in specific research questions for field and/or lab experiments. Hence, social simulation is a tool that both stimulates the interaction between scientific disciplines, and may stimulate theory development/specification within the behavioural sciences.

An increasing number of agent-based models is being used in a policy context. A recent inventory on the SIMSOC mailing list by Nigel Gilbert[8] resulted in a list of modelling projects that in some way were related to actual policy making. Topics included energy systems, littering, water management, crowd dynamics, financial crisis, health management, deforestation, industrial clustering, biogas use, military interventions, diffusion of electric cars, organization of an emergency centre, natural park management, postal service organization, urban design, introduction of renewable technology, and vaccination programmes. Whereas some models were actually being used by policymakers, in most instances, the models were being used to inform policy makers about the complexities in the system they were interacting with. The basic idea is that a better understanding of the complex dynamics of the system contributes to understanding how to manage these systems, even if they are unpredictable by nature. Here, a comparison can be made with sailing as a managerial process.

Sailing can be seen as a managerial challenge in using different forces that constantly change and interact in order to move the ship to a certain destination. In stable and calm weather conditions, it is quite well possible to set the sails in a certain position and fix the rudder, and make an accurate prediction where of the course the boat will follow. The situation becomes different when you enter more turbulent stages in the system, and strong and variable winds, in combination with bigger waves and streams, requiring the sailor to be very adaptive to the circumstances. A small deviation from the course, due to a gush or a wave, may alter the angle of the wind

---

[8] See mailing list SIMSOC@JISCMAIL.AC.UK. Mail distributed by Nigel Gilbert on December 14, 2013, subject: ABMs in action: second summary.

in the sail, which may give rise to further deviations of the course. This is typically a feedback process, and obviously an experienced sailor is well aware of all these dynamics, and, as a consequence, the sailor responds very adaptive to these small disturbances, yet keeps the long-term outcome—the destination port—also in mind.

The social systems that we are dealing with, in transitions, are way more complex than the sailing example. Yet, the underlying rational is the same: the better we learn to understand the dynamics of change, the better we will be capable of coping with turbulences in the process, whilst keeping the long-term goals in focus. Hence, policy aims such that the transition towards a sustainable energy future provides a reasonably clear picture of the direction we are aiming for, but the turbulences in the process towards this future are not well known. Where the sailor has a deep understanding of the dynamics that govern the behaviour of his boat, for policymakers, this understanding is often limited, as the opening example demonstrated.

Using agent-based models for policy would contribute to a better understanding and management of social complex phenomena. First, agent-based models will be useful in identifying under what conditions a social system will behave relatively stable (predictable) versus turbulent (unpredictable). This is critical for policy making, because in relatively stable situations, predictions can be made concerning the effects of policy, whereas in turbulent regimes, a more adaptive policy is recommended. Adaptive policy implies that the turbulent developments are being followed closely, and that policymakers try to block developments to grow in an undesired direction, and benefit and support beneficial developments. Second, if simulated agents are more realistic in the sense that they are equipped with different utilities/needs/preferences, the simulations will not only show what the possible behavioural developments are but also reveal the impact on a more psychological quality-of-life level. Whereas currently many policy models assess behavioural change from a more financial/economical drivers, agent-based models open a possibility to strengthen policy models by including additional outcomes. Examples would be outcomes relating to the stability and support in social networks, and general satisfaction levels.

Agent-based models, thus, can provide a richer and more complex representation of what may be happening within complex and highly dynamic situations, allowing for some of the real possibilities within the system to be explored. This exploration of possibilities can inform the risk analysis of policy, and help ensure that policymakers are ready for more of what the world may throw at them, for example, by having put in place custom-designed indicators that give them the soonest-possible indication that certain kinds of processes or structural changes are underway.

4.5 Conclusions

The bad news for policymakers is that predictive models perform worst exactly at the moment policymakers need them most—during turbulent stages. Yet, we observe that many policymakers, not being aware of the complex nature of the system they are interfering with, still have a mechanistic worldview, and base their decisions on classical predictions. This may be one of the reasons for scepticism by policymakers of any modelling approaches (see e.g. Waldherr and Wijermans 2013). Even nowadays, when complexity has turned into a buzzword, many policymakers still confuse this concept with "complicatedness", not embracing the essence and meaning of what complexity means for understanding social systems. As a consequence, still many policymakers are "Cartesian[9]" in their demand for better predictive models. On the other side, still many modellers working from a mechanistic perspective (e.g. linear and/or generic models), holding out the false hope of "scientifically" predictive models, look for more resources to incrementally improve their models, e.g. covering more variables. However, whereas it is sometimes justified to argue for the inclusion of more variables in a model, this will not contribute to a better predictive capacity of the model. As Scott Moss reports in his paper (Moss 2002), there are no reported correct real-time forecasts of the volatile clusters or the post-cluster levels in financial market indices or macroeconomic trade cycles, despite their incremental "refinement" over many years. Characteristically, they predict well in periods where nothing much changes, but miss all the "turning points" where structural change occurs.

Even if policymakers have some understanding of the complex nature of the systems they are managing, they still often respond with "I know it is complex, but how else can I decide policy except by using the numbers I have?", indicating that the numbers are often an important justification of decisions, even if people are aware of the uncertainties behind them. The example of the former minister in the introduction is a prototypical example of this decision making.

The challenge, hence, is not in trying to convince policymakers of the value of simulation models, but providing them with a deeper level understanding of complex systems. Here, simulation models can provide an important role by creating learning experiences. But before going to simulation models, it might be important to use a strong metaphor in anchoring the core idea of managing complex systems. Sailing offers an excellent metaphor here, because many people know the basics of sailing, and understand that it deals with the management of a ship in sometimes turbulent circumstances. What is critical in this metaphor is that in more turbulent conditions, the crew should become more adaptive to the developments in the system.

Agent-based simulation is increasingly being used as a modelling tool to explore the possibilities and potential impacts of policy making in complex systems. They are inherently possibilistic rather than probabilistic. However, the models being used are usually not very accessible for policymakers. Also, in the context of education, not many models are available that allow for an easy access to experiencing policy making in complex systems. In Chap. 13 of this book, Jager and Van der Vegt suggest using based gaming as a promising venue to make agent-based models more

---

[9] Descartes' mechanistic worldview implies that the universe works like a clockwork, and prediction is possible when one has knowledge of all the wheels, gears, and levers of the clockwork. In policy this translates as the viable society.

accessible in education and practical policy settings. A setting where valid games are being used to increase our understanding of the processes in complex management issues is expected to contribute to an improvement of the policy-making process in complex systems.

Acknowledgments   This chapter has been written in the context of the eGovPoliNet project. More information can be found on http://www.policy-community.eu/.

References

Boettiger C, Hastings A (2012) Quantifying limits to detection of early warning for critical transitions. J R Soc Interface 9(75):2527–2539

Campbell DT (1960) Blind variation and selective retention in creative thought as in other knowledge processes. Psychol Rev 67:380–400

Dai L, Vorselen D et al (2012) Generic indicators for loss of resilience before a tipping point leading to population collapse. Science 336(6085):1175–1177

Dakos V, Carpenter RA et al (2012) Methods for detecting early warnings of critical transitions in time series illustrated using simulated ecological data. PLoS ONE 7(7) e41010

Edmonds B (2000) The purpose and place of formal systems in the development of science. CPM report 00–75, MMU, UK (http://cfpm.org/cpmrep75.html)

Edmonds B (2001) The use of models—making MABS actually work. In: Moss S, Davidsson P (eds) Multi agent based simulation. Lecture Notes in Artificial Intelligence 1979. Springer, Berlin, pp 15–32

Edmonds B (2010) Bootstrapping knowledge about social phenomena using simulation models. J Artif Soc Soc Simul 13(1):8 (http://jasss.soc.surrey.ac.uk/13/1/8.html)

Edmonds B (2013) Complexity and context-dependency. Found Sci 18(4):745–755. doi:10.1007/s10699-012-9303-x

Galán JM, Izquierdo LR, Izquierdo SS, Santos JI, del Olmo R, López-Paredes A, Edmonds B (2009) Errors and artefacts in agent-based modelling. J Artif Soc Soc Simul 12(1):1 (http://jasss.soc.surrey.ac.uk/12/1/1.html)

Heisenberg W (1927) Ueber den anschaulichenInhalt der quantentheoretischen. Kinematik and Mechanik Zeitschriftfür Physik 43:172–198. English translation in (Wheeler and Zurek, 1983), pp 62–84

May RM (1976) Simple mathematical models with very complicated dynamics. Nature 261(5560):459–467

Moss S (2002) Policy analysis from first principles. Proc US Natl Acad Sci 99(Suppl 3):7267–7274

Scheffer et al (2009) Early warnings of critical transitions. Nature 461:53–59

Silver N (2012) The signal and the noise: why so many predictions fail-but some don't. Penguin, New York

Waldherr A, Wijermans N (2013) Communicating social simulation models to sceptical minds. J Artif Soc Soc Simul 16(4):13 (http://jasss.soc.surrey.ac.uk/16/4/13.html)

Chapter 5
From Building a Model to Adaptive Robust Decision Making Using Systems Modeling

Erik Pruyt

Abstract Starting from the state-of-the-art and recent evolutions in the field of system dynamics modeling and simulation, this chapter sketches a plausible near term future of the broader field of systems modeling and simulation. In the near term future, different systems modeling schools are expected to further integrate and accelerate the adoption of methods and techniques from related fields like policy analysis, data science, machine learning, and computer science. The resulting future state of the art of the modeling field is illustrated by three recent pilot projects. Each of these projects required further integration of different modeling and simulation approaches and related disciplines as discussed in this chapter. These examples also illustrate which gaps need to be filled in order to meet the expectations of real decision makers facing complex uncertain issues.

5.1 Introduction

Many systems, issues, and grand challenges are characterized by dynamic complexity, i.e., intricate time evolutionary behavior, often on multiple dimensions of interest. Many dynamically complex systems and issues are relatively well known, but have persisted for a long time due to the fact that their dynamic complexity makes them hard to understand and properly manage or solve. Other complex systems and issues—especially rapidly changing systems and future grand challenges—are largely unknown and unpredictable. Most unaided human beings are notoriously bad at dealing with dynamically complex issues—whether the issues dealt with are persistent or unknown. That is, without the help of computational approaches, most human beings are unable to assess potential dynamics of complex systems and issues, and are unable to assess the appropriateness of policies to manage or address them.

E. Pruyt (✉)
Faculty of Technology, Policy, and Management, Delft University of Technology, Delft,
The Netherlands
e-mail: E.Pruyt@tudelft.nl

Netherlands Institute for Advanced Study, Wassenaar, The Netherlands

© Springer International Publishing Switzerland 2015   75
M. Janssen et al. (eds.), *Policy Practice and Digital Science,*
Public Administration and Information Technology 10, DOI 10.1007/978-3-319-12784-2_5

Modeling and simulation is a field that develops and applies computational methods to study complex systems and solve problems related to complex issues. Over the past half century, multiple modeling methods for simulating such issues and for advising decision makers facing them have emerged or have been further developed. Examples include system dynamics (SD) modeling, discrete event simulation (DES), multi-actor systems modeling (MAS), agent-based modeling (ABM), and complex adaptive systems modeling (CAS). All too often, these developments have taken place in distinct fields, such as the SD field or the ABM field, developing into separate "schools," each ascribing dynamic complexity to the complex underlying mechanisms they focus on, such as feedback effects and accumulation effects in SD or heterogenous actor-specific (inter)actions in ABM. The isolated development within separate traditions has limited the potential to learn across fields and advance faster and more effectively towards the shared goal of understanding complex systems and supporting decision makers facing complex issues.

Recent evolutions in modeling and simulation together with the recent explosive growth in computational power, data, social media, and other evolutions in computer science have created new opportunities for model-based analysis and decision making. These internal and external evolutions are likely to break through silos of old, open up new opportunities for social simulation and model-based decision making, and stir up the broader field of systems modeling and simulation. Today, different modeling approaches are already used in parallel, in series, and in mixed form, and several hybrid approaches are emerging. But not only are different modeling traditions being mixed and matched in multiple ways, modeling and simulation fields have also started to adopt—or have accelerated their adoption of—useful methods and techniques from other disciplines including operations research, policy analysis, data analytics, machine learning, and computer science. The field of modeling and simulation is consequently turning into an interdisciplinary field in which various modeling schools and related disciplines are gradually being integrated. In practice, the blending process and the adoption of methodological innovations have just started. Although some ways to integrate systems modeling methods and many innovations have been demonstrated, further integration and massive adoption are still awaited. Moreover, other multi-methods and potential innovations are still in an experimental phase or are yet to be demonstrated and adopted.

In this chapter, some of these developments will be discussed, a picture of the near future state of the art of modeling and simulation is drawn, and a few examples of integrated systems modeling are briefly discussed. The SD method is used to illustrate these developments. Starting with a short introduction to the traditional SD method in Sect. 5.2, some recent and current innovations in SD are discussed in Sect. 5.3, resulting in a picture of the state of modeling and simulation in Sect. 5.4. A few examples are then briefly discussed in Sect. 5.5 to illustrate what these developments could result in and what the future state-of-the-art of systems modeling and simulation could look like. Finally, conclusions are drawn in Sect. 5.6.

5.2 System Dynamics Modeling and Simulation of Old

System dynamics was first developed in the second half of the 1950s by Jay W. Forrester and was further developed into a consistent method built on specific methodological choices[1]. It is a method for modeling and simulating dynamically complex systems or issues characterized by feedback effects and accumulation effects. Feedback means that the present and future of issues or systems, depend—through a chain of causal relations—on their own past. In SD models, system boundaries are set broadly enough to include all important feedback effects and generative mechanisms. Accumulation relates not only to building up real stocks—of people, items, (infra)structures, etc.,—but also to building up mental or other states. In SD models, stock variables and the underlying integral equations are used to group largely homogenous persons/items/… and keep track of their aggregated dynamics over time. Together, feedback and accumulation effects generate dynamically complex behavior both inside SD models and—so it is assumed in SD—in real systems.

Other important characteristic of SD are (i) the reliance on relatively enduring conceptual systems representations in people's minds, aka mental models (Doyle and Ford 1999, p. 414), as prime source of "rich" information (Forrester 1961; Doyle and Ford 1998); (ii) the use of causal loop diagrams and stock-flow diagrams to represent feedback and accumulation effects (Lane 2000); (iii) the use of credibility and fitness for purpose as main criteria for model validation (Barlas 1996); and (iv) the interpretation of simulation runs in terms of general behavior patterns, aka modes of behavior (Meadows and Robinson 1985).

In SD, the behavior of a system is to be explained by a dynamic hypothesis, i.e., a causal theory for the behavior (Lane 2000; Sterman 2000). This causal theory is formalized as a model that can be simulated to generate dynamic behavior. Simulating the model thus allows one to explore the link between the hypothesized system structure and the time evolutionary behavior arising out of it (Lane 2000).

Not surprisingly, these characteristics make SD particularly useful for dealing with complex systems or issues that are characterized by important system feedback effects and accumulation effects. SD modeling is mostly used to model core system structures or core structures underlying issues, to simulate their resulting behavior, and to study the link between the underlying causal structure of issues and models and the resulting behavior. SD models, which are mostly relatively small and manageable, thus allow for experimentation in a virtual laboratory. As a consequence, SD models are also extremely useful for model-based policy analysis, for designing adaptive policies (i.e., policies that automatically adapt to the circumstances), and for testing their policy robustness (i.e., whether they perform well enough across a large variety of circumstances).

---

[1] See Forrester (1991, 2007), Sterman (2007) for accounts of the inception of the SD field. See Sterman (2000), Pruyt (2013) for introductions to SD. And see Forrester (1961, 1969), Homer (2012) for well-known examples of traditional SD.

In terms of application domains, SD is used for studying many complex social–technical systems and solving policy problems in many application domains, for example, in health policy, resource policy, energy policy, environmental policy, housing policy, education policy, innovation policy, social–economic policy, and other public policy domains. But it is also used for studying all sorts of business dynamics problems, for strategic planning, for solving supply chain problems, etc.

At the inception of the SD method, SD models were almost entirely continuous, i.e., systems of differential equations, but over time more and more discrete and other noncontinuous elements crept in. Other evolutionary adaptations in line with ideas from the earliest days of the field, like the use of Group Model Building to elicit mental models of groups of stakeholders (Vennix 1996) or the use of SD models as engines for serious games, were also readily adopted by almost the entire field. But slightly more revolutionary innovations were not as easily and massively adopted. In other words, the identity and appearance of traditional SD was well established by the mid-1980s and does—at first sight—not seem to have changed fundamentally since then.

5.3 Recent Innovations and Expected Evolutions

5.3.1 Recent and Current Innovations

Looking in somewhat more detail at innovations within the SD field and its adoption of innovations from other fields shows that many—often seemingly more revolutionary—innovations have been introduced and demonstrated, but that they have not been massively adopted yet.

For instance, in terms of quantitative modeling, system dynamicists have invested in spatially specific SD modeling (Ruth and Pieper 1994; Struben 2005; BenDor and Kaza 2012), individual agent-based SD modeling as well as mixed and hybrid ABM-SD modeling (Castillo and Saysal 2005; Osgood 2009; Feola et al. 2012; Rahmandad and Sterman 2008), and micro–macro modeling (Fallah-Fini et al. 2014). Examples of recent developments in simulation setup and execution include model calibration and bootstrapping (Oliva 2003; Dogan 2007), different types of sampling (Fiddaman 2002; Ford 1990; Clemson et al. 1995; Islam and Pruyt 2014), multi-model and multi-method simulation (Pruyt and Kwakkel 2014; Moorlag 2014), and different types of optimization approaches used for a variety of purposes (Coyle 1985; Miller 1998; Coyle 1999; Graham and Ariza 1998; Hamarat et al. 2013, 2014). Recent innovations in model testing, analysis, and visualization of model outputs in SD include the development and application of new methods for sensitivity and uncertainty analysis (Hearne 2010; Eker et al. 2014), formal model analysis methods to study the link between structure and behavior (Kampmann and Oliva 2008, 2009; Saleh et al. 2010), methods for testing policy robustness across wide ranges of uncertainties (Lempert et al. 2003), statistical packages and screening techniques (Ford and Flynn 2005; Taylor et al. 2010), pattern testing and time series classification techniques

(Yücel and Barlas 2011; Yücel 2012; Sucullu and Yücel 2014; Islam and Pruyt 2014), and machine learning techniques (Pruyt et al. 2013; Kwakkel et al. 2014; Pruyt et al. 2014c). These methods and techniques can be used together with SD models to identify root causes of problems, to identify adaptive policies that properly address these root causes, to test and optimize the effectiveness of policies across wide ranges of assumptions (i.e., policy robustness), etc. From this perspective, these methods and techniques are actually just evolutionary innovations in line with early SD ideas. And large-scale adoption of the aforementioned innovations would allow the SD field, and by extension the larger systems modeling field, to move from "experiential art" to "computational science."

Most of the aforementioned innovations are actually integrated in particular SD approaches like in exploratory system dynamics modelling and analysis (ESDMA), which is an SD approach for studying dynamic complexity under deep uncertainty. Deep uncertainty could be defined as a situation in which analysts do not know or cannot agree on (i) an underlying model, (ii) probability distributions of key variables and parameters, and/or (iii) the value of alternative outcomes (Lempert et al. 2003). It is often encountered in situations characterized by either too little information or too much information (e.g., conflicting information or different worldviews). ESDMA is the combination of exploratory modeling and analysis (EMA), aka robust decision making, developed during the past two decades (Bankes 1993; Lempert et al. 2000; Bankes 2002; Lempert et al. 2006) and SD modeling. EMA is a research methodology for developing and using models to support decision making under deep uncertainty. It is not a modeling method, in spite of the fact that it requires computational models. EMA can be useful when relevant information that can be exploited by building computational models exists, but this information is insufficient to specify a single model that accurately describes system behavior (Kwakkel and Pruyt 2013a). In such situations, it is better to construct and use ensembles of plausible models since ensembles of models can capture more of the un/available information than any individual model (Bankes 2002). Ensembles of models can then be used to deal with model uncertainty, different perspectives, value diversity, inconsistent information, etc.—in short, with deep uncertainty.[2]

In EMA (and thus in ESDMA), the influence of a plethora of uncertainties, including method and model uncertainty, are systematically assessed and used to design policies: sampling and multi-model/multi-method simulation are used to generate ensembles of simulation runs to which time series classification and machine learning techniques are applied for generating insights. Multi-objective robust optimization (Hamarat et al. 2013, 2014) is used to identify policy levers and define policy triggers, and by doing so, support the design of adaptive robust policies. And regret-based approaches are used to test policy robustness across large ensembles of plausible runs (Lempert et al. 2003). EMA and ESDMA can be performed with TU Delft's

---

[2] For ESDMA, see among else Pruyt and Hamarat (2010), Logtens et al. (2012), Pruyt et al. (2013), Kwakkel and Pruyt (2013a, b), Kwakkel et al. (2013), Pruyt and Kwakkel (2014).

EMA workbench software, which is an open source tool[3] that integrates multi-method, multi-model, multi-policy simulation with data management, visualization, and analysis.

The latter is just one of the recent innovations in modeling and simulation software and platforms: online modeling and simulation platforms, online flight simulator and gaming platforms, and packages for making hybrid models have been developed too. And modeling and simulation across platforms will also become reality soon: the eXtensible Model Interchange LanguagE (XMILE) project (Diker and Allen 2005; Eberlein and Chichakly 2013) aims at facilitating the storage, sharing, and combination of simulation models and parts thereof across software packages and across modeling schools and may ease the interconnection with (real-time) databases, statistical and analytical software packages, and organizational information and communication technology (ICT) infrastructures. Note that this is already possible today with scripting languages and software packages with scripting capabilities like the aforementioned EMA workbench.

5.3.2   Current and Expected Evolutions

Three current evolutions are expected to further reinforce this shift from "experiential art" to "computational science."

The first evolution relates to the development of "smarter" methods, techniques, and tools (i.e., methods, techniques, and tools that provide more insights and deeper understanding at reduced computational cost). Similar to the development of formal model analysis techniques that smartened the traditional SD approach, new methods, techniques, and tools are currently being developed to smarten modeling and simulation approaches that rely on "brute force" sampling, for example, adaptive output-oriented sampling to span the space of possible dynamics (Islam and Pruyt 2014) or smarter machine learning techniques (Pruyt et al. 2013; Kwakkel et al. 2014; Pruyt et al. 2014c) and time series classification techniques (Yücel and Barlas 2011; Yücel 2012; Sucullu and Yücel 2014; Islam and Pruyt 2014), and (multi-objective) robust optimization techniques (Hamarat et al. 2013, 2014).

Partly related to the previous evolution are developments relates to "big data," data management, and data science. Although traditional SD modeling is sometimes called data-poor modeling, it does not mean it is, nor should be. SD software packages allow one to get data from, and write simulation runs to, databases. Moreover, data are also used in SD to calibrate parameters or bootstrap parameter ranges. But more could be done, especially in the era of "big data." Big data simply refers here to much more data than was until recently manageable. Big data requires data science techniques to make it manageable and useful. Data science may be used in

---

[3] The EMA workbench can be downloaded for free from http://simulation.tbm.tudelft.nl/ema-workbench/contents.html

modeling and simulation (i) to obtain useful inputs from data (e.g., from real-time big data sources), (ii) to analyze and interpret model-generated data (i.e., big artificial data), (iii) to compare simulated and real dynamics (i.e., for monitoring and control), and (iv) to infer parts of models from data (Pruyt et al. 2014c). Interestingly, data science techniques that are useful for obtaining useful inputs from data may also be made useful for analyzing and interpreting model-generated data, and vice versa. Online social media are interesting sources of real-world big data for modeling and simulation, both as inputs to models, to compare simulated and real dynamics, and to inform model development or model selection. There are many application domains in which the combination of data science and modeling and simulation would be beneficial. Examples, some of which are elaborated below, include policy making with regard to crime fighting, infectious diseases, cybersecurity, national safety and security, financial stress testing, energy transitions, and marketing.

Another urgently needed innovation relates to model-based empowerment of decision makers. Although existing flight simulator and gaming platforms are useful for developing and distributing educational flight simulators and games, and interfaces can be built in SD packages, using them to develop interfaces for real-world real-time decision making and integrating them into existing ICT systems is difficult and time consuming. In many cases, companies and organizations want these capabilities in-house, even in their boardroom, instead of being dependent on analyses by external or internal analysts. The latter requires user-friendly interfaces on top of (sets of) models possibly connected to real-time data sources. These interfaces should allow for experimentation, simulation, thoroughly analysis of simulation results, adaptive robust policy design, and policy robustness testing.

5.4 Future State of Practice of Systems Modeling and Simulation

These recent evolutions in modeling and simulation together with the recent explosive growth in computational power, data, social media, and other evolutions in computer science may herald the beginning of a new wave of innovation and adoption, moving the modeling and simulation field from building a single model to simultaneously simulating multiple models and uncertainties; from single method to multi-method and hybrid modeling and simulation; from modeling and simulation with sparse data to modeling and simulation with (near real-time) big data; from simulating and analyzing a few simulation runs to simulating and simultaneously analyzing well-selected ensembles of runs; from using models for intuitive policy testing to using models as instruments for designing adaptive robust policies; and from developing educational flight simulators to fully integrated decision support.

For each of the modeling schools, additional adaptations could be foreseen too. In case of SD, it may for example involve a shift from developing purely endogenous to largely endogenous models; from fully aggregated models to sufficiently spatially explicit and heterogenous models; from qualitative participatory modeling

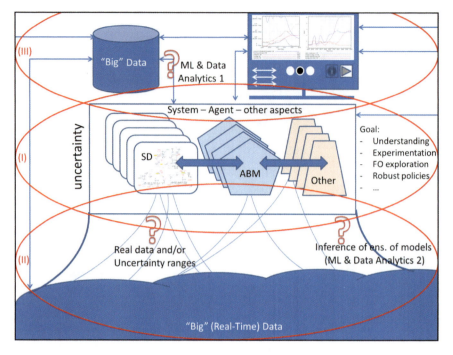

Fig. 5.1 Picture of the state of science/future state of the art of modeling and simulation

to quantitative participatory simulation; and from using SD to combining problem structuring and policy analysis tools, modeling and simulation, machine learning techniques, and (multi-objective) robust optimization.

Adoption of these recent, current, and expected innovations could result in the future state of the art[4] of systems modeling as displayed in Fig. 5.1. As indicated by (I) in Fig. 5.1, it will be possible to simultaneously use multiple hypotheses (i.e., simulation models from the same or different traditions or hybrids), for different goals including the search for deeper understanding and policy insights, experimentation in a virtual laboratory, future-oriented exploration, robust policy design, and robustness testing under deep uncertainty. Sets of simulation models may be used to represent different perspectives or plausible theories, to deal with methodological uncertainty, or to deal with a plethora of important characteristics (e.g., agent characteristics, feedback and accumulation effects, spatial and network effects) without necessarily having to integrate them in a single simulation model. The main advantages of using multiple models for doing so are that each of the models in the ensemble of models remains manageable and that the ensemble of simulation runs generated with the

---

[4] Given the fact that it takes a while before innovations are adopted by software developers and practitioners, this picture of the current state of science is at the same time a plausible picture of the medium term future of the field of modeling and simulation.

ensemble of models is likely to be more diverse which allows for testing policy robustness across a wider range of plausible futures.

Some of these models may be connected to real-time or near real-time data streams, and some models may even be inferred in part with smart data science tools from data sources (see (II) in Fig. 5.1). Storing the outputs of these simulation models in databases and applying data science techniques may enhance our understanding, may generate policy insights, and may allow for testing policy robustness across large multidimensional uncertainty spaces (see (III) in Fig. 5.1). And user-friendly interfaces on top of these interconnected models may eventually empower policy makers, enabling them to really do model-based policy making.

Note, however, that the integrated systems modeling approach sketched in Fig. 5.1 may only suit a limited set of goals, decision makers, and issues. Single model simulation properly serves many goals, decision makers, and issues well enough for multi-model/multi-method, data-rich, exploratory, policy-oriented approaches not to be required. However, there are most certainly goals, decision makers, and issues that do.

5.5 Examples

Although all of the above is possible today, it should be noted that this is the current state of science, not the state of common practice yet. Applying all these methods and techniques to real issues is still challenging, and shows where innovations are most needed. The following examples illustrate what is possible today as well as what the most important gaps are that remain to be filled.

The first example shows that relatively simple systems models simulated under deep uncertainty allow for generating useful ensembles of many simulation runs. Using methods and techniques from related disciplines to analyze the resulting artificial data sets helps to generate important policy insights. And simulation of policies across the ensembles allows to test for policy robustness. This first case nevertheless shows that there are opportunities for multi-method and hybrid approaches as well as for connecting systems models to real-time data streams.

The second example extends the first example towards a system-of-systems approach with many simulation models generating even larger ensembles of simulation runs. Smart sampling and scenario discovery techniques are then required to reduce the resulting data sets to manageable proportions.

The third example shows a recent attempt to develop a smart model-based decision-support system for dealing with another deeply uncertain issue. This example shows that it is almost possible to empower decision makers. Interfaces with advanced analytical capabilities as well as easier and better integration with existing ICT systems are required though. This example also illustrates the need for more advanced hybrid systems models as well as the need to connect systems models to real-time geo-spatial data.

5.5.1 Assessing the Risk, and Monitoring, of New Infectious Diseases

The first case, which is described in more detail in (Pruyt and Hamarat 2010; Pruyt et al. 2013), relates to assessing outbreaks of new flu variants. Outbreaks of new (variants of) infectious diseases are deeply uncertain. For example, in the first months after the first reports about the outbreak of a new flu variant in Mexico and the USA, much remained unknown about the possible dynamics and consequences of this possible epidemic/pandemic of the new flu variant, referred to today as new influenza A(H1N1)v. Table 5.1 shows that more and better information became available over time, but also that many uncertainties remained. However, even with these remaining uncertainties, it is possible to model and simulate this flu variant under deep uncertainty, for example with the simplistic simulation model displayed in Fig. 5.2, since flu outbreaks can be modeled.

Simulating this model thousands of times over very wide uncertainty ranges for each of the uncertain variables generates the 3D cloud of potential outbreaks displayed in Fig. 5.3a. In this figure, the worst flu peak (0–50 months) is displayed on the X-axis, the infected fraction during the worst flu peak (0–50 %) is displayed on the Y-axis, and the cumulative number of fatal cases in the Western world (0–50.000.000) is displayed on the Z-axis. This 3D plot shows that the most catastrophic outbreaks are likely to happen within the first year or during the first winter season following the outbreak. Using machine learning algorithms to explore this ensemble of simulation runs helps to generate important policy insights (e.g., which policy levers to address). Testing different variants of the same policy shows that adaptive policies outperform their static counterparts (compare Fig. 5.3b and c). Figure 5.3d finally shows that adaptive policies can be further improved using multi-objective robust optimization.

However, taking deep uncertainty seriously into account would require simulating more than a single model from a single modeling method: it would be better to simultaneously simulate CAS, ABM, SD, and hybrid models under deep uncertainty and use the resulting ensemble of simulation runs. Moreover, near real-time geospatial data (from twitter, medical records, etc.) may also be used in combination with simulation models, for example, to gradually reduce the ensemble of model-generated data. Both suggested improvements would be possible today.

5.5.2 Integrated Risk-Capability Analysis under Deep Uncertainty

The second example relates to risk assessment and capability planning for National Safety and Security. Since 2001, many nations have invested in the development of all-hazard integrated risk-capability assessment (IRCA) approaches. All-hazard IRCAs integrate scenario-based risk assessment, capability analysis, and capability-based planning approaches to reduce all sorts of risks—from natural hazards, over technical failures to malicious threats—by enhancing capabilities for dealing with

Table 5.1 Information and unknowns provided by the European Centre for Disease Prevention and Control (ECDC) from 24 April until 21 August

Date	24 April	30 April	08 May	20 May	12 June	20 July	21 August
Infectivity	Unknown	Unknown	Unknown	Unknown	Unknown	Unknown	Unknown
Ro	Unknown	Unknown	1–2; prob. 1.4–1.9	1–2; prob. 1.4–1.6	Unknown	–	[$R \leq 2$]
Immunity	Unknown	Unknown	Indications (elderly)	Idem	Idem	Idem	Idem
Virulence	Unknown	Unknown	Unknown	Unknown	Unknown	Mild and self-limiting	Idem
Incubation period	Unknown	Unknown	Long tail? (up to 8 days)	–	Median 3–4 days range 1–7 days	Idem	Idem
CFR Mexico	17%?	–	4%?	2%?	0.4–1.8%?	–	–
CFR USA	Unknown	Unknown	0.1%?	0.1%?	0.2%?	0.4%?	–
CFR[a] UK	Unknown	Unknown	Unknown	Unknown	Unknown	0.3%(–1%)?	0.1–0.2%?
Age distribution	Unknown	Unknown	Elderly less affected?	–	Skewed tow. younger	Idem	Idem
Antiviral suscep.	Unknown	Possible	Indications	–	–	–	–
% asymptomatic	Unknown	Unknown	Unknown	Unknown	Unknown	Indications	33–50%
Future?	Unknown	Unknown	Unknown	Unknown	Unknown	Unknown	Unknown

[a]CFR stands for case fatality ratio

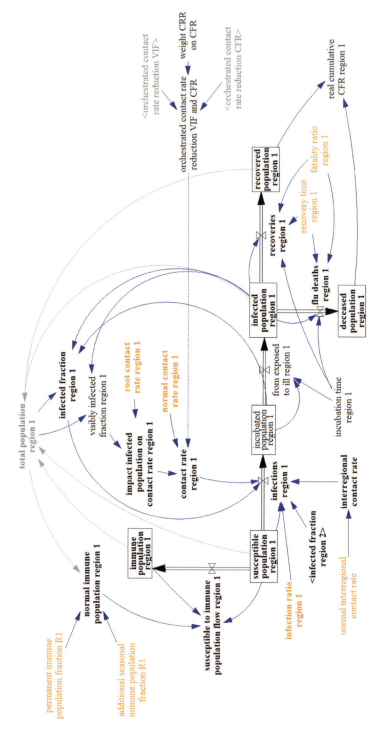

Fig. 5.2 Region 1 of a two-region system dynamics (SD) flu model

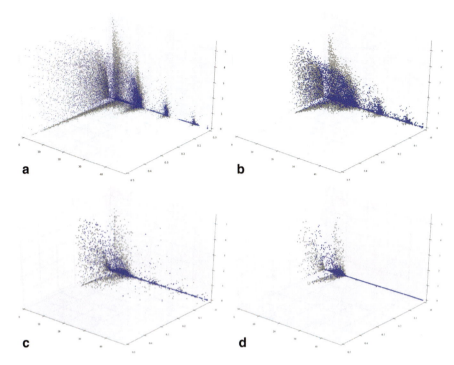

Fig. 5.3 3D scatter plots of 20,000 Latin-Hypercube samples for region 1 with X-axis: worst flu peak (0–50 months); Y-axis: infected fraction during the worst flu peak (0–50 %); Z-axis: fatal cases (0–5×10^7)

them. Current IRCAs mainly allow dealing with one or a few specific scenarios for a limited set of relatively simple event-based and relatively certain risks, but not for dealing with a plethora of risks that are highly uncertain and complex, combinations of measures and capabilities with uncertain and dynamic effects, and divergent opinions about degrees of (un)desirability of risks and capability investments.

The next generation model-based IRCAs may solve many of the shortcomings of the IRCAs that are currently being used. Figure 5.4 displays a next generation IRCA for dealing with all sorts of highly uncertain dynamic risks. This IRCA approach, described in more detail in Pruyt et al. (2012), combines EMA and modeling and simulation, both for the risk assessment and the capability analysis phases. First, risks—like outbreaks of new flu variants—are modeled and simulated many times across their multidimensional uncertainty spaces to generate an ensemble of plausible risk scenarios for each of the risks. Time series classification and machine learning techniques are then used to identify much smaller ensembles of exemplars that are representative for the larger ensembles. These ensembles of exemplars are then used as inputs to a generic capability analysis model. The capability analysis model is subsequently simulated for different capabilities strategies under deep uncertainty (i.e., simulating the uncertainty pertaining to their effectiveness) over all ensembles of exemplars to calculate the potential of capabilities strategies to reduce these risks.

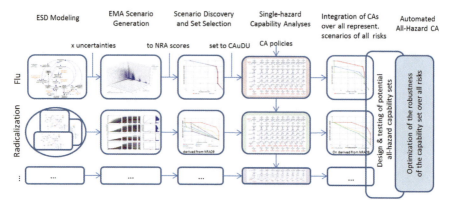

Fig. 5.4 Model-based integrated risk-capability analysis (IRCA)

Finally, multi-objective robust optimization helps to identify capabilities strategies that are robust.

Not only does this systems-of-systems approach allow to generate thousands of variants per risk type over many types of risks and to perform capability analyses across all sorts of risk and under uncertainty, it also allows one to find sets of capabilities that are effective across many uncertain risks. Hence, this integrated model-based approach allows for dealing with capabilities in an all-hazard way under deep uncertainty.

This approach is currently being smartened using adaptive output-oriented sampling techniques and new time-series classification methods that together help to identify the largest variety of dynamics with the minimal amount of simulations. Covering the largest variety of dynamics with the minimal amount of exemplars is desirable, for performing automated multi-hazard capability analysis over many risks is—due to the nature of the multi-objective robust optimization techniques used— computationally very expensive. This approach is also being changed from a multi-model approach into a multi-method approach. Whereas, until recently, sets of SD models were used; there are good reasons to extend this approach to other types of systems modeling approaches that may be better suited for particular risks or—using multiple approaches—help to deal with methodological uncertainty. Finally, settings of some of the risks and capabilities, as well as exogenous uncertainties, may also be fed with (near) real-world data.

5.5.3 Policing Under Deep Uncertainty

The third example relates to another deeply uncertain issue, high-impact crimes (HIC). An SD model and related tools (see Fig. 5.5) were developed some years ago in view of increasing the effectiveness of the fight against HIC, more specifically the fight against robbery and burglary. HICs require a systemic perspective and approach:

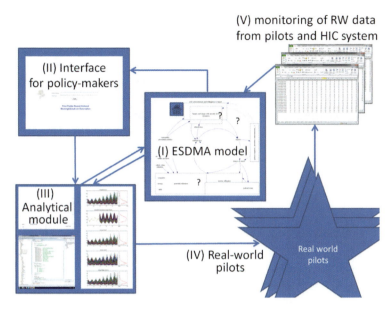

Fig. 5.5 (I) Exploratory system dynamics modelling and analysis (ESDMA) model, (II) interface for policy makers, (III) analytical module for analyzing the high-impact crimes (HIC)system under deep uncertainty, (IV) real-world pilots based on analyses, and (V) monitoring of real-world data from the pilots and the HIC system

These crimes are characterized by important systemic effects in time and space, such as learning and specialization effects, "waterbed effects" between different HICs and precincts, accumulations (prison time) and delays (in policing and jurisdiction), preventive effects, and other causal effects (ex-post preventive measures). HICs are also characterized by deep uncertainty: Most perpetrators are unknown and even though their archetypal crime-related habits may be known to some extent at some point in time, accurate time and geographically specific predictions cannot be made. At the same time, is part of the HIC system well known and is a lot of real-world information related to these crimes available.

Important players in the HIC system besides the police and (potential) perpetrators are potential victims (households and shopkeepers), partners in the judicial system (the public prosecution service, the prison system, etc.). Hence, the HIC system is dynamically complex, deeply uncertain, but also data rich, and contingent upon external conditions.

The main goals of this pilot project were to support strategic policy making under deep uncertainty and to test and monitor the effectiveness of policies to fight HIC. The SD model (I) was used as an engine behind the interface for policy makers (II) to explore plausible effects of policies under deep uncertainty and identify real-world pilots that could possibly increase the understanding about the system and effectiveness of interventions (III), to implement these pilots (IV), and monitor their outcomes (V). Real-world data from the pilots and improved understanding about the functioning of the real system allow for improving the model.

Today, a lot of real-world geo-spatial information related to HICs is available online and in (near) real time which allows to automatically update the data and model, and hence, increase its value for the policy makers. The model used in this project was an ESDMA model. That is, uncertainties were included by means of sets of plausible assumptions and uncertainty ranges. Although this could already be argued to be a multi-model approach, hybrid models or a multi-method approach would really be needed to deal more properly with systems, agents, and spatial characteristics. Moreover, better interfaces and connectors to existing ICT systems and databases would also be needed to turn this pilot into a real decision-support system that would allow chiefs of police to experiment in a virtual world connected to the real world, and to develop and test adaptive robust policies on the spot.

5.6   Conclusions

Recent and current evolutions in modeling and simulation together with the recent explosive growth in computational power, data, social media, and other evolutions in computer science have created new opportunities for model-based analysis and decision making.

Multi-method and hybrid modeling and simulation approaches are being developed to make existing modeling and simulation approaches appropriate for dealing with agent system characteristics, spatial and network aspects, deep uncertainty, and other important aspects. Data science and machine learning techniques are currently being developed into techniques that can provide useful inputs for simulation models as well as for building models. Machine learning algorithms, formal model analysis methods, analytical approaches, and new visualization techniques are being developed to make sense of models and generate useful policy insights. And methods and tools are being developed to turn intuitive policy making into model-based policy design. Some of these evolutions were discussed and illustrated in this chapter.

It was also argued and shown that easier connectors to databases, to social media, to other computer programs, and to ICT systems, as well as better interfacing software need to be developed to allow any systems modeler to turn systems models into real decision-support systems. Doing so would turn the art of modeling into the computational science of simulation. It would most likely also shift the focus of attention from building a model to using ensembles of systems models for adaptive robust decision making.

References

Bankes SC (1993) Exploratory modeling for policy analysis. Operat Res 41(3):435–449
Bankes SC (2002) Tools and techniques for developing policies for complex and uncertain systems. Proc Natl Acad Sci U S A 99(3):7263–7266

Barlas Y (1996) Formal aspects of model validity and validation in system dynamics. Syst Dyn Rev 12(3):183–210

BenDor TK, Kaza N (2012) A theory of spatial system archetypes. Syst Dyn Rev 28(2):109–130

Bryant BP, Lempert RJ (2010) Thinking inside the box: a participatory, computer-assisted approach to scenario discovery. Technol Forecast Soc Change 77(1):34–49

Castillo D, Saysel AK (2005) Simulation of common pool resource field experiments: a behavioral model of collective action. Ecol Econ 55(3):420–436

Clemson B, Tang Y, Pyne J, Unal R (1995) Efficient methods for sensitivity analysis. Syst Dyn Rev 11(1):31–49

Coyle GR (1985) The use of optimization methods for policy design in a system dynamics model. Syst Dyn Rev 1(1):81–91

Coyle GR (1999) Simulation by repeated optimisation. J Operational Res Society 50:429–438

Diker VG, Allen RB (2005) XMILE: towards an XML interchange language for system dynamics models. Syst Dyn Rev 21(4):351–359

Dogan G (2007) Bootstrapping for confidence interval estimation and hypothesis testing for parameters of system dynamics models. Syst Dyn Rev 23(4):415–436

Doyle JK, Ford DN (1998) Mental models concepts for system dynamics research. Syst Dyn Rev 14:3–29

Doyle JK, Ford DN (1999) Mental models concepts revisited: some clarifications and a reply to Lane. Syst Dyn Rev 15:411–415

Eberlein RL, Chichakly KJ (2013) XMILE: a new standard for system dynamics. Syst Dyn Rev 29(3):188–195

Eker S, Slinger JH, Daalen EC, Yücel G (2014) Sensitivity analysis of graphical functions. Syst Dyn Rev 30(3):186–205

Feola G, Gallati JA, Binder CR (2012) Exploring behavioural change through an agent-oriented system dynamics model: the use of personal protective equipment among pesticide applicators in Colombia. Syst Dyn Rev 28(1):69–93

Fallah-Fini S, Rahmandad R, Chen HJ, Wang Y (2014) Connecting micro dynamics and population distributions in system dynamics models. Syst Dyn Rev 29(4):197–215

Fiddaman TS (2002) Exploring policy options with a behavioral climate–economy model. Syst Dyn Rev 18(2):243–267.

Ford A (1990) Estimating the impact of efficiency standards on the uncertainty of the northwest electric system. Oper Res 38(4):580–597

Ford A, Flynn H (2005) Statistical screening of system dynamics models. Syst Dyn Rev 21(1): 273–303

Forrester JW (1961) Industrial dynamics. MIT Press, Cambridge (Waltham, MA: Pegasus Communications. AND Productivity Press: Portland, OR)

Forrester JW (1968) Principles of systems. Wright-Allen Press, Cambridge

Forrester JW (1969) Urban dynamics. MIT Press, Cambridge

Forrester JW (1991) The beginning of system dynamics. D-Note D-4165-1

Forrester JW (2007) System dynamics—a personal view of the first fifty years. Syst Dyn Rev 23(2–3):345–358

Graham AK, Ariza CA (2003) Dynamic, hard and strategic questions: using optimization to answer a marketing resource allocation question. Syst Dyn Rev 19(1):27–46

Hamarat C, Kwakkel JH, Pruyt E (2013) Adaptive robust design under deep uncertainty. Technol Forecast Soc Change 80(3):408–418

Hamarat C, Kwakkel JH, Pruyt E, Loonen ET (2014) An exploratory approach for adaptive policymaking by using multi-objective robust optimization. Simul Model Pract Theory 46:25–39

Hearne JW (2010) An automated method for extending sensitivity analysis to model functions. Nat Resour Model 23(2):107–120

Homer JB (2012) Models that matter: selected writings on system dynamics 1985–2010. Grapeseed Press, Barrytown

Islam T, Pruyt E (2014) An adaptive sampling method for examining the behavioral spectrum of long-term metal scarcity. In: Proceedings of the 32nd international conference of the System Dynamics Society. System Dynamics Society, Delft, The Netherlands

Kampmann CE, Oliva R (2008) Structural dominance analysis and theory building in system dynamics. Syst Res Behav Sci 25(4):505–519

Kampmann CE, Oliva R (2009) Analytical methods for structural dominance analysis in system dynamics. In: Meyers R (ed) Encyclopedia of complexity and systems science. Springer, New York, pp 8948–8967

Kwakkel JH, Auping WL, Pruyt E (2013) Dynamic scenario discovery under deep uncertainty: the future of copper. Technol Forecast Soc Change 80(4):789–800

Kwakkel JH, Auping WL, Pruyt E (2014) Comparing behavioral dynamics across models: the case of copper. In: Proceedings of the 32nd international conference of the System Dynamics Society. System Dynamics Society, Delft, The Netherlands

Kwakkel JH, Pruyt E (2013a) Using system dynamics for grand challenges: the ESDMA approach. Syst Res Behav Sci doi:10.1002/sres.2225

Kwakkel JH, Pruyt E (2013b) Exploratory modeling and analysis, an approach for model-based foresight under deep uncertainty. Technol Forecast Soc Change 80(3):419–431

Lane DC (2000) Diagramming conventions in system dynamics. J Opl Res Soc 51(2):241–245

Lempert RJ, Groves DG, Popper SW, Bankes SC (2006) A general, analytic method for generating robust strategies and narrative scenarios. Manag Sci 52(4): 514–528

Lempert RJ, Popper SW, Bankes SC (2003) Shaping the next one hundred years: new methods for quantitative, long-term policy analysis. RAND report MR-1626, The RAND Pardee Center, Santa Monica, CA

Lempert RJ, Schlesinger ME (2000) Robust strategies for abating climate change. Climat Change 45(3–4):387–401

Logtens T, Pruyt E, Gijsbers G (2012) Societal aging in the Netherlands: exploratory system dynamics modeling and analysis. In: Proceedings of the 30th international conference of the System Dynamics Society. System Dynamics Society, St.-Gallen, CH

Meadows DH, Robinson JM (1985) The electronic Oracle. Computer models and social decisions. Wiley, Chichester

Miller J (1998) Active nonlinear tests (ANTs) of complex simulation models. Manag Sci 44(6):820–830

Moorlag R (2014) Exploring the effects of shale gas development on natural gas markets: a multi-method approach. In: Proceedings of the 32nd international conference of the System Dynamics Society. System Dynamics Society, Delft, The Netherlands

Oliva R (2003) Model calibration as a testing strategy for system dynamics models. Eur J Operat Res 151(3):552–568

Osgood N (2009) Lightening the performance burden of individual-based models through dimensional analysis and scale modeling. Syst Dyn Rev 25(2):101–134

Pruyt E (2013) Small system dynamics models for big issues: triple jump towards real-world complexity. TU Delft Library, Delft. http://simulation.tbm.tudelft.nl/

Pruyt E, Cunningham SC, Kwakkel JH, de Bruijn JA (2014) From data-poor to data-rich: system dynamics in the era of big data. In: Proceedings of the 32nd international conference of the System Dynamics Society. System Dynamics Society, Delft, The Netherlands

Pruyt E, Hamarat C (2010) The influenza A(H1N1)v pandemic: an exploratory system dynamics approach. In: Proceedings of the 28th international conference of the System Dynamics Society. System Dynamics Society, Seoul, Korea

Pruyt E, Hamarat C, Kwakkel JH (2012) Integrated risk-capability analysis under deep uncertainty: an integrated ESDMA approach. In: Proceedings of the 30th international conference of the System Dynamics Society. System Dynamics Society, St.-Gallen

Pruyt E, Kwakkel JH (2014) Radicalization under deep uncertainty: a multi-model exploration of activism, extremism, and terrorism. Syst Dyn Rev 30:1–28 doi:10.1002/sdr.1510

Pruyt E, Kwakkel JH, Hamarat C (2013) Doing more with models: illustration of a system dynamics approach for exploring deeply uncertain issues, analyzing models, and designing adaptive robust policies. In: Proceedings of the 31st international conference of the System Dynamics Society. System Dynamics Society, Cambridge

Rahmandad H, Sterman JD (2008) Heterogeneity and network structure in the dynamics of diffusion: comparing agent-based and differential equation models. Manag Sci 54(5):998–1014

Ruth M, Pieper F (1994) Modeling spatial dynamics of sea-level rise in a coastal area. Syst Dyn Rev 10(4):375–389

Saleh M, Oliva R, Kampmann CE, Davidsen PI (2010) A comprehensive analytical approach for policy analysis of system dynamics models. Eur J Operat Res 203(3):673–683

Sterman JD (2000) Business dynamics: systems thinking and modeling for a complex world. Irwin/McGraw-Hill, New York

Sterman JD (ed) (2007) Exploring the next great frontier: system dynamics at fifty. Syst Dyn Rev 23(2–3):89–93

Struben J (2005) Space matters too! Mutualistic dynamics between hydrogen fuel cell vehicle demand and fueling infrastructure. In: Proceedings of the 2005 international conference of the System Dynamics Society. System Dynamics Society, Boston

Sucullu C, Yücel G (2014) Behavior analysis and testing software (BATS). In: Proceedings of the 32nd international conference of the System Dynamics Society. System Dynamics Society, Delft, The Netherlands

Taylor TRB, Ford DN, Ford A (2010) Improving model understanding using statistical screening. Syst Dyn Rev 26(1):73–87

van der Maaten LJP, Hinton GE (2008) Visualizing data using t-SNE. J Mach Learn Res 9:2579–2605

Vennix JAM (1996) Group model building. Facilitating team learning using system dynamics. Wiley, Chichester

Yücel G (2012) A novel way to measure (dis)similarity between model behaviors based on dynamic pattern features. In: Proceedings of the 30th international conference of the System Dynamics Society, St. Gallen, Switzerland, 22 July–26 July 2012

Yücel G, Barlas Y (2011) Automated parameter specification in dynamic feedback models based on behavior pattern features. Syst Dyn Rev 27(2):195–215

Chapter 6
Features and Added Value of Simulation Models Using Different Modelling Approaches Supporting Policy-Making: A Comparative Analysis

Dragana Majstorovic, Maria A. Wimmer, Roy Lay-Yee, Peter Davis and Petra Ahrweiler

Abstract Using computer simulations in examining, explaining and predicting social processes and relationships as well as measuring the possible impact of policies has become an important part of policy-making. This chapter presents a comparative analysis of simulation models utilised in the field of policy-making. Different models and modelling theories and approaches are examined and compared to each other with respect to their role in public decision-making processes. The analysis has shown that none of the theories alone is able to address all aspects of complex policy interactions, which indicates the need for the development of hybrid simulation models consisting of a combinatory set of models built on different modelling theories. Building such hybrid simulation models will also demand the development of new and more comprehensive simulation modelling platforms.

D. Majstorovic (✉) · M. A. Wimmer
University of Koblenz-Landau, Koblenz, Germany
e-mail: majstorovic@uni-koblenz.de

M. A. Wimmer
e-mail: wimmer@uni-koblenz.de

R. Lay-Yee · P. Davis
Centre of Methods and Policy Application in the Social Sciences (COMPASS Research Centre),
University of Auckland, Private Bag 92019, 1142 Auckland, New Zealand
e-mail: r.layyee@auckland.ac.nz

P. Davis
e-mail: pb.davis@auckland.ac.nz

P. Ahrweiler
EA European Academy of Technology and Innovation Assessment GmbH,
Bad Neuenahr-Ahrweiler, Germany
e-mail: Petra.Ahrweiler@ea-aw.de

© Springer International Publishing Switzerland 2015
M. Janssen et al. (eds.), *Policy Practice and Digital Science,*
Public Administration and Information Technology 10, DOI 10.1007/978-3-319-12784-2_6

6.1 Introduction

Using computer simulation as a tool in examining, explaining and predicting social processes and relationships started intensively during 1990s (Gilbert and Troitzsch 2005). Since 2000s, a growing recognition of simulation models playing a role in public decision modelling processes can be noted (van Egmond and Zeiss 2010). One reason for this increased attention is that simulation models enable the examination of complex social processes and interactions between different entities and the potential impact of policies. For example, simulation models can be used to examine the impact of measures such as school closure and vaccination in stopping the spread of influenza as the cases described in Sect. 3.1 and 3.2 demonstrate; or to examine the influence of different policies in the early years of life as the case outlined in Sect. 3.3 evidences.

This chapter presents a comparative analysis of different simulation models with respect to their role in public decision-making processes. The focus is on investigating the differences between simulation models and their underlying modelling theories in order to find variables that impact the effectiveness of the usage of simulation models in policy-making. The ultimate goal is to provide an understanding of the peculiarities and the added value of different kinds of simulation models generated on the basis of particular modelling approaches. The chapter also aims at giving indications of how existing approaches to policy simulation can and should be combined to effectively support public policy-making in a comprehensive way.

This comparative analysis was performed as part of the eGovPoliNet[1] initiative, which aims at developing an international multidisciplinary policy community in information and communication (ICT) solutions for governance and policy modelling. eGovPoliNet brings researchers from different disciplines and communities together for sharing ideas, discussing knowledge assets and developing joint research findings. The project fosters a multidisciplinary approach to investigate different concepts in policy modelling. In investigating these concepts, researchers from different disciplines (such as information systems, e-government and e-participation, computer science, social sciences, sociology, psychology, organisational sciences, administrative sciences, etc.) collaborate to study the—so far mostly mono-disciplinary—approaches towards policy modelling. With this approach, eGovPoliNet aims at contributing to overcoming the existing fragmentation of research in policy modelling across different disciplines.

The research carried out in this paper was based on the literature study of policy modelling approaches whereby the authors collaborated with expertise from their own academic background. On the other hand, a comparative analysis of five different simulation models was performed using a framework of comparison developed along the eGovPoliNet initiative. The selection of the cases was based on the authors'

---

[1] eGovPoliNet—Building a global multidisciplinary digital governance and policy modelling research.and practice community. See http://www.policy-community.eu/ (last access: 28th July 2014).

access to and involvement in generating the particular models. Accordingly, the respective authors also elaborated the individual descriptions of the simulation models. The subsequent comparison and synthesis of simulation models based on different modelling approaches was done in a collaborative way. Findings were developed jointly and present views of different disciplines concerning the role of simulation models in policy modelling as well as possible ways of advancement of the usage of combinations of simulation models and joint elaborations thereof.

The key research questions guiding the comparative investigation of different simulation models are twofold: (1) What particular modelling theories, frameworks and/or methods build the theoretical and methodical foundations of simulation models in policy modelling? (2) In what way do simulation models developed on the basis of different foundations (cf. question (1)) differ and what lessons can be drawn from using different simulation models in policy modelling? To answer research question (1), the different theoretical and methodical grounds of simulation approaches will be studied, while for research question (2), five different simulation models will be compared and analysed.

The chapter is organised as follows: Sect. 6.2 first provides an understanding of the key terms and subsequently examines three different and widely used theories and approaches to simulation modelling (system dynamics, micro-simulation and agent-based modelling (ABM)) in order to establish common grounds for the research context. Subsequently, a framework for the comparative analysis of simulation models based on these modelling paradigms is introduced and five different simulation models are analysed in Sect. 6.3 (VirSim, MicroSim, MEL-C, OCOPOMO's Kosice model and SKIN). Then in Sect. 6.4, these models are compared and discussed to extract features of usage, benefits and the main characteristics of specific approaches to simulation modelling in policy-making. Some reflections on the research and practice implications as well as further research needs are also drawn from the comparative analysis. We conclude with a reflection on the results and insights gathered in Sect. 6.5.

6.2   Foundations of Simulation Modelling

Gilbert and Troitzsch define a simulation model as 'a simplification—smaller, less detailed, less complex, or all of these together—of some other structure or system' (Gilbert and Troitzsch 2005). A simulation model is a computer program that captures the behaviour of a real-world system and its input and possible output processes. It relies on data from the real world to create an artificial one that mimics the original but upon which experiments can be performed (Gilbert and Troitzsch 2005. According to Gilbert and Troitzsch, simulation models are useful for many reasons—it is easier, less expensive and in many cases the only appropriate way (e.g. spreading of a disease) or only feasible way (e.g. the consequences of some policy decisions can be seen only many years ahead as is the case with urbanisation) of examining possible impacts of policies. The output of a simulation is a set of measurements describing the observable reactions and a performance of a real-world system. For example, simulation models may produce forecasts or projections as output into the future, hence supporting policy-making processes, while stakeholders could use simulation models as support tools in examining possible impacts of different policies(Gilbert and Troitzsch 2005. Simulation models can also be used for a better understanding of real-world processes and relationships (Gilbert and Troitzsch 2005, for entertainment (e.g. the simulation game MoPoS[2], where a player is a central bank governor), as well as for education and training purposes (e.g. the simulation model GAIM[3]). On a higher abstraction level, simulation models can even be used for the formalisation of social theories producing social science specifications (Gilbert and Troitzsch 2005).

Different paradigms (i.e. approaches and theories) to simulation modelling exist in the literature. They vary in aspects of the reality they model as well as in methods they use to produce a simulation model (Gilbert and Troitzsch 2005. Three approaches are considered in this chapter: system dynamics as a representative type of macro-simulation, ABM as a representative type of modelling social behaviour of groups, and micro-simulation focusing on modelling individual's evolution. These approaches have been selected as they are well-known and widely used.

The system dynamics approach models a situation at a global level to describe a real-world system using analytical means via systems of differential equations (Gilbert and Troitzsch 2005. A real-world system is described and analysed as a whole at the macro-level (Forrester 1961) and represented using flow diagrams and internal feedback loops (Harrison et al. 2007). Such a model does not require much data and the output of the model consists of plots describing behaviour and the changes of the initial values of the variables and parameters of the model over time. To describe behaviour of the real-world process accurately, a model needs to be run many times with different parameter values (Maria 1997). A typical use of system dynamics models is macro-economic modelling as well as for describing the impact of policies during, for example, a spread of a disease. According to (Astolfi et al. 2012), system dynamics models are well suited for predicting short-term policy impacts.

Complex policy issues require approaches that enable research synthesis and the use of systems thinking (Milne et al. 2014). Micro-simulation modelling has the potential to represent systems and processes in various social domains and to test their functioning for policy purposes (Anderson and Hicks 2011; Zaidi et al. 2009). A micro-simulation model is based on empirical individual-level data and it can account for social complexity, heterogeneity, and change (Orcutt 1957; Spielauer 2011). Micro-simulation operates at the level of individual units, each with a set of associated attributes as a starting point. A set of rules, for example equations derived from statistical analysis of (often multiple) survey data sets, is then applied in a stochastic manner to the starting sample to simulate changes in state or behaviour.

---

[2] MoPoS—A monetary Policy Simulation Game (Lengwiler 2004).
[3] GAIM—Gestione Accoglienza IMmigrati (Sedehi 2006) is used for the training of foreign intercultural mediators in the immigration housing management courses.

Modifications of influential factors can then be carried out to test hypothetical 'what if' scenarios on a key outcome of policy interest (Davis et al. 2010). Micro-simulation can integrate, and accommodate the manipulation of, and the effects of variables across multiple model equations (often derived from multiple data sources) in a single simulation run. Thus, each otherwise separate equation is given its social context and influence among the other equations, representing a system of interdependent social processes.

Gilbert defines ABM as 'a computational method that enables a researcher to create, analyse and experiment with models composed of agents that interact within an environment' (Gilbert 2007). In artificial intelligence, agents are 'self-contained programs that can control their own actions based on their perceptions of the operating environment' (Gilbert and Troitzsch 2005). Applied to social processes, agents are individuals or groups of individuals aware of their environment and at the same time proactive in interactions with each other and their surroundings. Agent-based simulation models capture and explain the behaviour of agents and the dynamics of their social interactions, and they usually do not assume future predictions (Srbljanovic and Skunca 2003, Gilbert and Troitzsch 2005). ABM is considered a powerful tool for developing, testing and formalising social theories and examining complex social interactions (Gilbert and Troitzsch 2005). For example, agent-based simulations are able to describe complex social phenomena at a global macro-level emerging from simple micro-level interactions between the agents (Srbljanovic and Skunca 2003). The application of ABM offers two major advantages (Gilbert and Troitzsch 2005): a capability to show from where collective phenomena come based on isolation of critical behaviour and the main agents, and a possibility to explore various alternatives of development.

Building a simulation model means developing a computer program either from scratch or from adapting existing models. To achieve this, tools such as AnyLogic[4], NetLogo[5], etc.[6] are being used. Prior to programming the simulation model, appropriate knowledge about the policy context that should be explored needs to be collected. Different literature provide indications of the steps in an ordered process as shown in Fig. 6.1. It is to be noted that not necessarily every step is carried out by a simulation modeller. Depending on the expertise of programmers or policy analysts, steps 1 and 2 are in some cases merged, or steps 3 and 4 are not differentiated. In the simplest case, an expert policy modeller might even just perform steps 1, 4 and 5. However, to support a wider understanding of policy modelling, the sharing of the overall concept of analysis and programming, and a higher quality of simulation models, the performance of all five steps is highly recommended.

The first three steps to generate a simulation model are to (1) collect source data, (2) to develop a conceptual model and (3) to design the simulation model. These

---

[4] http://www.anylogic.com/ (last access: 28th July 2014).
[5] http://ccl.northwestern.edu/netlogo/ (last access: 28th July 2014).
[6] A more detailed overview of tools and technologies supporting policy making is provided in (Kamateri et al. 2014).

Fig. 6.1 Generic steps for developing simulation models

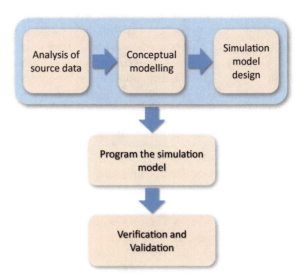

steps form the analytical work of policy modelling and can also be labelled 'policy analysis' and 'conceptual modelling'. The ways and methods to collect and *analyse source data* (step 1) depend on the type of simulation model to be generated and its underlying modelling paradigm. For example, micro-simulation is based on large amounts of representative data gathered on individuals; it considers characteristics of individuals and is able to reproduce social reality (Martini and Trivellato 1997). Micro-simulation is beneficial in predicting both short-term as well as long-term impacts of policies (Gilbert and Troitzsch 2005). System dynamics models the real-world system as a whole, i.e. at the macro-level (Forrester 1961) by using (a small set of) aggregated data. ABM is valuable for describing and explaining complex social interactions and behaviour, thus contributing to the understanding of a real-world social system and to a better management of different social processes (Gilbert and Troitzsch 2005). The focus is on groups and individuals interacting in a social system and the amount of data needed for developing the simulation model can be considered moderate. The particular approach of simulation modelling determines the complexity of data analysis (i.e. highly complex and intense for micro-simulation, moderate to high complexity for ABM (depending on the number of agents and the aggregation concept), and rather low for system dynamics). Inputs for data analysis are features, descriptions, relationships and specifications of the observed real-world system (Gilbert and Troitzsch 2005). Data analysis can be performed through many different ways ranging from qualitative and quantitative data analysis methods of the social sciences (Mayring 2011) to action research (Greenwood and Levin 2006), design research (Collins et al. 2004) and active stakeholder engagement using, e.g. scenario-building and online citizen participation methods (Wimmer et al. 2012). The second step—*conceptual modelling*—is not always explicitly implemented as already mentioned. It is a step that is widely used in action research and in design research. Newer approaches to policy modelling are based on the value of conceptualising a policy context and accordingly building conceptual models from the data analysed, as is, e.g. described in (Scherer et al. 2013). Since simulation models are simplifications of reality (Zeigler 1976), conceptual modelling, in practical terms, means to decide on which characteristics of the real-world system are to be included in a simulation model and which ones are not (Gilbert and Troitzsch 2005). In the third step—*design of the actual simulation model*—the programming of the simulation model is prepared by building a construct of the simulation model (again dependent on the modelling paradigm). The fourth step—*programming the simulation model*—involves putting hands on writing the code using a particular tool for programming. The fifth step—*verification and validation*—aims to check if a simulation model behaves as desired (i.e. verification) and whether the model describes the intended real-world system in a satisfactory way and gives reliable outputs (i.e. validation). Validation can be conducted by comparing known behaviour and parameters of the real-world system with the outputs of a simulation model (Maria 1997).

Based on the insights of different paradigms of simulation models, the next sections analyse and compare different models built on these theories and approaches.

6.3   Analysis of Simulation Models of Different Modelling Approaches

In this section, the analysis of five simulation models is presented with respect to their contribution to policy modelling in different public domains. The main goal is to describe and compare different simulation models in order to identify similarities and differences that suggest approaches, tools and techniques that are useful and effective in different policy modelling contexts. For the comparative analysis, eGov-PoliNet developed a framework which serves as a template to ensure comparability across particular aspects of study and to simplify understanding. The framework is divided into three parts: (1) abstract, which gives a brief summary of the model under investigation, and its context; (2) metadata, providing general information such as name of the model, developer, the publication date, background documents used in developing the model, references, tools needed to run the simulation model (for an ordinary user), and a reference to the source of the model; and (3) conceptual aspects of interest in the comparison such as disciplines involved in the model development, underlying theory, particular methods applied to develop the model, technical frameworks and tools used to develop the simulation model[7], application domain of the model, constraints of using the model in a particular way, examples of (re)use of the formal model (i.e. giving reference to policy cases and projects where the model

---

[7] A comparative analysis of tools and technical frameworks is provided in (Kamateri et al. 2014).

Table 6.1 Simulation models examined in the comparative analysis

Based on theory	Simulation model
System dynamics	VirSim—a model to support pandemic policy-making (cf. Sect. 6.3.1)
Micro-simulation	MicroSim—micro-simulation model: modelling the Swedish population (cf. Sect. 6.3.2)
	MEL-C—Modelling the early life-course (cf. Sect. 6.3.3)
Agent-based modelling (ABM)	OCOPOMO's Kosice case (cf. Sect. 6.3.4)
	SKIN—simulating knowledge dynamics in innovation networks (cf. Sect. 6.3.5)

is/was used), transferability of the simulation model in other domains or disciplinary contexts, and concluding recommendations on the model development and use).[8]

The simulation models studied in this chapter are based on the modelling paradigms presented in Sect. 6.2, namely system dynamics, micro-simulation, and ABM. Table 6.1 indicates the five simulation models examined in the comparative analysis and presented in the subsections below. It was not the aim of the authors to present an exhaustive list of models but rather a collection that is an informative choice of specific simulation models corresponding to different modelling theories. The models were chosen because the authors had the access to, and knowledge about these simulation models, and they were directly involved in the development of the simulation models analysed in Sect. 3.3, 3.4 and 3.5. The two models described in Sect. 3.1 and 3.2 are interesting for the comparison since they represent the same policy domain and use the same data but represent implementations of different modelling paradigms and methods.

The five simulation models are presented in the following subsections. The descriptions follow the structure suggested by the framework proposed by eGovPoliNet, i.e. abstract, metadata and conceptual aspects of interest. While the abstract is provided as a narrative paragraph, the metadata and conceptual aspects are each elaborated in a tabular form. The subsequent Sect. 6.4 provides a comparative discussion of the different models and their added value to policy modelling.

6.3.1 VirSim—A Model to Support Pandemic Policy-Making

VirSim simulates the spread of pandemic influenza and enables evaluating the effect of different policy measures (Fasth et al. 2010). The main goal is to find the most optimal policies connected to the starting time and the duration of school closure as

---

[8] The framework is published in Annex I to technical report D 4.2 of eGovPoliNet: Maria A. Wimmer and Dragana Majstorovic (Eds.): Synthesis Report of Knowledge Assets, including Visions (D 4.2). eGovPoliNet consortium, 2014, report available under http://www.policy-community.eu/results/public-deliverables/ (last access: 28th July 2014).

well as the pace and the vaccination coverage. Using the model, it is also possible to estimate public costs due to the absence of staff from work during sick leave. The model considers real population data in Sweden at both national and regional levels (Fasth et al. 2010). In VirSim, the population is divided into three age groups: individuals less than 20 years old, those between 20 and 59 years, and people aged 60 years and more. It is initially assumed that influenza spreads within and between groups with different probabilities. For each age group, a SEIR model (**S**usceptible, **E**xposed, **I**nfected, and **R**ecovered) is constructed, which represents the dynamics of spread of the disease. This means that a healthy person starts as a susceptible (S), becomes exposed (E), then infected (I) and, after some time recovered (R) (or dead). VirSim supports scenario analysis (i.e. 'what-if' analysis), which means that a user can combine a number of different parameters producing 'real' scenarios and examine the impact of policies while asking 'what could happen if we apply policy XY' (Fasth et al. 2010) (Table 6.2).

Table 6.2 Analysis of metadata and conceptual data of the simulation model VirSim

Metadata	
Name	VirSim
Developer	Tobias Fasth, Marcus Ihlar, Lisa Brouwers
Publication date	2010
Background documents	To segregate the Swedish population into three age groups: (Statistics Sweden (Statistiska centralbyrån, SCB 2009) To estimate frequency of social contacts between and within age groups: (Wallinga 2006) To decide on the duration of a latent period: (Carrat et al. 2008, Fraser et al. 2009)
Reference(s)	(Fasth et al. 2010)
Tools needed to run the model	Web browser, Internet
Source of the model	http://www.anylogic.com/articles/virsim-a-model-to-support-pandemic-policy-making (last access: 28th July 2014) http://people.dsv.su.se/~maih4743/VirSim/VirSim.html (needs Java Platform SE 7 U activated; last access: 28th July 2014)
Conceptual aspects	
Discipline(s)	Health science, Information technology/E-Government
Based on theory	System dynamics
Developed through method	SEIR model (**s**usceptible, **e**xposed, **i**nfected, **r**ecovered)
Technical framework/tools used for development	AnyLogic
Application domain(s)	Policy-making under pandemic influenza

Table 6.2 (continued)

Metadata	
Constraints of using the model in a particular way	The VirSim model does not take into account parameters that are also important for the transmission and spreading of the influenza virus, such as effect of weather and temperature conditions, geographical differences between regions as well as diverse social structures including travelling frequency, gender and hygiene habits. It is not possible to analyse many of the missing parameters since the underlying SEIR model and system dynamics method do not take into account social differences. Hence, the same infection probability was assigned to all people within the three age groups
Examples of use (projects/cases)	Policy-making under pandemic influenza in Sweden in 2009. Tested policies were vaccination and school closure (Fasth et al. 2010)
Transferability of formal model in other domains or disciplinary contexts	The initial values for all parameters are provided, for example, starting time of vaccination and the infection risk for different age groups, based on the documents and the data available in the time of the development of the model. However, VirSim allows for the change of all parameter values, including those initially assumed. This assures that the model is re-usable when other data become available. To our knowledge, the model is not transferable to other domains and contexts since it does not allow for a change of the parameters as such, their number, and the underlying differential equations
Concluding remarks on simulation model development and/or use	VirSim runs fast and a user can easily manipulate different parameters. However, the user interface does not include descriptions of the parameters; a user has to guess their meaning and a range of values, based on their names. In some cases, this is difficult, for example, for the parameter 'vaccination . . . starts after' with the initial value of 147—it is not clear for what the given initial value stands. Apart from this issue, the model is intuitive and easy to work with. The model is based on the scenario analysis—a user posts a question ('what could happen if we apply certain policy under certain conditions . . . ') and gets the answer in a form of suitable plots. This allows policy-making officials to discuss policies further towards finding the most suitable ones. To provide accurate and significant results, VirSim uses real population data in Sweden, at the national and regional level (Fasth et al. 2010). To use the simulation model in similar contexts, the model development should become flexible to support the definition of custom variables and at least some classes of differential equations that are suitable for modelling similar phenomena. Also, based on supported types of processes, the description of possible domains of application to which the model could be transferred would be helpful

6.3.2   MicroSim—Micro-simulation Model: Modelling the Swedish Population

According to Brouwers et al, MicroSim addresses the problem of the spread of influenza in Sweden. It is an event-driven micro-simulation model with discrete time steps of an hour, developed for exploring the impact of different intervention policies based on vaccination, isolation and social distancing. Each person living in Sweden was modelled in many details, including age, family status, employment details, and important geographical data, such as home and workplace coordinates. Such a modelling strategy provided a fine-grained differentiation between age groups, people's daily routines and their educational level. This enabled examining the spread of influenza through different social contacts as well as analysing the spatial spread of the disease within the time range of 1 h (Brouwers et al. 2009a, 2009b) (Table 6.3)

Table 6.3 Analysis of metadata and conceptual data of the simulation model MicroSim

Metadata	
Name	MicroSim—micro-simulation model: modelling the Swedish population
Developer	Lisa Brouwers, Martin Camitz, Baki Cakici, Kalle Mäkilä, Paul Saretok
Publication date	2009
Background documents	MicroSim uses registry data obtained from Statistics Sweden (Statistiska centralbyrån, SCB)[a] to generate the simulated population, in particular: National Population Register (2002) to describe age, marital status, children, employment, IDs father and mother; Employment Register (2002) to describe company, workplace, branch, municipality of the workplace for each individual; Employment Register (2002) to obtain family household coordinates, workplace coordinates, and school coordinates
Reference(s)	(Brouwers et al. 2009a, 2009b)
Tools needed to run the model	Executable that runs within C++ environment
Source of the model	Available on demand from http://arxiv.org/abs/0902.0901 (last access: 28th July 2014)
Conceptual aspects	
Discipline(s)	Health science, Information technology/E-Government
Based on theory	Micro-simulation
Developed through method	Population analysis
Framework/tools used for development	C++
Application domain(s)	Policy-making under pandemic influenza

Table 6.3 (continued)

Metadata	
Constraints of using the model in a particular way	The model relies on particular data from Sweden and therefore cannot be used for other countries. Also, due to possible migrations and changes in structure of Swedish population, the model has to be validated against new available data
Examples of use (projects/cases)	Policy-making under pandemic influenza in Sweden in Autumn of 2009
Transferability of formal model in other domains or disciplinary contexts	The model can be used as a basis for examining effects of different policies as well as dependencies in the real-world systems and processes based on social and geographical distributions
Concluding remarks on simulation model development and/or use	While micro-simulation models in general use only sample data of the population, MicroSim uses personal, employment and geographic data of the complete Swedish population (approximately 9 million people), which provides an explicit enhancement of the model's accuracy and reliability. Such detailed representation provides conditions suitable for realistic simulations of influenza outbreaks in Sweden. However, micro-simulation models based on the ontology of the population is not robust towards demographic changes in the social structure of a population

[a] http://www.scb.se (last access: 28th July 2014).

6.3.3 MEL-C—Modelling the Early Life-Course

MEL-C is a Knowledge-based Inquiry tool With Intervention modelling (KIWI) developed on the early life-course as a decision support aid to policy analysts and advisors in New Zealand. Underlying the tool is a dynamic discrete-time micro-simulation model using a social determinants framework to predict child outcomes, for which the key parameters have been estimated from existing longitudinal cohort studies in New Zealand, initially the Christchurch Health and Development Study. These parameters were applied to a starting sample synthesised from a combination of data from the national census and from the longitudinal studies. Thus a set of synthetic representative early life histories was created that reproduced patterns found in the original data. The tool can be interrogated with realistic policy scenarios by changing baseline features or parameters in the model and observing the effect on outcomes, for example, 'what if' the initial social determinants were different and what would be their impact. The model content, tool interface and inquiry system have been developed in cooperation with central government policy advisors drawn from the agencies with a special interest in the early life-course (Mannion et al. 2012) (Table 6.4).

Table 6.4 Analysis of metadata and conceptual data of the simulation model MEL-C

Metadata	
Name	MEL-C—modelling the early life-course
Developer	COMPASS[a]
Publication date	2014
Background documents	(Fergusson et al. 1989; Solar and Irwin 2010)
Reference(s)	(Mannion et al. 2012; Milne, et al. 2014; McLay et al. 2014; Lay-Yee et al. 2014)
Tools needed to run the model	The MEL-C executable, which includes JAMSIM (consisting of ASCAPE, JAVA and R) and simulation code run with R and tailored functions from the R Simario package developed by COMPASS
Source of the model	See http://code.google.com/p/jamsim/ for JASMIM (last access: 28th July 2014) See http://code.google.com/p/simario/ for R SIMARIO package (last access: 28th July 2014) MEL-C simulation model accessible on request from the COMPASS research centre
Conceptual aspects	
Discipline(s)	Social and health sciences (sociology, psychology, epidemiology), statistics, computer science, policy sciences
Based on theory	Child development, Social determinants of health, Micro-simulation
Developed through method	Regression analysis R and JAVA programming Micro-simulation modelling End-user engagement Cluster matching and data imputation
Framework/tools used for development	MEL-C as a single executable software application in which users can interrogate the model from the 'front end' and not need to deal with the 'behind-the-scenes' computer programs and statistical models. The tools used are: Eclipse, StatEt, Git control, Ivy. ASCAPE[b] and Jamsim[c] (JAVA) for front end Simario (R)[d] for execution of models
Application domain(s)	Early life-course, Health, Justice, Education, Social Policy, Policy scenarios, User interface
Constraints of using the model in a particular way	Limited by variables available in the source data sets. Relationships between variables are un-directional with no feedback. Scenarios tested involve changing the distribution of variables not the effects (e.g. the effect of X on Y). Potential geographical and period limits of data sources. Discrete time only
Examples of use (projects/cases)	Illustrative application to social determinants of health and end-user engagement

Table 6.4 (continued)

Metadata	
Transferability of formal model in other domains or disciplinary contexts	The model is of generic applicability in early life-course analysis. Subject to data availability and funding, it is possible to extend the model to later periods in the life-course and other domains. There may be other dynamic socio-demographic processes where this approach can be applied
Concluding remarks on simulation model development and/or use	The model is restricted to a notional 'evidence-based'/ science-informed approach to policy development. The model is conceptually predicated on the primacy of social determinants. The role of stakeholders is limited to the rather formal role of a policy advisor or analyst seeking to weigh different options within a prescribed range. The model is able to reproduce actualities and to produce plausible substantive results in scenario testing. The model has the great potential of combining a realistic data framework with estimates derived from meta-analyses, systematic reviews and other research sources. The model is a simplification of reality but is nevertheless a powerful source of information that can be interrogated by end-users and can be considered alongside other evidence for policy

[a] http://www.arts.auckland.ac.nz/en/about/ourresearch-1/research-centres-and-archives/centre-of-methods-and-policy-application-in-the-social-sciences-compass/about-compass.html (last access: 28th July 2014).
[b] http://ascape.sourceforge.net/ (last access: 28th July 2014).
[c] http://code.google.com/p/jamsim/ (last access: 28th July 2014).
[d] http://code.google.com/p/simario/ (last access: 28th July 2014).

6.3.4 Ocopomo's Kosice Case

Energy policy is increasingly receiving attention, especially in exploring renewable energy sources, energy saving and to raise awareness about energy policy among citizens. The aim of the simulation model developed for the Kosice self-governing region was to capture the behaviour of key stakeholders and decision-makers towards a new energy policy moving to better house insulation and to using renewable energy sources. The renewable energy policy case combined the scenario-method with ABM to explore social behaviour and interrelations between stakeholders, economic conditions of the region and realistic social dynamics. Based on the stakeholder inputs gathered through scenarios developed via an online e-participation platform, a conceptual model was developed which informed the agent-based simulation model. The simulation model helped to test the effectiveness of various policy options (e.g. to support better insulation of houses, to invest in renewable energy sources such as gas, coal, and biomass, etc.) (Wimmer et al. 2012). A particularity of the model is the possibility to trace evidence data provided in stakeholders' scenarios or background documents via a conceptual model to inform the simulation model. Accordingly it is possible for stakeholders to navigate from the simulation outputs back to the evidence input (Lotzmann and Wimmer 2013) (Table 6.5).

Table 6.5 Analysis of metadata and conceptual data of the simulation model developed in OCOPOMO's Kosice case

Metadata	
Name	OCOPOMO's Kosice case
Developer	Partners of the OCOPOMO consortium, involving University of Koblenz-Landau, Scott Moss Associates, Technical University of Kosice, Intersoft and Kosice Self-Governing Region (KSR)
Publication date	2013
Background documents	Based on the OCOPOMO approach (Wimmer et al. 2012) a number of background documents was used, such as: Analysis of structural funds (2007–2013) and Projects Approved in 2009 in KSR Energy policy of KSR (2007) Strategy of Renewable Energy Sources Utilization in KSR (2006) Demographic composition of the households (1996) Annual report 2009, Regulatory Office for Network Industries Regional Statistics Database (2010) Interviews with experts from KSR and local energy providers
Reference(s)	(Wimmer et al. 2012; Wimmer 2011; Lotzmann and Meyer 2011; Butka et al. 2011; Lotzmann and Wimmer 2013)
Tools needed to run the model	Collaborative e-participation platform for scenario generation and stakeholder engagement using the ALFRESCO[a] Web content management system (wiki for scenario generation, discussion, polling) DRAMS (Lotzmann and Meyer 2011)—the Declarative Rule-based Agent Modelling system, Consistent Conceptual Modelling Tool (CCD) (Scherer et al. 2013)
Source of the model	http://www.ocopomo.eu/results/software-and-models/software-and-model-artefacts/eclipse-based-tools-and-simulation-models (last access: 28th July 2014)
Conceptual aspects	
Discipline(s)	Social Science, Information Systems/E-Government
Based on theory	Agent-based modelling, Model-driven Architecture, Design Research, Stakeholder theory
Developed through method	Stakeholder engagement through online deliberation, qualitative analysis methods such as workshops and interviews, conceptual modelling using Consistent Conceptual Modelling (CCD), ontology development
Framework/tools used for development	Eclipse Modelling Framework (EMF)[b], Eclipse Graphical Modelling Framework (GMF)[c], Graphical Editing Framework (GEF)[d], Collaborative participation platform for scenario generation and stakeholder interaction ALFRESCO (wiki, discussion, voting), DRAMS—Declarative Rule-based Agent Modelling System, Consistent Conceptual Modelling (CCD) Tool
Application domain(s)	The simulation model is used for policy development in the field of energy with the focus on: • Energy efficiency • Decrease of energy consumption (heating) and improved insulation as well as wise spending of energy • Utilisation of renewable energy sources
Constraints of using the model in a particular way	Agent-based modelling is particularly applicable for examining social behaviour but cannot be the only source for policy-making.

Table 6.5 (continued)

Metadata	
Examples of use (projects/cases)	Renewable energy and heating in Kosice Self-Governing Region (KSG), Slovakia Housing policy in London, UK Knowledge transfer in Campania Region, Italy Parts of the OCOPOMO simulation environment are also used in the GLODERS project[e]
Transferability of formal model in other domains or disciplinary contexts	Natural conditions of the Kosice region, such as terrain, location of and distance from the renewable energy sources, concentration of housing, available infrastructure, influence the output of the model. Therefore, transferability is restricted, and the use of the model demands for updating the local and natural conditions of a region
Concluding remarks on simulation model development and/or use	The simulation model is evidence-based and built around the descriptions, expectations, interactions and beliefs of stakeholders in the policy-making process. The modelling process involved stakeholders who expressed their views and concerns on a policy via collaborative scenarios and e-participation tools. They acted as partners and researchers in the modelling process. A key feature of the OCOPOMO policy modelling approach is to engage stakeholders and to ensure traceability from evidence-based input of stakeholders in narrative text to simulation outputs generated through agent-based simulation. A lesson from using a declarative rule programming paradigm as implemented in DRAMS vs. the imperative paradigm in most ABM tools is that the declarative way is more difficult to program and less intuitive for programmers

[a] http://www.alfresco.com/?pi_ad_id=39517088287 (last access: 28th July 2014).
[b] https://www.eclipse.org/modeling/emf/ (last access: 28th July 2014).
[c] http://www.eclipse.org/modeling/gmp/ (last access: 28th July 2014).
[d] http://www.eclipse.org/gef/ (last access: 28th July 2014).
[e] http://www.gloders.eu/ (last access: 28th July 2014).

6.3.5 SKIN—Simulating Knowledge Dynamics in Innovation Networks

Simulating Knowledge Dynamics in Innovation Networks (SKIN) is an agent-based model used to understand innovation policy initiatives, which contain heterogeneous agents, who act and interact in a large-scale complex and changing social environment. The agents represent innovative actors who try to sell their innovations to other agents and end users but who also have to buy raw materials or more sophisticated inputs from other agents (or material suppliers) to produce their outputs. This basic model of a market is extended with a representation of the knowledge dynamics in and between the agents. Each agent tries to improve its innovation performance and its sales by improving its knowledge base through adaptation to user needs, incremental or radical learning, and co-operation and networking with other agents (Ahrweiler et al. 2004) (Table 6.6)

Table 6.6 Analysis of metadata and conceptual data of the simulation model SKIN

Metadata	
Name	Simulating knowledge dynamics in innovation networks (SKIN)
Developer	Gilbert, Nigel; Ahrweiler, Petra; Pyka, Andreas
Publication date	2001, with continuous updates since
Background documents	Literature from Evolutionary Economics, Economic Sociology, and Science and Technology Studies (see body of literature cited in the references as listed next)
Reference(s)	(Gilbert et al. 2001; Ahrweiler et al. 2004; Gilbert et al. 2007; Pyka et al. 2007; Scholz et al. 2010; Ahrweiler et al. 2011a, 2011b; Gilbert et al. 2014)
Tools needed to run the model	NetLogo (versions available in alternative languages such as Java) http://ccl.northwestern.edu/netlogo/ (last access: 28th July 2014)
Source of the model	http://cress.soc.surrey.ac.uk/SKIN/ (last access: 28th July 2014)
Conceptual aspects	
Discipline(s)	Economics, sociology, science and technology studies, policy research, business studies
Based on theory	Evolutionary Economics, Organisational Theory, Organisational Learning, Field Theory, Complex Systems Theory, Agent-based modelling
Developed through method	Theory formation, empirical research, implementing theoretical concepts and empirical insights, consistent conceptual modelling, agent-based modelling
Framework/tools used for development	NetLogo
Application domain(s)	Knowledge-intensive industries, EU framework programmes, national innovation policies, role of specific actors in innovation networks
Constraints of using the model in a particular way	SKIN is about knowledge and agent networks embedded in a dynamic environment. Not applicable if domain has nothing to do with it.
Examples of use (projects/cases)	EU projects: Simulating self-organizing innovation networks (SEIN)[a], 1998–2001 Network models, governance, and R&D collaboration networks (NEMO)[b], 2006–2009 Managing emerging technologies for economic impact (ManETEI)[c], 2010–2014 Using network analysis to monitor and track effects resulting from Changes in policy intervention and instruments, (SMART 2010/0025) 2010–2011 Governance of responsible research and innovation (GREAT)[d], 2013–2016

Table 6.6 (continued)

Metadata	
Transferability of formal model in other domains or disciplinary contexts	SKIN is a multi-disciplinary initiative (see above Discipline(s)) and is therefore used in various disciplinary contexts. However, as it is about knowledge and agent networks embedded in a dynamic environment, it is not applicable if the policy domain is not working with knowledge, innovation and agent networks
Concluding remarks on simulation model development and/or use	The advantages of using SKIN for policy modelling include: The experiments can be run many times to find statistically average behaviour. Experiments can be used to give an indication of the likely effects of a wide variety of policy measures Empirical 'Un-observables' such as the amount of knowledge generated, and the number of proposals started but abandoned before submission, can be measured by instrumenting the simulation The problems include determining: What are the ultimate policy objectives for the support of Research and Development? When were the policies being formulated and by whom? How can the research be presented so that it is interesting and comprehensible to a policy-making audience?

[a] http://ec.europa.eu/research/social-sciences/projects/097_en.html.
[b] http://cress.soc.surrey.ac.uk/SKIN/research/projects/nemo.
[c] http://lubswww.leeds.ac.uk/manetei/home/.
[d] http://www.great-project.eu/ (last access 28th July 2014).

6.4 Comparison of Simulation Models and Discussion of Added Value and Limitations of Particular Simulation Models

In Table 6.7, the key elements of the five simulation models introduced in Sect. 3 are compared using the comparison framework above, and summed up on the following aspects: publication date of the model, key aspects of the model, tools needed to run the model, discipline(s), simulation paradigm on which the model is based, method through which the model is developed, framework and/or tools used for the development of the model, application domain, constraints of using the model, examples of use, model's transferability to other domains, and limitations and suggestions.

As elaborated in Sect. 3.1, the VirSim simulation model examines the effect of different policies to the problem of influenza spread by using the SEIR model for modelling the population on a global (macro-) level. Over time, a person changes between the categories and this flow is described with a set of differential equations (Fasth et al. 2010). The model applies a system dynamics paradigm. The other example of the same policy domain, the micro-simulation model MicroSim as introduced in Sect. 3.2, applies a different modelling approach to the same problem, where each person is modelled in many details. The spread of influenza is therefore determined by many 'micro'-level factors.

Table 6.7 Comparison of simulation models

	VirSim	MicroSim	MEL-C	OCOPMO's Kosice case	SKIN
Publication date	2010	2009	2014	2013	2001, with frequent updates since
Key aspects	Simulates spread of pandemic influenza. Uses real population data in Sweden on national and regional level Runs fast and allows easy manipulation of values of predefined parameters Based on scenario analysis. Tested policies: vaccination and school closure	Simulates spread of pandemic influenza in Sweden Models complete Swedish population in many details including personal data, working data and household details	Knowledge-based inquiry tool with intervention modelling Decision support for early life-course Realistic policy scenarios. Developed in cooperation with central government policy advisors and the agencies relevant to the early life-course	Testing the effectiveness of public policies connected to renewable energy sources and energy saving under different conditions. Capturing the behaviour of key stakeholders in the decision-making process Simulation model evidence-based and built around the descriptions, expectations, interactions and beliefs of stakeholders. Stakeholders acting as partners in the modelling process Raising awareness about energy policy among citizens and stakeholders through scenario-based method with online e-participation platform Traceability of evidence inputs to inform the agent-based simulation model	For understanding innovation policy initiatives The experiments can be run many times to find statistically average behaviour and the likely effect of a wide variety of policies Empirical 'Un-observables' can be measured by instrumenting the model

Table 6.7 (continued)

	VirSim	MicroSim	MEL-C	OCOPOMO's Kosice case	SKIN
Tools needed to run the model	Web browser, Internet	Executable that runs within C++ environment	MEL-C executable, which includes JAMSIM (consisting of ASCAPE, JAVA and R) and simulation code run with R and tailored functions from the R Simario package	ALFRESCO web content management for stakeholder engagement CCD Tool and DRAMS for conceptual modelling and programming the model	NetLogo. Versions also in other languages, such as Java
Discipline(s)	Health science, information technology/ e-government	Health science, information technology/ e-government	Social and health sciences (sociology, psychology, epidemiology), statistics, computer science	Social science, information systems/e-government	Economics, sociology, science and technology studies, policy research, business studies
Simulation paradigm	System dynamics	Micro-simulation	Micro-simulation	Agent-based modelling	Agent-based modelling
Developed through method(s)	SEIR model	Population analysis, Micro-simulation modelling	Regression analysis, R and JAVA programming, Micro-simulation modelling, End-user engagement, Cluster matching and data imputation	Evidence-based OCOPOMO policy modelling process, involving stakeholder engagement, scenario-building, conceptual modelling, agent-based modelling using declarative rule engine	Theory formation, empirical research, implementing theoretical concepts and empirical insights, consistent conceptual modelling, agent-based modelling
Framework/ tools used for development	AnyLogic	C++ programming framework	Eclipse, StatEt, Git control, Ivy. ASCAPE and Jamsim (JAVA) for front end Simario (R) for execution of models	Eclipse with EMF, GMF, GEF, DRAMS, CCD Tool and CCD2DRAMS transformation tool ALFRESCO WCMS	NetLogo

Table 6.7 (continued)

	VirSim	MicroSim	MEL-C	OCOPMO's Kosice case	SKIN
Application domain	Health and social policy with focus on pandemic influenza	Health and social policy with focus on pandemic influenza	Health, Justice, Education, Social Policy with focus on early life-course	Energy policy with focus on user behaviour towards energy efficiency and renewables	Knowledge-intensive industries, European and National innovation policies
Constraints of the usage	Missing important parameters. To all people within age groups assigned same probability	Uses particular data from Sweden. Not robust to changes in the population data	Limited by available data sources. Un-directional relationships between variables with no feedback. Changing the distribution of variables not the effects. Discrete time only	Agent-based modelling applicable for examining social behaviour but cannot be the only source for policy-making. Model can become quite complex depending on the number of agents	Model applicable for a domain of knowledge and agent networks embedded in a dynamic environment
Examples of use	Policy-making under pandemic influenza in Sweden in 2009	Policy-making under pandemic influenza in Sweden in Autumn of 2009	Illustrative application to social determinants of health and end-user engagement	Energy policy to explore stakeholder behaviour in KSR, SK. Further models generated: Housing Policy in London, UK. Knowledge Transfer support in Campania Region, Italy	EU projects SEIN, NEMO, ManETEI, SMART, GREAT
Transferability and re-usability	Re-usable for other available data but not for other domains and contexts	Re-usable for examining policies based on demographics	Generic applicability in early life-course analysis. Possible to extend model to later periods in the life-course and to other domains. Other dynamic socio-demographic processes	Re-use limited to particular policy and regional context. Model can serve as a blueprint for new models	SKIN can be used in various disciplinary contexts working with knowledge and agent networks embedded in dynamic environments

Table 6.7 (continued)

	VirSim	MicroSim	MEL-C	OCOPMO's Kosice case	SKIN
Limitations of models/ suggestions for extensions	*Limitations*: model parameters and equations are fixed and cannot be modified *Suggestions*: Extend the model to support definition of custom variables Allow for modelling similar phenomena Allow for transferability to other domains	*Limitations*: the model is not robust towards demographic changes. *Suggestion*: allow for realistic simulation of influenza outbreaks	*Limitations*: restricted to a notional 'evidence-based'/science-informed approach conceptually predicated on the primacy of social determinants Limited role of stakeholders. *Suggestions*: Combination of a realistic data framework and estimates derived from trials and systematic reviews Useful for end-users	*Limitations*: Declarative rule engine not easy to program Conceptual and simulation model not easy to understand for end-users. *Suggestions*: Extend the CCD tool and transformation tool to connect to other ABM tools such as AnyLogic, NetLogo etc. Extend the model transformation to support also backward consistency from simulation model to conceptual model as programmers may change simulation code easily	*Limitations*: The ultimate policy objectives for the support of research and development need yet to be determined *Suggestions*: Important to develop methods of the research presentations to be interesting and comprehensible to a policy-making audience

The main advantage of system dynamics models is that they are fast to run and technologically not demanding while providing useful information about the real-world processes and insights into possible impacts of different macro-level policies. However, these models face a number of restrictions. For example, VirSim initially assumes infection probabilities where elderly people (age group 60 and more) have considerably fewer chances of being infected with influenza compared to the other two age groups (Fasth et al. 2010). However, the SEIR model that was applied cannot predict this and cannot explain why this occurs. The authors of VirSim used this result from the micro-simulation model MicroSim and assumed this phenomenon happens because of less social contacts of elderly people or some prior immunity. VirSim cannot explain this phenomenon because system dynamics does not include modelling of various social interactions and other similar dependencies between actors since all variables are averaged over particular groups or the population in general - in the case of VirSim within the members of a particular age group. Apart from the categories of people based on their age, VirSim cannot identify fine-grain groups that have higher probability to be infected. For example, a student has more chances to be exposed and therefore infected than a researcher working in the same university but more in the closed environment of an office while students usually have more frequent social interactions among their groups and communities. It is important to identify closed environments that have high risk of spreading influenza, for example boarding and nursing homes. From the policy modelling point of view, it is important to identify high-risk groups to start the vaccination from there. One could define refined categories of actors by defining more variables, but in general, it would not be possible to represent relations between subcategories, such as taxonomies or ontologies needed to represent social contacts or interactions among actors, due to the lack of representation apparatus in system dynamics models.

As Gilbert and Troitzsch argue, due to social complexity and non-linearity, it is difficult to describe processes and systems analytically. To be able to examine interactions between simulation units, other modelling techniques such as ABM or micro-simulation models need to be applied for exploring the social heterogeneity and structures (Gilbert and Troitzsch 2005).

Micro-simulation models, usually based on a weighted sum of a representative sample of the population, consider characteristics of individuals and are able to re-produce social reality (Martini and Trivellato 1997). They are beneficial in predicting both, short-term as well as long-term impact of policies (Gilbert and Troitzsch 2005). However, micro-simulation models are costly to build and complex, especially at the level of data analysis requirements. In the case of MicroSim, the Swedish population of approximately nine million people was modelled in many details (Brouwers et al. 2009). In addition, in 'simple' cases, especially in demographics, a micro-simulation model produces similar results as a system dynamics-based model (Gilbert and Troitzsch, 2005). This proved true in the case of MicroSim and VirSim: The lat-ter confirmed the results of the former, although with a greater difference between vaccination and non-vaccination results (The National Board of Health and Wel-fare 2011). According to Spielauer, micro-simulation is best to use when population heterogeneity matters; when there are too many possible combinations to split the population into a manageable number of groups; in situations when the micro level explains complex macro-behaviours, or when individual history is important for the model's outcomes (Spielauer 2011).

Although agent-based models lack clear predictive possibilities, they are considered a highly valuable tool for describing and explaining complex social interactions and behaviours, contributing to the understanding of real-world social systems and to a better management of different social processes. Schindler argues that agent-based simulations are capable of representing real-world systems, where small changes in parameter values induce big changes in the model's outputs. This property shifts attention from the importance of predictions of the system's future behaviour to the management of critical (social) processes responsible for the changes. However, agent-based simulations alone are not sufficient to model reality. Another possible problem is a high degree of freedom in modelling agents, which amplifies the importance of a proper validation of a simulation model (Schindler 2013).

While agent-based and micro-simulation models would be able to show that an elderly person has less infection probability, it is questionable whether they would be able to answer why an elderly person is less infected by influenza. Knowing 'why' can help in building a successful strategy for protection against the disease. It might happen that hidden variables and parameters influence this age group. For this reason, in order to model correct probabilities for different age groups, several authors suggest that uncertainty models, such as (dynamic) Bayesian models or Markov chains could be used. In addition, if the past should be also considered (for example, a person has less chances to be infected now because he/she was infected in the recent past), then we have to use more complex probability models, such as the Dempster–Shafer model (Ronald and Halpern 1991, Jameson 1996). Gilbert and Troitzsch argue that statistical models can also be used to predict values of some dependent variables. However, statistical models assume linear relationships between parameters, which becomes a restrictive assumption in the case of (complex) social systems (Gilbert and Troitzsch 2005).

Comparing the three different paradigms of social and policy modelling explored in this chapter, the three approaches can be examined according to the level of granularity they are focussing on, the complexity of the models, the demand for the amount of data needed to generate a valuable simulation model and whether social behaviour is modelled. Table 6.8 provides this comparison, which is adapted from (Gilbert and Troitzsch 2005). Micro-simulation models represent particular ontologies of the population or its representative subset based on individuals and are most demanding regarding data needed for developing a model. Agent-based models are less data demanding, less complex and well suited for representing groups of actors (which can represent individuals, groups as well as a system as a whole) and their social behaviour. ABM is the only one of the three paradigms studied which models social behaviour. However, social behaviour cannot be the only source for policy-making (Gilbert and Troitzsch 2005) Macro-models, in this chapter represented by system dynamics, are the least demanding—they model a situation at a global level and require the least data. Nevertheless, they are better for the analysis of short-term policy impacts than for longer-term perspectives (Astolfi et al. 2012).

Table 6.8 Comparison of simulation modelling theories along level of granularity, the complexity of the models, the amount of data needed to generate simulation models, and the modelling of social behaviour of agents

Simulation paradigm	Granularity	Complexity	Data needed	Behavioural
System dynamics	Macro-focusing on the system as a whole	Low	Aggregated data	No
Micro-simulation	Micro-focusing on individuals	High	High amount at individual level	No
Agent-based modelling	Micro-macro—focusing on interaction of agents (which can be individuals as well as a system)	Medium-high	Low to moderate (depending on the number of agents and the policy context)	Yes

The analysis of three different modelling paradigms with the comparison of five different simulation models has shown that each of the modelling approaches has strengths and weaknesses that constrain their usage in policy-making. For example, micro-simulation can be used for representing social structures while ABM examines interactions between the agents. Astolfi et al argue that none of the theories alone is able to address complex policy interactions (Astolfi et al. 2012). In consequence, a necessary step in the development of simulation modelling is to build and explore ways of maintaining complex simulation models consisting of a few sub-models built on different modelling theories, which communicate with each other by setting up and propagating particular parameters after each reasoning iteration (Astolfi et al. 2012). These hybrid models can be considered as modelling platforms or complex systems consisting of sub-models. Yet, it is necessary to study methodologies and possibilities of combining different modelling paradigms in order to provide reliable simulation platforms. Current research indicates this trend, as an example of micro-macro combination in a Chronic Disease Prevention Model developed in Australia shows (Brown et al. 2009). However, more research is needed to better understand the implications of combined modelling paradigms, to develop innovative simulation platforms that support easy adjustment and development of different models based on different modelling paradigms and to bring evangelists of particular modelling paradigms closer to each other to support mutual understanding and the exploration of the added value and benefits of particular simulation models. Further recommendations and indications of research needs include, but are not exhaustively listed:

- Providing guidelines for how to best choose and arrange a collection of smaller (sub) models each describing certain aspects of a given domain of modelling;
- Finding the junction points of those models of distinct modelling paradigms with each other by defining input and output parameters for each of the sub-models;
- Developing meta-models that reflect the combinatory use of distinct modelling approaches;

- Determining the workflow of a simulation process by means of, e.g. a sequence and timing of exchanging the input and output parameters between sub-models in a combined hybrid meta-model;
- Exploring more extensive engagement of stakeholders in the policy development[9];
- Developing more comprehensive simulation platforms that enable the combination of different simulation paradigms in an easy way.

6.5   Conclusions

In this chapter, we have examined and compared five different simulation models, which were built on three different modelling paradigms: system dynamics, micro-simulation, and ABM. The chapter first provided an overview of the main characteristics of each of the modelling paradigms and then described the five simulation models by outlining them according to a framework elaborated by eGovPoliNet for comparative analysis of knowledge assets. The simulation models are each suitable for representing different aspects of socio-political and/or socio-economic phenomena, such as demographic processes (education, social contacts, spread of diseases, etc.), innovation processes or natural resource consumptions (e.g. energy consumption). The comparison has revealed the major differences as well as added value and limitations of the different approaches and simulation models. Some lessons from the comparative analysis are that the main strengths of using simulation models in policy-making are the possibilities of exploring and creating understanding of real-world systems and relationships, of experimenting with new situations and of forecasting outputs of alternative policy options or situations based on the given values of parameters. Another key added value of simulation models in policy-making is that simulation models enable the exploration of social processes to evaluate potential impacts of alternative policy options on real-world situations and thus to identify the most suitable policy option.

Current paradigms of policy modelling using simulation models are however constrained by their particular focus. Yet, our real-world systems and social processes are complex and require the consideration of parameters at different levels: macro-level, micro-level as well as social behaviour and interconnections between actors. Accordingly, applying one singular approach to modelling a real-world problem is constrained by the particular modelling approach it focuses on: A simulation model of system dynamics may therefore lack precision and social interactions because the missing factors are not accounted for. While the demand for meeting the appropriate level of details included in a model's description, being not too complex and also not too simple, determines the success of a simulation model, there is a rising need for integrating and combining different modelling paradigms to accommodate the diverse aspects to be considered in complex social world policy contexts. Unifying

---

[9] A more detailed discussion of stakeholder engagement in policy making is given in (Helbig et al. 2014).

different modelling theories under an umbrella of comprehensive policy modelling platforms is a research need identified in this chapter. Such research should put forward a meta-model of how individual simulation paradigms can be combined, and suggestions of 'clever' junctions of individual smaller (and self-contained) simulation models dedicated to individual aspects to be modelled.

While this chapter selected three widely used simulation paradigms for the study, it does not claim to be exhaustive nor comprehensive. Further research is needed to extend the study to involve other important modelling approaches such as theory-based macro-economic forecasting for instance Dynamic Stochastic General Equilibrium (DSGE) modelling. DSGE is exemplified by the Global Economy Model (GEM) which provides support in policy analysis to central banks and the International Monetary Fund (IMF) (Bayoumi 2004). This will further add to understanding the scope and limitations of different modelling paradigms, as for example Farmer and Foley argue, too, that instead of DSGE models, agent-based models should be used to model the world economy (Farmer and Foley 2009). Thus, the authors of this chapter recognise the need to continue comparative analysis as carried out in this contribution and to expand the research to incorporate further modelling paradigms as well as other public policy domains. Insights gained will help build up better hybrid models of social simulation paradigms that are better able to cope with the complexity of our social and dynamic world systems and that are more reliable as they are covering the various social, policy and economic aspects at various levels of abstraction and giving consideration in a more comprehensive way. Accordingly, better social simulation modelling platforms will emerge.

References

Ahrweiler P, Pyka A, Gilbert N (2004) Simulating knowledge dynamics in innovation networks (SKIN). In: Leombruni R, Richiardi M (eds) The agent-based computational approach. World Scientific Press, Singapore, pp 284–296

Ahrweiler P, Gilbert N, Pyka, A (2011a) Agency and structure. A socials simulation of knowledge-intensive industries. Comput Math Org Theor 17(1):59–76

Ahrweiler P, Pyka A, Gilbert N (2011b) A new model for university-industry links in knowledge-based economies. J Prod Innov Manage 28(2):218–235

Anderson RE, Hicks C (2011) Highlights of contemporary microsimulation. Soc Sci Comput Rev 29(1):3–8

Astolfi R, Lorenzoni L, Oderkirk J (2012) A comparative analysis of health forecasting methods. OECD Health Working Papers, No. 59. OECD Publishing. doi:10.1787/18152015

Bayoumi T (2004) GEM: a new international macroeconomic model, Occasional Paper 239. Washington, D.C.: International Monetary Fund. http://213.154.74.164/invenio/record/12437/files/bayoumiop239.pdf. Accessed 29th July 2014

Brouwers L, Cakici B, Camitz M, Tegnell A, Boman M (2009a) Economic consequences to society of pandemic H1N1 influenza 2009– preliminary results for Sweden. Euro Surveillance 14(37):pii= 19333. http://www.eurosurveillance.org/ViewArticle.aspx?ArticleId = 19333 Accessed 29 July 2014

Brouwers L, Camitz M, Cakici B, Mäkilä K, Saretok P (2009b) MicroSim: modeling the Swedish Population. http://arxiv.org/abs/0902.0901. Accessed 29 July 2014

Brown L, Harris A, Picton M, Thurecht L, Yap M, Harding A et al. (2009). Linking micro-simulation and macro-economic models to estimate the economic impact of chronic disease prevention. In: Zaidi A, Harding A, Williamson P (eds) New frontiers in microsimulation modelling. Ashgate, European Centre Vienna, pp 527–556

Butka P, Mach M, Furdik K, Genci J (2011) Design of a system architecture for support of collaborative policy modelling processes. In: Proceedings of SACI 2011, 6th IEEE International Symposium on Applied Computational Intelligence and Informatics. Red Hook, NY, USA, Òbuda University, Hungary, IEEE, Curran Associates, Inc, pp 193–198

Carrat F, Vergu E, Ferguson N, Lemaitre M, Cauchemez S, Leach S, Valleron A (2008) Time lines of infection and disease in human influenza: a review of volunteer challenge studies. Am J Epidemiol 167(7):775–785

Collins A, Joseph D, Bielaczyc K (2004) Design research: theoretical and methodological issues. J Learn Sci 13(1):15–42

Davis P, Lay-Yee R, Pearson J (2010) Using micro-simulation to create a synthesized data set and test policy options: the case of health service effects under demographic ageing. Health Policy 97:267–274

Farmer JD, Foley D (2009) The economy needs agent-based modelling. Nature 460:685–686

Fasth T, Ihlar M, Brouwers L (2010) VirSim—a model to support pandemic policy making. PLOS Currents Influenza. 2010 Sep 22, 2: RRN1181. doi:10.1371/currents.RRN1181

Fergusson D, Horwood L, Shannon F, Lawton J (1989) The Christchurch child development study: a review of epidemiological findings. Paediatr Perinat Epidemiol 3:278–301

Forrester JW (1961) Industrial dynamics. MIT Press, Cambridge

Fraser C, Donnelly CSC, WP H, MD VK, TD H et al. (2009). WHO rapid pandemic assessment collaboration. Pandemic potential of a strain of influenza A (H1N1): early findings. Science 324(5934). PubMed PMID: 19433588, pp. 1557–1561

Gilbert N (2007) Agent-based models. Sage, London

Gilbert N, Troitzsch K (2005) Simulation for the social scientist. Open University Press, Maidenhead

Gilbert N, Pyka A, Ahrweiler P (2001) Innovation networks—a simulation approach. J Artif Soc Soc Simul 4(3)

Gilbert N, Ahrweiler P, Pyka A (2007) Learning in innovation networks—some simulation experiments. Physica A: Stat Mech Appl 374(1):100–109

Gilbert N, Ahrweiler P, Pyka A (2014) Simulating knowledge dynamics in innovation networks. Springer, Heidelberg

Greenwood DJ, Levin, M. (2006) Introduction to action research: social research for social change. Sage, Thousand Oaks

Harrison RJ, Lin Z, Carroll GR, Carley KM (2007) Simulation modeling in organizational and management research. Acad Manage Rev 32(4)1229–1245

Helbig N, Dawes SS, Dzhusupova Z, Klievink B, Mkude CG (2014) Stakeholder engagement in policy development: observations and lessons from international experience. In: Janssen M, Wimmer MA, Deljoo A (eds) Policy practice and digital science—integrating complex systems, social simulation and public administration in policy research. Springer Science, Berlin

Jameson A (1996) Numerical uncertainty management in user and student modeling: an overview of systems and issues. User modeling and user adapted interaction, 5, special issue on numerical uncertainty management in user and student modeling, pp 193–251

Kamateri E, Panopoulou E, Tambouris E, Tarabanis K, Ojo A, Lee D, Price D (2014) A comparative analysis of tools and technologies for policy making. In: Janssen M, Wimmer MA, Deljoo A (eds) Policy practice and digital science—integrating complex systems, social simulation and public administration in policy research. Springer Science, Berlin

Lay-Yee R, Milne B, Davis P, Pearson J, McLay J (2014) Determinants and disparities: a simulation approach to the case of child health care. Under Review

Lengwiler Y (2004) A monetary policy simulation game. J Econ Educ 35(2):175–183

Lotzmann U, Meyer R (2011) DRAMS—a declarative rule-based agent modelling system. In: Proceedings of 25th European Conference on Modelling and Simulation (pp 77–83)

Lotzmann U, Wimmer MA (2013) Evidence traces for multi-agent declarative rule-based policy simulation. In Proceedings of the 17th IEEE/ACM International Symposium on Distributed Simulation and Real Time Applications (DS-RT 2013). IEEE Computer Society, pp115–122

Mannion O, Lay-Yee R, Wrapson W, Davis P, Pearson J (2012) JAMSIM: a microsimulation modelling policy tool. J Artif Soc Soc Simul 15(1):8

Maria A (1997) Introduction to modelling and simulation. Proceedings of the 29th Conference on Winter Simulation, pp 7–13

Martini AP, Trivellato U (1997) The role of survey data in microsimulation models for social policy analysis. Labour 02/1997, 11(1):83–112. (doi:10.1111/1467–9914.00030)

Mayring P (2011) Qualitative Inhaltsanalyse: Grundlagen und Techniken. Beltz, Weinheim und Basel

McLay J, Lay-Yee R, Milne B et al (2014) Statistical modelling techniques for dynamic microsimulation: An empirical performance assessment. Under review

Milne BJ, Lay-Yee R, McLay J, Tobias MTP, Armstrong A, Lynn R et al (2014) A collaborative approach to bridging the research-policy gap through the development of policy advice software. Evid Policy 10(1):127–136

Orcutt G (1957) A new type of socio-economic system. Rev Econ Stat 39(2):116–123

Pyka A, Gilbert N, Ahrweiler P (2007) Simulating knowledge-generation and—distribution processes. Innov Collab Netw, Cybern Syst 38:667–693

Ronald F, Halpern JY (1991) Uncertainty, belief and probability. Computational Intell 7:160–173

Scherer S, Wimmer MA, Markisic S (2013) Bridging narrative scenario texts and formal policy modeling through conceptual policy modeling. Artif Intell Law 21(4):455–484

Schindler J (2013) About the uncertainties in model design and their effects: an illustration with a land-use model. J Artif Soc Soc Simul 16(4):6

Scholz R, Nokkala T, Ahrweiler P, Pyka A, Gilbert N (2010) The agent-based NEMO model (SKEIN): simulating European framework programmes. In: Ahrweiler P (ed) Innovation in complex social systems. Routledge Studies in Global Competition (pp 300–314)

Sedehi H (2006) GAIM (Gestione Accoglienza IMmigrati): a System Dynamics Model for Immigration "housing" Management. In: Proceedings of International Conference of the System Dynamics Society. Nijmegen, The Netherlands (pp 3359–3367)

Solar O, Irwin A (2010) A conceptual framework for action on the social determinants of health. Social Determinants of Health Discussion, Paper 2: Policy and Practice. World Health Organization, Geneva

Spielauer M (2011) What is social science microsimulation. Soc Sci Comput Rev 29(1):9–20

Srbljanovic A, Skunca O (2003) An introduction to agent-based modelling and simulation of social processes. Interdiscip Descr Complex Syst 1(1–2):1–8

Statistics Sweden (Statistiska centralbyrån, SCB). (2009). Sweden's population by sex and age on 31/12/2008. http://www.scb.se/Pages/TableAndChart____262460.aspx. Accessed 28 July 2014

The National Board of Health and Welfare. (2011). A(H1N1) 2009– An evaluation of Sweden's preparations for and management of the pandemic. Evaluation Report number 2011–8–4

van Egmond S., Zeiss R (2010) Modeling for policy science-based models as performative boundary objects for Dutch policy making. Sci Stud 23(1):58–78

Wallinga JTP (2006) Using data on social contacts to estimate age-specific transmission parameters for respiratory-spread infectious agents. Am J Epidemiol 164(10):936–944

Wimmer MA (2011) Open government in policy development: from collaborative scenario texts to formal policy models. Proceedings of 7th International Conference on Distributed Computing and Internet Technologies (ICDCIT—2011) (pp 76–91). Berlin, Springer

Wimmer MA, Scherer S, Moss S, Bicking M (2012) Method and tools to support stakeholder engagement in policy development. The OCOPOMO project. Int J Electron Gov Res 8(3):98–119

Zaidi A, Harding A, Williamson P (2009) New frontiers in microsimulation modeling (Public policy and social welfare. Ashgate Publishing Ltd, England

Zeigler B (1976) Theory of modeling and simulation. Wiley, New York

Chapter 7
A Comparative Analysis of Tools and Technologies for Policy Making

**Eleni Kamateri, Eleni Panopoulou, Efthimios Tambouris,
Konstantinos Tarabanis, Adegboyega Ojo, Deirdre Lee and David Price**

Abstract Latest advancements in information and communication technologies offer great opportunities for modernising policy making, i.e. increasing its efficiency, bringing it closer to all relevant actors, and enhancing its transparency and acceptance levels. In this context, this chapter aims to present, analyse, and discuss emerging information and communication technologies (ICT) tools and technologies presenting the potential to enhance policy making. The methodological approach includes the searching and identification of relevant tools and technologies, their systematic analysis and categorisation, and finally a discussion of potential usage and recommendations for enhancing policy making.

E. Kamateri (✉) · E. Panopoulou · E. Tambouris · K. Tarabanis
Information Technologies Institute, Centre for Research & Technology—Hellas,
Thessaloniki, Greece
e-mail: ekamater@iti.gr

E. Panopoulou
e-mail: epanopou@iti.gr

E. Tambouris · K. Tarabanis
University of Macedonia, Thessaloniki, Greece
e-mail: tambouris@iti.gr, tambouris@uom.gr

K. Tarabanis
e-mail: kat@iti.gr, kat@uom.gr

A. Ojo · D. Lee
INSIGHT Centre for Data Analytics, NUIG, Galway, Ireland
e-mail: adegboyega.ojo@deri.org

D. Lee
e-mail: deirdre.lee@deri.org

D. Price
Thoughtgraph Ltd, Somerset, UK
e-mail: david@debategraph.org

© Springer International Publishing Switzerland 2015   125
M. Janssen et al. (eds.), *Policy Practice and Digital Science,*
Public Administration and Information Technology 10, DOI 10.1007/978-3-319-12784-2_7

7.1 Introduction

Policy making may be defined as "the process by which governments translate their political vision into programmes and actions to deliver 'outcomes' desired changes in the real world" (UK Government 1999). Policy making encompasses any activity relevant to discussing political issues, identifying areas of improvement or solutions, creating and implementing laws and regulations, monitoring and evaluating current policies, etc.

Policy making is a multidisciplinary scientific field referring mainly to political science, but it may also refer to social, economics, statistics, information, and computer sciences. These diverse scientific fields are essential in order to perform policy making in a more effective and informed manner. Information and communication technologies (ICTs), specifically, have supported decision-making processes for many years. However, the current ICT advancements and good practices offer even greater opportunities for modernising policy making, i.e. increasing its efficiency, bringing it closer to all relevant actors and increasing participation, facilitating its internal processes (e.g. decision making), and enhancing its transparency and acceptance levels.

In this context, this chapter aims to present, analyse, and discuss emerging ICT tools and technologies presenting the potential to enhance policy making. Our approach includes searching and identification of relevant tools and technologies, their systematic analysis and categorisation, and finally a discussion of potential usage and recommendations for enhancing policy making. The chapter is structured in the following way: Sect. 7.2 describes our methodological approach, Sect. 7.3 provides the comparative analysis, and Sect. 7.4 discusses the findings and concludes the chapter.

Before proceeding to the rest of the chapter, we should provide further clarifications with regard to its scope. First, for work presented in this chapter, policy making is considered as a broad and continuous process that commences from the need to create a policy and ends when a policy is abandoned or replaced. In this context, the policy-making process is usually described with a circular-staged model called "the policy cycle". There are differences in the number, names, and boundaries of the stages adopted in each proposed policy cycle (e.g. Jann and Wegrich 2006; Northern Ireland Government 2013); however, every policy cycle includes an initiation stage, a drafting stage, an implementation stage, and an evaluation stage. The scope of our work refers to all these stages of the policy cycle.

Second, we consider all stakeholders relevant to policy making within the scope of work presented in this chapter. Obviously, the main actor involved in policy making is the government with its different roles, bodies, and institutions. However, noninstitutional actors are also involved such as political parties, political consultants and lobbyists, the media, nongovernmental organisations, civil organisations, and other interested parties depending also on the policy topic at hand. Last but not least, individual citizens are also actors of policy making; as the final policy recipients and beneficiaries, they should actively participate in policy making. Hence, in this chapter, we do not consider policy making as a close, internal government process, but rather as an open, deliberative process relevant to the whole society.

7.2 Methodology

In order to analyse the existing ICT tools and technologies that can be used to enhance the policy-making process, we adopted a simple methodology consisting of four main steps.

Before introducing the adopted methodology, we provide a short description with regard to the difference between ICT tools and technologies. ICT tools normally include software applications, web-based environments, and devices that facilitate the way we work, communicate, and solve problems. These are developed by individual software developers, big software providers, researchers, and scientists (Phang and Kankanhalli 2008). Technology, on the other hand, refers to knowledge and know-how, skills, processes, tools and/or practices.[1] Therefore, technology not only refers to tools but also the way we employ them to build new things. In the current survey, we organise the findings of our literature analysis based on tool categories.

Step 1: Identification During this step, we surveyed the current state of the art to identify ICT tools and technologies that have been (or have a clear potential to be) used to reinforce the policy-making process. These tools have been collected mainly from project deliverables, posts, electronic articles, conference papers, scientific journals, and own contacts and expertise.

In particular, we searched for tools and technologies that have been highlighted, used, or created by existing research and coordination projects in the area of e-government and policy modelling, i.e. CROSSOVER[2], e-Policy[3], FuturICT[4], OCOPOMO[5], COCKPIT[6] and UbiPol[7], OurSpace[8], PuzzledbyPolicy[9], etc. This investigation resulted in a collection of more than 30 ICT tools and technologies mainly coming from project deliverables, posts, electronic articles, conference papers, scientific journals, and own contacts and expertise.

Thereafter, we expanded our research on the web to include additional tools that were not previously identified. To this end, we tried multiple searches in the major research databases of computer science, e.g. Association for Computing Machinery (ACM) Digital Library and Google Scholar using a combination of different

---

[1] http://en.wikipedia.org/wiki/Technology.
[2] http://crossover-project.eu.
[3] http://www.epolicy-project.eu/node.
[4] http://www.futurict.eu.
[5] http://www.ocopomo.eu.
[6] http://www.cockpit-project.eu.
[7] http://www.ubipol.eu/.
[8] http://www.ep-ourspace.eu/.
[9] http://www.puzzledbypolicy.eu/.

keywords such as tools, technologies, policy modelling, online participation, engagement, government, policy making, decision making, policy formulation, etc. The references of the selected papers were checked and additional papers were found. Some of the journals that have been reviewed include *Government Information Quarterly*, *International Journal of Electronic Government Research*. In addition, we surveyed similar initiatives that summarise tools or/and methods, i.e. the Participation Compass[10] launched by Involve[11] (not-for-profit organisation in public participation), the ParticipateDB[12] by Intellitics[13], and the ReformCompass by Bertelsmann Stiftung[14] (providers of digital engagement solutions). The final result of this exercise was a list of 75 tools and technologies.

Step 2: Categorisation Analysing the identified tools and technologies, it was evident that most of them fall under a number of categories. We defined, therefore, 11 categories of tools and technologies for policy making. Each category has a specific application focus, e.g. opinion mining, serious games, etc., and may be further divided into one or more subcategories.

We then organised tools and technologies' analysis according to the defined categories. There are few cases, however, where the same tool could be classified under more than one category, i.e. in the case of visualisation and argumentation tools and in the case of serious games and simulation tools. In the first case, argumentation tools represent and structure arguments and debates, and usually exploit visual means in order to clearly represent the arguments. However, the main focus remains the representation of arguments. On the other hand, the visualisation tools present, in a graphical form, any type of input data. Thus, it was selected for the sake of simplicity to analyse each tool in one category according to its most prominent feature. Similar difficulties in categorisation have also arisen in the case of simulation tools and serious games. Serious games are created for educational and entertainment purposes, or for helping citizens to further understand some processes by playing the role of a key stakeholder. On the other hand, simulation tools are usually created on a more serious context (e.g. within a research project, taking into account accurate real-world data) in order to help real policy makers or governments to simulate long-term impacts of their actions. Therefore, the categorisation of tools in these two categories was made based on the context and the goal of the tool.

Step 3: Comparative Analysis A comparative analysis of identified ICT tools and technologies per category was then performed. Initially, we analysed tools' functionality to identify core capabilities per category. Then, we examined the key features for each tool. The outcome of this analysis is a comparative table for each category

---

[10] http://participationcompass.org/.
[11] http://www.involve.org.uk.
[12] http://participatedb.com/.
[13] http://www.intellitics.com/.
[14] http://www.reformkompass.de.

that shows, at a glance, an overview of different features found in each tool of the category.

Step 4: Conceptualisation During this step, we performed an overall discussion of the presented tools and technologies and their potential for enhancing policy making. To this end, we examined three main aspects for policy making—the type of facilitated activities, the type of targeted stakeholders, and the stages of the policy cycle. Finally, we drafted overall recommendations and conclusions.

7.3   Tools and Technologies for Policy Making

Based on the literature survey, we identified 11 main categories of ICT tools and technologies that can be used for policy making purposes as follows:

- *Visualisation tools* help users better understand data and provide a more meaningful view in context, especially by presenting data in a graphical form.
- *Argumentation tools* visualise the structure of complex argumentations and debates as a graphical network.
- *eParticipation tools* support the active engagement of citizens in social and political processes including, e.g. voting advice applications and deliberation tools.
- *Opinion mining tools* help analyse and make sense of thousands of public comments written in different application contexts.
- *Simulation tools* represent a real-world system or phenomenon and help users understand the system and the effects of potential actions in order to make better decisions.
- *Serious games* train users through simulation and virtual environments.
- *Tools specifically developed for policy makers* have been recently developed to facilitate the design and delivery of policies.
- *Persuasive tools* aim to change users' attitudes or behaviours.
- *Social network analysis (SNA) tools* analyse social connections and identify patterns that can be used to predict users' behaviour.
- *Big data analytics tools* support the entire big data exploitation process from discovering and preparing data sources, to integration, visualisation, analysis, and prediction.
- *Semantics and linked data tools* enable large amounts of data to become easily published, linked to other external datasets, and analysed.

We present an analysis of each category of tools and technologies in the rest of this section.[15]

---

[15] All tools mentioned in this section are summarized in the end of the chapter along with their links.

7.3.1 Visualisation Tools

Visualisation tools enable large amounts of "raw" data to become visually represented in an interpretable form. Moreover, they provide appropriate means to uncover patterns, relationships, and observations that would not be apparent from looking at it in a nonvisual format. Therefore, users can explore, analyse, and make sense of data that, otherwise, may be of limited value (Osimo and Mureddu 2012). Today, there are many data visualisation tools, desktop- or web-based, free or proprietary, that can be used to visualise and analyse raw data provided by the user. Examples include Google Charts, Visokio Omniscope, R, and Visualize Free. Besides visual presentation and exploration of raw data, they provide additional features such as data annotation (e.g. Visokio Omniscope), data handling, and other statistical computations on raw data (e.g. R).

Over recent years, geovisualisation (shortened form of the term geographic visualisation) has gained considerable momentum within the fields of geographic information systems (GIS), cartography, and spatial statistics. Some consider it to be a branch of data visualisation (Chang 2010). However, geovisualisation integrates different approaches including data visualisation, such as cartography, GIS, image analysis, exploratory data analysis, and dynamic animations, to provide visual exploration, analysis, synthesis, and presentation of *geospatial data* (MacEachren and Kraak 2001). Geovisualisation tools have been widely used to visualise societal statistics in combination with geographic data.

Several visualisation and geovisualisation tools have been developed to visualise and analyse demographic and social statistics in several countries across the world. Most tools are used for data coming from the USA. However, many efforts have been made, lately, to visualise statistics coming from all over the world (e.g. Google Public Data Explorer and World Bank eAtlas). The most important source of information for these tools is governmental reports which are made available by each state. Most tools support data transparency, mainly for downloading data and figures, while uploading of users' data is available only in few cases. Visualisation tools are organised into static and interactive based on a categorisation proposed for web-mapping tools (Kraak and Brown 2001). A static tool contains a figure or a map displayed as a static image (Mitchell 2005), while interactive tools allow users to access a set of functions to have some interaction with the tool or the map, such as zooming in and out (Mitchell 2005). Table 7.1 summarises well-known visualisation and geovisualisation tools and compares their main characteristics. In particular, the table provides information on: (a) the number and subject of indicators, e.g. if they deal with demographic, health, environmental, or other social issues, (b) the coverage, namely, the countries supported, (c) the period for which statistics are available, (d) data transparency, and (e) whether it is a static or interactive tool.

Table 7.1 Visualisation and geovisualisation tools for analyzing regional statistics

	Indicators and Topic	Coverage (countries)	Period	Data transparency	Static/ Interactive
Gapminder	> 400 Demographics, social, economic, environmental, health	> 200	Over the past 200 years	Download and upload	Interactive
Worldmapper	∼ 696 maps Demographics	All	N/A	Download (No custom maps)	Datasets, static
Dynamic Choropleth Maps	Multiple social, economic, and environmental	USA	N/A	Download (free to adjust the threshold criteria)	Interactive
DataPlace	∼ 2360 Demographics, health, arts, real estate	USA	After 1990	N/A	Interactive
Data Visualizer-World Bank	∼ 49 Social, economic, financial, IT, and environmental	209	1960–2007	N/A	Interactive
World Bank eAtlas	∼ 175 Development challenges	200	After 1960	Download and upload	Interactive
State Cancer Profiles	Demographic data related to cancer	USA	2006–2010	N/A	Interactive
Health Infoscape	Health conditions	USA	January 2005– July 2010	N/A	Interactive
OECD eXplorer	∼ 40 Demographics, economic, labour market, environment, social, and innovation	34 (335 large regions 1679 small regions)	1990–2005	Download and upload	Interactive (time animation) storytelling

Other tools investigated, but not included, in the above table include STATcompiler, Google Public Data Explorer, NComVA, Social Explorer (USA), PolicyMap (USA), All-Island Research Observatory (UK), and China Geo-Explorer II

Demographic, social, environmental, health, and other public data, provided by governmental and public authorities, in raw form, can be transformed and presented through visualisation and geovisualisation tools into a more interpretable way. Thus, information and current trends hidden in this data can easily become apparent. This can assist policy stakeholders and decision makers to make more informed decisions. In addition, incorporating geographical knowledge into planning and formation of social and political policies can help derive more accurate spatial decisions. Obvious fields where visualisation and geovisualisation tools can be applied for policy making are investment, population, housing, environmental assessment, public health, etc.

7.3.2   Argumentation Tools

Argumentation tools visualise the structure of complex arguments and debates as a graphical network. In particular, they allow a large number of stakeholders to participate, discuss, and contribute creative arguments and suggestions which then become visualised. This visual representation provides a better and deeper understanding of topics discussed. Thus, complex debates can become easily analysed, refined, or evaluated, e.g. by pinpointing possible gaps and inconsistencies or strong and weak points in the arguments, etc. (Benn and Macintosh 2011).

Table 7.2 summarises well-known argumentation tools and depicts their main characteristics (i.e. whether they are open source, whether they enable importing/exporting data, whether they are Web-based or collaborative, the argument framework, whether they support visual representation argumentation structure modification and manipulation of layouts). DebateGraph, Rationale, Cope It!, and bCisive constitute proprietary solutions, while Cohere, Araucaria, Compendium, and Carneades were developed during research studies within universities and research projects. Most argumentation tools enable users to share ideas and collaborate upon "wicked problems". For example, DebateGraph allows users to collaboratively modify the structure and the content of debate maps in the same way they can collaboratively edit a wiki. In addition, MindMeister and Compendium constitute desktop-based solutions that support collaborative argument analysis, while Mind-Meister and bCisive also enable real-time collaboration. Though most argumentation tools provide, even partially, a visual representation of discussions, only few support an easy layout manipulation; such tools are Compendium, Araucaria, Cohere, and DebateGraph. Besides argument analysis, argumentation tools offer additional features, such as argument reconstruction, discussion forums, argument evaluation, etc. For example, Araucaria and Argunet enable users to reconstruct and map debates, Cohere enables any content on the web to serve as a node of information in the argument map, and Rationale allows users to judge the strength of an argument by evaluating its elements. These judgments are also represented on the map. Similarly, Carneades allows users to evaluate and compare arguments as well as to apply proof standards. Finally, Cope It! supports a threaded discussion forum, while

Table 7.2 Argumentation tools. (Source: Benn and Macintosh 2011)

Tool	Open source	Import/ export	Web-based	Collab-orative	Argument frame-work	Visual represen-tation	Modify argument structure	Manipulate layouts
Araucaria	Yes	Yes	No	No	Walton, Toulmin, Wigmore, Classical	Partially	Yes	Partially
Argunet	Yes	Yes	Yes	Yes	Classical	Yes	Partially	N/A
Carneades	Yes	Yes	Yes	No	Walton	Partially	Yes	N/A
Cohere	Yes	Yes	Yes	Yes	IBIS	Yes	Partially	Partially
Compendium	Yes	Yes	No	Yes	IBIS	Yes	Partially	Partially
Cope_it!	N/A	No	Yes	Yes	IBIS	Yes	Partially	N/A
DebateGraph	No	No	Yes	Yes	Multiple (including IBIS)	Partially	Partially	Partially
Rationale	No	No	No	No	Classical	Partially	Partially	N/A
bCisive	No	No	Yes	Yes	IBIS	Partially	Partially	N/A
MindMeister	No	Yes	Yes	Yes	N/A	Yes	Yes	Partially

IBIS Issue-Based Information System

bCisive incorporates group planning, decision making, and team problem-solving capabilities.

Argumentation tools facilitate better-informed public debate, policy deliberation, and dialogue mapping on the web about complex political issues. For example, DebateGraph has been used by the Dutch Foreign Ministry in its recent consultation on its human rights policy[16], the UK Prime Minister's Office[17], and the White House's Open Government Brainstorming.[18] Compendium has been used in a case study for consultation on regional planning in southeast Queensland (Ohl 2008). Carneades has been developed during the European Estrella project[19] that aims to help both citizens and government officials to take part, more effectively, in dialogues for assessing claims and has been used in several applications.

---

[16] http://debategraph.org/MR
[17] http://debategraph.org/No10.
[18] http://debategraph.org/WH.
[19] http://www.estrellaproject.org/.

7.3.3 eParticipation Tools

eParticipation tools have been specifically developed to involve citizens in the policy-making process, i.e. to enable citizens to get informed, to provide feedback on different policy issues, and to get actively involved in decision making (Gramberger 2001). These tools are mainly based on Web 2.0 features including a variety of social networking tools such as discussion forums or message boards, wikis, electronic surveys or polls, e-petitions, online focus groups, and webcasting.

eParticipation may entail different types of involvement, which are supported by different tools and functionalities, ranging from the provision of information, to deliberation, community building and collaboration, active involvement through consultations, polling, and decision making. The International Association for Public Participation (IAP2) has produced a public participation spectrum[20], which shows how various techniques may be employed to increase the level of public impact.

Recently, eParticipation tools have been widely used by governmental and public authorities. Through actively engaging citizens, in the planning, design, and delivery process of public policies, they have moved towards improving democratic governance, preventing conflicts, and facilitating citizens' active participation in the solution of issues affecting their lives. Table 7.3 presents a set of such recently developed eParticipation tools.

7.3.4 Opinion Mining Tools

The Web's widespread use over the past decade has significantly increased the possibility for users to express their opinion. The users not only can post text messages now but also can see what other users have written about the same subject in a variety of communication channels across the Web. Moreover, with the advent of Twitter and Facebook, status updates, and posts about any subject have become the new norm in social networking. This user-generated content usually contains relevant information on the general sentiment of users concerning different topics including persons, products, institutions, or even governmental policies. Thus, an invaluable, yet scattered, source of public opinion has quickly become available.

Opinion-mining tools (or otherwise called sentiment analysis tools) perform a computational study of large quantities of textual contributions in order to gather, identify, extract, and determine the attitude expressed in them. This attitude may be users' judgment or evaluation, their affectual state (that is to say, the emotional state of the author when writing), or the intended emotional communication (that is to say, the emotional effect the author wishes to have on the reader; Stylios et al. 2010).

---

[20] Available at: http://www.iap2.org/associations/4748/files/spectrum.pdf.

Table 7.3 eParticipation tools developed to improve people involvement in government

	Typical actions	Examples
Citizen Space	Consultation and engagement software Create, organise, and publish public consultations across the net on complex policy documents Share consultation data openly in a structured way Provide a way to easily analyse consultation data (both qualitative and quantitative)	Used by government bodies to run e-consultations around the world
Adhocracy.de	Participation and voting software Present and discuss issues Collaborate (develop and work on texts together) Make proposals, gather, and evaluate proposals Add polls for decision making Vote on issues	Used in the Munich Open Government Day where citizens could propose policies, projects, and actions of the city
MixedInk.com	Collaborative writing software Large groups of people work together to write texts that express collective opinions Post ideas Combine ideas to make new versions Post comments and rate versions to bring the best ideas to the top	Used by the White House to let citizens draft collective policy recommendations for the Open Government Directive
Loomio.org	Decision making and collaborative software Initiate discussions and present proposals that can then be discussed, modified, and voted (Agree, Abstain, Disagree, or Block, along with a brief explanation of why) Change their position any time	Used by the Wellington City Council for discussion with their citizens
CitySourced	Mobile civil engagement platform Identify and report civic issues (graffiti, trash, potholes, etc.), and comment on existing ones	Used in San Francisco, Los Angeles, and several other cities in California
Puzzledbypolicy	Consultation and opinion mapping software Learn about policy issues concerning immigration in the European Union (EU) Give their voice Graphically compare their views on immigration with national and EU immigration policies as well as with the opinions of relevant stakeholders Encourage to join discussions on particular aspects of immigration policy they feel strongly about	Used by the Athens and Torino municipalities and other stakeholders in Tenerife, Hungary, and Slovenia

Table 7.3 (continued)

	Typical actions	Examples
Opinion Space	Opinion mapping software Collect and visualise user opinions on important issues and policies (rate five propositions on the chosen topic and type initial response to a discussion question) Show in a graphical "map" where user's opinions fall next to the opinions of other participants Display patterns, trends, and insights Employ the wisdom of crowds to identify the most insightful ideas	Used by US State Department to engage global online audiences on a variety of foreign policy issues
CivicEvolution.org	Collaboration platform Engage citizens in structured dialogue and deliberation and develop detailed community-written proposals to make constructive changes	Used by the City of Greater Geraldton, in Australia, to facilitate collaboration and deliberation among participants in participatory budgeting community panels
UbiPol	Mobile civil engagement platform Identify and report problems or suggestions Report policy issues	Used by TURKSAT, a publicly owned but privately operated company in affiliation with Ministry of Transportation in Turkey
OurSpace	Youth eParticipation platform Engage young people in the decision-making process Enable collaboration	European and National Youth Organisations already using OurSpace
Dialogue App	Set up a dialogue Share, rate, comment, and discuss ideas and bring the best ideas to the top	Department for Environment, Food and Rural Affairs in the UK is using Dialogue App to get thoughts, ideas and input on how to improve and formulate policy

In social media, opinion mining usually refers to the extraction of sentiments from unstructured text. The recognised sentiments are classified as positive, negative, and neutral, or of a more fine-grained sentiment classification scheme. Examples include Sentiment140, Sentimentor, Repustate, etc. Opinion-mining tools may also integrate a broad area of approaches including natural language processing, computational linguistics, and text mining. Text mining, for example, can provide a deeper analysis of contributions; it summarises contributions, helps highlight areas of agreement and disagreement, and identifies participants' main concerns—the level of support for draft proposals or suggestions for action that seem necessary to address. Opinion mining tools providing such approaches include DiscoverText, RapidMiner, and Weka.

Classifying statements is a common problem in opinion mining, and different techniques have been used to address this problem. These techniques follow two main approaches; those based on lexical resources and neutral-language processing (lexicon-based) and those employing machine-learning algorithms. Lexicon-based approaches rely on a sentiment lexicon—a collection of known and precompiled sentiment/opinion terms. These terms are words that are commonly used to express positive or negative sentiments, e.g. "excellent", "great", "poor", and "bad". The method basically counts the number of positive and negative terms, and decides accordingly the final sentiment. Machine-learning approaches that make use of syntactic and/or linguistic features and hybrid techniques are very common, with sentiment lexicons playing a key role in the majority of methods.

Table 7.4 presents several opinion mining tools that have been recently developed to analyse public opinions.

Opinion mining tools can help derive different inferences on quality control, public relations, reputation management, policy, strategy, etc. Therefore, opinion mining tools can be used to assist policy stakeholders and decision makers in making more informed decisions. In particular, knowing citizens' opinion about public and political issues, proposed government actions, and interventions or policies under formation can ensure more socially acceptable policies and decisions. Finally, gathering and analysing public opinion can enable us to understand how a certain community reacts to certain events and even try to discover patterns and predict their reactions to upcoming events based on their behaviour history (Maragoudakis et al. 2011).

7.3.5   Simulation Tools

Simulation tools are based on agent-based modelling. This is a recent technique that is used to model and reproduce complex systems. An agent-based system is formed by a set of interacting and autonomous "agents" (Macal and North 2005) that represent humans. Agents act and interact with their environment, including other agents, to achieve their objectives (Onggo 2010). Agents' behaviour is described by a set of simple rules. However, agents may also influence each other, learn from their experiences, and adapt their behaviour to be better suited to their environment. Above all, they operate autonomously, meaning that they decide whether or not to perform an operation, taking into account their goals and priorities, as well as the known context. The analysis of interactions between agents results at the creation of patterns that enable visualising and understanding the system or the phenomenon under investigation.

Table 7.4 Opinion mining tools

	Purpose	Sources	Classification
SwiftRiver	Aggregate, manage, filter, and validate web data Discover relationship and trends in data	Twitter, SMS, e-mail, and RSS feeds	Machine learning
DiscoverText	(Text analytics) Search, filter, collect, and classify data Generate insights	E-mail archives, social media content, and other document collections	Machine learning
Repustate	Categorise and visualise social media data Extract text sentiment Predict future trends	Twitter or Facebook Multiple languages	Machine learning
Opinion observer	(Opinion mining) Extract text sentiment Discover patterns	Web pages	Lexicon-based (feature category)
AIRC Sentiment Analyser	Extract text sentiment	N/A	Lexicon-based
Social Mention	Aggregate and analyse social media data Extract text sentiment Discover patterns	Blogs, comments, social media including Twitter, Facebook, Social bookmarks, microblogging services, Images, News, etc.	Lexicon-based
Umigon	Sentiment analysis	Twitter	Lexicon-based
Convey API	Sentiment analysis	Social media records	Machine learning Natural-language processing Statistical modelling
Sentiment140	Sentiment analysis for tweets on a subject or keyword	Twitter	Machine learning Natural-language processing
Sentimentor	Sentiment analysis for tweets on a subject	Twitter	Machine learning
Corpora's Applied Linguistics	Document summarisation and sentiment analysis	Documents	Natural-language processing in combination with an extensive English language lexicon
Attentio	Sentiment analysis	Blogs, news, and discussion forum sites	Lexicon-based Machine learning

Table 7.4 (continued)

	Purpose	Sources	Classification
Opinmind	Sentiment analysis of bloggers opinion	Blogs	Not available
ThinkUp	Archive and analyse social media life	Twitter and Facebook	Machine learning

In this sense, simulation tools are particularly suited to explore the complexity of social systems. A social system consists of a collection of individuals who interact directly or through their social environment. These individuals evolve autonomously as they are motivated by their own beliefs and personal goals, as well as the circumstances of their social environment. Simulating social systems and analysing the effects of individuals' interactions can result in the construction of social patterns (e.g. how society responds to a change) that can be used for policy analysis and planning as well as for participatory modelling (Bandini et al. 2009).

There are several general-purpose simulation tools. Most of them are open source and free to be accessed by anyone. Some of these are specially designed to focus on social systems. For example, Multi-Agent Simulation Suite (MASS) is a software package intended to enable modellers to simulate and study complex social environments. To this end, it models the individual together with its imperfections (e.g. limited cognitive or computational abilities), its idiosyncrasies, and personal interactions. Another tool focusing on the development of flexible models for living social agents is Repast.

An increasing number of tools for the simulation and analysis of social interactions has been developed in recent years. These aim to help policy stakeholders and decision makers to simulate the long-term impact of policy decisions. Table 7.5 presents such simulation tools that have been used in the field of health, environment, developmental policies, etc.

7.3.6   Serious Games

Agent-based modelling is used also in serious games, providing the opportunity for experiential and interactive learning and exploration of large uncertainties, divergent values, and complex situations through an engaging, active, and critical environment (Raybourn et al. 2005). Serious games enable players to learn from the accurate representations of real-world phenomena and the contextual information and knowledge and data embedded in the dynamics of the game. Abt (1987) defines serious games as games with "an explicit and carefully thought-out educational purpose and are not intended to be played primarily for amusement".

Table 7.5 Simulation tools simulating the long-term impact of policy decisions

	Purpose	Input	Interface	Scale
Threshold 21	Simulate the long-term impact of socioeconomic development policies	About 800 variables concerning economic, social, and environment factors	Flexible	Customisable to suit the needs of any sector and country
GLEaMviz	Simulate global epidemics	Detailed population, mobility, and epidemic–infection data (real-world data) Compartmentalised disease models	Visual tool for designing compartmental models	Thirty countries in 5 different continents
The Climate Rapid Overview and Decision-support Simulator (C-ROADS)	Simulate long-term climate impacts of policy scenarios to reduce greenhouse gas emissions (CO_2 concentration, temperature, sea-level rise)	Sources of historical data	Flexible equations are available and easily auditable	Six-region and 15-region mode
UrbanSim	Simulate the possible long-term effects of different policies on urban development (land use, transportation, and environmental planning)	Historical data	Flexible	Any country
Modelling the Early Life Course (MEL-C)	Simulate the effects of policy making in the early life course and issues concerning children and young people	Data from existing longitudinal studies to quantify the underlying determinants of progress in the early life course	Flexibly adapted for new data and parameter inputs	N/A
Global Buildings Performance Network (GBPN) Policy Comparative Tool	An interactive tool that enables users to compare the world's best practice policies for new buildings (residential and commercial)	N/A	N/A	N/A

Table 7.5 (continued)

	Purpose	Input	Interface	Scale
CLASP's Policy Analysis Modeling System (PAMS)	Forecast the impacts of energy efficiency standards and labelling programs Assess the benefits of policies, identify the most attractive targets for appliances, and efficiency levels	N/A	N/A	Support basic modelling inputs for over 150 countries Customisable where country-specific data is available
Scenario Modelling and Policy Assessment Tool (EUREAPA)	Model the effects of policies on environment, consumption, industry, and trade	Detailed carbon, ecological, and water footprint indicators	N/A	N/A
Budget simulator	Budget consultation platform that enables to adjust budget items and see the consequences of their allocations on council tax and service areas	N/A	Flexible	Any country

CLASP Comprehensive, Lightweight Application Security Process, *EUREAPA, MEL-C, C-ROADS*

In policy making, serious games provide the opportunity for players to assume roles of real-world critical stakeholders whose decisions rely on extensive data collected from the world around them. In this way, players get educated on the process of decision making as well as on the limitations and trade-offs involved in policy making. Serious games may be used in fields like defence, education, scientific exploration, health care, emergency management, city planning, engineering, religion, and politics (Caird-Daley et al. 2007).

Table 7.6 summarises a number of serious games aiming to tackle different social and political problems. In some of these, users assume the role of critical stakeholders. For example, in 2050 Pathways, users play as if they were the Energy and Climate Change Minister of the UK, while, in Democracy, users act as the president or the prime minister of a modern country. Other games enable users to apply policies/strategies and explore their potential impact. Such an example is the Maryland Budget Map Game that gives the option to make cost-cutting decisions and consider short-term and long-term budget effects. Serious games also help users gain virtual experiences for solving real-world problems. Thus, such games could be used to train citizens and public authorities on how to enforce a policy, e.g. a disaster or crisis management policy. For instance, Breakaway simulates critical incidents

Table 7.6 Serious games focusing on policy making

	Purpose	Features	Scope
2050 Pathways	Users act as the energy and climate change minister and explore the complex choices and trade-offs which the UK will have to make to reach the 80 % emission reduction targets by 2050, while matching energy demand and supply	It covers all parts of the economy and all greenhouse gas emissions Users create their emission reduction pathway, and see the impact using real scientific data	Scientific exploration and engineering
Democracy	Users are in the position of president (or prime minister) of a modern country and the objective of the game is to stay in power as long as possible	It recreates a modern political system as accurately as possible Users influence the voters and the country by putting in place policies	Education, political strategy
Maryland Budget Map Game	Users act as the administration and general assembly of a state Gives the options to make cost-cutting decisions, weigh revenue options, and consider short-term and long-term budget effects	It explains how budgeting decisions are made	Education, political strategy
NationStates—create your own country	Users build a nation and run it according to their political ideals and care for people	N/A	Entertainment, education
Breakaway(disaster management—incident commander)	Helps incident commanders and other public safety personnel train and plan for how they might respond to a wide range of critical incidents	It models acts of terrorism, school hostage situations, and natural disasters	Education, emergency management
The Social Simulator	Trains communications, policy, and frontline staff in a variety of sectors using a number of crisis scenarios Users use the language, tools, and norms of the social web for crisis response	It models terrorist attacks, a leaked report spreads anger about a government policy, etc.	Education, emergency management, political strategy

Table 7.6 (continued)

	Purpose	Features	Scope
CItyOne	Users are poised with a series of problems concerning energy, water, or commercial investments (such as banking and payment systems) and are asked to address specific challenges	Planner players think through the sorts of energy, water, or commercial investments that might be needed for particular urban environments in the years to come	Education, awareness
World Without Oil	Engages people concerned with the world's dependence on oil and both educate and move them to action and contribute "collective imagination"	Risks that oil extraction poses to our economy, climate, and quality of life	Awareness, public good
Urgent Evoke	Empowers people all over the world to come up with creative solutions to the most urgent social problems	N/A	Awareness
MP For A Week	Enables users to learn about the work of a member of parliament (MP) and key features of democracy in the UK	N/A	Education
Budget Hero	Allows players to build a balanced budget	Creates and tests a budget policy and sees the effects of those cuts or increased expenses on the federal budget	Education, political strategy

and risk scenarios and helps players train and plan their responses. Last, they improve imaginary thinking by exploring possible futures and sparking future-changing actions. For example, Urgent Evoke invites people to come up with creative solutions to the most urgent social problems. Other games focusing on a better world can be found in World-Changing Game[21] and Purposeful Games[22]; however, they are not included in Table 7.6 due to their loose connection with the policy-making process.

---

[21] http://www.scoop.it/t/world-changing-games.

[22] http://purposefulgames.info/.

Table 7.7 Political analysis tools

	Purpose	Features	Scope
PolicyMaker	Helps users to analyse, understand, and create effective strategies to promote point of view on any policy question or political issue	Conduct a stakeholder analysis Identify political dynamics of policy making Analyse systematically the supporters, why a policy may face opposition, and what strategies might help it be more effective Design political strategies to support a policy	Policy planning
Oracle Policy Automation for Social Services	Transform complex policies in human language Assess impact of policy changes by enabling what-if analysis of proposed amendments	It includes debugging, regression testing, policy simulation, and what-if analysis for policy changes	Policy delivery

7.3.7 Tools Specifically Developed for Policy Makers

Policy-making tools are designed to facilitate governments, industry, construction experts, and other stakeholders design and deliver national renovation policies and strategies. We present two illustrative examples of such tools in Table 7.7.

7.3.8 Persuasive Tools

Persuasive tools aim to change users' attitudes or behaviours, such as exercising more or sticking to medication, by enhancing feedback, persuasion and social influence, but not through coercion (Fogg 2002). Persuasive tools can be applied in policy making for promoting different political causes and enhancing policies' adoption by the public. The Behavioural Insights Team has published a paper on fraud, debt, and error that presents a completely new way of doing policy based on citizens' behavioural reactions (Behavioural Insights Teem; BIT 2012).

Until recently, only indirect efforts have been made to persuade or motivate citizens adopting a specific policy. For example, the USA[23] and Australia[24] have developed smartphone applications that enable taxpayers to keep up to date with their tax affairs. In addition, the Australian Tax Office offers a "Tax Receipt Log" app that makes it easier to keep up to date on expenses and tax receipts by using the

---

[23] http://www.irs.gov/uac/New-IRS2Go-Offers-Three-More-Features.

[24] http://www.taxreceiptlog.com/blog/gst/tax-calculator/.

phone camera to take a photo of a receipt, which is then processed and stored. These can serve as persuasive tools reminding citizens of their delayed fees or motivating them to ask for receipts for their purchases.[25]

7.3.9 Social Network Analysis Tools

A social network consists of nodes representing individual actors within the network and ties which represent relationships between the individuals. Social network analysis (SNA) tools facilitate the study of social structure, providing the means (methods) to determine if there are regular patterns in social relationships, and how these patterns may be related to attributes or behaviour (Tang et al. 2011). In addition, SNA could identify and map informal networks around any given issue. It can be used to identify who is connected to whom and thus adds value/does not add value, and who should be connected to whom to solve the issue at hand. It also identifies conflicts and broken links that need attention to facilitate more functional action-orientated relationships to achieve goals (Rowena 2010).

SNA can be used in policy making in order to identify a social network's patterns and key actors and try to influence these (and, therefore, their networks) by applying appropriate targeted policy interventions. For example, SNA could be used to think through and tackle social issues such as unemployment. To do this, SNA may pinpoint the most influential key actors relevant to entrepreneurship or employment (e.g. pioneering entrepreneurs, venture capitalists, etc.) and target these for promoting entrepreneurship or employment policies.

Magus Networker[26] was designed to illuminate complex, informal networks so that they become understandable. Powerful querying functions enable key patterns to be identified quickly, displaying where opportunities for improving performance can be developed.

7.3.10 Big Data Analytics Tools

Over the last decade, much information has gradually become open. Sources of such information include machine-operated sensors, video, digital images, e-mail, social media, and open data from government, research institutes, and nongovernmental organisations. The aim of open data movement is to make information freely available, without restrictions and in standard machine readable format (United Nations Department of Economic 2010).

---

[25] Due to the limited number of the identified tools for this category and the following ones, we decided not to summarise them in a table format.

[26] http://www.magus-toolbox.com/Networker/.

Open data create significant opportunities for achieving deeper and faster insights towards knowledge development, decision making and interdisciplinary collaboration. However, they have little value if people cannot use them. Thus, new tools and technologies were developed lately to address this problem. One of these technologies is big data analytics.

Big data analytics tools have emerged due to the increasing volume and variety of open data that became available on the web. The term big data refers to datasets so large and complex that are difficult to process using traditional data management and processing techniques.

Big data analytics tools aim to tackle several technological and analytical challenges, such as analysing unstructured data, uncovering hidden patterns, exploiting social media, making fast decisions on massive data volumes, etc. Furthermore, big data predictive analytics aim to unlock the value of big data and make predictions about future, or otherwise unknown events, in a near-real-time mode (Nyce 2007).

Big data analytics tools can be used by government agencies for information purposes, e.g. for understanding what people are saying about government, and which policies, services, or providers are attracting negative opinions and complaints. Moreover, they can find out what people are concerned about or looking for, e.g. from the Google Search application programming interface (API) or Google Trends, which record Google's search patterns of a huge number of internet users. Based on analysis of current and "historical" facts, they can develop accurate models and forecasts about the future.

In addition, big data can contribute to "smart" cities and governments and to transformational government. In particular, big and open data can foster collaboration; create real-time solutions to tackle challenges in agriculture, health, transportation, and more; promote greater openness; and introduce a new era of policy and decision making (Bertot et al. 2014).

Several applications utilising the power of big data are already available. An example is the case of an insurance company, named The Climate Corporation, which examines massive streams of climate data to assess future risk and current damage and provide insurance to farmers who can lock in profits even in the case of drought, excessive rains, or other adverse weather conditions.

Despite the wide adoption in the private sector, big data still have limited applications in policy making. One of the few initiatives is that of New Zealand, which has recently expressed their intention to reform and/or create new governmental services to improve people, society, and economy. In particular, the Ministry of Education in New Zealand is already processing population projections, building consent data, and school enrolment data to work out where new schools are needed. In addition, using geospatial, population, traffic, and travel-to-work information, it is possible to locate the best place for a hospital, school, or community facility, to serve communities most at need, or cut travel times. Moreover, Ministry of Social Development is using data to better learn which of its services get better outcomes for individuals and communities in order to waste less public expenditure on services that do not work and invest more on what does work (New Zealand Data Futures Forum).

7.3.11   Semantics and Linked Data Tools

Semantic technology enables users to enrich their documents and contents with machine-processable semantics of data that make use of metadata to enable more sophisticated data mining (Berners-Lee et al. 1999). The explicit representation of the semantics of data is accompanied by domain theories, namely ontologies. Linked data is based on semantic web philosophy and technologies, but, in contrast to the full-fledged semantic web vision, it is mainly about publishing structured data in Resource Description Framework (RDF) using uniform resource identifiers (URIs) rather than focusing on the ontological level or inferencing (Hausenblas 2009). Thus, linked data refer to the ability to link together different pieces of information published on the Web and the ability to directly reference to a specific piece of information (Cyganiak et al. 2011; Heath and Bizer 2011).

Responding to this trend, traditional content management systems (CMS) have been improved to support semantic technology and provide semantic lifting of the textual content (Auffret 2001). For example, new CMS enable users to (collaborative) elaborate their documents and online texts submitting comments and annotations (e.g. Enrycher, Annotea). In other cases, users can define and store data based on custom ontologies created by them (e.g. WebNotes). Furthermore, some CMS have tried to support linked data techniques such as automatic detection of entities such as persons, places, and locations, and their linking to external sources, e.g. to dbpedia descriptions of resources (e.g. Apache Stanbol). On the other hand, several tools have been created to address collaborative creation of ontologies (OntoMat-Annotizer, OntoGen).

Considering the recent shift towards massively offering open nonpersonal government data, one can easily understand the importance of linked data in the field of policy making (Kalampokis et al. 2011). One example of how Linked Open Data may be effectively used to inform discussions held by policy makers and others is the clean energy information portal, Reegle[27]. This portal interprets raw data in order to provide useful information and context for end users: It provides high-quality information on renewable energy efficiency and climate compatible development around the world as easily navigable graphs and tables with a lot of additional information at hand too.

7.4   Summary and Discussion

In the previous section, we presented emerging tools and technologies with the potential to enhance policy making. In this section, we would like to provide an overall discussion of this potential, especially with regard to three main aspects for policy making:

---

[27] http://www.w3.org/2012/06/pmod/report.

- The *main activities* facilitated by each tool and technology. Previous analysis showed that each tool category presents a different way for enhancing policy making. For example, some tools focus on providing information in a user-friendly manner, other tools promote deliberation, other tools are used to gauge public opinion, etc. Analysing this characteristic, we can draw conclusions on the different ways each emerging tool and technology may be used in policy making.
- The *stage of the policy cycle* facilitated by each tool and technology. It was previously mentioned that the policy making process is composed of a number of stages; these stages describe the policy life cycle. Analysing the "fit" of each tool and technology in the policy cycle stages promotes understanding of how each tool and technology can enhance the policy-making process. We will consider four main stages of the policy cycle as they were defined by Jann and Wegrich (2006): Agenda setting; policy formulation and decision making; implementation; evaluation and termination.
- The *stakeholder types* that can use each tool and technology. We categorise the previously identified stakeholders in policy making as follows: institutional stakeholders (i.e. the government), noninstitutional stakeholders (i.e. political parties, political consultants, and lobbyists, the media, nongovernmental organisations, civil organisations, and other interested parties), and the public. Analysing who of these stakeholder groups could use each tool and technology and in what ways, promotes understanding of how these tools and technologies can be adopted in policy making.

Following this, we examined each category of the identified tools and technologies with regard to these three aspects.

Visualisation tools are ideal mainly for information provision, namely for presenting data in a user-friendly, easy-to-grasp representation. These tools can be used in any stage of the policy cycle, wherever the need for demographic, social, or spatial data representation emerges. For example, they can be used during the decision-making stage in order to fine-tune new policies, during the implementation and evaluation stage in order to understand whether the application of a certain policy brought any changes or even during the agenda-setting stage in order to identify problems that should be addressed with policies. All types of stakeholders may be potential users of visualisation tools depending on the topic addressed and due to the fact that no specialisation is required in order to use and understand them.

Argumentation tools are ideal for structured deliberation, namely for discussing specific issues with the aim to reach a common understanding or a commonly accepted decision. As such, these tools can be useful in all stages of the policy cycle, whenever a targeted deliberation is needed; maybe they are more relevant for the agenda setting, the policy formulation and decision making, and the evaluation and termination stages where such discussions are usually performed. With regard to potential users, in principle, all stakeholders can use argumentation tools. However, previous experience in the field has shown that argumentation tools require a certain degree of logic and critical thinking. It is, therefore, not easy for the general public to productively use these tools without prior training (Tambouris et al. 2011 and Panopoulou et al. 2012). For this reason, argumentation tools may be more effectively used for somewhat "closed" deliberation groups targeting a specific issue within a certain policy field.

eParticipation tools are ideal for involving the public in the policy-making process. They refer to many different activities such as information provision, deliberation, consultation, gauging public opinion, citizen engagement, community building, etc. eParticipation tools may be initiated by an institutional stakeholder (top-down participation) or a noninstitutional stakeholder or even the public (bottom-up participation). Thus, all stakeholder types are potential users of these tools, although typical usage refers to interactions between the government and the public. Due to the wide spectrum of supported activities, eParticipation tools may be used in any stage of the policy cycle.

Opinion mining tools are ideal for gauging the public's opinions and sentiments, thus, they can be used in any stage of the policy cycle whenever such a service is needed. For example, they can be used for gauging the acceptance potential of a new policy or for detecting negative evaluations of a policy. Due to their technical complexity, opinion mining tools are better suited to be used by trained institutional stakeholders or noninstitutional stakeholders, but not the general public.

Simulation tools are useful in policy making for detecting and simulating social interactions and behaviour patterns. For example, they can be used for simulating the long-term impact of different policy alternatives and thus assist in the policy formulation and decision-making stage. Simulation tools are technically complex to implement; therefore, they are mostly suited for usage by a few specialised institutional or noninstitutional stakeholders.

Serious games are useful in policy making for educational purposes. They are mostly relevant to the policy formulation and decision-making stage of the policy cycle, as players may assume a stakeholder's role in order to explore different policy scenarios on a given topic and make relevant decisions. Serious games can also be used in the implementation stage of the policy cycle, for educating citizens on how to apply a certain state policy, e.g. a health or environmental policy. The main stakeholder group of serious games is the wide public.

The two tools included in our analysis that were specifically developed for policy makers are relevant to the policy formulation and decision-making stage and to the evaluation and termination stage of the policy cycle. Of course, their user group includes only institutional or noninstitutional stakeholders.

Persuasive tools can be used by institutional or noninstitutional stakeholders for influencing public attitudes and behaviours. Thus, it is mostly relevant to the implementation stage of the policy cycle, for strengthening policy adoption.

Social network analysis tools are useful for identifying key actors and social patterns relevant to specific policy areas. These can be used in the policy formulation and decision-making stage, and in the implementation stage of the policy cycle for deciding alternative policies or for strengthening policies' implementation. SNA is a complex process requiring specialised knowledge, thus it can only be used by trained institutional or non-institutional stakeholders.

Big data analytics tools can be useful in policy making for processing huge amounts of information and, through this, for detecting and predicting patterns and trends of the public. These activities are relevant to all stages of the policy cycle, maybe less relevant to the implementation stage. Nonetheless, the users of this technology can be the government per se or noninstitutional stakeholders interested in analysing data for a specific topic.

Semantics and linked data tools can be exploited for enhancing interoperability of government data and for creating linkages between open government data and social data. Thus, linked data tools can facilitate better understanding of social data and public opinion and better prediction of public reactions, e.g. to different policy alternatives. For this reason, semantics and linked data tools seem relevant to all stages of the policy cycle. Again, the specialty required for applying these technologies means that only institutional or noninstitutional stakeholders may be the immediate users of such technologies (Table 7.8).

The table above shows that a policy stakeholder has a number of different ICT tools and technologies at hand. From these, they could choose the most appropriate ICT mix depending on the targeted activity and policy-making stage. For example, we can draw the following conclusions:

- Visualisation tools, argumentation tools, opinion mining tools, big data, linked data, and eParticipation tools may be used at any point of the policy-making process depending on the activities needed.
- Serious games and persuasive tools are the most appropriate in order to strengthen the implementation stage and promote policy adoption.
- The policy formulation and decision-making stage of the policy cycle is the most frequently addressed stage. This is not surprising as this stage involves multiple and diverse activities such as scenario analysis, policy drafting, public consultations, and decision making.
- Visualisation tools, big data analytics tools, and linked data tools can help enhance provision and analysis of large amounts of information.
- A number of different technologies have emerged for detecting opinions, sentiments, trends, and other patterns of behaviour: opinion mining, simulation, social network analysis, big data analytics tools, and linked data tools. There is clearly a trend for using modern ICT towards analysing crowd knowledge already available online.
- For exploiting advanced tools and technologies expert skills are needed that can only be hired in the context of big (institutional or noninstitutional) organisations.
- For involving the public, visualisation tools, eParticipation tools, and serious games are the most appropriate choices.

Acknowledgments This work is partially funded by the European Commission within the 7th Framework Programme in the context of the eGovPoliNet project (http://www.policy-community.eu/) under grand agreement No. 288136.

Table 7.8 Potential of emerging tools and technologies for enhancing policy making

Tools and technologies	Main activities	Policy cycle stages	Stakeholder types
Visualisation tools	Information provision	All	All
Argumentation tools	Structured deliberation	All (possibly less in the implementation stage)	All (though not easy for untrained public)
eParticipation tools	Information provision, deliberation, gauging opinions, citizen engagement	All	All, typically for interaction between the public and the government
Opinion-mining tools	Gauging opinions and sentiments	All	Institutional or noninstitutional stakeholders
Simulation tools	Detecting and simulating social interactions and behaviour patterns	Policy formulation and decision making	Institutional or noninstitutional stakeholders
Serious games	Policy education	Policy formulation and decision making, implementation	The public
Tools specifically developed for policy makers	Policy analysis and assessment	Policy formulation and decision making, evaluation and termination	Institutional or noninstitutional stakeholders
Persuasive tools	Influencing public attitudes and behaviours	Mostly relevant to Implementation	Institutional or noninstitutional stakeholders
Social network analysis tools	Identifying key actors and social patterns	Policy formulation and decision making, implementation	Institutional or noninstitutional stakeholders
Big data analytics tools	Information processing, detecting and predicting patterns and trends	All (possibly less in the implementation stage)	Institutional or noninstitutional stakeholders
Semantics and linked data tools	Understand opinions, predict public reaction	All	Institutional or noninstitutional stakeholders

Appendix

Visualisation Tools

China Geo – Explorer II http://chinadataonline.org/cge
   Data Visualizer-World Bank http://devdata.worldbank.org/DataVisualizer
   DataPlace http://www.dataplace.org http://devdata.worldbank.org/DataVisualizer
   Dynamic Choropleth Maps http://www.turboperl.com/dcmaps.html
   e-Atlas of Global Development–World Bank http://data.worldbank.org/products/
data-visualization-tools/eatlas
   Gapminder http://www.gapminder.org/tag/trendalyzer
   Google Charts https://developers.google.com/chart
   Google Public Data Explorer http://www.google.com/publicdata/directory
   Health Infoscape http://senseable.mit.edu/healthinfoscape
   NComVA http://www.ncomva.com
   OECD eXplorer http://stats.oecd.org/OECDregionalstatistics
   PolicyMap http://www.policymap.com
   R http://www.r-project.org
   Social Explorer http://www.socialexplorer.com
   STATcompiler http://www.statcompiler.com
   State Cancer Profiles http://statecancerprofiles.cancer.gov/micromaps
   Visokio Omniscpoe http://www.visokio.com
   Visualize Free http://visualizefree.com
   Worldmapper http://www.worldmapper.org

Argumentation Tools

Araucaria http://araucaria.computing.dundee.ac.uk/doku.php
   Argunet http://www.argunet.org
   bCisive https://www.bcisiveonline.com
   Carneades http://carneades.github.io
   Cohere http://cohere.open.ac.uk
   Compendium http://compendium.open.ac.uk/institute
   Cope_it! http://copeit.cti.gr/Login/Default.aspx
   DebateGraph http://debategraph.org
   MindMeister http://www.mindmeister.com
   Rationale http://rationale.austhink.com

eParticipation Tools

Citizen Space https://www.citizenspace.com/info
   Adhocracy.de http://code.adhocracy.de/en

CitySourced https://www.citysourced.com
CivicEvolution.org http://civicevolution.org
Dialogue App http://www.dialogue-app.com/info/
Loomio.org https://www.loomio.org/
MixedInk.com http://www.mixedink.com
Opinion Space http://opinion.berkeley.edu
OurSpace http://www.ep-ourspace.eu/
Puzzledbypolicy http://www.puzzledbypolicy.eu
UbiPol http://www.ubipol.eu/

Opinion Mining Tools

AIRC Sentiment Analyzer http://airc-sentiment.org
   Attentio http://www.attentio.com
   Convey API https://developer.conveyapi.com
   Corpora's Applied Linguistics http://www.corporasoftware.com/products/
sentiment.aspx
   DiscoverText http://www.discovertext.com
   Opinion observer http://citeseerx.ist.psu.edu/viewdoc/summary?doi=10.1.1.79.
8899
   Opinmind http://www.opinmind.com
   Repustate https://www.repustate.com
   Sentimentor http://sentimentor.co.uk
   Sentiment140 http://www.sentiment140.com
   Social Mention http://socialmention.com
   SwiftRiver http://www.ushahidi.com/products/swiftriver-platform
   ThinkUp https://www.thinkup.com/
   Umigon http://www.umigon.com/

Agent-Based Modelling and Simulation Tools

Budget simulator http://www.budgetsimulator.com/info
   C-ROADS http://climateinteractive.org/simulations/C-ROADS
   CLASP's Policy Analysis Modeling System (PAMS) http://www.clasponline.org/
en/Tools/Tools/PolicyAnalysisModelingSystem
   EUREAPA tool https://www.eureapa.net/
   GLEaMviz http://www.gleamviz.org/simulator
   Global Buildings Performance Network (GBPN) Policy Comparative Tool
http://www.gbpn.org/databases-tools/purpose-policy-comparative-tool
   MASS http://mass.aitia.ai
   MEL-C http://code.google.com/p/jamsim

Repast http://repast.sourceforge.net
Threshold 21 http://www.millennium-institute.org/integrated_planning/tools/T21
UrbanSim http://www.urbansim.org/Main/WebHome

Serious Games

2050 Pathways https://www.gov.uk/2050-pathways-analysis
Breakaway (Disaster Management-Incident Commander) http://www.breakawayltd.com
Budget Hero http://www.marketplace.org/topics/economy/budget-hero
CItyOne http://www-01.ibm.com/software/solutions/soa/innov8/cityone/index.html
Democracy http://www.positech.co.uk/democracy
Maryland Budget Map Game http://iat.ubalt.edu/MDBudgetGame
MP For A Week http://www.parliament.uk/education/teaching-resources-lesson-plans/mp-for-a-week-game/
NationStates—create your own country http://www.nationstates.net
The Social Simulator http://www.socialsimulator.com
Urgent Evoke http://www.urgentevoke.com
World Without Oil http://worldwithoutoil.org

Policy-Making Tools

Oracle Policy Automation for Social Services http://www.oracle.com/us/industries/public-sector/059171.html
PolicyMaker http://www.polimap.com/default.html

Semantics and Linked Data Tools

Annotea http://www.w3.org/2001/Annotea
Apache Stanbol http://stanbol.apache.org
Enrycher http://ailab.ijs.si/tools/enrycher
OntoGen http://ontogen.ijs.si
OntoMat-Annotizer http://annotation.semanticweb.org/ontomat
Reegle http://www.reegle.info
WebNotes http://www.webnotes.net

References

Abt CC (1987) Serious games. University Press of America, Lanham (Cited in: Michael, D. and Chen, C. (2006). Serious games: games that educate, train and inform. Boston, MA: Thompson Course Technology, PTR)

Auffret M (2001) Content management makes sense—Part 1, delivering increased business value through semantic content management. J Knowl Manage Pract. http://www.tlainc.com/articl28.htm

Bandini S, Manzoni S, Vizzari G (2009) Agent-based modeling and simulation: an informatics perspective. J Artif Soc Soc Simul 12(4):4

Behavioural Insights Teem (BIT) (2012) Applying behavioural insights to reduce fraud, error and debt. Cabinet Office, London

Benn N, Macintosh A (2011) Argument visualization for eParticipation: towards a research agenda and prototype tool. In: Tambouris E, Macintosh A, de Bruijn H (eds) Electronic participation. Springer, Berlin, pp 60–73

Berners-Lee T, Fischetti M, Dertouzos M (1999) Weaving the web: the original design and ultimate destiny of the world wide web by its inventor. Harper, San Francisco

Bertot JC, Gorham U, Jaeger PT, Sarin LC, Choi H (2014) Big data, open government and e-government: issues, policies and recommendations. Inform Polity 19(1):5–16.

Caird-Daley A, Harris D, Bessell K, Lowe M (2007) Training decision making using serious games. Technical report. Human Factors Integration Defence Technology Centre. UK, HFIDTC/2/WP4.6.2/1

Chang KT (2010) Introduction to geographic information systems. McGraw-Hill, New York

Cyganiak R, Hausenblas M, McCuirc E (2011) Ocial statistics and the practice of data fidelity. In: Wood D (ed) Linking government data. Springer, Berlin, pp 135–151

Fogg BJ (2002) Persuasive technology: using computers to change what we think and do. Ubiquity, December: Article 5

Gramberger MR (2001) Citizens as partners. OECD handbook on information, consultation and public participation in policy-making. OECD, Paris, p 64

Hausenblas M (2009) Exploiting linked data to build web applications. IEEE Internet Comput 13(4):68–73

Heath T, Bizer C (2011) Linked data: evolving the web into a global data space. Synthesis lectures on the semantic web: theory and technology, vol 1:1. Morgan & Claypool, San Rafael, pp 1–136

Jann W, Wegrich K (2006) Theories of the policy cycle. In: Fischer F, Miller GJ, Sidney MS (eds) Handbook of public policy analysis: theory, politics, and methods. CRC Press, Boca Raton

Kalampokis E, Hausenblas M, Tarabanis K (2011) Combining social and government open data for participatory decision-making. In: Tambouris E, Macintosh A, de Brujin H (eds) Electronic participation. Springer, Berlin, pp 36–47

Kraak MJ, Brown A (eds) (2001). Web cartography: developments and prospects. Taylor & Francis, New York, p 213

Macal CM, North MJ (2005) Tutorial on agent-based modeling and simulation. In: Proceedings of the 37th conference on Winter simulation, pp 2–15. Winter Simulation Conference

MacEachren AM, Kraak MJ (2001) Research challenges in geovisualization. Cartogr Geogr Inf Sci 28(1):3–12

Maragoudakis M, Loukis E, Charalabidis Y (2011) A review of opinion mining methods for analyzing citizens' contributions in public policy debate. In: Maragoudakis M, Loukis E, Charalabidis Y (eds) Electronic participation. Springer, Berlin, pp 298–313

Mitchell T (2005) Web mapping illustrated. O'Reilly, Sebastopol

Northern Ireland Government (2013) A practical guide to policy making in Northern Ireland. http://www.ofmdfmni.gov.uk/practical-guide-policy-making.pdf. Accessed 22 Dec 2014

Nyce C (2007) Predictive analytics white paper. American Institute for Chartered Property Casualty Underwriters. Insurance Institute of America, pp 9–10

Ohl R (2008) Computer supported argument visualization: Modelling in consultative democracy around wicked problems. In: Okada A, Buckingham Shum S, Sherborne T (eds) Knowledge cartography: software tools and mapping techniques. Advanced information and knowledge processing series. Springer, London, pp 267–286

Onggo BS (2010) Running agent-based models on a discrete-event simulator. In: Proceedings of the 24th European Simulation and Modelling Conference, pp 51–55

Osimo D, Mureddu F (2012) Research challenge on visualization. W3C workshop on "Using Open Data: policy modeling, citizen empowerment, data journalism"

Panopoulou E, Dalakiouridou E, Tambouris E, Tarabanis K (2012) Citizens' evaluation of an online argument visualisation platform for eParticipation. In: Tambouris E, Macintosh A, Saebo O (eds) ePart 2012. Lecture Notes in Computer Science, vol 7444. Springer, Berlin, pp 49–60

Phang CW, Kankanhalli A (2008) A framework of ICT exploitation for e-participation initiatives. Commun ACM 51(12):128–132

Raybourn EM, Deagle ME, Mendini K, Heneghan J (2005) Adaptive thinking & leadership simulation game training for special forces officers. In: The interservice/industry training, simulation & education conference (I/ITSEC), vol 2005, no 1). National Training Systems Association

Rowena D (2010) Applying a systems-centered (SCT) approach and social network analysis (SNA) to citizen-centric behaviour change. http://www.rdaconsulting.net/LiteratureRetrieve. aspx?ID=42614

Stylios G, Christodoulakis D, Besharat J, Vonitsanou M, Kotrotsos I, Koumpouri A, Stamou S (2010) Public opinion mining for governmental decisions. Electron J e-Gov 8(2):203–214

Tambouris E, Dalakiouridou E, Panopoulou E, Tarabanis K (2011) Evaluation of an argument visualisation platform by experts and policy makers. In: Tambouris E, Macintosh A, de Bruijn H (eds) ePart 2011. Lecture Notes in Computer Science, vol 6847. Springer, Berlin, pp 73–84

Tang S, Yuan J, Mao X, Li X, Chen W, Dai G (2011) Relationship classification in large scale online social networks and its impact on information propagation. In proceeding of 30th IEEE International Conference on Computer Communications (INFOCOM), pp 2291–2299, IEEE

UK Government (1999) Modernising government. http://www.archive.official-documents.co.uk/ document/cm43/4310/4310.htm. Accessed 22 Dec 2014

United Nations Department of Economic (2010) United Nations e-government survey 2010: leveraging e-government at a time of financial and economic crisis, vol 10. United Nations Publications, Herndon

Chapter 8
Value Sensitive Design of Complex Product Systems

**Andreas Ligtvoet, Geerten van de Kaa, Theo Fens, Cees van Beers,
Paulier Herder and Jeroen van den Hoven**

Abstract We increasingly understand technical artefacts as components of complex product systems. These systems are designed, built, maintained, and deprecated by stakeholders with different interests. To maintain interoperability between components, standards are being developed. The standardisation process itself is, however, also influenced by different stakeholders.

In this chapter, we argue that a full, comprehensive overview of all relevant components of a system is increasingly difficult. The natural response to complex problems is to delve into details. We suggest that an opposite move towards a more abstract approach can be fruitful. We illustrate this by describing the development of smart meters in the Netherlands. A more explicit focus on the values that play a role for different stakeholders may avoid fruitless detours in the development of technologies. Policymakers would do well by not only addressing functional requirements but also taking individual and social values into consideration.

8.1 Complex Technology

Modern society is highly dependent on a number of infrastructures; electricity and telecommunications infrastructures are considered most critical (Luiijf and Klaver 2006). The desire to move towards a more sustainable energy system with a more decentralised structure, and with a focus on renewable energy sources such as solar energy and wind power, requires adjusting the existing, centralised electricity infrastructure. By adding information and communication technologies (ICT) to the electricity grid at all levels of the system—from high-voltage transformers to washing machines—each node in the network can decentrally respond to its neighbourhood while safeguarding the reliability of the whole system. The concept of such a new electricity infrastructure is known as the *smart grid*.

The smart grid concept implies a number of changes at various system levels (national transmission grid, local distribution grid, and residential connections;

A. Ligtvoet (✉) · G. van de Kaa · T. Fens · C. van Beers · P. Herder · J. van den Hoven
Faculty of Technology, Policy, and Management, Delft University of Technology,
Delft, The Netherlands
e-mail: a.ligtvoet@tudelft.nl

© Springer International Publishing Switzerland 2015   157
M. Janssen et al. (eds.), *Policy Practice and Digital Science*,
Public Administration and Information Technology 10, DOI 10.1007/978-3-319-12784-2_8

Morgan et al. 2009) with a large role for ICTs (Mulder et al. 2012). However, the precise technological constellation of smart grid systems is yet unknown, and a matter of discussion for politicians and policymakers, (systems) engineers and standardisation bodies, energy providers and distributors, knowledge institutes and telecommunication organisations, and citizen representatives.

Even when limiting ourselves to the residential realm the number of interrelated issues is vast. A case in point is the smart meter. This improved version of an electricity meter is seen as an important element for electricity grid optimisation that also allows for end-user efficiency through insight into consumption patterns (EC 2011). The most comprehensive version of such a device provides information about household energy consumption (accounting for decentral generation). The smart meter transmits this information to energy providers and/or distributors to improve their systems, and control of electric devices remotely, for example, to optimise the load of the distribution grid, or to switch off consumers who have not paid their bills. In practice, however, smart meter deployment is guided by various motives (e.g. fraud detection or improved billing) that have different technical requirements (AlAbdulkarim 2013). At the same time, it has become clear that the roll-out of smart meters can only be successful if the end users in households also recognise their benefits (Cuijpers and Koops 2013; Hierzinger et al. 2013). Until recently, this has not been the case and citizens have voiced concerns about issues including privacy (McDaniel and McLaughlin 2009) and health effects (Verbong et al. 2013; Hess and Coley 2012).

In this chapter, we take the position that technology development is driven by the needs and requirements of a wide range of stakeholders. Among these, technology developers and their competitors play an important role in shaping and standardising technologies. Other stakeholders, such as households, may have a less prominent role in determining the development of technologies, but at times play a significant role in the acceptance of the technology (Mitchell et al. 1997). It is important to identify all the stakeholders involved, and to understand their motives and values so that the technology development can be adjusted in a timely fashion. The Dutch smart metering history provides a cautionary tale as the needs of households end users, one of the main stakeholders, were not sufficiently taken into account. This was one of the main reasons that the Dutch Senate rejected the proposed Energy Bill in 2008 (Cuijpers and Koops 2013) which consequently delayed the roll-out of smart meters for several years.

We aim to shed light on the development process of the complex product system and examine to what extent value-sensitive design (VSD) could have avoided this delay. We employ a case study analysis of the standardisation[1] of smart metering in the Netherlands. We add insights from overlapping standards discussions in household automation and show that the interlinked nature of ICT, consumer products, energy systems, and home automation does not allow a strict delineation of technological

---

[1] We follow the definition of standardisation as proposed by de Vries (1999): An activity of establishing and recording a limited set of solutions to actual or potential matching problems, directed at benefits for the party of parties involved, balancing their needs and intending and expecting that these solutions will be repeatedly or continuously used, during a certain period, by a substantial number of the parties for whom they are meant.

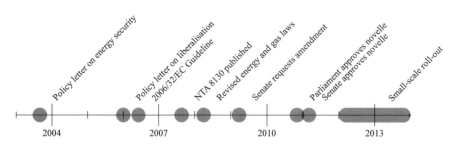

Fig. 8.1 Timeline of the smart meter policy process in the Netherlands

artefacts, and leads to an oversimplification of the issues at stake. We discuss to what extent earlier analysis of this information could have led to adjustments of standards such as the Dutch smart metering requirements (DSMR).

8.2 Smart Meters in the Netherlands

Early scholarly mentions of *intelligent* or *smart* meters suggest their (technical) development took place in the 1980s and 1990s (see e.g. Peddie 1988). As we are interested in official standardisation, we provide an overview of Dutch policies regarding smart meters (see also Fig. 8.1), its standardisation, and the stakeholders involved in this process.

Following a letter about security of energy supply from the Ministry of Economic Affairs to Dutch Parliament in 2003 (MinEZ 2003), SenterNovem, a ministry agency, was requested to investigate the standardisation, stakeholder involvement, and conduct a cost–benefit analysis on the roll-out of a smart meter infrastructure (Dijkstra et al. 2005). Demand-side response was seen as a major contribution to security of supply during peak electricity consumption. The Dutch standardisation institute Nederlands Normalisatie-Instituut (NEN) was commissioned to formulate and describe a national standard for smart meters. The societal cost–benefit analysis proved to be positive (a net gain of 1.2 billion €) with the citizens as main beneficiaries of the roll-out. Interestingly, in the ensuing stakeholder consultation, consumer representatives were not heavily involved: "The point of view of the consumer, individually as a household, or collective via housing corporations, Home Owners Association or Consumers Association was not a key issue" (Dijkstra et al. 2005). The other stakeholders—energy producers, energy suppliers, grid operators, metering companies, telecom, energy regulators—requested the ministry to clearly identify meter functionalities, expedite meter roll-out by setting a time frame, and provide regular consumption overviews (to make smart meters the only affordable solution).

Anticipating the EU Directive 2006/32/EC on on energy end use and energy services, the Ministry of Economic Affairs provided more information on smart meters requirements, citing billing administrative problems and the energy savings goals of the Commission as main arguments in favour of smart meters (MinEZ 2006). In 2007, NEN published the technical agreement NTA 8130, which set out a minimum set of requirements for smart metering. The organisation of grid operators (Netbeheer Nederland) took the lead in specifying these requirements, which became DSMR.

In 2008, the Ministry of Economic Affairs revised the electricity and gas bills that implemented the European directive. Grid operators became responsible for meter deployment, and energy providers were appointed the point of contact for consumers. This was supposed to increase clarity for consumers, efficiency, and create a level playing field for market parties. Consumers were required to cooperate in installing smart meters; not doing so would constitute an economic felony. After several rounds of reviews and discussions about privacy, and amendments as a response to the Dutch Data Protection Authority (Customs and Border Protection, CBP), the bills were passed by the Lower House of Parliament in July 2008. By that time, the smart meter and its privacy issues had gained wider public interest. Technical experts assessed possible security and privacy breaches of the meter, and legal experts deemed the proposed solution irreconcilable with the European Convention on Human Rights (Cuijpers and Koops 2013). When the bills were scrutinised by the Senate in 2009, it proposed amendments regarding the mandatory character of smart meters and revisions concerning consumer privacy.

The smart metering bill was amended into a voluntary roll-out of smart meters and reintroduced for political consideration in September 2010. The customer could now decline a smart meter and energy suppliers were required to give customers bimonthly statements with specific minimum information requirements. The grid operators set up uniform authorisation and authentication procedures to ensure that individual measurement data were only used for specific purposes and only after customer consent. The revised bills passed the Lower House of Parliament in November 2010 and was approved by the Senate in February 2011 (Hierzinger et al. 2013).

The Ministry of Economic Affairs agreed on a "small-scale" deployment of smart meters in 2012 and 2013. This 2-year period was used to test the practical implications of roll-out in approximately 400,000 households and to assess consumer response. A midterm review of the roll-out did not identify any major issues, with only 2–3 % of households rejecting the smart meter. At the end of 2013, there is still a political debate about whether the smart meter should be coupled with the functionality to switch off electricity and gas. In other countries, this was the main reason to install smart meters, but the Dutch Consumers' Association argued that remote-controlled switches would constitute a cyber threat on a nationwide scale. In its latest consultation round, the ministry seems to share this view.

Meanwhile, several stakeholders (notably hardware providers) argue that the Netherlands with its 8 million households and 750,000 small and medium enterprise connections is not large enough to make a customised smart meter financially feasible. They emphasise that the DSMR should be abandoned in favour of European standards.

8.3   Smart Meters as Complex Product Systems

A smart meter could be seen as an artefact that, like a pair of scissors, can be designed or bought on the market in relative isolation. However, our case study already indicates that the development of smart meters is contingent upon developments on international, national, and (inter)organisational levels. Literature on technology management has long conceptualised technological artefacts as subsystems that are linked together, as well as being a component of even larger systems (Clark 1985; Suarez 2004). Tidd (1995) calls these complex product systems, that have three distinctive characteristics:

- Systemic: the systems consist of numerous components and subsystems.
- Multiple interactions take place across different components, subsystems, and levels.
- Nondecomposable: the systems cannot be separated into their components without degrading performance.

This means that technologies, components, and interfaces incorporated in products are interdependent, and thus rely on standard interfaces, but also depend on different market segments and the range and specificity of performance criteria within these markets. This also means that technological designs, sponsored by different actors, compete for dominance through a process where economic, technological, and sociopolitical factors are intertwined (Rosenkopf and Tushman 1998). The more complex the product system, the greater is the number of actors needing to be aligned for a technological design, and thus the more complicated the actual design process becomes (Suarez 2004).

In the following sections, we indicate that the development of smart meters and home energy management systems (HEMS) is influenced by competing formal and industry standards (Sect. 8.3.1) and that a whole range of actors or stakeholders is involved in the development of these artefacts (Sect. 8.3.2). By combining these two analyses, a multifaced picture emerges.

8.3.1   Competing Standards

In the decision about smart meters and HEMS, competing formal and nonformal standards play a role. We have attempted to provide an overview of different standards that are related to these technologies in Table 8.1. This overview shows us that there are many options for the design of smart meters/HEMS components. Whereas, there may be some room for consolidation, some of the presented standards provide unique solutions to specific problems. As Gallagher (2007) indicates, it remains extremely difficult to pick "winners" ex ante.

Whereas smart metering falls under governmental regulation, the market for HEMS is not regulated. However, depending on the final specifications of the smart meter, some functionalities may overlap. Many different established and

Table 8.1 Overview of different (competing) standards in the converging technology realms

Component/Subcomponent	Competing standards
Smart meter	
Smart meter	NTA 8130, DRMS X.X, DLMS, IEC 62056-21, NEN-EN 13757, IEEE Std 1901, IEEE P1703, IEEE 1377, DLMS/COSEM standard (IEC 62056 / EN 13757-1), IEEE 802.15.4, Wired M-Bus, M-Bus protocol (EN 13757), 6LoWPAN, ANSI C12.18, IEC 61107
Communication systems	
Wired local area networks (application level)	Arcnet vs ATM vs CEPCA vs Ethernet vs FDDI vs Home plug and play vs homeplug vs hiperlan2 vs open air vs Passport vs Powerpacket, Smart Energy Profile 2, Universal Powerline Bus (UPB), DMX512
Wired local area networks (infrastructure level)	FRF vs MPLS/Framerelay vs Orthogonal frequency divising multiplexing vs Salutation vs SSERQ vs Token Bus vs Token Ring vs UPA
Wireless local area networks (infrastructure level)	HomeRF vs IEEE802.16 vs Open air vs IEEE802.11(Wifi), HiperLAN
Wireless personal area network	Bluetooth vs IEEE 802.15.3 vs IEEE 802.15.4 vs Irda vs Zigbee, Z-wave, 6LoWPAN
Power line communication	IEEE Std 1901-2010, HomePlug,G.hn(G.9960), PRIME, PLC-G3, IEC-61334 SFSK
Computer networks (wired)	USB vs Convergence bus vs Firewire vs IRDA
Mobile telecommunications	3G vs Dect vs GPRS vs GSM vs UMTS
Home automation systems	
Home networks	DLNA vs HANA vs HAVi vs HomeAPI vs HOMAPNA vs Moca vs UPnP, IEC/TS 62654, NEN-ISO/IEC 15045-1, ISO/IEC 14543-3-7, IEC 61970, IEEE 1905.1, ITU-T G.9960, CEA-2027-B, CEA-2033, CAN/CSA-ISO/IE, NEN-EN 50090-1, MultiSpeak, IEC 62457, H950 SystemLink
Home automation (wired and wireless)	CEA851 vs CEBus vs Echonet vs EHS vs HBS vs HES vs HGI vs HomeCNA vs HomeGate vs HPnP vs Lontalk vs Smarthouse, ISO/IEC 14543KNX, Zigbee, digitalSTROM, ISO/IEC TR 15044, EN 50090 (KNX/EIB)
Building automation	BACnet vs BatiBUS vs COBA vs DALI/IEC 60929 vs FND vs Instabus vs KNX vs Metasys vs MOCA vs Profibus vs Worldfip vs X10 vs Zigbee, NPR-CLC/TR 50491-6-3, ISO 16484-5BACnet NEN-EN 13321-1, NEN-EN 15232, ISO 16484-5, ISO 50001, ISO/IEC 18012-1, EnOcean, Modbus, oBIX
Consumer electronics	
Video	Displayport vs DVI vs HDMI vs Scart vs VESA vs VGA

Table 8.1 (continued)

Component/Subcomponent	Competing standards
Energy systems	
Heat/cold storage	NEN-EN-IEC 60531, NEN-EN-IEC 60379
Electric stationary storage batteries	J537, 1679-2010 IEEE
Electric car batteries	SAE J2847, SAE J2836/1-3, SAE J2931/5, SAE J2758, Smart Energy Profile (SEP 1.1), ASTM D 445, DIN 51 562 (part 1) , ISO 3105
Decentral electricity production systems	
Solar photovoltaics	IEC 61215, IEC 61646, UL 1703, IEC 60904
Small wind mills	DIN EN 61400-25-4, AGMA 6006-A03, NEN 6096
Micro CHPs	DIN 4709

newly emerging industries and product markets are involved in HEMS (den Hartog et al. 2004). We observe a convergence between established industries such as telecommunications, consumer electronics, and home automation (domotics) with new developments in energy industries: photovoltaics, micro heat and power, micro wind, storage, and home automation. ICT plays a crucial role at both national and local level. In the energy sector, integrating information technology with operational technology (IT/operations technology (OT) integration) is seen as a major development. In short, ICT is what makes a smart grid smart.

Actors that originate from the different converging industries develop and promote standards that enable communication not only for components within single industries but also for communication between components that originate in different industries (van de Kaa et al. 2009). van de Kaa et al. (2009) have performed a search for standards for home networking and present a graphical overview of these standards that originate in different converging industries. We use that graphical overview and have adapted it for the situation of HEMS (see Fig. 8.2).

While some of the standards mentioned in Fig. 8.2 clearly belong in one industry, we also see shifts taking place. We have indicated two of these shifts in the figure. Whereas Universal Serial Bus (USB) started off in the computer industry, it became increasingly used in consumer electronics, e.g. for allowing MP3 music files to be played on audio systems. Likewise, Digital Enhanced Cordless Telecommunications (DECT) was orginally a wireless telephony protocol, but was soon used in baby monitors, and since the development of the Ultra Low Energy variant in 2011 it is used in home appliances, security, healthcare, and energy monitoring applications that are battery powered.

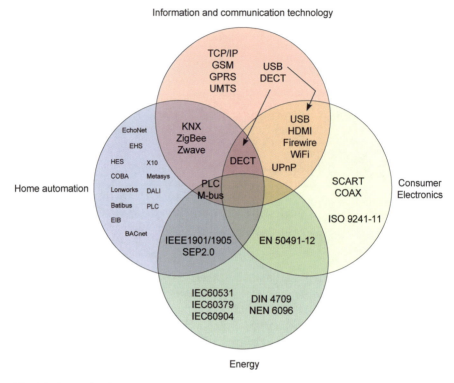

Fig. 8.2 Converging formal and industrial standards in the realm of home energy management

8.3.2 Actor or Stakeholder Analysis

The fact that industries are converging broadens the number of stakeholders involved in technical developments. Although many of the traditional players in the energy field still play a role, opportunities have been created for niche players to take on a larger role. de Vries et al. (2003) have identified search directions for stakeholder identification: production chain, physical systems and their designers, end users and related organisations, inspection agencies, regulators, research and consultancy, education, representative organizations, and organised groups of stakeholders. We take this categorisation as a starting point, but add *standardisation bodies* as an additional category. We have attempted to capture the interaction of electricity grid components within a value chain representation in Fig. 8.3.

1. We take the electricity production chain as a starting point. Important players are the distribution system operators (DSOs). In the Netherlands, these include the largest DSOs Alliander, Delta, Enexis, and Stedin. Other players are the energy production companies (e.g. Nuon and RWE/Essent), energy suppliers (which may be middlemen between production and consumption), and the national grid operator Tennet.

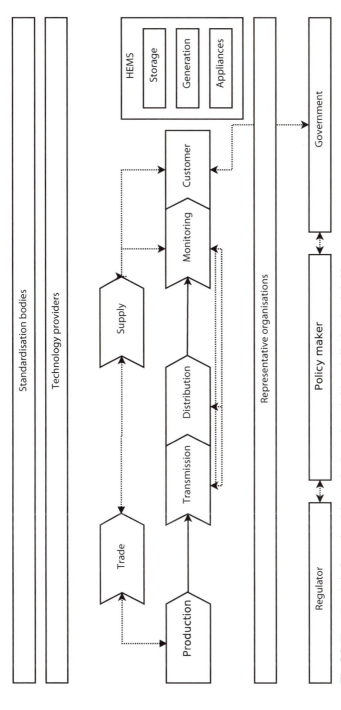

Fig. 8.3 The value chain from electricity production to households and all related stakeholders

2. Various technology providers are involved in the development and design of physical components that are part of the entire value chain. This includes companies such as Cisco Systems, IBM, Philips, Honeywell, and Siemens, meter companies such as Landis + Gyr, Echelon, Itron, and Iskra, and data managers and integrators such as Ferranti. Whereas some companies specifically focus on one aspect of the value chain, most have a broader involvement.
3. End users and related organisations are the actual home owners and tenants that may be organised in local groups such as local home owners' associations (e.g. owners of houses in the same building or street) or national groups such as Vereniging Eigen Huis (home owners association of the Netherlands). Expert consultation revealed that consumer representation in standardisation committees is rare in the Netherlands but in some countries such as the UK and Japan consumers are involved in standard development.
4. Important inspection agencies with regard to smart meters include not only Keuring van Elektrotechnische Materialen te Arnhem (KEMA), who are charged with organising Dutch meter inspections, but also NMi Certin and Verispect.
5. Regulators (Autoriteit Consument en Markt (ACM) Energiekamer) and policymakers (Ministry of Economic Affairs (Ministerie van Economische Zaken, EZ)) are involved heavily in the smart meter component. And also the European Union's policies have effect upon the Dutch smart meters and HEMS.
6. Universities, research institutes, and consultants play an important and major role in standardization for HEMS in the Netherlands. Noteworthy in this context are KEMA (who have provided several cost-benefit analyses) and Nederlandse Organisatie voor Toegepast Natuurwetenschappelijk Onderzoek (TNO; who have advised the Ministry and parliament). The Netherlands' national metrology institute Van Swinden Laboratory (VSL) takes a special role in this category, as it is charged with certifying the (tools for) inspection agencies. Other important stakeholders include IT consultancy firms.
7. The education category is less relevant for the identification of stakeholders for HEMS. Although a lot of universities are actively engaged in research relating to smart grids, active participation in standardisation is rare.
8. National representative organisations include consumer organisations such as the Consumers' Association (Consumentenbond). But also DSOs are represented by *Netbeheer Nederland* and energy producers are represented by *Energie Nederland*. At the European level, smart meter providers are represented by European Smart Metering Industry Group (ESMIG). For other networks, see below.
9. Standardisation bodies operate at different levels. Internationally, there are International Organization for Standardization (ISO), International Electrotechnical Commission (IEC), and International Telecommunication Union (ITU), at the European level Comité Européen de Normalisation (CEN), Comité Européen de Normalisation Électrotechnique (CENELEC), and European Telecommunications Standards Institute (ETSI), and at the national level NEN. See Sect. 8.3.3 below.

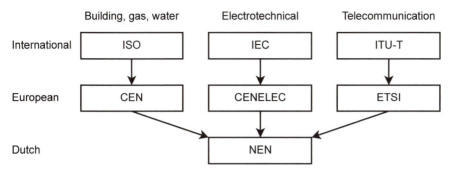

Fig. 8.4 Standardisation organisations in different technology fields at (inter)national levels

8.3.3   Networks of Stakeholders

Not only are the stakeholders mentioned in the previous section active in influencing policy but also are members of various standards organisations and consortia.

Noteworthy are international formal standardisation organisations ISO (general standards; related to smart meters buildings, gas, and water), International Electrotechnical Commission (IEC; electrotechnical standards), and International Telecommunication Union-Telecom Sector (ITU-T; telecommunication standards). These organisations also have standardisation organisation counterparts active on the European level (CEN, CENELEC, and ETSI), and at the national level (in the Netherlands this is NEN; see Fig. 8.4). Most standardisation organisations have different work groups or technical committees that develop standards for particular product markets and/or technical areas. Smart meters, for example, are covered by IEC technical committee TC13 and its CENELEC counterpart (conveniently named TC13). However, some aspects may be covered by other technical committees, such as TC57 on power systems management and associated information exchange. Members of these work groups are to a large extent drawn from industrial partners or industrial consortia. The members are, however, deemed to provide their expertise independent of their employers.

Next to the formal standardisation organisations, various consortia exist that develop and/or promote standards for components of HEMS. These standards may be based on formal standards, but used in a specific application area. Several subcomponents are combined to create a set of coherent components, some of which are not formal standards. In the field of HEMS, these consortia include:

- KNX Association—promoting a standard for home and building control
- ZigBee Alliance—promoting a wireless technology designed to address the unique needs of low-cost, low-power wireless sensor and control networks
- Salutation Consortium—promoting a service discovery and session management protocol providing information exchange among and between different wireless hand-held devices and office automation equipment.

- Echonet Consortium—promoting the development of basic software and hardware for home networks that can be used for remote control or monitoring of home appliances
- The Digital Living Network Alliance—publishing a common set of industry design guidelines that allow manufacturers to participate in a growing marketplace of networked devices.
- Smart Grids European Technology Platform—a European forum for the crystallisation of policy and technology research and development pathways for the smart grids sector.

8.4 Values in the Design of Technical Artefacts

The vast amount of standards and stakeholders involved makes an overview of the possible technological trajectories nearly impossible. We suggest that a focus on values and the notion of VSD allows for a more comprehensive view of smart meter and HEMS development.

Values are mentioned in a wide array of disciplines (e.g. philosophy, sociology, economics) and generally denote what something is worth, opinions about that worth, and/or moral principles (Dietz et al. 2005). Values are also described as "enduring beliefs that a specific mode of conduct is personally or socially preferable to an opposite or converse mode of conduct or end-state of existence" (Rokeach 1968). In decision making, values, which can be described as an abstract set of principles, allow us to resolve conflicts by suggesting which preferences are better. They provide us with criteria to distinguish options (see, e.g. Keeney 1994).

Values also play a role in the design and use of technological artefacts. Whereas historically technology may have been considered purely instrumental and value-free (Manders-Huits 2011), it has become clear that technological artefacts exhibit moral and political choices and consequences (even though the moral and political dimension may not be perceived by their designers and users). This means that the choice for a specific technology may imply a social and institutional order without which the technology might not work. Winner (1980) suggests that in "societies based on large, complex technological systems, . . . moral reasons other than those of practical necessity appear increasingly obsolete, 'idealistic,' and irrelevant. Whatever claims one may wish to make on behalf of liberty, justice, or equality can be immediately neutralized when confronted with arguments to the effect: 'Fine, but that's no way to run a railroad' (or steel mill, or airline, or communications system, and so on)". We would argue that the *smart grid* is one of those large, complex technological systems, for which the same argument holds.

8.4.1 Value-Sensitive Design

A stream of research that focuses on moral and political dimensions of technology and technology design is called *Value Sensitive Design (VSD)* (Friedman et al. 2002; Borning and Muller 2012). VSD seeks to be proactive to influence the design of technology early in and throughout the design process. It employs conceptual, empirical, and technical investigations (Friedman et al. 2008; van de Poel 2009):

- Conceptual investigations aim, for instance, at clarifying the values at stake, and at making trade-offs between the various values.
- Empirical investigations involve social scientific research on the understanding, contexts, and experiences of the people affected by technological designs.
- Technical investigations involve analysing current technical mechanisms and designs to assess how well they support particular values, and, conversely, identifying values, and then identifying and/or developing technical mechanisms and designs that can support those values.

Many of the technological examples addressed in VSD literature relate to ICTs (Friedman 1996; van den Hoven 2007; Friedman et al. 2008), which is why we expect the approach to be pertinent to smart meter/home/grid technologies. VSD started from the recognition that when designing information technologies, the predominant, traditional focus of engineers is on functionality, i.e. the efficiency, reliability, and affordability of (new) technologies—conform the practical necessity argument identified by Winner (1980). Furthermore, the point of reference is often the designer's own experiences, needs, and values. For example, it has been shown that software designers (unknowingly) design software that is more aligned with males than with females. Friedman (1996) also mentions an example of educational software that is geared towards the American competitive education system which is less successful in foreign classrooms, where cooperation is considered more important.

8.4.2 Values in Our Research

Although it is embedded in moral philosophy, VSD uses a broad sense of values: values refer to what persons, either singularly or collectively, consider important to their lives. However, the 56 personal values that the Schwartz Value Survey, commonly used in social sciences (Dietz et al. 2005), defines, might not relate to technological artefacts and technology use. For this study, we therefore focus on a subset that is often mentioned in VSD literature. Next to the already mentioned *functional* values (accountability, correctness, efficiency, environmental sustainability, legitimacy, reliability, safety, tractability), we address *social* values (cooperation, courtesy, democracy, freedom from bias, identity, participation, privacy, trust) and *individual* values (autonomy, calmness, economic development, informed consent, ownership, universal usability, welfare). Most of these values are defined in Fried-man et al. (2008). For the purposes of our research, we have translated these into broad definitions which can be found in Table 8.2.

We have attempted to identify the values that played a role in the development of smart meters (Ligtvoet et al. in press). Based on expert elicitation, the five most important values associated with smart meters are:

1. *Privacy*: The system allows users to determine which information about them is used and communicated.
2. *Correctness*: The system provides correct data or performs the correct function.
3. *Reliability*: The system fulfils its function without the need to monitor/control it.
4. *Informed consent*: The system allows its users to voluntarily agree to its activation, based on comprehensible information.
5. *Economic development*: The system is beneficial to its users' economic or financial status.

These results very closely match the general impression of the smart metering debate in the Netherlands. *Privacy* is a very important value that was virtually ignored at the start of the implementation process. As could be expected for a device that is designed to measure, the functional values of *correctness* and *reliability* are also ranked high. The individual values of *informed consent* and *economic development* emphasise that end users' needs should be taken into consideration.

An interesting and unexpected finding of our expert group discussion was that these values depend on the delineation of the system. The experts indicated that the important values actually shift when the smart meter is not only seen as a connected measuring device but also more as an energy management nexus for households. This generates a new ranking of values for HEMS:

1. *Economic development*: The system is beneficial to its users' economic or financial status.
2. *Universal usability*: The system can easily be operated by all users.
3. *Privacy*: The system allows users to determine which information about them is used and communicated.
4. *Autonomy*: The system allows its users to make their own choices and pursue their own goals.
5. *Reliability*: The system fulfils its function without the need to monitor/control it.

Here, we see a clear shift towards the individual and social values of the users and slightly less emphasis on the functional values of the technology. We believe that this corresponds with findings of Krishnamurti et al. (2012) and Balta-Ozkan et al. (2013). Compared with standalone smart meters, a clearly higher score was given for *participation* and *well being*, again emphasising the user experience. Also, the values *legitimacy* and *freedom from bias* became much less important. In the discussion, it became clear that HEMS are seen as a commercial consumer product, for which consumers are personally responsible.

Table 8.2 Overview of 23 values that we found in the value sensitive design literature

Value	Description
Accountability	The system allows for tracing the activities of individuals or institutions
Autonomy	The system allows for its users to make their own choices and choose their own goals
Calmness	The system promotes a peaceful and quiet state
Cooperation	The systems allows for its users to work together with others
Correctness	The systems processes the right information and performs the right actions
Courtesy	The system promotes treating people with politeness and consideration
Democracy	The system promotes the input of stakeholders
Economic development	The system is beneficial to the economic status/finances of its users
Efficiency	The system is effective given the inputs
Environmental sustainability	The system does not burden ecosystems, so that the needs of current generations do not hinder future generations
Freedom from bias	The system does not promote a select group of users at the cost of others
Identity	The system allows its users to maintain their identity, shape it, or change it if required
Informed consent	The systems allows its users to voluntarily make choices, based on arguments
Legitimacy	The system is deployed on a legal basis or has broad support
Ownership	The system facilitates ownership of an object or of information and allows its owner to derive income from it
Participation	The system promotes active participation of its users
Privacy	The system allows people to determine which information about the is used and communicated[a]
Reliability	The system fulfils its purpose without the need to control or maintain it
Safety and health	The system does not harm people
Tractability	The functioning of the system can be traced
Trust	The system promotes trust in itself and in its users
Universal usability	The system can be easily used by all (foreseen) users
Welfare	The system promotes physical, psychological, and material well-being

[a] We acknowledge that this is a limited definition of privacy

8.5 Discussion

8.5.1 From Values to Design Requirements

VSD purports to be a holistic approach that combines theory with empirics (Manders-Huits 2011). The identification of values should therefore be linked to the formulation of design requirements for complex product systems, in our case smart meters and HEMS.

The need for (elements of) *privacy* was addressed in the NTA8130 standard and the requirement of an encryption protocol was added. Functional requirements of *correctness* and *reliability* were already covered by the Dutch measurement code and no further requirements were necessary. *Informed consent* is not easily addressed from a technological standpoint, but it did prove important in the debate in the Senate. The solution was not technical, but procedural. The end user was given four options: no smart meter but an ordinary one, a smart meter that does not communicate, low-frequency communication, or high-frequency communication. The *economic development* was addressed by several cost-benefit assessments and a restriction of the metering tariff.

Given the nature of HEMS (i.e. more like a consumer product), the values associated with it should also be addressed in a slightly different way. The focus on *economic development* suggests a restriction in the price of the system and a clear indication of how much can be saved by installing such a system. *Universal usability* emphasises the need for easy-to-use interfaces: end users should not require an engineering degree to operate the system. *Privacy* remains an issue and requires communication channels to be secured—similar to (mobile) telecommunication and computing requirements. *Autonomy* suggests that the users should be in charge of their home energy management and automation: this is closely linked to ease of use. And finally, the system should be *reliable* like other consumer products.

We acknowledge that the current research has performed an ex post analysis of values and identified issues that were already resolved in the course of history of the Dutch smart meter (standard and requirements). The proof of the pudding would be an ex ante assessment and monitoring of the upcoming issues.

8.5.2 Values Salience

Our research has led us to question the extent to which values are important and identified, which one could call "values salience". Comparing smart meters to other technological systems such as communication systems or smart grids, we find that the meter has received quite some attention. (On the basis of our interviews, we believe that smart meters were initially only considered a technical issue.) We suggest that values salience relates to the *size* of the technical system according to an inverted U as shown in Fig. 8.5. This means that small technical components such as communication protocols attract little attention and the general public remains

Fig. 8.5 Values salience of a
technical component depends
on its size

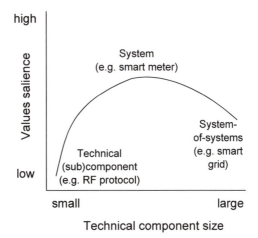

indifferent. The same argument holds for large systems such as an entire electricity grid—although the public may still be able to judge some of the importance of such an artefact for their own energy supply, they largely remain uninvolved. However, the level of the household, thus of the smart meter, is most visible to people and therefore their attention and ability to express values is much greater at this level.

8.5.3   Multidisciplinary Approach

Our research contributes to the literature on innovation management and standardisation (e.g. Schilling 1998, 2002; Suarez 2004; Sheremata 2004). Scholars in the area of innovation management and standardisation have attempted to explain standard dominance and draw from various areas of research including network economics and institutional economics (van de Kaa et al. 2011). They have come up with technology-, firm-, and environmental-level factors that explain standard dominance (Suarez 2004). In this chapter, we shed light on another level of analysis that is neglected in the literature: the end user. We provide a first illustration of the notion that societal acceptance of a platform will grow if a technological design is modified to changing user requirements related to ethical and societal values surrounding the technology. *Privacy* is the most salient value for the Dutch smart meter case, but *informed consent* also played an important role. Combining literature from philosophy and ethics on the one hand and technology management on the other hand, we provide a clearer view on the influence of factors relating to the end user. Future research could further explore the ex ante translation from identified values to actual design requirements.

8.6   Conclusion

Our case study of the development of smart metering and smart metering standards in the Netherlands shows the complexity of introducing new technologies in an existing sociotechnical system. We believe that our findings can be generalised, not only to other components of the *smart grid* but also to other systems-of-systems that are deployed and used by a wide array of stakeholders.

Current technological development is often so complex that stakeholders are unable to fully assess new technologies. Nor are they able to weigh the input of all stakeholders. First of all, because not all stakeholders are always involved and secondly, because people's opinions and beliefs change because of new information, insights, and experiences. Although the introduction of a new technical component may start off from a very functional and technical position, nontechnical issues (values) can be introduced by consumers' associations and other stakeholders.

It can be argued that a lack of consideration for these values can lead to a delay in the roll-out of new technologies. Even though technical solutions only seem to address technical problems, they influence society through the interconnected nature of modern infrastructures. Especially, when technology is "visible" at the household level, consumers or their representatives can be expected to have an opinion. For policymakers, it would be wise to foresee such stakeholder involvement and to address stakeholder values in an early stage.

The outcome of a values elicitation is a more balanced representation of the interests of all stakeholders, including end users: a combination of functional, social, and personal values. This focus on values may help designers in their search for better technical and functional specifications. However, such a design process is complicated by the fact that technical artefacts form an intricate part of larger systems-of-systems. As we have shown, depending on the system focus, the related values are somewhat different and there still may be some discussion to what extent an artefact serves a higher (system level) goal. This is certainly an area in which VSD could further develop and provide more guidance.

Acknowledgements This research was supported by Netherlands Organisation for Scientific Research (NWO) grant MVI-12-E02 on responsible innovation ("maatschappelijk verantwoord innoveren"). We are indebted to our valorisation committee (Gertjan van den Akker, Theo Borst, Johan Crols, Michiel Karskens, Gerrit Rietveld, Rick van der Tol, and Gerritjan Valk) for their insight and comments. We would also like to thank our interviewees: Johan Boekema, Coco Geluk, Tjakko Kruit, Erik Linschoten, Willem Strabbing, Jeike Wallinga, and Teus de Zwart.

References

AlAbdulkarim L (2013) Acceptance-by-design: elicitation of social requirements for intelligent infrastructures. Next generation infrastructures thesis 66, Delft University of Technology, the Netherlands
Balta-Ozkan N, Davidson R, Bicket M, Whitmarsh L (2013) Social barriers to the adoption of smart homes. Energy Policy 63:363–374

Borning A, Muller M (2012) Next steps for value sensitive design. In: CHI '12, Proceedings of the SIGCHI conference on human factors in computing systems. Austin, Texas, USA

Clark KB (1985) The interaction of design hierarchies and market concepts in technological evolution. Res Policy 14:235–251

Cuijpers C, Koops BJ (2013) Smart metering and privacy in Europe: lessons from the Dutch case . In: European data protection: coming of age, Chap. 12. Springer, Berlin, p 269

de Vries H (1999) Standardization, a business approach to the role of national standardization organizations. Kluwer Academic, Boston/Dordrecht/London

de Vries H Verheul H Willemse H (2003) Stakeholder identification in it standardization processes. In: Standard making: a critical research frontier for information systems, MISQ Special Issue Workshop

den Hartog F Baken N Keyson D Kwaaitaal J Snijders W (2004) Tackling the complexity of residential gateways in an unbundling value chain. In: 15th international symposium on services and local access, Edinburgh, Scotland

Dietz T, Fitzgerald A, Shwom R (2005) Environmental values. Annu Rev Environ Resour 30: 335–372

Dijkstra A, Leussink E, Siderius P (2005) Recommendation implementing smart metering infrastructure at small-scale customers. Technical Report FAS No. 1-2893 (SenterNovem: 4150), SenterNovem, Utrecht, the Netherlands

EC (2011) Definition, services, functionalities and benefits of smart grids. Commission staff working document SEC (2011) 463 final. European Commission, Brussels

Friedman B (1996) Value-sensitive design. Interactions November + December, pp 17–23

Friedman B, Kahn PH, Borning A (2002) Value sensitive design: theory and methods. Technical Report 02-12-01, Dept. of Computer Science and Engineering, University of Washington

Friedman B, Kahn PH, Borning A (2008) Value sensitive design and information systems. In: Himma KE, Tavani HT (eds) The handbook of information and computer ethics, Chap. 4. Wiley, Hoboken, pp 69–101.

Gallagher S (2007) The complementary role of dominant designs and industry standards. IEEE Trans Eng Manag 54(2):371–379

Hess DJ, Coley JS (2012) Wireless smart meters and public acceptance: the environment, limited choices, and precautionary politics. Public Underst Sci 23(6):688–702. doi:10.1177/0963662512464936. Published online 6 November 2012

Hierzinger R, Albu M, van Elburg H, Scott AJ, Lazicki A, Penttinen L, Puente F, Sale H (2013) European smart metering landscape report 2012 – update may 2013. Deliverable 2.1, SmartRegions, Vienna. www.smartregions.net

Keeney RL (1994) Using values in operations research. Oper Res 42(5):793–813

Krishnamurti T, Schwartz D, Davis A, Fischhoff B, de Bruin WB, Lester Lave JW (2012) Preparing for smart grid technologies: a behavioral decision research approach to understanding consumer expectations about smart meters. Energy Policy 41:790–797

Ligtvoet A, van de Kaa G, Fens T, van Beers C, Herder P, van den Hoven J (in press) Stakeholder values in home energy management. Sci Eng Ethics

Luiijf EA, Klaver MH (2006) Protection of the Dutch critical infrastructures. Int J Crit Infrastruct 2(2/3):201–214

Manders-Huits N (2011) What values in design? the challenge of incorporating moral values into design. Sci Eng Ethics 17(2):271–287

McDaniel P, McLaughlin S (2009) Security and privacy challenges in the smart grid. IEEE Secur Priv May/June:75–77

MinEZ (2003) Voorzienings- en leveringszekerheid energie. In: Brief van de Minister van Economische Zaken, Tweede Kamer, Tweede Kamer. The Hague, The Netherlands, 29023-1

MinEZ (2006) Liberalisering energiemarkten. In: Brief van de Minister van Economische Zaken, Tweede Kamer, Tweede Kamer. The Hague, The Netherlands, 28982-51

Mitchell RK, Agle BR, Wood DJ (1997) Toward a theory of stakeholder identification and salience: defining the principle of who and what really counts. Acad Manag Rev 22(4):853–886

Morgan MG, Apt J, Lave LB, Ilic MD, Sirbu M, Peha JM (2009) The many meanings of 'smart grid'. Technical Report, Department of Engineering and Policy, Carnegie Mellon University

Mulder W, Kumpavat K, Faasen C, Verheij F, Vaessen P (2012) Global inventory and analysis of smart grid demonstration projects. Technical Report, DNV Kema, Arnhem, the Netherlands

Peddie R (1988) Smart Meters, NATO ASI Series. In: Demand-side management and electricity end-use efficiency, vol III. Kluwer Academic, Dordrecht, pp 171–180

Rokeach M (1968) Beliefs, attitudes and values: a theory of organization and change. Jossey-Bass, San Francisco

Rosenkopf L, Tushman ML (1998) The coevolution of community networks and technology: lessons from the flight simulation industry. Ind Corp Change 7(2):311–346

Schilling MA (1998) Technological lockout: an integrative model of the economic and strategic factors driving technology success and failure. Acad Manag Rev 23(2):267–284

Schilling M (2002) Technology success and failure in winner-take-all markets: the impact of learning orientation, timing, and network externalities. Acad Manag J 45:387–398

Sheremata W (2004) Competing through innovation in network markets: strategies for challengers. Acad Manag Rev 29:359–377

Suarez FF (2004) Battles for technological dominance: an integrative framework. Res Policy 33:271–286

Tidd J (1995) Development of novel products through intraorganizational and interorganizational networks – the case of home automation. J Prod Innov Manag 12:307–322

van de Kaa G, den Hartog F, de Vries HJ (2009) Mapping standards for home networking. Comput Stand Interf 31:1175–1181

van de Kaa G, van den Ende J, de Vries HJ, van Heck E (2011) Factors for winning interface format battles: a review and synthesis of the literature. Technol Forecast Soc Change 78:1397–1411

van de Poel I (2009) Values in engineering design. In: Handbook of the philosophy of science, vol 9. Philosophy of Technology and Engineering Sciences, pp 973–1006

van den Hoven J (2007) ICT and value sensitive design. In: Goujon P, Lavelle S, Duquenoy P, Kimppa K, Laurent V (eds) The information society: innovations, legitimacy, ethics and democracy, IFIP International Federation for Information Processing, vol 233. Springer, Berlin, pp 67–72

Verbong GP, Beemsterboer S, Sengers F (2013) Smart grids or smart users? Involving users in developing a low carbon electricity economy. Energy Policy 52:117–125

Winner L (1980) Do arifacts have politics? Daedalus 109(1):121–136

Chapter 9
Stakeholder Engagement in Policy Development: Observations and Lessons from International Experience

Natalie Helbig, Sharon Dawes, Zamira Dzhusupova, Bram Klievink and Catherine Gerald Mkude

Abstract This chapter provides a starting point for better understanding how different approaches, tools, and technologies can support effective stakeholder participation in policy development. Participatory policy making involves stakeholders in various stages of the policy process and can focus on both the substance of the policy problem or on improving the tools and processes of policy development. We examine five international cases of stakeholder engagement in policy development to explore two questions: (1) what types of engagement tools and processes are useful for different stakeholders and contexts? And (2) what factors support the effective use of particular tools and technologies toward constructive outcomes? The cases address e-government strategic planning in a developing country, energy policy in a transitional economy, development of new technology and policy innovations in global trade, exploration of tools for policy-relevant evidence in early childhood decision making, and development of indicators for evaluating policy options in urban planning. Following a comparison of the cases, we discuss salient factors of stakeholder

N. Helbig (✉) · S. Dawes
Center for Technology in Government, University at Albany, 187 Wolf Road,
Suite 301, 12205 Albany, New York, USA
e-mail: nhelbig@ctg.albany.edu

S. Dawes
e-mail: sdawes@ctg.albany.edu

Z. Dzhusupova
Department of Public Administration and Development Management
United Nations Department of Economic and Social Affairs (UNDESA), New York, USA
e-mail: dzhusupova@un.org

B. Klievink
Faculty of Technology, Policy and Management, Delft University of Technology,
Jaffalaan 5, 2628 BX, Delft, The Netherlands
e-mail: a.j.klievink@tudelft.nl

C. G. Mkude
Institute for IS Research, University of Koblenz-Landau, Universitätsstr. 1,
56070 Koblenz, Germany
e-mail: cmkude@uni-koblenz.de

© Springer International Publishing Switzerland 2015   177
M. Janssen et al. (eds.), *Policy Practice and Digital Science,*
Public Administration and Information Technology 10, DOI 10.1007/978-3-319-12784-2_9

selection and representation, stakeholder support and education, the value of stakeholder engagement for dealing with complexity, and the usefulness of third-party experts for enhancing transparency and improving tools for engagement.

9.1 Introduction

Complex public problems are shared and dispersed across multiple organizations and domains (Kettl 2002). Consider, for example, the array of concerns associated with improving air quality or assuring the safety of food products. The formal governmental responses to these specific public needs are addressed through public policies. Policy might focus on different geographic locations, processes, or products, or could specify how certain outcomes are defined, observed, and assessed. Moreover, individuals, families, communities, industry, and government itself are all affected by policy choices, and they all have interests in both the decision-making process and the final decisions (Bryson 2004).

In light of seemingly intractable and complex social problems, public administrators have shifted toward governance activities that allow citizens and stakeholders to have deeper involvement in the policy-making process and the work of government (Bingham et al. 2005). Governance models which focus on quasi-legislative activities such as participatory budgeting, citizen juries, focus groups, roundtables, or town meetings (Bingham et al. 2005; Fishkin 1995) create opportunities for citizens and stakeholders to envision their future growth (Myers and Kitsuse 2000), clarify their own policy preferences, engage in dialogue on policy choices, or bring various groups to consensus on proposals (McAfee 2004). The models vary based on degree of involvement by the general population, whether they occur in public spaces, if the stakeholders are actually empowered, and whether they lead to tangible outcomes (Bingham et al. 2005).

Stakeholder engagement objectives may also vary by their point of connection with the policy process (Fung 2006). The policy process is complex and there are many different ways to conceptualize how it works. The stages heuristic of public policy making is one of the most broadly accepted (Sabatier 1991). Although the utility of the stages model has limits, and numerous advances in theories and methods for understanding the policy process have been made, the stages heuristic continues to offer useful conceptualizations (Jenkins-Smith and Sabatier 1993). While specification and content of the stages vary somewhat throughout the literature, however (as shown in Fig. 9.1), models often comprise some combination of problem identification, agenda setting, formulation, adoption, implementation, and policy evaluation (Lasswell 1951; Easton 1965; Jones 1977). More recent conceptualizations involve feedback across the various stages.

Research in both the public and private sectors has identified a number of benefits associated with stakeholder engagement in governance. Stakeholders' interests illuminate the multiplicity of factors that underlie policy problems, decisions, and implementation. Direct engagement of stakeholders increases public understanding

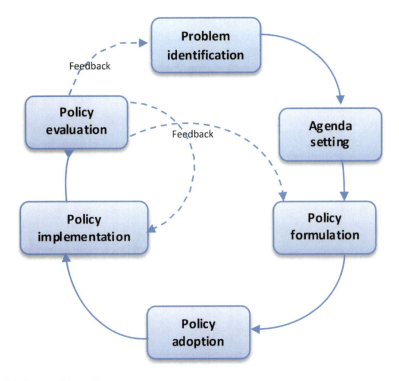

Fig. 9.1 Stages of the policy process

of the issues and the consequences of different choices. Accordingly, engagement generates more options for policies or actions. Engagement brings more information into the deliberation process from different kinds of stakeholders so that decisions are more likely to avoid unintended consequences and fit better into existing contexts. Engagement also reveals both conflicts and agreements among different stakeholder groups. While taking stakeholders into account is a crucial aspect of solving public problems, policy development includes both powerful and powerless stakeholders within the process (Bryson 2004). Some stakeholders have the power, knowledge, or resources to affect the policy content, while others are relatively powerless but nevertheless are affected, sometimes in dramatic ways (Brugha and Varvasovszky 2000). Thus, open and evenhanded stakeholder engagement, especially among those with conflicting viewpoints, can sometimes resolve differences and build trust in the policy-making process and help secure public acceptance of decisions (e.g., Klievink et al. 2012).

In the past 20 years, specialized technologies, electronic communication, and advanced analytical, modeling, and simulation techniques have been developed to support governance processes. Administrators, analysts, and planners must decide how and when to engage citizens and stakeholders in governance, particularly during the different stages of policy making. They must also consider which mechanisms to use for managing the relationships (Bryson 2004) and must select from a variety of tools and techniques. In this chapter, we begin to explore two questions: (1) What types of engagement tools and processes are useful for different stakeholders and contexts? And (2) what factors support the effective use of particular tools and technologies toward constructive outcomes?

The next sections start by reviewing the foundational elements of stakeholder theory and its relation to governance, including a summary of tools and techniques used to identify stakeholders and analyze stakeholder interests and ways to classify types of engagement. We then offer five case stories of stakeholder engagement in complex and dynamic settings across the world including e-government strategic planning in a developing country, exploring different uses of evidence in early childhood decision making, developing technology and policy innovations in global trade, and involving citizens in the design of energy policy and transportation planning. The cases vary in both policy content and the extent to which newer technologies were used to deal with the complexity of the engagement process, their accessibility and understandability to outsiders, and the advantages and disadvantages they offer to expert stakeholders as compared to laymen. We then compare the cases, discuss their similarities and differences, and conclude with a discussion of the usefulness of different tools and processes for different stakeholders and contexts and the factors that support their effectiveness.

9.2 Foundations of Stakeholder Engagement

Stakeholder engagement, as a concept, originated within organizational studies as an approach to managing corporations (Freeman 2010; Bingham et al. 2005; Donaldson and Preston 1995; Mitchell et al. 1997). This approach has since been adapted for use by public sector organizations to highlight the importance of stakeholders in various aspects of the policy-making process (Bingham et al. 2005). Bingham et al. (2005) situate stakeholders as part of "new governance" concepts where government actively involves citizens as stakeholders in decision making through activities such as deliberative democracy, participatory budgeting, or collaborative policy making. Research on stakeholder inclusion in government processes has been found to enhance accountability, efficiency in decision-making processes, and good governance (Ackerman 2004; Flak and Rose 2005; Yetano et al. 2010). The growing popularity of stakeholder analysis reflects an increasing recognition of stakeholder influences on decision-making processes (Brugha and Varvasovszky 2000).

9.2.1 Defining Stakeholders

The term "stakeholder" is defined differently by different disciplines. Most definitions mention similar stakeholder categories such as companies and their employees or external entities such as suppliers, customers, governments, or creditors. In the public sector, the definition of stakeholder emphasizes categories of citizens defined by demographic characteristics, life stages, interest groups, or organizational boundaries (Bingham et al. 2005; Ackerman 2004; Yetano et al. 2010). Stakeholders can be both internal to the government (e.g., the government organizations responsible for policy implementation) and external to it (e.g., the industries, communities, or individuals to be affected by government actions or rules).

In this chapter, we use Freeman's (1984) definition of stakeholder as any group or individual who can affect or is affected by the achievement of an organization's objectives. In the public sector, "organization" is understood to mean a government entity or body with responsibility for public policies or services. In the simplest terms, those who can affect or may be affected by a policy can be considered stakeholders in that policy. In traditional expert-based approaches to policy making, the needs of stakeholders are indirectly addressed by public agencies and acknowledged experts (Bijlsma et al. 2011; De Marchi 2003). In these expert-based approaches, internal and external stakeholders may be consulted, but in participatory approaches, stakeholders are not only consulted but are also involved in a structured way to influence problem framing, policy analysis, and decision making. Bijlsma et al. (2011) define participatory policy development as the "influence of stakeholder involvement on the development of substance in policy development, notably the framing of the policy problem, the policy analysis and design, and the creation and use of knowledge" (p. 51).

9.2.2   Stakeholder Identification and Analysis

Stakeholder identification and analysis is an important first phase in stakeholder engagement processes (Freeman 2010). Analysis typically involves five steps (Kennon et al. 2009): identifying stakeholders, understanding and managing stakeholders, setting goals, identifying the costs of engagement, and evaluating and revisiting the analysis. Through these various steps, an analysis helps to distinguish stakeholders from non-stakeholders and to identify the ways that stakeholders need to be engaged during different parts of the policy cycle. Over time, the mix of stakeholders in a particular policy issue is likely to change, as new stakeholders may join the engagement activities, while others may drop out (Elias et al. 2002) or shift among different types. Joining, dropping out, or moving among types thus dynamically changes the configuration and analysis of stakeholders over time.

Various techniques for stakeholder identification and analysis are reviewed in the literature. These techniques focus attention on the interrelations of groups or organizations with respect to their interests in, or impacts on policies within, a broader political, economic, and cultural context. These techniques also provide ways for analysts to understand stakeholder power, influence, needs, and conflicts of interest. Bryson (2004) characterized stakeholder identification as an iterative process highlighting the need to determine the purpose of involving stakeholders and cautioning that these purposes may change over time. He describes a stage approach to selecting stakeholders: someone or a small group responsible for the policy analysis develops an initial stakeholder list as a starting point for thinking about which stakeholders are missing. Brainstorming and the use of interviews, questionnaires, focus groups, or other information-gathering techniques can be used to expand the list. Bryson (2004) notes "this staged process embodies a kind of technical, political, and ethical rationality" (p. 29). He also lists a variety of analysis techniques, such as power and influence grids (Eden and Ackermann 1998), bases of power diagrams (Bryson et al. 2002), stakeholder–issue interrelationship diagrams (Bryant 2003), problem-frame stakeholder maps (Anderson et al. 1999), ethical analysis grids (Lewis 1991), or policy attractiveness versus stakeholder capability grids (Bryson et al. 1986). Each of these tools is used in different situations to help understand and identify various aspects of stakeholder interests.

9.2.3 Stakeholder Engagement

Stakeholder engagement methods are the means by which stakeholder views, information, and opinions are elicited, or by which stakeholders are involved in decision making. Engagement can take various forms. The International Association for Public Participation identified five levels of stakeholder engagement: (IAP2 2007). At the simplest level, *informing,* stakeholders are merely informed, for example, via websites, fact sheets, newsletters, or allowing visitors to observe policy discussions. The level of engagement in this form is very low and suitable only to engage those stakeholders with low urgency, influence, importance, or interest (Bryson 2004). Various methods are available for *consulting,* including conducting interviews, administering surveys to gather information, opening up draft policy documents for public comment, or using Web 2.0 tools to gather ideas. The main goal of this form of engagement is to elicit the views and interests, as well as the salient information that stakeholders have with regard to the policy concern.

Involving stakeholders is a more intensive engagement where stakeholders work together during the policy development process. Some tools used to ensure that ideas, interests, and concerns are consistently understood and addressed include scenario building (Wimmer et al. 2012), engaging panels of experts such as the Delphi method (Linstone and Turoff 1975), or group model building that includes simulating policy choices, games, or role playing (Andersen et al. 2007; Vennix et al. 1996). Models, simulations, or scenarios can be used as boundary objects (Black and Andersen 2012; Star and Griesemer 1989) to enable diverse sets of stakeholders to have a shared experience and to exchange localized or specialized knowledge in order to learn, create common understanding, and identify alternative choices. All these levels focus on the flow of information among actors, but the direction and intensity vary.

The most intense engagement is realized through full collaboration with or even empowerment of stakeholders. In the IAP2 spectrum of public participation, *collaboration* means stakeholders' advice and recommendations will be incorporated in the final decisions to a maximum extent (IAP2 2007). *Empowerment* means that the final decision making is actually in the hands of the public. Realistically, collaboration and empowerment exist within institutional and legal parameters. For example, the policy-making body (usually a government agency) will need to put some constraints or boundaries around the policy options that comport with the limits of its legal authority. For both levels, consensus-building approaches are essential. This can be done through citizen juries (Smith and en Wales 2000), the enactment of a stakeholder board (urbanAPI[1]; Klievink et al. 2012), or by setting up living labs (Tan et al. 2011; Higgins and Klein 2011) in which stakeholders collaboratively develop, implement, and evaluate solutions within a given context. All of these approaches not only assist in incorporating stakeholders' views into the policy process but also enhance acceptance by stakeholders because they were part of the deliberation process (e.g., see Klievink and Lucassen 2013).

9.3 Cases

Below we offer five case stories about stakeholder engagement in policy making. The cases were recommended by a diverse set of eGovPoliNet consortium partners who shared an interest in tools and techniques to support the policy process. The main goal of the case stories is to highlight the roles that stakeholders can play in policy development and to discuss how different methods, tools, and technologies could be used for engaging stakeholders in the policy process. Each case describes a situation where stakeholders were involved in the problem definition, agenda setting, and formulation stages of the policy cycle. In all cases, a trusted third party, generally university researchers, facilitated the process and applied the tools. The cases vary in policy content and in the extent of technology use in the engagement process. They represent different policy domains, and governments at different stages of development with different political systems. The first three cases focus on substantive policy choices for e-government strategic planning, alternative energy policy, and global trade inspection. The last two concentrate on stakeholder involvement in improving tools to support the policy-making process. Of those, the first focuses on connecting policy makers and modelers in building a supportive framework for assessing early childhood programs and second involves stakeholders in defining assessment indicators to be built into a model that supports urban planning decisions.

In this section, we describe these diverse situations as the foundation for the comparison presented in Sect. 9.4 where we identify similarities and differences that suggest approaches, tools, and techniques that are useful and effective in different contexts and with different kinds of stakeholders.

For each case below, we present the key characteristics of the policy-making situation and assess the purpose of stakeholder engagement. With respect to stakeholder

---

[1] UrbanAPI is an EC FP7 project focused on interactive analysis, simulation, and visualization tools for agile urban policy implementation http://www.urbanapi.eu/.

identification and analysis, we cover both the identification of stakeholders (types) involved and the methods used for identification and analysis. With respect to stakeholder engagement (see Sect. 9.2.3), we analyze the engagement approach followed in each case, as well as the type of participation and the methods of stakeholder engagement. We also inventory which tools and technologies were used and describe the results and outcomes of each engagement process.

9.3.1 E-Government Strategic Planning in Afghanistan

The EGOV.AF project was a joint initiative of the Afghanistan Ministry of Communications and Information Technology (MCIT) and the United Nations University–International Institute for Software Technology–Center for Electronic Governance (UNU-IIST-EGOV). One goal of EGOV.AF was to develop a nationally owned EGOV strategy and program (Dzhusupova et al. 2011). In many developing countries, two major challenges to long-term sustainability of e-government initiatives exist: (1) too much reliance on donor funding (Ali and Weerakkody 2009) and (2) lack of understanding regarding citizen demand for e-government services (Basu 2004). To mitigate these challenges, a strategy of the EGOV.AF project was to reach out to stakeholders in a systematic way before putting together a national e-government policy. Afghanistan is one of the poorest countries in the world (World Bank 2012) plagued by a recent history of war and conflict, with a significant digital divide between rural and urban areas. Thus, identifying important stakeholders and understanding their interests, expectations, capacity, and influence were very important, but also very difficult.

In 2011, the UNU-IIST-EGOV team engaged in action research with the MCIT through the development of a stakeholder analysis tool and execution of a series of stakeholder identification exercises, analyses, and workshops. The MCIT was the project owner and lead agency, while the UNU-IIST-EGOV provided mentorship, additional experience, expertise to apply stakeholder analysis tools and engagement methods, and capacity to facilitate the process.

Historically, standard exercises at the MCIT around e-government planning had focused only on consultation with technology stakeholders, such as consulting companies. Initially, the MCIT did not see the value in involving citizens, local provinces, international organizations, academics, or nonprofit organizations that focus on governance. The case was made by UNU to engage people outside of government to address several factors: Many of the nonprofit organizations are advocates for transparency and good governance, donor organizations assert influence over the process through special programs and funding, and the provincial governments work closely and most directly with citizens.

To expand MCIT's limited understanding of this broad set of stakeholders, they conducted a series of consultation and involvement activities. The first instance of engagement with stakeholders was a survey that asked questions about their interests, needs, activities, and conditions. The team also collected additional contextual information from websites and professional contacts. The second stage of engagement occurred after the analysis of the survey. Using the stakeholder analysis tool developed by UNU, the MCIT identified from the survey results a set of interested and relevant stakeholders, defined the roles for major stakeholders in the policy process, and developed communication strategies. Later these stakeholders were invited to attend two stakeholder workshops. One workshop was designed as a "visioning" exercise and another designed to elicit "strategy development." During the workshops, MCIT and UNU-IIST-EGOV were able to provide participants with general knowledge about approaches and methodologies regarding strategy development, provided examples from other countries, and facilitated discussions focused on e-government in the local Afghanistan context. Participants in the workshops were encouraged to share their ideas and to discuss and prioritize strategic goals and tasks for e-government based on the mutual consensus among them. The last stage of the stakeholder engagement was to complete a series of face-to-face meetings and e-mails in which the MCIT collected suggestions on strategic actions. Additional feedback was taken through an e-forum set up on the government website to collect comments on a draft national strategy.

The key result of the overall project was the successful completion of a nationally owned EGOV vision and strategy agreed upon by most important stakeholders. The most critical points of the vision and strategy were to better respond to Afghan citizens' expectations that e-government would bring convenient public services, transparency, accountability, and responsiveness and would help to deter widespread corruption. The project provided evidence that stakeholder engagement in national-level planning processes was possible, and that involving stakeholders can increase commitment, build consensus, and demonstrate transparency and openness in the strategic e-government planning process.

9.3.2   Renewable Energy Policy for Kosice, Slovakia

The process of developing an energy policy in Kosice self-governing region (KSR) in Slovakia is surrounded by political, economic, and environmental challenges. High dependency on imported energy from Russia and Ukraine, presented KSR with economic and political vulnerabilities. The emergence of domestic small to medium enterprises (SMEs) within the energy sector has provided new opportunities for employment and new technologies for utilizing local energy sources. Control of energy production with respect to emissions also impacted the policy-making environment. Any change in the sources of energy would likely affect the pricing of energy consumption and directly affect citizens and businesses. This case not only is a matter for policy makers and the authorities devising new energy policies but also affects the KSR government entities, energy importing companies, local SMEs, and citizens. Creating a new policy in such an environment required considerations of a wide variety of stakeholders; the goal was to ensure the new policy would be realistic, supported, and agreed upon.

This case describes a pilot of the Open Collaboration for Policy Modeling (OCOPOMO) project.[2] The main objective of the OCOPOMO project was to develop an online environment for, and information and communications technology (ICT) tools for, policy modeling in collaboration with stakeholders (Wimmer et al. 2012). Presenting complex information on policy choices for renewable energy requires some technical expertise and is influenced by individual beliefs. The pilot project in Kosice focused on capturing stakeholders' views on alternative renewable sources of energy versus traditional energy production and consumption. It provided an understanding of various choices in relation to different policies for promoting the use of renewable energy, the perceived market potential for different energy sources, barriers hindering different kinds of energy generation in the region, and the motivating factors leading citizens and companies towards renewable energy sources. It also provided an early understanding of employment, financial, and environmental impacts of any potential policy (Furdík et al. 2010). This pilot was the first time that Kosice used advanced ICTs in policy making and the first time the region involved a range of stakeholders other than policy makers, experts, and key representatives from private heat producers and distribution companies.

The project team met with regional government committees and identified and analyzed relevant stakeholders ranging from heating producers to distribution companies, building construction experts to technology experts, to household associations, citizens, and city employees. Desk research and surveys were used to identify the stakeholders, their roles, and expectations in the engagement process. The local authorities were mainly responsible for identifying the stakeholders. The project team and the local government applied action research to engage these stakeholders in the process and involvement was by invitation only. Several methods of engagement were used. Workshops were used to clarify tasks and expectations of stakeholders in the engagement process. Collaborative scenario development enabled stakeholders to provide evidence documents and to generate scenarios related to the policy problem. This method also allowed stakeholders to collaborate among themselves by exchanging views and concerns about the policy problem and possible solutions. Conceptual modeling transformed stakeholder-generated scenarios and evidences into formal policy models for simulation and then transformed the model-based scenarios into narrative scenarios to enable understanding of simulation results to stakeholders and steer further collaboration on the results. This process was iterative as new scenarios emerging from the discussions of results could be evaluated and simulated again.

The stakeholders first met with the project team and were given a tutorial of how the OCOPOMO online platform is used and they were free to use the platform for about 1 month. The online platform provided background and supporting materials to inform stakeholders of the different policy options available. After reviewing existing options, stakeholders could propose several scenarios—for example, they could propose a type of renewable energy and discuss what should be done from the stakeholder's own perspective. Scenarios, based on these stakeholder proposals,

---

[2] http://www.ocopomo.eu/in-a-nutshell/piloting-cases/kosice-self-governing-region-slovakia.

were later turned into formal policy models for simulation. The consistent conceptual description (CCD) tool was used to perform this task.

The next phase began almost 1 year later with another face-to-face meeting to inform stakeholders of the purpose of the second iteration. Given the length of time between the first exercise and the second, some stakeholders were involved in the first face-to-face one but not the second, and some started in the second. In the second iteration, stakeholders were presented with simulation results of their policy choices. Additional background documents were provided to help educate them such as a return on investment (ROI) of different energy sources proposed. Stakeholders, particularly policy owners, provided comments on the model-based scenarios and then published one new evidence-based scenario. The topics which were most discussed leading to the new scenario included detailed technical pros and cons of a local versus central heating system, ROIs, legislation proposed by heat producers that would affect customers who decided to disconnect from the central heating system, and financial tools for investments in building renovation or installation of new heat sources.

The project was successful in highlighting the need for and usefulness of more innovative approaches to policy development processes. These innovative approaches proved to be particularly important with diverse stakeholders with different interests in an existing problem and potential solutions (Wimmer et al. 2012). The added value of OCOPOMO to traditional approaches is the added confidence for policy makers about the expected outcomes of a policy in respect to stakeholders involved. Moreover, the stakeholder engagement process in Kosice was positively viewed by the stakeholders themselves. It enabled better understanding of the policy problem through background documents provided in the platform, and it also provided a tool where different stakeholders' views and expectations could be explicitly captured.

9.3.3 Redesigning the European Union's Inspection Capability for International Trade

The European Union (EU) is implementing a risk-based approach (RBA) policy to government supervision of international trade lanes. As part of this approach, the risk posed by cargo entering and leaving the EU is analyzed on the basis of cargo information submitted electronically in a single declaration by operators prior to departure or arrival. However, this policy can only be effective if the data that circulate among the supply chain partners are accurate, timely, and of sufficient quality to be relied upon, which is currently not the case (Hesketh 2010). This case draws from two projects: Extended Single Window (ESW): Information Gateway to Europe, funded by the Dutch Institute for Advanced Logistics (DINALOG), and common assessment and analysis of risk in global supply chains (CASSANDRA), funded by the 7th Framework Program of the European Commission. The goal of both projects was to improve supply chain visibility.

Transparency is important for both government and commercial interests; it relates to having access to the transaction data necessary to know what is actually happening in the supply chain. However, major challenges exist in today's global supply chains, including lack of trust and understanding between public and private entities and among private entities (Klievink et al. 2012) about existing laws and ways of working among EU countries and other countries. Without the involvement of international trading businesses and other stakeholders, and without their active contribution to data sharing solutions that enable the RBA policy, the policy will not lead to the intended results for government and may lead to unnecessary increases in the administrative burden of legitimate traders.

To overcome these challenges, the project team assembled an international consortium of government bodies that included multiple European customs organizations, in addition to universities, IT providers, logistics operators, and standardization bodies. The project team conducted desk research and a survey based on Bryson (2004) to elicit stakeholders' interests, urgency, influence, and importance. The total number of entities involved in international supply chains is so large that it was necessary to choose stakeholders that would reasonably represent the range of actors. Therefore, selection was based on criticality and representativeness. For example, the consortium involved representatives of a several very large and medium-sized freight forwarders. This was done to ensure different perspectives within this stakeholder group without having to involve the hundreds of parties that can be involved with the cargo on any single ship. Stakeholders were also grouped according to trade lanes. This approach limited the total number of actors by using the trade lane as a boundary. To ensure diversity in interests, ten different global trade lanes were modeled, including lanes between Shenzhen (China) and Felixstowe (UK), Penang (Malaysia) and Rotterdam (the Netherlands), Alexandria (Egypt) and Barcelona (Spain), and Bremerhaven (Germany) and Charleston (USA). Using this method, the stakeholders were able to see the common themes across trade lanes that are important for each of the key stakeholder groups.

In order to engage stakeholders to innovate within a real-life setting, a living lab approach was used. Tan et al. (2011) describe a living lab methodology as bringing together multiple stakeholders, across multiple locations, and seeing stakeholders as co-innovators. A living lab methodology is suitable for situations where a neutral party, often academics, acts as honest brokers to bring the different stakeholders to consensus. Each living lab group used real trade lanes to model the physical flow of data, information system landscape, and administrative burden in order to configure, demonstrate, and refine the entire system with the stakeholders. The consortium team created visual models and data-flow diagrams of the existing and to-be situations to enable the stakeholders to sort out the policy and data-sharing issues among themselves. Another goal was for stakeholders to come to common understanding of their respective situations, ultimately joining up different systems of different stakeholders in order to capture the data they collectively needed. The overall dataset was visualized in a dashboard with role-based access. The dashboard enabled discussion of how the system would impact the day-to-day processes of the various businesses and inspection authorities.

Involving stakeholders early helped increase commitment and consensus to this initiative. However, decision making remained relatively slow due to the considerable time it takes to design technical tools, models, and diagrams, and to constantly update them to reflect the feedback from stakeholders' advice and recommendations. By providing a comprehensive overview of the roles, the data sources, and the work processes using them, parties came to an understanding of how the innovations were used. Through this, they over time build trust towards those potential vulnerabilities that the innovation might bring, would not be exploited. This facilitated acceptance and uptake by the various stakeholder groups. In addition, not all of the potential answers the living lab groups provided are also enabled by existing European legislation. Alignment between the business stakeholder groups, national governments, and European bodies is still needed. One of the outcomes of the project is therefore a consensus-based agenda for further policy development.

9.3.4   Understanding Child Health Outcomes in New Zealand

The next case examines the Modelling the Early Life-Course (MEL-C) project in New Zealand, which was supported by a public good research grant provided to researchers at the University of Auckland, New Zealand (Milne et al. 2014). Life-course studies examine "the biological, behavioral and psychosocial pathways that operate across an individual's life course, as well as across generations, to influence the development of chronic diseases" (Ben-Shlomo and Kuh 2002). An abundance of research evidence can be found about the early life course of children and the determinants of health. The goal of the project was to develop a decision support software tool for policy makers to test different policy scenarios against realistic data and to consider this evidence alongside other policy-relevant information such as politics, other evaluations, or expert consultations. The main purpose was not to develop a specific policy but to develop a process and tool for better identification and use of data in this policy domain.

In an environment where a great deal of information about a policy exists, the tool is meant to help bridge the research–policy translation gap (Milne et al. 2014). The lack of research evidence uptake by policy makers is well documented (Lomas 2007; Van Egmond et al. 2011). One main factor is the lack of uptake in the "translation gap"—characterized as the mismatch between the knowledge that research produces and the knowledge that policy makers want (Milne et al. 2014). Milne et al. (2014) identify two solutions to bridge the gap—knowledge brokers (Frost et al. 2012; Knight and Lightowler 2010; Lomas 2007) and research–policy partnerships (Best and Holmes 2010; Van Egmond et al. 2011). Knowledge brokers act as translators, turning the research evidence into information that is easily understood and usable by policy makers. Research–policy partnerships involve a more intense interaction between both groups, where they work together to produce the evidence needed for policy purposes. Previous work focused on database interventions aimed at knowledge translation where all relevant documents synthesizing research results could be found (Milne et al. 2014). However, with the online databases the onus is still on policy makers to search for relevant papers, assess their content for relevance, and evaluate their importance for the policy question under consideration. The MEL-C project took a different approach with a decision-support tool "where the evidence is embedded in a working model and can be interrogated to address specific policy questions" (p. 8).

Using a micro-simulation model, the tool incorporates longitudinal data to determine the normal transition of children through their life course and the impact of policy interventions on their outcomes. Two representatives each from four New Zealand government ministries—Health, Education, Justice, and Social Development—formed a "policy reference group" for the project (Milne et al. 2014). The representatives were selected because they represented people who could understand the aims of the project and were data and technology savvy. Thus, the boundary for engagement was limited to the translation gap, and did not extend to the behavior of the children modeled within the system. The main strategy for involving policy makers was to hold regular, face-to-face meetings for almost 2 years to discuss the development of the MEL-C tool, including the simulation model and graphical user interface. The discussions were facilitated and documented by the task leader for end-user engagement.

The simulation model was shown to stakeholders who then provided feedback and became collaborators in the development of user interfaces and the types of key policy questions that the model needed to be able to address. The results of this specialized form of stakeholder engagement included a much more useful decision-support tool than might have been developed otherwise, an ongoing process of collaborative refinement, and a set of potential users and advocates for the tool.

Results of the model are beginning to be explored. For example, for child health service use outcomes it was found that appreciable improvement was only effected by modifying multiple determinants; structural determinants (e.g., ethnicity, family structure) were relatively more important than intermediary determinants (e.g., over-crowding, parental smoking) as potential policy levers; there was a social gradient of effect; and interventions bestowed the greatest benefit to the most disadvantaged groups with a corresponding reduction in disparities between the worst-off and the best-off (Lay-Yee et al. 2014).

9.3.5 Transportation and Urban Planning Indicator Development in the USA

Understanding how choices today will impact life in the future is a major concern for policy making in any area. In transportation and urban planning, it is even more important because the infrastructure created is not easily changed, once roads and buildings are built and patterns of living start to evolve around them. The urban planning context is fraught with different stakeholders who often have fundamentally opposing beliefs and value systems (Pace 1990; Borning et al. 2005). They embody widely divergent opinions regarding urban development and land use. Each stakeholder group is likely to have their own philosophies about different forms of land use in urban environments, and different views about how long-term planning should occur, what situations constitute problematic conditions, what solutions should be sought for those problems, and what constitutes successful outcomes.

Under these contentious conditions, advanced computer simulation tools that show the long-term potential effects of different choices can contribute to legitimation of the policy process as well as to well-considered decisions. However, in order to achieve this, the model itself must be considered legitimate. In other words, its structure, inputs, processes, and outputs must be transparent and understandable to all stakeholders. Our last case, UrbanSim, is a land-use modeling system, developed over the past 20 years, that helps policy makers and stakeholders understand the 20–30-year impacts of different choices regarding land use and transportation on community outcomes including effects on the economy and the environment. It has been used widely in the USA and Europe and is of growing interest globally. The system not only estimates the direct effects of different infrastructure and policy choices but also estimates how individual and group responses to those choices will affect the outcomes (Borning et al. 2005; Borning et al. 2008).

UrbanSim simulation results are mainly presented to users as indicators. These indicators are variables that convey information about an attribute of the system at a given time. Indicators in UrbanSim include such variables as the population density in different neighborhoods, the ratio of car trips to bus trips for the region, and the projected cost of land per acre in different parts of the region. These and other indicators are presented under different possible scenarios over the course of the full simulation, generally 30 years. Indicator values are presented in tables, graphs, charts, or maps (Friedman et al. 2008). These indicators allow stakeholders to assess and compare the results of different policy scenarios on a consistent set of dimensions. For example, if a city has the goal of supporting more walkable densely populated urban neighborhoods as an alternative to sprawl surrounding the city center, then changes in the "population density" indicator in different neighborhoods could be used to assess the simulated outcomes of different policies over time (Borning et al. 2005).

In recent years, enhancements to UrbanSim have concentrated on making the model more realistic and meaningful to stakeholders by expanding, categorizing, and differentiating the stakeholder values represented by the indicators. The UrbanSim team had two goals: to make advocacy for different views more explicit and contextualized, and to improve the overall legitimacy of the system by incorporating these values in a wider range of indicators in the simulations. The involvement of stakeholders, essentially a process of codevelopment of the model, was guided by an overarching theory of value sensitive design (Friedman 1997). A key feature of value sensitive design is designing technology that accounts for human values with an emphasis on representing direct and indirect stakeholders (Borning et al. 2005).

The UrbanSim team partnered with three local organizations in the Seattle, Washington, region to develop and test new ways of expressing their values to model users through the choice of indicators and related technical information. The partners (a government agency, a business association, and an environmental group) were selected to represent a range of known issues and stakeholder views about development in the region. The goal was to create for each group a narrative value indicator perspective that explained the values of most importance to that group and to select, define, and incorporate key indicators representing those views in the model. Stakeholders were convened in separate groups so that they could work independently to formulate their indicator perspectives. This was an important design choice because the goal was to present each group's values and desires by essentially telling a story advocating particular values and criteria for evaluating policy outcomes (Borning et al 2005). The team engaged each stakeholder group through a series of face-to-face meetings and semi-structured interviews to help them craft and write both narratives and descriptions of indicators that closely matched their core values and views.

To assess the extent to which these approaches enhanced the legitimation of the model, a separate group of citizen evaluators reviewed each grouping of stakeholder-selected indicators and along with associated technical documentation as well as the indicators in the system as a whole. They considered coherence, informativeness, usefulness for supporting diverse opinions, usefulness for advocating for differing views and values, and usefulness for supporting the democratic process. The evaluation showed positive scores on all measures and also produced additional findings about the usefulness of different kinds of information (technical compared to advocacy), the importance of explicitly presenting and balancing diverse views, and the overall perception of transparency and lack of bias in the modeling system itself.

9.4   Case Comparison

Table 9.1 presents key elements of each case story based on the following points of comparison: (a) situation and approach, (b) types of stakeholders and type of participation, (c) methods for stakeholder identification, (d) methods for stakeholder engagement, (e) tools and technologies used, and (f) results.

Table 9.1 Case comparison

	Case 1	Case 2	Case 3	Case 4	Case 5
Policy area	E-government	Renewable energy	International trade	Child health	Urban planning
Length of project	1 year	3 years	3 years	5 years	1 year
Primary country (ies)	Afghanistan	Slovakia	European Union and trading partners	New Zealand	USA
Development status	Developing	Transition	Developed and developing	Developed	Developed
Level of government	National	Municipal	Multinational	National	Regional
Approach	*Action research—* involving trusted 3rd party facilitates new connections between stakeholders and government	*Action research—* involving collaborative scenario building through an online tool, supplemented with in-person meetings	*Action research—* creation of a living lab where stakeholders themselves, facilitated by 3rd parties, developed solutions and implement them	*Research–practice partnership—* researchers and policy makers worked together through iterative discussion, demonstration, and enhancements	*Action research—* using value-sensitive design where stakeholder values are made explicit in the codevelopment of enhancements to the technology and model system
Purpose of stakeholder engagement	Ensure ownership, commitment, and transparency, in pursuit of *balancing stakeholders' interests*	*Build consensus to* support a realistic policy that would be widely accepted	Attune the system towards the interests and existing practices of the stakeholders, thereby *building commitment and supporting consensus among stakeholders to new policies*	*Facilitate synthesis of research findings and improve the usefulness and usability of a decision-support tool* for policy makers	*Enhance the legitimacy of a modeling system* used in contentious policy areas

Table 9.1 (continued)

	Case 1	Case 2	Case 3	Case 4	Case 5
Stakeholder types involved	Representatives from central government, local governments, public service providers, IT and consulting firms, NGOs, universities, think tanks, resource centers; international organizations (donors and sponsors)	Policy makers, representatives from energy-related companies, expert groups, representatives from citizens and housing associations	Involvement of "exemplary" actors from main stakeholder groups: government, international traders, IT solution providers, standards organizations	Expert group drawn from public agencies responsible for children's health	Representatives of selected nonprofit, government, and business interests known to have strong views of development in the region
Method for identifying stakeholders	Online surveys; interviews; analysis of interests, needs, and capabilities	Desk research, survey research, qualitative and quantitative data analysis. Face-to-face meetings	Detailed stakeholder map for specific trade lanes (including commercial, government, logistics, and information functions)	Convenience sample of policy makers in the domain known to the developers	Convenience sample of organizations known to represent a range of views about urban development in the region
Type of participation	Involving	Involving	Involving/collaboration	Involving	Involving
Method of stakeholder engagement	Face-to-face workshops	Face-to-face workshops; collaborative scenario building	Face-to-face meetings; consensus-building workshops; interviews; joint specification of trade lane and of solution	Face-to-face meetings between developers and policy maker/users	Separate face-to-face meetings, interviews, joint document preparation with each stakeholder
Tools and technologies used	Stakeholder analysis tool; online forum; e-mail	OCOPOMO platform and consistent conceptual description (CCD)	Visual models; data-flow diagrams; logistics-flow diagrams; games	Micro-simulation modeling	Simulation model

Table 9.1 (continued)

	Case 1	Case 2	Case 3	Case 4	Case 5
Results/outcomes of engagement process	Increased commitment and consensus among key stakeholders	The stakeholder engagement process was perceived among stakeholders as a useful and an important process in policy analysis	A dedicated group innovation setting enabled the stakeholders to better understand the needs between them, which enables "trust" and propagate solutions that were not possible a year ago	The engagement facilitated the development of a decision-support tool for policy making	A framework and template for defining, presenting, and incorporating value-based indicators in the model
	Increased transparency and openness of the strategic planning process	Engagement enabled understanding of the policy case among stakeholders, and the tool facilitated the sharing of views to support stakeholders' views in a new policy	Making stakeholders part of the fact-finding and solution-development process supported commitment of stakeholders to the solution	This engagement also established a group who were able to be early adopters of the decision-support tool, and who are able to advocate for it	A method that allows different stakeholders to advocate for different values, but for all stakeholders to view the implications of those values in a standard set of agreed-upon indicators that measure their long-term effects
			Joint process supports consensus among stakeholders (at least in the same trade lane)		

9.5 Discussion

In this section, we return to our two guiding questions: What types of engagement tools and processes are useful for different stakeholders and contexts? And what factors support the effective use of particular tools and technologies toward constructive outcomes? The extant literature reveals a rich history of examining the role of participation in democratic theory and complex governance (Fung 2006; Fung et al. 2007). Various analytical tools in the literature address participant selection, modes of communication, and involvement and many of these were present in the cases. The cases confirm previous research regarding the importance of stakeholders and the need for careful and goal-oriented stakeholder selection and engagement. The cases also demonstrate the importance of support and education for participants and the role of trusted facilitators, contributing to the knowledge in this field. This section presents the key findings of our case comparison.

Identifying and Representing Relevant Stakeholders New governance means bringing in stakeholders who are not traditionally part of the policy-making process. Fung (2006) describes a continuum of types of stakeholders in new governance, including state representatives (described as expert administrators or elected representatives) and mini-publics (described as professional and lay stakeholders with organized interests). Professionals are paid participants (such as lobbyists) or not-for-profit organizations. Lay stakeholders are those who volunteer their services such as individuals serving on school councils or neighborhood associations. The cases show that effective stakeholder engagement requires a nuanced understanding of who are the relevant stakeholders with respect to the specific goal of the engagement. Each case represents a complex policy area where the different stakeholders selected or invited to engage in the policy process represented particular aspects or viewpoints about a complex problem. Our study confirms that stakeholder analysis helps policy makers understand differences in stakeholder behavior, intentions, preferences, interrelations, and interests. It also helps them assess the influence and resources different stakeholders bring to decision-making or implementation processes (Varvasovszky and Brugha 2000). We found that ordinary citizens were seldom involved in these cases. Despite the common rhetoric of "citizen" participation, the cases show how it is often impractical to engage members of the public or representatives of the full range of relevant stakeholders. In these situations, policy modelers and policy makers needed to appreciate the limitations of stakeholder engagement and aim for results that take advantage of less-than-complete stakeholder participation.

For example, in the UrbanSim case, only three organizations participated in the codevelopment of new indicators. The modelers did not treat these stakeholder views as complete or definitive but rather they used this limited experience to create a value-based indicator framework to guide further development of new indicators and future applications of the UrbanSim model. In the international trade case, the main stakeholder groups were each represented by up to four "exemplary" actors. In this way, the key positions of these groups were reasonably well represented in the various activities in the project. These representative actors also served as a starting point to identify specific trade lanes where innovations could take place, and thereby also created awareness of other stakeholders that play a role in those trade lanes. In the Kosice energy policy case, stakeholder identification was done using a technique similar to that proposed by Bryson (2004). The local government was mainly responsible for identifying relevant stakeholders that were invited to the engagement process. Other complementary techniques such as surveys were used to assess stakeholders' roles and expectations. In the international trade case, similar techniques were applied.

Providing for Participant Support and Education In order to participate in meaningful ways, stakeholders in our cases needed to be educated regarding the purpose of the engagement, the processes and tools to be used, and the ways in which stakeholder input would be considered. For all the cases presented, stakeholders, including those that were often not directly involved in policy making (e.g., citizens, smaller companies), were made aware of the policy problem in some depth, presented with opportunities to deliberate the different policy choices, and presented with the information necessary to understand the expected outcome from implementation of different policy options.

In the case of EGOV Afghanistan, stakeholders were provided with the results of an EGOV readiness assessment exercise for them to understand the crucial problems to be solved through the implementation of a national e-government policy. Workshops offered them general knowledge about approaches and methodologies for strategy development. In Kosice, participants were provided with the energy policy problem and background documents for additional information about the policy such as the energy conceptions proposed for various cities in the region and studies of ROI for various combinations of heat energy sources. The descriptive scenarios and background documents were important for stakeholders to understand the policy issue, its boundaries, and its challenges. In UrbanSim, the stakeholders were guided through the process of creating narrative value statements as well as ways to describe and document indicators in accurate, neutral language. All of these education and support activities made the stakeholders' deliberations and input more usable and more relevant to the problem at hand.

Using Stakeholder Engagement Methods to Reveal and Explain Complex Policy Problems and Contexts Our cases illustrated that stakeholder engagement is an important process in policy development as evidenced in the literature reviewed in Sect. 9.2.3. Engagement helped in all cases to assure that policy processes and policy decisions were well grounded and responsive to both social values and practical needs. Action research and living labs helped assure that involvement was not based on an oversimplified view of the policy problem, Different tools acted as boundary objects to facilitate knowledge sharing, consensus building, listening, and negotiating. Models of many kinds were used to break down complex processes and revise mental models.

In very intractable public problems like trade lanes, in order to understand how various actors would be affected by different policy options, it was important to understand how information flowed between actors. The specificity of the models used, as well as their comprehensiveness in representing the actual situation, facilitated a focused debate between businesses and government agencies, forcing each party to be clear about their precise activities and relevant policy concerns. As a result, no stakeholder could hide behind a policy that allegedly forced or blocked a certain solution, and the consensus process could focus on the policy options that were feasible in practice. The Kosice energy policy problem required a balance of diverse interests of stakeholders both supplying and consuming energy. This presented policy makers with challenges in identifying and engaging those interests that will affect the implementation of the new policy. Collaborative scenario building engaged both categories of stakeholders. This method was particularly important for policy makers to increase the level of certainty of the policy choice by understanding the intersecting interests of these stakeholders. Formal policy modeling and simulation were also important to inform all stakeholders and policy makers of the different possible outcomes of their scenarios. In the child health case, stakeholders were educated about the concepts and assumptions underlying the policy-modeling tool being developed. They also learned from each other about the policy questions of greatest importance to child health and development. The methods used in these cases are similar to those identified in literature (Andersen et al. 2007; Vennix et al. 1996) and can be employed to contribute to many different policy development efforts.

Using Trusted Third Parties to Enhance Transparency of the Process and Improve the Tools of Engagement Negotiating, brokering, and collaboration skills and expertise with engagement tools are all essential for achieving new forms of governance (Bingham et al. 2005). The tools and technologies used in our cases have different characteristics that affect choice and suitability, including available expertise and financial resources, level of participation, type of policy problem, and the geographic location or dispersion of stakeholders. The cases also address a factor that is less often critically addressed, namely the ways that "trusted" third parties, such as researchers, are used in stakeholder engagement. In these situations, researchers were not only doing academic research on engagement but also crafting, testing, and improving meaningful tools toward practical outcomes. As "brokers" in the process, researchers and the tools and technologies they use can inhibit or promote better models of engagement in policy making and governance.

In the case of EGOV Afghanistan, the use of online surveys by the UNU-IIST team solved the issue of trying to reach a distributed set of stakeholders separated by geography and also provided a confidential way to gather information about stakeholder interests, while the stakeholder analysis tool provided by UNU-IIST helped MCIT to understand stakeholder preferences and concerns and to assess their potential to influence the policy process. The technology tools used were not intended to "socialize" the interests of stakeholders but to gather intelligence by a trusted third party that could be used in the strategic planning process. By comparison, the intention of the online OCOPOMO platform used in the Kosice case was to bring the stakeholders themselves into a virtual meeting place where they could see the interests of other stakeholders. This technology choice, implemented by expert researchers, was intended to facilitate knowledge sharing in a multidirectional way.

In the UrbanSim case, the stakeholders' values and interests were intentionally developed in isolation from one another because the goal was to represent the distinct values of each stakeholder type within the model. The simulation mechanism, built by the academic experts, could then model and report indicators showing how these different interests might interact over time. In the international trade case, a neutral party designed the modeling approach and helped the stakeholder groups in each trade lane model their own existing situations. This approach facilitated joint problem identification and solution development. In the New Zealand child health case, researchers helped policy makers discover policy-relevant material while the policy makers helped the researchers understand what formats and other factors made that material relevant and usable. Each example demonstrates the role of trusted, independent experts who can select technology options, tools, and techniques that introduce transparency into the process and are technically and practically suitable to the situation. The researchers/modelers were trusted independent brokers who gathered data, facilitated engagement, and built models or systems to transparently reflect the reality of the stakeholders.

9.6 Conclusion

All of the cases we reviewed above used an active approach, assisted by third-party experts, to bring stakeholders together in workshops, through a collaboration platform, or in living labs to support interaction in problem identification, codevelopment of solutions, and foundations for gaining commitment or consensus by different types of stakeholders. These experiences go well beyond eliciting stakeholders' positions and requirements, leaving the interpretation and balancing to be done by the policy maker independently. The approaches used in these cases supported the stakeholders directly in gaining a shared understanding of the problem, providing some insight into the position and reasoning of other stakeholders, laying the groundwork for potential negotiation or other ways to find common ground with respect to the policy issue, and in some cases establishing or reinforcing trust among different stakeholders as well as trust in the participation process. In line with the literature on this topic, the cases also illustrate some of the cautions and limitations of stakeholder engagement, with particular emphasis on the realistic limits of involvement and representation, and the consequent necessity to match stakeholder selection and engagement methods to a well-defined goal within the larger policy process.

We find that a careful identification of stakeholders is required, and the selection depends on the goals of engaging stakeholders. The appropriate selection of stakeholders to involve can evolve over time, the identification and engagement of stakeholders is a continuous process, as Bryson (2004) suggests. To illustrate this in one of the cases, in the international trade case, the process started with a set of stakeholders needed to identify and initiate the demonstration trade lanes. These provided grounds for further identifying other stakeholders that play a role in those trade lanes or that were relevant to the initial set of stakeholders. These needed to be engaged also in order to meet the goals of engaging stakeholders. The goals themselves can also evolve along the changing stakeholder involvement. In this case, especially in the beginning, stakeholders were involved to elicit their views and interests in the matter, whereas during the process this shifted toward engaging stakeholders to ensure commitment and to facilitate building consensus among the stakeholders. There are similarities among the cases such as the use of surveys and convenience sampling as methods to identify stakeholders, face-to-face meetings, and workshops as methods of engagement and use of modeling techniques as tools and technologies. Although the literature provides various available methods and techniques used in stakeholder engagement processes, the cases illustrate that the approaches, tools, and technologies selected in each case are highly influenced by the purposes and expected outcomes of the engagement effort. Therefore, we emphasize that every stakeholder engagement needs to be tailored with well-selected processes and tools that suit the overall purpose and expected outcomes.

As frequently highlighted in the literature, stakeholders' involvement in policy processes can help build consensus by balancing stakeholder interests and preferences, increasing their commitment for policy implementation, and ensuring transparency and openness of the process. Often, these advantages of stakeholder engagement are linked to the idea of empowering stakeholders as much as possible (i.e., stakeholders make key decisions). However, our study shows that all of these advantages can also be gained by *involving* stakeholders, with less emphasis on empowerment. We posit that these benefits can be realized when stakeholders understand their roles and the objectives of their engagement, enabling them to bring their own interests to the table while also gaining an understanding of other interests and factors that influence decisions and results. Therefore, our findings on the importance of offering support and education for participants in order to enable them to understand their role and the engagement process are an important contribution to the literature. In a similar vein, the role that trusted (third-party) facilitators could play in the engagement process is often underestimated in the literature, but is clearly an important ingredient in the cases presented in this chapter.

Tools can take many different forms, some using technology and some not—the important factor is to match the tool to the objective and the capabilities of the stakeholders involved. Making this match requires an understanding of the capabilities of the stakeholders to use such tools and technologies, sometimes also in a specific country context. Furthermore, as the UrbanSim and child health case shows, stakeholders can not only contribute to policy analysis and choices but also make significant contributions to improving the effectiveness of policy processes, and the validity and usability of models, and other tools.

Based on these findings, our study offers some practical insights for policy makers (and researchers) that want to engage stakeholders for policy development. The first critical step is identification of salient stakeholders or stakeholder types. The literature reviewed in this chapter as well as the five cases offer various approaches to identify stakeholders. As concluded above, the method used to identify stakeholders is closely related to the intended purpose of stakeholder engagement. For example, when aiming to learn from stakeholders about a specific domain, a convenience sample of relevant actors is a suitable method. However, if the goal is to ensure commitment or to build consensus, the methods employed need to be rigorous in identifying all key stakeholder groups. Desk research, surveys, interviews, and stakeholder or interests mapping tools are useful approaches to do this. Iterative stakeholder identification often helps create a more complete array of relevant stakeholders. Our research in combination with the relevant literature also shows other purposes for stakeholder engagement that guide the selection of stakeholder types. For example, transparency of the process, facilitating adoption, improving usefulness and usability of tools, and enhancing legitimacy are purposes of stakeholder engagement we found in the cases.

Once the relevant stakeholders have been identified and the objective of involving them is clear, the approach to stakeholder engagement needs to be selected. Whereas the literature presents various options, all the cases we covered were in an advanced stage and almost all employed some form of action research, in which stakeholders (especially practitioners and policy makers) worked closely with each other and with researchers in a collaborative way. This was found in all cases, as all cases were focused on *involving* stakeholders. In case the objective is to primarily *inform* or *consult* stakeholders, other approaches are more suitable, and some suggestions have been provided in the background section. When involving stakeholders, policy makers and researchers will have to carefully consider what role the engaged stakeholders will have; involving stakeholders to work in real-world complexity as much as possible will benefit from action research or living labs, but requires that the material, objectives, activities, etc. be carefully prepared and designed, as stakeholders do not always have a clear idea of what their involvement should look like or contribute to. On the other hand, complexity can also be broken down to make the matter more comprehensible for stakeholders. For this, modeling tools and simulations can be used for both purposes. In either case, tools and models can function as boundary objects that stakeholders can view, discuss, or manipulate to better understand how a particular decision might play out. However, the conceptual capacity stakeholders that will need to have affects the kind and amount of work that should go into preparing the engagement.

While much remains to be learned about stakeholder engagement in policy modeling, this chapter provides a starting point for better understanding how different approaches, tools, and technologies can support effective stakeholder participation toward better policy choices and outcomes. The cases presented here demonstrate that stakeholder engagement processes, tools, and technologies are versatile and useful to both policy makers and the stakeholders themselves. With careful selection and application, they can work in a wide variety of situations including different policy domains and kinds of problems, different political systems, and different levels of social and economic development.

Acknowledgment This comparison and analysis was conducted as a collaborative activity of the eGovPoliNet Project, funded through the European Commission Framework 7 Program as agreement FP7-ICT-2011–288136, and supported by US National Science Foundation (NSF) grant

IIS-0540069 to explore policy modeling and governance through an international consortium of research institutions. Ideas and opinions expressed by the authors do not necessarily represent those of all eGovPoliNet partners.

We also gratefully acknowledge the information and reference material provided by Peter Davis and Barry Milne of the COMPASS Center at the University of Auckland regarding the New Zealand case, and Alan Borning at the University of Washington regarding the UrbanSim case.

References

Ackerman J (2004) Co-governance for accountability: beyond "exit" and "voice". World Dev 32(3):447–463

Ali M, Weerakkody V (2009) The impact of national culture on e-government implementation: a comparison case study. Proceedings of the 15th Americas Conference on Information Systems, San Francisco, California, 6–9 August 2009

Anderson SR, Bryson JM, Crosby BC (1999) Leadership for the common good fieldbook. University of Minnesota Extension Service, St. Paul

Andersen DA, Vennix J, Richardson G, Rouwette E (2007) Group model building: problem structuring, policy simulation and decision support. J Oper Res Soc 58(5):691–694

Basu S (2004) E-government and developing countries: an overview. Int'l Rev L Comp Tech 18(1):109–132

Ben-Shlomo Y, Kuh D (2002) A life course approach to chronic disease epidemiology: conceptual models, empirical challenges and interdisciplinary perspectives. Int'l J Epidemiol 31(2):285–293

Best A, Holmes B (2010) Systems thinking, knowledge and action: towards better models and methods. Evid Policy 6(2):145–159

Bijlsma RM, Bots PW, Wolters HA, Hoekstra AY (2011) An empirical analysis of stakeholders' influence on policy development: the role of uncertainty handling. Ecol Soc 16(1):51

Bingham LB, Nabatchi T, O'Leary R (2005) The new governance: practices and processes for stakeholder and citizen participation in the work of government. Public Adm Rev 65(5):547–558

Black LJ, Andersen DF (2012) Using visual representations as boundary objects to resolve conflict in collaborative model-building approaches. Syst Res Behav Sci 29(2):194–208

Borning A, Friedman B, Davis J, Lin P (2005) Informing public deliberation: value sensitive design of indicators for a large-scale urban simulation. Proceedings of the 9th European Conference on Computer-Supported Cooperative Work (ECSCW) (pp 449–468), Paris, September

Borning A, Waddell P, Förster R (2008) UrbanSim: using simulation to inform public deliberation and decision-making. In: Hsinchun Chen et al. (eds) Digital government: e-government research, case studies, and implementation. Springer-Verlag, New York, pp 439–463

Brugha R, Varvasovszky Z (2000) Stakeholder analysis: a review. Health Policy Plan 15(3):239–246

Bryant J (2003) The six dilemmas of collaboration: inter-organisational relationships as drama. Chichester: Wiley

Bryson J 2004 What to do when stakeholders matter. Public Manag Rev 6(1):21–53

Bryson J, Freeman RE, Roering W (1986) Strategic planning in the public sector: approaches and directions. In B. Checkoway (ed) Strategic perspectives on planning practice. Lexington Books, Lexington

Bryson JM, Cunningham GL, Lokkesmoe KJ (2002) What to do when stakeholders matter: the case of problem formulation for the African American men project of Hennepin County, Minnesota. Public Admin Rev 62(5):568–584

De Marchi B (2003) Public participation and risk governance. Sci Public Policy 30(3):171–176

Donaldson T, Preston LE (1995) The stakeholder theory of the corporation: concepts, evidence, and implications. Acad Manage Rev 20(1):65–91

Dzhusupova Z, Janowski T, Ojo A, Estevez E (2011) Sustaining electronic governance programs in developing countries. In: Proceedings of the 11th European Conference on eGovernment (ECEG 2011), pp 203–212

Easton D (1965) A systems analysis of political life. Wiley, New York

Eden C, Ackermann F (1998) Making strategy: the journey of strategic management. Sage, London

Elias AA, Cavana RY, Jackson LS (2002) Stakeholder analysis for R & D project management. R&D Manag 32(4):301–310

Flak LS, Rose R (2005) Stakeholder governance: adapting stakeholder theory to e-government. Commun Assoc Inf Syst 16(1):31

Fishkin JS (1995) The voice of the people: public opinion and democracy. Yale University Press, London

Freeman RE (1984) Strategic management: a stakeholder approach. Pitman, Boston

Freeman RE (2010) Strategic management: a stakeholder approach. Cambridge University Press, Cambridge

Friedman B (ed) (1997) Human values and the design of computer technology. Cambridge University Press, New York (CSLI, Stanford)

Friedman B, Borning A, Davis JL, Gill BT, Kahn Jr PH, Kriplean T, Lin P (2008) Laying the foundations for public participation and value advocacy: interaction design for a large scale urban simulation. In: Proceedings of the 2008 international conference on digital government research (pp 305–314). Digital Government Society of North America

Frost H, Geddes R, Haw S, Jackson CA, Jepson R, Mooney JD, Frank J (2012) Experiences of knowledge brokering for evidence-informed public health policy and practice: three years of the Scottish Collaboration for Public Health Research and Policy. Evid Policy 8(3):347–359

Fung A (2006) Varieties of participation in complex governance. Public Adm Rev 66(s1):66–75

Fung A, Graham M, Weil D (2007) Full disclosure: the perils and promise of transparency. Cambridge University Press, Cambridge

Furdík K, Sabol T, Dulinová V (2010) Policy modelling supported by e-participation ICT tools. In: MeTTeG'10. Proceedings of the 4th international conference on methodologies, technologies and tools enabling e-government. University of Applied Sciences, Northwestern Switzerland, Olten (pp 135–146)

Hesketh D (2010) Weaknesses in the supply chain: who packed the box? World Cust J 4(2):3–20

Higgins A, Klein S (2011) Introduction to the living lab approach. In: Tan Y-H, Bjørn Andersen N, Klein S, Rukanova B (eds) Accelerating global supply chains with IT-innovation. ITAIDE tools and methods. Springer, Berlin, pp 31–36

IAP2 (2007) IAP2 spectrum of public participation. International Association for Public Participation. http://www.iap2.org. Accessed 24 Dec 2013

Jenkins-Smith HC, Sabatier PA (1993) The study of public policy processes. In: Sabatier PA, Jenkins-Smith HC (eds) Policy change and learning. An advocacy coalition approach. Westview Press, Boulder

Jones C (1977) An introduction to the study of public policy, 3rd ed. Wadsworth, Belmont

Kennon N, Howden P, Hartley M (2009) Who really matters? A stakeholder analysis tool. Ext Farming Syst J 5(2):9–17

Kettl DF (2002) The transformation of governance: public administration for twenty-first century America. John Hopkins University Press, Baltimore

Klievink B, Lucassen I (2013) Facilitating adoption of international information infrastructures: a Living Labs approach. Lect Notes Comput Sci 8074:250–261

Klievink B, Janssen M, Tan Y-H (2012) A stakeholder analysis of business-to-government information sharing: the governance of a public-private platform. Int'l J Electron Gov Res 8(4):54–64

Knight C, Lightowler C (2010) Reflections of 'knowledge exchange professionals' in the social sciences: emerging opportunities and challenges for university-based knowledge brokers. Evid Policy 6(4):543–556

Lasswell HD (1951) The policy orientation. The policy sciences. Stanford University Press, Stanford, pp 13–14

Lay-Yee R, Milne B, Davis P, Pearson J, McLay J (2014) Determinants and disparities: a simulation approach to the case of child health care, submitted to Social Science and Medicine

Lewis C (1991) The ethics challenge in public service: a problem-solving guide. San Francisco: Jossey-Bass

Linstone H, Turoff M (1975) The Delphi method: techniques and applications. Addison-Wesley, London

Lomas J (2007) The in-between world of knowledge brokering. BMJ 334(7585):129

McAfee N (2004) Three models of democratic deliberation. J Specul Philos 18(1):44–59

Milne BJ, Lay-Yee R, Thomas J, Tobias M, Tuohy P, Armstrong A, Lynn R, Pearson J, Mannion O, Davis P (2014) A collaborative approach to bridging the research-policy gap through the development of policy advice software. Evid Policy 10(1):127–136

Mitchell RK, Agle BR, Wood DJ (1997) Toward a theory of stakeholder identification and salience: defining the principle of who and what really counts. Acad Manage Rev 22(4):853–886

Myers D, Kitsuse A (2000) Constructing the future in planning: a survey of theories and tools. J Plan Educ Res 19(3):221–231

Pace RC (1990) Personalized and depersonalized conflict in small group discussions: an examination of differentiation. Small Gr Res 21(1):79–96

Sabatier PA (1991) Toward better theories of the policy process. PS 24:147–156. doi:10.2307/419923

Smith G, en Wales C (2000) Citizens' juries and deliberative democracy. Polit Stud 48(1):51–65

Star SL, Griesemer J (1989) Institutional ecology, translations, and boundary objects: amateurs and professionals in Berkeley's Museum of Vertebrate Zoology, 1907–1939. Soc Stud Sci 19:387–420

Tan YH, Bjørn-Andersen N, Klein S, Rukanova B (2011) Accelerating global supply chains with IT-innovation: ITAIDE tools and methods. Springer, Berlin

Van Egmond S, Bekker M, Bal R, van der Grinten T (2011) Connecting evidence and policy: bringing researchers and policy makers together for effective evidence-based health policy in the Netherlands: a case study. Evid Policy 7(1):25–39

Varvasovszky Z, Brugha R (2000) A stakeholder analysis. Health Policy Plann 15(3):338–345

Vennix JAM, Akkermans HA, Rouwette E (1996) Group model-building to facilitate organizational change: an exploratory study. Syst Dyn Rev 12(1):39–58

Wimmer MA, Scherer S, Moss S, Bicking M (2012) Method and tools to support stakeholder engagement in policy development: the OCOPOMO Project. Int'l J Electron Gov Res 8(3):98–119

World Bank (2012) World development indicators 2012. World Bank Publications, Washington, DC

Yetano A, Royo A, Acerete B (2010) What Is driving the increasing presence of citizen participation initiatives? Environ Plann C 28(5):783–802

Chapter 10
Values in Computational Models Revalued

The Influence of Designing Computational Models on Public Decision-Making Processes

Rebecca Moody and Lasse Gerrits

Abstract This chapter aims to add to the technology debate in the sense that it aims to research the role of values and trust in computational models in the policy process. Six case studies in which a computational model was used within a complex policy context were research for the role values play within these models. Conclusions deal with the role of the designer of the model, the number of different actors, the amount of trust already present, and the question of agency by humans or technology. Additionally, margins of error within the model are discussed as well as authority by one actor over others concerning the model.

10.1 Introduction

Policy makers are tasked with making decisions on issues characterized as wicked problems because of controversies, unknown relationships between causes and consequences, and (consequently) uncertain futures. From this perspective, it would be desirable to map the decisions and their possible outcomes prior to the actual decision making because that would generate certainty in ambiguous situations. Broadly speaking, this provides the motive for using computational modeling for policy making as expressed in, e.g., policy informatics. Although there are computational models that are ready off-the-shelf, it is more common to work with models "modded off-the-shelf" (MOTS) or even tailor-made models to suit specific questions and conditions. As such, the model itself becomes part of the decision-making process during the acquisition.

We observe that this phase, during which scope, functionality, and deployment are determined by commissioning actors and designers, is essential to the way the models influence policy making. Although it may be assumed that such models are neutral or value-free, they are not because of the changes that designer and client

R. Moody (✉) · L. Gerrits
Department of Public Administration, Erasmus University Rotterdam,
P.O. Box 1738, 3000 DR Rotterdam, The Netherlands
e-mail:moody@fsw.eur.nl

L. Gerrits
e-mail:gerrits@fsw.eur.nl

© Springer International Publishing Switzerland 2015   205
M. Janssen et al. (eds.), *Policy Practice and Digital Science,*
Public Administration and Information Technology 10, DOI 10.1007/978-3-319-12784-2_10

introduce to the original model. This chapter aims to shed light on the relationships between computational models and policy making by looking at the role *values* play in commissioning, designing, and using such models in policy making. We will rely on the notions set forward in the technology debate in order to understand the way technical design can be perceived by actors and used in policy making. These notions will also be used in our analysis in order to understand the way actors within the policy process reach conclusions based on the models. We will primarily look at the perception of the models in terms of values on which we will elaborate below. We carried out a secondary analysis of case study data we collected for other research (Gerrits 2008; Moody 2010). The case studies concern: (1) predicting effects of deepening operations in rivers in Belgium and the Netherlands and (2) in Germany; (3) determining flood risk prediction in Germany and the Netherlands; (4) determining the implementation of congestion charging in the UK; (5) predicting and containing the outbreak of live stock diseases in Germany; (6) predicting particular matter concentrations in the Netherlands. The chapter is structured as follows. We will first discuss the theoretical background of our analysis by looking at autonomy of technology and technology as being deterministic, blending notions from the technology debate with notions from public administration and public policy in Sect. 10.2. The methodological approach is discussed in Sect. 10.3, the case studies in Sect. 10.4, the analysis in Sect. 10.5, and the conclusions in Sect. 10.6.

10.2 Technological Perceptions: The Debate

To understand the implications of the design of computational models it is necessary to understand the underlying assumptions of the design process. The way modelers design different models can be viewed from different viewpoints as pointed out in the technology debate. This is an ongoing debate in philosophy of science as well as in sociology and technical studies. The technology debate revolves around technology and humans, technology and society, and technology itself. It reflects on questions of who drives technology: Are humans the drivers of technology or does technology drive humans? Does technology possess any values of its own and are these values given to technology by humans or does technology have no values whatsoever and is it completely neutral? What is the relationship between technology and society, does technology constitute society or is it the other way around?

A large number of authors have described the technology debate and placed their opinion (see: Smith and Marx 1994; Scharff and Dusek 2003; Kaplan 2004). In the technology debate, several issues are discussed. A central issue is who masters the other, do humans master over technology, or does technology control humans? Another key theme is the question whether technology is autonomous and determines its own causality. Another key feature is whether technology incorporates values or should be seen as neutral. Finally, the relationship between technology and society is important—which drives the other? A number of standpoints within the technology debate can be identified. For the sake of briefness, we will only look at social constructivism and technological determinism and technological instrumentalism.

Within technological determinism, it is believed that technology is not neutral or value-free. Technology can be good or bad or a mixture of both—this goes for effects as well as consequences. These consequences may not be dependent on the desired goal but are dependent on the technology. Technological development, therefore, does not depend primarily on the intention of the user but is fixed within the technology itself, it is inevitable and cannot be steered or controlled by humans. Agency here is not given to the human user but is attributed to technology. It is argued that certain political and social norms and values are hidden inside the technology. Therefore, the technology will bring about consequences according to these norms and values (Ellul 1954, 1990; Zuboff 1988; Heilbroner 1967, 1994; Winner 1977, 1980, 1983, 1993).

In social construction of technology, the viewpoint held is that choices need to be made in the design and the direction of technology. Economy, society, institutions, and culture shape the direction and scope of technological development, the form of technology, the practice, and the outcome of technological change. Agency in this approach is given back to humans. Technology is neither seen as autonomous nor does it have a fixed outcome with inevitable consequences. All technology is seen as a human construct and is thus shaped, or made by humans (Bijker 1993, 1995; Hoff 2000).

What is very important in understanding the approach of social construction of technology is the technological frame. This technological frame consists of goals, problems, problem-solving strategies, requirements to be met by problem solutions, current theories, tacit knowledge, testing procedures, design methods and criteria, users practice perceived substitution function, and exemplary artifacts (Bijker 1995). The technological frame is thus the set of rules, ideas, and meanings within a group and it determines the interaction between the members of a group. This means the technological frame determines which meaning a group will attribute to a technology (Bijker 1995).

Within technological instrumentalism, technology is seen as a neutral and value-free tool. This means a number of things. Firstly, that the technology can be used to any end. Secondly, this means that technology is indifferent to politics. The technology can simply be used in any social or political context since it is not intertwined with any context. Thirdly, technology is viewed as being rational. It is based on causal propositions; it can therefore be transferred into any other context as well. Finally, technology is seen as universal, it stands under the same norm of efficiency in any and every context (Feenberg 1991). Within the approach of technological instrumentalism, technology is not attributed with any agency. This means that technology itself cannot account for any form of causality; humans cause this causality. Technological progress, therefore, is viewed as desired progress since it is the human actor who pursues it (Bekkers et al. 2005). Technology is developed and implemented with the purpose of achieving one's goal and the technology serves as a means to achieve this goal.

Authors within all positions agree, however, to the point that in computer technology it becomes very difficult to model the real world. Reality is composed of infinite variables and relationships that pose practical limits to what data can be processed. Computer models, their designers, and users all are bound in the degree of rationality they can display. Among others, Simon (1976, 1957), Dror (1968); Lindblom (1959), and March and Simon (1993) recognized that public decision makers limit the number of options they consider because of this cognitive limitation. While with computer models it is assumed by many that this bound in rationality can be lifted, it can also be argued that this is not necessarily the case (Moody 2010).

10.3   Technology and Public Decision Making

The argument above means that synoptic decision making where the model maps decision outcomes, to be followed up by the actual decision, its implementation and possible feedback, is too optimistic an approach. It assumes that a model would deliver (nonbiased) data, which is judged by decision makers to generate alternatives, of which the best alternative is chosen and consequently carried out (March and Simon 1993; Winner 1977; Beniger 1986; Goodhue et al. 1992; Chen 2005). It is then assumed that a computational model is a value-free tool that will provide a neutral oversight of all available alternatives with their consequences. Therefore, it is believed by some that these models will decrease the bounds in rationality that decision makers face and that public policy making will become a more rational process in which all consequences are foreseen prior to decision making (Ware 2000; Moody 2010; Beniger 1986; Goodhue et al. 1992).

This line of reasoning corresponds with the technological instrumentalist viewpoint. However, while public decision making is also a political process in practice, we see that computational models, next to not being able to include all variables needed for complete consequences, also suffer from limits on the side of political values. It must be noted that the designer of the model is not a neutral object either and becomes able to influence the model (Winner 1977; Chen 2005; Ware 2000; Wright 2008). Known margins of error can be manipulated toward political values and the necessary choice which needs to be made on which variables to include in the model is value-driven as well.

The question we need to ask ourselves here is not only whether computational models are a value-free or neutral tool, but moreover who or what determines the values within these models. Technological determinists would argue that values are inherent for the models themselves, and the outcomes of the model are fixed before use. Social constructivists would argue that the models would be attributed with value through a process of using the model. We want to take this reasoning a step further, without taking position in the debate, and look at who designs the model, who decides which variables should be put into the model, and which variables should be excluded. Who decides what the functionality of the model is—what is it able to do and what not—and how do policy makers react to this?

While the above demonstrates that the topic on values in a computational model is a very loaded and complex topic to begin with, we find that next to the complexity in the model itself in terms of values, the process of policy making deals with additional values and its own complicatedness. We have to also address the complexity in the actual decision-making process because of the multiple actors with diverging norms, beliefs, and interests. Following the previously stated and driving on outcomes and hypotheses of previous research (Gerrits 2008; Moody 2010) we find that in dealing with values in computational models and public policy, some core characteristics can be identified:

1. The values attributed to the data on which the computational model is based. These values can be subdivided into:
   a. The dominant ideas actors hold on these data, for example, are the data correct, are they trustworthy? (Trust)
   b. The margin of error in the data and how this margin of error is communicated to policy makers. Are they aware of the correct margin of error, do they understand what this implies, do they feel this is an acceptable margin? (Margins of error)
2. The values attributed to the model itself, this can be subdivided into:
   a. The organization that owns or commissions the model. Is there one organization who owns the model, or are there clusters of organizations owning the model, if so, do they share the same values? (Ownership)
   b. Perceptions and values toward the model itself by designers, owners, and other actors. Do they trust the model, do they feel the outcomes the model produces are correct? (Beliefs)
3. The values within the decision-making process, this can be subdivided into:
   a. Who is the organization which makes the final decision on policy? Are they codependent on other organizations in order to be able to make the decision or do they have sole authority? (Authority)
   b. Are there other actors involved in the policy making? These actors do not necessarily need to have the authority to make the decisions but are present in a policy arena or community affecting the decision or the reception of this decision. Are there many of such actors? (Multiactors)

In the analysis of the cases, these are the core characteristics to be analyzed.

10.4 Methodology

As mentioned above, we carried out a secondary analysis on original case studies by us. This was done to change the perspective of our original analysis, which dealt more with outcomes instead of process. The selected cases share three basic characteristics. Firstly, they all featured new tailor-made computational models that were deployed for the first time in the case. Secondly, all cases concern policy issues with the natural or built environment. Thirdly, all cases concern highly complex and controversial issues.

10.5   Case Studies

The case studies are presented in this section. Each case has a brief introduction. The main characteristics are presented in Table 10.1. An overview of the stakeholders in each case can be found in Table 10.2.

Case 1: Morphological Predictions in the Westerschelde (Belgium and the Netherlands)   The Westerschelde estuary runs from the Belgian port of Antwerpen through the Netherlands before ending at the North Sea coast. The estuary has a limited depth and the Antwerpen port authorities were seeking ways to deepen the main channel in the estuary to facilitate larger ships and thus promote economic growth. However, the estuary is Dutch territory and the Dutch authorities are reluctant to facilitate the wishes of their Belgian counterparts. They regard the estuary as a fragile complex system that has a high ecological value and fear that the ecology could be destroyed by yet another deepening operation. The estuary consists of multiple channels through which the tide flows. Those channels are considered pivotal to the very specific and rare estuarine ecology of which very few remain across Europe. Negotiations starting in the early 2000s included the extensive use of computational models to assess the extent to which a deepening would harm the multichannel morphology of the riverbed and with that the ecological value. Research was jointly commissioned by the Dutch and Belgian authorities. A Dutch research institute, Deltares (formerly WL-Delft Hydraulics), was the main contractor, with a small number of subcontractors. It deployed two computational models: Sobek, which is modified off-the-shelf; and Delft3d, which was a brand-new model and considered the more advanced but less tested model of the two. Both models were used to simulate the consequences of dredging operations. The results of Sobek seemed more robust but were considered relatively crude, while the results of Delft3d appeared more advanced but featured more model and outcome uncertainty.

Case 2: Morphological Predictions in the Unterelbe (Germany)   Like the Westerschelde, the German Unterelbe is also an estuary that gives access to a major European seaport. It runs from the port of Hamburg through the federal states Niedersachsen and Schleswig–Holstein before flowing into the North Sea. Similar to the first case, the port authorities are seeking for a deepening of the main channel to facilitate larger ships. Such a deepening was carried out in the 1990s but had resulted in severe (partly) unforeseen and unwanted changes to the estuary that many people felt had harmed the ecological state. Here it appears as if the desire to deepen the estuary had influenced the outcomes of the computational model. The ensuing societal and political protests, from both nongovernmental organizations (NGOs) and the federal states except Hamburg itself, led to a different approach when considering a new deepening in early 2000. The Hamburg port authorities and the Hamburg Senate commissioned the research to the federal research institute Bundesanstalt für Wasserbau (BAW). This institute collected the relevant data and built its own model in-house to generate directions for dredging and ecological development.

Table 10.1 Overview of the main characteristics of the case studies

Case number	Values in data				Values in the model				Values in the decision-making process			
	Trust		Margin of error		Ownership		Beliefs		Authority		Multiactors	
	Trust in data	Distrust in data	High	Low	Monopoly for an organization	Open to more actors	Trust in the model	Distrust in the model	Held by one organization	Held by more organizations	Large number of actors	Small number of actors
1	X		X		X		X		X		X	
2	X		X			X	X			X	X	
3	X		X		X		X			X	X	
4	X		X		X		X		X		X	
5		X	X		X			X	X			
6		X	X			X		X		X	X	

Table 10.2 Overview of relevant stakeholders per case

Case no.	Actors involved, including societal stakeholders
1	Bureau Getijdenwateren, Havenbedrijf Antwerpen, Ministerie van Verkeer en Waterstaat, Office BeNeLux, Provincie Zeeland, Port of Antwerp Expert Team, ProSes, Rijksinstituut voor Kust en Zee, Rijkswaterstaat Directie Zeeland, Waterschap Zeeuwse Eilanden, WL Borgerhout, WL Delft Hydraulics, Zeeuwse Milieufederatie
2	ARGE-Elbe, BUND Hamburg, Bundesanstalt für Stadtentwicklung und Umwelt, Bundesanstalt für Wasserbau und Schifffahrt, Hamburg Hafen und Logistik AG, Hamburg Port Authority, Handelskammer Hamburg, Landkreis Stade, NABU Hamburg, Rettet die Elbe, Senat Hamburg
3	Ministerie van Verkeer en Waterstaat, Rijkswaterstaat, Taskforce Management Overstromingen, Municipalities Netherlands, Gemeenten Municipalities Germany, Waterboards, Citizens, Royal Haskoning, Provinces Germany
4	City of London, Transport for London, Citizens, National Alliance against Tolls
5	Friedrich Loeffler Institute, Bundeslanden, Universities, Veterinarians, Citizens
6	Provinces Netherlands, Municipalities Netherlands,Rijks Instituut Volksgezondheid en Milieu, Landelijk Meetnet Luchtkwaliteit, environmental organizations

Because of the belief that it should be seen as neutral in the controversial debate, BAW took the unusual decision to make its data and the model parameters available to any third party interested to replicate the results or to develop different models. Consequently, NGOs used the data to model their own particular version of the dredging works and their consequences. They arrived at different conclusions, which meant that the commissioning actors were obliged to engage in a dialogue about the future of the estuary. This slowed down and altered the original plans.

Case 3: Flood-Risk Prediction (Germany and the Netherlands)   In the last 2 years, it was decided to run one application in the Netherlands and Germany with the goal of predicting and managing floods from rivers. Before this, applications and authorities were divided on the subject. The application named FLood Information and WArning System (FLIWAS) was to integrate different applications and organizations to make sure water management and flood prediction could be done more efficiently. FLIWAS was developed and the application will predict on the basis of weather conditions, satellite data, past results, and the height of the water whether a flood will occur and what the damage would be in terms of economics, damage to landscape and lives. Also, the application is able to calculate proper evacuation routes. The implementation of the application has resulted in the water sector becoming more integrated and being able to communicate to policy makers what the result of certain actions are. It is now more the case than before that water management professionals are invited to the negotiation table in matters of urban planning, where they are able, on the basis of predictions and scenario sketching to convince governments that some plans might not be wise.

Case 4: Determining the Implementation of Congestion Charging in London (UK) The city of London has had a large problem with congestion. In order to find a solution to this congestion problem the local government has come up with a plan to reduce congestion by imposing a charge on all vehicles that enter the zone in which the congestion is worst. A computational model was used to determine where this zone should be so the location of the zone would be most effective in not only reducing congestion but also gaining the government enough money to reinvest in public transportation and cycling facilities. On the basis of traffic data, alternative routes, and public transportation plans the organization Traffic for London had decided on a zone in which the measures are implemented. The application to do so finds its basis in scenario sketching so different alternatives of the location of the zone could be viewed with their effects.

Case 5: Predicting and Containing the Outbreak of Livestock Diseases (Germany) Due to European regulations and after the outbreak of mouth and foot disease in the 1990s which caused significant financial damage, the German government decided to centralize all information on contagious livestock diseases into one application, TSN (TierSeuchenNachrichten). The application holds information on farms and animals. Further, the application will make scenarios on how to contain and prevent outbreaks of contagious diseases. On the basis of the contagiousness of the disease, the estimated health of animals, natural borders, wind and weather conditions, and the location of farms, a decision can be taken on what measures to take. These measures include the killing of the animals, vaccination of the animals, or installing a buffer zone in which no traffic is allowed. The German government appointed the Friedrich Loeffler Institute with the task to develop and manage the application.

Case 6: Predicting Particular Matter Concentrations (the Netherlands) Particulate matter in recent years has become an issue more and more prone to attention. Due to European regulations, the countries in the EU are to make sure the concentration of particulate matter in the air does not exceed a set norm. Therefore, whether buildings and roads can be built becomes dependent on this norm, not only for the effect on air quality by the building process but also for the effect of the plans once in use. Applications have been made to predict the potential concentrations of particulate matter after implementation of building plans, the outcome of the prediction determines whether a building can be built. The problem in this case lies in the fact that the way to calculate particulate matter to begin with is unclear, scientists are not sure of the calculation as of now, the health effects are not clear as well, just like the prediction itself. Furthermore, other NGOs have made their own application to predict concentrations, in which mostly the outcome differs significantly from the applications local governments use. This causes each building process to be reevaluated for their legitimacy, and this causes a lot of distrust.

10.6 Analysis

When analyzing our empirical data on the basis of the core characteristics earlier established we find a number of things. These will be discussed below.

Values in Data We have distinguished in trust and margin of error and there are some trends to be discovered in our six cases. First, we find that the trust and the reliance on the data in the model are large in the cases 1–4 and low in the cases 5 and 6. In order to explain this we must realize that this in fact has no causal relation to the data itself but to the cases in specific and the actors involved. What we find is that in cases 1–4 the actors involved in the cases share a common goal and common values, in the cases 5 and 6 there are several groups of actors with different goals. The trust an actor has in the data can, therefore, be explained by the trust and common values and goals he has with other actors. When there are different goals among actors or groups of actors, we find that the trust in the data itself in the model decreases. When relating this back to our theoretical notions we find that a determinist viewpoint would be difficult to hold since the trust in the data does not depend on the manner of collection of data or on the model itself but on the diversity of the goals and values of actors involved. It must be noted however, that each of the actors, both in the cases in which there is trust in the data as well as those cases without trust in the data themselves do hold a deterministic viewpoint. They feel that the data will lead to better solutions in cases 1–4 and in cases 5–6 they believe the data will only lead to a politically motivated outcome serving another actor.

When looking at the margins of error we find that the margins of error are relatively high in all cases. This can be explained by the large number of variables within the cases and their complex interrelation. In all cases, those actors involved acknowledge these errors but also realize that politicians want to hear a nominal "yes" or "no" answer. Therefore, these margins of errors disappear in the communication between the experts and policy makers as the experts simplify the presentation of their results. While the trust in the data and the reliance on the model is high in most of our cases, we still find a high margin of error which is only acknowledged by actors in cases in which the trust in the data is low. This shows us that the objective margin of error will only be perceived as a "problem" or an "issue that needs to be taken into account," when there is little trust in data. Not only are these margins emphasized but also on the basis of these margins actors accuse each other of manipulation of the model and the data for their own political goal. Taking this into account it can be concluded that for both the trust in the data and the margins of error, the group of actors and their goals, are determinant for the course of the process. When actors agree on goals the trust in the data is high and margins of error are neither communicated, nor seen as a problem. When actors do not agree on the political goal, trust is low, the margins of error are emphasized, and the manipulability of the data is communicated very frequently.

Values in the Model When we look at the values in the model itself, we have distinguished between *ownership* and *beliefs*. In terms of ownership, it can be found that most models, except for the case 6 are owned and developed by one organization. Therefore, it is the case that they have a monopoly on the information generated by the model, which grants them the power to use this monopoly in terms of decision making. Only in cases 2 and 6 we see that other actors use the data and the information to build their own model. In both cases, this has led to conflict. We also find that in case 5 some issues of ownership have occurred, but these issues were only addressed by actors not sharing the same political goal as the actors who owned the application, they were not granted access, while other actors who did agree with the political goals of the owner were granted access. What this leads us to conclude is that ownership by actors who share different political goals will lead to a conflictuous process of policy making. The manner of ownership or monopolization of a model by a (group of) actor(s) with the same political goal, therefore, does influence the outcome of the policy-making process as well as the process itself.

In terms of beliefs or trust in the model, we find the same results as for trust in the data, which would appear logical. The explanation of why some models are trusted and others are not, is the same explanation as for the trust in the data. In cases with actors with different goals, the trust in the model is generally low, the situation is conflictuous, and those opposed do not trust the model and accuse the owner of the model of distrustfulness, using the application for their own political, motivation, and manipulation of the model so their preferred outcome will prevail. Here as well we find that actors individually hold a fairly deterministic viewpoint regarding the model in question. Additionally, it shows us that data in the model and the model itself cannot be seen separate from each other in terms of trust.

Values in the Decision-Making Process   When we look at the values of the decision-making process we have distinguished between *authority* and *multiactor setting*. We can find that in terms of authority an interesting situation exists. In some cases, cases 1, 4, and 5, there is a clear line of authority. In these cases, it is agreed upon who should provide the data, the model, and the results on the basis of which policy should be made. In most cases, this is institutionally arranged, by legally making one organization responsible. In some cases, this is arranged by a code of conduct in which all agree this to be the organization dealing with this topic. In the cases 2, 3, and 6, we find that there is no clear agreement on who holds authority. This can be explained by the idea that more than one organization is using the same data but reaches different policy conclusions based on this data which eroded authority (cases 2 and 6) or by monopolization issues, in which one organization used to hold authority over policy decisions but because of the emergence of the model and the monopolization of this information authority has become blurred (case 3). The lack of clear lines of authority accounts for a situation of conflict, different actors are trying to use the outcomes of the models for their own political goals. A very social constructivist situation in which technological frames of actors create a situation in which they believe the outcome of the model supports their claims, policy solutions, and goals.

A final factor is the number of actors and their relation with one another. Naturally, a number of different interests can be found in each case and a clear trend on this variable is not to be found, it seems to be rather case specific. In case 1, we see that there is a high number of actors involved in the decision-making process and that the diversity of the actors regarding their political goals and convictions is also high. This complicates the decision-making process. Case 2 shows that the number of actors involved is somewhat low in the first case but the main authorities share the same convictions, which ostensibly simplifies the decision-making process. The fact that opponents have organized themselves efficiently and have had access to the same data but with different results means that in the end the decision making was as tiresome as in the first case. Cases 3 and 5 provide us with insight on how a group of actors can become very powerful in the decision-making process because they have the monopoly on the information. In case 4, it becomes clear that institutional arrangements can reduce complexity since only one organization has formal authority. Finally, case 6 tells us that the lack of trust, the enormous difference in political opinion, and the lack of one owner and authority make decision making so complex that a decision that is seen as legitimate by all actors becomes impossible. In general, taking the previous part of the analysis into account it shows that the actual number of different actors has no influence, it is the number of different goals they hold.

10.7   Conclusions

This chapter aims to answer the question how the designing and using models and the communication between designer and policy maker influences the process of public decision making in terms of values. Analysis of the six cases shows that this influence is considerable. We find that a large diversity exists within the cases on the different values we have evaluated and that the impact of these values, perceptions, and beliefs is very important for the process of policy making. This is because when actors think and believe the same things, they tend to think that their work encompasses all possible variety. In other words, being of the same mindset triggers unintentional selective blindness. Consequently, the models are not under close scrutiny and decisions made using a certain model reflect the biases that were unintentionally programmed into the model. For example, in the case of predicting the outbreak of livestock diseases, it appeared that the option "clearing of animals" could never be a feasible outcome of the model, whereas in reality it could be a possible answer.

A high diversity in actors raises a situation of conflict as multiple actors bring forward their own perspectives that are in many cases only partly convergent and downright contradictory in some cases. In other words, higher diversity leads to more obvious clashes of goals, beliefs, and values. The models that are used and the results that the models generate are being questioned more explicitly and openly, consequently leading to a higher perceived complexity as it becomes much more difficult to reach a quick conclusion. Diversity or lack, thereof, is partly a design feature of the institutional dimension, partly an unintentional process between actors who trust and believe each other. As a design feature it emerges when the commissioning, developing, and using models are clustered around one or a limited set of tightly coupled actors. Such a concentration of power, where both the research and the final decision are strongly linked, causes the actors to develop a bias towards their own ideas. Whether this link is institutionally determined or not, does not influence this. The models are consequently used as such. When such close links are contested or absent, the diversity raises because of the possibility of questioning current ideas and beliefs. As an unintentional process, it emerges when actors develop relationships of trust and belief. Although actors are not aware of it, such relationships still promote convergence of thinking, thus decreasing contradictory ideas.

If anything, the current research shows that models and data never speak for itself. On the contrary, they are heavily influenced by the social dynamics of the context they are developed in. Not only, as social constructivists claim, because of the values attributed to the models while they were used in their own political and institutional context but also as the technological determinists argue, because of the values in the model itself. They have been put there by the designers' choice, often unintentionally; however, public policy makers are unaware of these choices. This leads us to conclude that computational models have a very large influence on the decisions that are made, as our case study shows. Following this we can argue that the potential power of these models within public decision making is substantial. Even though throughout this chapter we have argued that humans do have agency over technology our case studies show that this agency at some points is limited to the designer of the application and not to the public decision maker using the application in order to come to a decision. This raises questions for the future in which we ask ourselves that when computational models are normative because they cannot mimic full reality and instead reflect the developers' and users' ideas, what this means for those elected officials using the computational model for decision making. We observed often that belief in the model as the right descriptor and predictor of reality was almost absolute at the level of policy makers. "If it has a number it must be true." We argue that this number is as much a reflection of the developers' ideas as it reflects reality.

Furthermore, we can conclude that not only the designer of the model is able to place values into the model but these values are also incorporated by the users of the application. Not because through a technological frame, they attribute a certain meaning to a technology but because the data in the model itself is not flawless. This means that is possible that models used by different actors generate entirely different outcomes. It is not as much a design flaw of the model but rather a consequence of the complexity of values of data and models. However, public decision makers are often unaware of this and regard the model as being neutral and value-free. Designers often in their communication with public decision makers are trying to simplify their message and are trying to hide the normative biases.

Concluding, we can state that while the technology debate remains an ongoing debate, in terms of computational models and public decision making it is also important to research the relationship between the designer of the model and the public policy maker, the role of the designer and its interaction with end users and policy makers should be further researched. The nature of this relationship accounts partly for a more deterministic or more social constructivist view on the side of the public policy maker regarding technology. Therefore, this chapter cannot conclude whether technology should be viewed in either a social constructivist manner or a deterministic manner, but can conclude that different actors view the same technology in different epistemological manners.

References

Bekkers V, Lips M, Zuurmond A (2005) De maatschappelijke en politiek-bestuurlijke positionering van ICT in het openbaar bestuur. In: Lips M, Bekkers V, Zuurmond A (eds) ICT en openbaar bestuur: implicaties en uitdagingen van technologische toepassingen voor de overheid. Lemma, Utrecht, pp 17–46

Beniger JR (1986) The control revolution: technological and economic origins of the information society. Harvard University Press, Cambridge

Bijker WE (1993) Do not despair: there is life after constructivism. Sci Technol Hum Values 18(1):113–138

Bijker WE (1995) Of bicycles, bakelites, and bulbs: toward a theory of sociotechnical change. MIT Press, Cambridge

Chen C (2005) Top 10 unsolved information visualization problems. IEEE Comput Graph Appl July/August: 12–16

Dror Y (1968) Public policy making reexamined. Chandler, San Francisco

Ellul J (1954) The 'autonomy' of the technological phenomenon. In: Scharff RC, Dusek V (eds) Philosophy of technology: the technological condition. An anthology. Blackwell, Malden. pp 386–397

Ellul J (1990) The technological bluff. William B. Eerdmans, Grand Rapids

Feenberg A (1991) Critical theory of technology. Oxford University Press, New York

Gerrits L (2008) The gentle art of coevolution. Erasmus Universiteit Rotterdam, Rotterdam

Goodhue DL, Kirsch LJ, Quillard JA, Wybo MD (1992) Strategic data planning: lessons from the field. MIS Quart 16(1):11–35

Heilbroner RL (1967) Do machines make history? In: Scharff RC, Dusek V (eds) Philosophy of technology. The technological condition. An anthology. Blackwell, Malden, pp 398–404

Heilbroner RL (1994) Technological determinism revisited. In: Smith MR, Marx L (eds) Does technology drive history? The dilemma of technological determinism. MIT Press, Cambridge, pp. 67–78

Hoff J (2000) Technology and social change. The path between technological determinism, social constructivism and new institutionalism. In: Hoff J, Horrocks I, Tops P (eds) Democratic governance and new technology: technologically mediated innovations in political practice in western Europe. Routledge/ECPR Studies in European Political Science, London, pp 13–32

Kaplan DM (ed) (2004) Readings in the philosophy of technology. Rowman & Littlefield, Lanham

Lindblom CE (1959) The science of 'muddling through'. Public Admin Rev 19(1):79–88

March JG, Simon HA (1993) Organizations. Blackwell, Cambridge

Moody R (2010) Mapping power. Geographical information systems, agenda-setting and policy design. Erasmus University Rotterdam, Rotterdam

Scharff RC, Dusek V (eds) (2003) Philosophy of technology. The technological condition. An anthology. Blackwell, Malden

Simon HA (1957) Models of man: social and rational. Mathematical essays on rational human behavior in a social setting. Wiley, New York

Simon HA (1976) Administrative behavior. A study of decision-making processes in administrative organization. Free Press, New York

Smith MR, Marx L (eds) (1994) Does technology drive history? The dilemma of technological determinism. MIT Press, Cambridge

Ware C (2000) Information visualization: perception for design. Morgan Kaufmann, San Francisco
Winner L (1977) Autonomous technology: Technics-out-of-control as a theme in political thought. MIT Press, Cambridge
Winner L (1980) Do artifacts have politics? Daedalus 109(1):121–138
Winner L (1983) Technologies as forms of life. In: Kaplan DM (ed) Readings in the philosophy of technology. Rowman & Littlefield, Lanham, pp 103–113
Winner L (1993) Upon opening the black box and finding it empty: social constructivism and the philosophy of science. Sci Technol Hum Values 18(3):362–378
Wright R (2008) Data visualization In: Fuller M (eds) Software studies: a lexicon. MIT Press, Cambridge, pp 78–86
Zuboff S (1988) In the age of the smart machine: the future of work and power. Basic, New York

Chapter 11
The Psychological Drivers of Bureaucracy: Protecting the Societal Goals of an Organization

Tjeerd C. Andringa

> Bureaucracy is the art of making the possible impossible
> –Javier Pascual Salcedo
> A democracy which makes or even effectively prepares for
> modern, scientific war must necessarily cease to be democratic.
> No country can be really well prepared for modern war unless it
> is governed by a tyrant, at the head of a highly trained and
> perfectly obedient bureaucracy.
> –Aldous Huxley
> Whether the mask is labeled fascism, democracy, or dictatorship
> of the proletariat, our great adversary remains the
> apparatus—the bureaucracy, the police, the military. Not the
> one facing us across the frontier of the battle lines, which is not
> so much our enemy as our brothers' enemy, but the one that calls
> itself our protector and makes us its slaves. No matter what the
> circumstances, the worst betrayal will always be to subordinate
> ourselves to this apparatus and to trample underfoot, in its
> service, all human values in ourselves and in others.
> –Simone Weil

Abstract This chapter addresses the psychological enablers of bureaucracy and ways to protect bureaucrats and society from its adverse effects. All organizations benefit from formalization, but a bureaucracy is defined by the dominance of coercive formalization. Since bureaucrats are not bureaucratic among friends, one might ask what changes someone at work into a bureaucrat and why do bureaucrats and bureaucratic organizations exhibit their characteristic behaviors?

The pattern of behavior arises from fundamental psychology and in particular (1) our capacity for habitual behavior, (2) the difference between intelligence as manifestation of the coping mode of cognition and understanding as manifestation of the pervasive optimization mode, and (3) the phenomenon of authoritarianism as the need for external authority through a lack of understanding of one's living environment. The combination of these phenomena leads to a formal definition, the "Bureaucratic Dynamic," in which the prevalence of coercive formalization scales

T. C. Andringa (✉)
University College Groningen, Institute of Artificial Intelligence and Cognitive Engineering (ALICE), University of Groningen, Broerstraat 5, 9700 AB, Groningen, the Netherlands
e-mail: t.c.andringa@rug.nl

© Springer International Publishing Switzerland 2015
M. Janssen et al. (eds.), *Policy Practice and Digital Science*,
Public Administration and Information Technology 10, DOI 10.1007/978-3-319-12784-2_11

with "institutional ignorance" (as measure of how well workers understand the consequence of their own (in)actions, both within the organization as well on the wider society) and "worker cost of failure."

Modern organizational theory has become progressively more aware of the inefficiencies and dangers of bureaucracy. The framework developed in this paper can be applied to protect society, organizations, and workers from the adverse effects of bureaucracy. Yet while non-bureaucratic organizations can produce excellence, they also rely on it and are therefore somewhat fragile. Improved protective measures can be developed using the framework developed in this chapter.

11.1 Introduction

In 2005 a Dutch insurance company aired a television commercial[1] in which they showed a mother and daughter trying to collect their "purple crocodile" at a lost-and-found department. The clerk reaches for the missing object form—just next to the huge purple crocodile—and hands it to the mother to be filled in. After a few attempts the form is filled-in to the clerk's satisfaction and he instructs the family to collect the missing object the next morning between 9 and 10 a.m. "But it's there" the mother remarks. "Yes it is there" the clerk responds with an empty expression to this completely irrelevant remark.

Clearly, the original societal role of this lost-and-found department was replaced by a new goal: procedural correctness, irrespective of the state of the world and the implications of following procedure. The commercial ended with the remark that less bureaucracy is preferable.

We all know these blatant examples of bureaucracy, where form and procedure have become stultifying, any genuine empathy and human decency is absent, and the organization is no longer serving its original purpose efficiently. Yet the most shocking, albeit not normally acknowledged, aspect of these examples is that bureaucrats—outside the direct working environment—are just regular law-abiding individuals who might do volunteer work and who will gladly return something without insisting on a form to fill in first: *among friends no-one is a bureaucrat.*

I consider bureaucracy and bureaucratic mindsets as suboptimal or even pathological for the organization because it has adopted self-serving goals in favor of its original societal goal and for the bureaucrat because he or she is reduced—at work—to a shadow of his or her full human potential. This paper addresses the psychological reasoning on which this opinion is based.

Administration is not necessarily bureaucratic. And formalization—the extent of written rules, procedures, and instructions—can both help and hinder the overall functioning of the organization. In this chapter, I define bureaucracy as the dominance of *coercive formalization* within professional organizations. Coercive formalization

---

[1] https://www.youtube.com/watch?v = 2Rw27vcTHRw

takes away autonomy and changes a worker into the direction of an automaton: someone who can be easily replaced by information technology or a robot.

All human activities benefit from some form of formalization. Formalization allows automating routine tasks, to agree on how to collaborate, determine when and how tasks should be executed, and when they are finished. As such, procedures should not be changed too often so that they become and remain a stable basis for organizational functioning. Yet procedures should also not be too static and too strictly adhered to so that they lead to stultification, suboptimal task execution, and, above all, to loosing track of the societal goals of an organization. These are all signs of bureaucracy.

The bulk of this chapter comprises the formulation of a psychological framework that explains the phenomenology of bureaucratic and non-bureaucratic organizations. This framework is based on the two cognitive modes—the coping mode and the pervasive optimization mode—that we defined in an earlier paper on Learning Autonomy (Andringa et al. 2013). Since bureaucracy has a lot to do with preventing worker autonomy, it is not surprising that our paper contains relevant ideas. What I found quite surprising, and highly relevant, was how well the "coping mode of cognition" fitted with the bureaucracy literature (Adler and Borys 1996; Weber 1978). In Learning Autonomy we had addressed the phenomenon of authoritarianism: the need for and acceptance of centralized or group authority. In this chapter I show that bureaucracy is a manifestation of authoritarianism in the context of professional organizations. Based on the defining characteristics of authoritarianism, I predict the incentives for coercive formalization, and with that the incentive for bureaucracy, as follows:

Incentive for coercive formalization = Institutional ignorance × Worker cost of failure

I call this the Bureaucratic Dynamic. Maximizing "institutional ignorance" and "Worker cost of failure" leads, via psychological mechanisms outlined below, inevitably to more bureaucracy. Fortunately, minimizing these will reduce bureaucracy. I predict that this formula can be used as an effective means to improve our understanding of the phenomenon, to improve effective anti-bureaucracy measures, and to expose ineffective ones.

This chapter provides a transdisciplinary approach of bureaucracy. Transdisciplinarity entails that I will ignore traditional (and often quite arbitrary) disciplinary boundaries and I will address multiple description levels; in particular a number of subdisciplines of psychology (fundamental science level), organizational research (applied science level), policy (normative level), and ethical considerations (value level) (Max-Neef 2005).

I start in Sect. 11.1, with an interdisciplinary analysis addressing how the diversity of bureaucracy can be understood through the degree and the type of coercive and enabling formalization. This analysis outlines many manifestations of bureaucracy that, together with the observation that no one is a bureaucrat among friends, demand a psychological explanation.

Section 11.2, forms the fundamental science bulk of this chapter. In it, I start with habits as effective and goal realizing activities that require only a minimal involvement of the higher faculties of mind because the behavior originates from and is guided by the (work) environment. This is followed by the observation that the two modes of thought we have defined in our earlier paper on Learning Autonomy (Andringa et al. 2013) match bureaucratic and non-bureaucratic strategies. The two modes differ in the locus of authority: external for bureaucracy and internalized for non-bureaucratic approaches. The centrality of the concept of authority becomes even clearer when I change the perspective to political psychology and in particular to the opposition authoritarians–libertarians. These groups of people differ in whether or not they (*unconsciously*) consider the complexity of the world too high to act adequately and feel comfortable. The shared feelings of inadequacy motivate them to instill order through coercive formalization and group or centralized authority: a phenomenon known as the "Authoritarian Dynamic." This dynamic, in this chapter, applied in the context of professional organizations, drives the growth or demise of bureaucracy according to the "Bureaucratic Dynamic." Section 11.2 closes with a short reflection on the (serious) detrimental effects of bureaucracy might have on bureaucrats (value level).

This chapter closes with a shorter section on how three modern management paradigms (applied science and policy level) can be classified according to the prevalence of the coping or the pervasive optimization mode. This entails, in some sense, that experiential evidence has already discovered what I argue from a psychologically informed perspective. Yet this perspective complements and enriches the experientially acquired understanding. I then direct attention to non-bureaucratic or "libertarian" organizations. One crucial aspect of these is that they not only are able to deliver pervasive optimization of all organizational roles, they also depend on it. This entails that they are fragile and easily wrecked by workers with insufficient institutional understanding. I give examples of how this degradation process typically occurs and indicate a number of "red flags." I end the chapter with a number of conclusions and observations.

11.2   Characteristics of Bureaucracy

This section is based on the analysis of organizations with different types, levels and forms of bureaucracy by Adler and Borys (1996). They provide an insightful and fairly comprehensive analysis of bureaucracy and its diverse forms. In addition Adler and Borys propose a structured typology of organizations that matches very well with our recent paper on open-ended (lifespan) development and in particularly with the development of bounded or full autonomy (Andringa et al. 2013). Taken together, these two articles provide an interesting generalized perspective on bureaucracy and, in general, on some foundational perspectives on human autonomy and human organizations.

Adler and Borys address the issue of worker autonomy in many different examples and remark "that much of the literature on the sociology of scientists and engineers asserts that employees in these occupations typically aspire to high levels of autonomy in their work and that bureaucratic formalization undermines their commitment and innovation effectiveness." Yet other employees might benefit from bureaucratic formalization. Consequently:

> Organizational research presents two conflicting views of the human attitudinal or outcomes of bureaucracy. According to the negative view, the bureaucratic form of organization stifles creativity, fosters dissatisfaction, and demotivates employees. According to the positive view, it provides needed guidance and clarifies responsibilities, thereby easing role stress and helping individuals be and feel more effective.

In terms of autonomy, it seems that the bureaucratic form of organization stultifies the functioning of highly autonomous and motivated employees, while it actually provides the less autonomous employees guidance and effectiveness in roles in which they would otherwise not be able to function. So bureaucracy *constrains* the autonomous employees, but *enables* the less autonomous to contribute more effectively. Accordingly, Adler and Borys conclude that the study "of the functions and effects of bureaucracy has split correspondingly with one branch focused on its power to enforce compliance from employees assumed to be recalcitrant or irresponsible and the other branch focused on bureaucracy's technical efficiency."

Based on this observation and a number of examples, Adler and Borys propose two structural dimensions for organizations: the *type of formalization*, spanning a continuum from coercive to enabling, and the *degree of formalization* from low to high. This leads to a two-dimensional representation with four quadrants resulting from the intersection of the axes as depicted in Fig. 11.1. The degree of bureaucracy is represented by the diagonal connecting a high degree of coercive formalization—characteristic of a highly bureaucratic or "mechanistic" organization—to a low degree of enabling formalization in the non-bureaucratic, or "organic," organization. The other diagonal corresponds to a highly centralized, or "autocratic," organization or a decentralized "enabling bureaucracy."

The key component of this organizational typology is formalization and Adler and Borys describe many different aspects of formalization. A number of these are summarized in Table 11.1.

It will be clear from Table 11.1 that some degree of suitable formalization is highly beneficial, and probably defining for any organization and as such is broadly supported. Yet, too much formalization or formalization of an unsuitable kind will be detrimental for the employees and the way the organization realizes its societal mission and as such enacts its *raison d'être*.

Adler and Borys couple the two types of formalization—coercive and enabling—to perspectives on the organization. The "enabling approach" considers *workers as sources of skill and intelligence to be activated*. This works, of course, for workers who enjoy to be challenged, who aspire to develop their skills, and who feel a personal or shared pride regarding the work they are performing. In the "coercive approach" *workers are treated as sources of problems to be eliminated*. In this approach the opportunism and autonomy of workers (skilled or not) is to be feared and it leads almost inevitably to a deskilling approach. Deskilling is, of course, resented by those who consider work autonomy and skill-development essential for personal growth, but for the less skilled and probably more insecure workers, who know they will not be able to contribute effectively without strict and firm guidance, the coercive approach

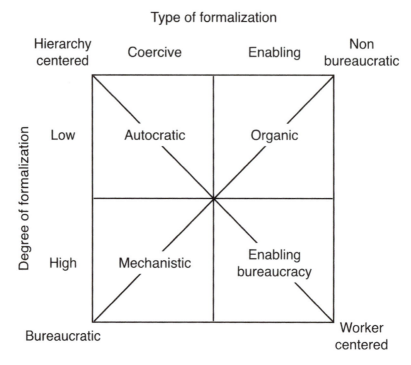

Fig. 11.1 Types of organization. (Based on Fig. 1 in Adler and Borys (1996))

is a way to contribute on a higher professional level than they would otherwise be able to achieve. Adler and Borys provide many properties of coercive and enabling formalization, which are summarized in Table 11.2.

As Table 11.2 shows, the basic logic of the coercive approach is to curtail the scope of behavioral options of workers through *centralized* and/or (corrective) *group* authority. In contrast, the basic logic of the enabling approach is to use diversity of insights and independent judgment of all employees to improve all aspects of the organization (in the context of all its roles and obligations). As such the enabling approach relies on a combination of group authority and individual authority. But note that the role of group authority differs between the two approaches: in the coercive approach it is to signal and correct any deviant behavior, while in the enabling approach it is a means to aggregate organizational understanding in a common mode of working.

Asymmetries in power, of course, promote the coercive approach, but the same holds for ignoring or actively suppressing the skills and knowledge of the workers since this almost inevitably impoverishes the understanding of the organization and as such it leads to organizations that progressively become out-of-sync with reality: instead the organization creates its own peculiar realities based on whatever pleases the power structure, which progressively makes it more difficult to apply the observations, knowledge, and insights of the workers for the proper execution of the organization's societal role.

Table 11.1 Positive and negative aspects of formalization. (Based on Adler and Borys (1996))

Negative effects of formalization:	Positive effects of formalization:
Higher absences	Formalization can increase efficiency
Propensity to leave organization	Embrace of well-designed procedure facilitates task
Physical and psychological stress	Performance and pride on workmanship
Reduced innovation	Reduction of role conflict and role ambiguity
Reduced job satisfaction	Increased work satisfaction
Reduced commitment to the organization	Reduction of feelings of alienation and stress
	Can help innovation if it capture lessons of prior
Lower motivation	Experience or help coordination of larger-scale projects
	broad preference and benefits for routine tasks
Formalization is disfavored if:	Formalization is favored if:
Rules benefit managers: especially when rules are also used to sanction	Work is considered as a cooperative endeavor rather than the abrogation of autonomy
Bad rules/procedures:	Good rules/procedures:
Resented	Taken for granted
If possible ignored or avoided	Hardly noticed

Adler and Borys couple the motivations (Deci and Ryan 1987) to participate in the organization to the type of formalization. The coercive formalization corresponds to external (authority enforced, fear of punishment, rule compliance) or introjected motivation (internal or esteem-based pressures to avoid harm) because it does not tap into whatever is intrinsically motivating for the employees. The enabling formalization does just that: it allows motivation based on identification with personal importance or compliance with personal goals. It might even allow intrinsic motivation in the form of completely unconstrained and self-determined activities that involve highly enjoyable states like flow and play.

These motivations—in this order—have been coupled to the perceived locus of causality (PLOC), which reflects the degree the individual or some external authority or influence originates the behavior (Ryan and Connell 1989). It is a measure of autonomy and agency. The more autonomous the behavior, the more it is endorsed by the whole self and is experienced as action for which one is responsible (Deci and Ryan 1987). In particular for activities with an external PLOC individuals do not really feel a personal responsibility and probably no moral responsibility as well. This then suggests that it is possible to realize highly unethical goals by promoting the coercive form of formalization: the workers will not feel any sense of responsibility. This explains why bureaucracies (or more general hierarchical organizations subject to coercive formalization, such as the military, intelligence agencies, or some multinationals) are so often involved in atrocities. Aldous Huxley's quote at the beginning of this chapter acknowledges this as well.

Table 11.2 Properties of coercive and enabling formalization

Coercive formalization	Enabling formalization
Basic attitude	Basic attitude
Workers as sources of problems to be eliminated. Opportunism of workers to be feared: deskilling approach	Workers as a source of skill and intelligence to be activated
Key properties:	*Key properties:*
The formal system (e.g., organogram) is leading, workers exist to serve their role	The formal system exists to enable and support the workers in executing the societal function of the organization
Deviation from the protocol is suspect	Deviations from procedure decided by the workers
Procedures often non-transparent to keep knowledge about the organization from the employees to prevent "creative interaction"	Deviations from the protocol signals the need for better procedures or methods and are a learning opportunity
Procedures as assertions of duties (not to help)	Procedures help to explain key components and codifying best practices
"Global transparency" highly asymmetric, with procedures that, for example, help to realize a panopticon (so that employees know that superiors can monitor them at any time)	Procedures to provide insight into personal performance
Global transparency of the organization is a source of employee initiative and as such a risk to be minimized	Global transparency provides insight in the role of processes in the broader context of the organization as necessary source of innovation and improvement for the whole organization
Procedures define, in detail, a sequence of steps to be followed and force the employee to ask approval for any deviation of the protocol (such as skipping unnecessary steps)	
Forces promoting the coercive formalization:	*Forces promoting the enabling formalization:*
Asymmetries in power	Societal preference for enabling formalization
Absence of reality checks associated with an inward focus in which local conflicts become more important than organizational goals	A necessity of a very complex task environment (such as in times of competitive pressure)
The results of automation (whatever ICT produces) needs to be communicated and followed-up to the letter	Automation first replaces routine operations (their formalization become part of the ICT) and leads to a demand for more skilled employees
Motivation type:	*Motivation type:*
External (authority enforced, fear of punishment, rule compliance)	Intrinsic motivation (completely self-determined activities)
Introjected motivation (internal or esteem-based pressures to avoid harm)	Identified (with personal importance) or integrated (compliance with personal goals)

In this section I have outlined a number of properties of bureaucracies for which I will propose the psychological underpinnings in Sect. 11.3. This section will focus on why the phenomena outlined before, emerge *inevitably* from basic psychology.

11.3 Psychological Roots of Bureaucracy

11.3.1 Habits

Since the formalization, and therefore automation, of behavior is an integral part of bureaucracy it makes sense to address the topic of habits and habitual behavior because the psychological term "habit" refers to an automatic response to a specific situation (Ouellette and Wood 2003; Wood and Neal 2009). The ability to behave habitually is a wonderful thing, because it means that we have learned to do something so efficiently that our minds are kept free for other things. Habits can be nested so that for example, the habit of driving can be part of daily, weekly, monthly, or yearly routines.

Habits are well-trained perception–action relations that are efficiently combined so that they address our daily affairs with minimal mental effort and their combination may lead to an endless variety of effective, while still seemingly effortless, behaviors. During the execution of a habit it is the environment that determines your actions: if there is a door on your path, you open it. You will not normally initiate the door opening behavior without a door. You can of course, willingly, try to activate door-opening behavior in the middle of a lawn. But nothing in the lawn-environment will activate this particular behavior. This holds for steak cutting, hair combing, wall painting, and turning the page of a newspaper: you can do it whenever you want, but it is only productive (and looks less silly) if you let the environment activate the desired behavior. That is the reason why each habit is activated in situations that provide the affordances to activate the behavior.

The way we respond to *social or work* situations is also for a large part habitual. In particular we find "that mental content activated in the course of perceiving one's social environment automatically creates behavioral tendencies" (Bargh 2010). The first time we encounter some situation we might not know what to do and to give it all our attention to decide on appropriate behavior, but after a few times practice, the situation is neither novel nor challenging and we respond habitually and according to, for example, the stereotypes activated by the environment. Because of the flexibility of habitual components and because of the minimal mental effort it costs to combine them adaptively, most of our daily activities are habitual, which is good because during habit execution we are left with ample opportunities to direct our attention to interesting, useful, or important things.

William James, one of the first and still one of the greatest psychologists, had much to say on habits. In fact he addresses the topic of habits as one of the foundations of psychology. And what is relevant for this chapter, he explicitly defined habit, 125 years ago, as the flywheel that keeps society (and the organizations that constitute it) stable (James 1890, p 16–17).

> Habit is thus the enormous flywheel of society, its most precious conservative agent. It alone is what keeps us all within the bounds of ordinance, and saves the children of fortune from the

envious uprisings of the poor. It alone prevents the hardest and the most repulsive walks of life from being deserted by those who are brought up to tread therein. It keeps the fisherman and the deckhand at sea through the winter; it holds the miner in its darkness, and nails the countryman to its log-cabin and its lonely farm through all the months of snow; it protects us from invasion by the natives of the desert and the frozen zone. It dooms us all to fight out the battle of life upon the lines of our nurture or our early choice, and to make the best of a pursuit that disagrees, because there is no other for which we are fitted, and it is too late to begin again.

So habits do not only free our minds for more important things they also keep us within the bounds of the status quo or pursuits once started. Habits are not a genetic inevitability, but are the result of the way we are raised, educated, and introduced in our professional lives. James defines the role of education therefore in terms of acquiring habits.

> The great thing, then, in all education, is *to make our nervous system our ally instead of our enemy*. It is to fund and capitalize our acquisitions, and live at ease upon the interest of the fund. *For this we must make automatic and habitual, as early as possible, as many useful actions as we can*, **and guard against the growing into ways that are likely to be disadvantageous to us, as we should guard against the plague**. The more of the details of our daily life we can hand over to the effortless custody of automatism, the more our higher powers of mind will be set free for their own proper work.

The original text had an emphasis in italic, here I have added an emphasis in bold to focus on the fact that habits may not necessarily be beneficial to us, they might in fact be more beneficial to whoever has defined the status quo and now benefits from the habitual continuation of that status quo. This status quo can typically be some sort of working or living environment that has not been designed by the individual himself, but results from some reasoning that is predominantly or wholly beyond the individual's understanding. In a situation like this we have, as far as work is concerned, no "opportunities to direct our attention to interesting, useful, or important things." In these conditions habitual behavior dominates the work floor and very little of the behavior that characterizes the individual in the rest of its life is visible.

This already explains part of the bureaucratic syndrome by answering, at least partially, the question "What shuts down so much of a bureaucrat's mental capabilities?" The partial answer is that a difficult to understand environment that effectively activates habitual behavior leads to the activation of habitual behavior while denying the bureaucrat self-selected opportunities of intrinsic interest, usefulness, or importance. Consequently, absent the understanding of their significance in the bigger scheme of things, the true bureaucrat has no real responsibilities other than maintaining the conditions in which habitual functioning is facilitated, which is exactly what I saw in the introductory example.

The conclusion that the bureaucrat's single or main—self-imposed—responsibility is to uphold the conditions for its own habitual functioning explains to a large degree the stability of bureaucracies. But note that this is especially the case for work environments that exceed the scope of understanding of workers and management: only here they have no choice but to uphold the conditions in which they function habitually. With sufficient organizational understanding, workers and management can break this cycle. We will return to this topic in the subsection on "Authoritarianism" (Sect. 11.3).

11.3.2   Two Modes of Thought

The previous subsection already separated a habitual mode of thought, which requires very little attentional control, and forms of cognition that are not (yet) habitual because they do require highly focused attention, for example because they are new, ever changing, or otherwise engaging or challenging. This opposition arises from two large families of cognitive phenomena that McGilchrist (2010) (with extensive justification and highly compelling historical support) couples to the left and right brain hemispheres. In a recent paper (Andringa et al. 2013) we generalized McGilchrist's interpretations as two complementary modes of cognition: the *coping mode* and the *pervasive optimization mode*.[2]

The coping mode is concerned with control: with preventing things (the whole world actually) from spinning out of control. Problem solving and the suppression of interfering diversity are central concepts for this mode. The pervasive optimization mode on the other hand is, as the name suggests, concerned with the optimization of all processes in the context of everything else. Where the coping mode is concerned with the problems of the here and the now, the pervasive optimization mode is concerned with promoting the likeliness of beneficial states in the near and distant future; both here and elsewhere, and for yourself (body and mind) as well as the rest of the world (family and friends, and the natural and social environment). Where the coping mode is highly focused and aims at tangible results in a structured and predictable way, the pervasive optimization mode is much more diffuse; it has no sequential demands and does not necessarily lead to directly tangible results. It does however set-up, in a statistical sense, the conditions for an unproblematic future. The coping mode relies on situational control and *intelligent* problem solving skills. The pervasive optimization mode relies on a broad *understanding* of the world and its dynamics in combination with the skills to relate to and work with these dynamics (Andringa et al. 2013).

The concept of "intelligence," especially as conceptualized and measured in an IQ-test, summarizes the coping mode because it measures one's ability to produce standardized and expected answers to self-contained problems. Intelligence is proven through the ability to solve problems posed by others. The minimal capacity to do this is simply by reproducing and applying appropriate formal operations without understanding neither the problem nor the situation that gave rise to it. This rule-application ability—apparent as formalization—is capitalized on in a stereotypical bureaucracy.

This can be contrasted to the concept of "understanding"—according to the New Oxford Dictionary "the ability to perceive the significance, explanation, or cause of

---

[2] The term pervasive-optimization mode has been introduced in this paper. In Andringa et al. (2013) we did not use a single term and we described this mode as cognition for exploration, disorder, or possibility. In a recent paper "Cognition From Life" (Andringa et al. 2015) we introduced the term cocreation mode of cognition. We decided to use the term pervasive-optimization mode in this paper since the term co-creation mode requires additional explanation.

(something)"—which captures strengths of the pervasive optimization mode. If you understand something you can use it not only reproductively or in a scripted way, but you know how to apply it in novel and open application domains. Consequently you can prove your depth and breadth of understanding through realizing novel or nonstandard results in the world. Conversely you proof your *lack* of understanding by making a mess of your live (indicating the utter failure of pervasive optimization). Another way to proof your lack of understanding is by reducing your life to an existence where very little novel or nonstandard happens (e.g., the extension of a bureaucratic attitude to the rest of life). In positive terms, the discovery of relations (between everything) and the detection of possibilities (in oneself, in others, at work, or in the whole of the environment) is strength of the pervasive optimization mode.

Returning to the example I started with. A bureaucrat is unlikely to act bureaucratically when not at work and especially not while among friends. The pervasive optimization mode seems, therefore, the default mode, while the coping mode is a fall-back mode that shines when the pervasive optimization mode was unable to prevent immanent or pressing problems. Interpreted as such, a bureaucracy is a working environment that forces (coerces) employees into a problem-solving, problem-preventing, or problem-control mode: the coping mode.

As outlined in our earlier paper on Learning Autonomy (Andringa et al. 2013), the pervasive optimization mode assumes autonomous participation in an open, dynamic, and infinite world of nested processes that form dynamically stable and continually evolving entities: the real continually developing and never fully graspable world. For the pervasive optimization mode of being, truth is defined as accordance with reality, which is to be tested by acting in the world; as such understanding and experiences are essentially subjective. This mode of being is particularly effective in situations where new aspects of the dynamics of the world are to be investigated to expand one's thought-action repertoire (Fredrickson and Branigan 2005) and where novel and creative solutions are appropriate.

In contrast, the coping mode assumes a closed, static, and self-contained (and therefore finite) world, in which entities are symbolic, discrete, and abstract and in which perfect solutions may be possible. It is also a mode in which one is an "objective" observer instead of a participant. It is the world as represented in a computer program: highly functional, perfectly repeatable, and subject to rational considerations, but ultimately devoid of life. In this mode of being, truth is defined as the result of consistent reasoning and consensually agreed on linguistically shared and presented facts. This mode of being is particularly effective in situations in which (immediate) problems have to be solved or addressed in a detached, rational, standardized, and communicable way. Bureaucracies, but also scientific communication, are typical examples of this.

Because the coping mode assumes a closed, static, and self-contained (and therefore finite) world it needs an external influence to maintain the conditions in which it can function in the first place. As we argued in Learning Autonomy, *authorities— defined as processes or agents that create, maintain, and influence the conditions in which agents exist—fulfill this role*. The authority for the left hemispheric coping mode is either its own right hemisphere or some external authority such as parents, leaders, governments, or cultural influences in the broadest possible sense. In practice, it is a combination of internal and external authority, and it defaults to external authority whenever the right hemisphere is unable to act as reliable authority. Put differently, when the right hemisphere is unable to generate a sufficient level of understanding of the situation, it cannot remain in the lead and the left hemisphere becomes dominant at the cost of surrendering autonomy to some (actually any) external authority. Importantly, this switch is subconscious. Still we can become aware of it through metacognition (like observing a change of emotions and/or a change in attitude or strategy). We will return to the role of *understanding* in the section on authoritarianism.

Table 11.3 provides a summary of properties ascribed to the coping and the pervasive optimization mode. It is based on Table 11.1 of Andringa et al. (2013), which in turn is based on Chap. 1 of McGilchrist (2010). The remarks in *italic* are examples of a bureaucratic (for the coping mode) and a non-bureaucratic (for the pervasive optimization mode) interpretation of these properties. It will be clear from Table 11.3 that the strengths of the coping mode can be used to illustrate typical and/or extreme bureaucratic functioning, while the pervasive optimization mode can be used to illustrate a non-bureaucratic alternative. Note that the original table was intended as a summary of left and right hemispheric strengths to be used in a quite different context: that it can be used to illustrate typical properties of bureaucratic and non-bureaucratic organizations, is a serendipitous observation that I consider highly meaningful.

11.3.3 Authoritarianism

At the end of the last subsection, authority was defined as the ability to create, maintain, influence, or exploit a living environment (Andringa et al. 2013). This entails that whenever individuals do not know how to self-maintain proper living conditions, they must rely on some sort of "authority" to keep living conditions within manageable bounds. This need for authority scales inversely with the scope of inadequacy: the more pervasive the inadequacy, the greater the need for and role of authority. Conversely, the better individuals cope with and maintain their own living environment—the more they have internalized authority—the less they need external authorities. This essential (and existential) need for authority is the defining characteristic of the concept of authoritarianism.

Within the domain of political psychology people with a strong need for authority are known as *authoritarians* and those who do not as *libertarians* (Stenner 2005, 2009, 2009). Authoritarians prefer (centralized) group authority and uniformity, while libertarians prefer (decentralized) individual authority and diversity. The structure and properties of authoritarian behavior have been studied in detail in "The Authoritarian Dynamic" by Princeton researcher Karen Stenner (2005). Authoritarianism is characterized by a strong tendency to maximize oneness (via centralized or group control) and sameness (via common standards), especially in conditions where the things that make us one and the same—common authority and shared values—appear to be under threat.

Table 11.3 Cognitive modes define organizations. Comparing properties of the coping mode of cognition (attributed to the left hemisphere) and the pervasive optimization mode (attributed to the right hemisphere). Associated with each topic, in italic, a bureaucratic interpretation for the coping mode and a non-bureaucratic interpretation for the pervasive optimization mode. (Based on Andringa et al. 2013)

Topic	Coping mode of cognition (Left hemisphere) *Bureaucratic interpretation*	Pervasive optimization mode of cognition (Right hemisphere) *Non-bureaucratic interpretation*
Main concern	Principal concern is utility	Prioritizes what actually is and what concerns us
	Technically qualified personnel is able to use these utilities to the max	*The organization adapts itself flexibly and effectively to the current situation*
	The world as a resource	
	The client should support ("feed") and comply with the bureaucracy irrespective its functioning	
Scope	Local short-term view	Bigger picture (broader, long-term view). Draws attention from the edges of awareness
	Focus on short term solutions	*Everything that the organization can contribute to the larger world is potentially important*
	Deal with what it knows	
	Only what is officially entered in the bureaucracy is exists	
Attitude towards world	Representing the world: the world as a copy that exists in a conceptual form, suitable for manipulation	Experiencing the world: the world as it is, open for novelty and whatever exists apart from ourselves, without preconceptions and not focusing on what it already knows
	Strong focus on rules and procedure in combination with record keeping and written (explicit) communication. Only what can be represented within the bureaucracy exists and is subject to manipulation	*The organization in all its functions can adapt to what "the world brings"*

Table 11.3 (continued)

Topic	Coping mode of cognition (Left hemisphere) *Bureaucratic interpretation*	Pervasive optimization mode of cognition (Right hemisphere) *Non-bureaucratic interpretation*
Interests	Interested in the familiar and the known, difficulty with disengaging from the familiar	Interested in the novel
	Forms and procedures form the only object of interest	*Always interested in ways to adapt the organization to a changing and developing world*
	Concerned with what it knows	Concerned with what it experiences
	What cannot be dealt with in the bureaucracy does not exist	New information, new skills, emotional engagement
	Concerned with man-made objects	*Competence development of workers is not scripted but develops on the job through individual experience and development. Works should be inherently rewarding*
	Because these are typically static and for a particular use	
	Nonliving objects specialist. Living entities as tools or instruments	More concerned with living individuals. Living individuals as other individuals
	People and animals reduced to numbers that can manipulated in a similar way as other resources	*Each individual customer has to be treated in the way most suitable for the individual*

Table 11.3 (continued)

Topic	Coping mode of cognition (Left hemisphere) *Bureaucratic interpretation*	Pervasive optimization mode of cognition (Right hemisphere) *Non-bureaucratic interpretation*
Strengths	Thoroughly known and familiar	Gathering new information
	Standardized task execution by specialists	*Improve understanding of all relevant processes and aspects of the job*
	Efficient in routine situations and familiar skills	Good when prediction is difficult
	Training to reduce error frequency	*Flexible task execution by generalists*
	Prioritizes the expected and generates expectations	Anomaly (individuality) detector: individuals
	Help standard customers first, irrespective of urgency	*Adapt organization to the situation*
	Things made fixed and equivalent: types. All that is re-presented as over-familiar, inauthentic, lifeless categories	More efficiently when initial assumptions need to be revised or when old information needs to be distinguished from new information. All that is "present" as new, authentic, and individuated
	Equate people with (case) numbers. Guaranteed equality in treatment of all cases	*The ability to guarantee that the societal goal is contributed to, irrespective the situation or the customer*
Preferences	Preferences for things that are represented as relatively invariant across specific instances, allowing for abstracted types or classes of things	Preference for things that exist in the world. Sensitive to what distinguishes different instances of similar type from each other.
	People (including bureaucrats) should adapt to the bureaucracy. Not vice versa	*The organization adapts itself flexibly to the situation and/or changes in the situation*
Attention type	Local narrowly selective (highly) focused attention	Broad, global and flexible attention
	Only spend time on formal roles and formal procedures. Unable (and uninterested) to foresee consequences	*Spend time on the role and impact of the organization in the context of the larger society*

Table 11.3 (continued)

Topic	Coping mode of cognition (Left hemisphere) *Bureaucratic interpretation*	Pervasive optimization mode of cognition (Right hemisphere) *Non-bureaucratic interpretation*
Construction of world	Start with pieces and put these together. Bottom-up	Start from the whole and go, if required, into detail. Top-down
	Organize along formal roles and work-breakdown structure	*Start with societal role of the organization*
Representation of objects	Preference to re-present categories of things, and generic, nonspecific objects	Individual unique instances of things and individual generic objects: individuals are Gestalt wholes
	People and tasks as numbers or cases. Variations between cases suppressed	*Uniqueness of people and tasks defines the approach. Variation between cases as guideline*
Solution limitations	Problem solving: single solution and latch on to that	Array of possible solutions, which remain life when alternatives are explored
	All activities framed as problem-solving with a single optimal solution	*Activities are framed as a continual optimization process of the whole organization given its societal role*
	Deny inconsistencies. Suppressing not currently relevant relations	Actively watching for discrepancies
	Mismatches between bureaucratic reality and actual reality are settled in favor of the bureaucratic reality	*Discrepancies between reality and expectations seen as a learning opportunity*
Preferred knowledge type	Affinity with public knowledge	Personal knowledge
	Decisions based on written record	*Decisions based on individual experience and understanding*
Main emotions	Emotions associated with competition, rivalry, individual-self- believe (positive and negative)	All emotions. Emotions related to bonding and empathy
	Emotions associated with bureaucratic infighting, preserving one's public face, competition within and between department	*Emotions associated with the functioning of the whole organization and its customers*
Empathy	Unconcerned with others and their feelings	Empathic identification. Self-awareness, empathy, identification with others
	Rationality highest personal virtue. Career advancement on the basis of objective (not personal) criteria	*Integrity and moral behavior highest moral value. The organization aims to prevent adverse consequences of its behavior*

Table 11.4 Child rearing qualities used to determine authoritarianism

Authoritarians Children should:	Libertarians Children should:
Should obey parents	Be responsible for their actions
Have good manners	Have good sense and sound judgment
Be neat and clean	Be interested in how and why things happen
Have respect for elders	Think for themselves
Follow the rules	Follow their own conscience

Stenner (2005) used the 5 two-option questions about child rearing values to determine the degree of authoritarianism that are depicted in Table 11.4.

The difference between the answers that authoritarians and libertarians choose is qualitative: authoritarians teach children *to behave in certain proscribed ways* and to obey external authorities (elders, parents, norms), libertarians teach children *how to understand the world and how to act responsibly and autonomously*. The difference between authoritarians and libertarians is, therefore, neither ideological nor political: it depends on a combination of two aspects (1) internal or external authority, and (2) the depth and pervasiveness of understanding of the *current* living environment. Authoritarianism is, therefore, both, a personality trait and a state-of-being that is manifested in some situations, but not in others: the more individuals are brought into situations they do not (have learned to) understand and the more they are pressured to act, the more they will exhibit authoritarian behavior (See subsection Authoritarian Dynamic).

The child rearing qualities reflect the conditions that were identified for the left hemispheric coping mode and the right hemispheric pervasive optimization mode. As such it makes sense to interpret authoritarian behavior as behavior guided by the logic of the coping mode and libertarian behavior as behavior guided by the pervasive optimization mode. It also follows that bureaucracy is a manifestation of authoritarianism. Which also explains the reason why even strong bureaucrats are never bureaucratic among friends: here they are responsible for their own actions, expected to have a good sense and sound judgment, to be interested in others, to think and decide for themselves, and to follow their conscience. It is just that their working environment forces them out of this mode and into the coping mode.

11.3.4 Two Attitudes Toward a Complex World

According to Stenner (2009) authoritarians *are not endeavoring to avoid complex thinking so much as a complex world*. Authoritarians are just as intelligent as libertarians[3], but they understand the world more shallowly and less pervasively. Consequently, two individuals can experience and interpret a shared world quite differently. If it is experienced as too complex to comfortably deal with, one is in a coping or authoritarian mode of being. Consequently one's highest priority is to eliminate all sources of diversity to bring complexity down to manageable levels. And this can explain why people in the authoritarian mode take control over decision processes and become subtly or overtly intolerant to uncontrolled diversity through, for example, coercive formalization. It is not because they think they can do it better—although they might be convinced of that—but because of a strong unconscious urge to establish a larger measure of control over the situation with the aim to simplify it.

In the libertarian or pervasive optimization mode the complexity of the world is well below daily coping capacity and where authoritarians see problems they see opportunities. This can actually be problematic because realizing these opportunities is bound to lead to further social or organizational complexification that might aggravate authoritarians even further. Libertarians are therefore, quite unwittingly, major sources of feelings of inadequacy in authoritarians.

And this leads to a one-sided resentment—a shared and therefore unifying emotion—toward anything beyond coping capacity among authoritarians of which libertarians are typically completely unaware. In fact encroaching bureaucracy can be interpreted as a (low-intensity) war between two ways of facing reality. While libertarians are unaware of any war being fought (because they fail to see any need for it), they can be blamed for co-creating a complex world surpassing authoritarian coping capabilities. And authoritarians, with their limited understanding, share a deep anxiety and are highly motivated to do something about it collectively.

This subconscious anxiety motivates to oppose all sources of complexity, unpredictability, novelty, and growth that complexify, confuse, and destabilize an ordered and predictable state of affairs. In fact people in an authoritarian mode want to distance themselves from all of these things and the people (e.g., immigrants, homosexuals, libertarians) that embody or promote them. One driving emotion is disgust (Frijda 1986; Inbar et al. 2009): the urge to distance oneself from an unhealthy or otherwise harmful object, activity, person, or influence. Authoritarians in this state speak quite frankly and clearly about the moral decline that they see all around them and that disgusts them (and often enough explicitly worded). And they are quite motivated to do something about it. Vocal moral outrage about the organization losing its values and morals (typically in response to some gentle questions about the state of the organization) is an indication of an organization ready to become dominated by an authoritarian mindset and the associated urge to bring the complexity of the world/organization back to within coping capacity.

---

[3] Authoritarians might value intelligence more than libertarians. For example more than half of the 21 Nazi Nuremburg defendants had a superior intelligence (belonging to the most intelligent 3 to 0.2 %) and only one had average intelligence (Zillmer et al. 2013). This suggests that authoritarians select on intelligence.

In fact this same process seems to occur on a societal scale during revolutions. In his seminal book on revolutions in the nineteenth and twentieth century, Billington (1980) explicitly mentions the revolutionary's strong motivation to reduce complexity when he concludes:

> The fascinating fact is that most revolutionaries sought the simple, almost banal aims of modern secular men generally. What was unique was their intensity and commitment to realizing them.

Billington concludes that popular revolutions invariably aim to bring society back to a simpler state of affairs. Those revolutions, equally invariably, seem to coincide with periods of increased intolerance (against moral violators, freethinkers, or libertarians) and the rise of bureaucracy will not be surprising. It is all part of the same dynamic.

11.3.5 The Authoritarian Dynamic

This complexity reducing dynamic has a name: it is called the Authoritarian Dynamic (conform the name of Stenner's 2005 book). In its original form it was formulated for the domain of Political Psychology as the correlation:

Intolerance = Authoritarianism × Threat

In this "formula" "Intolerance" refers to intolerance to diversity and in particular intolerance to (perceived) violations of norms or the normative order. "Authoritarianism" initially (Stenner 2005) referred to how often one chooses the left-side answers of Table 11.4, which in turn is a (crude) measure of the shallowness of understanding of the world and the need for external (central or group) authority to create or maintain a world in which one feels adequate. "Threat" refers to the perceived threat and/or abundance of indicators of moral decline. The multiplication symbol " × " refers to the "AND"-condition entailing that for "intolerance to diversity" to become prominent *both* authoritarian disposition and perceived threat are required to build up the motivation to restore order through intolerance (or coercive formalization).

Note that this combination of (1) a low level of understanding of the world— ignorance— and (2) the threat-induced significance of acting appropriately leads to deep feelings of personal inadequacy. This entails that the fundamental driver of the authoritarian dynamic can be reformulated as the "Ignorance Dynamic."

Motivation to restore personal adequacy = Ignorance × Cost of failure to act appropriately

The deep feelings of personal inadequacy can—from the perspective of the Authoritarian—only be improved through the realization of a more tightly controlled and less diverse world. Interestingly, violence researcher Gilligan (1997) argues that shame, due to the public display of personal failure to act appropriately, is the root cause of all violence. This is yet another perspective on the coercive nature of intolerance.

There is a perfectly viable alternative approach to improve one's deep feelings of personal inadequacy, but, unfortunately, authoritarians generally do not come up with this among themselves. This alternative is to educate oneself out of feelings of personal inadequacy through acquiring a deeper and more pervasive understanding as a basis for more advanced strategies. Shallow understanding in combination with normal or good intelligence prevents this. The strength of the coping mode's "intelligent" ways of treating problems as self-contained (such as the problems in an IQ-test) leads authoritarians to redefine or ignore reality until it fits with their current solution repertoire.

This is another way to understand authoritarian intolerance. It is intolerance against anything opposing successful coping with an existing solution repertoire. It is therefore also intolerance against advanced strategies—based on a deeper and more pervasive understanding—that are not (yet) fully understood. Only when the threat level and the "cost of failure to act appropriately" diminish, these coping strategies can be replaced by pervasive optimization strategies. This entails that whoever controls the threat-level, controls the level of intolerance to diversity and growth, the moment intolerance becomes dominant, and the number of people in an authoritarian mode.

The Authoritarian Dynamic can be defined on the level of the individual as well as on a group or even societal level. A single authoritarian in an organization will defer its own authority to the more skilled and knowledgeable around. But the same authoritarian in a context with more authoritarians will be highly motivated to collectively adopt and enforce measures, i.e., introduce coercive formalization, expected to reduce situational complexity and personal inadequacy. Actually a small, but highly motivated, fraction of a society might start a revolution to (re)turn to a simpler, more controlled, and better understood world according to Billington's (1980) conclusions.

For example one of the slogans of the French revolution *Liberté, égalité, fraternité (freedom, equality, brotherhood)*, which became the French national motto a century later, is appealing to the libertarian values of diversity and individual authority. Yet it is also consistent with an urge to a simpler and better understood state of affairs, where people are more equal (similar), more brotherly responsible for each other (more able to keep each other to the norm), and free to define new (narrower) social norms. In this light it is not at all surprising that the French Revolution included a period called "the Reign of Terror" in which all perceived opposition to the revolution was punished at the guillotine. It was the period of about a year in a highly chaotic revolutionary decade in which intolerance peaked.

Yet the intolerance to diversity of anxious authoritarians is a normal coping response to a situation of which the complexity has developed out of coping capacity of some fraction (per definition the authoritarian fraction) of the population. It is their good and democratic right to do something about a situation that they perceive as highly troublesome. The problem is that their understanding of society, compared to the libertarian fraction, is lower and this may easily lead to the adoption of suboptimal or counterproductive strategies. Yet, the feelings of inadequacy and anxiety that authoritarians share and that unite them are genuine and these deserve to be taken very seriously. Ideally they should not be ignored or derided by libertarians, although they neither share nor understand their outlook on reality.

The more pervasive and deeper understanding of libertarians should allow them to understand authoritarians much better than vice versa. This entails that the libertarian fraction of society, at least in principle, holds the keys to the way the authoritarian dynamic will play out. Libertarians can influence the perceived complexity of society through coaching, education, and media and they can in some cases respond adequately to the threats perceived and moral decline experienced by authoritarians. Simply taking these seriously and addressing the root causes may result in a society in which considerably less people are in the authoritarian mode. In such a society many more people feel adequate because they are adequate social actors. The ensuing equality in personal adequacy ensures that most are in the pervasive optimization mode. This equality enhances overall wellbeing (Wilkinson 2006; Wilkinson and Pickett 2009) and it minimizes the probability of a concerted action by authoritarians to overthrow the (morally depraved) status quo in favor of a simpler, but also more regimented and less free society.

11.3.6   The Bureaucratic Dynamic

I will now come to the core and title of this chapter. How to formulate the psychological enablers of bureaucracy most succinctly? If bureaucracy is a manifestation of authoritarianism, i.e., the prevalence of the coping mode of thought, within professional organizations, something similar to the Authoritarian Dynamic or the "Ignorance Dynamic" should hold. Of course it must be adapted to the particular context of professional organizations.

My proposal, as variant of the Ignorance and Authoritarian Dynamic, for a "Bureaucratic Dynamic" is as follows:

Incentive for coercive formalization
= Bureaucracy incentive = Institutional ignorance × Worker cost of failure

In this "formula" the role of "intolerance" and "motivation to restore personal adequacy" is played by either the "Incentive for coercive formalization" or the "Bureaucracy incentive" as described by Adler and Borys (1996) and summarized in the left column of Table 11.2. The role of "Authoritarianism" and "Ignorance" is played by "Institutional ignorance." This is a measure of how well workers understand the consequences of their own actions, both within the organization and on the wider society. Directly associated is their need (often a demand) for guidance in every nonstandard activity. The role of "Threat" and "Cost of failure to act appropriately" is played by "Worker cost of failure." In the case of bureaucracy, the threat is not moral decline, but failing at the job and publicly being revealed as professionally inadequate. This threat pertains as much to the worker making the mistake, as it does to the superior who will be shamed because (s)he did not have the department under control.

Here, again, we have a combination of two factors: (1) institutional ignorance leads to an abundance of opportunities to fail and (2) (high) cost of failure. The prevalence and seriousness of failure now becomes *the* measure of personal inadequacy. As in the "Ignorance Dynamic" the right side of the Bureaucratic Dynamic corresponds to deep feelings of personal inadequacy that "can only be improved through the realization of a more manageable world," which, according to the logic of the coping mode, is through coercive formalization.

The Bureaucratic Dynamic, formulated like this, explains both the basic attitude and all the key properties of coercive formalization so characteristic of bureaucracy (see Table 11.2). Workers are seen as sources of problems to be eliminated, and opportunism of ("fools" as) workers is to be feared. A formal system of complex procedure and guidelines—all strengths of the coping mode of cognition—replaces worker's intelligence, skills, and improvisation ability. Deviations from protocol become suspect. To prevent the natural tendency of workers to use their "good sense and sound judgment" the whole organization is made nontransparent and whatever global transparency exists is made highly asymmetrical so that superiors at any moment can, but not necessarily do, monitor workers so that workers self-impose limits on their behavior.

In this process capable workers loose their intrinsic motivation ("The job is no longer fulfilling and it impedes my personal development") and identified motivation ("The job is no longer important and its results not satisfying"). These motivations are replaced by introjected motivation ("I'd better do it otherwise I'll face unpleasant consequences") and external motivation ("I have no choice," "The protocol says so," "The computer says so," *Befehl ist Befehl*). Quickly enough this state of being becomes habitual. The result is an individual that while at work, has shut down half of its intellectual potential, is stuck in a situation with minimal personal growth potential, and is reduced to an automaton-like shadow of a fully functioning human being.

11.3.7 The Psychological Effects on the Bureaucrat

While bureaucracy is annoying and frustrating for the client and costly for society, its effects might be worse for the bureaucrat. Compared to a worker in a non-bureaucratic organization, the bureaucrat misses many opportunities to engage in inherently fulfilling activities, to enjoy meaningful activities, to help others, to contribute undeniably to a better society, and in general to give meaning and significance to life.

What happens to the bureaucrat if these high-level human needs cannot be compensated in the rest of life? What level of life quality will result? Somewhat alarmingly, the pattern of these effects resembles those of torture. For example, torture victim therapist Leanh Nguyen (2007) concludes the following:

> The most terrible, and intractable, legacy of torture is the killing of desire—that is, of curiosity, of the impulse for connection and meaning making, of the capacity for mutuality, of the tolerance for ambiguity and ambivalence.

This description sounds eerily similar to the description of someone indefinitely locked in the coping mode of cognition. This quote describes a complete inability to experience curiosity, joy, play, and interpersonal contact. An inability for playful sensemaking associated with intrinsic motivation. This is replaced by a constant need for the certainty and formal clarity. It is as if the pervasive optimization mode has become inaccessible. Does not this resemble the automaton like bureaucrat in the introductory example?

This comparison between bureaucracy and torture might, at first glance seem a bit over the top, but remember that both are about subduing the individual to external authority (just as slavery by the way). Individual autonomy may well be a defining characteristic for health (see Andringa and Lanser (2013) for the role of freedom over mind-states in sound annoyance). From that perspective it makes sense to consider bureaucracy as a low, but prolonged, level of psychological torture that like full-blown torture, may have a profound and long lasting influence on bureaucrats and by extension on society. As far as I know, this topic has not deserved the attention it should have.

11.3.8 Summary of the Psychological Roots of Bureaucracy

In Sect. 2, the psychological enablers of bureaucracy, I have progressively developed the psychological foundations of bureaucracy by addressing a number of complementary perspectives from different psychological specialisms. I will summarize its main results here.

Step one involved the notion of habits. During habitual behavior it is the environment that drives behavior. Habits free the higher faculties of mind during routine tasks and have as such great benefits. If, however, the use of the higher faculties of mind is discouraged at work, the result is something of an automaton: a half-empty human shell performing routine tasks, but devoid of compassion, empathy, and understanding.

In the section called "Two modes of thought" I showed that (proto)typical bureaucratic behaviors fit perfectly with the coping mode of cognition (Table 11.3). The coping mode is characterized by intelligently solving self-contained problems, while the pervasive optimization mode is characterized by ever-improving one's understanding of the diversity of the world. This leads to two different attitudes toward "authority." For the coping mode some (typically external) authority must limit and constrain the world so that one's existing solution repertoire can be applied. In the pervasive optimization mode the individual internalizes the role of authority and becomes progressively more self-deciding and autonomous as understanding becomes more pervasive and deep.

To study the interplay between authority and understanding, I discussed the phenomenon of authoritarianism as defined by Stenner (2005). This led to the identification of two attitudes toward the world: the libertarian attitude in which the world is full of possibilities and an authoritarian attitude in which a lack of understanding of the world leads to anxiety and feelings of personal inadequacy of which libertarians are generally unaware. These feelings unify and motivate authoritarians to oppose all sources of complexity, unpredictability, novelty, and growth that complexify, confuse, and destabilize a predictable state of affairs. This drives encroaching bureaucracy.

The emergence of intolerance to (ill-understood) diversity has been summarized in the "Authoritarian Dynamic" in which "intolerance" scales with the level of ignorance (authoritarianism) and "threat-level" as a measure of the significance of not understanding one's world. Together these lead to a sense of personal inadequacy. The strength of the coping mode's "intelligent" ways of treating all problems as self-contained (such as the problems in an IQ-test) leads authoritarians to redefine or ignore reality until it fits with their current solution repertoire.

The digression into political psychology allowed the formulation of a "Bureaucratic Dynamic." The role of intolerance to diversity is apparent as the prominence of coercive formalization. Conform the Authoritarian Dynamic, this scales with the product of "institutional ignorance" and "worker cost of failure." Public shaming in case of failure is a measure of worker's inadequacy as a professional and the manager's inadequacy both as a leader and as a person. This leads, again according to the logic of the coping mode, to the worker accepting (or demanding) and the manager instilling more coercive formalization.

However, in this process workers lose their intrinsic motivation and become gradually more extrinsically motivated and the work becomes more and more habitual. The workers have shut down half of their intellectual potential and are stuck in a situation with minimal personal growth potential.

This then, finally, leads me to question whether the psychological effects on bureaucracy on bureaucrats might be an ignored, yet imminently important, psychological and societal problem. The third and last section of this chapter will not focus on this problem, but on how the societal goals of organizations can be protected from bureaucracy. Fortunately this may also protect workers from the (likely) adverse effects of bureaucracy.

11.4 Protecting the Societal Goals of an Organization

The subtitle of this chapter is "Protecting the societal goals of an organization." This section addresses this topic for nonprofit organizations because these have a social mission. In the introductory example the original societal role of the lost-and-found department was replaced by a new goal: procedural correctness, irrespective of the state of the world and the implications of following the procedure. As I have outlined in the previous section this is the result of the coping mode running amok in an organization conform the "Bureaucratic Dynamic." This entails that this section will firstly address a number of management paradigms in relation to their societal goals and bureaucracy, secondly it describes core features of non-bureaucratic or libertarian organizations, and thirdly it formulates safeguards against encroaching bureaucracy. This chapter ends with some reflections and conclusions.

11.4.1 Management Paradigms for Nonprofits

As summarized at the end of the previous section, the psychology of *not* understanding one's world and in particular ignorance about one's working environment and not overseeing the consequences (both adverse and beneficial) of one's activities leads to encroaching bureaucracy through the generation of more self-centered goals of complexity reduction that progressively erode the focus on the original societal goals of an organization. For nonprofit organizations, of which the mission aims at the achievement of social purposes rather than in generating revenues, this entails that they gradually delegitimize themselves through making their own stability and survival more important than their original *social raison d'être* (Moore 2000). Yet depending on the management paradigm, nonprofits run this risk to varying degrees.

Stoker (2006) describes and summarizes three management paradigms that neatly fit a progression from organizations based on coping mode rationality to the rationality of the pervasive optimization mode. I will describe all three.

11.4.1.1 Traditional Public Management

Traditional public management follows the typical Weberian early twentieth-century template (Weber 1978) in which bureaucracy delivers organizational effectiveness through four features that Stoker (2006) summarizes as follows:

> The first is the placing of officials in a defined *hierarchical* division of labor. The central feature of bureaucracy is the *systematic* division of labor whereby *complex* administrative *problems* are broken down into *manageable and repetitive tasks*, each the province of a particular office. A second core feature is that officials are employed within a full-time *career structure* in which *continuity* and *long-term advancement* is emphasized. Third, the work of bureaucrats is conducted according to *prescribed rules without arbitrariness or favoritism* and preferably with a *written record*. Finally, officials are appointed on merit. Indeed they become *experts by training for their function* and in turn *control access, information, and knowledge in their defined area of responsibility*.

The italic emphasis has been added to indicate concepts arising from the logic of the coping mode.

11.4.1.2 New Public Management

New public management arose as an alternative to the observation "that public service organizations tend to be neither efficient in terms of saving public money nor responsive to consumer needs" (Stoker 2006). As a result it did not arise from positive motivations, but as a solution to the problems of bureaucracy. Stoker describes this as follows.

> The solution is to fragment monopolistic public service structures and develop incentives and tools to influence the way that they operate. Key reforms include the introduction of a purchaser-provider divide within organizations and the development of performance targets

and incentives. The aim is to create an organizational home for the client or consumer voice within the system to challenge the power of producers. Consumers or their surrogate representatives, commissioners, would have the power to purchase the services they required and measure performance. The achievement of better performance would be aided by arms-length systems of inspection and regulation to check not only the spending of public money but also the delivery of public services against demanding targets.

New public management then seeks to dismantle the bureaucratic pillar of the Weberian model of traditional public administration. Out with the large, multipurpose hierarchical bureaucracies, new public management proclaims, and in with lean, flat, autonomous organizations drawn from the public and private sectors and steered by a tight central leadership corps

So the key improvement compared to the traditional model is the explicit role and importance of the societal function of the organization, but in this case limited to specific performance targets to be delivered by lean, flat, and autonomous organizations of which the performance indicators are still fully under control of some sort of central leadership that is supposed to represent public and private sector interests.

New public management is clearly aware of important drawbacks of Weberian bureaucracy, yet it is still guided by the logic of the coping mode. However, it has some indicators of the pervasive optimization mode such as greater worker autonomy (within the tight constraints of performance indicators) and some, albeit indirect, representation of consumers and other beneficiaries of the delivered services.

11.4.1.3   Public Value Management

Public value management (Moore 2000) is an emerging new management paradigm that is not so much a response to an existing paradigm but a formulation of the role of nonprofits in modern society (Stoker 2006). Public value management is succinctly formulated as a public value scorecard (Moore 2003) in which an organization should balance (1) the public value produced by the organization, (2) the legitimacy and support enjoyed by the organization, and (3) the operational capacity to achieve its results. In the public value scorecard the performance indicators are translated as measures of performance. Moore (2003) describes these as follows.

Some of the measures are those we associate with the public value produced by the organization—the extent to which it achieves its mission, the benefits it delivers to clients, and the social outcomes it achieves.

Others are associated with the legitimacy and support enjoyed by the organization—the extent to which "authorizers" and "contributors" beyond those who benefit from the organization remain willing to license and support the enterprise. These measures can, to some degree, be viewed as important because they indicate the capacity of the organization to stay in operation over time. But these measures can also be viewed to some degree as measures of value creation in themselves. This is particularly true if we recognize that some part of the value created by nonprofit organizations lies in the opportunities it affords to public spirited individuals to contribute to causes they care about, and another part lies in the capacity of the nonprofit organization to link contributing individuals to one another in a common effort to realized shared social goals.

Still others are associated with the operational capacity the nonprofit organization is relying on to achieve its results. This includes not only measures of organizational output, but also of organizational efficiency and fiscal integrity. It also includes measures of staff morale and capacity, and the quality of the working relationships with partner organizations. And, it includes the capacity of the organization to learn and adapt and innovate over time.

Where the Weberian bureaucracy follows the logic of the coping mode, these measures read as the pervasive optimization mode specified to the context of nonprofit organizations.

The public value scorecard was a response to an earlier score card: Kaplan's (Kaplan and Norton 1996) Balanced Scorecard, for the new public management paradigm through its focus on financial and efficiency measures. The Public Value Scorecard differs in a number of central aspects that are characteristic of the pervasive optimization mode. Moore (2000) formulates these differences as follows.

First, in the public value scorecard, the *ultimate value to be produced by the organization is measured in non-financial terms*. Financial performance is understood as the means to an end rather than an end itself. The end in itself is denominated in *non-financial social terms*. It also notes that the value produced by the organization may not lie simply in the satisfaction of individual clients. It can lie, instead, in *the achievement of desired aggregate social outcomes* of one kind or another.

Second, the public value scorecard focuses attention not just on those customers who pay for the service, or the clients who benefit from the organization's operations; it *focuses as well on the third party payers and other authorizers and legitimators* of the nonprofit enterprise. These people are important because it is they who provide some of the wherewithal that the organization needs to achieve its results, and *whose satisfaction lies in the achievement of aggregate social states as well as in the benefits delivered to individual clients.*

Third, the public value scorecard focuses attention on productive capabilities for achieving large social results outside the boundary of the organization itself. Other organizations existing in a particular industry are viewed *not as competitors* for market share, *but instead as partners and co-producers* whose efforts should be combined with the effort of the nonprofit enterprise to produce *the largest combined effect* on the problem that they are *jointly trying to solve*. In short, a nonprofit organization should measure its performance not only by its ability to increase its market share, but also by *its ability to strengthen the industry as a whole*.

Again I have added emphasis in italic to stress some the core concepts of this approach. The reader can combine these with the italic remarks in the right column of Table 11.3 that interprets the strong points of the pervasive optimization mode in organizational terms. It will be clear that this description matches the properties of the pervasive optimization mode.

Stoker (2006) concludes that public value management rests "on a fuller and rounder vision of humanity than does either traditional public administration or new public management." He identifies a key difference, namely the role of motivation, when he concludes:

Ultimately, the strength of public value management is seen to rest on its ability to point to a motivational force that does not solely rely on rules or incentives to drive public service practice and reform. People are, it suggests, motivated by their involvement in networks and partnerships, that is, their relationships with others formed in the context of mutual respect and shared learning. Building successful relationships is the key to networked governance and the core objective of the management needed to support it.

In terms of motivation, the public value management relies on the power of identified ("I find it important") and intrinsic ("I enjoy doing it") motivation. And this can be contrasted to the bureaucratic extreme in which the motivations are mainly extrinsic ("I have no choice") or introjected ("I'd better do it otherwise I face negative consequences"). The positive motivations are associated with (not only) experiential learning (Andringa et al. 2013; Vygotskiĭ 1978) and the growth of organization understanding, which is, conform the Bureaucratic Dynamic, the key protector against institutional ignorance.

11.4.1.4 Summarizing Key Properties of the Three Management Paradigms

Table 11.5 provides a summary, adapted from Stoker (2006), to which I have added six rows describing properties in terms of the strengths of the coping and the pervasive optimization mode.

11.4.2 Libertarian Organizations

Until now I have focused mostly on bureaucracy and the personal, organizational, and societal manifestations of the coping mode. But how does the pervasive optimization mode manifest itself in the context of organizations? Stoker (2006) notes that for public value management to work the motivation of workers needs to be "intrinsic" or "identified," which complies with the organic organization type identified by Adler and Borys (1996). Alternatively one might call organizations that realize this "Libertarian organizations" because the members are dominated by intrinsic and identified motivation, understand what they are doing, are autonomous self-deciders, and, in summary, rely mostly on the pervasive optimization mode of cognition.

Organizational structures that effectively contribute to an ever-changing real world of dangers and opportunities need flexible access to the available competence and enthusiasm. Libertarian organizations must therefore match the available competences and institutional understanding to whatever the world demands of the organization. Where authoritarian organizations realize (at best) proscribed results and predictable mediocrity, libertarian organizations can realize personal growth, institutional excellence, and with that effective contributions to the wider society. They are truly optimizing pervasively.

In libertarian organizations the formal hierarky is as important as in a bureaucracy, but its role is quite different: it has to manage autonomy instead of enforcing compliance. For superiors who know how to manage motivations and how to convey the role of the organization in society, this is not at all demanding because the very autonomy and commitment of a healthy libertarian organization ensures that it can deal with stability (where efficiency and organizational optimization are priorities) and change (where protection of quality and the realization of opportunities are prominent).

Table 11.5 Management paradigms. (Adapted from Stoker (2006), which is based on Kelly et al. (2002). The lowest 6 rows have been added as interpretations of the original table in terms of the discourse of this chapter.)

Key objectives	Traditional public administration	New public management	Public value management
Role of managers	Politically provided inputs; services monitored through bureaucratic oversight	Managing inputs and out- puts in a way that ensures economy and responsiveness to consumers	The overarching goal is achieving public value that in turn involves greater effectiveness in tackling the problems that the public most cares about; stretches from service delivery to system maintenance
Definition of public interest	To ensure that rules and appropriate procedures are followed	To help define and meet agreed performance targets	To play an active role in steering networks of deliberation and delivery and maintain the overall capacity of the system
Approach to public service ethos	By politicians or experts; little in the way of public input	Aggregation of individual preferences, in practice captured by senior politicians or managers supported by evidence about customer choice	Individual and public preferences produced through a complex process of interaction that involves deliberative reflection over inputs and opportunity costs
Preferred system for service delivery	Public sector has monopoly on service ethos, and all public bodies have it	Skeptical of public sector ethos (leads to inefficiency and empire building); favors customer service	No one sector has a monopoly on public service ethos; maintaining relationships through shared values is seen as essential
Contribution of the democratic process	Hierarchical department or self-regulating profession	Private sector or tightly defined arms-length public agency	Menu of alternatives selected pragmatically and a reflexive approach to intervention mechanisms to achieve outputs
Interpretation in terms of cognitive modes	Typical of the coping mode	Aware of limitations of the coping mode	Transition to the pervasive optimization mode
Role of worker	Skilled obedience	Responsible for assigned tasks and maintaining skills. Customer oriented	Co-responsible for societal role execution and the adaptation of the organization's changing societal demands

Table 11.5 (continued)

Key objectives	Traditional public administration	New public management	Public value management
Skills of worker	Precision in role execution (aimed at error prevention)	Deep understanding of tasks and role skills	Deep understanding of role skills and broad understanding of impact of own activities on public value
Motivations	Extrinsic and introjected	Extrinsic, introjected, identified, and intrinsic. Role of motivation not central	Identified and intrinsic. Essential role of motivation
Attitude to work	Obedient and unengaged	Professional development	Personal development

In healthy libertarian organizations everyone develops in terms of (institutional) understanding. This entails that eventually everyone can "play" a diversity of formal and functional roles. Basically the only real requirements for a healthy libertarian organization is that everyone in the organization has roles that are often intrinsically motivating, are generally satisfying, and that do not exceed understanding capacity. An organization that satisfies these conditions will remain in a pervasive optimization mode, even in the face of great organizational or societal challenges.

Table 11.6 provides a selection of properties of libertarian organizations formulated to promote the pervasive optimization mode in organizations.

11.4.3   The Dynamics of Encroaching Bureaucracy

We have probably all been members of a team that functioned amazingly well for a time, but then started to dysfunction and eventually disintegrated. This is because excellence is fragile: it not only delivers pervasive optimization, but also depends on it. In his analysis of how twentieth-century (American) bureaucrats took over education from teachers, Labaree (2011) describes how the "*pedagogically* progressive" vision of education—child-centered, inquiry based, and personally engaging—is a fragile hot-house flower because it depends on broadly realized favorable conditions (i.e., successful pervasive optimization). In contrast, the "*administrative* progressive" vision of education is a weed because it grows under difficult conditions such as erratic funding, poorly prepared teachers, high turnover, dated textbooks, etc. It is robust "because its primary goal is to be useful in the narrowest sense of the term: It aims for survival rather than beauty."

Labaree accounts a "battle" between the philosopher John Dewey and educational reformer David Snedden. As proponent of the pedagogically progressive vision, John Dewey formulated a complex and nuanced narrative of education as a means to make "workers the masters of their own industrial fate." In contrast, David Snedden as the champion of the administrative progressive approach, saw education as vocational

Table 11.6 Properties of libertarian organizations. Intended to stimulate the pervasive optimization mode of cognition

Topic	Property
Vision	A "lived" vision of the goals and roles of the organization is widely shared. It allows everyone in the organization to contribute to its realization via well-formulated procedures and competent improvisation alike
	Approach the organization holistically: optimize everything in context of the whole; prevent at all cost strict compartmentalization of responsibilities and information, because specialism and other forms of close-mindedness are seeds of stagnation and corruption
Motivation	Promote and ensure a predominance of intrinsic and identified motivations
	Allow people to be happy or enthusiastic about what they have done well and allow them to repair and learn from mistakes
Competences	Focus on pervasive competence development
	Promote a deep insight in the societal effects of individual work and the organization as a whole
	Stimulate overlapping competences to ensure organizational redundancy, optimization opportunities, more timely services, and enhanced work satisfaction
	Distribute responsibilities according to available competences, interests, ambitions, and enthusiasm. Ignore hierarchical considerations
	Be alert of indications of low competence, stagnated development, insensitivity to adverse consequences of (in)action, low inherent motivation, low commitment to the organization and the services it should provide (e.g., 9-to-5 mentality), and indicators of lack of enthusiasm
Autonomy	The task of management is to manage worker autonomy
	Competent autonomy of workers is success indicator
	Put real responsibility in *every* job description and allow a diversification or responsibilities as competence grows
	Stimulate expertise, but prevent specialization
Information	Develop an open information infrastructure
	Allow for ample opportunities for unstructured information sharing
	The Scottish proverb "When the heart is full the tongue will speak" will ensure that really important information will be shared

training in preparation for a life of servitude. As a narrow-minded authoritarian, he understood the world in dualisms and countered nuanced arguments by ignoring them and by repeating reasonable sounding dogma. Labaree (2011) concludes:

> Therefore, the administrative progressive movement was able to become firmly established and positioned for growth because of Snedden's flame throwing. Put another way, a useful idiot, who says things that resonate with the emerging ideas of his era and helps clear the ideological way for the rhetorical reframing of a major institution, can have vastly more influence than a great thinker, who makes a nuanced and prescient argument that is out of tune with his times and too complex to fit on a battle standard.

This is how authoritarians gain control. Not by the quality of argument, but by focusing the discussion, by subtly reinterpreting the goals of an organization in a less rich manner, by ignoring nuances or replacing them by similar sounding oppositions, and by gradually marginalizing and deriding opposition. When authoritarians have gained control they start simplifying, harmonizing, focusing, and reorganizing the organization according to Billington's (1980) observations on revolutions. The rhetoric is a convenient tool. But the real objective, albeit rarely acknowledged, is a simpler, more controlled, and better understood world. Authoritarians bring the complexity of the world, or in this case national education, down to *their* level of understanding of it.

This process matches the Bureaucratic Dynamic that we have formulated.

Incentive for coercive formalization
= Bureaucracy incentive = Institutional ignorance × Worker cost of failure

The true drivers of the bureaucratization process are feelings of personal inadequacy among workers. In the case of educators like Snedden, these feelings arose from being lost in the complex world of education in which responsibilities are unclear and the means to realize them even more. The resulting personal anxiety motivates workers to reestablish their sense of adequacy whenever possible: at work they are now in an authoritarian mode. Their colleagues who *do* understand their responsibilities and know how to realize them feel no anxiety. They are and remain in a libertarian mode and are generally unaware of the severity of the anxiety in their (now) authoritarian colleagues.

The authoritarians gravitate toward each other and start to formulate and promote a simplified understanding of the roles and aims of the organization. The libertarian opposition against this simplified understanding is of course based on a fuller understanding of the roles and aims of the organization. But these arguments have no impact on the authoritarians because, in their eyes, the arguments are addressing irrelevancies with no relation of their new, simplified, and more tangible understanding of the organization's scope and aims. While the libertarians waste their time and energy with progressively more nuanced arguments, the authoritarians find each other and may at some point take control over the organization.

When they do, they make their level of "institutional ignorance" the norm. And because they are in the coping mode they will realize this norm according to the logic of the coping mode (Table 11.3, left side). This will, according to the Bureaucratic Dynamic, lead to the introduction of more "coercive formalization" and a shift from being as professional as possible to producing tangible measureable outcomes and preventing errors in realizing these. Preventing worker failure and publicly displayed inadequacy becomes more important than professional success.

At the same time the libertarians in the organization discover that many of the things they used to do—and which still make sense given the logic of the pervasive optimization mode—are no longer officially endorsed because they are incompatible with the new simplified norm. In fact the old way of working has become a liability if it hinders the realization of the new, more tangible, performance measures. What used to be the highest indicators of professionalism, are now costly ways to fail as a worker. The new professionalism is rule compliance and not organizational excellence.

Much of what the libertarian worker motivated, is no longer officially or practically part of the organization's core business. The moment the new management initiates a reorganization, of course according to the logic of the coping mode, the libertarians are faced with a dilemma: leave with professional dignity or succumb to the new normal and deskill and comply. Whatever the libertarian chooses, the result is the same: increased institutional ignorance.

11.4.4 Preventing Bureaucracy

I had the doubtful honor to witness such a process in my university. Only two individuals at key positions in the hierarchy drove the process. Fortunately, it was followed by repair measures when the whole process overshot and the organizational costs became too high. This happened after some highly skilled and motivated colleagues had left and others were on sick-leave. At that point workers simply refused to take further responsibility and the department almost stopped functioning. This paper is informed by witnessing this process. Without understanding bureaucracy as well as I do now, the unfolding process was very difficult to counter. Yet it is possible to devise effective protective measures. In Table 11.7 I have formulated a number of "Red Flags" as indicators of encroaching bureaucracy that may be helpful to stop a bureaucratization process before it becomes self-reinforcing.

According to the Bureaucratic Dynamic, the best protection against bureaucratization is preventing worker (including management) ignorance and promoting worker professionalism instead of preventing worker error. A truly healthy and resilient organization maintains a sufficient level of institutional understanding and worker autonomy so that no one feels inadequate and every one contributes to the realization of the organizations *full* societal goals and not only to a single or a few "key performance objectives." Yet as the analysis of the three management paradigms shows, institutional understanding improves over time. For example, the new public value management paradigm starts from the logic of the pervasive optimization mode instead of the logic of the coping mode as would have been the natural Weberian option a century ago.

A future informed public might not accept the products of a bureaucratic organization because it demonstrates, for all to witness, that its management and workers do not quite understand what they are doing. In addition, if my expectation is substantiated that bureaucracy leads to high personal and societal costs for bureaucrats, future societies might simply not accept bureaucracy because it signifies a pathological state of affairs of which the immediate costs are apparent as reduced quality and efficiency, while the full personal and societal costs are deferred to future generations. In fact sustainability arguments might drive this.

Table 11.7 Red flags. Early indicators disrupting the pervasive optimization mode

	Red Flags
Mission	The absence of a shared, living vision about the organization's goals in a larger societal context
	The advance of a simplified and more focused interpretation of the organizations mission, typically as a limited number of "key performance objectives"
Leaders	Leaders insensitive to reasoned and nuanced arguments by competent individuals at any position in the organization
	Leaders only sensitive to arguments related to goal achievement or procedure. Realizable goals are preferred over desirable goals
	Leaders preferring obedience over autonomy and who curtail work-floor autonomy
	Bureaucrats promoted to key positions
Competences	Neglect of work-floor competences
	Demotivation of highly autonomous, competent and committed co-workers
	Gradual deterioration of quality of the working environment and worker motivation
	The most competent and committed coworkers leave
	Standardization at the cost of curtailing of essential/useful diversity
Uniformization	Strong focus on formalities while neglecting (or indefinitely) postponing content
	Compartmentalization of information and plans
	Mediocracy facilitated

11.4.5 Conclusion and Reflection

In some sense this chapter is about the difference between intelligence and understanding as manifestations of, respectively, the coping and the pervasive optimization mode of cognition. Understanding proofs itself as the ability to set up, in a statistical sense, the conditions for an unproblematic future and an interesting and fulfilling life. Failure to do so leads to problematic situations to be solved intelligently. While understanding shines in an open world, intelligence assumes a closed world of self-contained problems to be addressed with an existing solution repertoire. Anything in the way of the solution will be ignored or coercively made irrelevant. While understanding manifests itself through fostering empathic relations, intelligence, as a last line of defense, is self-protective, impersonal, and ruthless.

Without understanding the consequences of one's activities, work is bureaucratic. Since no one is bureaucratic while not at work and especially not among friends, it is the work environment that activates bureaucratic behavior. In this chapter, I have shown that bureaucracy in all it facets can be understood from basic psychology. Bureaucratic behavior is habitual or intelligent rule following. The bureaucrat obediently performs activities that it understands superficially and values marginally, but that it does not endorse or feels responsible for. As such the bureaucrat appears and acts as a dehumanized automaton. It is a pitiful state of being.

The psychological enabler of bureaucracy is a sense of personal inadequacy among workers resulting from not understanding their work and its consequences. This activates the coping mode of cognition and with that an urge to bring the complexity of the working environment down to more manageable levels through promoting coercive formalization. This process can be summarized as the Bureaucratic Dynamic, which states that the prevalence of coercive formalization depends on the combination of "Institutional Ignorance" and "Worker cost of failure."

Fortunately, in the last century society became gradually more aware of the effects and dangers of bureaucracy. New public management arose as a response to curtail the adverse effects of Weberian bureaucracy as defining aspect of traditional public management. Because it is still based on the coping mode of cognition it will not become a bureaucracy-free alternative. New value management however arises from the logic of the pervasive optimization mode and it *has* the potential to achieve organizational excellence without bureaucracy.

Anti-bureaucratic measures should not only focus on the reduction of the number of rules and regulations because this still follows the logic of the coping mode. It should instead focus on motivating workers to understand their professional roles and to learn to oversee the impact of their activities; not only on the organization, but also on the wider society. This understanding will lead to a reevaluation of the role of formalization and will erode the need for coercive formalization. The organization will no longer focus on preventing errors, but on optimizing the multifaceted societal roles of the organization in ways that are experienced as important, worthwhile, and intrinsically motivating for its workers. Yet organizations that function like this are somewhat fragile and may be eroded from the inside by a fraction of workers that still have an impoverished understanding of the organization and its societal roles. It will be important to develop safeguards to prevent this.

Current anti-bureaucratic awareness stems from the observation that bureaucratic organizations are neither efficient in terms of saving public money nor responsive to consumer needs. Future research may however proof important adverse effects of bureaucracy on bureaucrats and on society as a whole. This may expose bureaucracy for what I think it is: a pathological state of human organization, with equally serious adverse consequences for the bureaucrat and society as a whole.

In the course of writing this chapter I was struck by the consistency and complementarity of disparate scientific results. Science produces wonderful observations and generates deep insights, but it has difficulty in combining these if they originate from different domains. The transdisciplinary framework presented in this chapter allowed far reaching conclusions through the combination of a number of these observations and insights.

For example the work of Adler and Borys (1996) and especially their conceptualization of bureaucracy, in terms of the degree and type of formalization (enabling or coercive), gained theoretical support. The stability of bureaucracies can be explained through the link between bureaucracy and habitual behavior, since bureaucrats feel a self-imposed responsibility to maintain the condition in which their habitual functioning is guaranteed. Furthermore, McGilchrist's (2010) description of the way the two brain hemispheres understand the world and our conceptualization of the pervasive optimization mode and the coping mode (Andringa et al. 2013), seems to predict how non-bureaucratic and bureaucratic organizations micromanage. This was a serendipitous finding that I consider highly relevant. In addition Stenner's (2005) conceptualization of authoritarianism—as having a problem with a complex world (and not with complex thinking)—helped to understand the psychological motivators of bureaucracy in terms of feelings of personal inadequacy. Finally, Billington's (1980) observations about revolutions always aiming for simplicity, helped to understand why well-functioning non-bureaucratic organizations might be eroded from the inside and turn into a bureaucracy.

All in all, it seems to me that bureaucracy is not just a phenomenon that occurs in professional organizations. Instead it is just one of many manifestations of the interplay between understanding and intelligence that are important for every aspect of live.

Appendix

Some core properties of the bureaucratic syndrome (authoritarian dominated) and the non-bureaucratic syndrome (libertarian dominated organizations).

Topic	Bureaucratic syndrome	Non-bureaucratic syndrome
Key properties		
Organizational goals	Societal goals of the organization are only adhered in name, but neither understood nor clearly implemented	Development of a broadly shared vision about the societal reason d'être of the organization and the way to realize it
Overall strategy	Stimulating sameness and oneness through standardization and obedience	Continual skilled improvisation on the basis of a shared vision and well-chosen procedures
Competence	Ignoring, discouraging, and demoralizing competent "subordinates." Deskilling	Relying on and fostering all proven and budding competencies in the organization
Autonomy	Subordinate autonomy is not an option. Obedience is more important than competence	Autonomy and competence development of subordinates expected
Content	Complete disregard of content while favoring form	Content is leading, form a means
Organizational development	Structures and procedures adapt to the lowest competence level	Everyone is expected to learn and grow towards autonomous roles in organization

Topic	Bureaucratic syndrome	Non-bureaucratic syndrome
Main conflicts		
Stability versus development	Stability and other forms of high predictability leading. This defines the organization	The workers in the organization are constantly developing their skills in order to improve all aspects of the societal role of the organization (i.e., quality and efficiency)
Form versus optimization	Obsessed with form and formalisms. Centralized optimization of standardized and narrowly defined responsibilities	Actively eliciting creative and decentralized optimization of organizational goals. Disregard of form when counter-productive
Standardization versus diversity	Obsession with standardization and curtailing diversity, at the cost of quality if quality entails diversity	Concerned with the overall optimization of all work processes in context, of which both standardization and increasing diversity are options
Error versus learning	Obsessed with preventing errors and mistakes. The organization redefines itself to produce what it can, not what it should; "race to the bottom"	Error and correction after error part of continual creative optimization of work processes
Short versus long term	Exclusively short-term (form) oriented, neither care for nor understanding of mid of long term goals. However, what is short- or mid-terms depends on the role in the organization	Optimization, by all workers. on all time-scales and all dimensions of success
Structural properties		
Role of hierarchy	Hierarchy formalized and inflexible, based on assumed (but never fully checked) competence of superiors	Hierarchy task dependent, and therefore flexible and competence-based
Perception of authorities	Authorities never fundamentally questioned	Incompetent authorities not accepted, but coached or dismissed
Locus of control	Formation of stable authoritarian cliques, who take control over the institutional change processes to prevent further complexity	Loosely and varyingly linked libertarians at control positions.
Measures of success	Performance measures redefined to what is delivered	Performance measure based on what should be delivered (given reason d'être)
Accountability	Suppression of all forms of accountability at the higher levels and prevention of errors and retribution in case of error at the lower levels	Accountability part of normal institutional learning and competence building

Topic	Bureaucratic syndrome	Non-bureaucratic syndrome
Emotions		
Overall role	Rationality and "objectivity" leading. Emotions treated as irrelevant source of variation, to be suppressed	Central role of positive emotions (compassion, enthusiasm, interest) as key motivators; prominent negative emotions indicative of organizational failure
Emotion of workers	Motivating emotion negative: activities guided by the fear of losing control or being shamed publically	Motivating emotion positive: activities aimed at realizing shared benefits including personal development
Emotions of co-workers	Utter disregard of the feelings and emotional wellbeing of coworkers	Strong focus on the creation of optimal working condition in which coworkers feel optimally motivated to give their best

References

Adler PS, Borys B (1996) Two types of bureaucracy: Enabling and coercive. Adm Sci Q 41(1):61–89

Andringa TC, Lanser JJ (2013) How pleasant sounds promote and annoying sounds impede health: a cognitive approach. Int J Environ Res Public Health 10(4):1439–1461. doi:10.3390/ijerph10041439

Andringa TC, van den bosch KA, Vlaskamp C (2013) Learning autonomy in two or three steps: linking open-ended development, authority, and agency to motivation. Front Psychol 18. doi:10.3389/fpsyg.2013.00766

Andringa TC, van den Bosch KA, Wijermans F (2015) Cognition from life: The two modes of cognition that underlie moral behavior. Frontiers in Theoretical and Philosophical Psychology (Accepted)

Bargh JA (2010). Bypassing the will: towards demystifying the nonconscious control of social behavior. In: Hassin R, Uleman J, Bargh J (Eds) The new unconscious. Oxford University Press, New York, pp 37–58

Billington JH (1980) Fire in the minds of men. Basic Books, New York

Deci E, Ryan RM (1987) The support of autonomy and the control of behavior. J Pers Soc Psychol 53(6):1024–1037

Fredrickson BL, Branigan C (2005) Positive emotions broaden the scope of attention and thoughtâŁłaction repertoires. Cognit Emot 19(3):313–332. doi:10.1080/02699930441000238

Frijda N (1986) The emotions. Cambridge University Press, Cambridge

Gilligan J (1997) Violence: reflections on a national epidemic. Vintage Books, New York

Inbar Y, Pizarro DA, Bloom P (2009) Conservatives are more easily disgusted than liberals. Cognit Emot 23(4):714–725. doi:10.1080/02699930802110007

James W, McDermott JJ (1978) The writings of William James: A comprehensive edition, including an annotated bibliography updated through 1977. University of Chicago Press, Chicago

Kaplan RS, Norton DP (1996) Using the balanced scorecard as a strategic management system. Retrieved from https://noppa.tkk.fi/noppa/kurssi/tu-22.1500/luennot/TU-22_1500_pre-reading_1_kaplan_norton_1996_.pdf

Kelly G, Mulgan G, Muers S (2002) Creating public value. London. Retrieved from http://webarchive.nationalarchives.gov.uk/20100416132449/http:/www.cabinetoffice.gov.uk/media/cabinetoffice/strategy/assets/public_value2.pdf. Accessed 14 March 2015

Labaree D (2011) How Dewey lost: The victory of David Snedden and social efficiency in the reform of American education. In: Tröhler D, Schlag T, Ostervalder F (Eds) Pragmatism and modernities. Sense Publishers, Rotterdam

Max-Neef MA (2005) Foundations of transdisciplinarity. Ecol Econ 53(1):5–16. doi:10.1016/j.ecolecon.2005.01.014

McGilchrist I (2010) The master and his emissary: the divided brain and the making of the Western world. Yale University Press, New Haven

Moore MH (2000) Managing for value: organizational strategy in for-profit, nonprofit, and governmental organizations 29(suppl 1):183–208. doi:10.1177/089976400773746391

Moore MH (2003) The public value scorecard: a rejoinder and an alternative to "strategic performance measurement and management in non-profit organizations" by Robert Kaplan, 23. doi:10.2139/ssrn.402880

Nguyen L (2007) The question of survival: The death of desire and the weight of life. Am J Psychoanal 67:53–67

Ouellette JA, Wood W (2003) Habit and intention in everyday life: the multiple processes by which past behavior predicts future behavior. Psychol Bull 124(1): 54–74

Ryan RM, Connell JP (1989) Perceived locus of causality and internalization: Examining reasons for acting in two domains. J Pers Psychol 57(5):749–761. doi:10.1037/0022-3514.57.5.749

Stenner K (2005) The authoritarian dynamic (1 edn). Cambridge University Press, New York

Stenner K (2009a) Three kinds of "conservatism". Psychol Inq 20(2):142–159. doi:10.1080/10478400903028615

Stenner K (2009b) "Conservatism," context-dependence, and cognitive incapacity. Psychol Inq 20(2):189–195

Stoker G (2006) Public value management a new narrative for networked governance? Am Rev Public Adm 36(1):41–57. doi:10.1177/0275074005282583

Vygotskiĭ LLS (1978) Mind in society: The development of higher psychological processes. In: Cole M, John-Steiner V, Scribner S, Souberman E (Eds) Harvard University Press, London

Weber M (1978) Economy and society. University of California Press, Berkeley

Wilkinson R (2006) Why is violence more common where inequality is greater? Ann N Y Acad Sci 1036(1):1–12. doi:10.1196/annals.1330.001

Wilkinson R, Pickett K (2009) The spirit level: why more equal societies almost always do better. Health.Gov.Au

Wood W, Neal D (2009) The habitual consumer. J Consum Psychol 19(4):579–592. doi:10.1016/j.jcps.2009.08.003

Zillmer EA, Harrower M, Ritzler BA, Archer RP (2013) The quest for the Nazi personality. Routledge, Hillsdale, New Jersey

Chapter 12
Active and Passive Crowdsourcing in Government

Euripidis Loukis and Yannis Charalabidis

Abstract Crowdsourcing ideas have been developed and initially applied in the private sector, first in the creative and design industries, and subsequently in many other industries, aiming to exploit the 'collective wisdom' in order to perform difficult problem solving and design activities. It was much later that government agencies started experimenting with crowdsourcing, aiming to collect from citizens information, knowledge, opinions and ideas concerning difficult social problems, and important public policies they were designing for addressing them. Therefore, it is necessary to develop approaches, and knowledge in general concerning the efficient and effective application of crowdsourcing ideas in government, taking into account its special needs and specificities. This chapter contributes to filling this research gap, by presenting two novel approaches in this direction, which have been developed through extensive previous relevant research of the authors: a first one for 'active crowdsourcing', and a second one for 'passive crowdsourcing' by government agencies. Both of them are based on innovative ways of using the recently emerged and highly popular Web 2.0 social media in a highly automated manner through their application programming interfaces (API). For each of these approaches, the basic idea is initially described, followed by the architecture of the required information and communications technology (ICT) infrastructure, and finally a process model for its practical application.

12.1 Introduction

The capability of a large network of people, termed as 'crowd', networked through web technologies, to perform difficult problem solving and design activities, which were previously performed exclusively by professionals, has been initially recognized by private sector management researchers and practitioners, leading to the development of crowdsourcing (Brabham 2008; Howe 2008). Crowdsourcing ideas

E. Loukis (✉) · Y. Charalabidis
University of the Aegean, Samos, Greece
e-mail: eloukis@aegean.gr

Y. Charalabidis
e-mail: yannisx@aegean.gr

© Springer International Publishing Switzerland 2015   261
M. Janssen et al. (eds.), *Policy Practice and Digital Science,*
Public Administration and Information Technology 10, DOI 10.1007/978-3-319-12784-2_12

have been initially applied in the private sector, first in the creative and design industries, and subsequently in many other industries, aiming to exploit the 'collective wisdom' (Surowiecki 2004) in order to perform difficult problem solving and design activities. This has resulted in the development of a considerable body of knowledge on how crowdsourcing can be efficiently and effectively performed in the private sector (comprehensive reviews are provided by Rouse 2010; Hetmank 2013; Pedersen et al. 2013; Tarrell et al. 2013). It was much later that government agencies started experimenting with crowdsourcing, aiming to collect from citizens information, knowledge, opinions and ideas concerning difficult problems they were facing, and important public policies they were designing, through some first 'citizensourcing' initiatives (Hilgers and Ihl 2010; Nam 2012). So there is still limited knowledge on how crowdsourcing can be efficiently and effectively performed in the special context of the public sector, much less than in the private sector. Therefore, extensive research is required for the development of approaches and methodologies for the efficient and effective application of crowdsourcing ideas in government for supporting problem solving and policy making, taking into account its special needs and specificities. This is quite important, taking into account that social problems have become highly complex and 'wicked', with multiple and heterogeneous stakeholders having different problem views, values and objectives (Rittel and Weber 1973; Kunzand Rittel 1979); previous research has concluded that information and communications technology (ICT) can be very useful for gaining a better understanding of the main elements of such problems (e.g. issues, alternatives, advantages and disadvantages perceived by various stakeholder groups; Conklin and Begeman 1989; Conklin 2003; Loukis and Wimmer 2012).

This chapter contributes to filling this research gap, by presenting two approaches in this direction, which have been developed through extensive previous relevant research of the authors: a first approach for 'active crowdsourcing' (in which government has an active role, posing a particular social problem or public policy direction, and soliciting relevant information, knowledge, opinions and ideas from citizens), and a second one for 'passive crowdsourcing' (in which government has a more passive role, collecting and analyzing content on a specific topic or public policy that has been freely generated by citizens in various sources, which is then subjected to sophisticated processing). Both of them are based on innovative ways of using the recently emerged and highly popular Web 2.0 social media in a highly automated manner through their application programming interfaces (API) (which are libraries provided by all social media, including specifications for routines, data structures, object classes, and variables, in order to access parts of their functionalities and incorporate them in other applications).

In particular, the first of them is based on a central ICT platform, which can publish various types of discussion stimulating content concerning a social problem or a public policy under formulation to multiple social media simultaneously, and also collect from them data on citizens' interactions with this content (e.g. views, ratings, votes, comments, etc.), both using the API of the utilized social media. Finally, these interaction data undergo various types of advanced processing (e.g. calculation of analytics, opinion mining, and simulation modelling) in this central system, in order to exploit them to support drawing conclusions from them. This approach has been developed mainly as part of the research project PADGETS ('Policy Gadgets Mashing Underlying Group Knowledge in Web 2.0 Media'—www.padgets.eu), which has been partially funded by the European Commission.

The second passive crowdsourcing approach is based on a different type of central ICT platform, which can automatically search in numerous predefined Web 2.0 sources (e.g. blogs and microblogs, news sharing sites, online forums, etc.), using their API, for content on a domain of government activity or a public policy under formulation, which has been created by citizens freely, without any initiation, stimulation or moderation through government postings. Through advanced processing and analysis of this content in the above platform (using opinion and argument extraction, sentiment analysis and argument summarization techniques), conclusions can be drawn concerning the needs, issues, opinions, proposals and arguments of citizens on this domain of government activity or public policy under formulation. This approach is developed as part of the research project NOMAD ('Policy Formulation and Validation through Non-moderated Crowdsourcing'—www.nomad-project.eu/), which is partially funded by the European Commission.

The two approaches presented in this chapter combine elements from management sciences (concerning crowdsourcing approaches), political sciences (concerning wicked social problems) and technological sciences (concerning social media capabilities and API), in order to support problem solving and policy-making activities of government agencies. We expect that the findings of this research will be interesting and useful to both researchers and practitioners of these three disciplines who are dealing with the public sector. It should be noted that governments have been traditionally collecting content created by various social actors about domains of government activity, social problems or public policies under formulation using various traditional (offline) practices (e.g. collecting relevant extracts from newspapers); furthermore, they actively solicited relevant opinions and ideas from citizens (through various offline and online citizens' consultation channels). However, the proposed approaches allow government agencies to perform such activities more extensively and intensively at a lower cost, reaching easily wider and more diverse and geographically dispersed groups of citizens' (e.g. collecting relevant content not only from a small number of top newspapers but also from numerous bigger or smaller newspapers, blogs, Facebook accounts, etc.; also, interacting actively with many more citizens than the few ones participating in government consultations),so that they can gradually achieve mature levels of crowdsourcing. Furthermore, the proposed approaches allow overcoming the usual 'information overload' problems of the traditional practices, as they include sophisticated processing of the collected content that extracts the main points of it.

This chapter is organized in seven sections. In 'Background' our background is presented, and then in 'Research Method' the research methodology is outlined. Next, the two proposed approaches for passive and active crowdsourcing by government agencies are described in 'An Active Crowdsourcing Approach' and 'A Passive Crowdsourcing Approach', respectively. A comparison of them, also with the 'classical' is presented in 'Comparisons', while in the final 'Conclusion' our conclusions are summarized.

12.2 Background

12.2.1 Crowdsourcing

The great potential of the 'collective intelligence', defined as a 'form of universally distributed intelligence, constantly enhanced, coordinated in real time, and resulting in the effective mobilization of skills', (Levy 1997), to contribute to difficult problem solving and design activities has lead to the emergence of crowdsourcing and its adoption, initially in the private sector, and subsequently (still experimentally) in the public sector as well. Crowdsourcing is defined as 'the act of a company or institution taking a function once performed by employees and outsourcing it to an undefined (and generally large) network of people in the form of an open call' (Howe 2006), or as 'a new web-based business model that harnesses the creative solutions of a distributed network of individuals', in order to exploit 'collective wisdom' and mine fresh ideas from large numbers of individuals (Brabham 2008). While the use of the collective intelligence of a large group of people as a help for solving difficult problems is an approach that has been used for long time (Surowiecki 2004; Howe 2008), it is only recently that crowdsourcing started being widely adopted as a means of obtaining external expertise, accessing the collective wisdom and creativities resident in the virtual crowd. The capabilities provided by the development and wide dissemination of ICT seem to have played an important role for this, as they allow the efficient participation and interaction of numerous and geographically dispersed individuals, and also the analysis of their contributions (Geiger 2012; Zhao and Zhu 2012; Majchrzak and Malhotra 2013). Brabham (2008), based on the analysis of several cases of crowd wisdom at work, which resulted in successful solutions emerging from a large body of solvers, concludes that 'under the right circumstances, groups are remarkably intelligent, and are often smarter than the smartest people in them', due to the diversity of opinion, independence, decentralization and aggregation that characterize such a crowd.

Crowdsourcing started being applied initially in the creative and design industries, and then it expanded into other private sector industries, for solving both mundane and highly complex tasks. It gradually becomes a useful method for attracting an interested and motivated group of individuals, which can provide solutions superior in quality and quantity to those produced by highly knowledgeable professionals. Such a crowd can solve scientific problems that big corporate R&D groups cannot solve, outperform in-house experienced geophysicists of mining companies, design original t-shirts resulting in very high sales, and produce highly successful commercials and fresh stock photography against a strong competition from professional firms (Surowiecki 2004; Howe 2006, 2008; Brabham 2008, 2012). This can result in a paradigm shift and new design and problem solving practices in many industries.

For these reasons there has been significant research interest on crowdsourcing, which has resulted in a considerable body of knowledge on how crowdsourcing can be efficiently and effectively performed in the private sector; reviews of this literature are provided by Rouse (2010), Hetmank (2013), Pedersen et al. (2013) and Tarrell et al. (2013). Initially this research focused on analyzing successful cases, while later it started generalizing, based on the experience of multiple cases, in order to identify patterns and trends in this area and also to develop effective crowdsourcing practices. A typical example in this direction is the study by Brabham (2012), which, based on the analysis of several case studies, identifies four dominant crowdsourcing approaches: (i) the knowledge discovery and management approach (= an organization tasks crowd with finding and reporting information and knowledge on a particular topic), (ii) the broadcast search approach (= an organization tries to find somebody who has experience with solving a rather narrow and rare empirical problem), (iii) the peer-vetted creative production approach (= an organization tasks crowd with creating and selecting creative ideas), and (iv) the distributed human intelligence tasking (= an organization tasks crowd with analyzing large amounts of information). Hetmank (2013), based on a review of crowdsourcing literature, identifies a basic process model of it, which consists of ten activities: define task, set time period, state reward, recruit participants, assign tasks, accept crowd contributions, combine submissions, select solution, evaluate submissions and finally grant rewards. Also, he identifies a basic pattern with respect to the structure of crowdsourcing Information System (IS), which includes four main components that perform user management (providing capabilities for user registration, user evaluation, user group formation and coordination), task management (providing capabilities for task design and assignment), contribution management (providing capabilities for contributions evaluation and selection) and workflow management (providing capabilities for defining and managing workflows), respectively. Furthermore, there are some studies that attempt to generalize the experience gained from successful applications of crowdsourcing ideas in order to develop effective practices for motivating individuals to participate (Brabham 2009; Stewart et al. 2009).

Rouse (2010), based on a review of relevant literature, distinguishes between two types of crowdsourcing with respect to participants' motivation: (i) individualistic (aiming to provide benefits to specific persons and firms), (ii) community oriented (aiming to benefit a community of some kind, through ideas and proposals), and (iii) mixed (combinations of the above). Furthermore, she proceeds with identifying seven more detailed types of participant motivations: learning, direct compensation, self-marketing, social status, instrumental motivation (= motivation to solve a personal or firm problem, or to address a personal/firm need), altruism (= motivation to help the community without personal benefit) and token compensation (= earning a small monetary prize or gift). Also, the same publication concludes that many of the benefits of crowdsourcing described in the literature are similar to those of the 'mainstream' outsourcing: cost savings, contracts and payments that are outcome based (rather than paid 'per hour'), and access to capabilities not held in-house; an additional benefit of crowdsourcing, which is not provided by outsourcing, is the capacity to exploit knowledge and skills of volunteers who might not, otherwise, contribute. However, at the same time it is emphasized that—as with all outsourcing—the decision to crowdsource should only be made after considering all the production, coordination and transaction costs, and the potential risks. Many of the highly publicized crowdsourcing successes have been achieved by organizations with substantial project management and new product/services development systems and capabilities, which lead to low levels of crowdsourcing coordination and transaction costs.

12.2.2   Public Sector Application

Crowdsourcing ideas, as mentioned above, have been initially developed and applied in the private sector, however later some government agencies started experimenting with them. Highly influential for this have been central top-down initiatives in several countries, such as the 'Open Government Directive' in the USA (Executive Office of the President 2009). It defines transparency, participation and collaboration as the main pillars of open government:

a. Transparency promotes accountability by providing the public with information about what the government is doing.
b. Participation allows members of the public to contribute ideas and expertise so that their government can benefit from information and knowledge that is widely dispersed in society, in order to design better policies.
c. Collaboration improves the effectiveness of government by encouraging partnerships and cooperation within the federal government, across levels of government, and between the government and private institutions.

Crowdsourcing can be quite valuable for promoting and developing two of these three main pillars of open government: participation and collaboration. This has lead government organizations, initially, in the USA and later in other countries as well, to proceed to some first crowdsourcing initiatives, having various forms of 'citizensourcing' for collecting information on citizens' needs and for the solution of difficult problems. These initiatives motivated some first research in this area, which aims to analyze these initiatives in order to learn from them, and to identify common patterns and trends (Lukensmeyer and Torres 2008; Hilgers and Ihl 2010; Nam 2012). Lukensmeyer and Torres (2008) conclude that citizen sourcing may become a new source of policy advice, enabling policy makers to bring together divergent ideas that would not come from traditional sources of policy advice; furthermore, it may change the government's perspective on the public from an understanding of citizens as 'users and choosers' of government programs and services to 'makers and shapers' of policies and decisions. Hilgers and Ihl (2010) developed a high-level framework for the application of citizen sourcing by government agencies, which consists of three tiers:

1. Citizen ideation and innovation: this first tier focuses on the exploitation of the general potential of knowledge and creativity within the citizenry to enhance the quality of government decisions and policies, through various methods, such as consultations and idea and innovation contests.
2. Collaborative administration: the second tier explicitly addresses the integration of citizens for enhancing existing public administrative processes.
3. Collaborative democracy: this tier includes new ways of collaboration to improve and expand public participation within the policy process, including the incorporation of public values into decisions, improving the quality of decisions, building trust in institutions and educating citizens.

Nam (2012), based on the study of citizen-sourcing initiatives in the USA, developed a framework for the description and analysis of such initiatives, which consists of three dimensions: purpose (it can be for image making, information creation, service co-production, problem solving and policy-making advice), collective intelligence type (professionals' knowledge or nonprofessionals' innovative ideas), and government 2.0 strategy (it can be contest, wiki, social networking, or social rating and voting).

However, since public-sector crowdsourcing is still in its infancy, having much less maturity than private-sector crowdsourcing, further research is required in this area; its main priority should be the development of approaches and methodologies for the efficient and effective application of crowdsourcing ideas in government for supporting problem solving and policy making, taking into account its special needs and specificities. They should focus on addressing the inherent difficulties of modern policy making, which are caused by the complex and 'wicked' nature of social problems (Rittel and Weber 1973; Kunz and Rittel 1979), enabling a better and deeper understanding of the main elements of them (e.g. issues, alternatives, advantages and disadvantages perceived by various stakeholder groups; Conklin and Begeman 1989; Conklin 2003; Loukis and Wimmer 2012).

12.3   Research Method

The development of the two proposed approaches for active and passive crowdsourcing, respectively, was performed through close cooperation with public sector employees experienced in public policy making, using both qualitative and quantitative techniques: semi-structured focus group discussions, scenarios development and questionnaire surveys.

12.3.1   Active Crowdsourcing

The development of our active crowdsourcing approach (described in 'An Active Crowdsourcing Approach') included the following six phases (for more details on them see DeliverableD2.1 'Padget Design and Decision Model for Policy Making' of the PADGETS project accessible in its website www.padgets.eu):

a. Initially three semi-structured focus group discussions were conducted in the three government agencies participating in the PADGETS project (mentioned in the introductory section) as user partners (Center for eGovernance Development (Slovenia), ICT Observatory (Greece), Piedmont Regional Government (Italy)), which aimed at obtaining an understanding of their policy-making processes, the degree and form of public participation in them, and also their needs for and interest in ICT support.

b. The main themes of the above semi-structured focus group discussions were used for the design of a questionnaire, which was filled in and returned to us through e-mail by another four government agencies (City of Regensburg (Germany), World Heritage Coordination (Germany), North Lincolnshire Council (UK), IT Inkubator Ostbayern GmbH (Germany)), which have some form of close cooperation with the above three user partners of PADGETS project. This allowed us to obtain the above information from a wider group of government agencies, and cover a variety of government levels (national, regional and local).

c. Based on the information collected in the above first two phases the main idea of the active crowdsourcing approach was formulated: combined use of multiple social media for consultation with citizens on a social problem or public policy of interest, and sophisticated processing of relevant content generated by citizens.

d. Three application scenarios were developed in cooperation with the above three user partners of PADGETS project concerning the application of the above main idea for a specific problem/policy of high interest. Each of these scenarios described which social media should be used and how, what content should be posted to them, and also how various types of citizens' interactions with it (e.g. views, likes, comments, retweets, etc.) should be monitored and exploited, and what analytics would be useful to be computed from them.

e. Finally, a survey was conducted, using a shorter online questionnaire, concerning the required functionality from an ICT tool supporting the use of social media for such multiple social media consultation. It was distributed by personnel of the three user partners involved in the PADGETS project to colleagues from the same or other government agencies, who have working experience in public policy making, and finally was filled in by 60 persons.

f. Based on the outcomes of the above phases C, D and E, we designed this government active crowdsourcing approach in more detail, and then the required ICT infrastructure and its application process model (described in 'Description', 'ICT Infrastructure' and 'Application Process Model', respectively).

12.3.2 Passive Crowdsourcing

The development of our passive crowdsourcing approach (described in 'A Passive Crowdsourcing Approach') included the following seven phases (for more details on them see Deliverable D2.1 'Padget Report on User Requirements' of the NOMAD project in its website www.nomad-project.eu/):

1. Initially the main idea was developed, in cooperation with the user partners of the NOMAD project (Greek Parliament, Austrian Parliament, European Academy of Allergy and Clinical Immunology), based on the digital reputation and brand management ideas from the private sector (e.g. see Ziegler and Skubacz 2006): passive retrieval of content that has been generated by citizens freely (without any initiation, stimulation or moderation through government postings) in numerous Web 2.0 sources (e.g. blogs and microblogs, news sharing sites, online

forums, etc.) on a specific topic, problem or public policy, and then sophisticated processing of this content using opinion mining techniques.

2. Four application scenarios of this idea were developed by the above user partners of the NOMAD project. Each application scenario constitutes a detailed realistic example of how this passive croudsourcingidea could be applied for supporting the formulation of a particular public policy, and describes how various types of users involved in this might use an ICT platform that implements this idea.

3. A questionnaire was distributed electronically to a sample population of potential users, which included questions concerning: (a) respondent's personal information, (b) general citizens' participation information (in his/her organization), (c) current use of social media in policy-making processes, (d) general assessment of this ideaand and (e) specific relevant requirements.

4. Organization of focus groups and workshops with the participation of potential users. This allowed in-depth discussion among people experienced in the design of public policies, with different backgrounds and mentalities, about this new idea, and also ways and processes of its practical application, required relevant ICT functionalities and at the same time possible problems and barriers.

5. Organization of in-depth interviews based of a series of fixed questions concerning attitudes towards this new idea, its usefulness and applicability.

6. A review of systems that offer at least a part of the above ICT functionalities (e.g. for content retrieval, opinion mining, etc.).

7. Based on the outcomes of the above phases we designed this government passive crowdsourcing approach in more detail, then its application process model and finally the required ICT infrastructure (as described in 'Description', 'Application Process Model' and 'ICT Infrastructure', respectively).

12.4 An Active Crowdsourcing Approach

12.4.1 Description

The proposed active crowdsourcing approach is based on the centralized automated publishing of multimedia content (e.g. a short text, a longer description, images, videos, etc.) concerning a social problem of interest or a public policy under formulation to the accounts of a government agency in multiple social media (e.g. Facebook, Twitter, YouTube, Picasa and Blogger), in order to actively stimulate discussions on it. As mentioned in 'Introduction' and 'Background' social problems have become highly complex and 'wicked', with multiple and heterogeneous stakeholders having different problem views, values and objectives (Rittel and Weber 1973; Kunz and Rittel 1979; Conklin 2003), so in order to address this inherent difficulty our methodology uses multiple social media, with each of them attracting different groups of citizens. Throughout these social media consultations we continuously retrieve and monitor various types of citizens' interactions with the content we have posted (e.g. views, likes, ratings, comments and retweets), and finally we process these interactions in order to support drawing conclusions from them. Both content posting and interactions' continuous retrieval are performed in a highly automated manner using the API of these social media from a central ICT platform, in which also processing and results presentation takes place.

In particular, a government agency policy maker, through a web-based dashboard or a mobile phone application, initiates a campaign concerning a specific topic, problem or policy in multiple social media. For this purpose, he/she creates relevant multimedia content (e.g. short and longer topic description, images, videos, etc.), which are then automatically published in the corresponding social media (e.g. in the Twitter the short-topic description, in Blogger the longer one, in YouTube the video, in Picasa the images, etc.) by a central platform. The citizens will view this content, and interact with it (in all the ways that each social media platform allows), either through these social media, or through a mobile phone application. Then, these interactions will be automatically retrieved and shown continuously to the policy maker, through the above web-based dashboard or mobile phone application, so that appropriate interventions can be made (i.e. new content can be published) if necessary. Finally, after the end of the campaign, sophisticated processing of all citizens' interactions with the above content will be performed in this central ICT platform, using a variety of techniques (e.g. calculation of web analytics and opinion mining), in order to provide useful analytics that support government decision and policy making. In Fig. 12.1, this active crowdsourcing approach is illustrated.

The practical application of the above approach will lead to a collection of large amounts of content generated by citizens in various Web 2.0 social media concerning the particular topic, problem or policy we have defined through our initial postings. So it will be of critical importance to use highly sophisticated methods of automated processing this content, in order to offer substantial support to government agencies policy makers in drawing conclusions from it . Part of this citizens-generated content is numeric (e.g. numbers of views, likes, retweets, comments, ratings, etc.), so it can be used for the calculation of various analytics. However, a large part of this content is in textual form, so opinion mining, defined as the advanced processing of text in order to extract sentiments, feelings, opinions and emotions (for a review of them see Maragoudakis et al. 2011), will be a critical technology for processing it and maximizing knowledge extraction from it. The development and use of opinion mining first started in the private sector, as firms wanted to analyze comments and reviews about their products, which had been entered by their customers in various websites, in order to draw conclusions as to whether customers like the specific products or not (through sentiment analysis techniques), the particular features of the products that have been commented (through issues extraction techniques) and the orientations (positive, negative or neutral) of these comments (through sentiment analysis techniques). These ideas can be applied in the public sector as well, since citizens' comments are a valuable source of information that can be quite useful for government decision and policy making: it is important to identify the main issues posed by citizens (through issues extraction) on a particular topic, problem or policy making we are interested in, and also the corresponding sentiments or feelings (positive, neutral or negative—through sentiment analysis). More details about this active crowdsourcing approach are provided by Charalabidis and Loukis (2012), Ferro et al. (2013) and Charalabidis et al. (2014a).

Fig. 12.1 An approach for
active crowdsourcing in
government

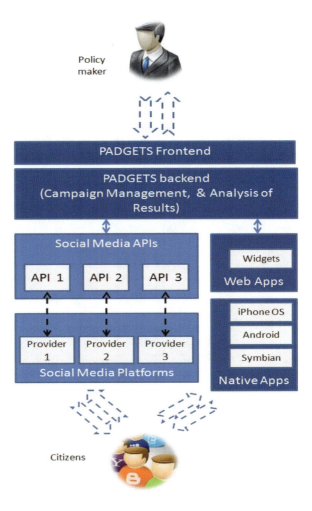

12.4.2 ICT Infrastructure

An ICT platform has been developed for the practical application of the above approach, which provides all required functionalities to two main types of users of it: government agencies' policy makers and citizens. In particular, a 'policy makers dashboard' (accessible through a web-based or a mobile interface (Android mobile application)) enables government agencies' policy makers:

1. To create a multiple social media campaign, by defining its topic, the starting and ending date/time, the social media accounts to be used, and the relevant messages and multimedia content to be posted to them
2. To monitor continuously citizens' comments on the messages; in Fig. 12.2, we can see this part of the web-based policy-makers' interface, which is structured

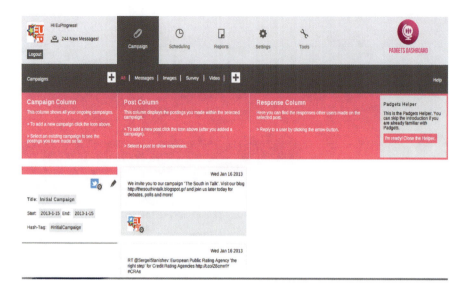

Fig. 12.2 Policy-makers' interface for viewing active campaigns, messages and citizens' feedback

    in three columns: in the first column, the active campaigns are shown, while by selecting one of them in the second column are shown the corresponding messages posted by the policy maker (the initial, and the subsequent ones), and finally by selecting one of these messages in the third column are shown citizens' comments on it (textual feedback stream)

3. And after the end of the campaign to view (as graphics and visualizations) a set of analytics and opinion mining results, which are produced by the decision support component of the platform (described later in this section) for the whole campaign.

The citizens can see the initial content of each campaign, and also other citizens' interactions with it (e.g. textual comments), either through the interfaces of the corresponding social media, or through a mobile interface (Android mobile application) or a widget, which enables citizens to view active campaigns, and by selecting one of them to view all policy maker and citizens' comments on it, or add a new comment.

    The technological architecture of this ICT platform is shown in Fig. 12.3. We can see that it consists of two main areas:

1. The front-end area, which provides the abovementioned web interface to the policy makers, and also the mobile application and widget interfaces to both policy makers and citizens.

2. The back-end area, which includes three components: the first of them perfoms publishing of various content types in multiple social media through the second component, which consists of connectors with the utilized social media, while the third component performs aggregation/analysis of citizens interactions with

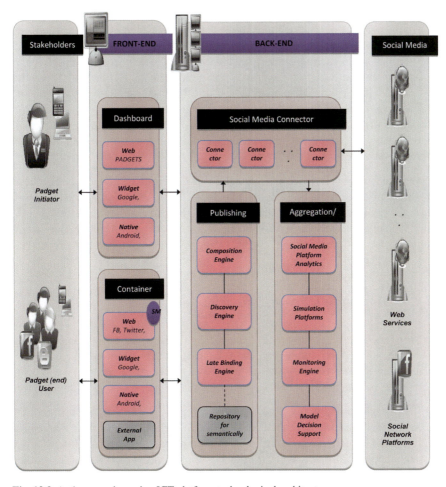

Fig. 12.3 Active crowdsourcing ICT platform technological architecture

the above-published content in these social media, retrieved through the second component; it consists of one subcomponent that allows continuous monitoring of these citizens interactions, and several subcomponents that provide analytics for government policy-makers' decision support.

One of these subcomponents collects and processes the 'raw analytics' provided by the analytics engines of the utilized social media. Another subcomponent provides more advanced analytics, which concern citizens' textual inputs (e.g. blog postings, comments, opinions, etc.), processing them using opinion mining techniques (Maragoudakis et al. 2011). In particular, it performs the following three types of tasks:

- Classification of an opinionated text (e.g. a blog post) as expressing a positive, negative or neutral opinion (this is referred to as document-level sentiment analysis).
- Classification of each sentence in a such a text, first as subjective or objective (i.e. determination of whether it expresses an opinion or not), and for each subjective sentence (i.e. expressing an opinion) classification as positive, negative or neutral (this is known as sentence-level sentiment analysis).
- Extraction of specific issues commented by the author of a text, and for each issue to identify its orientation as positive, negative or neutral (this is referred to as feature-level sentiment analysis).

Another subcomponent performs simulation modelling (Charalabidis et al. 2011), having mainly two objectives: estimation of the outcomes of various citizens' proposals on the public policies under discussion, and also forecasting the future levels of citizens' interest in and awareness of these policies. The simulation modelling takes as input various indicators produced by the other two aforementioned subcomponents.

12.4.3 Application Process Model

Furthermore, an application process model for this active crowdsourcing approach has been developed. It provides a model of the process to be followed by government agencies for the practical application of it, which includes a sequence of specific activities to be executed:

1. The policy maker initially setsup a policy campaign, using the capabilities of the central ICT platform described above, through a graphical user interface
2. Then he/she creates textual content for this campaign (both short and longer policy statements), and also can add various types of multimedia content to it (e.g. policy images, video, etc.)
3. And finally defines the multiple social media accounts to be used in this campaign
4. And views a preview of the campaign in each of them
5. The campaign is launched by publishing the above content (in each of these multiple social media will be automatically published the appropriate part of the above content, e.g. in the Twitter will be published the short policy statement, in Blogger the longer one, in YouTube the video, in Picasa the images, etc.).
6. Citizens interact with the published content in various ways in these social media (in the particular ways each of them allows): they access and see this content, rate it and make some comments on it, retransmit it in their networks, etc
7. The above citizens' interactions are automatically retrieved continuously from all the used social media in the central ICT platform, and after the end of the campaign are processed there using various advanced techniques (as described above), in order to calculate useful analytics that provide assistance and support to the policy maker.
8. The results are sent immediately to the policy maker, by e-mail or SMS message.

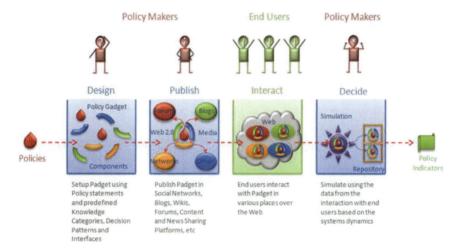

Fig. 12.4 A typical application scenario of the active crowdsourcing ICT approach

In Fig. 12.4, we can see a typical application scenario of this active crowdsourcing approach.

12.5   A Passive Crowdsourcing Approach

12.5.1   Description

The proposed passive crowdsourcing approach is based on the exploitation of the extensive political content created in multiple Web 2.0 sources (e.g. blogs and microblogs, news sharing sites, and online forums) by citizens freely (= without active stimulation through some government posting) concerning various domains of government activity and public policies. An ICT platform automatically retrieves this content from these Web 2.0 sources using their API, and then processes it using sophisticated linguistic processing techniques in order to extract from it relevant issues, proposals and arguments. So in this approach government is not active in conducting crowdsourcing (as it is in the active crowdsourcing approach presented in the previous section, by posing to citizens particular discussion topics, problems or policies), but it remains passive (just 'listening' to what citizens discuss, and analyzing the content they freely produce in order to extract knowledge from it). Taking into account the highly complex and 'wicked' nature of modern social problems, which usually have multiple and heterogeneous stakeholders with different problem views, values and objectives (Rittel and Weber 1973; Kunz and Rittel 1979; Conklin 2003), our passive crowdsourcing approach uses multiple Web 2.0 content sources, with diverse political perspectives and orientations.

In particular, this passive crowdsourcing approach includes three stages, which are illustrated in Fig. 12.5. The first stage, called 'Listen', includes listening and monitoring what citizens say concerning a domain of government activity (e.g. higher education) or a public policy under formulation (e.g. a new policy on higher education) in a large set of Web 2.0 sources $S_1, S_2, \ldots, S_N$ defined by the policy maker. For this purpose a 'focused crawler' is used, which is a program that browses the above sources in an automated and organized manner, and retrieves solely content that is relevant to the specific topic of interest.

The second stage, called 'Analyse', includes advanced processing and analysis of the retrieved content, from which are identified relevant issues, proposals and arguments expressed by citizens. As the majority of this content is in textual form, this stage makes use of advanced linguistic processing techniques (for a review of them, see Maragoudakis et al. (2011)). In particular, each content unit retrieved by the crawler will go through a series of automated processing steps:

- *Language detection*, which will recognize the language used in it.
- *Opinion and argument extraction*, using appropriate semantic similarity measures and inference mechanisms that allow the identification of elements of the analyzed content which are pertinent to the particular domain or policy.
- *Sentiment analysis*, using smart sentiment classifiers that recognize the polarity (positive, neutral, and negative) of the elements identified above.
- *Argument summarization*, using appropriate algorithms for generating qualitative information about opposing arguments, in the form of anonymity-preserving and automatically generated summaries.

The third stage, called 'Receive', aims to present to the end-user (policy maker) the knowledge acquired from the previous stages in a complete, coherent and usable manner. The platform will provide an aggregated view of the results of the above processing, their polarity, their association with various policy concepts and statements, and also statistical indications of their significance and impact. For this purpose visual analytics (Wong and Thomas 2004; Thomas and Cook 2005; Keim et al. 2010) will be used, so that policy makers can view visualizations of the results of previous stages, and easily understand them with minimal cognitive effort (e.g. in a familiar word cloud form), which is quite important due to the high information overload the policy makers usually experience.

The knowledge gained through this passive crowdsourcing (e.g. issues, proposals and arguments concerning a domain of government activity or a policy under formulation) can be used in order to formulate more specific questions, positions or proposals about the particular policy and then solicit citizens' feedback and contributions on them through more 'active' forms of communication. This can be achieved through 'active crowdsourcing', i.e. by making relevant stimulating postings (based on the findings from passive crowdsourcing) to various social media (e.g. blogs, Twitter, Facebook, YouTube, etc.), and also to official government e-participation websites, in order to collect citizens' interactions with this content (e.g. ratings, votes, comments, etc.). Therefore, the proposed 'passive crowdsourcing' approach

Fig. 12.5 The three stages of the government passive crowdsourcing approach

can be combined with the 'active crowdsourcing' approach described in the previous section, in order to increase its effectiveness. More details about this passive crowdsourcing approach are provided by Charalabidis et al. (2014b).

12.5.2 Application Process Model

Extensive effort was required in order to design how the above passive crowdsourcing concept can be practically applied by government agencies and work efficiently, and formulate an apropriate process model for its application. So we will describe first this aspect of it, and then the required ICT infrastructure in the following 'ICT Infrastructure' (since the latter has been to a large extent based on the former). There was wide agreement that since the domains of government activity and the public policies for them are quite complex and multidimensional entities, it is not possible to search for content on them in the predefined Web 2.0 sources using just a small number of keyworks. So it was concluded that the best solution for addressing this complexity is to develop a model of the specific domain, for which a policy is intended, which will consist of the main terms of it and the relations among them (a kind of 'structured thesaurus' of this domain). An example of such a domain model for the energy domain, which has been developed based on the documents of the 'Greek Strategy for Energy Planning', is shown below in Fig. 12.6.

Based on such a domain model we can then build a policy model, by adding to the nodes of the former: (a) the 'policy statements' (= the specific policy objectives and actions/interventions that a policy includes) and also (b) positive and negative arguments in favour or against them, respectively. An example of such a policy model for the energy domain is shown in Fig. 12.7 (including three policy objectives, one concerning the whole national energy planning, and two concerning the renewable energy sources, six positive arguments and nine negative ones).

These two models (domain and policy ones) can be used for searching for and retrieving relevant content concerning the main terms of a domain, or the policy statements and the arguments of a policy. This search has to be performed at regular time intervals in order to keep the retrieved content updated, and the results should be stored in a database, and then undergo the advanced processing mentioned in the previous section (in the 'Analyse' stage), the results of which will be also stored in the same database. The authorized policy makers will have the capability at any time to explore the results of this advanced processing stored in the above database, and

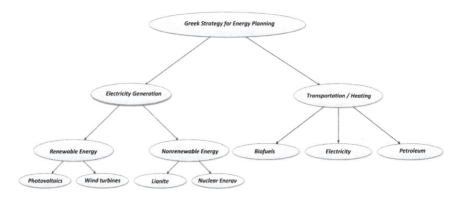

Fig. 12.6 Energy domain model

view various visualization of them, e.g. the most frequently mentioned terms-topics with respect to a particular domain or policy model (e.g. in a tag cloud form).

Also, most of the potential users we interviewed mentioned that it is important to view citizens' sentiment with respect to these frequently mentioned terms-topics (i.e. whether citizens regard each of them as positive, negative or neutral), or even with respect to the individual policy statements and arguments of a policy model. Furthermore, our interviewees noted that all the above (i.e. frequently mentioned terms-topics and sentiments) may differ significantly between different citizens groups (e.g. between age, gender, education and region groups), so policy makers should have the capability to view them for particular citizens' groups, or to view comparisons between different citizens' groups. Furthermore, since public stance changes rapidly, it was mentioned that policy makers should have the capability to view all the above information for particular user-defined time periods, or to compare between different time periods, while future forecasts of them would be quite useful.

Based on the above, a model of the process to be followed by government agencies for the practical application of this passive crowdsourcing approach was developed. It includes the following nine activities:

1. Development of a domain model
2. Development of a policy model
3. Definition of Web 2.0 content sources
4. Search of these content sources at regular time intervals
5. Process retrieved content and store results in a database
6. Policy maker views polarized tag glouds with the most frequently mentioned terms-topics with respect to a particular domain or policy model and the corresponding sentiments for a predefined time period.
7. Policy maker views the sentiments with respect to the individual policy statements and arguments of a policy model.
8. Policy maker views the above for particular citizens' groups, and then makes comparisons between different citizens' groups, or with other time periods.
9. Policy maker views short-term future forecasts of the above.

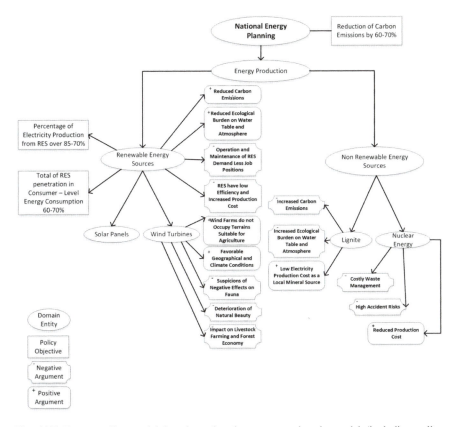

Fig. 12.7 Energy policy model based on the above energy domain model (including policy statements and arguments)

Finally, we identified four roles which are required for the practical application of this process model:

- Domain models author: this role will create domain models and also modify existing ones.
- Policy models author: this role will create policy models based on existing domain models (= add to their nodes policy statements and argumentations) and also modify existing ones.
- End user/policy maker: this role will view the results of processing the content retrieved from the Web 2.0 sources in all the abovementioned forms.
- Platform administrator: this role will have full access to all platform functionalities, monitor platform operation, manage the set of users accessing the platform and their access rights to the offered services and functionalities.

12.5.3 ICT Infrastructure

Based on the above application process model, we proceeded to the design of the functional architecture of the required ICT platform. In particular, we defined in more detail the functionality to be provided to each of the above four roles:

1. *Domain models author*
   - Creation of new domain models (= definition of main terms of the domain and the relations among them).
   - Modification of existing domain models.
   - Import of external domain models (e.g. having the form of ontology files in OWL).
   - Export of domain models (e.g. in the form of ontology files in OWL).
2. *Policy models author*
   - Access to domain models.
   - Creation of new policy models (using existing domain models, by adding policy statements and arguments to their nodes).
   - Modification of existing policy models.
   - Import of external policy models (e.g. having the form of ontology files in OWL).
   - Export of policy models (e.g. in the form of ontology files in OWL).
3. *End user/policy maker*
   - View the most frequently mentioned terms-topics with respect to a particular domain or policy model for a predefined time period, citizens' group and sources subset (see Fig. 12.8 for a first design of the corresponding screen).
   - View sentiment for these terms-topics.
   - View sentiment for each policy statement and argument of a particular model.
   - View differentiations of the above over time.
   - View differentiations of the above across citizens' groups.
   - View differentiations of the above across sources subsets.
   - View short-term future projections of the above.
4. *Platform administrator*
   - Users and roles management.
   - Domain and policy roles management.
   - Monitoring and administration of all platform services.

Based on the above functional architecture of the platform, its technological architecture was designed. The objective of this design was to provide this functionality with an acceptable response time. Since this could not be achieved through online retrieval of content from a large number of sources (e.g. numerous blogs, news websites, Facebook, Youtube and Twitter accounts) and processing of it at the time a user initiates a search, the only solution was to perform a scan of the predefined sources at some regular time intervals (e.g. every 6 h) in order to retrieve new content, store it in a database and then process it and store the results in the same database. Whenever the user performs a search, the results will be produced in a very short time, using this database. This separation between sources scanning and content processing on one

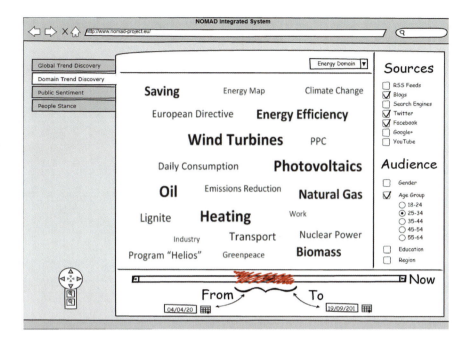

Fig. 12.8 View of the most frequently mentioned terms-topics with respect to a particular domain or policy model for a predefined time period, citizens' group and sources subset

hand, and users' searches processing on the other, allows a low response time and at the same time sufficiently 'fresh' content for policy makers (i.e. allows addressing these two conflicting requirements).

The above design leads to a three layers' technological architecture of the platform, which consists of a storage layer, a processing layer and a presentation layer, and is shown in Fig. 12.9. Each of them includes a number of components, performing different tasks, which act as services coordinated by an orchestration component.

In particular, the *data storage layer* includes the repositories where the raw and processed content is stored:

- The *content repository*: it stores the raw content retrieved from the Web 2.0 sources, the cleaned content derived from the raw data, the content uploaded by users and the results of the linguistic analysis associated with each content unit.
- The *model repository*: it stores in a structured form the domain and policy models entered by users with domain expert and policy advisor roles.
- The *metadata repository*: it stores the metadata retrieved or calculated for our sources.
- The *thematic catalogues*: it stores a representation of the thematic categories used by the platform in order to characterize each content unit.
- The *users repository*: it contains information about the roles and the users of the platform.

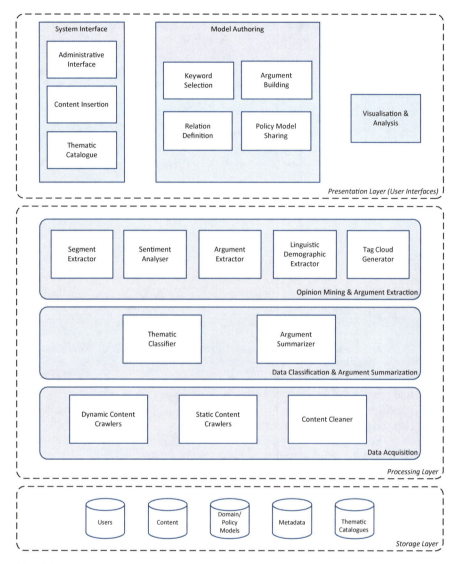

Fig. 12.9 Passive crowdsourcing ICT platform technological architecture

The *processing layer* includes all the components that retrieve and process the content from the predefined sources, which are organized in three sub-layers:

- The *data acquisition layer*, which includes the crawling components for fetching content from the sources, using their APIs, as well as the modules responsible for cleaning the fetched content and obtaining the actual textual information from it (static content crawlers, dynamic content crawlers and content cleaner).
- The *data classification and argument summarization layer*, which includes (a) the thematic classifier, which processes the available content and associates it

with one more of the defined thematic categories in the thematic catalogues, and (b) the result summarizer, which processes the available results and provides a summarization that allows their presentation in a condensed manner.

- The *argument extraction and opinion mining layer*, which includes all the components that process the available content and extract segments, arguments and sentiments (segment extractor, argument extractor, sentiment analyzer, linguistic demographic extractor, tag cloud generator).

The *presentation layer* includes all the components that either require input from the user or present to him/her the results:

- The *thematic catalogue* interface, for entering or updating the available thematic categories and also terms associated with each category.
- The *keyword selection* interface, which allows entering keywords/terms for creating domain models.
- The *relation definition* interface, which allows the user to introduce relations between the above keywords/terms for the definition of domain models.
- The *argument building* interface, which allows the user to insert in natural language statements and arguments supporting or objecting to policy statements of policy models.
- The *policy model sharing* interface, which provides a catalogue of the policy models created by the user and allows defining them as visible to others.
- The *admin interface*, which provides the means to an administrator to manage the configurable aspects of the system.
- The *visualisation and analysis module*, which utilizes the results of the processing layer in order to provide the user with a view of domain and policy models, and also various visualizations of the results of users' searches, enabling also the selection of sources, demographic characteristics and time periods.

The domain and policy modelling components of the presentation layer (thematic catalogue, keyword selection, relation definition, argument building and policy model sharing interfaces) will be based on the ELEON Ontology Authoring and Enrichment Environment (http://www.iit.demokritos.gr/ eleon), developed by the National Center for Scientific Research 'Demokritos', which participates as a partner in the NOMAD project. It supports editing ontologies and relating such ontologies with linguistic resources that can be used to extract structured ontological information from text, and also supports the author with a number of innovative methods for ontology checking (Bilidas et al. 2007) and autocompletion (Konstantopoulos et al. 2011). The sentiment analyser will be based on existing tools developed by 'Demokritos' as well (Rentoumi et al. 2009; Rentoumi et al. 2010), which are based on algorithms that take into account various intricacies of the language forms commonly used in the context of user-generated web content, such as metaphors, nuances, irony, etc. For the summarization task the 'n-gram graph framework' (Giannakopoulos et al. 2008; Giannakopoulos and Karkaletsis 2009) will be used, which is a statistical, domain agnostic and language-independent framework that allows the analysis of texts as character n-gram graphs.

12.6 Comparisons

In this section, we make a comparison between the two proposed crowdsourcing approaches, and also with the private and public sector crowdsourcing patterns reported in the literature (outlined in 'Background'), identifying similarities and differences.

Both approaches adopt two of the four crowdsourcing approaches identified by Brabham (2012): mainly 'knowledge discovery' and secondarily 'creative production'. From the four public sector specific crowdsourcing purposes identified by Nam (2012) they focus mainly on 'information creation', and secondarily on 'problem solving' and 'policy making advice'; also from the two types of collective intelligence mentioned in the same study both approaches aim at 'nonprofessionals innovative ideas' and much less at 'professionals knowledge'. With respect to participants' motivation, from the two main motivation types identified by Rouse (2010) both approaches are based mainly on citizens' 'community oriented' motivations and much less on 'individualistic' ones (since none of the two approaches is based on the monetary or other types of rewards used in private sector crowdsourcing); also, from the seven more detailed participants' motivations identified in the same study the 'altruism', 'instrumental motivation' and 'social status' seem to be ones our approaches mainly rely on. Finally from the four organizer benefits identified in the same study, both methodologies aim to provide to adopting government agencies 'access to capabilities not held in-house' and 'capacity to exploit knowledge and skills of volunteers who might not otherwise contribute', but not 'cost savings' or 'contracts and payments that are outcome based'.

With respect to the required ICT infrastructures it should be noted that the one of our active crowdsourcing approach—described in 'ICT Infrastructure'—has some similarities with the typical crowdsourcing IS (which according to Hetmank (2013)) includes user, task, contribution and workflow management components), but also important differences as well. In particular, this active crowdsourcing ICT platform includes 'task management' components (that enable setting-up a campaign and creating/adding multimedia content to it) and 'contribution management' components (processing citizens' interactions with the above content in the utilized social media). However, it does not include 'user management' components (as the management of the citizens participating in our campaigns is conducted through our social media accounts) and 'workflow management' ones. Also the process model we have developed for the application of this active crowdsourcing approach—described in 'Application Process Model'—has some similarities with the typical crowdsourcing process model (according to Hetmank (2013)), but also important differences as well. In particular, this application process model includes four out of the ten activities of this typical crowdsourcing process model (define task, set time period, accept crowd contributions, and combine submissions), however most of them in a quite different form. However, the former does not include the remaining six activities of the latter (state reward, recruit participants, assign tasks, select solution, evaluate submissions and finally grant rewards), due to inherent differences of our active crowdsourcing approach from the mainstream crowdsourcing (e.g. lack of reward and specific task assignments, participants management through our accounts in the utilized social media, lack of individual submissions evaluation, etc.).

On the contrary, both the application process model of our passive crowdsourcing approach and also the structure and components of the required ICT platform are quite different from the one of the typical crowdsourcing approaches, which has been identified by Hetmank (2013). In particular, our passive crowdsourcing approach does not include any of the main tasks of the mainstream crowdsourcing (problem definition, open call for contributions, search for and motivation of contributors, evaluation of contributions, and finally reward of the most successful of them), but has a quite different task structure (including domain and policy modelling, definition of the Web 2.0 sources to be used, automated content retrieval and sophisticated processing of the retrieved content, which do not exist in mainstream crowdsourcing). For this reason, its application process model—described in 5.2—is quite different from the one of the typical crowdsourcing. Also, the passive crowdsourcing ICT platform we have designed—described in 5.3—includes 'contribution management' components (allowing advanced linguistic processing of the textual content retrieved from multiple Web 2.0 sources), but not 'task management', 'user management' and 'workflow management' ones. This new passive crowdsourcing approach requires more extensive and complex ICT infrastructures than the existing crowdsourcing approaches, which are based on the use of API of numerous Web 2.0 sources, in combination with advanced linguistic processing techniques.

12.7 Conclusions

Crowdsourcing has been initially developed and applied in the private sector, and later introduced in the public sector (still in experimental mode). Therefore, there is limited knowledge concerning the efficient and effective application of crowdsourcing ideas in government, taking into account its special needs and specificities, much less than in the private sector. This chapter contributes to filling this gap, presenting two approaches for this purpose: a first one for 'active crowdsourcing', and a second one for 'passive crowdsourcing' by government agencies. The foundations of both come from management sciences (crowdsourcing research), political sciences (wicked social problems research) and technological sciences (social media capabilities and API). For each of these approaches has been presented the basic idea, the architecture of the required ICT infrastructure, and its application process model.

A common characteristic of the two proposed government crowdsourcing approaches is that they do not include competitive contest among the participants and monetary or other types of rewards, as in private sector crowdsourcing, but mainly collaboration among citizens for knowledge and innovative ideas creation. Also they both rely mainly on community-oriented motivations of the participants and not on individualistic ones. They aim to provide to adopting government agencies not benefits associated with 'cost savings' or 'contracts and payments that are outcome based' (as in the mainstream private sector crowdsourcing), but benefits concerning

Table 12.1 Similarities and differences between the proposed active and passive crowdsourcing approaches

Similarities
Both approaches exploit multiple Web 2.0 social media simultaneously
In a centrally managed manner based on a central platform
Fully automatically using their API
And then both make sophisticated processing of the collected content, in order to extract the main points from it, in order to reduce the 'information overload' of government decision makers
They both aim to provide to government agencies access to resources (e.g. information, knowledge, ideas, and skills) not available in-house
But without competitive contests and monetary rewards (which are quite usual in private sector crowdsourcing)
Relying both on community oriented motivations of the participants and not on individualistic ones
Differences
The active crowdsourcing approach uses the accounts of the particular government agency in several social, while the passive crowdsourcing approach goes beyond them, using other accounts, blogs, websites, etc., not belonging to government agencies
Also the former actively stimulates discussions and content generation by citizens on specific topics (through government postings and content), while the latter does not: it passively collects content created by citizens freely, without any initiation, stimulation or moderation through government postings
The initial preparation—content generation requirements for the application of the passive crowdsourcing approach (= creation of domain and policy models) are much higher than the ones of active crowdsourcing
The processing of the collected content has to undergo much more sophisticated processing in the case of the passive crowdsourcing approach than in the active crowdsourcing one
And also the required ICT infrastructure for the active crowdsourcing approach, and its application model are more similar to the ones of the mainstream private sector crowdsourcing than the passive crowdsourcing approach

'access to capabilities not held in-house' and 'capacity to exploit knowledge and skills of volunteers who might not otherwise contribute'. However, while for our active crowdsourcing approach the required ICT infrastructure and its application process model have some similarities with the ones of the mainstream private sector crowdsourcing (also important differences as well), our passive crowdsourcing approach requires quite different forms of ICT infrastructure and application process model from the ones of the mainstream crowdsourcing. The similarities and differences between the two proposed approaches are summarized below in Table 12.1. However, it should be noted that these two approaches are not mutually exclusive, but can be combined: the results of passive crowdsourcing can be used for guiding active crowdsourcing on the most important of the identified issues and problems, or even for organizing relevant discussions in government e-consultation spaces.

From a first evaluation we have conducted for the active crowdsourcing approach based on pilot applications (see Ferro et al. 2013; Charalabidis et al. 2014a), it has been concluded that it constitutes a time and cost efficient mechanism of reaching wide and diverse audiences, and stimulating and motivating them to think about social problems and public policies under formulation, and provide relevant information, knowledge, ideas and opinions. Furthermore, it enables identifying the main issues perceived by citizens with respect to a particular social problem or domain of government activity, and collecting from them interesting ideas on possible solutions and directions of government activity. However, our pilot applications have shown that the above information generated from such multiple social media crowdsourcing might be not be at the level of depth and detail required by government agencies. So in order to achieve a higher level of detail, and more discussion depth in general, a series of such multiple social media consultations might be required, each of them focused on particular subtopics and/or participants. Another risk of this active crowdsourcing approach is that it can lead to unproductive discussions among like-minded individuals belonging to the network of the government policy maker who initiated the consultation; such discussions are characterized by low diversity of opinions and perspectives, low productivity of knowledge and ideas, and in general limited creativity. Therefore, for the effective application of this crowdsourcing approach it is of critical importance to build large and diverse networks for these social media consultations; for his purpose, we can combine networks of several government agencies, and also politicians, preferably from different political parties and orientations, and also invite additional interested and knowledgeable individuals and civil society organizations. Our passive crowdsourcing approach is currently under evaluation based on pilot applications.

The research presented in this chapter has interesting implications for research and practice. It opens up new directions of multidisciplinary research concerning the application of crowdsourcing ideas in government, taking into account its special needs and specificities, and also for the development of advanced ICT infrastructures for this purpose, and appropriate application process models. With respect to government practice, it provides to government agencies advanced, efficient and effective methods and ICT tools, in order to conduct 'citizen sourcing', and collect useful information, knowledge, ideas and opinions from citizen, and the society in general, so that it can finally design better, more socially rooted, balanced and realistic public policies for addressing the growing problems of modern societies. Such tools can be for government policy makers valuable 'sensors', allowing the early identification of new problems, needs, ideas and trends in the society, so that appropriate policy responses can be developed. It is important that such approaches are gradually introduced and integrated in the policy formulation processes and practices, which can lead to a significant 'renewal' of them.

Further research is required concerning the multidimensional evaluation of the two proposed government crowdsourcing methodologies, through various 'real-life' applications (aiming at conducting crowdsourcing for various types of problems and public policies), and using various theoretical foundations and lenses from multiple disciplines. Also, it would be interesting to conduct research towards the development of contest oriented government crowdsourcing methodologies, which include definition of a more specific task to be performed, competition among participants and monetary or other types of rewards.

References

Bilidas D, Theologou M, Karkaletsis V (2007) Enriching OWL ontologies with linguistic and user-related annotations: the ELEON system. Proceedings of IEEE international conference on tools with artificial intelligence (ICTAI-07), Patras, Greece

Brabham DC (2008) Crowdsourcing as a model for problem solving an introduction and cases. Convergence: Int J Res New Media Tech 14(1):75–90

Brabham DC (2009) Moving the crowd at threadless—motivations for participation in a crowdsourcing application. Inf Commun Soc 13(8):1122–1145

Brabham DC (2012) Crowdsourcing: a model for leveraging online communities. In: Delwiche A, Henderson J (eds) The Routledge handbook of participative cultures. Routledge, New York

Charalabidis Y, Loukis E (2012) Participative public policy making through multiple social media platforms utilization. Int J Electron Gov Res 8(3):78–97

Charalabidis Y, Loukis E, Androutsopoulou A (2011) Enhancing participative policy making through simulation modelling—a state of the art review. Proceedings of the European Mediterranean Conference on Information Systems (EMCIS) 2011, Athens, Greece

Charalabidis Y, Loukis E, Androutsopoulou A (2014a) Fostering social innovation through multiple social media combination. Inf Syst Manage 31(3):225–239

Charalabidis Y, Loukis E, Androutsopoulou A, Karkaletsis V, Triantafillou A (2014b) Passive crowdsourcing in government using social media. Transform Gov: People Process Policy 8(2):283–308

Conklin J (2003) Dialog mapping: reflections on an industrial strength case study. In: Kirschner P, Shum SB, Carr C (eds) Visualizing argumentation: software tools for collaborative and educational sense-making. Springer, London

Conklin J, Begeman M (1989) gIBIS: a tool for all reasons. J Am Soc Inf Sci 40(3):200–213

Executive Office of the President (2009) Memorandum for the Heads of Executive Departments and Agencies: Open Government Directive. http://www.whitehouse.gov/open/documents/open-government-directive. Accessed 14 July 2014

Ferro E, Loukis E, Charalabidis Y, Osella M (2013) Policy making 2.0: from theory to practice. Gov Inf Quart 30(4):359–368

Geiger D, Rosemann M, Fielt Er, and Schader M (2012). Crowdsourcing information systems—definition typology, and design. Proceedings of international conference on information systems (ICIS) 2012, Orlando, USA

Giannakopoulos G, Karkaletsis V (2009) N-gram graphs: representing documents and document sets in summary system evaluation. Proceedings of text analysis conference TAC 2009.Text analysis conference (TAC) 2009, November 16–17, 2009, Gaithersburg, Maryland, USA

Giannakopoulos G, Karkaletsis V, Vouros G, Stamatopoulos P (2008) Summarization system evaluation revisited: N-gram graphs. ACM Trans Speech Lang Process 5(3):1–39

Hetmank L (2013) Components and functions of crowdsourcing systems—a systematic literature review. Wirtschaftsinformatik Proceedings 2013

Hilgers D, Ihl C (2010) Citizensourcing: applying the concept of open innovation to the public sector. Int J Public Participation 4(1):67–88

Howe J (2006) The rise of crowdsourcing. Wired 14(6). http://www.wired.com/wired/archive/14.06/crowds.html. Accessed 14 July 2014

Howe J (2008) Crowdsourcing, why the power of the crowd is driving the future of business. Crown Business, New York

Keim DA, Kohlhammer J, Ellis GP, Mansmann F (2010) Mastering the information age—solving problems with visual analytics. Eurographics, Germany

Konstantopoulos S, Karkaletsis V, Vogiatzis V, Bilidas D (2011) Authoring semantic and linguistic knowledge for the dynamic generation of personalized descriptions. In: Sporleder C et al (eds) Language technology for cultural heritage. Springer, Berlin

Kunz W, Rittel H (1979) Issues as elements of information systems. Working Paper No 131. University of California, Berkley

Levy P (1997) Collective intelligence: mankind's emerging world in cyberspace. Plenum, New York

Lukensmeyer CJ, Torres LH (2008) Citizensourcing: citizen participation in a networked nation. In: Yang K, Bergrud E (eds) Civic engagement in a network society. Information Age Publishing, Charlotte, pp 207–233

Loukis E, Wimmer M (2012) A multi-method evaluation of different models of structured electronic consultation on government policies. Inf Syst Manage 29(4):284–294

Majchrzak A, Malhotra A (2013) Towards an information systems perspective and research agenda on crowdsourcing for innovation. J Strategic Inf Syst 22:257–268

Maragoudakis M, Loukis E, Charalabidis Y (2011) A review of opinion mining methods for analyzing citizens' contributions in public policy debate. Proceedings of IFIP 3rd international conference on e-participation—ePart 2011, August 29–September 1, 2011, Delft, The Netherlands

Nam T (2012) Suggesting frameworks of citizen-sourcing via government 2.0. Gov Inf Quart 29:12–20

Pedersen J, Kocsis D, Tripathi A, Tarrell A, Weerakoon A, Tahmasbi N, Xiong J, Deng W, Oh O, Vreede GJd. (2013) Conceptual foundations of crowdsourcing: a review of IS research. Proceedings of the 46th annual Hawaii international conference on system sciences, Maui, HI, USA.

Rentoumi V, Giannakopoulos G, Karkaletsis V, Vouros G (2009) Sentiment analysis of figurative language using a word sense disambiguation approach. Proceedings of RANLP 2009

Rentoumi V, Petrakis S, Karkaletsis V, Vouros G (2010) A collaborative system for sentiment analysis. Proceedings of SETN 2010.

Rouse AC (2010) A preliminary taxonomy of crowdsourcing. Proceedings of the Austalasian conference on information systems (ACIS) 2010, Paper 76.

Rittel HWJ, Weber MM (1973) Dilemmas in a general theory of planning. Policy Sci 4(2):155–169

Stewart O, Huerta J, Sader M (2009) Designing crowdsourcing community for the enterprise. Proceedings of the ACM SIGKDD workshop on human computation, New York, USA

Surowiecki J (2004) The wisdom of crowds: why the many are smarter than the few and how collective wisdom shapes business, economies, societies, and nations. Doubleday, New York

Tarrell A, Tahmasbi N, Kocsis D, Tripathi A, Pedersen J, Xiong J, Oh O, Vreede GJd (2013) Crowdsourcing: A snapshot of published research. Proceedings of the nineteenth Americas conference on information systems (AMCIS) 2013, Chicago, Illinois, USA

Thomas J, Cook K (eds) (2005) Illuminating the path: research and development agenda for visual analytics. IEEE, Los Alamitos

Wong PC, Thomas J (2004) Visual analytics. IEEE Comput Gr Appl 24(5):20–21

Zhao Y, Zhu Q (2012) Evaluation on crowdsourcing research: current status and future direction. Inf Syst Frontier 16(3):417–434

Ziegler CN, Skubacz M (2006) Towards automated reputation and brand monitoring on the web. Proceedings of IEEE/WIC/ACM international conference on Web intelligence 2006, Hong Kong

Chapter 13
Management of Complex Systems: Toward Agent-Based Gaming for Policy

Wander Jager and Gerben van der Vegt

Abstract In this chapter, we discuss the implications of complexities in societal systems for management. After discussing some essential features of complex systems, we discuss the current focus of managers and management theory on prediction and the problems arising from this perspective. A short overview is given of the leadership and management literature, identifying what information is lacking concerning the management of complex systems. Next agent-based gaming, which allows for modeling a virtual and autonomous population in a computer-game setting, is introduced as a tool to explore the possibilities to manage complex systems. The chapter concludes with a research agenda for management and leadership in complex systems.

13.1 Introduction

The Dexia bank run, which started with a tweet, and Project X Haren, that started with an open invitation on Facebook, demonstrate that social interactions may give rise to developments that spin out of control. In many different areas, managers in both the public and private sectors have to deal with the management of such complex behaving systems, e.g., the transition in the energy system, the development toward sustainability of our society, the developments in our health care system and the robustness of our financial–economic system, to name a few. Complexity theory applied to social systems contributes to our understanding of the mechanisms driving the sometimes turbulent developments in such social systems. It explains how the interactions between many individual agents may result in sometimes surprising processes of self-organization. In Chap. 4, Jager and Edmonds explained the principles of social complexity in more detail. A relevant contribution of the social complexity perspective is that it explains under what conditions a social system is rather predictable, and under what conditions it may start behaving turbulently,

W. Jager (✉)
Groningen Center of Social Complexity Studies, University of Groningen, Groningen, The Netherlands
e-mail: w.jager@rug.nl

G. van der Vegt
Faculty of Economics and Business, University of Groningen, Groningen, The Netherlands

© Springer International Publishing Switzerland 2015   291
M. Janssen et al. (eds.), *Policy Practice and Digital Science,*
Public Administration and Information Technology 10, DOI 10.1007/978-3-319-12784-2_13

making prediction in a classical sense impossible. For example, the car market has been a relatively predictable market for many years. For many brands and models, estimations of sales were being made that often lived up to their expectations. However, the introduction of hybrid and electric cars in the existing market resulted in turbulences. One example would be that in 2013 virtually all produced Mitsubishi Outlander PHEV (plug-in hybrid electric vehicle) models were shipped to the Netherlands due to a beneficial financial regime in that country. In 2014, the sales of this model dropped significantly[1]. It can be imagined that with the introduction of newer, more radical designs, such as the Google driverless car and new systems of car-sharing that utilize web based sharing tools new uncertainties are introduced in the car-market that may give rise to large turbulences and unpredictability in the market. In a way this reflects the uncertainties of a century ago when steam and gasoline were two viable and competing sources of propulsion.

Besides technological aspects, social aspects are also critical in the success or failure of introducing a new product or technology. Uncertainty, social norms, the spreading of rumors through social networks, and the behavior and opinions of role models all have significant effects on the success or failure and contribute to the turbulence during the introduction of new technology. Although social mechanisms underlying social complex phenomena have been identified in many social–scientific studies, the management of developments in turbulent systems remains problematic. At the same time, the more social interaction takes place in a system, which is usually the case with the introduction of radical new technology, the more turbulently it can behave, and the more important effective management of the system becomes. Yet little is known about the effective management of complex systems' behavior. It is precisely in such turbulent situations where good management can result in favorable outcomes. However, bad management may result in disasters hitting the news, such as failed evacuation plans, civil war, or power shortages. Hence, the question—if we can develop a tool to identify managerial leadership styles that help better manage complex social systems—seems a highly relevant one.

13.2 Simulating Social Complex Phenomena

In improving our understanding of how social complex systems can be managed, the first step is getting a better understanding of how interactions between people may give rise to social complex phenomena. Due to the large scale of many social systems and the often unique events that happen, experimentation with real populations is not possible. However, it is possible to experiment with computer simulated populations of artificial people, through so-called agent-based modeling (ABM, see e.g., Chap. 4). This methodology has proven to be a suitable approach in exploring the dynamics of social complex systems and is gaining momentum in many disciplines (e.g., Gilbert

---

[1] In December 2013 4988 Mitsubishi Outlander PHEV were registered, against 83 in January 2014 (Kane 2014).

and Troitzsch 2005). In ABMs, agents are connected in a network and follow simple rules that are programmed at the individual level. In a model to investigate a particular social system, these rules can be derived from a more general behavioral theory as well as specific data originating from the field.

An example is the model of Van Eck et al. (2011), where the role of opinion leaders on the diffusion of a new product was explored. In an empirical study, they found that opinion leaders had a more central network position, possess more accurate knowledge about a product, and tend to be less susceptible to norms and more innovative. Implementing this in an agent-based model opened the possibility of introducing new products in a simulated market and comparing the effects of the presence versus absence of such opinion leaders in the system. The simulation experiments demonstrated that opinion leaders increase the speed of the information stream and the adoption process itself. Furthermore, they increase the maximum adoption percentage. The simulation model thus suggests that targeting these opinion leaders might be a viable marketing strategy.

ABM makes it possible to conduct many experiments and explore the conditions under which social systems start behaving turbulent, which implies that the social system gets into a state where fast and unforeseen developments take place, such as in fashion dynamics or social conflicts. ABM also allows for exploring how individuals change their behavior over time due to social interactions and allows for the identification of the key individuals in a social network. Interestingly, it opens the possibility to explore how certain management strategies would perform in different conditions of turbulence.

13.3 Managing Social Complex Phenomena

From a social scientific experimental perspective, one would suggest running experimental designs as to identify the effects of different strategies. Comparing different interventions in a simulation model would yield information on what interventions are most effective. However, whereas empirically validated ABMs clearly provide a relevant perspective on identifying the social complexities in many social systems, their application in experimentally testing the effects of operational management strategies remains problematic in turbulent conditions. Two key reasons cause that experimentation with predefined leadership interventions are problematic.

First, in a turbulent system the effects of a specific management strategy may vary considerably. This is because in one simulation run such a strategy may be on spot with the developments that take place in the simulation, whereas in another simulation run the same timing of that specific strategy may be very inconvenient. As a result, specific management strategies may have different consequences, making it difficult to draw conclusions about their effectiveness.

Relaxing the experimental rigor of adopting certain management strategies at an identical moment in the simulation would allow for tracking the developments in the simulation and adopting the strategy at a moment that seems most effective. This implies that the experimentation bears an adaptive character, responding with the manipulation on developments in the simulation run as they evolve. However, here we run into the problem that in understanding effective management of a system it is not sufficient to study specific leadership behaviors in isolation. Rather, the management of social complex phenomena often implies that a sequence of behaviors takes place, and that (unforeseen) responses of other stakeholders have to be addressed as well. In regular experimental designs as used in the social sciences, this would result in an exponential growth of possible strategies to be tested. For example, given a simulated simple market with ten competing products, a manager trying to stimulate the sales of an "innovative green" product may decide on pricing, quality of the product, and type of marketing. Each of these elements already implies a choice from a wide array of possibilities. In selecting one possibility, the other product managers have an equal number of possibilities that even interact with each other. Many decision-making contexts are much more complex than this example, as they involve many stakeholders with different and sometimes conflicting goals, different valuations, and perspectives on outcomes, and different responsibilities and influencing power. And realizing that many complex social processes may span longer periods of time (e.g., years), it is clear that testing the effect of particular strategies in managing turbulent behaving social systems is not feasible in ABMs.

However, on a more aggregate level we may identify consistent patterns in managerial behavior, such as being adaptive to change, collecting information, and having a long-term perspective. These can be understood as a management or leadership *style,* and we hypothesize that these styles are far less divergent than operational management strategies, so that their effectiveness may be observed from the interaction between managers and a complex social system.

13.4   Leadership and Management in Complex Systems

The dominant paradigm in leadership research has been to examine the relationships between leadership styles, such as task- and relationship-oriented behavior (Bass 1990), and the outcomes of these behaviors, including follower attitudes (satisfaction, commitment, trust), behaviors (extra effort, cooperation, organizational citizenship behavior), and performance or unit level outcomes, like group cohesion, collective efficacy, and unit performance. Within this paradigm, the vast majority of studies has examined such relationships at a single period in time and has ignored the dynamic character of most of these relationships. In the field of leadership studies, this state of affairs is unfortunate because: (1) the effectiveness of specific leadership behaviors may depend on their timing, and (2) because leadership essentially represents a dynamic influence process between leader and followers that unfolds over time (Uhl-Bien and Marion 2009). Scholars have, therefore, recently started to develop theoretical frameworks that address these shortcomings, and now focused on team leadership as a dynamic process necessitating adaptive changes in leader behavior.

Kozlowski et al. (2008) proposed that the effects of certain leadership styles and actions may depend on their timing. They developed a team leadership framework that portrays team development as a cyclical and dynamic process, which requires leaders to adapt their leadership style to the various phases of team development and to the different adaptation needs of the team at each phase. This means that certain leadership actions and interventions may lead to desirable outcomes at a certain phase of the relationship but not in another phase. The theoretical framework proposes that for leaders to be adaptive, they must be aware of the key contingencies that necessitate shifts in leadership behavior, and they must possess the underlying skills needed to help the team resolve challenges. In these models, the leader has two major responsibilities or functions.

One leadership function is instructional and regulatory in nature. By responding to variations in team tasks by goal setting, performance monitoring, diagnosis, and feedback, the leader may help or stimulate team members to develop the knowledge and skills that contribute to team effectiveness. Leadership behaviors associated with this leadership function are transactional, structure-initiating, monitoring, authoritative, and directive leadership.

The second leadership function is developmental. As teams acquire the necessary knowledge and skills, the leader role shifts to help the team develop progressively more complex skills and capabilities (Kozlowski et al. 2008). Leadership behaviors associated with this leadership function are transformational, consideration, coaching, empowerment, facilitative, and participative leadership. Over time, this dual-pronged leadership process is hypothesized to yield team-level regulation and adaptive teams.

Other scholars have developed theoretical frameworks that explicitly conceptualize leadership as a dynamic influence process between leaders and followers. They suggest that leadership has to be understood as a reciprocal interaction process between leaders and followers, taking into consideration the characteristics, actions, and reactions of both sides (Collinson 2005). Uhl-Bien et al. (2007), for example, have proposed complexity leadership theory (CLT) as a model of team leadership consistent with this line of thinking. According to CLT, the question is how leaders might enable and coordinate the dynamic interactions between interdependent individuals without suppressing their adaptive and creative capacity. It distinguishes between three leadership functions that are important in this regard: adaptive, administrative, and enabling leadership. Adaptive leadership refers to the creative and learning actions that emerge from the interactions between team members; it is an informal, emergent dynamic that occurs among interacting individuals. Administrative leadership refers to the actions of persons in formal managerial roles who plan and coordinate activities to accomplish organizationally prescribed outcomes in an efficient and effective manner; it is about structuring tasks, planning, building a vision, allocating resources, and managing crises. Enabling leadership is behavior aimed at creating appropriate conditions to foster effective adaptive leadership in places where innovation and adaptability are needed, and facilitating the flow of knowledge and creativity from adaptive structures into administrative structures.

Enabling leadership tailors the behaviors of administrative and adaptive leadership so that they can effectively function in tandem with one another.

Although leadership scholars have acknowledged the dynamic nature of leadership and have started to develop models and frameworks to organize and describe the factors that are important, empirical research testing these models is scarce. The reason for the lack of research on dynamic leadership processes is that it requires a different approach than the traditional research methods employed in leadership research. Even multiwave studies are at best a series of time-spaced sequential snapshots and do not capture the dynamic relationships between inputs and outcomes over time. Serious gaming may provide a suitable tool to enable real-time observation of leadership processes: longitudinal methods for the real-time tracking of leadership relationships and consequences as they evolve over time.

13.5   Serious Gaming

Serious gaming is well equipped as a tool to experiment with and train people for situations that are less easy to practice in reality (e.g., Lisk et al. 2012). The flight simulator is the most renowned serious game in this context, offering the possibility to develop and maintain the skills to deal with all kinds of flying events, starting with routine flights and ending with co-occurrences of rare events that in reality often lead to disaster. One of the main advantages in studying and training behavior is that the behavior of a person can be observed and tracked over time, offering precise and controlled measurements, and allowing for detailed evaluations of the behavior. Currently gaming is widely adopted in military training, and increasingly being used in testing, for example, the organization of firefighting departments, new product introductions (marketing), the optimal crowd streams in cities and stadiums, and managing traffic flows. Leaving the implementation of strategies to real people interacting with the model thus has the advantage of creating a plausible managerial environment, as real people manage the system.

Up till now, serious games that are being used to study and train leadership and management were based on deterministic models. The basic principle here is that the player is confronted with a choice, and depending on the selection, a predefined scenario path is picked. Whereas the multitude of choices creates a large landscape of possible routes through the game, the game is deterministic by nature. This implies that current games are not capable of capturing the social complex phenomena mentioned earlier that emerge as the result of many autonomous interacting agents. Yet for testing leadership and management in social complex systems over time, it is critical to include these social complexities in a gaming setting. Whereas several scientists within the ABM community identified gaming as a tool to explore and forecast developments in complex systems (e.g., Arai et al. 2006; Guyot and Honiden 2006), it has not been used to study leadership and management of social complex systems. Considering that especially turbulent developments in social systems can be problematic and require effective leadership, and observing that management science lacks a suitable tool to study this, we propose to use *agent-based gaming* as a new tool to study leadership and management behavior of real people in a controlled simulated complex environment.

13.6 Agent-Based Games for Testing Leadership and Management

To study the management of social complex phenomena we propose developing agent-based games that includes an autonomously behaving artificial population. Players will perform a management task in this game, allowing us to experimentally test under what system characteristics a specific management strategy or leadership style performs best. We hypothesize that in systems that are more turbulent, an adaptive and people-oriented style will outperform conservative and outcome-oriented styles. More adaptivity prevents unwanted lock-ins to emerge, and a people-oriented style will translate in better relations, and thus performance in the long run. However, we also hypothesize that a long-term goal orientation is critical in efficient leadership/management. Just concentrating on adapting to short-term developments may cause that the long-term goals are neglected, which may also be a sign of ineffective management. Hence, our basic hypothesis is that effective management of social complex systems requires a strong adaptive capacity for responding to short-term developments combined with a clear long-term perspective of the goals to reach. For example, in stimulating the adoption of more sustainable technologies, one should be very alert on what is currently happening in the market, and responding to threats and identifying opportunities, but at the same time one should have a clear vision of how the successful diffusion of sustainable technology creates future conditions for further developments.

Currently, several practice-oriented agent-based simulation models have been developed that are aimed to support policy making. A recent inventory initiated by Gilbert[2] demonstrated that dozens of simulation models are being used in practical settings. In many instances, the contributions remain at a more conceptual level, providing the practitioners with a deeper understanding of the complexities of the system they are interacting with, and the implications for policy making. If practitioners actually interact with a model it usually requires close guidance by the modelers because of the expertise required to interact with the interface.

It is our stand that the use of social simulation models, and their application in studies exploring managerial and leadership styles, is necessary to work toward interfaces that make it easier and more intuitive to interact with the simulation tool. In the gaming industry, many developments took place, and as a result there is an

---

[2] On 04-12-2013, Gilbert sent out an e-mail on the SIMSOC list asking for examples of ABMs that have actually been used to support policy decision making or for other purposes "in the real world."

abundance of games that create a very convincing environment in which it is relatively easy to operate, to learn what the behavioral options are, and most importantly, to create an experience of "flow" in the players that keeps them motivated to continue playing the game. Important here is that the behavior of simulated agents and the environment one interacts with provide a sufficiently realistic experience.

Whereas for amusement games convincing graphics are essential to create a flow, and we emphasize the importance of developing high-quality interfaces for agent-based games, the applicability of appeal of these serious games resides primarily in the realism of the behavioral dynamics that are being simulated. This implies that the behaviors as displayed by the artificial agents should reflect the behavior that can be observed in reality. The consumat approach has specifically been designed to capture a number of main processes of human behavior and has been used in a variety of applications (see e.g., Jager 2000; Jager et al. 2000). Figure 13.1 gives an overview of the components in the consumat framework.

A simulated agent, when satisfied and certain, may continue repeating itself many times. Only if the satisfaction drops, and/or the uncertainty rises, the consumat may switch to using a different decisional strategy. If this results in an increase in satisfaction and the uncertainty is reduced, the agent may return to a new habitual behavior.

Agents differ concerning their uncertainty tolerance (when to engage in social processing) and aspiration level (when is an agent dissatisfied). The agents also differ concerning the relative importance of the needs that determine their satisfaction (individual preferences). As a consequence, an action directed on a specific agent may result in different responses depending on the type and state of an agent. Agents also have different abilities, such as financial means, which determine if a behavior is possible to perform.

The consumat approach has been used to guide the modeling of different agent-based models, such as fashion dynamics (Janssen and Jager 2001), transitions in a society (Jager et al. 2000), sustainable life styles (Bravo et al. 2013), farmer crop choice behavior (Mialhe et al. 2012; Speelman 2014), and currently projects are addressing the diffusion of light-emitting diode (LED) household lighting (Schoenmacker 2014) and electric cars (Jager et al. 2014).

A key attribute of the artificial population in our proposed agent-based gaming approach is that the agents are linked in a social network, where some agents have more links and influence than other agents. This implies that experiences of agents are being communicated through the social network as information exchange and normative influences, and may give rise to the emergence of precisely those social complexities and turbulences where we want to study management and leadership. Depending on the requirements of the topic to be modeled, one can implement static or dynamic networks (see e.g., Squazzoni et al. 2013). For example, in developing a game directed at the diffusion of new energy technology one could use a static network with a number of actors having many contacts, representing influential opinion leaders. However, in developing a model to experiment with the emergence of extremism it is essential to include dynamic networks that allow for clusters of agents that separate from mainstream society.

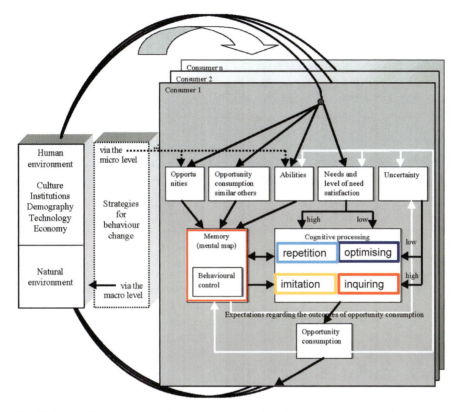

Fig. 13.1 How different factors influence one another and result in behavior (opportunity consumption), which aggregates over all simulated consumers and results in macrolevel outcomes that set the conditions for a next behavioral cycle. In the consumat approach, the agents have existence needs (e.g., food, income), social needs (group belongingness and status), and identity needs (personal preferences, taste). To select a behavior an agent can employ four different types of decisional strategies, depending on its satisfaction and uncertainty. A satisfied and certain agent will *repeat* its previous demand, which captures habitual behavior/routine maintenance. A satisfied but uncertain agent will *imitate* the demand of a similar other in its network, which reflects normative compliance (fashion). A dissatisfied and certain agent will evaluate all possible demands and select the one providing the best outcomes (*optimizing*). And finally, a dissatisfied and uncertain agent will *inquire* the demands other agents had and copy this demand if the outcomes are expected to be better (social learning).

13.7   Single and Multiplayer Settings

A player confronted with an agent-based game using this approach will experience realistic behavioral dynamics. First, because the consequences and impacts of policy decisions will be communicated through the network of agents, which may elicit far fetching effects, treating one person wrong may elicit a cascade of negative information, whereas convincing an opinion leader of the benefits of, e.g., an energy-efficient device may stimulate the social diffusion of this device. Players thus learn how their policies may spread through the social system and may develop strategies that use these social forces. This also implies that a player becomes aware of the fact that his/her policy action may spread through society and hence may have long-term effects on other agents beyond those directly affected in the here and now.

A second valuable outcome of using such a model is that the player not only observes the impact of policy measures in the diffusion of products of the changing of behavior but also sees what is happening with the level of need satisfaction of different groups of agents. Hence, a deeper insight is generated concerning the effects of policy on well-being and it can be observed if well-being drops, so measures can be taken before a decrease in well-being results in negative behavior.

Up till now, we mentioned the players as an individual interacting with the simulation model. And indeed it is very well possible to let an individual interact with the simulation tool, both in training, teaching, and experimentation settings. However, many social complex systems are being managed by multiple stakeholders. In developing agent-based models several researchers already include different stakeholders in the model building stages and also in the playing of the game, which were often cardboard games (e.g., Barreteau et al. 2001). In the context of gaming, it is already a common practice to use multiplayer settings. An example is World of Warcraft (WoW), an Internet-based war game that started in 1994 as a simple computer game and transformed into a massively multiplayer online role-playing game (MMORPG), where over 7 million people are playing. A very relevant attribute of WoW that makes it very appealing to play is the possibility to join a team of people in accomplishing a mission. Here similarities in interest and complementary in skills may lead to effective teams. These teams are often in competition with other teams and often conflicts arise, which are being settled in fights.

In managing social complex systems often the same social structures can be observed as in WoW and similar games. Decisions by a firm or organization are made by groups of people having different and often complementary competences, and they often have other and sometimes conflicting interests than other companies and organizations. For agent-based gaming, a same venue can be created as in such games. Instead of single players, a team may be composed, and it can be studied what team compositions function well in managing turbulent situations in social complex systems. It depends on the issue at stake if multiple teams are a relevant extension of the agent-based game.

An example of a single group agent-based game would be a crowd managing game. Here an artificial crowd can be modeled (see e.g., Wijermans et al. 2013), which is gathering at a specific environment, such as a city center or a stadium. The crowd can be given a general motivation, e.g., demonstrating, watching a performance, of attending a soccer match, and a distribution can be given of the behavioral tendencies of the simulated agents, e.g., in terms of aggression motivation. The players can be a police task force that is composed of people in the field and a command level. At the field level, a number of players will represent law-enforcement in the field. These players will move in the environment and have a perception of the local environment that is limited. They can interact with the simulated civilians. Here the agent-based architecture allows for a realistic response of the simulated people, such as obeying orders, discussing and changing of arousal, or engaging in aggressive behavior. Essential is that the behavior of an artificial agent will affect the behavior of other agents as well, which may lead to cascade effects. For example, if a policeman decides to hit an agent, nearby agents will experience a higher arousal upon observing a fellow agent being hit, and will probably have a higher tendency to either flee or engage in aggressive behavior. In the game policemen can also communicate with each other using a radio system (which can be blurred or fail in game scenarios). At the command level, the player (which can be a group of people) has a generic overview of the festival terrain, but they rely on the reports of the field-level players for the interpretation of what is happening. The command level can give orders to the field-level concerning their position and actions. Hence, they may decide to have law enforcement as couples in the crowd, or cluster them in a line to block an area. Also, they can give orders to the field-level players, such as arresting a civilian. Such a single team game can be played to study optimal group compositions, learn about how to manage turbulent situations in groups and as a practice tool. Also, such a game can be played in a specific location on a confined time slot.

A multiple agent-based group game can target social complex systems where different groups are interacting with the agent population, but are having different and sometimes conflicting interests. An example would be a team that is trying to stimulate the diffusion of electric cars, which implies experts on technical possibilities, economical viability, infrastructural development, and marketing and communication. Experts from these different domains have to develop and manage a joint proposition toward segments in an artificial consumer base. At the same time, comparable teams can work on fuel-propelled cars, and thus compete with the electric team for market share. Using a realistic artificial population that is based on empirical data will provide a simulated environment where these different teams can operate. Because in these settings is becomes impractical to meet in a specific location on a confined time slot, it seems more realistic to implement multigroup agent-based games as Internet games where different teams can operate quite independently, but are being confronted with the implications of each other's actions. In the multigroup game teams also have to identify the strategy of competitors, and adapt to that, which adds to the complexity of the game.

13.8   Experimentation with Management

The proposed game setting allows for measuring different task- and relationship-oriented behaviors of the players. Critical factors to track are adaptive speed, information collection, orientation on agent behavior, orientation on competitor behavior, and overall performance in terms of reaching predefined goals and agent satisfaction. Experimentation will be possible to show the relation between the managerial/leadership style of the player(s), and its success in turbulent settings. It will also be possible as a *post measurement* to ask the players for their understanding of the dynamics of the system using the methodology of Endsley (1995) and Edwards et al. (2006), which focuses on measuring situation awareness in complex situations and the identification of relations. This will contribute also to a more qualitative indication of the extent to which they understand the complex nature of the game and the best styles and strategies within social complex systems. Experiments thus are capable of showing: (1) what leadership and managerial styles perform best in conditions of varying complexity (single vs. multi player) and the type of population (importance of social need), (2) how task- and relationship-oriented behavior, adaptive speed, information collection, agent, and competitor orientation relate to performance in management under different conditions of complexity, and (3) what leadership and managerial styles are more effective in developing an understanding of the system.

13.9   Conclusions and Discussion

In this chapter, we discussed how agent-based gaming may provide a methodology to study effective management and leadership on social complex systems. Because the major challenges in our society often deal with behavior change of large populations and social complex processes, turbulent developments are common. This proposed direction of development of methodology may contribute to a better understanding of how our species can manage common behavior, both among ourselves and in interaction with our habitat. A critical contribution will be the formalization of some main principles of human behavior in an integrated model, which subsequently allows for interaction with an artificial but realistically behaving population. This will facilitate the transfer of behavioral insights into the realm of policy testing and will contribute to the development of the required knowledge on how to manage social complex behaving systems. Currently, the respective fields of social simulation, management science, and gaming technology seem developed far enough to make such an endeavor possible, but, considering agent-based gaming projects will require the interaction between many different actors, also, here turbulences can be expected.

Acknowledgment   This chapter has been written in the context of the eGovPoliNet project. More information can be found on http://www.policy-community.eu/

References

Arai K, Deguchi H, Matsui H, (2006) Agent-based modeling meets gaming simulation. Springer, Japan

Barreteau O, Bousquet F, Attonaty JM (2001) Role-playing games for opening the black box of multi-agent systems: method and lessons of its application to Senegal River Valley irrigated systems. J Artif Soc Soc Simul 4(2):12 (http://www.soc.surrey.ac.uk/JASSS/4/2/5.html)

Bass BM (1990) Bass & Stogdill's handbook of leadership: theory, research, and managerial applications, 3rd ed. Free Press, New York

Bravo G, Vallino E, Cerutti AK, Pairotti MB (2013) Alternative scenarios of green consumption in Italy: an empirically grounded model. Environ Model Softw 47:225–234

Collinson D (2005) Dialectics of leadership. Hum Relat 58:1419–1442.

Endsley (1995) Measurement of situation awareness in dynamic systems. Hum Factor 37(1):65–84.

Edwards, BD, Day, EA, Arthur, W Jr, Bell, ST (2006) Relationships among team ability composition, team mental models, and team performance. J Appl Psychol 91(3):727–736.

Gilbert N, Troitzsch KG (2005) Simulation for the social scientist. Open University Press, Buckingham.

Guyot P, Honiden S (2006) Agent-based participatory simulations: merging multi-agent systems and role-playing games. J Artif Soc Soc Simul 9(4):8. http://jasss.soc.surrey.ac.uk/9/4/8.html

Jager W (2000) Modelling consumer behavior. Doctoral thesis. Groningen, University of Groningen, Centre for Environmental and Traffic psychology

Jager W, Janssen MA, De Vries HJM, De Greef J, Vlek CAJ (2000) Behaviour in commons dilemmas: homo economicus and homo psychologicus in an ecological-economic model. Ecol Econ 35:357–380

Jager W, Janssen M, Bockarjova M (2014). Diffusion dynamics of electric cars and adaptive policy: towards an empirical based simulation. Adv Soc Simul 229:259–270

Janssen MA, W Jager (2001) Fashions, habits and changing preferences: simulation of psychological factors affecting market dynamics. J Econ Psychol 22:745–772

Kane M (2014) Sales of plug in vehicles in the Netherlands drop off big time. Insideeves.com. http://insideevs.com/sales-of-plug-in-vehicles-in-the-netherlands-drop-off-big-time/ retrieved on 08–07–2014

Kozlowski SWJ, Watola DJ, Nowakowski JM, Kim BH, Botero IC (2008) Developing adaptive teams: a theory of dynamic team leadership. In E Salas, GF Goodwin, CS Burke (eds) Team effectiveness in complex organizations: cross-disciplinary perspectives and approaches. Psychology Press, New York.

Lisk TC, Kaplancali UT, Riggio RE (2012) Leadership in multiplayer online gaming environments. Simul Gaming 43(1):133–149.

Mialhe F, Becuc N, Gunnelld Y, (2012) An agent-based model for analyzing land use dynamics in response to farmer behaviour and environmental change in the Pampanga delta (Philippines). Agric Ecosyst Environ 161(2012):55–69.

Schoenmacker GH (2014) Agent-based consumer modelling of the Dutch lighting market. Master Thesis Department of Artificial Intelligence Faculty of Mathematics and Natural Sciences, University of Groningen.

Speelman EN (2014) Gaming and simulation to explore resilience of contested agricultural landscapes. Doctoral Thesis, Wageningen University, Farming Systems Ecology

Squazzoni F, Jager W, Edmonds B (2013) Social simulation in the social sciences: a brief overview. Soc Sci Comput Rev. First published on December 6, 2013. doi:10.1177/0894439313512975

Uhl-Bien M, Marion, R (2009) Complexity leadership in bureaucratic forms of organizing: a meso model. Leadersh Q 20:631–650

Uhl-Bien M, Marion R, McKelvey B (2007) Complexity leadership theory: shifting leadership from the industrial age to the knowledge era. Leadersh Q 18:298–318.

Van Eck PS, Jager W, Leeflang PSH (2011) Opinion leaders' role in innovation diffusion: a simulation study. J Prod Innov Manag 28:187–203

Wijermans W, Jorna R, Jager W, Van Vliet T, Adang O (2013) CROSS: modelling crowd behaviour with social-cognitive agents. J Artif Soc Soc Simul 16(4):1

Chapter 14
The Role of Microsimulation in the Development of Public Policy

Roy Lay-Yee and Gerry Cotterell

Abstract This chapter seeks to provide a brief introduction to the method of microsimulation and its utility for the development of public policy. Since the inception of microsimulation in the 1950s, its use for policy purposes has extended from the economic to other domains as data availability and technological advances have burgeoned. There has also been growing demand in recent times to address increasingly complex policy issues that require new approaches. Microsimulation focuses on modelling individual units and the micro-level processes that affect their development, be they people's lives or other trajectories. It comes in various types, for example along the dimensions of arithmetical or behavioural, and static or dynamic. It has its own distinctive model-building process, which relies on empirical data and derived parameters with an insertion of chance to simulate realistic distributions. The particular utility of microsimulation for policy development lies in its ability to combine multiple sources of information in a single contextualised model to answer 'what if' questions on complex social phenomena and issues.

14.1 Introduction

This chapter provides an introduction to the method of microsimulation and its role in the development of public policy. The chapter firstly provides a brief history of microsimulation, which tracks the development of this method since its inception in the 1950s. This is followed by an explanation of microsimulation itself, the differences between its various types, and the model-building procedure. We end with assessing the utility of microsimulation for policy development, and setting out its strengths and weaknesses as a method for this purpose. We describe a case study taken from a dynamic microsimulation model of the early life course developed in New Zealand. In the Appendix, we provide selected examples of a number of other existing microsimulation models in use from around the world.

R. Lay-Yee (✉) · G. Cotterell
Centre of Methods and Policy Application in the Social Sciences (COMPASS Research Centre),
University of Auckland, Private Bag 92019, 1142 Auckland, New Zealand
e-mail: r.layyee@auckland.ac.nz

© Springer International Publishing Switzerland 2015
M. Janssen et al. (eds.), *Policy Practice and Digital Science*,
Public Administration and Information Technology 10, DOI 10.1007/978-3-319-12784-2_14

14.2   A Brief History

The academic literature generally acknowledges the pioneering work of Guy Orcutt in his 1957 paper, 'A new type of socio-economic system', as providing the foundation for the field of microsimulation. In his paper, Orcutt posited that microsimulation models consisting of 'various sorts of interacting units which receive inputs and generate outputs' (Orcutt 1957, p. 117) could be used to investigate 'what would happen given specified external conditions and governmental actions' (Orcutt 1957, p. 122). Even today, Orcutt's prescient ideas still provide a relevant blueprint for modelling. However, the potential of this new approach was slow to materialise because of limitations in computing power and the lack of suitable data.

As these respective limitations were gradually overcome with the rise of technology and data collection, the use of microsimulation increased. In the 1970s, microsimulation models were being used in the USA to assist the development of social policy (Citro and Hanusek 1991), and by 1990 'microsimulation had become widespread enough in the domain of tax and transfer analysis' (Anderson and Hicks 2011, p. 1). Merz identified six major microsimulation projects in the USA and Europe in the 1980s, growing to 18 in the 1970s and then to 33 in the 1980s (Merz 1991). Further rapid advances in computing power, along with information sharing, served to increase the use of microsimulation modelling, and in 2005, the International Microsimulation Association was formed (Anderson and Hicks 2011, p. 1; http://www.microsimulation.org/). Microsimulation models have historically been employed for tax and transfer policy purposes (Harding 1996; Gupta and Kapur 2000; Harding and Gupta 2007), but their use has extended to other social domains (Gupta and Harding 2007). In recent times, there has been growing demand for new approaches to address increasingly complex policy issues. However, even today, despite the advances in technology and data availability, microsimulation projects typically require large investments of time and resources.

14.3   What Is Microsimulation?

As a form of social simulation, the microsimulation variant can be seen to be located between and contrasted with system dynamics—with a macro focus and low complexity—on one side, and agent-based modelling—with a behavioural focus often relying on notional rules—on the other (Gilbert and Troitzsch 2005). Based on the use of empirical individual-level data, it can potentially account for complexity, heterogeneity, and change (Orcutt 1957; Spielauer 2011).

The core of microsimulation has been defined as 'a means of modelling real life events by simulating the actions of the individual units that make up the system where the events occur' (Brown and Harding 2002), and as 'computer-simulation of a society in which the population is represented by a large sample of its individual members and their behaviours' (Spielauer 2011). This has been broadened to encompass its role in policy so that 'microsimulation models are computer programs that simulate aggregate and distributional effects of a policy, by implementing the provisions of the policy on a representative sample of individuals and families, and then summing up the results across individual units using population weights' (Martini and Trivellato 1997, p. 84). Microsimulation models are based on individual-level data, or microdata relating to the characteristics and behaviours of individuals. The method endeavours to approximate an experiment whereby the potential range of outcomes is 'simulated or imputed on the basis of a set of assumptions about the behavioural reactions of individuals following changes… brought about by the introduction of a policy' (Zucchelli et al. 2012, p. 3).

The microsimulation method relies on data from the real world to create an artificial one that mimics the original, but upon which virtual experiments can be carried out (Gilbert and Troitzsch 2005). Microsimulation operates at the level of individual units, for example people, each possessing a set of associated attributes as a starting point. A set of rules, for example equations derived from statistical analysis of (often multiple) survey data sets, is then applied in a stochastic manner to each and every individual in the starting sample to simulate changes in state or behaviour. Such a model (Rutter et al. 2011; Spielauer 2007) can essentially generate a set of diverse synthetic biographies for the base sample of individuals. Modifications of influential factors can then be carried out to test hypothetical 'what if' scenarios on a key outcome of policy interest (Davis et al. 2010). Simulation at the micro level enables the assessment of the impact of potential policy changes for subgroups as well as aggregates of the population. Microsimulation has the capability to integrate, and accommodate the manipulation of, the effects of variables across multiple model equations (often derived from multiple data sources) in a single simulation run. Thus, each otherwise separate equation is given its context and influence among the other equations, representing a system of interdependent social processes.

Last but not least, the human and technology requirements for implementing microsimulation are demanding, especially in relation to forming a team with multidisciplinary skills, finding relevant data sources (for inputs), and deploying computer hardware and software (for implementation and outputs) (Cassells et al. 2006).

In summary, the essential characteristics of microsimulation are: the use of empirical micro-level data both to form a starting sample and from which to derive equations to drive the simulation forward; the integration of data and equations from disparate sources; the use of a stochastic simulation process that generates both aggregate and distributional effects; and the facility to be able to manipulate the underpinning model to test counterfactuals or policy scenarios.

14.4 Types of Microsimulation

There exists a range of types of microsimulation for policy purposes, which can be categorised on various dimensions. Zucchelli et al. propose a taxonomy that comprises 'arithmetical versus behavioural models and static versus dynamic models'

(Zucchelli et al. 2012, p. 6). The primary features of each of these types are outlined below:

1. *Arithmetical* microsimulation models are typically run to estimate distributional and budgetary change occurring as a response to changes in taxes, benefits, and wages. These models ignore the behavioural responses by individuals to the policy change being examined. For example, in the case of a model simulating tax and benefit changes, the simulation mimics adjustments to real disposable income following a policy change, and assumes that the behaviour of the individual does not change (Bourguignon and Spadro 2006). Such models are useful in highlighting the impact of reforms, and in ascertaining those who benefit and those who lose from the modelled reforms, along with their characteristics (Zucchelli et al. 2012).

2. In contrast, *behavioural* microsimulation takes into account changes in the behaviour of the individuals in the simulation in response to the policy parameters modified. For example, changes to tax-benefit policy introduced into a model are considered to impact on the options favouring the individual, and may lead to a change in the amount of labour they choose to supply (Zucchelli et al. 2012, p. 8).

3. *Static* simulation models restrict their analysis to a single point in time or a set of points in time, without modelling the processes that drive the changes over time (Spielauer 2011, p. 2). Thus static models evaluate the putative state of each individual under a changed set of policy rules (Brown and Harding 2002). Static models are typically used to model changes in taxes and social security benefits. A data-based static microsimulation model consists of two parts: (1) a baseline database—containing information on individual or family/household units, particularly sociodemographic characteristics and economic information that bears a relationship with a set of policies; and (2) a set of accounting rules—computer language instructions that produce for each unit the results of, for example, alternative tax or transfer policies and procedures (Martini and Trivellato 1997).

4. 'Dynamically ageing microsimulation models, on the other hand, involve updating each attribute for each micro-unit for each time interval' (Brown and Harding 2002, p. 3.). *Dynamic* microsimulation models are constructed using either stochastic or deterministic algorithms. If the former, then the model is 'based on conditional probabilities that certain economic or social conditions or processes will exist or occur' (Brown and Harding 2002, p. 3.). If the latter, it is rule-based so that a condition will trigger a state or event. Spielauer argues that behaviours studied in dynamic microsimulation are of two types: 'behaviour that produces events that take place over time such as demographic events, for example, marriage, divorce, death, and economic events such as leaving the labour force', and 'behaviour producing feedback reactions of individuals and/or families to changes in external circumstances, notably to changes in public policies' (Spielauer 2011, p. 4).

Distinctions can be made among dynamic microsimulation models themselves depending on the nature of the starting sample of individuals and the process by which it is aged (Spielauer 2011).

(a) Actual *or* synthetic starting sample, i.e. the starting sample comes from an actual survey, *or* it is synthesised from various data sources;

(b) Open *or* closed population, i.e. other individuals can be introduced to the starting sample as the simulation progresses, *or* membership of the sample is fixed;

(c) Cohort *or* population, i.e. a cross-sectional sample that is aged and eventually dies out, or a sample of the population whose representativeness is maintained over time;

(d) Discrete time *or* continuous time, i.e. individuals' characteristics are simulated at fixed time intervals, for example yearly, *or* their characteristics are assigned and can change at any time;

(e) Case-based *or* time-based, i.e. each individual's life course is simulated independently from beginning to end, *or* all individuals have their characteristics updated at the same time points.

The taxonomy of Zucchelli et al. (2012) is useful to policymakers in choosing the type of microsimulation model to support their decisions. For example, if they wanted to take into account the impact of not only a policy change but also changes in individual behaviour due to that policy change, then the model of choice would be the 'behavioural' type rather than the more straightforward 'arithmetical' type. Similarly, if the policy interest was in changes over time, then the 'dynamic' type would be more appropriate than the 'static' type.

14.5 The Process of Microsimulation

The process of building a microsimulation model follows several linked stages and components (Caro et al. 2012; Cassells et al. 2006; Zaidi and Rake 2001). This process is not strictly sequential—as presented for exposition—but branched and iterative where steps may be overlapping or repeated until the model is functioning as required. A case study is described in Sect. 14.8.

1. *Conceptualisation*—considerations
    (a) Setting clear objectives delineating the focus and scope of the model, e.g. what processes and variables to include;
    (b) Deciding on the level of simplicity or complexity of the model;
    (c) Ensuring that the framework accounts for core processes of the phenomenon being modelled so that the simulation sufficiently matches reality;
    (d) Recognising that proper configuring of model structure and pathways is critical to the success of the model's application for projection or scenario testing;
    (e) Balancing the dual goals of explanation and prediction of the phenomenon of interest.

2. *Computing platform*—considerations (Percival 2007; Scott 2003)
   (a) Following good IT practice, e.g. best-practice guidelines and standards, software selection, testing regime, and computing facilities;
   (b) Procuring adequate and sufficient resources to sustain a project;
   (c) Building a developer and user platform that is fit for purpose, reliable, and well supported, and that ideally can be maintained and repurposed for further studies.
3. Data integration—considerations
   (a) Identifying and accessing various data sources relevant to the phenomenon of interest, i.e. quantitative, qualitative, findings from other studies, or guesstimates;
   (b) Generating data to form the starting file (initial conditions) from which the simulation proceeds;
   (c) Generating parameters (e.g. from data analyses) to inform the rules that drive the simulation;
   (d) Combining both data and parameters into a cohesive model, and as inputs to the simulation engine.
4. Implementation—steps
   (a) Initialisation, presimulation—setting up model specifications, the starting file, and procedures;
   (b) Simulation—invokes a stochastic process—in which a (transition) probability is compared to a number from a random draw to assign a state or behaviour to a unit or individual;
   (c) Validation—comparing simulation results against both internal and external benchmarks;
   (d) Calibration (before simulation) or alignment (after simulation) of simulation results to benchmarks.
5. Application
   (a) Projection of the current state into the future assuming that inherent features of the status quo remain the same;
   (b) Simulating the impact of potential policy change or intervention over time, i.e. posing and testing scenarios, by altering relevant features of the model and observing flow-on effects.

14.6 Is Microsimulation Useful for Policy Development?

Complex policy issues require approaches that enable research synthesis and use systems thinking (Grimshaw et al. 2012; Lobb and Colditz 2013; Milne et al. 2014). Large sums of money are spent on public policy sometimes without a clear understanding of how they will impact on or benefit different groups in the population. Anchored in empirical data, microsimulation modelling has the potential to represent systems and processes in various social domains and to test their functioning for policy purposes (Anderson and Hicks 2011; Zaidi et al. 2009). By attempting to mimic an experiment, it is a relatively cost-effective means of testing policy options to ensure defective polices are not implemented (Mitton et al. 2000). Microsimulation has been primarily used for investigating the effects of tax and benefit policies but its use is spreading rapidly to other domains such as health policy (Glied and Tilipman 2010; Ringel et al. 2010; Rutter et al. 2011).

Microsimulation techniques bring a range of benefits to social policy modelling, including the ability to change a greater variety of parameters independently and the capacity to provide considerably more accurate estimates and detailed projections of the distributional effects of changes. Two key advantages of microsimulation models are that: (1) they can replicate the complexity of the policy structures, transfers, and settings; and (2) they can be used to forecast the outcomes of policy changes and 'what if' scenarios (i.e. the counterfactual where the results describe what, under specified conditions, may happen to particular individuals and groups) (Brown and Harding 2002).

Microsimulation models are important tools for the development of policy for other reasons. Policy evaluation is typically undertaken 'by ex-post techniques which by definition are used to evaluate the impact of interventions and programmes following their implementation' (Zucchelli et al. 2012, p. 2). Use of microsimulation removes the need to collect information after the implementation of the policy—allows the testing of a wide range of scenarios—with the range only being limited by the data that are available. Microsimulation also allows ex ante examination of the impact of policies before their implementation under different conditions. In this role, the models can be used to assist in recognising ineffectual policies prior to their implementation (Zucchelli et al. 2012).

A microsimulation model, as a policy decision-making support tool, is ideally implemented in a software package that can be interrogated by policymakers in their workplace as the need arises (Milne et al. 2014). However, it is a major undertaking, adding another layer of complexity, to make such a model transparent and accessible to end users. Not only does the package need to accommodate the simulation code but it must also contain a user-friendly graphical interface and adequate user documentation. Then there are the challenging requirements of delivering on-site deployment, and end-user training and support.

Despite resource barriers to implementation, microsimulation models hold much promise for policy development. In the Appendix, we provide a selection of well-known microsimulation models used for policy purposes from around the world. In Sect. 14.8, we also present a case study from New Zealand.

14.7 Strengths and Weaknesses

'To simulate a society realistically requires detailed data, complicated models, fast computers, and extensive testing' (Spielauer 2011, p. 1).

The primary strength of microsimulation techniques is their use of actual individual-level data, which allows them to reproduce social reality and the intricacy of policy structures. The model can then be used to estimate the outcomes of 'what if' scenarios (Brown and Harding 2002, p. 4). The benefit of such models is dependent on the circumstances in which they are used.

Spielauer notes that microsimulation is certainly the preferred modelling choice in three situations: (1) if population heterogeneity matters and if there are too many possible combinations of considered characteristics to split the population into a manageable number of groups; (2) if behaviours are complex at the macro level but better understood at the micro level; and (3) if individual histories matter, that is, when processes possess memory (Spielauer 2011, pp. 6–8).

1. The strengths of microsimulation for policy purposes can be summed up as follows:
    (a) Can provide another piece to the jigsaw complementing other forms of evidence;
    (b) Can tackle problems perhaps intractable by conventional means of analysis and interpretation;
    (c) Can model processes or pathways that may be identified for and amenable to policy intervention;
    (d) Can account for social complexity, heterogeneity, and change in its use of rich micro data for modelling;
    (e) Can combine relevant information from disparate data sources into a cohesive whole to form the substantive content of the model;
    (f) Can be used to carry out virtual experiments by altering features of the model and observing changes to outcomes, i.e. testing policy scenarios with various underlying assumptions;
    (g) Can produce both aggregate and distributional results—a property derived from the use of individual-level data—and allows subgroup analysis that can inform the targeting of policy interventions.
2. There are typical weaknesses of the microsimulation method that are not necessarily inherent given more sophisticated modelling.
    (a) Macro social outcomes tend to be merely a mechanical aggregation of micro ones—the macro is not greater than the sum of the micro parts;
    (b) There is no creative emergence of macro social phenomena from micro ones;
    (c) There is no interaction between individuals or their trajectories;
    (d) There may be no feedback loops or reciprocal effects where changes in individual behaviour may modify policy impacts;
    (e) Models tend to be predictive rather than explanatory—this may improve the accuracy of projections but may hamper substantive scenario testing;
    (f) Pathways tend to be simplified and may miss important elements;
    (g) True individual behaviour, e.g. motivation or intention, tends to be neglected in favour of external manifestations, e.g. working longer hours;
    (h) There tends to be no influence of exogenous macro factors (e.g. economic climate) that may provide a broader societal context for the model;
    (i) There is high demand for data and computer technology.

14.8   A Case Study: Modelling the Early Life Course

We present a case study describing the prototype of a dynamic microsimulation model (nicknamed MEL-C) developed by the COMPASS Research Centre (Centre of Methods and Policy Application in the Social Science) at The University of Auckland, New Zealand (www.compass.auckland.ac.nz). The full 5-year project (2008–2013) was funded by the Ministry of Business, Innovation and Employment to produce a microsimulation-based policy tool to model aspects of the early life course, particularly focusing on family factors that influence child outcomes (Milne et al. 2014). End users from government agencies were involved at an early stage to ensure policy-relevant issues would be addressed and to facilitate ultimate usage of the tool. The prototype model reported here was based on data from a single longitudinal study of children while the full model incorporates data and parameters from the New Zealand 2006 Census and various longitudinal studies. The emphasis here will be on the methodology related to dynamic microsimulation modelling and how it can be used to test policy-relevant scenarios.

14.8.1   Aim

The overall aim of the project was to construct and apply a computer-based model in a New Zealand setting designed to represent social outcomes in early childhood— e.g. related to health or education—and enable experimentation on the impact of changing family factors—e.g. socioeconomic status (Lay-Yee et al. In Press). The construction of the model followed a framework (Fig. 14.1) where structural factors related to social advantage or disadvantage fundamentally influence intermediary family factors and final outcomes (Solar and Irwin 2010). Any specific factor may have a direct or an indirect effect, through a mediating factor, on the outcome.

14.8.2   Methods

We employed a behavioural dynamic microsimulation model reflecting a life course perspective (Fig. 14.2). According to the typology introduced in Sect. 14.4, this dynamic model had the following features: it used an 'actual' starting sample of children, a birth 'cohort', which was 'closed' to new entrants and where mortality was considered ignorable; and it was organised as 'discrete-time' with annual time steps in the simulation process, and 'time-based' with the updating of individual attributes occurring at the same time for all individuals in the sample.

   In order to build an empirically realistic model, our prototype used longitudinal data on a cohort of 1017 children born in Christchurch, New Zealand in 1977 and followed to age 13 (Christchurch Health and Development Study or CHDS) (Fergusson et al. 1989; Gibb et al. 2012). The CHDS data were used for three purposes:

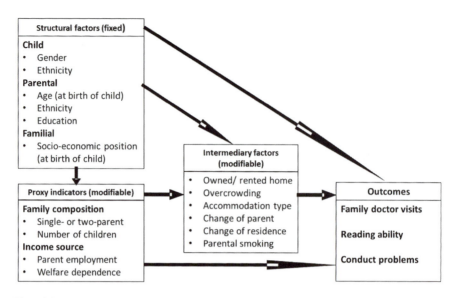

Fig. 14.1 Model of structural and intermediary influences on child outcomes

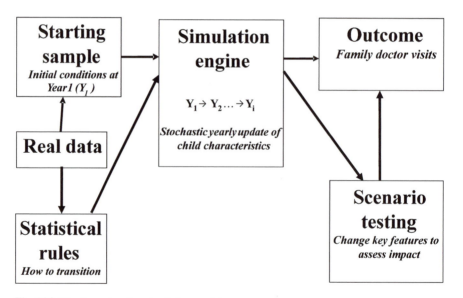

Fig. 14.2 The dynamic microsimulation model

(1) to form a starting sample providing initial conditions to the simulation, (2) to generate statistically derived simulation rules, and (3) to provide benchmarks with which simulated results could be compared to gauge reproducibility. Data manipulation and statistical analysis were carried out using SAS (SAS Institute 2013) and R (R Development Core Team 2013). The simulation was implemented in JAVA and R

(Mannion et al. 2012). Underlying tools for the graphical user interface, 'Jamsim', can be found at *http://code.google.com/p/jamsim/* and for the simulation engine, 'Simario', at *http://code.google.com/p/simario/*.

We applied statistically derived rules to age the cohort from birth to 13 years and so create a virtual cohort composed of representative synthetic histories approximating the original sample data (McLay et al. unpublished manuscript under review). The simulation model required firstly a critical sequencing of steps within each annual cycle and secondly dynamic transitions from year to year. Each step or transition can be seen to be governed by a submodel with the full model consisting of an ordered series of submodels. Each time-variant factor was predicted and in turn was a potential predictor to a successive time-variant outcome in the cycle. Successive submodels included both time-variant and time-invariant predictors from preceding submodels. Dynamic transition was achieved by the use of time-variant predictors including, where justified, a lagged dependent variable (state in current year depends on state in previous year). Thus, for any given individual, a persistent link from year to year enabled the generation of a coherent trajectory through the life course.

14.8.3   Implementing the Simulation

Our discrete-time model used a starting sample comprising data on a cohort of children at birth. The simulation process for each subsequent year followed a sequence of steps from structural through intermediary factors to the final outcomes. Each time-variant attribute (in turn) for an individual child was updated each year using a statistically derived probability and Monte Carlo simulation. The simulated estimates were the average results of 100 runs with a different random seed specified for each run. We calculated 95 % confidence intervals around simulated estimates by taking the 2.5 and 97.5 percentiles on the distribution of the means from the 100 runs. Validation of the simulated results was carried out by comparison to the actual real world CHDS data as borne out over the first 13 years of the life course with the test being whether the simulation model was able to reproduce a similar distribution of outcomes to the original longitudinal data.

14.8.4   Scenario Testing

Ultimately, the model could be used to produce projections into the future or be interrogated to assess the likely effects of changing various social factors and their pattern across groups. What if there was a policy intervention that could improve family factors and what would be its impact on outcomes for children? We attempted to answer this 'what if' question by testing various scenarios. We used scenario testing as a form of counterfactual reasoning where we simulated a potential outcome by varying relevant (single or multiple) factors of interest in the starting sample, e.g.

aspects of family socioeconomic status, while holding other initial factors constant, and then observing change to the outcome, e.g. health service use, compared to baseline.

14.9   Conclusion

Microsimulation employs a systems approach, which can take into account social complexity, heterogeneity, and change. Microsimulation relies on the availability and quality of individual-level data that are representative of the target population. These data can come from various sources, which microsimulation can potentially combine into a cohesive whole. Microsimulation also relies on the incorporation of parameters for the core processes underlying the system of interest. Thus, a virtual (and realistic) world can be created, on which experiments can be undertaken and scenarios tested. Such a model is a simplification of reality but is nevertheless a powerful source of indicative information that can be used alongside other evidence for policy.

The future of microsimulation is bound with that of computational social science in general (Conte et al. 2012). The exponential growth in digital data availability, allied with burgeoning computational capacity to handle these data, offers unparalleled opportunities to model social systems and processes. This also comes with challenges notably developing frameworks that better address features which have typically been weak in the microsimulation approach: the macro–micro link, the emergence of social phenomena, social interaction, and reciprocal effects. Such enhanced models will be increasingly valuable in supporting policy practice in a complex and rapidly changing social world.

Acknowledgements   The Modelling the Early Life Course (MEL-C) project was funded by the Ministry of Business, Innovation and Employment. Data were made available by the Christchurch Health and Development Study, University of Otago.

Appendix

Examples of Usage for Policy   This section highlights a number of existing microsimulation models used for policy purposes. The list is not intended to be exhaustive, merely to provide an indication of the broad sweep of models in use across various domains and countries. There are useful reviews and compendia of existing microsimulation models that describe their features in more detail (for example: Li and O'Donoghue 2012; O'Donoghue 2001).

APPSIM (Australian Population and Policy Simulation Model)   APPSIM, developed by the National Centre for Social and Economic Modelling (NATSEM), is a dynamic model which simulates the life cycle of 200,000 individuals (1 % sample of census) from 2001 to 2050. It shows how the Australian population develops over time under various scenarios, and allows the social and fiscal impacts of policy changes over time to be simulated.

URL: http://www.natsem.canberra.edu.au/models/appsim/

EUROMOD (Europe)   EUROMOD, based at the Institute for Social & Economic Research, University of Essex, is a static tax-benefit model for the European Union (2000s). It enables researchers and policy analysts to calculate, in a comparable manner, the effects of taxes and benefits on household incomes and work incentives for the population of each country and for the European Union as a whole.

URL: https://www.iser.essex.ac.uk/euromod/

FEM (Future Elderly Model—USA)   FEM, developed by the RAND Roybal Center for Health Policy Simulation, is a demographic and economic simulation model designed to predict the future costs and health status of the elderly and explore the implications for policy. It uses a representative sample of 100,000 Medicare beneficiaries aged 65 and over drawn from the Medicare Current Beneficiary Surveys. Each beneficiary in the sample is linked to Medicare claims records to track actual medical care use and costs over time.

URL: http://www.rand.org/labor/roybalhp/projects/health_status/fem.html

LIFEPATHS (Canada)   LIFEPATHS, developed by Statistics Canada, is a dynamic model of individuals and families from an 1872 birth cohort, to today. It creates synthetic life histories from birth to death that are representative of the history of Canada's population. It can be used to evaluate government programmes, or to analyse societal issues of a longitudinal nature, e.g. intergenerational equity.

URL: http://www.statcan.gc.ca/microsimulation/lifepaths/lifepaths-eng.htm

MIDAS (Microsimulation for the Development of Adequacy and Sustainability— Belgium, Germany, Italy)   MIDAS is a dynamic population model. Starting from a cross-sectional dataset representing a population of all ages at a certain point in time (early 2000s), the life spans of individuals are simulated over time. So new individuals are born, go through school, marry or cohabit, enter the labour market, divorce, retire, and finally, die. During their active years, they build up pension rights, which result in a pension benefit when they retire.

URL: http://www.plan.be/publications/Publication_det.php?lang=en&TM=30& KeyPub=781

POHEM (Population Health Model—Canada)   POHEM is a dynamic microsimulation model intended to represent the lifecycle dynamics of the population. The simulation creates and ages a large sample until death. The life trajectory of each simulated person unfolds by exposure to different health events. The model combines data from a wide range of sources, including cross-sectional and longitudinal surveys, cancer registries, hospitalisation databases, vital statistics, census data, and treatment cost data as well as parameters in the published literature.

URL: http://www.statcan.gc.ca/microsimulation/health-sante/health-sante-eng.
htm#a2

SADNAP (Social Affairs Department of the Netherlands Ageing and Pensions)
SADNAP is a dynamic microsimulation model for estimating the financial and economic implications of an ageing population and evaluating the redistributive effects
of policy options. It simulates the life paths of a sample of the Dutch population
using transition probabilities on demographic events. The model uses administrative
data sets on pension entitlements and payments.
    URL: http://ima.natsem.canberra.edu.au/IJM/V4_1/Volume%204%20Issue%
201/5_IJM2011_van_Sonsbeek_CORRECTED_GD_JMS.pdf

STINMOD (Static Incomes Model—Australia)   STINMOD is a static microsimulation model of Australia's income tax and transfer system, developed by NATSEM.
The model is mostly used to analyse the distributional and individual impacts of
income tax and income support policies and to estimate the fiscal and distributional
impacts of policy reform.
    URL: http://www.natsem.canberra.edu.au/models/stinmod/

References

Anderson RE, Hicks C (2011) Highlights of contemporary microsimulation. Soc Sci Comput Rev
    29(1):3–8
Bourguignon F, Spadaro A (2006) Microsimulation as a tool for evaluating redistribution policies.
    J Econ Inequal 4:77–106
Brown L, Harding A (2002) Social modeling and public policy: application of microsimulation
    modeling in Australia. J Artif Soc Soc Simul 5(4):6
Caro JJ, Briggs AH, Siebert U, Kuntz KM (2012) Modelling good research practices—overview:
    A report of the ISPOR-SMDM Modeling Good Research Practices Task Force-1. Med Decis
    Making 32:667–677
Cassells R, Harding A, Kelly S (2006) Problems and prospects for dynamic microsimulation: A
    review and lessons for APPSIM. Discussion Paper no. 63. National Centre for Social and
    Economic Modeling, University of Canberra
Citro CF, Hanusek EA (eds) (1991) The uses of microsimulation modeling, vol 1. Review and
    recommendations. National Academy Press, Washington DC
Conte R, Gilbert N, Bonelli G, Cioffi-Revilla C, Deffuant G, Kertesz J, Loreto V, Moat S, Nadal J-P,
    Sanchez A, Nowak A, Flache A, San Miguel M, Helbing D (2012) Manifesto of computational
    social science. Eur Phys J Spec Top 214:325–346
Davis P, Lay-Yee R, Pearson J (2010) Using micro-simulation to create a synthesized data set and
    test policy options: the case of health service effects under demographic ageing. Health Policy
    97:267–274
Fergusson DM, Horwood LJ, Shannon FT, Lawton JM (1989) The Christchurch Child Development
    Study: A review of epidemiological findings. Paediatr Perinat Epidemiol 3:278–301
Gibb SJ, Fergusson DM, Horwood LJ (2012) Childhood family income and life outcomes
    in adulthood: findings from a 30-year longitudinal study in New Zealand. Soc Sci Med
    74:1979–1986
Gilbert N, Troitzsch K (2005) Simulation for the social scientist. Open University Press, Maidenhead
Glied S, Tilipman N (2010) Simulation modeling of health care policy. Annu Rev Publ Health
    31:439–455

Grimshaw M, Eccles MP, Lavis JN, Hill SJ, Squires JE (2012) Knowledge translation of research findings. Implement Sci 7:50 doi:10.1186/1748–5908-7–50

Gupta A, Harding A (eds) (2007) Modelling our future: population ageing, health and aged care. Elsevier, Amsterdam

Gupta A, Kapur V (eds) (2000) Microsimulation in government policy and forecasting. North-Holland, Amsterdam

Harding A (ed) (1996) Microsimulation and public policy. Contributions to Economic Analysis Series. North-Holland, Amsterdam

Harding A, Gupta A (eds) (2007) Modelling our future: population ageing, social security and taxation. Elsevier, Amsterdam

Lay-Yee R, Milne B, Davis P, Pearson J, McLay J. (In Press) Determinants and disparities: a simulation approach to the case of child health care. Social Science and Medicine

Li J, O'Donoghue C (2012) A methodological survey of dynamic microsimulation models. UNU-Merit Working Paper #2012–002. Maastricht University

Lobb R, Colditz GA (2013) Implementation science and its application to population health. Annu Rev Publ Health 34:235–251

Mannion O, Lay-Yee R, Wrapson W, Davis P, Pearson J (2012) JAMSIM: a microsimulation modeling policy tool. J Artifi Soc Soc Simul 15(1):8. Retrieved from http://jasss.soc.surrey.ac.uk/15/1/8.html. Accessed 18 Dec 2014

Martini A, Trivellato U (1997) The role of survey data in microsimulation models for social policy analysis. Labour 11(1):83–112

McLay J, Lay-Yee R, Milne B, Davis P. Statistical modelling techniques for dynamic microsimulation: An empirical performance assessment. *Unpublished manuscript under review*

Merz J (1991) Microsimulation—A survey of principles, developments and applications. Intern J Forecast 7(1):77–104

Milne BJ, Lay-Yee R, McLay J, Tobias M, Tuohy P, Armstrong A, Lynn R, Davis P, Pearson J, Mannion O (2014) A collaborative approach to bridging the research-policy gap through the development of policy advice software. Evidence Policy 10(1):127–136

Mitton L, Sutherland H, Weeks M (2000) Microsimulation modelling for policy analysis: challenges and innovations. Cambridge University Press, Cambridge

O'Donoghue C (2001) Dynamic microsimulation: A survey. Brazilian Electronic J Econ 4(2):77

Orcutt G (1957) A new type of socio-economic system. Rev Econ Stat 39(2):116–23

Percival R (2007) APPSIM—Software selection and data structures. Working Paper. National Centre for Social and Economic Modeling, University of Canberra

R Development Core Team (2014) R: A language and environment for statistical computing. R Foundation for Statistical Computing, Vienna. Retrieved from http://www.R-project.org. Accessed 18 Dec 2014

Ringel JS, Eibner C, Girosi F, Cordova A, McGlynn EA (2010) Modeling health care policy alternatives. Health Serv Res 45:1541–1558

Rutter CM, Zaslavsky AM, Feuer EJ (2011) Dynamic microsimulation models for health outcomes. Med Decis Making 31(1):10–18

SAS Institute Inc. (2013) SAS 9.2. 2014. Cary, NC, USA: SAS Institute Inc. Retrieved from http://www.sas.com. Accessed 18 Dec 2014

Scott A (2003) A computing strategy for SAGE: 2. Programming considerations. Technical Note no. 3. Citeseer, London

Solar O, Irwin AA (2010) A conceptual framework for action on the social determinants of health. World Health Organization, Geneva. Discussion paper 2

Spielauer M. (2007) Dynamic microsimulation of health care demand, health care finance and the economic impact of health behaviours: survey and review. Intern J Microsimul 1(1):35–53

Spielauer M (2011) What is social science microsimulation? Soc Sci Comput Rev 29(1):9–20

Zaidi A, Rake K (2001) Dynamic microsimulation models: A review and some lessons for SAGE. Discussion Paper no. 2. Citeseer, London

Zaidi A, Harding A, Williamson P (eds) (2009) New frontiers in microsimulation modeling. Public policy and social welfare, vol 36. Ashgate, England
Zucchelli E, Jones AM, Rice N (2012) The evaluation of health policies through dynamic microsimulation methods. Intern J Microsimul 5(1):2–20

Chapter 15
Visual Decision Support for Policy Making: Advancing Policy Analysis with Visualization

Tobias Ruppert, Jens Dambruch, Michel Krämer, Tina Balke, Marco Gavanelli, Stefano Bragaglia, Federico Chesani, Michela Milano and Jörn Kohlhammer

Abstract Today's politicians are confronted with new information technologies to tackle complex decision-making problems. In order to make sustainable decisions, a profound analysis of societal problems and possible solutions (policy options) needs to be performed. In this policy-analysis process, different stakeholders are involved. Besides internal direct advisors of the policy makers (policy analysts), external experts from different scientific disciplines can support evidence-based decision making. Despite the alleged importance of scientific advice in the policy-making process, it is observed that scientific results are often not used. In this work, a concept is described that supports the collaboration between scientists and politicians. We

T. Ruppert (✉) · J. Dambruch · M. Krämer
Fraunhofer Institute for Computer Graphics Research, Darmstadt, Germany
e-mail: tobias.ruppert@igd.fraunhofer.de

J. Dambruch
e-mail: jens.dambruch@igd.fraunhofer.de

M. Krämer
e-mail: michel.kraemer@igd.fraunhofer.de

J. Kohlhammer
GRIS, TU Darmstadt & Fraunhofer IGD, Darmstadt, Germany
e-mail: joern.kohlhammer@igd.fraunhofer.de

T. Balke
University of Surrey, Surrey, UK
e-mail: t.balke@surrey.ac.uk

M. Gavanelli
University of Ferrara, Ferrara, Italy
e-mail: marco.gavanelli@unife.it

S. Bragaglia · F. Chesani · M. Milano
University of Bologna, Bologna, Italy
e-mail: stefano.bragaglia@unibo.it

F. Chesani
e-mail: federico.chesani@unibo.it

M. Milano
e-mail: michela.milano@unibo.it

M. Janssen et al. (eds.), *Policy Practice and Digital Science,*
Public Administration and Information Technology 10, DOI 10.1007/978-3-319-12784-2_15

propose a science–policy interface that is realized by including information visualization in the policy-analysis process. Therefore, we identify synergy effects between both fields and introduce a methodology for addressing the current challenges of science–policy interfaces with visualization. Finally, we describe three exemplary case studies carried out in European research projects that instantiate the concept of this approach.

15.1 Introduction

The increasing complexity of societal and economic problems in the past decades has brought new challenges to politicians. In order to make sustainable decisions, a profound analysis of the problems and possible solutions has to be performed. The process addressing this challenge, often referred to as policy analysis, is one of the most critical steps in the policy-making process. The creation and analysis of alternative solutions (i.e., policy options) to a public problem remain a complex and challenging task with many different stakeholders involved.

From our experience in European research projects in the field of policy modeling, there mainly exist two methods to make decisions on a profound knowledge basis: data-driven and model-driven approaches. Prominent data-driven methods in the policy-making domain include social media analysis, text analysis (like opinion mining, hot topic sensing, and topic summarization), and statistical data analyses approaches. In this chapter, we focus on model-driven approaches that aim at reflecting complex real-world dependencies between social, environmental, and economical factors that have to be included in the analysis process. The application of these complex models in policy analysis helps to improve decision making by providing insight into the impacts that new policies may induce. To build these complex models, policy analysts often need to collaborate with external experts consulted as advisors. Due to different expertises of these stakeholders, the whole process may suffer from knowledge gaps. This implies challenges to be addressed.

In this chapter, we introduce a concept for visual decision support systems to support the policy analysis stages of the policy-making cycle. These systems include information visualization and visual analytics as possible solutions to bridge knowledge gaps between stakeholders involved in the policy-making process. The methods can help non-IT experts to get access to complex computational models. The coupling of visualization techniques and computational models supports different stakeholders in the policy-making process. The standard policy cycle will build the foundation of identifying the need for objective analysis in the entire policy-making cycle. Therefore, we characterize the main stakeholders in the process, and identify knowledge gaps between these roles. We emphasize the merits of including visualization techniques into the policy-analysis process, and describe visualization as a facet bridging the knowledge gaps in a collaborative policy-making life cycle. After describing our concept, best practices and research approaches will be discussed that have already implemented aspects of our concepts in European research projects. These approaches are implemented into decision-support systems that include visual interfaces to complex models and enable policy makers, policy analysts, etc. to participate in the analysis of policy options.

15.2 Background

In the following, we first give an introduction to information visualization and related fields. The goal is to provide an overview of the capabilities that these research fields offer for policy making. Second, the discipline of policy analysis is characterized. With this introduction, we intend to harmonize the terminology, summarize different perspectives on the discipline, and identify open problems and challenges that inhibit the field.

15.2.1 Information Visualization and Visual Analytics

Information visualization is defined as "the use of computer-supported interactive, visual representations of abstract data to amplify cognition" (Card et al. 1999). In this definition, several aspects of information visualization are highlighted. First of all, as a research discipline from computer science, its solutions are provided as software. Second, these software solutions address the visual representation of data through visual artifacts or diagrams. The artifacts consist of basic visual elements that have been presented in the theory of graphics by Bertin (1983). In contrast to the static visual representation, information visualization deals with the interactive visual representation of data. Hence, an important aspect lies in the possibility of the user to interact with graphics generated by the software. Zoom and filter operations on the data are examples for user interaction. As a further aspect, information visualization deals with abstract data in contrast to scientific data. While scientific data are typically physically based reflecting at least some geometric information, abstract data such as economic data or document collections are not. Finally, the goal of information visualization is to amplify cognition. Cognition is defined as the acquisition of knowledge and insight about the world (Card et al. 1999). With information visualization, the user is enabled to gain knowledge about the internal structure of the data and causal relationships in it. Thereby, vision as the human sense with the highest bandwidth is exploited to support the comprehension of information. "Visual representations and interaction techniques take advantage of the human eye's broad bandwidth pathway into the mind to allow users to see, explore, and understand large amounts of information at once" (Thomas and Cook 2005).

Following Stephen Few, the purpose of information visualization is to support the exploration, sensemaking, and communication of data (Few 2009). Extracted from his work, Fig. 15.1 provides an overview of the broader data visualization field. Here, the activities addressed by data visualization are exploration and sensemaking

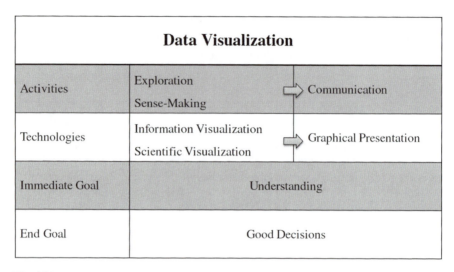

Fig. 15.1 A characterization of data visualization by Stephen Few (2009). Distinction between activities addressed by data visualization. Exploration and sensemaking as analysis tasks. Communication as knowledge transfer task. Technologies differ with respect to presented data (information visualization for abstract data and scientific visualization for physically based data) and interaction capabilities of the technologies, e.g., graphical presentation does not imply user interaction. Understanding of provided information as intermediate goal. Good decisions based on derived knowledge as the end goal

as analysis tasks, and communication as knowledge transfer task. While exploration and sensemaking have the goal to extract knowledge from data, the purpose of communication is the transfer and presentation of these analysis outcomes. The applied data visualization technologies in Fig. 15.1 are information visualization, on which we focus in this approach: scientific visualization and graphical presentation. Information visualization can be used for both analysis and presentation. However, the choice of information visualization techniques and their use will differ with the task, data, and users involved. As an intermediate goal, data visualization attempts to support the understanding of the information hidden in the massive amounts of data. The ultimate goal is to support good decision making based on the knowledge extracted from the data.

Information visualization emerged from research in human–computer interaction, computer science, graphics, visual design, psychology, and business methods (Shneiderman and Bederson 2003). It allows to intuitively access results of complex models, even for nonexperts, while not being limited to intrinsic application fields. In fact, information visualization is increasingly considered as critical component in scientific research, data mining, digital libraries, financial data analysis, manufacturing production control, market studies, and drug discovery (Shneiderman and Bederson 2003).

The growing amount of data collected and produced in modern society contain hidden knowledge that needs to be considered in decision making. Due to the data's

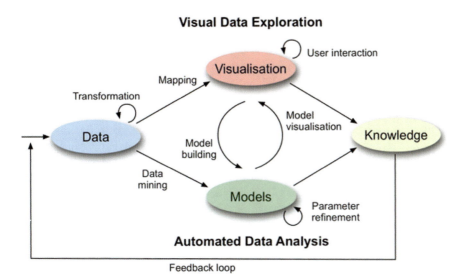

Fig. 15.2 Visual analytics process adapted from Keim et al. (2008). Connecting the information visualization (*top*) and the data mining (*bottom*) processes

volume and complexity information, visualization can no longer be applied alone. A new research discipline within information visualization was introduced. *Visual analytics* is defined as "the science of analytical reasoning facilitated by interactive visual interfaces" (Thomas and Cook 2005). The goal of visual analytics research is the creation of tools and techniques to enable the user to (a) synthesize information and derive insight from massive, dynamic, ambiguous, and often conflicting data, (b) detect the expected and discover the unexpected, (c) provide timely, defensible, and understandable assessments, and (d) communicate assessment effectively for action. In contrast to pure information visualization, visual analytics combines interactive visualization with automated data analysis methods to provide scalable interactive decision support.

Figure 15.2 shows an adaptation of Keim's widely accepted process model for visual analytics (Keim et al. 2008). The visual data exploration process from information visualization (upper part), and automated data analysis methods (lower part) are combined to one visual, and interactive analysis process model. The user is directly included in the model by interactive access to the process steps. This generic process model makes visual analytics applicable to a variety of data-oriented research fields such as engineering, financial analysis, public safety and security, environment and climate change, as well as socioeconomic applications and policy analysis, respectively. The scope of visual analytics can also be described in terms of the incorporated information and communication technologies (ICT) key technologies like information visualization, data mining, knowledge discovery or modeling, and simulation (Keim et al. 2008). In its framework program seven, the European commission (EC) emphasized visualization as a key technology in the objective for ICT for governance and policy modeling (European Commission 2010).

Recently, methodologies on how to design and implement information visualization and visual analytics solutions for data-driven challenges of domain specialists have been presented (Munzner 2009; Sedlmair et al. 2012). Due to their reflection upon practical experiences of hundreds of information visualization and visual analytics research papers, the value of the introduced methodologies is widely recognized. In these methodologies, visualization researchers are guided in how to analyze a specific real-world problem faced by domain experts, how to design visualization systems that support solving this problem, and how to validate the design. Considering information visualization validation, we refer to Lam et al. (2012).

Recent approaches in visual analytics focus on the questions how to simplify the access to the analysis functionality of visual analytics techniques, and on how to present analysis results. This includes the analysis process with its intermediate steps, and the findings derived with the visual analytics techniques (Kosara and Mackinlay 2013).

Information visualization and visual analytics approaches in the policy analysis domain are still surprisingly scarce compared to the number of approaches presented in other analysis-driven fields (Kohlhammer et al. 2012). Still, the policy analysis domain is an ecosystem with a variety of involved stakeholders that intend to collaborate in the best possible way. This outlines policy analysis as an interesting application field for information visualization.

15.2.2   Policy Analysis

Policy analysis as a discipline of the policy sciences was introduced by Laswell and Lernen in their work "The Policy Sciences" in 1951 (Schneider and Janning 2006). It was interpreted as societal problem-solving discipline with the higher goal to support rational decisions in policy making (Blum and Schubert 2009). The main breach of this approach erased from the experience that decisions solely based on rational perspectives (positivism) are not sufficiently considering external factors within real-world scenarios. From this experience, post-positivism approaches evolved (Fischer et al. 2007). With this change of perspectives, the profession of the policy analysts had to be newly interpreted (Howlett and Wellstead 2009).

The knowledge background of policy analysts has to cover different facets ranging from policy science, social science, and economical science, to computer science (Göttrik 2009). The main objective of policy analysts is to provide scientific advice to policy makers during their political decision-making process. This process is also defined as the policy cycle (Blum and Schubert 2009). The policy cycle introduced by Jones (1970) and Anderson (1975) is depicted in Fig. 15.3.

It consists of five succeeding stages: problem identification and agenda setting, policy formulation, policy adoption, policy implementation, and policy evaluation. In the first stage, public problems are identified and the political agenda is set by

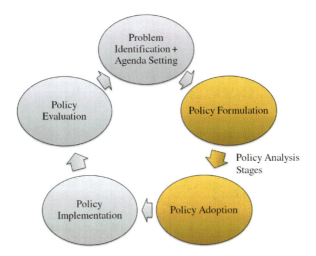

Fig. 15.3 Policy cycle adapted from Jones (1970) and Anderson (1975). Policy analysis is mainly conducted in the policy formulation and the policy adoption stage. While in the policy formulation stage, alternative solutions to a given problem are defined; in the policy adoption stage, one of these solutions (policy options) is selected for implementation. In a broader sense, policy analysis can also be conducted in the other stages of the cycle. However, in this work, we focus on the pre-decision phase before a policy is implemented

prioritizing societal problems. In the second stage, alternative solutions to these problems are explored and evaluated. In the third stage, these policy options are compared, and it is decided which option to choose. In the fourth stage, the selected policy option is implemented through legal process. In the final stage of the cycle, the implemented policy is evaluated with respect to the objectives defined in the first stage of the cycle.

Within the policy cycle, especially the policy formulation phase is supported by the policy analysts' expertise. "Policy formulation clearly is a critical phase of the policy process. Certainly designing the alternatives that decision makers will consider directly influences the ultimate policy choice" (Fischer et al. 2007).

More precisely, policy formulation is about choosing from different types of policy options those that can be used to address particular policy problems. Then, these choices are analyzed in terms of both their technical and political feasibility, with an eye to reducing their number to a small set of alternative courses of action that can be laid out for decision makers at the next stage of the policy process (Howlett et al. 1995).

Despite the expected importance of considering scientific knowledge in the policy formulation phase, a main deficit of policy making is recognized: the *policy paradox* describes the asymmetry between the amount of knowledge generated by scientific experts, and the actual amount of knowledge effectively used in the decision-making process (Shulock 1999). Among others, this paradox evolved from the following obstacles:

Limitations of scientific approaches: The impacts of societal processes are highly complex. The scientific models attempting to simulate reality are seldom precise or accurate. Furthermore, in most cases this uncertainty is not communicated to the user. This fails to raise the awareness of the model's uncertainty and, as a consequence, reduces the credibility of scientific outputs (Hove 2007; Schneider 2008; Göttrik 2009).

Isolation, complexity, and ephemerality of political processes: The policy cycles move faster than the research cycles (Schneider 2008; Howlett and Wellstead 2009). Some of the most frequent problems that policy analysts mention are lack of time, resources, and the ignoring of information (Howlett and Wellstead 2009).

Subjectivity of stakeholders: Different facets of subjectivity influence scientific experts and advisors. Human subjectivity is induced by individual, cultural, and religious values (Hove 2007). Economic subjectivity is induced since the advisors and scientific experts may be influenced by their employer (Dobuzinskis et al. 2005). Moreover, political subjectivity may be induced due to an affiliation to political parties (Greven 2008).

Concepts have been introduced to address these problems, which evolve from bringing two contrary systems, politics and science, together. Most of these concepts can be summarized under the term science–policy interface. Janse defines the science–policy interface as "the point at which science and policy meet and act on each other" (Janse 2008). The positive aspects out of this are: (a) rationality and legitimation through knowledge in politics, (b) exploration of policy alternatives with focus on cause and effect, (c) communication between two fields—e.g., research assignment and scientific advice. In order to realize these aspects, the concept of "knowledge brokers" is propagated. Their goal is to mediate between the two systems (Howlett and Wellstead 2009). Still, these concepts contain the risk of subjectivity described above. As a consequence, the propagation of a mere technocratic model has to be replaced by a concept with high interaction possibilities between knowledge and decision makers as mentioned in Göttrik (2009). In our approach, we will lay out how information visualization may support this concept.

15.3 Approach

In this section, we describe our approach of using visual decision support systems as the means to bridge gaps in policy analysis. A first version of this concept can be found in our previous work (Ruppert et al. 2013a). In the following, we characterize the stakeholder involved in the policy-analysis process. Then we provide more detail about the policy-analysis process with its challenges, and provide a concept how to address these challenges. As the last part of this approach, we summarize the advantages of our concept with regards to enhanced policy making.

15.3.1 Characterization of Stakeholders

As described in Sect. 15.2, several stakeholders involved in the policy-making process can be identified.

Policy makers are the final decision makers in the policy-analysis process. They decide which societal problems appear on the political agenda, and by which policy option they are finally tackled. In most cases, policy makers do not have the time and the technical background to execute the policy analysis by themselves. For making profound decisions, they have advisors, namely policy analysts, who conduct the analysis, and provide summaries of the analysis in the form of reports, or presentations. Still, in the agenda setting and problem definition stage, policy makers decide which public problems appear on the political agenda, and how these problems are defined. Requirements for the analysis of policy options are derived from this problem definition. After the analysis process, policy makers finally decide which of the generated policy options will be implemented.

Policy analysts (or policy advisors) are the coordinator of the policy analysis. Their goal is to conceptualize the problem based on the requirements defined by the policy maker. Then, they have to identify information sources, and consult external advisors that assist in analyzing the problem. Finally, the policy analyst provides alternative solutions (policy options) to the policy maker via a report or presentation.

Modeling experts are in most cases external advisors recruited by the policy analyst. They have profound knowledge in modeling techniques. Expertise in the policy domain is not necessarily required from modeling experts. Still, the models have to be adapted to the policy domain, which can be realized by translating the problem to the model domain or by defining technical requirements on the model. The adapted model supports the policy analysis by producing outcomes—e.g., impact of possible actions that are the basis for the generation of policy options.

Domain experts are optional stakeholders in our concept. In many cases, the analytical models have to be fed with domain knowledge and data. If neither the modeling expert nor the policy analyst can provide this information, a domain expert has to be consulted. The domain expert does not necessarily have expertise in policy analysis or modeling techniques but rather contributes as an information provider.

Public stakeholders are not explicitly considered in our concept. Still, they play an increasingly important role in the policy-making process. By realizing an intuitive visual access to complex models for the analysis of policy options, even nonexperts like most citizens may be involved in the policy analysis. This will increase the transparency of the whole policy-making process, improve democracy, and increase the trust in the policy makers. An example of how public stakeholders can be included in the policy analysis is described in the case study of the urban agile policy implementation (urbanAPI) project in Sect. 15.4.3.

A further stakeholder that is not explicitly included in our concept is the role of the *politician*. From our perspective, politicians influence various of the above stakeholders and sometimes even play their roles. For example, the agenda setting and thereby the work of the policy maker is influenced by politicians. Moreover, they may act as a neutral (or public) stakeholder observing the potential solutions generated through science–policy interfaces. Furthermore, the acquisition of external advisors, the work of the policy analyst, may be influenced by politicians. Due to this heterogeneity, we do not explicitly define the role of the politician in this approach. However, we want to point out their influences.

These different stakeholders need to collaborate in the policy-analysis process to generate policy options that will later be implemented to tackle societal problems. Due to the stakeholders' different backgrounds and knowledge, the collaboration is a challenge to be addressed by science–policy interfaces. In the next section, we show how information visualization technology may be applied as supporting component of science–policy interfaces.

15.3.2 Bridging Knowledge Gaps with Information Visualization

We now sketch how the policy-analysis process is usually conducted. This is based on the literature review presented in Sect. 15.2 and our experience with projects in the field of policy modeling. After characterizing the process, we introduce a method to include visualization into policy analysis to bridge the knowledge gaps between different stakeholders involved.

At the beginning of each policy-analysis process, a public problem is identified that is put on the political agenda. It is mostly described in a more or less abstract way by the policy maker. In order to generate policy options that tackle this problem, policy analysts (policy advisors) are consulted. These policy analysts (a) gather information to provide policy options by themselves, or (b) ask external experts for help in analyzing the problem. Often, these external experts have a scientific background. They provide models that help in isolating the problem, and simulating the potential impact of generated policy options on societal, environmental, and economic aspects. The extracted knowledge provided by scientific experts is summarized by the policy analyst, most likely as a written report, as described in Weimer and Vining (2005). This report is presented to the policy maker textually, or as a presentation. It contains policy options to tackle the defined problem as well as an analysis of the impacts that each of these options inhibit. Based on this knowledge, the policy maker has to decide which option to choose. Alternatively, another iteration of the process can be requested by refining some parts of the problem definition. The upper part of Fig. 15.4 summarizes this process in a simplified way.

Our approach extends the "classical" policy-analysis process with information visualization technology. As described above, the generation of policy options is enriched by including scientific knowledge, in terms of information extracted from data or scientific models, into the process. This information and the models can in most cases be represented by computational models. However, the complexity of these models impedes the usage of the underlying knowledge for policy analysis. In order to simplify the access to computational models developed by policy analysts,

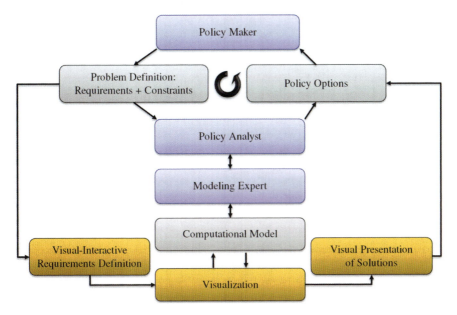

Fig. 15.4 Visual support model for policy analysis. The upper part denotes the policy analysis process which is conducted in the policy formulation stage of the policy cycle (cf. Fig. 15.3). Visualization is introduced into the process in order to support the analysis of policy options

or in most cases external scientific experts, we propose to connect information visualization techniques to these models. In this way, the complexity of the models can be hidden in the computational back end, while only the information necessary for providing user input (e.g., control parameters, etc.) and analyzing the model output (e.g., simulation results, statistical measures, etc.) is displayed on the screen. The most crucial aspect of this concept is that non-IT expert users can visually interact with computational models and execute their own analysis. Hence, the policy analyst and the policy maker can define their requirements and constraints via a visual interface (see Fig. 15.4, left side). They can "experiment" with different settings, and generate alternative model outputs (see Fig. 15.4, right side). As another aspect, due to the similar representation of the model, the different stakeholders can validate the models' utility and usability with visualization technology. For example, the policy maker can detect aspects not covered yet by the model, that the modeling expert might include in an improved model. The communication of results is facilitated, since all stakeholders work with the same visual representation.

To achieve a user-centered system that combines computational models with information visualization capabilities, several steps have to be undertaken. In the following, we propose a possible development cycle based on the concept of Andrews (2008). Before the visualization design process, the policy maker and the policy analyst have to define the societal problem (agenda setting) and identify relevant external experts that may support the decision-making process. We propose to include visualization experts in the process from the very beginning, since they have to help in conducting the requirement analysis. The steps that follow are:

Phase before design: In this phase, the requirement analysis has to be conducted. That includes the characterization of the (policy) domain, the needs of the users (e.g., policy maker, policy analyst, etc.), and an abstraction of the tasks the users want to achieve (e.g., generation of policy option, impact analysis, etc.). Furthermore, together with the scientific experts, computational models that may help in solving the tasks have to be defined.

Phase during design: In this phase, the information gathered in the previous step have to be summarized and structured. The data exchange interfaces to the computational models have to be specified. Furthermore, an initial design of the visualization tool has to be developed. Therefore, the interaction design, and the visual encodings of the underlying data has to be created.

Phase during implementation: In this phase, the initial design is implemented into software. This software will be implemented in an iterative process together with the user. Intermediate versions of the software will be shown to the users and improved based on the users' feedback regarding initial and upcoming requirements.

Phase after implementation: In the phase after the implementation, the system will be deployed, and tested regarding usability and utility. It will be measured whether the users can solve their tasks with the system, and how easy and intuitive it is adopted by the user.

The method presented here supports the design process whose main purpose is to find the right kind of visualization for the given problem. Note that there is no one-size-fits-all solution for information visualization. There are visualizations that work better as others in certain use cases but fail otherwise. If we generalize this problem to notations—i.e., ways to express information, either visually or textually—we can refer to Green who states, "a notation is never absolutely good, therefore, but only in relation to certain tasks" (Green 1989). Indeed, the question whether general visuals are appropriate for policy analysis is difficult since policy analysis usually involves many tasks (cf. Whitley 1997). However, visualizations tailored to a specific problem can help stakeholders understand its complexity. Gilmore and Green summarize this connection between a visual and the ability of stakeholders to solve a certain problem based on this visual in their match–mismatch hypothesis (Gilmore and Green 1984). They state that every notation (i.e., visualization) highlights certain aspects of a problem while it hides others (Whitley 1997). The match–mismatch problem implies that for every task different kinds of visualizations have to be used. That is also the reason why the case studies presented in Sect. 15.4 differ from each other in terms of visualization methods and why they cannot be generalized. For further readings about design processes in information visualization and visual analytics, we recommend, among others, the approaches by Sedlmair et al. (2012) and Munzner (2009).

15.3.3   Synergy Effects of Applying Information Visualization to Policy Analysis

In order to address the challenges imposed on science–policy interfaces, we proposed the inclusion of information visualization techniques within policy making (see Fig. 15.4). Hereby, information visualization serves as an important component of the science–policy interface itself. The following aspects can be resolved with this integration:

Communication. The communication between science and policy fields will be facilitated. Visualization may serve as a mediator of information between two distinct environments. Through the similar visual appearances of the system, different stakeholders may discuss issues on the same visually presented information basis. Thereby, the interaction of scientists and policy analysts with the policy-making process will be supported.

Complexity: Through the abstraction of user tasks and interactions with scientific models, the complexity of the underlying models may be reduced. With visualization, the complexity of scientific models can be executed on the machine side, while the degrees of freedom in form of parameters for their execution can be intuitively displayed on the screen. Visual interfaces provide the information on the level of detail needed by the respective user role.

Subjectivity: The aspect of subjectivity can be reduced since different stakeholders get access to the same information provided in an "objective" way via information visualization techniques. Hence, the provided information can be discussed among the stakeholders to balance subjective interpretations of the findings.

Validation: The outcomes of the policy-analysis process can be transparently presented to all involved stakeholders including public stakeholders. That way, decisions can be justified since they have been made based on an objective analysis. This can improve the trust in scientific results and political decision making.

Transparency and reproducibility of results: Public stakeholders (e.g., journalists, interest groups, etc.) can generate analysis results with the same tool and therefore better understand the rational background of political decisions.

15.4   Case Studies

In the following, we present three case studies that have already implemented aspects of our concept within European research projects. The target of each case study is briefly described. Relevant stakeholders are identified, and their roles in the process are characterized. In each approach, scientists have developed a computational model to support policy makers and policy analysts in their decision-making process. To simplify the access to these models, visual interfaces have been designed that have been developed by information visualization experts. The models and the visual interfaces to them are described. Finally, for each case study, findings are presented that substantiate the benefits of our concept. The three case studies covered the following scenarios:

1. Optimization: the optimization of regional energy plans considering environmental, economical, and social impacts (cf. Sect. 15.4.1).
2. Social simulation: the simulation of the impact of different policy instruments on the adoption of photovoltaic (PV) panels at household level (cf. Sect. 15.4.2).
3. Urban planning: the integration of heterogeneous data sources (simulation results, user input, etc.) in collaborative urban planning scenarios (cf. Sect. 15.4.3).

15.4.1 Optimization

The first case study presented comes from the ePolicy[1] project, whose main aim is to support policy makers in taking transparent, informed, and well-assessed decisions. The ePolicy goal is to develop a decision support system assisting the policy maker in understanding the impact of her decisions on the environment, the economy, and the society. The specific case study of ePolicy is the regional energy plan of the Emilia-Romagna region in Italy, in its part concerning the renewable energy share.

The design of a policy for regional planning is followed, as prescribed by European regulations, by an environmental assessment of the devised plan. Traditionally, the policy maker decides a policy, possibly with allocation of the available funds to chapters, and the plan is submitted to an environmental expert to be assessed. In the Emilia-Romagna region, the assessment is performed by using the so-called coaxial matrices (Cagnoli 2010) that are a development of the Leopold matrix (Leopold 1971). The information contained in the plan is usually very high level and misses many details, so the environmental assessment is usually only qualitative. One of the coaxial matrices links the possible actions that are taken in a plan with their environmental pressures providing information on how much each of the activities impacts on the environment. Current coaxial matrices consider 93 activities that range from building new constructions (buildings, sewers, factories, bridges, yards, etc.) to energy plants (PV, biomasses, coal, etc.) to moving materials (waste, dangerous materials, etc.) to installing infrastructures (pylons, wires, cables, etc.). Activities can have various impacts (or pressures) on the environment: e.g., a thermoelectric power plant emits pollutants or greenhouse gases in the atmosphere, consumes water, etc. The environmental pressures, then, modify the environment, and in particular, some environmental indicators called receptors: the emission of air pollutants changes the receptor quality of the air, while the emission of greenhouse gases impacts on the climate change. A second matrix links environmental pressures with environmental receptors. Both matrices contain qualitative values: the impacts can be high, medium,

---

[1] http://www.epolicy-project.eu/.

or low (or null). By considering the plan devised by the policy maker, and elaborating the environmental matrices on a large spreadsheet, the environmental expert is able to point out critical aspects of the plan.

However, even if there are important critical aspects in the plan, the effort for building a new plan, and reassessing it is so high that only small variations can be done. Moreover, although European regulations state that two or more alternative plans should be compared and environmentally assessed, this is rarely done in practice due to the difficulties and costs of designing alternative plans; in some cases, the devised plan is compared to the do-nothing case (the absence of a plan), but devising actual alternative plans and comparing them is usually out of reach.

15.4.1.1   Involved Stakeholders

The involved stakeholders in this research are primarily two. One is a policy analyst, an expert in the energy field. She is responsible for devising the Regional Energy Plan for the Emilia-Romagna region of Italy. Basically, she has the possibility of stating the minimum amount of energy to be produced and constraints limiting the minimum and maximum amount of energy to be produced by each renewable energy source given the regional characteristics and some political choices. As output, the policy analyst could obtain a number of alternative scenarios for the energy plan that can be easily compared.

The second is the domain expert that in this case is an environmental expert whose main task is the configuration of the system. For example, the coaxial matrices are inserted into the system by environmental expert who studies the impact of activities on the environment.

The system being tailored on a specific policy domain needs a modeling expert whose main aim is to (a) define the decisions that should be taken in the regional plan, (b) state the constraints tightening possible combinations of decisions, and (c) specify objective functions defining the evaluation metrics for the policy.

15.4.1.2   Underlying Technologies

In order to overcome the difficulties in current practices, and improve current methodologies, we developed a constraint-based application for performing automatically the environmental assessment of a plan (Gavanelli et al. 2010). In this way, the assessment phase could be performed easily and in a very short time, and the environmental impact of different, alternative plans could be quickly compared.

However, the real challenge was the integration of the two phases: planning and environmental assessment. A unique constraint model to perform both the planning and the environmental assessment was later proposed (Gavanelli et al. 2013).

The constraint model included not only the coaxial matrices needed for environmental assessment but also the cost of each activity, so that a global cost of the plan could be computed. Some of the activities are of primary importance for the given type of plan: For example, power plants are the main activities considered in an energy plan. On the other hand, power plants require infrastructures to be performed; although these secondary activities are not the main aim of the given plan, they can have an impact on the environment, and should be considered in the assessment. For example, thermoelectric plants require power lines, pipelines (for oil, gas, or steam), cooling systems, roads, etc., while a hydroelectric power plant may require the construction of a dam or other hydraulic works. The construction of such facilities has a significant impact on the wildlife, or on the wellness of people living nearby.

Other aspects taken into consideration in the constraint model are the minimum and maximum amount of each energy source, the required energy production (in terms of both electrical energy and thermal energy), and the amount of energy produced in a year for a given energy source.

The constraint model can be used to generate a single plan, e.g., optimizing an objective function. Examples of objective functions are the minimization of the cost, the maximization of the produced energy, the maximization of some environmental receptor (for example, one can compute the plan that improves most the quality of the air in the region), or a linear combination of these.

In case the policy maker wants to optimize more than one objective function, the constraint model can be used to compute a set of solutions. If two objectives are given, one solution can be the optimum for the first objective, another one for the second objective. Moreover, a series of plans in between can be found that are nondominated, i.e., for which there exists no other plan that improves both objective functions. The set of nondominated points is called the Pareto front. In such a way, it is easy to generate and compare alternative plans. Moreover, the considered alternative plans are not simply the absence of a plan, but they are the result of an optimization, and, in particular, represent plans for which it is impossible to improve one objective without sacrificing another objective.

15.4.1.3 Visual Design

We embedded the global optimizer component into a web interface that takes as input the bounds for each energy source, the objective functions to be optimized, and the number of plans that should be compared (see Fig. 15.5).

The global optimization component computes the Pareto front of the solutions that optimize the declared objectives. The visualization module provides the computed energy plans in several views. An overview shows the Pareto front through the different objective functions in a scatter plot view. The plans are also compared through bar graphs showing the amount of energy produced by each source. Each of the computed plan can be monitored in a single view providing details about this plan (see Fig. 15.6).

The environmental expert also suggested to add to the interface a set of dashboards: for each plan, they show the three environmental receptors with the best and worst values; in this way, one gets immediately the idea of which environmental aspects are most critical for this plan, and which are improved. For a more detailed description and evaluation of the visual interface, we refer to Ruppert et al. (2013b).

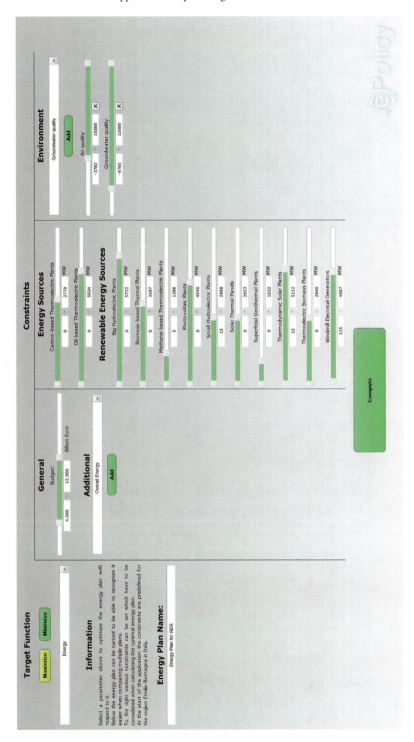

Fig. 15.5 The visual interface for providing the input to the optimization component

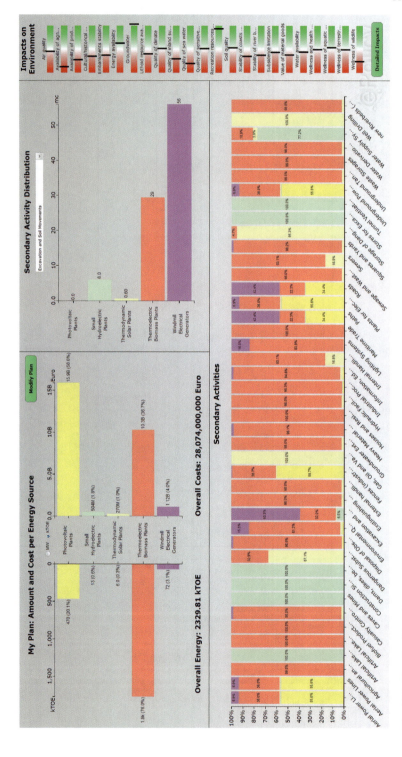

Fig. 15.6 The visual interface providing detailed information about a calculated plan

15.4.1.4 Findings

The developed system provides a number of features that enable a better policy-making process. First of all, it enables the policy analyst to compare different scenarios on demand, evaluating their strengths and weaknesses from an environmental and economic perspective.

Second, the domain expert that configures the system can insert and update the coaxial matrices and activity costs. As new technologies evolve, the impact of activities on the environment might change and coaxial matrices as well as costs can be consequently updated.

Finally, the system enables a more transparent decision process empowering a participatory and collaborative approach to public policy making. Citizens and stakeholders can get an explanation and a reason why some choices have been done.

15.4.2 Social Simulation

One further area of research, which has become important for supporting the policy-making process in recent years, is the area of social simulation (Brenner and Werker 2009). Social simulation is a research field that applies computational methods to study issues in the social sciences. One of its main aims thereby is to bridge the gap between the descriptive approach used in the social sciences and the formal approach sometimes used in the computer sciences, by moving the focus on the processes/mechanisms/behaviors that build the social reality (Edmonds et al. 2007). The goal of social simulation is to study this (complex) social reality in order to understand it better—and in case of policy making—to be able to influence and shape this social reality in a better way.

In the EU-funded ePolicy project, a social simulation was used to analyze the impact of different policy instruments on the adoption of PV panels at a household level. The social simulation logically is to be used by policy makers and policy analysts after the planning step on the regional level (also referred to as global level in the project). Once planning goals have been determined, through optimization (e.g., with respect to minimum costs, maximum CO_2 reduction, minimum disruption, etc.) and decisions on how to allocate the budget to policy instruments in order to achieve these goals at the level of the region have been made, it is then necessary to apply the policy instruments.

However, what is an optimal policy at the regional level may not be locally or individually optimal. Thus, some (incentive) mechanism is needed to enforce the policy—one cannot assume that individual agents will adopt the desired behaviors of their own accord. These potential policy instruments could reach from fiscal incentives, via tax incentives and different tariffs to legislation for example. All options have disadvantages, and which is best is not clear and will vary from case to case. In order to be able to assess effects of the different policy instruments on individual households better, a multilevel agent-based model has been developed that allows policy makers to explore the consequences of different types of policy instrument and thus enable them to make better choices.

In the social simulation (software), agents represent the main actors, the individual households. They are given behavioral rules modeling their likely individual responses to policy instruments (including the effect of influences from other actors, e.g., as a result of collective actions, imitation etc.). The overall response to the simulated policy instruments will be measured to inform policy makers.

15.4.2.1   Stakeholders

In the policy-making process, typically a large number of different stakeholders can be involved with a social simulation, including the mentioned policy makers, policy analysts, domain and modeling experts as well as public stakeholders.

In the social simulator of the ePolicy project in particular, four stakeholder groups thereby have been focused on:

- *Policy analysts* and *policy makers* that use the simulation to derive new information and knowledge about the modeled system (possibly in order to make policy decisions).
- *Domain* and *modeling experts* who are required in order to build the model both in terms of the technical implementation as well as the contribution of domain knowledge required for conceptualizing the simulation model. The domain experts thereby were asked to provide domain knowledge about the behavior of households with respect to PV as well as demographic information of the households to be modeled. The modeling expert's task was to translate this domain knowledge into agent rules and to incorporate the provided demographic household information (mainly data) into the simulation setup.

In this case study, we are mainly looking into the first group, i.e., policy analysts and policy makers and will consider the second group (i.e., domain and modeling experts) as suppliers of tools for them.

15.4.2.2   Underlying Technologies

The term social simulation can have several types of simulation and modeling of which agent-based modeling (ABM) is the most popular one.

An ABM "is a computational method that enables a researcher to create, analyze, and experiment with models composed of agents that interact within an environment (Abdou et al. 2012)."

There are several important elements in this description. First, the model is composed of autonomous and heterogeneous agents. That is, there are many simulated individuals with different properties and decision-making rules. In ePolicy for example, properties include geographic location, PV, and policy instrument knowledge as well as housing and financial situation, and rules include PV prevalence at which the individual will consider gathering information about PV because they might install panels.

Second, these agents interact within an environment. That is, the individuals are able to perceive the situation in which they find themselves take that situation into account in their decisions and take actions that affect the environment. Continuing the example, the individuals are able to perceive the PV prevalence in their location, which allows them to check their perception of PV and the respective policy instruments.

Finally, ABM is a computational method that simulates interactions over time. Simulations allow "what if" questions to be tested quickly, cheaply, and without the ethical problems of setting up experiments. Provided the key interactions are properly represented in the model, the simulation can explore the consequences of different actions. In the policy context, for example, different policy situations can be explored and better understood. Modeling a system thereby is often understood as a first step to understanding the system to be modeled better.

It is important to recognize, however, that the results of a simulation run will not be suitable for forecasting (Antunes et al. 2008). The model is a simplified representation of the key relationships that exist in the real world. That simplification is what makes the model useful—knowledge about the real world can be captured and its consequences can be understood—but the model will not be detailed enough to support specific claims. In the terminology of Heath et al. (2009), the model is a mediator "used primarily to establish the capability of the conceptual model to represent the system and to then gain some insight into the system's characteristics and behaviors" so as to understand potential implications of different scenarios.

As a result, one of the main problems with respect to the different stakeholders in a social simulation is to help them to understand the advantages and limits of a social simulation and its results in a better way.

That is why, in addition to an easy user interaction with the social simulation in general, it is important to help—by means of visual representation—the developers (domain and modeling experts) to communicate the limitations and assumptions of the simulation (and their impact on the simulation results) to the policy analysts and decision makers.

15.4.2.3 Visual Design

For better understanding what is considered "useful and easy to use" for the potential users of the social simulator, we designed a questionnaire which was given to representatives of potential user groups (including the regional policy makers, as well as PV companies interested in the reaction of households to different incentives fostering the uptake of PV panels).

Besides the obvious requirement that the social simulator must allow to analyze the update of PV by individual households based on different policy instruments, the main result of the questionnaire was that the users want to be able to look at individual subregions (e.g., their electoral region) of the Emilia-Romagna region

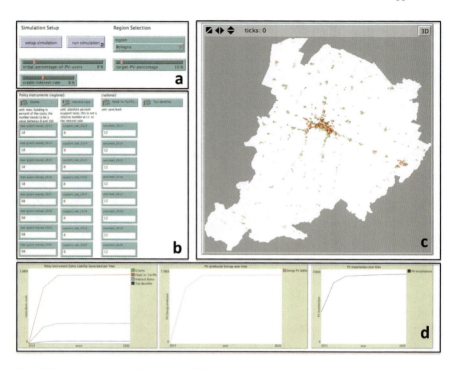

Fig. 15.7 Social simulation interface: (**a**) input parameters, (**b**) policy instruments to be chosen, (**c**) geographic representation of photovoltaic adoption, (**d**) output of simulation: costs per policy instrument (*left*), energy produced by photovoltaic panels (*middle*), number of panels installed (*right*)

and want to be able to look at both regional as well as national policy instruments. For these policy instruments, they want to be able to specify funding levels. With respect to the output, in particular adoption rates, the resulting energy production from PV and the costs associated with the adoption (per policy instrument) were of interest to the users. Furthermore, the speed of the simulation was mentioned as one attribute that can influence the utilization of the simulator.

Based on the above described user requirements, the social simulator shown in Fig. 15.7 was developed for the ePolicy project.

The social simulator interface consists of four areas, which will now be explained in more detail. Starting at the top left, as shown in Fig. 15.7a, the first area is composed of two buttons labeled *setup simulation* and *run simulation* as well as several sliders and a drop-down menu for specifying parameters of the simulation.

As indicated by their labels, the first of the purple buttons sets up the simulation with all specified parameters and the different decision entities, whereas the second one can be used to run it. Running the simulation without setting it up beforehand is not possible, thus it is strictly necessary to press the setup button before running the simulation. The parameters that can be specified by the user for the setup include the region to be simulated (via the drop-down menu; as this is a proof-of-concept prototype currently available only for the Emilia-Romagna and the Bologna region), the initial percentage of people having PV (initial-percentage-of-PV-users slider), the average interest rate for credits in percent (credit-interest-rate slider) as well as the target percentage of people who should have PV (target-PV-percentage slider).

In addition to these parameters, the users can specify which policy instruments should be available to the households being simulated. We thereby distinguish two regional and two national policy instruments all shown in Fig. 15.7b:

1. investment grants
2. contributions to interest rates for loans individuals have to take in order to finance a PV
3. feed-in tariffs, and
4. tax deductions on the PV investment.

For each of these instruments, using the on–off switches, the user can specify whether the instrument shall be considered (on) or not (off position of the switch). Furthermore, for each instrument the user can specify the size of the support by the policy instrument.

On the top right-hand side of the simulation interface, a third area can be seen, which shows the geographic representation (in form of a map) of the PV adoption. Before setup, this map is black. However, once the region the user is interested in has been defined in the setup process (and this setup process has been completed), it changes to a map showing the selected region. In the map, for easier orientation, different red shades are used to reflect population densities (with darker red shades representing higher population densities and lighter shades lower densities). The example map shown in Fig. 15.7c displays the map of the Bologna region. Furthermore, in each area where the previously specified target PV threshold is met, a green dot is shown to indicate this success.

The social simulation can be run by clicking on *run simulation* after the setup of the simulation is completed. A message announcing this setup completion is displayed at the end of the setup process. When the simulation is running, the area at the bottom of the simulator interface shows the results of the simulation in form of three plots displaying outputs of the simulation run over time: costs per policy instrument (left), energy produced by PV panels (middle), number of panels installed (right; cf. Fig. 15.7d). These plots were indicated as desired plots by the policy makers questioned about the interface. The screens show the liabilities the policy instruments have generated in a particular (per instrument)[2], the total number of PV installations over time, and the energy produced by these PV panels in terms of kilowatt hour.

---

[2] "Liability generated" that in a given year, also generated future liabilities will be shown. In terms of feed-in tariffs this means that all costs/liabilities resulting from the long-term (e.g., 30 years) feed-in-tariff contracts are completely in the year they were generated in.

15.4.2.4 Findings

During the requirement analysis with the users of the simulation system it became clear that an intuitive visual interface to the simulation model is of high relevance. The users want to "play" with parameters of the computational model to simulate the PV adoption depending on the policy instruments chosen. That way, the simulation becomes more accessible to them compared to a written report that only statically describes the outcomes of the simulation for a number of given parameterizations.

15.4.3 Urban Planning

The EC-funded project urbanAPI[3] is seeking for ICT-enabled tools that support the policy-making process in modern urban planning—hence the project's full name "Interactive Analysis, Simulation and Visualization Tools for Urban Agile Policy Implementation." UrbanAPI supports both sides in the urban policy and governance system: the policy making and practitioner side as well as the stakeholders and the public. UrbanAPI provides a tool set that enables the city planning authorities to effectively use interactive simulation and visualization instruments, and additionally facilitates direct participation of stakeholders and citizens.

The term agile is used to express the interaction with the different stakeholders, in particular the public. Krämer et al. amend the policy cycle from Fig. 15.3 and replace policy adoption with a more general stakeholder engagement phase (Krämer et al. 2013). They propose that all stakeholders—urban planners, decision makers as well as citizens—participate in discussing policies in order to find alternatives and finally achieve consent.

Policy making in the area of urban planning works quite similarly to the general process described in Sect. 15.2.2. The policy cycle describes the process of formulating, implementing, and evaluating policies as it is done nowadays. In the area of urban planning, however, this process has recently started to change. The top-down driven policy-making process is gradually transforming to one that is working bottom up. In Europe, for example, citizens and other stakeholders request to participate in political decisions more and more often. Experience from the past has shown that modern urban planning cannot be done at the municipal administration level alone anymore without risking public discontent. Additionally, stakeholders often have a different view on certain issues. Incorporating their ideas and proposals can improve the policy-making process and finally lead to policies experiencing higher acceptance within the public.

Obviously, involving a large number of stakeholders in the discussion requires provisioning of participation tools that are widely accessible. ICT tools developed in the urbanAPI project are web based and run in a typical Internet browser.

---

[3] http://www.urbanapi.eu/.

In the following, we describe the different types of stakeholders in the area of urban planning and their respective needs and requirements. We then present the ICT-enabled tools developed in urbanAPI and their underlying techniques and visual design.

15.4.3.1 Involved Stakeholders

In the context of the urbanAPI project, a thorough process of requirements gathering for ICT-enabled tools as mentioned above was carried out (Kahn and Ludlow 2013), which contributed a lot of information to application development (Dambruch et al. 2013) in the project. The stakeholder's requirements were analyzed and also which types of stakeholders are typically involved or are to be additionally addressed. The term stakeholder refers in this context to individuals or an organization that has a vested interest in the results of urban planning and also the process of policy modeling itself.

In addition to the stakeholders from Chap. 3, several other stakeholder groups were identified. The main target audience as already mentioned are:

- *Policy analysts*, the typical end users, who will actually operate the software applications to provide information, reports, etc.
- *Domain experts* such as architects, environmentalists, traffic planners, and urban planners
- *Policy makers*, the functional or political beneficiaries of the information generated by the applications for strategic planning
- *Citizen*s as there is a growing demand for public participation

The interests of the users are manifold and distinct in several ways. This is countered by a requirements engineering approach which lead to an exhaustive amount of use cases elaborated together with the four case study cities Bologna (Italy), Ruse (Bulgaria), Vienna (Austria), and Vitoria-Gasteiz (Spain). Three levels of stakeholder involvement have been identified, each is targeted with a specific application.

On the city quarter or neighborhood level, a 3D virtual reality application can be used to visualize alternative planning scenarios and support evaluations by using Internet technology to target to a broader audience, e.g., general public or citizens. By using interactive web technology, it is also possible to gather direct feedback on several topics without additional efforts.

On the citywide level, the public motion explorer provides additional information about the real movement of citizens over the daytime and therefore contributes to the analysis phase, and finally, can also be used in the evaluation phase to asses the impact of measures taken on the behavior.

Finally, on a region-wide level, the urban growth simulation combines several layers of socioeconomic and spatial information to create simulations of the possibilities of future developments which can be used to define indicators and possible hazardous conditions for the evaluation phase.

15.4.3.2 Underlying Techniques

In Gebetsroither (2009) and Krämer and Kehlenbach (2013), the authors show how a state-of-the-art *agent-based simulation model* can be applied to urban change simulation and contribute to urban policy analysis. The simulation includes geo-spatial data as well as socioeconomic data to model the phenomena of urbanization together with some rules to describe a likely human behavior.

The *public motion explorer* application, described in Loibl and Peters-Anders (2012), uses data logged by mobile devices while connected to a radio tower. Basically, modern smart phones have the capability to provide location information based on global positioning system (GPS), but often this functionality is disabled or the information is not logged due to regulations and privacy protection issues. On the other hand, the location and movement information can be derived, if the location of the radio tower to which a device is connected is known, but with a much coarser resolution. There are also some other side effects connected to this approach which have to be identified and corrected by preprocessing and data cleansing to eliminate potential hazards.

With the processed device data the application can provide answers to questions such as "Where are the people from district x at noon?" or "Where do the people in district x at noon come from?"

15.4.3.3 Visual Design

In the context of the urbanAPI project *3D visualization* plays an important role in several aspects. First, a 3D city model is a natural way to visualize changes and alternative designs for a visual impact assessment. The transfer to a virtual digital domain is straightforward, but depending on the data available. For example, if a sophisticated 3D city model is available, an architect can provide a virtual 3D model of a new building project. This building model can then be integrated and a visual impact assessment, such as the analysis how the new building would cast his shadow on other existing buildings, can be done.

Second, enabling the users to leave some feedback directly in the 3D visualization, or at least on the same website, opens up new possibilities in interaction. For example, the users can change a 3D scenario by putting in some custom objects which seem to be appropriate for them. Other options can be the inclusion of textual feedback or filling out some questionnaires about the scenarios.

Finally, the 3D scenario can provide an integrated view of several crosscutting concerns of all applications. For example, the simulation results from the urban growth simulation can be related to the public motion analysis tracks in the 3D city model.

The benefits of such an integrated view is that data can be interpreted in a context that is a more concrete and visually compelling, thus easier to understand by people with non-IT background. It can also be used to amend city planning scenarios and impact assessment for planned actions.

To achieve the aspects above the software design decision was taken to build a web-based portal application (Dambruch et al. 2013) which is based on a concept that uses reusable and customizable components. The components we created are designed to fulfill the requirements and use cases identified in (Kahn and Ludlow 2013), but they are generalized and easily customizable in such a way, that also other use cases can be fulfilled. All components can be arranged visually on the web pages that are created for the evaluation projects. Especially, the adoption of a role-based security concept for the users gives a lot of flexibility to address different target audiences. The policy analysis can therefore tailor the visualization to the level of expertise and, for example, can include additional information. On the other hand, confidentiality of information can be assured. So, it is easy to map the stakeholders into several user groups to which different access rights may be granted. For example, citizens may not be granted to change things, but only to annotate designs for a certain project. Moreover, the portal software provides many components off the shelf such as content management systems or blogs which can be used together with the 3D components to improve the user experience further.

Two of the prominent use cases are an architectural competition scenario and a comparison of design alternatives. In both cases, the stakeholders should have the possibility to place some annotation on an arbitrary point in the 3D scene. Also, the position of the viewer should cover several perspectives, such as viewing the scene as a pedestrian or getting an overview from a helicopter perspective. However, the key advantage of the applications is that the viewer can move interactively by just clicking and moving the mouse or a similar gesture on a touch device to move around in the 3D scene freely.

The next level of interaction is to leave some feedback by directly putting some annotations in the 3D scene. Whenever a user places an annotation, the exact position of the viewer along with the point the user was looking at when placing the annotation is recorded, so that the planner can easily take the point of view of the users. The user has the option to enter simple text in a pop-up window that is put directly into the 3D display, therefore not requiring distractive mouse movements to enter the text. Other components can access the annotations made and present it in a different format, which may be more appropriate, for example, a list view.

The third level is then to modify the 3D scene itself by placing additional or removing existing objects.

In Fig. 15.8, an example for the design comparison use case is given. The page displayed is made up of four components: The two 3D components are prominently placed side by side, each using the same basic 3D city model but with alternative buildings proposed. On the lower left side, a navigation bar with interesting perspectives is given which navigates both 3D views in sync. On the lower right side, a simple vote component is placed, so that stakeholders can select which alternative they like best.

Fig. 15.8 A portal page displaying an A/B comparison of design alternatives

15.4.3.4   Findings

The traditional policy-making process in the area of urban planning is transforming from a top-down approach to one that works bottom-up. The public's demands have changed and people want to take part in political discourse more and more often. However, at the moment policies are only discussed on a political level and citizens are rather informed than involved. At the same time, there is a gap in the availability of urban planning to anybody outside the city administration.

ICT tools such as the web-based solution of urbanAPI help mitigate this problem. Results of complex calculations such as the public motion analysis and the agent-based urban change simulation are visualized in a way that is understandable by non-IT personnel. The 3D visualization adds attractiveness that increases acceptance of the solution among the citizens. At the same time, the solution allows stakeholders to participate in the discussion by contributing feedback or new ideas. This happens in a controlled environment as the web-based portal application is highly configurable and individual modules can be customized, enabled, or disabled by the urban planners according to the scenario they wish to present and according to the degree of participation they are aiming for.

Within the time frame of the urbanAPI project, the developed tools are regularly evaluated in depth by users from the partner cities of Bologna (Italy), Ruse (Bulgaria), Vienna (Austria), and Vitoria-Gasteiz (Spain). We were able to derive the following results from these evaluations which we consider key for the success of ICT-enabled tools in participatory urban planning.

- The *data quality* has to be reasonably high. The 3D visualization has to be appealing in order to improve acceptance by citizens. This is only possible if it is based on high-quality geo-spatial data like textured 3D building models or high-resolution digital terrain models and aerial images. While many European cities already maintain a 3D city model, at the moment they often miss textures or fine geometrical details which would make the visualization more realistic.
- *Usability* plays an important role for ICT tools that are made available to a large audience. The tools can only gain high acceptance if they can be used easily and without barriers. The user interface has to be clear and understandable. The software should allow stakeholders to participate and contribute without too much effort. Otherwise, the software will not be used and the advantages of participatory urban planning are lost.
- In addition to that, the ICT tools have to be *portable* in order to run on a wide range of systems from desktop PCs to tablets and mobile devices. This improves the acceptance and lowers the barriers, which stakeholders have to take before they can participate in urban planning.

15.4.4 Summary of Case Studies

Figure 15.9 summarizes the presented case studies with a short task description, the applied modeling techniques, the relevant data types, the implemented visualization techniques, and the involved stakeholder. The table shows that the selected case study differ in nearly all of these characteristics. From this, we conclude that for policy analysis a broad range of scenarios exist that need to be tackled with different strategies. We already stated that a one-fits-all-solution from the field of information visualization does not exist. For each problem addressed in a case study, a specific solution needs to be designed in order to support the users in the best possible way. The heterogeneity of case studies in the field of policy analysis even amplifies this fact. Therefore, we strongly recommend to conduct a precise problem characterization and analysis of tasks to be solved with the technologies prior to their implementation. For this, all relevant stakeholders need to be involved. Design study methodologies in the field of information visualization and visual analytics already address this challenge. However, from our point of view these methodologies need to be adapted to the specific characteristics of policy analysis.

	Case Study 1: Optimization	Case Study 2: Social Simulation	Case Study 3: Urban Planning
Description	define optimal regional energy plan considering conflicting aspects	measure the impact of governmental subsidy strategies on public behavior	eParticipation for urban planning
Modeling Technique(s)	optimization	agent-based simulation	geo-spatial data modeling, agent-based simulation
Data Type	quantitative data	geo-spatial data	geo-spatial data, socio-economic data
Visualization Technique(s)	bar charts	maps, line charts	3D city model
Involved Stakeholders	Policy Analyst Domain Expert Modeling Expert	Policy Analyst Policy Maker Domain Expert Modeling Expert	Policy Analysts Domain Experts Policy Makers Public Stakeholder

Fig. 15.9 Summary of case studies

15.5   Conclusion

In this work, we presented a novel approach to tackle the challenges of the policy paradox. This paradox describes the fact that despite the acknowledged importance of scientific evidence for political decision making, the knowledge gained from scientific disciplines is seldom considered in policy making. In our approach, we proposed a concept that addresses this problem by introducing information visualization technologies to the policy-analysis field. Therefore, we described the disciplines of information visualization and policy analysis. We also identified capabilities provided by information visualization and challenges faced by policy analysis.

Information visualization is defined as "the use of computer-supported interactive, visual representations of abstract data to amplify cognition." Its purpose is the exploration, sensemaking, and communication of knowledge hidden in data. Policy analysis deals with the analysis of societal problems, and alternative policy options to be chosen by policy makers that may serve as solutions to these problems. For the generation of these policy options, scientific advice is proposed. The main challenges of policy analysis lie in an effective exploration, and sensemaking of policy options by the policy analysts, as well as a comprehensible communication of the analysis results to the policy makers who finally decide upon the options to be chosen.

From the capabilities of information visualization on the one hand, and the challenges of policy analysis on the other hand, we identified synergy effects resulting from the combination of these two fields. With this motivation, we proposed a method how to apply information visualization to the field of policy analysis. Therefore, we identified relevant stakeholders in the policy-making process. We defined possible collaborations between these stakeholders and hurdles that have to be faced. Finally, we sketched a methodology how to structure the development of such science–policy interfaces supported by information visualization.

As a last facet of our contribution, we presented three case studies that have been conducted in two European research projects dedicated to the field of policy modeling. These studies basically implemented the concept described in this approach. In the case studies, technologies from the scientific fields of agent-based simulation, optimization, and geo-spatial data modeling have been applied to the field of policy making in order to generate and analyze policy options for a given societal problem. All case studies provided access to the computational models by information visualization technologies. This enabled even non-IT experts to interact with complex models and generate policy options. Moreover, the visualization tools could be used to communicate and discuss the results derived from the policy analysis. The case studies showed that our provided concept can serve as an approach to further explore the synergy effects between information visualization and policy analysis. We believe that our provided concept stimulates and motivates further research and discussions in this new, interesting, and not yet extensively studied interdisciplinary field.

Acknowledgments   Research presented here is partly carried out within the project "urbanAPI" (Interactive Analysis, Simulation and Visualisation Tools for Urban Agile Policy Implementation), and "ePolicy"(Engineering the Policy-Making Life Cycle) funded from the 7th Framework Program of the European Commission, call identifier: FP7-ICT-2011-7, under the grant agreement no: 288577 (urbanAPI), and no: 288147 (ePolicy), started in October 2011.

References

Abdou M, Hamill L, Gilbert N (2012) Designing and building an agent-based model. In: Heppenstall AJ , Crooks AT, See LM, Batty M (eds) Agent-based models of geographical systems. Springer, Belmont, pp 141–165

Anderson JE (1975) Public policymaking, 7th edn. (2010). Wadsworth, Belmont

Andrews K (2008) Evaluation comes in many guises. In: BELIV'08 Workshop, CHI 2008. Florence, pp 8–10

Antunes L, Respício A, Balsa J, Coelho H (2008) Policy decision support through social simulation. In: Adam F, Humphreys P (eds) Encyclopedia of decision making and decision support technologies. IGI Global, Hershey, pp 716–723

Bertin J (1983) Semiology of graphics. University of Wisconsin Press, Madison

Blum S, Schubert K (2009) Politikfeldanalyse. VS Verlag für Sozialwissenschaften, Wiesbaden

Brenner T, Werker C (2009) Policy advice derived from simulation models. J Artif Soc Soc Simul 12(4):2

Cagnoli P (2010) VAS. Valutazione ambientale strategica. Dario Flaccovio, Palermo

Card S, Mackinlay J, Shneiderman B (eds) (1999) Readings in information visualization: using vision to think. Morgan Kaufann, San Francisco

Dambruch J, Peters-Anders J, Gebetsroither E (2013) User interface elements documentation—deliverable 3.2 of the project "urbanAPI" (interactive analysis, simulation and visualisation tools for urban agile policy implementation). http://www.urbanapi.eu/cgi-bin/download.pl?f=172.pdf

Dobuzinskis L, Howlett M, Laycock D (2005) Policy analysis in Canada: the state of the art. University of Toronto Press, Toronto

Edmonds B, Hernandez C, Troitzsch KG (2007) Social simulation: technologies, advances and new discoveries. IGI Global, Hershey

European Commission (2010) 7th framework programme for research and technological development

Few S (2009) Now you see it: simple visualization techniques for quantitative analysis. Analytics Press, Oakland

Fischer F, Miller G, Sidney M (2007) Handbook of public policy analysis: theory, politics, and methods. CRC Press, Boca Raton

Gavanelli M, Riguzzi F, Milano M, Cagnoli P (2010) Logic-based decision support for strategic environmental assessment. Theory practice of logic programming, 26th International Conference on Logic Programming (ICLP'10) (Special Issue, vol. 10, issue no. 4–6, pp 643–658)

Gavanelli, M, Riguzzi F, Milano M, Cagnoli P (2013) Constraint and optimization techniques for supporting policy making. In: Yu T, Chawla N, Simoff S (eds) Computational intelligent data analysis for sustainable development, data mining and knowledge discovery series, Chap. 12. Chapman & Hall/CRC, Boca Raton

Gebetsroither E (2009) Combining multi-agent systems modelling and system dynamics modelling in theory and practice. PhD thesis, Alpen-Adria-Universität Klagenfurt, Faculty of technical sciences

Gilmore DJ, Green TRG (1984) Comprehension and recall of miniature programs. Int J Man-Mach Stud 21(1):31–48

Göttrik W (2009) Politikberatung und Politikgestaltung. In: Schubert K, Bandelow NC (eds) Lehrbuch der Politikfeldanalyse 2.0. Oldenbourg Wissenschaftsverlag, München

Green TRG (1989) Cognitive dimensions of notations. In: Sutcliffe A, Macaulay L (eds) People and computers V. Cambridge University Press, Cambridge, pp 443–460

Greven MT (2008) Politik als Problemlösung - und als vernachlässigte Problemursache: Anmerkungen zur Policy-Forschung. In: Janning F, Toens K (eds) Die Zukunft der Policy-Forschung. Theorien, Methoden, Anwendungen. VS Verlag für Sozialwissenschaften, Wiesbaden

Heath B, Hill R, Ciarallo F (2009) A survey of agent-based modeling practices (January 1998 to July 2008). J Artif Soc Soc Simul 12(4):9

Hove Svd (2007) A rationale for science-policy interfaces. Futures 39:807–826

Howlett M, Ramesh M, Perl A (1995) Studying public policy: policy cycles and policy subsystems. Oxford University Press, Oxford

Howlett M, Wellstead A (2009) Re-visiting Meltsner: policy advice systems and the multi-dimensional nature of professional policy analysis. Available at SSRN 1546251

Janse G (2008) Communication between forest scientists and forest policy-makers in Europe: a survey on both sides of the science/policy interface. For Policy Econ 10:183–194

Jones CO (1970) An introduction to the study of public policy, 3rd edn. (1984). Brooks/Cole Publishing Co., Monterey

Kahn Z, Ludlow D (2013) User requirements definition—deliverable 2.1 of the project "urbanAPI" (interactive analysis, simulation and visualisation tools for urban agile policy implementation). http://www.urbanapi.eu/cgi-bin/download.pl?f=190.pdf

Keim D, Andrienko G, Fekete JD, Görg C, Kohlhammer J, Melançon G (2008) Visual analytics: definition, process, and challenges. In: Information visualization. Springer, Berlin

Kohlhammer J, Nazemi K, Ruppert T, Burkhardt D (2012) Toward visualization in policy modeling. Comput Graph Appl IEEE 32(5):84–89

Kosara R, Mackinlay J (2013) Storytelling: the next step for visualization. Computer 46(5): 44–50

Krämer M, Kehlenbach A (2013) Interactive, GPU-based urban growth simulation for agile urban policy modelling. In: Rekdalsbakken W, Bye R, Zhang H (eds) Proceedings of the 27th European Conference on Modelling and Simulation (ECMS). European Council for Modelling and Simulation, Ålesund, Norway, pp 75–81

Krämer M, Ludlow D, Khan Z (2013) Domain-specific languages for agile urban policy modelling. In: Rekdalsbakken W, Bye R, Zhang H (eds) Proceedings of the 27th European Conference on Modelling and Simulation (ECMS). European Council for Modelling and Simulation, Ålesund, Norway, pp 673–680

Lam H, Bertini E, Isenberg P, Plaisant C, Carpendale S (2012) Empirical studies in information visualization: Seven scenarios. IEEE Trans Vis Comput Graph 18:1520–1536

Leopold L (1971) A procedure for evaluating environmental impact. In: United States Geological Surve, Geological Survey Circular No. 645

Loibl W, Peters-Anders J (2012) Mobile phone data as source to discover spatial activity and motion patterns. In: GI Forum 2012: Geovisualization, Society and Learning. Wichman, pp 524–533

Munzner T (2009) A nested model for visualization design and validation. IEEE Trans Vis Comput Graph 15(6):921–928

Ruppert T, Bernard J, Kohlhammer J (2013a) Bridging knowledge gaps in policy analysis with information visualization. In: Proceedings of IFIP Conference on Electronic Government. Koblenz, Germany

Ruppert T, Bernard J, Ulmer A, Kuijper A, Kohlhammer J (2013b) Visual access to optimization problems in strategic environmental assessment. In: International Symposium on Visual Computing ISVC. Las Vegas, USA, pp 361–372

Schneider V (2008) Komplexität, politische Steuerung, und evidenz-basiertes Policy-Making. In: Janning F, Toens K (eds) Die Zukunft der Policy-Forschung. Theorien, Methoden, Anwendungen. VS Verlag für Sozialwissenschaften, Wiesbaden

Schneider V, Janning F (2006) Politikfeldanalyse. Akteure, Diskurse und Netzwerke in der öffentlichen Politik. VS Verlag für Sozialwissenschaften, Wiesbaden

Sedlmair M, Meyer MD, Munzner T (2012) Design study methodology: reflections from the trenches and the stacks. IEEE Trans Vis Comput Graph 18:2431–2440

Shneiderman B, Bederson B (2003) The craft of information visualization: readings and reflections. Morgan Kaufmann, San Francisco

Shulock N (1999) The paradox of policy analysis: if it is not used, why do we produce so much of it? J Policy Anal Manag 18(2):226–244

Thomas JJ, Cook KA (2005) Illuminating the path: the research and development agenda for visual analytics. IEEE Computer Society Press, Los Alamitos

Weimer DL, Vining AR (2005) Policy analysis: concepts and practice. Prentice Hall, Upper Saddle River

Whitley KN (1997) Visual programming languages and the empirical evidence for and against. J Vis Lang Comput 8(1):109–142

Chapter 16
Analysis of Five Policy Cases in the Field of Energy Policy

Dominik Bär, Maria A. Wimmer, Jozef Glova, Anastasia Papazafeiropoulou and Laurence Brooks

Abstract While the twentieth century is considered as the century of population explosion and burning of fossil fuels, environmental policies and the transition to effectively use renewable energy sources have become a priority of strategies in regions, countries and internationally. Different projects have been initiated to study the best suitable transition process towards renewable energy. In addition, an increasing number of climate change and energy policies is being formulated and released at distinct levels of governments. Many of these policies and projects pursue the aim of switching from energy sources like fossil fuels or nuclear power to renewable energy sources like solar, wind or water. The aim of this chapter is to provide foundations of policy implementation and particular methods as well as to investigate five policy implementation cases through a comparative analysis.

16.1 Introduction

The twentieth century was the century of population explosion and burning of fossil fuels, which led to the highest pollution in history causing climate change and biodiversity loss (Helm 2000). However, the pollution and its consequences have only been recognised in the recent decades and environmental policies are now of high

M. A. Wimmer (✉) · D. Bär
University of Koblenz-Landau, Koblenz, Germany
e-mail: wimmer@uni-koblenz.de

D. Bär
e-mail: dbaer@uni-koblenz.de

J. Glova
Technical University Kosice, Kosice, Slovakia
e-mail: jozef.glova@tuke.sk

A. Papazafeiropoulou · L. Brooks
Brunel University, Uxbridge, UK
e-mail: Anastasia.Papazafeiropoulou@brunel.ac.uk

L. Brooks
e-mail: Laurence.Brooks@brunel.ac.uk

© Springer International Publishing Switzerland 2015   355
M. Janssen et al. (eds.), *Policy Practice and Digital Science,*
Public Administration and Information Technology 10, DOI 10.1007/978-3-319-12784-2_16

priority to society, companies and policymakers (Helm 2000). Owing to this, governments all over the world have launched projects to improve the climate situation. The problem scope dealt with in this chapter concerns climate change and policies dealing with topics like sustainable energy management and the use of renewable energy sources. Many projects pursue the aim of switching from energy sources like fossil fuels or nuclear power to renewable energy sources like solar, wind or water. So on the one hand, the aim of policies is to replace polluting ways of power production with green technologies and, on the other hand, to reduce energy consumption by using innovative technologies.

Climate change affects the whole world and is a very huge organisational, technical and financial challenge, which is why industrial countries are expected to take responsibility and initiatives to counteract the current climate development. In the cause of this, these countries may serve as role models for other countries to join in improving the climate situation.

In this chapter, five projects and cases dealing with policies of climate change and energy use are investigated. First, a theoretical ground is provided about policy implementation like theories of policy implementation or methods of implementation in order to establish a common understanding. Subsequently, the projects are investigated and analysed via comparative analysis, performed in the frame of the eGovPoliNet[1] initiative. The selection of the policy cases was based on the authors' access to information of the cases of policy implementation. A framework[2] has been developed for the comparative analysis that supports pointing out major aspects and core information about the projects in order to have a brief overview and to make the projects comparable to each other. The framework provides a set of categories which need to be filled in to describe and analyse the projects, starting from an abstract and objectives, which gives both a brief summary of the policy case under investigation and its context and objectives, followed by a tabular overview structured along (a) metadata providing general information such as name and duration of the project, type of project (piloting case of a project or implementation project), domain (i.e. referring to the particular sector the policy is dealing with) and references; and (b) conceptual aspects of interest in the comparison providing more specific information such as specific policy domain and particular policy addressed, targeted users and/or stakeholders, an indication of the complexity of the policy case, theories used to develop the policy, methods used, supporting technology frameworks and tools use[3], simulation models developed[4], project outcome, links to other projects, transferability of solutions and techniques as well as concluding recommendations of the

---

[1] eGovPoliNet—Building a global multidisciplinary digital governance and policy modelling research and practice community. See http://www.policy-community.eu/ (last access: 28 July 2014).
[2] The framework is published in Annex I to technical report D 4.2 of eGovPoliNet: Maria A. Wimmer and Dragana Majstorovic (Eds.): Synthesis Report of Knowledge Assets, including Visions (D 4.2). eGovPoliNet consortium, 2014, report available under http://www.policy-community.eu/results/public-deliverables/ (last access: 28 July 2014).
[3] A comparative analysis of tools and technologies is provided in Kamateri et al. (2014).
[4] A comparative analysis of simulation models is provided in Majstorovic et al. (2014).

project or case. Based on the identified information from the comparative analysis, the projects are briefly discussed and compared to each other. Moreover, the results and benefits of the projects are described and the possibility of transferring the used approaches to other domains, projects or cases is investigated.

The following three research questions drive the comparative investigations of projects and cases: (1) what approaches of policy modelling are used in implementing public policies, how do these approaches differ and are these approaches best fit for the purposes of the policy cases? (2) How can the implications of selecting a particular approach to ensure successful policy implementation be measured and what lessons can be drawn from the case analyses? (3) How easily can the approaches of the policy cases investigated in the chapter be adopted to other countries, other policy domains and even other thematic policy areas?

The chapter is structured as follows: In Sect. 16.2, theoretical grounds and definitions about policy implementation are given in order to provide a common understanding and an overview of the purpose of policy implementation as well as of policy instruments used in climate change and renewable energy policy. Thereafter, the comparative analysis framework is introduced regarding its structure and content. Using this framework, projects and cases of the field are analysed in Sect. 16.4 and subsequently discussed and compared to each other, including a brief reflection of research and practice implications, and further research needs (Sect. 16.5). The chapter ends with some concluding remarks in Sect. 16.6.

16.2 Theoretical Grounds of Policy Implementation

Buse et al. argue that policy implementation refers to the execution of a formulated policy, which means turning theory into practice. When turning policy into practice, it is common to observe a gap between formulated and implemented policy as the policymakers hand over the responsibility for the implementation to policy implementers who may have a different understanding of the policy (Buse et al. 2012). The policy formulation is seen as a political activity and the implementation as technical, administrative or managerial activity. The gap between policymakers and policy implementers causes a lack of control from the policymaker view regarding the way the policy is implemented.

Implementation of public policy is always serving a purpose and is put in place in order to change things for the better and improve situations that seem to be problematic. There are different ways that decisions for a policymaking process to start take place (Lindblom 1968). An obvious but not always the most common way is through public demands. These are demands from the general public (known as "bottom up" initiatives) and can be very influential especially for important issues such as public health and safety. Nowadays, the general public is educated and informed at a level that gives them the power to be able to mobilize and in some cases demand changes at a public policy level. Another reason that policy implementation is starting to formulate is pressure from special interest groups that can influence policies promoting public welfare. For example, chambers of commerce are typically supporting interest of their business members, while Green Peace will express concerns and will try to address environmental issues, promoting the implementation of public policies for environmental protection (Portney and Stavins 2000).

According to the policy cycle, the implementation of a policy follows some basic steps such as agenda setting (problem identification), policy formulation, decision-making, implementation and evaluation (Nakamura 1987). The first stage of this cycle where the problem is identified is the stage where the purpose of the policy is formulated and is recognised as the starting point of the cycle. During this agenda setting, all stakeholders are or need to be participating and voicing concerns as well as possible remedies for the problem at hand. This stage was typically initiated in the past by government agencies but latest studies show that a number of other entities influence this stage (Young and Mendizabal 2009). These could be the media, think tanks, policy research institutes and other academic or business organisations.

The final outcome of the agenda setting stage is a purpose statement where policymakers state the problem as well as the desired outcome of the proposed strategy. Examples of such statements can be details of a costal policy and its desired outcomes (NZPCS 2010). The desired outcomes of policymaking are always aiming at improving the problem area in question and ultimately improve the welfare of citizens at large.

An important but not always well-executed stage of the policy implementation cycle is that of the evaluation of the policy outcomes. This is the time when the designers of a public policy have finalised the implementation and are in a position to evaluate whether the actions taken improved the situation and contributed to the welfare of the target population. Evaluation is a retrospective assessment of government initiatives, and it usually measures the success of activities that they are still taking place and are ongoing. Evaluation seems to be a controversial and hard-to-implement strategy that needs to be based on peoples' perceptions, opinions and judgments while at the same time needs to be objective enough to provide some insights into the complexities of public interventions (Vedug 1997).

As this chapter focuses on policy cases of climate change and renewable energy policies, the next two sections introduce instruments used in these two policy domains for steering and governing.

16.2.1 Instruments for Climate Change Policy

For the implementation and application of climate and energy policies, Oikonomou and Jepma present different instruments. They acknowledge that categorizations of policies differ within literature and therefore they make use of general studies from OECD, IPCC, etc. They have identified the following policy instruments (Oikonomou and Jepma 2007):

Table 16.1 Typology of policy instruments for global climate change summarised from Stavins (1997)

Types of instruments Categories	Command-and-control (and voluntary in domestic)	Market-based
Domestic	Energy efficiency standards Product prohibitions Voluntary agreements	Charges, fees and taxes (carbon taxes, taxes on fossil fuels, other energy taxes) Tradable rights (tradable carbon rights, tradable "emission reduction" credits)
International	Uniform energy efficiency standards Fixed national emission limits	Charges, fees and taxes (harmonized domestic taxes, uniform international tax) Tradable rights (international tradable permits, joint implementation)

- *Financial measures,* where the government can change the cost of energy through taxation and subsidy policies. The following types of taxation are distinguished: emission charges/taxes, user charges, and product charges/taxes.
- *Legal or regulatory instruments,* where governments can set legal requirements with financial penalties for non-compliance.
- *Organisational measures* are commitments undertaken by power producers or industries in consultation or negotiation.
- *Certificates or marketable* (tradable) *permits or quotas.*

Stavins identifies two distinct categories of policy instruments that are particular in global climate change: The first category—domestic policy instruments—enables individual nations to achieve their specific national or local targets and goals. The second category—bilateral, multilateral or global (or in general international) instruments—can be employed jointly by groups of nations (Stavins 1997). The author developed a typology of these two categories of policy instruments for global climate change which is summarised in Table 16.1.

16.2.2   Policy Instruments for Renewable Energy

Energy policy is closely linked to climate change as the energy sector has high potential for reducing greenhouse gas (GHG) emissions. There is no universal policy prescription for supporting renewable energy. Particular nations are typically unique. The most suitable policy instruments in one country may not be appropriate for another country. Instead of a single policy to achieve all of the policy objectives, it is more useful to consider a policy portfolio approach or a policy toolkit. Policy instruments are means by which policy objectives are pursued (Howlett 2009). Azuela and Barroso (2011) and IPCC (2012) put forward in the following five categories of policy instruments for renewable energy:

- *Regulations and standards* can promote renewable energy via direct support (with policy objectives in removal of non-economic barriers and in increasing demand for renewable energy) and indirect support (with policy objective in restrictions on fossil fuel power).
- *Quantity instruments*—market-based instruments that define a specific target or absolute quantity for renewable energy production.
- *Price instruments*—reduce cost- and pricing-related barriers by establishing favourable price regimes for renewable energy relative to other sources of power generation, e.g. fiscal incentives (production/investment tax credits, public investment, loans or grants; capital subsidy, grant or rebate; increase in taxes on fossil fuels; reductions in sales, energy, CO_2, value-added tax (VAT) or other taxes) and feed-in tariffs (a preferential tariff; guaranteed purchase of the electricity produced for a specified period; guaranteed access to the grid).
- *Public procurement*—governments are often a very large energy consumer, whereby their purchasing and procurement decisions affect the market.
- *Auction*—an auction is a selection process to allocate goods and services competitively, based on a financial offer. Specifically in a "reverse auction", electricity generators bid their supply to distribution companies and the process is designed to select the lowest prices. Auctions can be a very attractive mechanism for attracting new renewable energy supply.

16.3 Approaches to Policy Implementation

Policies can be implemented in different ways. Subsequently, four approaches of policy implementation are presented: top-down approach, bottom-up approach, macro- and micro-implementation and principal–agent theory. They exemplarily point out how policies can be implemented, what actors are involved along the implementation process and how they affect the policy, its implementation and outcome.

16.3.1 Top-Down Approach

The top-down approach was developed between the 1960s and 1970s by policy analysts in order to provide policymakers with a better understanding of how to minimise the gap between the formulated and the implemented policy (Buse et al. 2012). This approach describes a linear process from policy formulation to implementation, where policies are communicated from policymakers to executing entities like authorities, which turn the policy into practice. To successfully implement a policy, the policy goals need to be clearly described and understood by all involved actors. Moreover, the required resources for the implementation need to be available, a communication and command chain needs to be established and the whole implementation process needs to be controlled (Pressman and Wildavsky 1984).

The top-down approach may be criticised as it focuses mainly on the decision and on policymakers while it does not sufficiently include other involved actors and factors that are part of the policy implementation process. The implementation is seen as an administrative process and does not include the expertise of local experts who eventually implement the policy. Thus, the approach is difficult to apply in situations that are not driven by a single leading actor but where multiple actors participate in the policy implementation process (Buse et al. 2012). For this approach, Gunn formulated ten pre-conditions which should be fulfilled to successfully implement a policy (Gunn 1978 and Hogwood and Gunn 1984). However, Buse et al. criticize that hardly all pre-conditions could be fulfilled at once and that policy implementation in reality is too complex and thus cannot be covered with the top-down approach and its pre-conditions (Buse et al. 2012).

16.3.2 Bottom-Up Approach

The bottom-up approach was developed from the criticism of the top-down approach, which focuses on policymakers and neglects the other actors involved in the implementation process. The bottom-up approach focuses on policy implementers as they play an important role in the policy implementation process as active participants who give feedback to the policymakers and have high influence on the actual policy implementation (Buse et al. 2012). Lipsky studied the behaviour of "street-level bureaucrats" (teachers, doctors, nurses, etc.) in relation to their clients in the 1970s (Lipsky 1980). In his studies, Lipsky showed that even people in highly rule-bound environments could reshape parts of public central policy for their own ends (Buse et al. 2012). In consequence of these findings, researchers found that even if all pre-conditions for the top-down approach (see Gunn 1978) were fulfilled, policies could still be implemented in a way which was not planned by the policymakers (Buse et al. 2012).

16.3.3 Macro- and Micro-implementation

When governments execute policies in order to influence local authorities, it is called macro-implementation (Berman 1978). However, local authorities need to transfer governmental policies into their own local policies, which is then called micro-implementation. This approach can be understood as a two-phase implementation method. In the first phase, the overall policy is made by governmental policymakers in order to address certain issues and to pursue defined goals. Local authorities and policymakers then need to adopt the overall policy and transform it into a policy that is manageable and suited for local application. This transformation process may lead to a gap between the formulated governmental policy and the executed local policy, which makes this approach quite similar to the bottom-up and top-down approaches respectively. All these approaches carry the risk of a mismatch between formulated and implemented policy as is extensively elaborated, e.g. in James et al. (1999).

16.3.4 Principal–Agent Theory

According to Buse et al., the principal–agent theory argues an "implementation gap" as the inevitable consequence of the governmental institution structure. Policy- and decision-makers ("principals") delegate responsibility for the implementation of policies to their officials ("agents"), whom they cannot completely monitor and control. These "agents" have discretion in how they work on implementing the policy and may also see themselves from a different view than the policymakers. Thereby policy implementers may interpret the policy in a different way than the policy formulators which leads to implementing the policy in a different way than it was actually meant to be implemented (Buse et al. 2012).

Policy implementation is a complex process that is influenced by many actors (Turnpenny et al. 2005). From its formulation until its implementation, the policy passes through different levels of authorities and is handled by different actors. It is formulated by governmental policymakers and then passed on to local policymakers and authorities who have to adapt the overall policy in order to implement it successfully in their local structures. Along this implementation process, governmental policymakers are not completely able to monitor and control the implementation, as local policymakers need to take care of local policy peculiarities. Moreover, the local policymakers may understand the overall policy in a different way than it is meant to be understood. These factors, often inevitable, lead to a so-called implementation gap (James et al. 1999). This gap is the consequence of the different understandings and backgrounds of the actors who are involved in the implementation process of the policy. This issue needs to be addressed in order to minimise the gap between formulated and implemented policy, so that policies are implemented the way they are meant to be implemented.

In the next section, five different cases of policy implementation are being studied and compared to investigate the three research questions formulated in the introductory chapter. The theoretical foundations presented in Sect. 16.2 and the distinct approaches introduced in this section provide the underlying understanding for the comparative analysis of cases of climate change and renewable energy policy.

16.4   Investigating Five Cases of Climate Change and Renewable Energy Policy

Based on the research foundations and investigation of distinct approaches to policy implementation, the projects and cases introduced in this section provide examples of how policies are being implemented or how the implementation process of policies concerning climate change and energy matters is supported. In order to analyse the projects and cases and to describe them in detail, the framework developed in eGovPoliNet as outlined in the introductory section is used (i.e. describing the cases along abstract and objectives, metadata and relevant conceptual aspects). This framework offers the possibility to point out major aspects and characteristics of the projects and cases and to make them comparable along those aspects. The five cases chosen and analysed via the comparative analysis template are:

- Assessing the EU policy package on climate change and renewables
- German nuclear phase-out and energy transition policy
- KNOWBRIDGE: Cross-border knowledge bridge in the renewable energy sources (RES) cluster in East Slovakia and North Hungary
- Kosice Self-governing Region's (KSR's) strategy for the use of renewable energy resources
- MODEL: Management of domains related to energy in local authorities

The projects and cases have been selected on the basis of relevance for the domain of study of this chapter and of sufficient access to information to carry out the comparative analysis.

16.4.1   Assessing the EU Policy Package on Climate Change and Renewables

Abstract: As stated by Capros et al., the EU aims to reduce GHG emissions at least by 20 % in 2020 compared to 1990. Likewise, 20 % of energy needs should be covered through renewable energy sources—see EU (2007). The research of Capros et al. developed an energy model to assess the range of policy options that were debated to meet the two targets of the EU policy. Options of the energy policy explore and assess trading of renewable targets, carbon trading in power plants and industry and the use of the Clean Development Mechanism to improve cost-efficiency. In the research assessment of the EU energy policy, the authors also examined fairness by analysing the distribution of emission reduction in the non-emission trading sector, the distribution of CO_2 allowances in the emission trading sector and the reallocation of renewable targets across Member States. The authors assess the overall costs of meeting both targets being in the range of 0.4–0.6 % of gross domestic product (GDP) in 2020 for the EU as a whole. It is also argued that the redistribution mechanisms employed would significantly improve fairness compared to a cost-effective solution (Capros et al. 2011).

The main objectives of the EU policy package on climate change and renewables contain (Capros et al. 2011; EU 2007):

- Reducing unilaterally GHG by 20 % in 2020 compared to 1990 levels (including an offer to increase this target to −30 % given a sufficiently ambitious international agreement)
- Supplying 20 % of energy needs by 2020 from RES, including the use of 10 % renewable energy in transport
- Giving priority to energy efficiency in all energy domains

The assessment study of Capros et al. aimed at developing and testing an energy model to assess the range of policy options discussed to meet the two targets of the EU policy (Capros et al. 2011). Table 16.2 outlines the main aspects of the EU policy package and the respective assessment study of Capros et al. (2011).

16.4.2   German Nuclear Phase-Out and Energy Transition Policy

Abstract: Following the Fukushima disaster in Japan in March 2011, the German chancellor Merkel declared a 3-month moratorium on nuclear power plants, in which checks took place and nuclear policy was reconsidered. Subsequently, all eight nuclear power reactors which began operation in 1980 or earlier were immediately shut down. Although the Reactor Safety Commission reported that all German reactors were basically safe with regard to natural or man-made dysfunction, the government decided to shut down the nine remaining reactors until 2022 and approved construction of new coal and gas-fired plants despite retaining its CO_2 emission reduction targets, as well as expanding wind energy. Germany was expected to be dependent on energy imports after the shutdown of the first eight reactors but it still kept exporting energy as the energy production from wind, solar and hydro keeps growing. So far, the use of renewable sources is quite expensive and shouldered by tax payers and consumers. Moreover, it is dependent on wind and sunlight which are not always available (Moore 2013).[5]

The main objectives of Germany's nuclear phase-out and energy transition policy can be summed up as:[6]

- To accelerate the transformation of Germany's energy system to RES (nuclear power serving only as "bridging technology" to transform)

---

[5] See also the following two websites (last access: 30 July 2014): http://www.dw.de/power-exports-peak-despite-nuclear-phase-out/a-16370444 and http://energytransition.de/.

[6] See also the following two websites (last access: 30 July 2014): http://www.dw.de/power-exports-peak-despite-nuclear-phase-out/a-16370444 and http://energytransition.de/.

Table 16.2 Analysis of metadata and conceptual aspects of the study assessing the EU policy package on climate change and renewables

Metadata	
Name	Assessment of EU policy package on climate change and renewables
Duration	EU policy package: 2007–2020
Domain	Climate change and energy sectors
Project type	Policy implementation (of EU policy package) and assessment (for the research study)
Reference(s)	For the EU climate and energy policy package: EU (2007, 2008) and online under: http://ec.europa.eu/clima/policies/package/index_en.htm (last access: 30 July 2014) For the assessment study: Capros et al. (2011), PRIMES model of NTUA (http://www.e3mlab.ntua.gr/index.php?option=com_content&view=category&id=35%3Aprimes&Itemid=80&layout=default&lang=en, last access 30 July 2014), GAINS model of IIASA (http://www.iiasa.ac.at/rains/C&E_package.html?sb=19, last access 30 July 2014)
Conceptual aspects	
Implementing which policy	Energy policy (emissions and renewable energy sources)
Users/Stakeholders	European Commission, EU Member States, industry, general public
Complexity	Very high due to involvement of different actors and dependency of many interrelated factors
Theory(s) used[a]	Macro-modelling with PRIMES energy system model, which implements partial equilibrium (energy system and markets); and with GAINS model of IIASA, which models non-CO_2 GHGs and derives emissions of non-CO_2 GHGs from a series of activity indicators, referring among others to agriculture and to specific industrial processes
Method(s) used[a]	Scenario modelling and simulation modelling (cross-modelling of interacting targets) 150 energy scenarios with different carbon and RES values were investigated by using the PRIMES model for the period 2005–2030 for all EU Member States
Supportive technology frameworks and tools used[a]	PRIMES energy system model of NTUA GAINS model of IIASA
Model(s) generated[a]	PRIMES model, GAINS (greenhouse gas—air pollution interactions and synergies) model
Project outcome[a]	Eleven scenarios with different starting positions and influences Analysis of the different scenarios

Table 16.2 (continued)

Conceptual aspects	
Transferability of solutions and techniques[a]	Partially given as the models can serve as blueprints for similar models and as source for exploring further aspects of climate change and energy policy. The transferability is, however, restricted to the very policy domain
Concluding recommendations of the project[a]	Meeting the targets in the EU is an ambitious effort and requires considerable adjustments in how energy is consumed and produced Energy efficiency improvement is clearly the most cost-effective way for meeting the targets and must be the main driver of changes RES are of crucially important to implement the policy The compliance costs to meet both targets is estimated to be in a range between 0.4 and 0.6 % of GDP of the EU in 2020

GAINS Greenhouse Gas and Air Pollution Interactions and Synergies, *GHGs* greenhouse gases, *IIASA* International Institute for Applied Systems Analysis, *NTUA* National Technical University of Athens, *RES* renewable energy sources
[a]These entries provide analysis data regarding the assessment study but not for the EU policy package itself

- To shut down all nuclear power plants in Germany by 2022. The shutdown dates for the remaining reactors are: by 2015, Grafenrheinfeld; by 2017, Gundremmingen B; by 2019, Philippsburg 2; by 2021, Grohnde, Gundremmingen C and Brokdorf; and by 2022, the three youngest nuclear power stations, Isar 2, Emsland and Neckarwestheim 2.
- To find reliable alternative energy sources to coal power plants, which are still needed to close energy gaps
- To switch to renewable energy (sources; solar, wind, hydro)

Table 16.3 sums up the major metadata and conceptual aspects of the German nuclear phase-out and energy transition policy.

16.4.3 KNOWBRIDGE: Cross-Border Knowledge Bridge in the RES Cluster in East Slovakia and North Hungary

Abstract: The KNOWBRIDGE project is one of the three agreed initiatives of the cross-border Hungarian–Slovakian region, and it aims to increase and strengthen the capacity of the research potential of two cross-border and convergence regions: the KSR in Slovakia and the Borsod–Abaúj–Zemplén region in Hungary. KNOWBRIDGE is supporting the development of a new innovative cross-border research-driven cluster in the area of RES and associating research entities, enterprises and regional authorities. The major activities in the project are analysis, mentoring and integration of research agendas and the definition of a Joint Action Plan in order to support regional authorities and at the same time take account of the

Table 16.3 Analysis of metadata and conceptual aspects of the German nuclear phase-out and energy transition policy

Metadata	
Name	German nuclear phase-out and energy transition policy
Duration	06/2011–2022
Domain	Energy sector
Project type	Policy implementing
Reference(s)	http://www.dw.de/power-exports-peak-despite-nuclear-phase-out/a-16370444 (last access: 30 July 2014) http://energytransition.de/ (last access: 30 July 2014) http://www.bundesregierung.de/Content/DE/StatischeSeiten/Breg/Energiekonzept/05-kernenergie.html (last access: 30 July 2014) http://www.greenpeace.de/themen/energiewende (last access: 30 July 2014) (Moore 2013; Morris and Pehnt 2012)
Conceptual aspects	
Implementing which policy	Energy policy (nuclear phase-out and transition to renewable energy sources)
Users/Stakeholders	German politicians, energy providers and energy service sector, industry, general public
Complexity	Very high due to the involvement of many different actors and the complexity of providing a balanced as well as target oriented implementation of the nuclear phase-out and transition to renewable energies The high complexity requires very extensive and accurate planning
Theory(s) used	Not successful in retrieving relevant information
Method(s) used	Not successful in retrieving relevant information
Supportive technology frameworks tools and used	Monitoring system to monitor the policy implementation (annual reports on progress and examination by expert commission)
Model(s) generated	Various by distinct institutions, yet no insights to what kinds of models were generated as only the results are shown and discussed in the various literature studied
Project outcome	Germany will become one of the world's most efficient, most innovative and greenest economies Shutdown of all nuclear reactors by 2022 Growing engagement in renewable energy (source) development, which also contributes to jobs and economic growth Germany is setting standards with its energy concept for the EU and globally

Table 16.3 (continued)

Conceptual aspects	
Transferability of solutions and techniques	Germany serves as a role model for other countries (in Europe and worldwide) on the way to a cleaner and more sustainable energy system
Concluding recommen-dations of the project	Morris and Pehnt (2012) conclude the following nine key findings of implementing the nuclear phase-out and the energy transition in German in their report, which serve also as overall recommendations in this comparison:
	The German energy transition is an ambitious, but feasible undertaking
	The German energy transition is driven by citizens and communities
	The energy transition is Germany's largest post-war infrastructure project. It strengthens its economy and creates new jobs
	With the energy transition, Germany aims to not only keep its industrial base, but make it fit for a greener future
	Regulation and open markets provide investment certainty and allow small business to compete with large corporations
	Germany demonstrates that fighting climate change and phasing out nuclear power can be two sides of the same coin
	The German energy transition is broader than often discussed. It not only includes renewable electricity, but also changes to energy use in the transportation and housing sectors
	The German energy transition is here to stay
	The energy transition is affordable for Germany, and it will likely be even more affordable for other countries

interest of the private companies operating in the RES branch and of the research and development institutions. Therewith, a good basis for a triple helix concept is promoted.[7]

The objectives of KNOWBRIDGE are as follows[8]:

- To increase the overall capacities of regional players in northern Hungary and eastern Slovakia in enhancing science and technology-based development in cross-border context
- To improve links between regional authorities, research entities and local business community in two cross-border regions
- To promote development of specific goals for regional and cross-border research and technological development (RTD) policies
- To enhance common partnership of regional authorities, research entities and business community in national and European initiatives

[7] See http://www.knowbridge.eu/index.php (last access: 29 July 2014) and http://cordis.europa.eu/result/report/rcn/54725_en.html (last access: 29 July 2014).
[8] See http://www.knowbridge.eu/index.php (last access: 29 July 2014) and http://cordis.europa.eu/result/report/rcn/54725_en.html (last access: 29 July 2014).

- To foster trans-national (cross-border) cooperation between regional partners
- To further develop the research-driven cluster in the area of RES
- To develop joint action plans in order to increase regional economic competitive-
  ness through research and technological development activities in the defined area
  of RES
- To exploit synergies between regional national and Community programmes for
  research and economic development in cross-border environment
- To promote the reduction of CO_2 emissions in two cross-border regions

Table 16.4 provides insights into the KNOWBRIDGE project along the analysis
framework of eGovPoliNet.

16.4.4 KSR's Strategy for the Use of Renewable Energy Sources

Abstract: The KSR (Slovakia) aims at supporting the utilisation of renewable energy
sources, at achieving a better energy efficiency and at decreasing the energy consumption overall. In order to support these policy goals, KSR has participated in the
Open Collaboration for Policy Modelling (OCOPOMO) project[9] as a case study to
explore innovative approaches to policy modelling and exploration, and especially
to explore the views and attitudes of the various stakeholders in this sensitive policy context. OCOPOMO's Kosice policy model focuses on stakeholder views, on
different alternative renewable sources of energy, as well as on the traditional energy production and consumption culture in the region. A particular focus is put on
policy instruments and patterns for promoting the use of renewable energy, for best
assessing the perceived market potential of each specific kind of energy source, for
understanding the contractual, social and technical barriers hindering a specific kind
of technology for energy generation in the Kosice region, and for understanding the
motivating factors for citizens and companies to use RES while at the same time increasing energy efficiency by e.g. better insulation of buildings (Scherer et al. 2013;
Wimmer et al. 2012).

In order to achieve a widely accepted energy policy, KSR argues that regional
energy development should prioritise the development of renewable energy sources,
and policies should in particular focus on building infrastructures that particularly
support these goals.

In Table 16.5, we analyse the policy formulation case along the eGovPoliNet
framework to provide further details.

---

[9] www.ocopomo.eu (last access: 31 July 2014).

Table 16.4 Analysis of metadata and conceptual aspects of KNOWBRIDGE in the RES Cluster in East Slovakia and North Hungary

Metadata	
Name	KNOWBRIDGE: The Cross-border Knowledge Bridge in the RES Cluster in East Slovakia and North Hungary
Duration	2009–2012
Domain	Energy sector
Project type	EC co-funded project case study supporting policy formulation through a new way of innovative collaboration among key actors of governments, energy industry and research institutions
Reference(s)	http://www.knowbridge.eu/index.php (last access: 29 July 2014) http://cordis.europa.eu/result/report/rcn/54725_en.html (last access: 29 July 2014)
Conceptual aspects	
Implementing which policy	Supporting the research potential and the collaboration of governments with relevant actors of the energy sector and of research institutions of two cross-border and convergence regions in order to better exploring synergies and building up of capacities in the domain of renewable energy sources
Users/Stakeholders	Regional governments and politicians of the East Slovakian Košice Self-governing Region and of the North Hungarian Borsod–Abaúj–Zemplén region, energy providers, researchers
Complexity	Rather high due to the involvement of different actors with their specific interests and due to the complexity of the RES domain
Theory(s) used	Not successful in retrieving relevant information
Method(s) used	Desk research and participatory methods to develop and evaluate a research-driven cluster in the RES sector Joint framework with toolbox for analysis and benchmarking of the local RES sector and the cross-border cluster as well as for developing the Joint Action Plan and Business Plans Guidelines and reports SWOT analyses
Supportive technology frameworks and tools used	Not successful in retrieving relevant information
Project outcome	Reports on best practices and trends in the areas of (1) national and regional economic and technological development focused on RES, (2) RTD support policies and (3) knowledge creation, transfer between business entities through networking Methodological toolbox for Joint Action Plan and Business Plan preparation

Table 16.4 (continued)

Conceptual aspects	
	Financial tools and approaches for RTD funding
	Report on energy efficient technologies and technological development in RES
	Report on energy solution responding to SMEs specific energy demands in the region
	SWOT analyses in local RES
	Joint Action Plan for cross-border cluster in RES
	Mutual learning models elaboration
Links to other projects	Relevant related projects of policy implementation in the domain of climate change and RES are:
	http://www.arr.sk/?projekty&gid=19 (last access: 29 July 2014)
	http://www.cogitaproject.eu/index.php/en/ (last access: 29 July 2014)
	http://www.huskroua-cbc.net/en/ (last access: 29 July 2014)
Transferability of solutions and techniques	Methodological toolbox for analysis and benchmarking and methodological toolbox for Joint Action Plan and Business Plan is adoptable and adjustable for other cross-border activities in the area of RES
Concluding recommendations of the project	The project serves as a good blueprint of (1) cross-border collaborations of regions and (2) of collaboration of different actors in policy planning
	The methodological toolboxes can serve similar projects in their planning
	It is yet to be monitored and evaluated how the policy plans, joint action plan and business plan will be implemented in order to maintain and keep the network of actors sustainably active and successful, especially as EC-funding is in general a temporary investment

RES renewable energy sources, *RTD* research and technological development, *SWOT* strengths, weaknesses, opportunities and threats

16.4.5   MODEL: Management of Domains Related to Energy in Local Authorities

Abstract: MODEL stands for "Management of Domains Related to Energy in Local Authorities". The project aims at reducing the energy gap in the EU and beyond by helping volunteer local authorities become models for their own citizens and other municipalities. MODEL has started in 2007 with the support of the Intelligent Energy Europe programme and has set up a common methodology that was implemented in 43 pilot cities from new EU Member States and Candidate Countries so far. The main objective is that cities become models for citizens and other municipalities regarding energy management.

Table 16.5 Analysis of metadata and conceptual aspects of KSR's strategy for the use of RES

Metadata	
Name	Kosice Self-governing Region's strategy for the use of renewable energy sources
Duration	2010–2013
Domain	Energy sector
Project type	Pilot case of policy formulation of the OCOPOMO project
Reference(s)	http://www.ocopomo.eu/ (last access: 29 July 2014), (Scherer et al. 2013; Wimmer et al. 2012) An analysis of the software modelling approach of OCOPOMO and the Kosice case is also provided in Majstorovic et al. (2014)
Conceptual aspects	
Implementing which policy	Energy policy with focus on the increased use of RES as well as a better insulation of buildings
Users/Stakeholders	Government officials of the Self-governing Region of Kosice, energy provider, owners of houses and buildings, citizens and companies as energy consumers
Complexity	Rather complex because of the involvement of distinct actors and policy objectives
Theory(s) used	Complexity theory, agent-based modelling, stakeholder engagement theory, design research and meta-modelling
Method(s) used	Online consultation and engagement of stakeholders, scenario building, conceptual modelling, agent-based modelling, qualitative data analysis and coding through ontology development, provenance information conveyed from narrative scenarios to formal simulation models through a traceability concept using text annotation and UUID
Supportive technology frameworks and tools used	Eclipse modelling framework Collaboration and scenario editing tool (CSET) based on Alfresco Web content management system Consistent conceptual description tool (CCD Tool), CCD2DRAMS Tool, declarative rule-based agent-modelling system (DRAMS)—all based on eclipse modelling framework Simulation analysis tool
Model(s) used	Conceptual model as domain ontology, meta-models of conceptual model and simulation model, simulation models of Kosice policy via DRAMS Various conceptual models using UML modelling techniques

Table 16.5 (continued)

Conceptual aspects	
Project outcome	The project explored policy alternatives generated by stakeholders in scenarios in order to understand the behavioural aspects of the stakeholders involved towards policy options. Policy options explored were among others: generating clean power using regional resources; reducing CO_2, generating new job opportunities if investments in renewables are being made, increasing energy efficiency and decrease energy consumption through: (1) integration of new heating technologies (cogeneration, heat pumps), (2) better insulation of buildings, (3) switching to a natural gas fuel for public transportation by bus, (4) investment in municipal boiler house with integrated cogeneration unit fuelled by biomass, (5) advisory services for citizens and their awareness raising, (6) cooperation with private companies and local actors on the development and (7) the implementation of a city energy strategy
Links to other projects	Campania regional knowledge transfer case: http://www.ocopomo.eu/in-a-nutshell/piloting-cases/campania-region-italy (last access: 29 July 2014) London housing policy case: http://www.ocopomo.eu/in-a-nutshell/piloting-cases/greater-london-authority-gla (last access: 29 July 2014) Use of OCOPOMO tools in GLODERS: http://www.gloders.eu (last access: 31 July 2014)
Transferability of solutions and techniques	Basic approach transferable to different policy environment where stakeholder engagement is important, conceptual modelling shall facilitate the transformation of narrative text inputs of evidences to inform policy simulation models, and simulation models in DRAMS can serve as blueprints for new policy simulation models based on DRAMS
Concluding recommendations of the project	The lessons from the project case are that clear priorities (heat energy savings, refurbishment of public buildings, use of local renewable energy sources etc.) are of prime importance Also a strong focus should be built on more intensively caring about the energy savings in order to care for climate change issues Cooperation with experts from the energy domain is important to develop suitable policy models City membership in the Association of Sustainable Energy Municipalities—CITENERGO—facilitated the exchange of experiences and cooperation with other Slovak cities active in the energy field

CCD consistent conceptual description, *CSET* collaboration and scenario editing tool, *DRAMS* declarative rule-based agent-modelling system, *KSR* Kosice Self-governing Region, *OCOPOMO* Open Collaboration for Policy Modelling, *RES* renewable energy sources

Table 16.6 provides insights into the metadata and conceptual particularities of this project.

16.5   Comparison and Lessons from Analysis

The five projects and cases described in Sect. 16.5 are mainly focused on renewable energy sources. Besides, the change from fossil fuels and nuclear power to renewable energy sources is a topic, as well as the responsible handling and consumption of energy. The central aim of the projects and policy implementation cases is the advancement of the use of renewable energy sources, the simultaneous decrease of energy consumption and thereby the improvement of the overall energy efficiency. These aims are pursued on the one hand by developing concepts and strategies on a policymaking level and on the other hand by actively supporting cities and communities in improving their energy efficiency. Some projects clearly defined goals with dates and figures to be accomplished, like shutting down all nuclear reactors in Germany until 2022, or reducing CO_2 emission by 20 % until 2020 while increasing green energy production by 20 % simultaneously (cf. Sect. 16.4.1). Other projects like OCOPOMO's KSR case or the MODEL project developed and evaluated long-term strategies for the continuous improvement of energy efficiency and change of energy sources, which are actively carried out for interested communities and guided via frameworks for the practical application. The projects selected vary between ones that aim to pursue precise goals and projects that investigate issues and possible scenarios and policy alternatives to solve these problems. Based on these simulations and analysis, new action plans can be elaborated to achieve formulated goals.

The comparative analysis template proves to be well suited to analyse and compare projects and cases implementing policies. It provides a quick and compact overview and the essential facts can be compared to each other in an easy way. However, it turned out that in some cases, relevant information cannot be retrieved for some element of comparison, hence the fields were left with no information.

In terms of research and practice implications, the analysis shows that nowadays there are various alternatives for environment-friendly energy production like solar, water or hydro. Unfortunately, the awareness of the benefit that these technologies offer seems to be too small so that many governments, authorities and policymakers are not convinced to foster the use of them. A reason for that is may be that these technologies are very expensive so far and the way to lower the costs and thereby make these technologies more attractive for use needs yet to be figured out. Accordingly, there is still quite a field of research and more examples of the KNOWBRIDGE cluster should be fostered.

A big step in bringing about a progress in the counteraction of climate change is to involve the consumers, i.e. the citizens, governments and the industry sector more strongly in order to create awareness about the situation of energy production and consumption as well as the contribution of certain energy technologies to climate change.

Table 16.6 Analysis of metadata and conceptual aspects of the MODEL project

Metadata	
Name	MODEL: management of domains related to energy in local authorities
Duration	2007–2010
Domain	Energy sector
Project type	Policy implementation
Reference(s)	http://www.energymodel.eu/spip.php?page=index_en (last access: 29 July 2014) http://www.energymodel.eu/IMG/pdf/List_of_MODEL_pilot_cities_2009.12.02.pdf (last access: 29 July 2014)
Conceptual aspects	
Implementing which policy	Energy sustainability policy
Users/Stakeholders	43 pilot cities from 10 new EU Member States and Croatia Association Municipal Energy Efficiency Network EcoEnergy, Bulgaria Center for Energy Efficiency (EnEffect), Bulgaria Energetski Institut HrvojePozar (EIHP), Croatia PORSENNA o.p.s., Czech Republic SocialasEkonomikasFonds, Latvia Kaunas Regional Energy Agency, Lithuania, Norway Association of Municipalities Polish Network "EnergieCités" (PNEC), Poland AsociatiaOra_eEnergieRomânia, Romania RazvojnaAgencijaSinergijad.o.o., Slovenia
Complexity	Complexity is rather high due the complexity of energy resource management
Theory(s) used	Not successful in retrieving relevant information
Method(s) used	Process management in supporting planning, implementing and evaluating activities to improve local energy efficiency Common framework methodology (CFM) for the development, implementation and evaluation of municipal energy programmes Municipal energy programmes and annual action plans Guidelines for the preparatory phase, the development phase and the implementation/ monitoring and evaluation phase
Supportive technology frameworks and tools used	Not successful in retrieving relevant information
Project outcome	Common framework methodology (CFM) implemented by participating cities in order to adopt energy programmes

Table 16.6 (continued)

Conceptual aspects	
	Raised awareness and engagement in sustainable energy management amongst all pilot cities
Links to other projects	http://ec.europa.eu/energy/intelligent/ (last access: 29 July 2014) http://www.energy-cities.eu/spip.php?page=index_en (last access: 29 July 2014)
Transferability of solutions and techniques	The common framework methodology (CFM) is adoptable and adjustable for interested cities. It provides a guideline to implement sustainable energy management
Concluding recommend	It is important to convince responsible representatives of the benefits sustainable energy management can provide, since it may be difficult to realise and it may be time-consuming

CFM common framework methodology

16.6   Conclusions

Climate change and the transition to renewable energy sources has become a serious policy issue that affects all forms of life on earth. While the awareness of this situation is continuously growing, big measures are needed to counteract pollution, global warming and the resulting climate change. Policymakers and researchers, together with the industry sector and the citizens, need to develop strategies, programmes and policies that support a greener energy production and consumption.

As indicated in the EU policy package on climate change and renewables as well as in the German energy transition policy, the plan is to switch from fossil fuels and nuclear power to greener energy production, which can be realised by using renewable energy sources such as wind and water for example. There are projects thatare role models like the German nuclear phase-out or, the MODEL project or the KNOWBRIDGE project, showing that switching to renewable energy sources is possible and sustainable. Unfortunately, this development goes on rather slowly and is not accepted in many parts of the world. Therefore, there is still a great necessity to carry out the dialogue about climate change and possibilities to counteract it across the whole world. Moreover, the financial issue concerning greener energy production and consumption needs to be handled. So far, the use of renewable energy sources is very expensive and funded by taxpayers and consumers, which might also be a reason for the slow progress.

References

Azuela GE, Barroso LA (2011) Design and performance of policy instruments to promote the development of renewable energy: emerging experience in selected developing countries. Energy and mining sector board discussion paper, Washington, DC

Berman P (1978) The study of macro and micro implementation of social policy. Retrieved from RAND Corporation paper series: http://www.rand.org/pubs/papers/P6071.html. Accessed 30 July 2014

Buse K, Mays N, Walt G (2012) Making health policy. McGraw-Hill International, Berkshire

Capros P, Mantzos L, Parousos L, Tasios N, Klaassen G, Van Ierland T (2011) Analysis of the EU policy package on climate change and renewables. Energy Policy 39:1476–1485

EU (2007) Limiting global climate change to 2 degrees Celsius—the way ahead for 2020 and beyond. COM (2007) 2 final, Brussels

EU (2008) 20 20 by 2020: Europe's climate change opportunity. COM (2008) 30, Brussels

Gunn L (1978) Why is implementation so difficult? Manag Serv Gov 33:169–176

Helm D (2000) Environmental policy: objectives, Instruments, and Implementation. Oxford University Press, Oxford

Hogwood BW, Gunn LA (1984) Policy analysis for the real world. Oxford University Press, Oxford

Howlett M (2009) Governance modes, policy regimes and operational plans: a multi-level nested model of policy instrument choice and policy design. Policy Sci 42(1):73–89

IPCC (2012) Renewable energy sources and climate change mitigation. Cambridge University Press, New York

James P, Ghobadian A, Viney H, Liu J (1999) Addressing the divergence between environmental strategy formulation and implementation. Manag Decis 37(4):338–348

Kamateri E, Panopoulou E, Tambouris E, Tarabanis K, Ojo A, Lee D, Price D (2014) Chapter 7: a comparative analysis of tools and technologies for policy making. In Janssen M, Wimmer MA, Deljoo A (eds) Policy practice and digital science—integrating complex systems, social simulation and public administration in policy research. Springer Science, London

Lindblom C (1968) The policy making process. Prentice Hall, Englewood Cliffs

Lipsky M (1980) Street-level bureaucracy: the dilemmas of the individual in public service. Russell Sage Foundation, New York

Majstorovic D, Wimmer MA, Lay-Yee R, Davis P, Ahrweiler P (2014) Features and added value of simulation models using different modelling approaches supporting policy-making: a comparative analysis. In Janssen M, Wimmer MA, Deljoo A (eds) Policy practice and digital science—integrating complex systems, social simulation and public administration in policy research. Springer Sciences, London

Moore J (2013) How much precaution is too much? http://www.lse.ac.uk/IPA/images/Documents/PublicSphere/2013/4-germany-nuclear-phaseout-2012.pdf. Accessed 30 July 2014

Morris C, Pehnt M (2012) Energy transition. The German energiewende—7: key findings. Heinrich Böll Stiftung. http://energytransition.de/wp-content/themes/boell/pdf/en/German-Energy-Transition_en_Key-Findings.pdf. Accessed 30 July 2014

Nakamura R (1987) The textbook policy process and implementation research. Rev Policy Res 7(1):142–154

NZPCS (2010) New Zealand costal policy statement 2010. National implementation plan. http://www.doc.govt.nz/Documents/conservation/marine-and-coastal/coastal-management/nz-coastal-policy-final-implementation-plan.pdf. Accessed 29 July 2014

Oikonomou V, Jepma CJ (2007) A framework on interactions of climate and energy policy instruments. Springer Science + Business Media B.V., Berlin

Portney P, Stavins R (2000) Public policies for environmental protection. RFF Press, Washington, DC

Pressman JL, Wildavsky A (1984) Implementation. University of California Press, Oakland

Scherer S, Wimmer MA, Markisic S (2013) Bridging narrative scenario texts and formal policy modeling through conceptual policy modeling. Artif Intel Law 21(4):455–484

Stavins RN (1997) Policy instruments for climate change: how can national governments address a global problem? The University of Chicago Legal Forum, pp. 293–329

Turnpenny J, Haxeltine A, Lorenzoni I, O'Riordan T, Jones M (2005) Mapping actors involved in climate change policy networks in the UK. Retrieved from Tyndall Centre for Climate

Change Research, Working Paper No. 8. http://www.tyndall.ac.uk/sites/default/files/wp66.pdf. Accessed 30 July 2014

Vedug E (1997) Public policy and programme evaluation. Transaction, New Jersey

Wimmer MA, Scherer S, Moss S, Bicking M (2012) Method and tools to support stakeholder engagement in policy development. The OCOPOMO Project. Int J Electron Gov Res 8(3): 98–119

Young J, Mendizabal E (2009). Helping researchers become policy entrepreneurs. Retrieved from Overseas Development Institute, London. http://www.odi.org/sites/odi.org.uk/files/odi-assets/publications-opinion-files/1730.pdf. Accessed 29 July 2014

Chapter 17
Challenges to Policy-Making in Developing Countries and the Roles of Emerging Tools, Methods and Instruments: Experiences from Saint Petersburg

Dmitrii Trutnev, Lyudmila Vidyasova and Andrei Chugunov

Abstract Informational and analytical activities, as well as forecasting for the processes of socioeconomic development, should be an important element of all levels of governmental administration.

This chapter describes the development of information-analytical systems and situational centres in Russia in chronological order. The most ambitious Russian project concerning the implementation of effective analytics in the public sector—the system "Administration"—is described in detail, including its advantages and disadvantages. The management of territorial development necessitates the development of regional information-analytical systems. The authors gave as an example an algorithm used in information analysis, used in the Saint Petersburg administration.

17.1 Introduction

Informational and analytical activities, as well as forecasting for the processes of socioeconomic development, should be an important element at all levels of governmental administration. The development of methods and tools to support government decision-making on the basis of the analysis of information has a long history and their use has traditionally been included as a component of national development programmes, including the programme for the development of the information society in Russia, its regions and, in particular, Saint Petersburg.

This chapter presents a brief overview of the history, and the current state of the implementation of information processing techniques and practices for the purpose of public administration in the Russian Federation. The purpose of this chapter is to describe the chronology of information-analytical systems use in Russia and to identify the key challenges and the developments that will be faced by the government.

D. Trutnev (✉) · L. Vidyasova · A. Chugunov
ITMO University, St. Petersburg, Russia
e-mail: trutnev@egov-center.ru

© Springer International Publishing Switzerland 2015   379
M. Janssen et al. (eds.), *Policy Practice and Digital Science,*
Public Administration and Information Technology 10, DOI 10.1007/978-3-319-12784-2_17

The chapter consists of five sections. Section 17.1 describes the development of analytical centres in the Russian Federation over time. Section 17.2 includes data about the implementation of situational administration theory in Russia. Section 17.3 consists of the information about the functions of the information system, "Administration". Section 17.4 explains the regional aspects of the implementation of information-analytical systems. The section "Conclusions" outlines the challenges and the developments that are faced by the government.

17.2   Analytical Centres in the Russian Federation

It is believed that the first theoretical approaches and practical developments related to the implementation of socioeconomic processes information-analytical system were implemented in the early 1970s by Beer Stafford—the father of management cybernetics. Viable system model (VSM) was described in the book, *Brain of the Firm* (Stafford 1994). A special section in the book is devoted to the project "Cybersyn", implemented in Chile during the Allende government. B. Stafford was invited as a research director and chief designer of the operations room.

The control programme for established system (Cyberstrider) was written by Chilean experts in collaboration with the British scientists. With the telex system, 500 enterprises were connected into the network Cybernet. All the information in real-time situational came in the centre located at the Presidential Palace "La Moneda" (Santiago). The system has been implemented on the mainframe IBM360, and associated peripheral equipment. The system was provided for four levels of administration: the enterprise, industry, economy and global, and it had a functioning feedback. In the logic of the system, the algorithm that determines the sequence of solutions emerging organizational problems was laid. If the problem was not resolved at the lowest level for a certain period of time, then it was automatically escalated to a higher level of decision making (to global—the level of the President).

It can be assumed that the project "Cybersyn" was the first experience of the legitimate use of "e-participation" methods across the state. This information system was an important element of the Allende's political reforms. It allowed citizens to participate in shaping public policies, see the feedback and have a sense of their involvement in the processes of formation of political and economic reforms. The sub-system "Cyberfolk" provided citizens the opportunity to have real-time communication with groups of decision makers, thereby ensuring the participation in this process. This experiment, which can be termed as the implementation of direct democracy experiment, was conducted in urban Tome and Mejillones. Municipalities of both cities were connected with people and houses, indoor TV allowed to view information-sharing session of the Municipal Council and to participate in them. Residents were allowed to vote during the meeting by placing them in analogue devices.

The "Cybersyn" has proved itself as a very effective. For example, in 1972 only through the actions of the Situation Centre was organized food supply to Santiago during a large-scale strike of truck drivers. After the coup in 1973 and the overthrow of Allende system's control centre, "Cybersyn" was eliminated.

At the same time in the Soviet Union, a similar plan for basic task—going development of national accounting systems and automated data processing (OGAS—the nationwide automated system—more detail below) was implemented. It was a system focused on automated management of the economy of the USSR. The system was based on the principles of cybernetics and included computer network linking the data collection centres located in all regions of the country. The magnitude of these two systems (even in the number of business entities), of course, is difficult to compare, but OGAS did not aim to provide an interactive cooperation between authorities and the population.

In 1965, in the USSR, the transition from territorial economic management system in the industry took place. The need for a combination of sectoral and territorial principles set challenges to the authorities responsible for planning and ensuring the supply of industrial enterprises and organizations of various products. Complex tasks associated with the functions of operational planning and management of the current material flows between the entities of industrial activity through the territorial system were successfully carried out by OGAS. The establishment of production and economic ties between enterprises was one of the main tasks for OGAS. It allowed to form an optimal structure for marco technology production process throughout the USSR and exercised operational control over its implementation.

Tasks associated with the forecasting and management of the socioeconomic development of the country (region, city, industry, enterprise, etc.) with the use of information technologies were already established in the Soviet Union in the 1970–1980s. The concept of the National Automated System (NAS) was designed under the guidance of the well-known Soviet researcher and expert on the implementation of sophisticated computer systems, Glushkov (1987a). NAS was implemented as a distributed hierarchically organized (vertically and horizontally integrated) system of data centres that provide access to databases through various communication channels (Kiriyenko 2012). The components of this system included major institutional entities, such as the State Automated System of Scientific and Technical Information (SASSTI), uniting branches of institutes of scientific and technical information, and regional centres of scientific and technical information (CSTI). A telecommunications infrastructure, uniting institutions of the USSR Academy of Sciences ("Academset") and other programmes dealing with administration tasks, was created and developed in the 1980s. In particular, at that time, automated systems of information processing for policy makers (ASIPPM) established within the Union, as well as the Republican automated administration systems (RAAS), were actively developed. All these works were conducted within the NAS concept and were technically implemented in systems based on the mainframes of the EC and EM series (Russian names of IBM360 and PDP11 analogues). The system worked successfully and its results were widely used to control the USSR's planned economy, but its operations came to a halt in the early 1990s during the break-up of the Soviet Union's administrative system and the transition to a market economy. In the same period, due to the collapse of the USSR, many international creative teams involved in the creation and development of the methodological and mathematical support for these systems also collapsed. However, the theories and practices of the development and operation of large analytical information systems that had been developed formed the basis for many regional and municipal informatization projects implemented in the 1990s and 2000s (Mikheyev 2001).

It should also be noted that in the 1970s and 1980s, the Soviet Union built a multilevel hierarchic system for the collection and processing of data on various aspects of the socioeconomic development of the country. For example, the total amount of economic data was 120–170 billion units a year (and only 7 % of these were national statistics data). In the USSR State Planning Committee, the total amount of indicators reached 2 million in the 1970s (Maiminas 1971). These data and indicators were used in economic administration systems and the organization of planning not only at the union, sectoral and regional levels but also in the design of international programmes by the Council for Mutual Economic Assistance (COMECON—a coordinating inter-governmental body of the socialist bloc). Of course, the main objective of the indicator systems was to provide information support for directive planning in the Soviet Union, however, in the 1970 and 1980s scientific research was also carried out by focussing on the creation of a system of integral and functional lifestyle social indicators, with a view to forecasting social processes (Afanasiev 1975).

The history of the establishment of most of the think tanks in the public administration started in the mid-1990s. The first structures which served as the basis for the formation of the institutional and personnel capacity of the centres, as a part of the system of providing analytical support to the Russian President, were created in 1990 (Timofeyeva 2004). From the second half of the 1980s to the first part of 1990s, the necessity of basing administration on planning, and not of a historical and directive nature, but instead involving forecasting was quite acute. In the spring of 1990, study groups were formed to provide advice to the government on economic issues by people close to Boris Yeltsin (at that time he was the chairman of the State Committee for Cconstruction and Architecture of the USSR). Sometime later (in the summer of 1990), Boris Yeltsin (who by that time had become the chairman of the Supreme Soviet of the Russian Soviet Federative Socialist Republic (RSFSR)) formed a political advisory council (which later came to be known as the Supreme Coordination and Consultation Council), which analysed political information, developed plans to counter the Union Centre and forged ties with the regions.

These analytical groups became a part of the Russian President's administration in August 1991. The Information and Analytical Centre, operated as a part of the Russian President's administration from March 1992 to February 1993, was transformed into various structures from February 1993 to April 1994: the Analytical Centre on General Policy and the Analytical Centre on Social and Economic Policy (Handbook of Analytical Centers 1994). This was followed by several more transformations from 2000 to 2004, whereby these structures were finally transformed into the expert department and the department for press services and information, which provide up-to-date informational and analytical functions to the President's administration.

Among the expert and analytical groups, the Analytical Centre of the Government of the Russian Federation has the longest history. It was established in December 2005 and became the successor of the previous governmental centres of expertise: the Working Centre of Economic Reforms and the Centre on Prevailing Economic Situation and Forecasting which, in its turn, was formed on the basis of the Main Computing Centre of the USSR State Planning Committee (operated from 1959 to 1991).

The system providing analytical support to the government authorities also includes informational and analytical structures of the legislative bodies: the Federation Council and the State Duma of the Federal Assembly of the Russian Federation.

The activities, which may be attributed to this type of task, are also carried out at the municipal level. Municipal information and analysis centres focus on the tasks of managing the development of territories and, in some cases, also carry out projects related to the forecasting of some areas of such developments.

In addition to the analytical centres of the government's supreme bodies, independent analytical structures which can be roughly divided into two groups, analytical centres specializing in forecasting of electoral outcomes and other types of forecasting, are also engaged in political forecasting.

Currently, in the sphere of state and municipal administration, the tasks associated with the provision of informational and analytical support to the decision-making process are often associated with the creation and use of situational centres, which have become quite popular in recent years.

17.3 Situational Centres and the Development of the Theory of Situational Administration

Obvious successes in the fields of the computer processing of texts of natural language, high-quality functions for searching documents, tracking dynamic management objects, solving problems of pattern recognition, simulation modelling, statistical data processing and solving transport tasks were evident in Russia in the late 1980s. Developers increasingly focused on studying the adaptive properties of information systems using simulations of human mental activity during discourse and decision making. (Raykov 2009) notes that in the early 1990s, in Russia, "seeds of the theory of situational administration fell on fertile corporate soil and gave abundant shoots in the form of systems of strategic management, information technologies for resource planning, re-engineering, situational centers". In the mid-1990s, the business actively introduced intellectual information technologies of analytical processing of large volumes of information and decision support technologies which came from abroad (Novikova and Demidov 2012).

The first prototype for a situational centre in the Soviet Union was the operational headquarters established to mitigate the Chernobyl disaster in 1986. The situational centre of the Ministry of Emergency Situations was created on the basis of solutions and techniques of information collection and processing developed in this centre. One more situational centre, the Security Council for the Russian President, was created in 1994, and the Russian President's Situational Centre was opened in February 1996. The system of situational centres was created in all representative offices of the president in the federal districts and information sharing between the federal and regional levels of governance was organized in the 2000s. Some regions created situational centres; however, not all of them have a well-developed system of informational and analytical support for decision-making processes and are often used for video conferencing with both federal agencies and, in some regions, with local self-administration authorities.

In 2009, the Russian President approved, with Decree No. 536 of 12.05.2009, "The Basics of Strategic Planning in the Russian Federation" providing for the establishment in the Russian state authorities of a distributed system of situational centres interacting under a single set of regulations.

An important area in the development of the functionality of the situational centres is the geographic information systems (GIS) that provide the possibility for visualizing various information, its analysis (understanding and highlighting the main factors, causes and possible consequences) and forecasts drawn up on the basis of the completed analyses, and subsequent developments with strategic decision planning (Novikova and Demidov 2012).

One of the major problems which services, which provide informational and analytical support to the decision-making process, face is the effect of "big data": They are often so big that they are difficult to handle. Experts estimate that up to 90 % of the data stored in modern information systems are not used. It is no coincidence that there is a demand for data scientists who establish relationships and transform data into useful information; the ability of modern systems to process both structured data (mainly from relational database management systems) and semi-structured data (text, audio and video) is quite important. Decision makers at any time should be able to request information about the current state of affairs: interactively or in the form of a report. Consequently, the situational centre is transformed into an analytical one, which operates on a permanent basis. In addition, it is not so important where information systems are stored, in the data centre or in the cloud. Thus, the effectiveness of decisions made largely depends on the availability of analytical services in the situational centre. However, its creation, the training of its personnel, methodological support to activities and the acquisition of informational and analytical systems would cost much more than a well-equipped conference room (Situational Centers at the Service of the State 2012).

17.4 State Automated System "Administration"

The state automated system "Administration" (Site SAS "Administration" 2003) is positioned as one of the most ambitious projects to implement analytical systems in the Russian public sector.

SAS "Administration" is a unified distributed state information system for collecting, recording, processing and analysing data contained in state and municipal information resources, the official state statistics data and any other information needed to support administrative decisions in the sphere of public administration.

The SAS "Administration" structure includes classic business intelligence tools and data discovery modules (online analytical processing (OLAP), scheduled reporting), and an advanced analytics unit: modelling, forecasting, time series analysis and score cards. Units at the technological level include a data store designer, units to retrieve data from external sources (extract, transform, load, ETL), records of normative and reference information, an application development environment (software development kit, SDK), units dealing with business graphics, metadata management modules, administration and information security, an application server and web services.

In 2009 and 2010, the Federal Target Programme "Electronic Russia" allocated 550 million rubles for the development of SAS "Administration"; in 2011, 75 million rubles were spent on updating the system, and in 2012 about 70 million rubles more. Despite quite substantial investments, the project is far from complete, and the basic problems lie rather at the institutional level: who will fill the system with data and how reliable will they be? Sceptics have also questioned whether this decision will be claimed by functional customers, which are the first persons of the government. CNews Analytics (Analytics in Government Structures 2013) says that this is a common problem for all analytical systems in the public sector: they are created according to the interests of the senior management and should be a tool for decision making. However, to do this, the user (i.e. the decision makers) should have appropriate professional skills and the profession of an analyst is objectively different from the profession of a manager. However, all analysis reports have one substantial drawback: They provide information about the past that has already happened, while managers have to make decisions about the future.

The aims and objectives of SAS "Administration" are defined in the Decree of the government of the Russian Federation dated December 25, 2009, No. 1088 (SAS Administration 2003). Its objectives include:

1. The provision of informational and analytical support to the decision-making processes of the supreme bodies of state power on issues related to public administration, as well as the planning of the activities of these bodies.
2. The monitoring, analysis and control of the execution of decisions made by these bodies, the implementation of the main activities of the government of the Russian Federation, the implementation of priority national projects, the implementation of measures to rehabilitate the Russian economy, processes occurring in the real sector of the economy, finance and banking and social spheres, the social and economic development of the regions of the Russian Federation and the effectiveness of the regional state authorities.

SAS "Administration" is a set of information systems and information resources implemented as a three-level structure:

1. *The first level (central information system)*: a set of information systems which collect, process, store and disseminate information which comes from the second and third levels of SAS "Administration".
2. *The second level (departmental)*: information systems of the federal bodies of the executive power which are a part of SAS "Administration", and whose information resources are designed to be used in making management decisions in the sphere of public administration, and the information resources of other information systems, which need to be integrated into SAS "Administration" in accordance with the functional requirements given to it.
3. *The third level (regional)*: information resources of information system of bodies of state power of the regions of the Russian Federation, which need to be integrated into SAS "Administration" in accordance with the functional requirements that it has been set.

SAS "Administration" provides the following functions:

1. Collection of data for administrative decision making in the public administration from departmental and regional information systems and other information systems, which need to be integrated into SAS "Administration" in accordance with the functional requirements that it has been set.
2. Systematization and analysis:
    (a) Information about the level of the socioeconomic development of the Russian Federation and its regions, including comparisons with world statistics.
    (b) Information about the efficiency of the activities of the federal bodies of state power and the bodies of state power of the regions of the Russian Federation.
    (c) Information about the implementation of programmes, projects and activities implemented at the expense of the federal budget.
    (d) Information about budgetary forecasts and the use of the federal budget, including information about the use of cash of the federal budget and fiscal reports on the main spending units of the federal budget.
    (e) State official statistical information collected in accordance with the federal plan of statistical work.
    (f) Cartographic information and related data, about regions and resources in the Russian Federation.
    (g) Reference data in departmental information systems.
    (h) Other information which users of SAS "Administration" need.

It is no exaggeration to call SAS "Administration" the most controversial information technology (IT) system ever created in Russia. It is based on a simple and nice idea, to monitor from Moscow indicators of the activities of officials all over the country, and has faced quite a number of problems. The system is now in its 8th year, yet still there have been no visible results.

Speaking about SAS "Administration", in November 2010 at the CNews Forum, Konstantin Noskov, Director of the government IT department, stated that "so far, the work has been at the level of departmental systems or such topical systems as the Olympics project, priority national projects, and we have failed to reach the level of inter-departmental integration". Rostelecom launched gas-u.ru portal in the spring of 2011. However, there was not much information on the portal: Only five federal agencies provided data from their information systems to SAS "Administration". An expanded meeting of the Government Commission in April 2012 represented a milestone event, which brought together more than 100 officials. The event was chaired by Aleksey Polyakov, head of the government IT department. In the minutes of the meeting, there were a number of interesting points:

1. The federal authorities were advised to immediately appoint persons responsible for SAS "Administration" at the level of deputy heads and submit to the Ministry of Economic Development technological maps of inter-departmental interactions (TMIDI, describing the data which departments should provide to the system).
2. Some departments, among which were the developers of SAS "Administration", the Ministry of Communications, the Federal Treasury and the Federal Guard Service, said they had no need for the information from the system.
3. The commission pointed out that it was impossible to receive information from other authorities bypassing SAS "Administration".

However, all activity waned in May. A new government appeared in Russia and the system was forgotten for almost half a year.

A new concept of SAS "Administration" 2012 summarized the results of the previous period. In particular, it was noted that not all of the declared plans had been implemented. The objectives of SAS "Administration" were achieved, in that a limited list of the functional tasks of the supreme bodies of power was ensured. Prototypes of the information systems to support the activities of the prime minister and the head of the government office required a deeper individual development. A universal tool for the collection and analysis of data in the area of public administration to support decision making, and to support the monitoring and control of the making of decisions, etc. was not designed.

According to the authors of the document, the creation of a fully functional system was hampered by a lack of universally approved data formats, standards and protocols, unified normative and technical requirements for public information systems, regulations on inter-departmental documents and information sharing, established deadlines, mechanisms and the responsibility for the provision of data of the executive bodies to the "Administration" system.

Thus, at the end of 2012, information and analytical support of the activities of state bodies still had "a number of systemic weaknesses and pending issues: the information flow between federal and regional authorities was repeatedly duplicated, data updates and degree of detail were low, which, in its turn, made it difficult to apply modern methods of data processing and analysis, project management". The variety of technologies for collecting, processing and storing data by various government agencies significantly increased barriers to inter-departmental information exchanges, and the exchange between the authorities themselves existed only on paper.

The authors divided the concept of the further development of the system into three phases. In 2012, a system for data collection for providers that do not have the technical ability to provide them (primarily, in regions with low levels of information its necessary to provide data form via Internet browser) was to be created, the procedures for maintenance of a unified registry database were to be regulated, and an exchange mechanism via SAS "Administration" using inter-departmental electronic interaction systems (SIDEIS), etc. was to be established.

In 2013, an expansion of the composition of information resources that interact with the system and the composition of its users was planned, and the automation of data uploading from SAS "Administration" into Contour sub-system was planned, designed for use by senior persons in the state apparatus. It was created by the federal guard system (FGS).

Finally, in 2014, the connection of non-governmental sources of information to SAS "Administration" was planned to ensure the possibility of embedding third-party developer software into the system portal. Upon completion of these phases, the authors promised to create a register of state databases, increase the share of state systems integrated into SAS "Administration" to at least 70 % and to decrease by the same number the duplication of information flows. The authors of the concept do not promise to connect all the regions to the system, only "to provide for the possibility of access".

Experts, with whom Journal CNews discussed the prospects of SAS "Administration", are largely sceptical. "The functional customer of this resource is unknown", says an IT head of one of the federal agencies. "It was planned to take some data from agencies and put them up onto some panels for the first persons. But, do they need it? The first persons do not have the time to use these panels. In addition, it is not possible to determine the accuracy of the data as there is no mechanism of verification. Regions may submit any figures that are of benefit to them, and everyone will be sure, that's true". "Before you upload data to SAS "Administration" it is necessary to establish order in source information systems", adds another source of CNews. "Regions and federal agencies with high-quality databases can be counted on one hand". (Why SAS "Administration" did not take off 2013).

17.5   Other Policy-Making Tools and Techniques

All of the above apply to the forms of tools designed to support the administrative decisions of federal authorities, the creation of which was financed from the national budget. Solutions, centrally generated up to the 1990s, were designated to carry out the reporting and planning tasks of practically all levels of state, municipal and district administration. After the collapse of the Soviet Union, in the process of the transition to a market economy, and the provision to municipalities of all levels of some economic freedom and administration powers, the need to implement and use tools and techniques to enhance the effectiveness of administration solutions arose but there was a failure to develop and actively create and use these. In the 2000s, Russia began the systematic construction of the "vertical power structure", resulting in the practical loss of freedom of choice in political and economic decision making

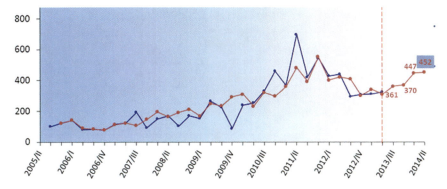

Fig. 17.1 Number of crimes

on the part of the regional and local authorities. For this reason, one may count, among 83 constituent entities of the Federation and more than 23,000 municipalities of all levels, only a few dozen examples of analytical IT tools used for policy-making.

One of the examples is the use of simulation tools in drug trafficking to generate programmes to counter crime in this area.

In relation to the task of evaluating processes such as drug addiction or drug trafficking, it is important to understand that the absolute values of the indicators of departmental statistics rarely reflect the process itself. Thus, the number of recorded crimes characterizes rather the registration and response system than the actual crime rate. Therefore, an important task is to model and estimate the value of the so-called latency of crimes, i.e. the number of hidden and unregistered crimes. This allows us to come closer to a real assessment of the situation in a region and to identify the factors which affect changes in crime rates.

For the purpose of assessing the actual number of drug users, a mathematical model was created, taking into account the interdependence of such indicators as information concerning seizures of illicit trafficking, registered cases of drug addiction, opinion polls data and the intensity of the debate on drug-related topics in social networks. As a result, estimates were obtained which show that the actual number of persons taking drugs at least once in their lifetime exceeds the registered number by 50 times. This discrepancy describes the process as highly latent, which is an obstacle to obtaining a high accuracy of modelling and forecasting when using the above-mentioned sources of information, therefore, measures were proposed to reduce latency, for example, compulsory testing for drug traces in pupils, students, drivers and public employees. However, these measures have not been taken, possibly because of fears that the reported cases of drug consumption are indirectly punishable under the criminal code and the very fact of such a discovery may lead to negative consequences for the system of identification and apprehension.

Even with the low accuracy of the model, the forecast of the development of the level of crime based on retrospective data provides the possibility of identifying trends and offers explanations of changes in dynamics (Fig. 17.1). For example,

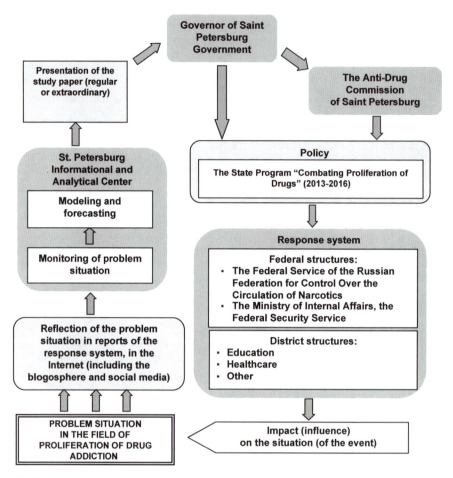

Fig. 17.2 Organizational tools for decision making and the response system according to results of informational and analytical activities on topics related to combating spread of drug addiction in Saint Petersburg

increases in recorded crime until 2011 were caused by increased migration from Central Asia and the reduction is a consequence of a series of municipal anti-drug programmes implemented in Saint Petersburg. The forecast predicting a growth in crime in 2013–2014 was due to a delay in the implementation of further anti-drug programmes.

The place of modelling and forecasting in the overall system of organizational tools to combat the spread of drug addiction in Saint Petersburg is shown in Fig. 17.2.

This example is one of the few successful examples of the practical application of the tools for modelling social or economic processes used for the purpose of policy formation and operational decision making.

17.6 Conclusions

Analysis of the literature and projects' performance in the field of information-analytical systems application in Russian for the improvement of socioeconomic processes leads to the following conclusions:

1. Systems of situational centres and federal vertically oriented systems ("Administration") are actively developing in the last 5 years, but they are not integrated into decision-making procedures. These systems are used in crisis situations and for "brainstorming" in the elaboration and adoption of government programmes (or report generation), but their abilities are still clearly underestimate by decision makers.
2. The existing resources and capabilities of situational centres are not fully leveraging. According to expert opinion, 90% of the existing situation centers are used only as a space for video conferencing. Only occasionally it used as a multidimensional view of data and multivariate analysis, as well as methods of situational modelling and forecasting.
3. There are serious problems with the financing for research (related to the development of situational forecasting and modeling), rarely to solving external experts. Meanwhile, in the USA, a separate budget line is allocated to finance the development of situational centres. Special federal contract system for the management of intellectual property used in the management decisions also operates separately.

As a recommendation, which can alleviate these problems and gradually increase the effectiveness of the functioning of information and analytical systems in government in the Russian Federation, the experts include the following:

1. To link the problem of information-analytical systems in government with the priorities of the state policy to improve the functioning of the state and municipal government.
2. More active involvement in the development associated with situational modeling and prediction, network expert community building.
3. The inclusion of information systems of this class in the list of public information resources, denoting requirements as to the actual system, and to a set of information sources and operational updates related to this activity with the development of open government data (Open Gov Data).
4. Maintaining up-to-date bank of simulation results and ensuring the coordination of research in the field of simulation, in order to improve linkages between the models for the authorities, industries and regions (the Russian Federation, the industry, the Federal District, the subject of the Federation, the municipality).

References

Analytics in Government Structures: Approaches and Solutions (2013) IT in government bodies 2013: review. CNews analytics. http://www.cnews.ru/reviews/free/gov2013/articles/analitika_v_gosstrukturah_podhody_i_resheniya/

Afanasiev VG (1975) Social information and administration of society. Political literature. Moscow, 408 p

Glushkov VM (1987a) Some problems of use of computing machines for administration of social processes. Retrieved from: http://ogas.kiev.ua/glushkov/nekotorye-problemy-yspolzovanyya-vychyslytelnyh-mashyn-dlya-upravlenyya-sotsyalnymy-protses

Glushkov VM (1987b) Basics of paperless informatics. Nauka, Moscow, p. 552

Handbook of Analytical Centers (1994) Limits of power: annex to journal "XX century and the world", 1. Retrieved from: http://old.russ.ru/antolog/predely/1/econen.htm

Kiriyenko VE (2012) IT systems of local government godies: from NAS to information society. Tomsk. Retrieved from: http://www.asdg.ru/upload/isomsu.pdf

Maiminas EZ (1971) Planning processes in economy: information aspect. Economy. Moscow, 392 p

Mikheyev YuA (2001) Public administration system in information society and information and communication technologies. VNIIPVTI, Moscow

Novikova E, Demidov N (2012) Means of intellectual analysis and modeling of sophisticated processes as a key tool for situational management. Connect 3:46–51 (Retrieved from: http://www.ситцентр.рф/pressa/novikova.pdf)

Raykov A (2009) Thorny path of intellectual information technologies. Retrieved from: http://www.strf.ru/material.aspx?CatalogId†=392&d_no=19326#.UsJW7LS6lOA

Raykov AN (2009) Converged management and decision support. ICAR Publishing House, Moscow, p. 245

Site SAS "Administration" (2003) Retrieved from: http://www.gas-u.ru/docs/doc/show/2.35.htm

Situational Centers at the Service of the State (2012) IT in government bodies 2012: review. CNews Analytics. http://www.cnews.ru/reviews/free/gov2012/articles/articles6.shtml

Stafford B (1994) Brain of the firm, 2nd ed. Wiley. ISBN 978-0471948391

Timofeyeva MA (2004) Institutions of political forecast in modern russia. Political analysis. Reports of the Center of Empirical Political Studies of Saint Petersburg State University. Issued 5. Ed. by G.P. Artyomov. Saint Petersburg: Publishing House of Saint Petersburg University, 81–89. http://philosophy.spbu.ru/userfiles/politanalise/Politanalise05.doc

Why SAS "Administration" did not take off (2013) CNews analytics. http://www.cnews.ru/reviews/?2013/07/08/534778

Chapter 18
Sustainable Urban Development, Governance and Policy: A Comparative Overview of EU Policies and Projects

Diego Navarra and Simona Milio

Abstract This chapter will provide a comparative overview of existing policies and projects to achieve energy efficiency in the European Union (EU) region delivering a concise overview of the contribution of e-government to energy efficiency in view of climate change. A system dynamics (SD) model is also presented to show how good urban policy and governance can support extant as well as future information and communications technology (ICT) projects in order to reduce energy usage, rehabilitate the housing stock and promote sustainable urban development. An additional contribution of the chapter is to show the role and significance of the cadastre to sustainable urban development e-government projects and the key characteristics of future policy and projects towards the European 2050 Agenda.

18.1 Introduction

What are the key characteristics of successful European initiatives in sustainable urban governance? And how can e-government projects encourage sustainable urban development in view of climate change? This chapter will identify the multidisciplinary dimensions of e-government projects in energy efficiency and present representative cases and experiences from different areas of the European Union (EU) in order to identify the key characteristics of future policy (including funding policy) that should be considered in practical developments and sustainability projects linked to the European 2050 policy agenda in different areas of the highly diverse European region. We find that, for the vast majority, existing and previous projects taking place in the EU (see Appendix 1) have been primarily centred around what we might consider as monodisciplinary approaches (i.e. approaches used from

D. Navarra (✉)
Studio Navarra, 25 Cleveland Gardens, London W2 6DE, UK
e-mail: diego@studionavarra.co.uk

S. Milio
London School of Economics, Houghton Street, London WC2A 2AE, UK
e-mail: s.milio@lse.ac.uk

© Springer International Publishing Switzerland 2015   393
M. Janssen et al. (eds.), *Policy Practice and Digital Science,*
Public Administration and Information Technology 10, DOI 10.1007/978-3-319-12784-2_18

a scientific discipline or subdisciplines without consulting any other discipline), emphasizing IT solutions as tools to reduce energy consumption, or information and communications technology (ICT) systems and energy efficiency management systems in buildings to monitor and transmit consumption data, rarely integrated or interoperable. At the same time energy and ICT systems (such as in energy trading and performance management) have become increasingly interdependent and complex.

Greenhouse gases (GHGs) emissions (which are a major determinant of climate change) typically come from energy supply, transport and industry in urban areas (Parry and IPPC 2007). Urban and industrial energy use in particular accounts for 80 % of all GHG emission in the EU and it is at the root of climate change and most air pollution. 'About 30–40 % of the total energy consumption in western countries is assigned to buildings. About 50 % of these refer to the energy consumption for indoor air conditioning (heating and cooling)' (Pulselli et al. 2009). Regarding the effects of climate change on the built environment Roberts (2008) clarifies that buildings play an important role in both adaptation and mitigation. Therefore, we argue that sustainable urban development, governance and policies informed by interdisciplinary approaches addressing future integrated energy monitoring and production needs can greatly contribute not only to improvements in energy efficiency but also facilitate mitigation and adaptation of urban areas to climate change.

18.2   Literature Review on EU Energy Security and ICT Policy

The point of departure of the EU's (European Commission 2007) energy policy is threefold: combating climate change, limiting the EU's external vulnerability to imported hydrocarbons, and promoting growth and jobs, thereby providing secure and affordable energy to consumers. The main focus of the EU's policy is to move towards a single global regime and the mainstreaming of climate into other policies, which will be assigned 20 % of the entire 2014–2020 EU budget. The focus at the urban level is to produce the greatest results in energy efficiency integrating three sectors:

1. Urban energy production and use, by supporting policies aimed at establishing standards for increasing the efficiency of existing buildings, supporting new energy efficient developments and conservation plans so as to minimize the use and production of fossil fuel-based electricity generation (OECD 1995).
2. Urban transport and mobility, by strengthening and implementing green transport policies aimed at increasing the share of cleaner transport options, such as public transportation for urban travel, zero-emissions vehicles (such as bicycles) and car sharing schemes (European Commission 1996).
3. Urban ICT, potentially affecting both of the sectors above and also the overall potential contribution to the reduction of urban CO_2 emissions in electricity production, use as well as in the construction of a dedicated city-wide ICT infrastructure for the evaluation of energy efficiency.

The EU has also developed a methodology to evaluate energy efficiency, relying on Internet-based ICT: the eeMeasure. The methodology is based on experimental projects carried out in public buildings and social dwellings. eeMeasure provides a first example of a European e-government policy aiming to increase energy efficiency using a common data collection approach and a single software system to collect and accommodate energy savings data across the pilot projects in both residential as well as nonresidential buildings. According to the eeMeasure website (eeMeasure 2014b) there are currently two ICT methodologies to measure energy efficiency: the residential methodology and the nonresidential methodology.

Both methodologies are based on the International Performance Measurement and Verification Protocol, a framework used to determine water and energy costs associated with energy conservation measures (IPMVP 2002). eeMeasure methodologies are developed from the experience of current and previous ICT projects which include approximately 10,000 social dwellings and 30 public buildings (such as hospitals and schools). The residential methodology is applicable only to dwellings and generally assumes a monthly measurement period. The main objectives of the eeMeasure methodologies are to: allow EU and related project parties to collect data in a centralized database, to produce better quantitative analyses of the energy saving potential of ICT solutions in residential and nonresidential buildings, to facilitate the evaluation of behavioural changes occurring due to ICT solutions, and to better public awareness about energy efficiency and ICT solutions (eeMeasure 2014a).

It is possible to distinguish between three main areas of data collection to measure energy efficiency in the pilot projects. Data collected to measure energy efficiency statistically (i.e. estimation, calculation, parameters, demand response and avoided CO_2 emissions) data collected to measure and quantify impact assessment (energy savings vs. socioeconomic status, energy savings vs. nationality, energy savings vs. cost of energy, physical and mental perception of comfort, perceived usability/usefulness of ICT solution) and finally qualitative data collected to understand behaviour: such as changes in energy use and habits. Reinforcing factors are those consequences of actions that give individuals positive or negative feedback for continuing their behaviour. These include information about the impacts of past behaviour (e.g. lower energy bill), feedback of peers, advice, and feedback by powerful actors. Enabling factors are the external constraints on behaviour. These factors allow new behaviour to be realized.

eeMeasure also collects data with respect to: (a) socio-demographic characteristics of tenants, (b) energy consumption behaviour, (c) ecological awareness: attitudes and knowledge, (d) user acceptance concerning consumption feedback services, (e) interest in the service and reasons for non-usage of passive users. The above are considered together with behaviour and motivation influencing factors. These factors are awareness, knowledge, social influence, attitude, perceived capabilities and intention. For people to intentionally change their energy behaviour, they must become aware of their energy use, pay notice to it, and be informed about the consequences. They must then be motivated to use the available information and instruments to control their energy use (International Energy Agency 2008; European Commission 2005; Hildyard 2011; Social Market Foundation 2003; United Nations 2004; World Bank 2013).

The eeMeasure's database includes a control building design methodology. In a control building design methodology the data is collected over the same period in time, both in the control and experimental groups, while experiencing differing influences on their behaviour such as a tightening credit crunch or a lengthening of school holidays. Control buildings are used to represent also the future exploitation of potential energy saving interventions using ICT. The calculation of energy saving is the result of the difference between the estimated nonintervention consumption in the control group and the measured energy consumption in the treatment (or experimental) group in the reporting period.

Appendix 1 outlines the pilot projects implementing the above-mentioned methodology (and related policies) in the European region. The listed projects have been selected based on the significance of the methodology which will be derived for the European region. However, we also feel that their significance could be further if a significant discussion about how their possible application to entire urban areas could produce the same impacts and expected results. Thus, extending and integrating the data generated from those initial projects also with existing and new databases within the public administration could be a way to develop an even greater set of innovative services and solutions which can increase resource use awareness and resource management in all key energy forms.

Nevertheless, the eeMeasure methodology remains confined to a handful of projects, these are still to be completed, and afterwards the question about how to expand the scope of the methodology beyond individual buildings to become applicable to entire urban areas will remain of interest. In fact, even if visible progress towards the conceptual identification of ICT enablers of energy efficiency has been made (see Fig. 18.1), thanks to intelligent monitoring systems within homes, or at the level if individual buildings, a great diversity of technologies and solutions adopted, a coherent set of results or policies applicable to the EU region is still lacking.

Essentially, the EU policy towards the funding of the eeMeasure methodology and related pilot projects developments can be linked to the first phase of EU support, centred around a first recognition of the potential role ICTs can play in improving energy performance, yet without an actual assessment of such technologies, if we exclude the outline in Table 18.1 providing some estimates from the ITU on the benefits of ICT solutions (ITU 2009).

However, up to a quarter of heat generated in houses can be lost though buildings' roof and can account for much of total energy consumption in urban areas resulting in higher fuel and energy consumption as well as higher levels of emissions that can negatively affect climate change. Accurate visualizations of thermal loss data in buildings can, therefore, provide a first important step towards heat-loss maps giving both a view of energy use at peak times as well as the possibility to identify urban areas mostly affected by heat loss. In that context, cadastral and land administration organizations (as will be illustrated) could have a fundamental role to play as part of a wider e-government policy initiative able to address simultaneously both the phenomena of urban energy efficiency and security as well as climate change, which are closely related to each other.

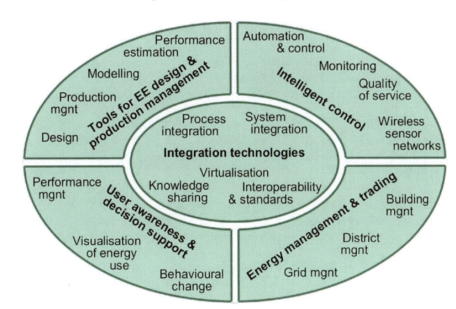

Fig. 18.1 The five different ICT enablers of energy efficiency identified by European strategic research Roadmap to ICT enabled Energy-Efficiency in Buildings and constructions (REEB) (2010)

Table 18.1 ICT solutions and benefits. (Source: ITU 2009)

ICT solutions	Benefits
Telework	Telework by 10 % of workers in the EU-25 countries will reduce CO_2 by 22 million t annually
Audio-conference	Replacement of conferences by audio-conferences once a year by workers in the EU-25 countries will reduce CO_2 by 2.128 million t annually
Videoconference	Replacement of 20 % of business trips with videoconferences in the EU-25 countries will reduce CO_2 by 22.35 million t annually
Online phone billing	Online billing to all households with Internet access in the EU-15 countries and all mobile phone subscribers in the EU-25 countries will reduce CO_2 by 1.03 million t annually
Web-based tax returns	Filing tax returns over the Internet by all (193 million) workers in the EU-25 countries will reduce CO_2 by 195,790 t annually

18.3 Case Studies

We now present four detailed case studies providing the comparative overview of existing EU policies and projects to achieve energy efficiency. These are: integrating energy efficiency and urban sustainability in Nordic Europe, the Dutch Kadaster, the Solar Atlas of Berlin and the Sicilian 'Carta del Sole'. The cases have been selected based on their realized and future potential for sustainable urban development, as well as to show the diversity and differences in the application of EU energy security and climate change policies

18.3.1 Integrating Energy Efficiency and Urban Sustainability

Northern Europe is regularly at the top of the green cities ranking according to the 2012 'Sustainable Cities Report' (Sustainable cities 2012) launched at the RIO+20 United Nations Conference in Sustainable Development. Already in 2003, Oslo received the European Sustainable City Award, while Copenhagen is famous for the strong municipal character and national policies for the creation of an excellent record on environmental issues. Stockholm was given the European Green Capital Award in 2010. Unsurprisingly, the Economist Intelligence Unit named the city as the greenest in Europe in 2011.

In the Nordic region, Finland is considered the country where urban sustainability takes a national as well as a municipal character. Helsinki is rated top on environmental politics in the European Green Cities Index and has been lauded for its active citizens, who are aware of environmental matters and support of Helsinki's environmental policy. The city displays an excellent record on air quality, waste utilization and construction. Its energy production is also extremely efficient at up to 90 % of all new developments, making lower emissions more achievable.

Other experiences in Finland include the City of Oulu, which is already a leader in energy-efficient building construction and city planning. Like in Helsinki, more than 90 % of new houses use low-energy buildings. The goal is that all new houses will be 'passive houses' by 2015, using zero energy building principles, and carbon neutral by 2020. Again in Finland, the city of Tampere launched the ECO2 project, emphasizing climate and energy issues in the city. The eco-efficiency of new urban plans is assessed comprehensively and energy system analyses in new areas are made. All new buildings in Tampere have to be at least energy class A from the beginning of 2012. Tampere hosts also Finland's first passive energy day care centre, which started its operation in the beginning of 2012 and the new information centre for energy efficiency in construction and housing.

A useful set of metrics to measure urban sustainability and energy efficiency has been developed by the city of Amsterdam and is known as the Amsterdam Sustainability Index (ASI). Please see Fig. 18.2 displaying the index indicators used the city of Amsterdam to measure urban sustainability.

According to the ASI urban sustainability is measured through: (a) energy savings achieved by locally produced sustainable energy and the efficient use of fossil fuels, which reduce also CO_2 emissions within the city; (b) mobility and air quality (Amsterdam is expected to be an accessible city on condition that our transport system is sustainable); (c) sustainable innovative economy (international companies choose Amsterdam because doing sustainable business in Amsterdam is worthwhile); (d) materials and consumers: Amsterdam is a liveable city where citizens and companies use raw materials in an effective way, live and act in a sustainable way and where the municipal organization itself demonstrates this approach. Low emissions energy systems, the harvesting of rainwater and clean water supply and sewage are just as important.

Pillars	Indicator	Indicators specified	Source
General indicators	CO_2 emissions per inhabitant	Annual CO_2 emissions in tonnes of CO_2 per inhabitant	Amsterdam Department for Research and Statistics
	NO_x emissions per inhabitant	Average concentration NO_2 + average concentration NO, data from ten measuring stations	Amsterdam Health Department
Climate and Energy	Energy use (households) per inhabitant	Annual energy use inhabitants in GJ per inhabitant	Liander, grid company
	Sustainable energy production per inhabitant (inverse)	Annual sustainable energy production in GJ per inhabitant	Amsterdam Climate and Energy Bureau
Sustainable Mobility and Air Quality	Bicycle share in modal split (inverse)	Percentage of bicycles in total movement of bicycles + mopeds + motorbikes + cars on the Singelgracht	Amsterdam Department of Transport and Infrastructure
	Share clean truck and lorries (inverse)	Percentage of trucks and lorries with Euro 4 or cleaner engine	TNO, research institute
Sustainable Innovative Economy	Attractiveness of Amsterdam for new companies	Ranking in European Cities Monitor (ECM)	Cushman & Wakefield
	Energy use per added value	Use of electricity and natural gas in MJ per euro added value	Liander, TNO and Amsterdam Department for Research and Statistics
Materials and Consumers	Amount of residual household waste per inhabitant	Residual waste from households in kg per inhabitant	Amsterdam Waste and Energy Company
	Liveability indicator (inverse)	Value between 1 and 10 given by inhabitants when asked: 'How satisfied are you with your own neighbourhood?'	Amsterdam Department for Research and Statistics

Fig. 18.2 The Amsterdam Sustainability Index. (Sustainable cities 2012)

Please note from the figure that climate and energy are considered to be part of the same pillar, likewise for indicators used to measure progress due to their high level of interdependency. It should also be noted that although the ASI provides and interesting benchmarking to measure the progress towards sustainability in an urban area, in Europe climate change related pressures will also affect rural environments and natural habitats driven also by human land use requirements, pollution and resource exploitation in urban areas. Progress towards urban sustainability (or the lack of it) could have severe impacts well beyond urban areas and not only as a consequence of decreasing water volume, higher temperatures and higher intensity rainfall. Hence, the role of national and municipal policies should not be underestimated. Anything from the promotion of ecological high-tech jobs, the redevelopment of brownfields, the diversity and ecological quality of services, access to low emissions public transport, pedestrian and bicycle systems and incentives for the construction of innovative house types can improve urban sustainability. However, policies shall also be carried forward by those organizations which can have a significant role in achieving the expected results. Albeit considering the fresh challenges which climate change presents not many countries have yet successfully experimented with overarching policy response collaborations with dedicated governance arrangements involving both the public and private sector organizations. According to climate tracker (WWF 2010) all of the EU 27 countries have failed on their developments in climate and energy policies on the way to achieving their goals towards 2050.

And while ICT can have a valuable role to play in sustainable urban development, yet no common understanding currently exists about the way in which the progress and future direction of existing policies and projects should be evaluated in terms of energy efficiency. The remaining of the chapter will emphasize the need of effective inter-institutional collaboration to establish effective data gathering and analysis systems able to cater for the integration and management of energy usage data with ICT able not only to monitor energy efficiency, but also to evaluate entire urban areas according to their energy labels, as well as to contribute to the policies which can stimulate sustainable urban development. Therefore, how can the vast amounts of data collected provide useful information to decision and policy makers and to support future sustainable policy and project initiatives in the EU? In other words, what is and what could be the contribution of e-government to energy efficiency in the EU?

18.3.2 The Dutch Kadaster

As one of the signatory parties to the Kyoto Protocol, the Netherlands' government recognizes the urgency and scale of the global climate challenge: its goal is a 30 % reduction in GHG emissions by 2020, relative to the benchmark year of 1990, preferably as part of a European effort. In view of the fact that 50 % of the land area in the Netherlands is located below sea level, it is no surprise that coping with the rising average seawater level, the higher run-off and discharge predictions for the major rivers and extreme precipitation forecasts is a priority. However, the government realizes that measures to cope with water management should be coupled to measures on land use, nature conservation, urbanization, transport and recreation. Therefore, the National Adaptation Policy is based on the concept of integrated land-use planning, which combines objectives of sustainable coastal defense measures, supplemented by robust river water systems, sustainable cities, climate-proof buildings and climate-proof agriculture. The Dutch Kadaster also supports land acquisition by the government in order to implement anti-flooding measures. The land consolidation expertise available at Kadaster is put into practice when the government aims at realizing better climate-proof agricultural business structures as well as subcatchments for river water. As a consequence of sea level rise, seawater will also penetrate further into the estuaries of the Rhine and Meuse, causing salt intrusion leading to high salt concentrations. In this area as well, Kadaster provides relevant land information to support land-based anti-salinization spatial planning.

Since January 1, 2008, legislation has entered into effect that requires an energy label to be available at the time of transactions related to the construction, sale or letting of houses and buildings. The energy label issued for a specific house provides information about the energy consumed during its standardized use. The registration of energy labels of buildings is a result of the implementation of the Energy Performance Building Directive (EPBD). In this directive, the EU has implemented the obligation to make an energy performance certificate for residential and utility buildings available for the prospective owner. This obligation was implemented with the direct aim of promoting the energy performance of buildings and is effective for all member states of the EU (Brounen et al. 2011).

In the Netherlands, this legislation has been implemented since January 2008. An energy label is now required during sale, letting or construction transactions of real estate. The energy labels are registered in the registers of the Dutch Cadastre and as such publicly available. These energy labels form a new category in the land registers. To date, the Dutch Kadaster has registered about 50,000 labels. Starting with the core data, cadastral parcels, buildings and ownership rights it is possible to attach relevant information attributes and design these into coherent and tailor-made information packages. These information packages can be used in the context of the policy issues as for climate change policies and energy policies (Vranken and Broekhof 2012). The energy labels are open for public inspection, as is all cadastral data. Kadaster supports the government in providing not only all information about land tenure, value and use of land and houses, but also about public properties and environmental limitations regarding use, noise, soil pollution and nuisance.

18.3.3   The Solar Atlas of Berlin

Another interesting European case study of the application of ICT for the efficient use of energy and to foster the development of renewable sources of energy is the Solar Atlas of Berlin. It is based on initial calculations for the German city of Berlin, which suggested that about two thirds of the entire energy consumption and small businesses could be generated on the city's roofs.

The implementation of the Solar Atlas of Berlin has three main objectives: the first objective is to display the location of existing solar installations in the city; the second objective is to visualize the potential of the solar industry in Berlin and finally the third objective is to highlight rooftops suitable for solar panel installation. In order to calculate the city's potential for solar energy production and installations down to the individual building a comprehensive and realistic 3D city model integrated to the solar atlas was developed. According to the project's description (Berlin Partner 2011): 'to create the model, the city's about 500,000 buildings in area of 890 km^2 were surveyed using aerial photography, and their roofs were measured with lasers. In addition, detailed models were created for about 80 landmarks, five of which can even be explored from the inside (Olympic Stadium, Sony Center, The Reichstag Building, DZ-Bank, and the Central Train Station)'.

For each suitable area the 3D model allows the calculation of solar energy potential by combining data on insulation, roof size, potential electricity generation, potential CO_2 savings, power in kilowatts and investment volume. This makes it possible for both owners and investors in real estate to find out whether or not the roof of a building is suitable for use as a source of energy, and whether or not such an investment would be sensible. The atlas, which was especially designed and developed for home and business owners, was first implemented in two pilot areas with a total of 19 km^2, is now online and free to access by residents.

18.3.4   The Sicilian 'Carta del Sole'

The Southern European region has to our knowledge (with the notable exception of Spain) not yet produced a lighthouse project or initiative which can be seen as to epitomize the direction set by the European roadmap to 2050. Nevertheless, it is worthwhile mentioning the Sicilian 'Carta del Sole', ten rules which were under-signed in 2012 by a number of industry and public sector representatives as well as the then candidates to the regional presidency. The ideas contained in those rules included the practical development of a variety of plants for distributed energy production also from citizens, public organizations and small and medium-sized enterprises (SMEs), centered around thermodynamic solar concentration, an idea conceived by an Italian Nobel Laureate, thanks to the aid of European structural funds.

Sicily has always been a problematic area of Europe, characterized by the diffi-culty of developing projects able to make use of assigned European resources, thus the Sicilian 'Carta del Sole' and its signatory parties pledged for an action plan aimed at broad environmental sustainability policies with the intention of supporting eco-nomic development with specific calls to be published by 2015. No action has so far followed. Regulations in support of integrated solutions in buildings are lacking, administrative procedures remain highly bureaucratized and complex and credit fa-cilities supporting the diffusion of energy efficiency based on the increased use of renewable sources of energy are longed for.

It might then come as a surprise that at the same time the most modern European plant for the production of electricity with thermodynamic concentrated solar power based on the idea of Carlo Rubbia, an Italian Nobel Laureate, was opened in the same region in 2010. Therefore, Sicily provides an interesting case of the challenges faced by Southern European regions to fully take on the developments which the availability of solar resources can support. In particular, large areas of the public administration remain unaware of the needs and skills needed to support distributed energy production and the innovations required in the existing housing stock in support of the necessary improvements in urban sustainability are also not always known from citizens. Finally, one of the most striking issues is the regional government's lack of action in support of a signed agreement which could crucially ratify, with the availability of the needed resources from the European structural funds, the necessary projects in furtherance an innovative model of sustainable urban development. The former could at the same time become a test-bed for European regions in a similar situation, also to ascertain the extent to which the applicability of European policies and funding mechanisms can be applied from the rooms of Brussels to diverse social and economic realities.

18.4 Policy Implications for Future EU Funding Policy and Projects' Evaluation

Beyond ICT, e-government can be used in a broad range of city functions that can directly impact urban sustainability as well indirectly produce economic recovery dynamics. These include urban policy development, planning and citizen engagement; public works, infrastructure development and maintenance (including transport planning and road and highway management); land administration; cadastral survey; environmental protection; coastal, ports and marine management; law enforcement and security; public health management; visualization of urban environment, demographic trends and social conditions for use by elected officials and citizens; and last but not least the evaluation and monitoring of cities energy efficiency (Navarra and van der Molen 2010, 2014).

The case studies presented in this chapter show that future EU funding policy and the evaluation of projects aimed at increasing sustainability and energy efficiency in urban areas should become more interdisciplinary and holistic. In doing so, it is important also to recognize, beyond ICT, what are the key components of future policies and projects developments. In the future, the role and significance of cadastre and land registration organizations as part of a wider e-government system for the monitoring, assessment and evaluation of urban energy efficiency needs to be highlighted.

The role and significance of the cadastre and land registration authorities to sustainable urban development rests with the usefulness of the large-scale cadastral map as a tool able to expose a 'representation of the human scale of land use and how people are connected to their land' (Williamson et al. 2010). As it is possible to see from Fig. 18.3, the digital cadastral representation of the human scale of the built environment and the cognitive understanding of land use patterns in peoples' farms, businesses, homes, and other developments form the core cadastral information sets,

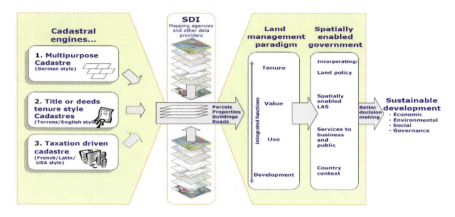

Fig. 18.3 Significance of the cadastre. (Williamson et al. 2010)

can enable a country to build an overall administrative framework to deliver sustainable urban development when well established within e-government projects, as shown in the previous case study.

The key question would then be: which approach or method could be adopted to make sense of the data produced from the integration of such large-scale databases resulting from the interinstitutional collaborations necessary to deliver according to new future funding priorities and to increase policy effectiveness?

Multiple indicators for assessing the contribution of ICT to energy efficiency should consider also the political nature of the development and management of ICT. This introduces a further difficulty to understand not only the cost of such information and value of the services that rely on them, but also of the effectiveness of the processes using ICT to provide these services, which together with informational elements have also distinct technological and social qualities. As a consequence, the contribution of ICT should be both conceived and evaluated with an apt interdisciplinary approach and a sound data validation and integration approach which can enable energy efficiency and help ascertain and create the conditions for replication of e-government initiatives on a large scale across Europe.

Navarra and Bianchi (2013) demonstrated how system dynamics (SD) modelling can be used in complex systems such as e-government policy and ICT systems as an aid to support territorial analysis, planning and governance, sustainable performance in urban areas and the assessment of policy outcomes. The approach is relevant for application in renewable energy, efficiency, the design and exploitation of urban energy, water and waste management infrastructure and the alignment of different stakeholders involved. Therefore, the methodological approach adapted from Navarra and Bianchi (2013) is considered to be especially relevant for this chapter.

The advantage of using this approach is placing performance measures into the broader context of the system, responding to the reality that even simple policy and process changes to impact specific outputs and outcomes are not likely to be that 'simple' in reality. The main focus is on the wider system, and policy implications

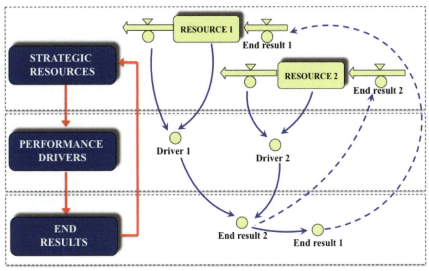

Fig. 18.4 A dynamic performance management view. (Bianchi 2012; Navarra and Bianchi 2013)

for each player can be taken by the light of the responses that the observed system's behaviour is likely to give, as a consequence of changes in its structure. SD can then be used to enrich performance management in local government, focusing specifically on how the development of conceptual and simulation models can foster a common shared view of the relevant system and the expected end results among stakeholders. This approach is especially suitable when the number and range of stakeholders involved in making decisions influencing strategic resource dynamics—and, therefore, the relevant system's performance—are located in several organizational units and institutions within a given territorial area, as it is the case of the e-government policies and projects of interest in this study.

Figure 18.4 illustrates how in SD the end-results provide an endogenous source in an organization to the accumulation and depletion processes affecting (political as well as) strategic resources. In fact, they can be modelled as in- or outflows, which change over a given time span the corresponding stocks of strategic resources, as a result of actions implemented by decision makers.

End-results that most synthetically measure the overall organizational performance, are flows affecting the accumulation of corresponding strategic resources that cannot be purchased. These are: (1) resources generated by management routines, and (2) financial resources. Figure 18.4 also highlights that *performance drivers* are a measure of factors on which to act in order to affect the final performance. For instance, if related to an end-result such as the number of new business initiatives undertaken in a urban area in a given time span, corresponding performance drivers could be associated with the (financial and sociopolitical) perceived stability of a region, and to the perceived transparency and promptness of the public sector (e.g. in terms of authorization protocols or supply of various services, such as those related to security, transportation, social assistance, housing). On the other hand, energy efficiency improvements could result from combining software, hardware, data provision and a web-portal service that enables free-of-charge, automatic assessment of domestic waste-heat footprints by simply clicking on a house in easily accessible map interface. Although the closest as a pilot project in Europe is to such an ambition is currently developed by the Netherlands Cadastre, if successful in the future a similar approach could also be used also to evaluate energy efficiency of an entire city at a glance.

Such a pilot could also identify the top 10,000-plus hottest houses in an area, enabling planners and policy makers to evaluate and compare the energy efficiency of different communities allowing them to formulate more informed advice, for instance for sponsoring energy-saving retro-fit incentives, focused repairs on weaker parts of a roof and to verify the effectiveness of post-renovation. Citizens can enter information about the material of the roof directly to determine the material's emissivity: a measure of the material's ability to radiate absorbed energy, which in turn allows accurate, and house-specific energy consumption and saving modelling. Finally, an intuitive graphical user interface can enable the retrieval of house area from the city's cadastral data and determines a fuel table model, which can be used to estimate the costs per day of heating based on the roof's temperature using several types of fuel, but also total monetary and GHG footprint costs and savings per year for each house.

18.5 Concluding Remarks

The examples from successful European experiences in urban sustainability and energy efficiency show some similarities: (1) a strong municipal vision for the city as a green-hub based around economic, social and cultural growth, according to nature's ability to sustain that growth ecologically; (2) focussed efforts on improving transport sustainability; (3) a dynamic approach to model possible areas of environmental impact or improvement; (4) an integrated e-government system, consideration of the environment in budgets and excellent planning, reporting and monitoring. The main policy implications of this brief chapter, therefore, are:

- Cadastral data can be incorporated in e-government and to calculate the integrated energy performance of buildings, for sponsoring energy saving retro-fit incentives and changes in taxation for communities with high heat loss and accurate house-specific energy modelling and to produce consistent and reliable evaluations of energy use in buildings for compliance with building regulations, for building energy performance certification purposes.
- Interinstitutional arrangements, legal frameworks, fiscal incentives, processes, standards and deliver meaningful information to citizens and decision makers should be promoted as key approaches to the use of government and non-government data for climate change mitigation and adaption policies, projects and for sustainable urban development dynamics in the future (Navarra and Bianchi 2013).

In conclusion, to encourage sustainable urban development in view of climate change and to promote energy efficiency, cadastres as part of government should enhance the development of focused policy measures with the aid of ICT in three main areas of urban sustainability adaptation and mitigation: infrastructure planning, energy efficiency and green building developments. Innovative ecosystems combining complex systems integration across the public and private sector in specific e-government projects built centred on good governance arrangements and interinstitutional collaboration are an essential first step towards the achievement of greater energy efficiency in urban areas. Nevertheless, further studies will be needed in order to improve our understanding of the relatively unknown impact e-government can have on behavioural change, which can also support even greater energy efficiency and resilience in urban areas.

18.6   Appendix 1: Selected EU Policies and Projects in E-Government and Energy Efficiency

Name of project	Web reference	Description
3eHouses—saving energy & environment across Europe	www.3ehouses.eu	Objectives: the project aims at implementing and testing an integrated and replicable ICT-based solution
		Expected results: to bring a significant reduction of 25 % of energy consumption in European social housing by providing tenants with feedback on actual consumption and by offering personalized advice for improving their EE and increasing the share of RES
		Impact: the project will monitor and transmit consumption data to Energy Services Companies which could enable real-time energy audits in order to perform more accurate refurbishment decisions as well as maintenance operations
BECA—balanced European conservation approach—ICT services for resource saving in social housing	www.beca-project.eu	Objectives: the project addresses the need to reduce energy consumption in European social housing by a very significant amount to meet overall emission reduction targets
		Expected results: to substantially reduce peak and overall demand for energy and water across EU social housing, BECA will develop a full set of innovative services for resource use awareness and resource management. Impact: balance is achieved by addressing not only energy but water, by including all key energy forms—electricity, gas and heating—and by including strong activities in Eastern Europe as well as in the North, South and West of the EU

Name of project	Web reference	Description
Best Energy—Built Environment Sustainability and Technology in Energy	www.bestenergy project.eu	Objectives: the project aims to integrate building and lighting technology and state-of-the-art ICT technology into innovative control and monitoring systems
		The main objective of this project is to improve the energy efficiency in public buildings and street public lighting, by the ICT-based centralized monitoring and management of the energy consumption and production, and to provide decision makers with the necessary tools to be able to plan energy saving measures
		Expected results and impact: to achieve an energy consumption reduction of 12 % in buildings and 30 % in public lighting systems
e3SOHO—ICT services for Energy Efficiency in European Social Housing	www.e3soho.eu	Objectives: the project aims at implementing and testing an integrated and replicable ICT-based solution
		Expected results: to bring a significant reduction of 25 % of energy consumption in European social housing by providing tenants with feedback on actual consumption and by offering personalized advice for improving their EE and increasing the share of RES
		Impact: the project will monitor and transmit consumption data to Energy Services Companies which could enable real-time energy audits in order to perform more accurate refurbishment decisions as well as maintenance operations
EDISON—Energy Distribution Infrastructure for Ssl Operative Networks	www.project-edison.eu	Objectives: the project aims to demonstrate, under real operational conditions, that a smart lighting system improves energy efficiency, reduces CO_2 emissions and encourages the use of small-scale renewable energy sources in European public buildings (e.g. schools, museums, administrative offices, hospitals, etc.)
		Expected results: to realize a smart energy platform (SEP), mainly aimed at delivering an efficient lighting system. This combination is able to provide more than 60 % reduction in on-going electricity costs, and is also able to reduce building maintenance costs. Measurement and analysis tools and metering indicators of energy performance, acting to demonstrate clear energy savings, have a relevant role in the Pilots
		Impact: the goal of the experimental actions is to validate the effectiveness of the proposed ICT (SEP) solution for smart lighting, to serve as showcases to these technologies, and to facilitate their wider uptake and replication

Name of project	Web reference	Description
eSESH—Saving Energy in Social Housing with ICT	www.esesh.eu	Objectives: the project aims to design, develop and pilot new solutions to enable sustained reductions in energy consumption across European social housing
		Expected results: providing usable ICT-based services for energy management (EMS) and energy awareness (EAS) directly to tenants, providing effective ICT monitoring and control of local generation of power and heat and by providing social housing providers, regional and national government with the data they need to optimize their energy-related policy and investment decisions at national, regional and organizational level
		Impact: the project will help Europe meet emission targets by achieving a significant reduction of energy consumption in European social housing
GREEN@Hospital— web-based enerGy management system foR the optimization of the EnErgy coNsumption in Hospitals	www.greenhospital-project.eu	Objectives: the project aims at integrating the latest ICT solutions in order to obtain a significant energy saving in existing hospital buildings, through a better management of energy resources and losses reduction
		Expected results: the realization of web-based energy management and control systems—web-EMCS—which integrates monitors and controls multiple buildings systems at the component level. Four different hospitals have been selected across Europe to take part in the pilot in order to demonstrate the validity of the proposed solution under real operating conditions
		Impact: the study will be the basis for possible replications of the solutions taking into account savings and return of investments
HosPilot—efficient energy efficiency control in hospitals	www.hospilot.eu	Objectives: the project is envisioned as an expert system providing—to the technical advisor or facility manager of a hospital—information on possibilities for energy saving by making educated choices between different available technical improvements for lighting and HVAC
		Expected results: energy conservation
		Impact: estimated payback period/ total cost of ownership, or, if this is not possible to access without an in-situ investigation, the relative installation difficulty

Name of project	Web reference	Description
ICE WISH— demonstrating through Intelligent	www.ice-wish.eu	Objectives: to design, integrate and pilot an innovative solution for social housing, using mature and interactive ICT
Control (smart metering, wireless technology, cloud computing, and user-oriented display information), energy and water wastage reductions in European Social Housing		Expected results and impact: to enable sustained reductions of energy and water consumption of at least 15 % below the current practice, without compromising living conditions, across 300 social dwellings in ten European countries, with latitudes ranging from 56 to 38°N
LiTES: Led-based intelligent street lighting for energy saving	www.lites-project.eu	Objectives: to deliver an intelligent public street lighting service using solid-state lights LED in order to reduce energy consumption
		Expected results: manufacturing the LED technology and the embedded intelligence, it is significant energy saving potential up to 70 %. The core element of the solution is the dimming of the lamp depending on the environment; a set of embedded sensors measures ambient light, temperature, current, and detect motion
		Impact: output data of sensors is then processed by the embedded intelligence allowing optimum regulation of light levels
Save energy	www.ict4saveen ergy.eu	Objectives: address the challenge of behaviour transformation through the use of ICT (serious game and real-time information) as an enabler of energy efficiency in five public building in five European cities—Helsinki, Leiden, Lisbon, Luleå and Manchester
		Expected results and impact: to provide an engaging virtual environment for users, citizens and policy makers to gain awareness, understanding and experience associated with energy saving attitudes

Name of project	Web reference	Description
SHOWE-IT—real-life trial in Social Housing, of Water and Energy efficiency ICT services	www.showe-it.eu	Objectives: the project aims to reduce energy and water consumption in social housing against (for all stakeholders) favourable conditions, by creating a win–win situation where the different stakeholders all have something to gain
		Expected results: this project should prove the attribution that ICT solutions could make to create these circumstances and help to create situations for replication that will be attractive and accepted on a large scale across Europe. To make the results of the project also financially viable we expect to need savings of around 20 % in consumption
		Impact: SHOWE-IT consists of three pilot sites in Rochdale (UK), St Etienne (FR) and Botkyrka (SE) where a total of 211 households will be provided with human-centred, ICT enabled services to save energy and water
SMARTBUILD— Implementing smart ICT concepts for energy efficiency in public buildings	www.smartbuild.eu	Objectives and expected results: the project will be implemented in existing public buildings in Germany, Italy, Slovenia and Greece in order to reach energy savings in annual and peak consumption up to 35 % and to provide social–economic benefits to building users, to building managers, to public authorities and to distributor network operators
		Impact: The "Far Echo" ICT system has already been installed and successfully tested for more than 1 year in Italy. The "Far Echo" ICT system will be implemented in each pilot building according to the building characteristics and National standards
SMARTSPACES— Saving energy in Europe's public buildings using ICT	www.smartspaces. eu	Objectives: the project enables public authorities in Europe significantly to improve their management of energy in the buildings they occupy
		Expected results: The SMARTSPACES energy optimization service exploits the potential of ICT including smart metering for significant energy saving in public buildings
		Impact: The implementation of operational services includes 11 pilot sites with more than 550 buildings in 8 countries with almost 20,000 professionals and staff users and reaching more than 6,000,000 visitors annually. The project is cofunded by the European Commission within the CIP ICT Policy Support Programme

Name of project	Web reference	Description
VerySchool—Valuable EneRgY for a smart School	www.veryschool.eu	Objectives: the project is a result-oriented project focused on Pilot demonstration and validation actions, with the Energy Action Navigator (EAN) at the core of the development
		Expected results: engage the subset of schools in the building domain developing a fundamental understanding of ISO 50001 international standard and a business process for systematic Energy Management Programme (EMP) in schools, with specification of the requirements for establishing, implementing, maintaining and improving the energy management system (EnMS) in the form of a more efficient and sustainable energy
		Impact: to be effective in energy management (in schools, and beyond) the VERYSchool project develops a roadmap on how to bring ICT solutions with cutting edge technologies and action management, that matches the specific needs of schools
EnergyTic—Technology, Information and Communication services for engaging social housing residents in energy and water efficiency	www.energy-tic.eu	Objectives: a demonstration project that will put into practice innovative ICT solutions available in different countries (France, Spain and later on a third cluster). Expected results and impact: providing the end-users with an easy to understand/intuitive solution allowing him to monitor and adapt its energy and water consumption
SMART CAMPUS—building-user learning interaction for energy efficiency	greensmartcampus.eu	Objectives: the project aims at the development of services and applications supported by a data gathering platform
		Expected results and impact: to integrate real-time information systems and intelligent energy management systems that drive a bidirectional learning process such that the user learns how to interact with the building and the building learns how to interact with the user in a more energy efficient way

18.7   Appendix 2: Research Projects Identified by REEB as Being Relevant for the ICT as a Motor Project

Name of project	Web reference	Description
AIM	http://www.ict-aim.eu/home.html	A novel architecture for modelling, virtualizing and managing the energy use of household appliances. The main objective is to foster a harmonized technology for profiling and managing the energy use of appliances at home. AIM seeks to introduce energy monitoring and management mechanisms in the home network and to provide a proper service creation environment to serve virtualization of energy use, with the final aim of offering users a number of stand-alone and operator services Duration: 2008–2010
ADDRESS	http://www.addressfp7.org/index.html	Acronym for 'Active Distribution network with full integration of Demand and distributed energy RESourceS' ADDRESS wants to study, develop and validate solutions to enable active demand and exploit its benefits To enable active demand ADDRESS intends to: – Develop technical solutions both at the consumer's premises and the power system level – Identify the possible barriers against active demand development and develop recommendations and solutions to remove these barriers considering economic, regulatory, societal and cultural aspects To exploit the benefits of active demand ADDRESS will: – Identify the potential benefits for the different power system participants – Develop appropriate markets and contractual mechanisms to manage the new scenarios – Study and propose accompanying measures to deal with societal, cultural and behavioural aspects. Duration: 2008–2012

Name of project	Web reference	Description
BeAware	http://www.energyaware ness.eu/beaware/about/	BeAware studies how ubiquitous information can turn energy consumers into active players by developing: an open and capillary infrastructure wirelessly sensing energy use at appliance level in the home and mobile interaction to integrate energy use profiles into users' everyday life. Value added service platforms and models are provided where consumers can act on ubiquitous energy information and energy producers and other actors gain new business opportunities. The prime challenge in BeAware is to provide consumers with a new kind of feedback about electricity conservation and turn them into active and responsible consumers Duration 2008–2011
BeyWatch	http://www.beywatch.eu/ about.php	Building Energy Watcher' aims to design, develop and evaluate an innovative, energy-aware and user-centric solution, able to provide intelligent energy monitoring/control and power demand balancing at home/building and neighbourhood level Duration 2008–2010
BuildWise	http://zuse.ucc.ie/buildwise/	The objective of this project is to specify, design and validate a data management technology platform that will support integrated energy and environmental management in buildings utilizing a combination of wireless sensor network technologies, an integrated data model and data mining methods and technologies. Energy and environmental performance management systems for residential buildings do not exist and consist of an ad hoc integration of wired building management systems and monitoring and targeting systems for nonresidential buildings. These systems are unsophisticated and do not easily lend themselves to cost-effective retrofit or integration with other enterprise management systems. Duration 2007–2010

References

Berlin Partner (2011) Berlin Solar Atlas. http://www.businesslocationcenter.de/en/3d/B/seite0.jsp. Accessed 23 Feb 2011

Bianchi Carmine (2012) Enhancing performance management and sustainable organizational growth through system dynamics modeling. In: Groesser SN, Zeier R (eds) Systemic management for intelligent organizations: Concepts, model-based approaches, and applications. Heidelberg, Springer-Publishing

Brounen D, Kok N, Quigley JM (2011) Residential energy use and conservation: economics and demographics. Eur Econ Rev 56:931–945 eeMeasure (Producer) (2014a) Definition of methodologies. http://www.3ehouses.eu/sites/default/files/3e-HOUSES_-_Deliverable_1_2_Definition_of_Methodologies_v12Annex.pdf. Accessed 22 Dec 2014

eeMeasure (2014b) Methodologies. http://eemeasure.smartspaces.eu/eemeasure/generalUser/methodology. Accessed 22 Dec 2014

European Commission (1996) Energy savings in urban transport. Luxembourg Brussels: Office for the Official Publications of the European Community; European Commission, Directorate General I–External Economic Relations. Tacis Information Office. Tacis Technical Dissemination Project

European Commission (2005) Directorate-general for energy and transport. Doing more with less: green paper on energy efficiency. Luxembourg: Office for Official Publications of the European Communities

European Commission (2007) An energy policy for Europe. http://ec.europa.eu/energy/energy_policy/doc/01_energy_policy_for_europe_en.pdf. Accessed 22 Dec 2014

Hildyard L (2011) Delivering energy efficiency in London: practical options for London boroughs to engage with the green deal and energy company obligation. Future of London, London

International Energy Agency (2008) Assessing measures of energy efficiency performance and their application in industry. http://www.iea.org/publications/freepublications/publication/jprg_info_paper-1.pdf

IPMVP (2002) Concepts and options for determining energy and water savings, Vol I. I. P. M. V. P. Committee (ed) http://www.nrel.gov/docs/fy02osti/31505.pdf. Accessed 22 Dec 2014

ITU (2009) Report to TSAG, Focus Group on ICT and Climate Change, April 28–30 Meeting. http://www.itu.int/ITU-T/focusgroups/climate/. Accessed 22 Dec 2014

Navarra DD, Bianchi C (2013) Territorial governance, e-governance and sustainable development policy: a system dynamics approach. Paper presented at the IIFP EGOV 2013, Koblenz

Navarra D, van der Molen P (2010) A global perspective on the role of cadastres in greening urban real estate markets. Paper presented at the UNECE-UBA Conference on Greening Real Estate Markets, Dessau, Germany

Navarra D, van der Molen P (2014) A global perspective on cadastres and Geo-ICT for sustainable urban governance in view of climate change. ACE Archit City Environ 24(8):58–72

OECD (1995) Urban energy handbook: good local practice. Organisation for Economic Co-operation and Development, Paris

Parry ML, Intergovernmental Panel on Climate Change. Working Group II (2007) Climate Change 2007: impacts, adaptation and vulnerability: contribution of Working Group II to the fourth assessment report of the Intergovernmental Panel on Climate Change. Cambridge, U.K.; New York: Cambridge University Press

Pulselli RM, Simonchi E, Marchettini N (2009) Energy and energy based cost-benefit evaluation of building envelopes. Build Environ 44:920–928

REEB (2010) ICT-based energy efficiency in construction—best practices guide REEB European strategic research roadmap to ICT enabled energy efficiency in buildings and constructions. http://ec.europa.eu/information_society/activities/sustainable_growth/docs/sb_publications/reeb_ee_construction.pdf. Accessed 22 Dec 2014

Roberts S (2008) Effects of climate change on the built environment. Energy Policy 36:4552–4557

Social Market Foundation (2003) Household energy efficiency: meeting the challenges. Social Market Foundation, London

Sustainable cities (2012) Building cities for the future

United Nations (2004) Economic and Social Commission for Asia and the Pacific. End-use energy efficiency and promotion of a sustainable energy future. New York: United Nations

Vranken M, Broekhof S (2012) Contribution of Cadastral Information to Climate Change Policy in The Netherlands. Paper presented at the FIG Working Week on Knowing to Manage the Territory, Protect the Environment, Evaluate the Cultural Heritage, Rome, Italy

Williamson I, Enemark S, Wallace J, Rajabifard A (2010) Land administration systems for sustainable development. San Diego

World Bank (2013) Energy efficiency: lessons learned from success stories

WWF (2010) Climate policy tracker for the European Union

Chapter 19
eParticipation, Simulation Exercise and Leadership Training in Nigeria: Bridging the Digital Divide

Tanko Ahmed

> *... behind every technology is somebody who is using it and this somebody is a society ...*
> Ernesto Che Guevara de La Serna (1963)

Abstract The digital divide remains formidable in scaling information and communication technology (ICT)-enabled opportunities for effective leadership and development in countries lagging behind. In a country like Nigeria, leadership and development challenges often hinge on the lack of effective coordination beneficial of eParticipation. This chapter discusses the application and practice of eParticipation in simulation exercise for leadership training in Nigeria. The Crisis Game, a simulation exercise, of the Nigeria's National Institute for Policy and Strategic Studies (NIPSS) provides a case study with the theme of political zoning. Three major theories of structuration, institutional and actor-network are used to ascertain the significance of eParticipation in bridging digital divide. Its findings include low level and inadequate utilization of ICT devices and processes for eParticipation at the highest level of leadership training in Nigeria. The chapter recommends stronger institutionalization of ICT support; public enlightenment; collaborative research on eParticipation; and legislation for enhancing eParticipation capability in bridging global digital divide.

19.1 Introduction

19.1.1 Background

The *digital divide*, based on accessibility to information and communication technology (ICT), remains formidable in scaling opportunities for countries lagging behind. The practice of eParticipation provides an avenue for adaptation, application and

T. Ahmed (✉)
National Institute for Policy and Strategic Studies (NIPSS), Kuru, Jos, Nigeria
e-mail: ta_mamuda@yahoo.com

© Springer International Publishing Switzerland 2015   417
M. Janssen et al. (eds.), *Policy Practice and Digital Science,*
Public Administration and Information Technology 10, DOI 10.1007/978-3-319-12784-2_19

utilization of ICT, as subset of eGovernance, in the realm of eDemocracy. This arrangement depicts a context and need for bridging existing digital gap within and across countries in global context.

This *divide* arises from the technological backwardness of developing countries in contrast with advancement in developed countries. A revolutionary call for acquisition and application of technology for societal building and development came from Ernesto Che Guevara de La Serna (1963):

> ... every technology should be used to the benefit of the greatest number of people so that we can build the society of the future, no matter what name it may be called. Guevara (1963)

As the world moves at a faster and voluminous pace, the need to acquire technology and the skill to use it is increasing at the rate beyond those societies that are unable to remedy their inadequacies. The essence of bridging the digital divide therefore rests on the systematic application of ICT capacity building through eParticipation. The challenges and opportunities in achieving this provides the impetus for this work.

The challenges to meet this pressure are enormous, but not insurmountable. The means to remedy such challenges are abundantly available in ICT-supported processes like eParticipation. The ICT is an enabler, as well as an equalizer, only if deliberate efforts are made to utilize its inherent opportunities. It is pertinent to view eParticipation as seemly beyond the immediate access of individuals and institutions. As cited in preceding sections of this work, however, the opportunities are indeed within reach through ideas and practices expressed at local to global fora.

The United Nations (UN), in support of countries at lower level of the emerging information age, organized World Summits on Information Society (WSIS) in Geneva and Tunis, in 2003 and 2005, respectively. This decade-long activity has so far instituted strong attempts towards building a people-oriented information society for all. The UN Millennium Development Goals (MDGs) also aim at making half of the world's population to have ICT access by 2015 (UN–ITU 2011). Thus, it behooves for ICT-based solutions in eParticipation to echoed at various global fora (Phang and Kankanhalli 2008; Butka et al. 2010) reflective of local to global structure of the digital divide.

19.1.2   Literature Flow

Literature on eParticipation tends to flow in multi-access stream, allowing for group contribution and utilization, mostly intensified by the UN–WSIS approach. A case in view is the Third International Federation for Information Processing held in the Netherlands at Delft, August/September 2011, with proceedings well circulated across the globe at all levels. Lee and Kim (2013) recognize that growing body of literature make emphasis on eParticipation as means of facilitating greater citizen participation. The eGovPoliNet, the policy community, aims at building a global multidisciplinary digital government and policy research and practice (eGovPoliNet 2014). This work contributes to a project by the *eGovPoliNet* on ICT-based or digital solution for governance and policy by bringing to light the need to bridge the gap in local to global digital divide.

19.1.3   Statement of the Problem

Nigeria is a developing country, diverse and divided, where challenges in governance and overall democratic practices often hinge on effective coordination. Imobighe (1988, p. 4) opine that Nigerian leaders are not adequately conversant with techniques of effective coordination. This situation can be improved by application of 'eParticipation' principles and practice, particularly in leadership training for policymakers. This chapter discusses the application of eParticipation principles and practice in 'simulation exercise' for 'leadership training'. The Crisis game, a simulation exercise, of National Institute for Policy and Strategic Studies (NIPSS) is dealt as a case study on eParticipation, with the theme of 'political zoning'.

19.1.4   Aim and Objectives

The chapter focuses on the use of innovative instruments and technologies as solution to policy problems through eParticipation as a contribution to bridging the digital divide. Its points of inquiry include:

a. What are the concepts and relationships of digital divide, eParticipation, simulation exercise, crisis game, leadership training, and political zoning?
b. How eParticipation is applicable to simulation exercises?
c. To what extent eParticipation in leadership training can contribute in bridging the digital divide?
d. What recommendations can be proffered in promoting eParticipation for eGovernance in the realm of eDemocracy in Nigeria?

19.1.5   Significance

The significance of this chapter is on the need to bridge the digital divide, from personal to local, national and global eParticipation, as a subset of e-government in the realm of eDemocracy. Its findings and recommendations would serve to improve much needed leadership skills for national development in Nigeria. It will also open grounds for scholarly and professional dialogue, understanding, and further research on the way forward in the field of eParticipation. It is hoped that the digital divide will close ranks from its lowest to the highest across the world, in a 'glocal' context.

19.2   Theoretical Framework

19.2.1   Major Theories in eParticipation

Major theories associated with application of *eParticipation* in activities of capacity building include the structuration, institutional, and actor-network. These theories address how ways of doing things affect the way such things are done. Islam (2008) suggests a framework for an effective eParticipation model applicable to any country targeting some essential common elements for universal applicability. This is based on some theories and lessons learned from eParticipation practices in both developing and developed countries in the digital divide architecture. A triad of structuration, institutional, and actor-network are explained and constructed into a thrust, as follows:

a) **Structuration Theory**

Structural theory suggests that human activity and larger structures relate with each other in such a way that structures are produced or altered by new ways and means (Gauntlett 2002). The local to global structure of the digital divide is a construct which can be produced or altered by applied principles of eParticipation, especially associated with institutional practices. This is expressed in the earlier UNs' WSIS cited above.

b) **Institutional Theory**

Institutional theory asserts that institutional environment influence the development of formal structures by diffusion of innovative structures http://faculty. babson.edu. Captured in the process of leadership training module, the tenets of this theory combine to impart eParticipation to beneficiaries as they engage in an interactive actor-network activities or exercise.

c) **Actor-Network Theory**

Actor-network theory treats individual objects as part of larger structure, mapping relations between things and meanings, in a network of relations (Latour 1987, 1999, 2005; Law and Hassard 2005). A situation of simulated exercise exposes participants to a network of relations consolidating bottom-up connectivity capable of bridging gaps in the global digital divide architecture.

19.2.2   A Theoretical Framework

The above framework yields to the propositions that complex situations may appear simpler than expected based on a construct view of the observer (Schmidhuber 1997; Chater 1999; Chater and Vitany 2003; Dessalles 2010). In this wise, the interlock of the structuration, institutional and actor-network theories would generate principles

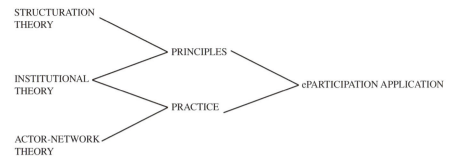

Fig. 19.1 Construct of '3 Theory' framework for application of eParticipation

and practice as common denominators. This construct in turn serves as a theoretical framework as presented in Fig. 19.1.

This proposition is used to test and apply the hypothesis that eParticipation can bridge the digital divide. The interplay of the major theories at hand attempts to validate this assumption in the case of eParticipation application to simulation exercise in leadership training in Nigeria.

19.2.3 A Hypothesis

Seen from the above theoretical prospect, the interlocking theories tend to generate principles and practices for application of eParticipation. Thus, this chapter hypothesizes that eParticipation application to simulation exercise for leadership training would enhance the bridging of digital divide.

19.3 Methodology

The method of study is mainly based on desk and library research, review of existing literature and analysis of acquired data. Focused group and individual interviews were conducted on stakeholders within the NIPSS. The chapter also examines empirical data used in the NIPSS simulation exercise on 'political zoning in Nigeria' to draw realistic conclusions. The theoretical framework is systematically applied and tested on the transmitted hypothesis downstream.

19.4   Conceptual Discourse

19.4.1   Digital Divide

Digital divide denotes the inequality of access to ICT or difference in opportunities available to people who have access and those who do not. The term applies more to inequalities between individuals, households, businesses, and geographical areas at different socioeconomic and other demographic scale categories (Norris 2001; Patricia 2003; US-NTIA 1995). Global Digital Divide, however, applies at the scale of nations as units of analysis, referring to gap between developing and developed countries (Chinn and Fairlie 2004). The two terms of digital divide and global digital divide may be represented in vertical and horizontal dimensions, respectively.

Buente and Robbin (2008) and Hilbert (2011) outline different angles in conceptualizing digital divide. They include subjects, characteristics, means, intensity, and purpose of connectivity corresponding to inquiries of 'who', 'which', 'what', 'how' and 'why'. Huang and Chen (2010) add the dynamics of evolution to address the questions of whether and when. These approaches and inquiries provide a framework for discourse on eParticipation and simulation exercise as follows:

a. Subjects of connectivity (who), including individuals, organizations, institutions, etc.;
b. Characteristics or attributes (which) including demography, socioeconomic variables, geography, etc.;
c. Means (what) including equipment like telephone, Internet, television, radio, etc.;
d. Intensity (how) including usage, access, interactivity, innovation, etc.;
e. Purpose (why) including reason, cause, justification, etc.; and
f. Dynamics of evolution (whether and when) including gap, utilization, development, etc.

Selhofer and Huesing (2002) had earlier considered 'digital divide' as a modern version of the knowledge gap theory. The acquisition, access and utility of ICT are therefore very crucial to eParticipation in its entire ramification. This work focuses on ICT-supported activities expressed as eParticipation.

19.4.2   eParticipation

The letter 'e' signifies 'electronic', relating to computer application, use, access or practice. Participation refers to the act of taking part in joint activities for the purpose of reaching a common goal. eParticipation involves the adaptation, application and utilization of modern ICT equipment, practices, or processes in activities. The term is generally defined as 'ICT-supported participation in processes involved in government and governance (Avdic et al. 2007), including administration, service delivery, decision making and policy making'.

Macintosh (2004) posits eParticipation to include the use of ICT to broaden and deepen political participation by enabling citizens to connect with one another. Clift (2003) encapsulates eParticipation as subset of e-government in the realm of eDemocracy for political processes at individual, local, state, regions, nations and global levels. Fraser (2006) reflects on the complexities arising from large number of different participation areas, stakeholders, levels of engagement, stages in policy making which characterize research and application. In this way, eParticipation becomes the threshold for digital circuit 'effect' or contact point. The subjects, characteristics, means, intensity and purpose of connectivity, all come to bear on eParticipation, particularly in its principles and practices of applications. One of such levels of application is found in the conduct of simulation exercise.

19.4.3   Simulation Exercise

Simulation is the production of essential features of something as an aid to study or training; while exercise refers to tasks designed and performed as a way of practice and improving skills and procedures of doing things. Simulation exercise is a training exercise in which participants perform same or all of the actions they would take in the event of plan activation, http://securemediastorage.co.uk/glossary.

Trends in training and education are replacing formal and extensive theoretical development with simulation exercises that develop ideas based on practical real-world situation (Biehler 1985; Gordon and Gordon 1992; Hogg 1992; Moore 1992). In some instances, entire course modules are zeroed into simulation exercises, for more practical benefits (Lipson 1997). This is demonstrated in the senior executive course module of NIPSS in which the Crisis Game simulation exercise is designed and introduced to inculcate leadership skills to its participants (Imobighe 1988, p. 4).

19.4.4   Crisis Game

Crisis is a situation or period in which things are uncertain, difficult or painful, especially a time when action must be taken to avoid complete disaster or breakdown. Game refers to competitive activity with rules in which participants strive or compete for scores or accomplishment of tasks. Crisis games are aspects of crisis management training in which participants deal or work through simulated crises to learn how to solve or cope with problems as they arise.

The purpose of Crisis Game at NIPSS is to simulate a crisis situation in order to equip participants of the senior executive course with skills to manage and resolve real-life crises. It is a decision-making tool designed for use by policymakers whose decisions usually have far-reaching effects on the polity. The convener of the NIPSS program, Imobighe (1988) elucidated that 'crisis game is to strategic studies what clinical work is to the study of medicine' (p. 5).

Crisis Games, as simulation exercises, are conducted for purpose of governance and policy modelling local-to-global implications. An example is the Unified Quest simulations conducted by the US Army War College with participants ranging from military officers to professors. Gardner (2008) reported a fictitious Nigerian scenario set in 2013 depicting a near collapse of government as rival factions vie for power. This is not irrelevant to the theme of 'political zoning' adopted for the NIPSS Crisis Game 2011.

19.4.5 Political Zoning

The word political concerns balance in power relationship especially in a group, organization or country. *Zoning* refers to the principle of using subsections of particular area, like a country, divided for purposes of rational or rotational benefits. Political zoning embraces allotment, ration, rotation or sharing of offices or positions amongst contending interests within or amongst groupings like political parties and institutions of governance.

In Nigeria, zoning carries an extensive usage from the inception of the country to the present six geopolitical zones structure on which the current debate on zoning is staged. Thus, the issue of zoning is critical in the general schemes and activities of governance in Nigeria, and a delicate subject, not easy to contain. Further, extension on the concept and practice of zoning in Nigerian politics include administrative and legal expression of federal character, quota system, catchment areas, localization of projects, etc. *Political zoning* in Nigeria is a rooted and institutionalized practice requiring skills necessary for effective leadership. The NIPSS Crisis Game theme on political zoning provides for roles, units and tempo in exercise of eParticipation application for leadership training.

19.4.6 Leadership Training

Leadership is the ability to guide, direct or influence people in the accomplishment of set tasks. Training is the process of teaching or learning a skill or job. Leadership training or leadership development refers to any activity that enhances the quality of leadership within an individual or organization, http://en.wikipedia.org/wiki/Leadership_training. Leadership development is defined as an intentional effort to provide leaders and emerging leaders with opportunities to learn, grow and change, with skills to function effectively, www.hillconsultinggroup.org.

Imobighe (1988) assesses Nigerian crops of leaders and pronounced that:

> ...it has not been evident that the country's leaders are adequately conversant with the techniques of crisis management. In most cases, they have relied on chance; and hardly were their responses based on any thorough and systematic appreciation of the mechanics for handling the relevant events. (pp. 3–4)

The need for leadership development in Nigeria necessitated the establishment of the NIPSS in 1979. Within the NIPSS senior executive course is the Crisis Game described as 'crisis game simulation' and considered as the 'crowning event' of the programme (Imobighe 1988).

19.5 Application of eParticipation in Simulation Exercise

19.5.1 Digital Opportunity Index (DOI)

The Digital Opportunity Index (DOI) operates on an e-index based on internationally accepted ICT indicators. The DOI is a standard tool for assessment of ICT performance within and across countries. These indicators are clustered into three main headings of opportunity, infrastructure and utilization applicable to the principles and application of eParticipation. For example, simulation exercises are administered on selected themes in scenarios activated by subjects, attributes, means, intensity and purpose for which they are staged. These exercises are designed to simulate state-of-play environment with briefs, timeframe, roles, locations, tempo and equipment similar to those encountered in real life.

19.5.2 Features of eParticipation Applications in Simulation Exercise

Individual or institutional participants, as *subjects* of simulation exercise, include persons or agencies charged with responsibilities for decision and policymaking and implementation. They bring forth the *attributes* of group dynamics in governance; utilization of the *means* through available equipment and skills; face the *intensity* of interactivity; and *purpose* of justified actions. The application of eParticipation to simulation exercise involves the use of modern ICT equipment, principles, practices and processes as tools.

19.5.3 Tools of eParticipation in Simulation Exercise

Simulation exercises are supported with tools ranging from ordinary electronic gadgets like television sets, radio equipment, recorders, cameras, and other audio visual aids to higher and more sophisticated computer-based applications. They include networking, Internet and systems like the Web 2.0., which allows users to interact and collaborate with each other in a social media dialogue in real time http://scholar.googleusercontent.com. DiNucci (1999, pp. 221–222) describes this methodology as 'the ether through which interactivity happens'.

19.5.4   Examples of eParticipation Applications

These tools of eParticipation represent the architecture for real-time simulation exercises. An example is the EU's 'Seventh Framework Programme (FP7) or ICT Challenge 7 in support of governance and policy modelling http://cordis.europa.eu. Other examples include simulation exercises like the US Army War College 'Unified Quested' earlier cited, which employ the use of tools and processes similar to requirements for the Crisis Simulation Games of the NIPSS leadership training module. This aspect of eParticipation within the NIPSS Crisis Game component signifies the application of principles and practices of eParticipation in simulation exercise in leadership training in Nigeria. In theoretical sense, therefore, such processes also deal with how ways of doing things affect the way they are done, as seen in the NIPSS Crisis Game.

19.6   Leadership Training in Nigeria at the NIPSS

19.6.1   The NIPSS

The NIPSS is the premier leadership training institution in Nigeria with dual mandate of policy research and training of senior executives. It was born out of the need to improve government service delivery, or public administration. Its emergence as a government 'think tank' was also associated with the need to coordinate the ever-increasing complexity in government activities (Eleazu 1978, pp. 5–7).

The Institute conducts policy research for government and trains senior executives in policymaking and implementation skills. It serves as a centre where representatives from all walks of the Nigerian national life could come together. Its activities include research, lectures, workshops, seminars and other action-oriented courses, studies and conferences, to analyse and exchange views on long-term national goals. Its aims and objectives include the conduct of courses for top-level policymakers and executors; and research into social, cultural, economic, political, scientific, technological, security and other problems for their solutions. Additionally, the Institute conducts seminars, workshops and other action-oriented programmes for leaders and potential leaders.

Participants going to NIPSS include professionals at the apex of their various careers spread across public and private sector. For example, the NIPSS senior executive course No. 33 of 2011 consisted of 65 participants drawn from the military, security agencies, diplomats, federal and states civil service, academia, trade unions, associations, professional bodies and the organized private sector. The participants were subjected to rigours of leadership training module on strategic studies, policy analysis, public administration, fieldwork and crowned with a Crisis Simulation Game.

19.6.2   *The NIPSS Crisis Simulation Game*

The NIPSS Crisis Simulation Game is conducted by an expert as convener and assisted by a Planning and Monitoring Committee supported by a logistics secretariat. The game is not a drama, so no script is necessary, but players are briefed on a theme, rules, roles and units' allocation and scenario. Participants are encouraged to show commitment and dedication in making the event as real as possible. To accomplish all these, both organizers and players are encouraged to employ equipment, particularly electronic gadgets for enhancement of performance.

At its initial stages, the NIPSS Crisis Game was supported with primary electronics like microphones, cameras, television sets, recorders, video players and public address systems. The trend in electronic advancement and easier access to services and processes brought in new equipment like mobile or smart phones, computer platforms, social media and the Internet capable of enhancing eParticipation. An assessment of the NIPSS Crisis Game 2011 on application of principles and practice of eParticipation would determine its level on the global digital divide architecture and the way to bridge it.

19.6.3   *An Assessment*

Computer literacy and skills, the knowledge and ability to utilize computers and related technology efficiently, are critical to eParticipation application. Calfee (1982) describes computer literacy as the starting point for knowledge required for participation in the computer age or eParticipation. The global digital divide architecture portrays developed countries with higher and more advanced computer literacy than developing countries. It is on this basis that the application of eParticipation principles and practice in bottom-up structure, as seen in the NIPSS Crisis Game, is assessed.

Equipment and applications used in the NIPSS Crisis Game are inferior to the more advanced Web 2.0 employed in similar exercises in developed Europe and America. The US Army War College 'Unified Quest' game, for example, employs the best, highest and most efficient means for achieving desired effect (Gardner 2008). Also, in a Focused Group interview with the NIPSS ICT Unit the following facts were revealed:

a. Course participants and staff were excited with the roles, tempo, and process of the game, but lack computer skills;
b. The game could have been better if adequate equipment and practices are provided;
c. No deliberate effort was made to provide higher equipment and special skills for upgrading of the Crisis Game programme;
d. Those in charge of budgeting do not take computerization of the institute very critical; and

e. The use of individual initiatives for use of smart phones, data mining software, and new methods were not logically pursued.

The above predicaments were compounded by low computer literacy of 50 % amongst both participants and staff of NIPSS, likened to an impasse of a catch-22 circumstance. This outcome, emanating from the lower skills of both the players and organizers, add up to amplify the gap in digital divide from the bottom level of the Institute.

19.6.4 Findings

Major findings associated with the above assessment indicate the manifestation of the structuration, institutional and actor-network theories used in the work, as follows:

a. That a gap has been established as proof of global digital divide architecture and the existence of a 'break point' or threshold from which efforts on bridging can be implemented. It proves that human activity and larger structure relate with each other in such a way that structures are produced or altered by new ways and means, reflecting the tenets of the *structuration theory;*
b. The NIPSS staff and course participants are willing and eager to improve epartic-ipate in the Crisis Game process by diffusion of innovative structures and relevant environmental influence seen in the assumptions of *institutional theory;* and
c. However, lost opportunities for bridging the digital divide were at the same time incurred due to lack of initiative and willingness to change, on the side of the conveners of the NIPSS Crisis Game. This exhibits weakness in network of relationships associated with the *actor-network theory.*

19.7 Conclusion

This chapter sets out to discuss the application of eParticipation principles and practice to simulation exercise in leadership training in Nigeria. It conceptualized associated key terms, explained and utilized relevant theories, applied principles and explained practices of eParticipation. It analysed the NIPSS Crisis Game for leadership training in Nigeria and outlined some challenges and opportunities. The digital divide remains formidable in scaling ICT-enabled opportunities for effective leadership and development in countries lagging behind. In a diverse and divided country like Nigeria, leadership and development challenges often hinge on effective coordination, beneficial of eParticipation principles and practice.

This chapter also discusses the application of eParticipation principles and practice in 'simulation exercise' for 'leadership training' in Nigeria. The 'Crisis Game', a simulation exercise of the NIPSS is treated as case study with the theme of 'political zoning'. The chapter employs three major theories of structuration, institutional and actor-network to ascertain the significance of eParticipation for leadership capacity building. Its findings include low level and inadequate utilization of ICT equipment and processes for eParticipation at highest level of leadership training in Nigeria.

What appeared to be like a local 'sink hole' in loss of opportunity for eParticipation application in the NIPSS Crisis Simulation Game may be the nucleus of a 'black hole' in global context. The work concludes that the opportunities in eParticipation, eGovernment and eDemocracy can expand e-applications from local to global spheres. In these ways and means, the bridging of the gap in digital divide, is feasible and will make the entire world a better place. That is, the bridging of digital divide requires deliberate, but systemic eParticipation at the lowest point for *behind every technology is somebody who is using it and this somebody is a society.*

For these to be achieved, the following recommendations are proffered:

a. eParticipation should be made accessible by global centres of activities in more developed countries, to enhance vertical and horizontal coverage across the world;
b. Local efforts in eGovernance should be intensified by less developed countries through basic and systematic eParticipation at individual, local, national, regional and global levels;
c. Individual citizens, particularly government officials, should be encouraged and provided with eParticipation skills for improved performance and general betterment of society;
d. Domestication and enactment of legislations and conventions on eParticipation, eGovernance and eDemocracy would enhance efforts at local, national, regional and global levels; and
e. The UN, the African Union, the ECOWAS, and other global efforts like the eGovPoliNet should continue to be involved in the promotion of eParticipation at the grassroots.

References

Avdic A, Hedstrom K, Rose J, Gronlund A (eds) (2007) Understanding eParticipation: contemporary PhD eParticipation research in Europe. http://www.diva-portal.org/smash/get/diva2:135074/FULLTEXT01.pdf. Accessed 4 Feb 2014

Biehler R (1985) Interrelation between computers, statistics, and teaching mathematics. Paper presented at the Influence of computers and informatics on mathematics and its teaching meeting, Strasbourg, Germany. http://www.dartmouth.edu/chance/teaching_aids/IASE/12.Lipson.pdf. Accessed 2 Feb 2014

Buente W, Robbin A (2008) Trends in internet information behavior: 2000–2004. J Am Soc Inf Technol 59(11):1743–1760. (http://www.interscience.wiley.com. Accessed 24 Jan 2014)

Butka P et al (2010) Use of e-Participation tools for support of policy modelling at regional level. The 5th Mediterranean conference on information systems, September 12–14, Tel Aviv Yaffo, Israel. http://web.tuke.sk/fei-cit/Butka/publications.html. Accessed 24 Jan 2014

Calfee RC (1982) Literacy and illiteracy: teaching the non-reader to survive in the modern world. Ann Dyslexia 32:71–91. http://www.unilorin.edu.ng/publications/asolorundare/-Computer_Literacy_and_Nigeria's_Educational_Advancement_(NXPowerlite).pdf. Accessed

10 Feb 2014. (In Olorundare SA (1988) Computer literacy and Nigeria's educational advancement: some basis considerations. J Edu Media Technol 1(5):350–366)

Chater N (1999) The search for simplicity: a fundamental cognitive principle? Quat J Exp Psychol 52(A):273–302

Chater N, Vitani P (2003) Simplicity: a unifying principle in cognitive science? Trends Cogn Sci 7(1):19–22

Chinn MD, Fairlie RW (2004) The determinants of the global digital divide: a cross-country analysis of computer and Internet penetration. Economic Growth Centre. http://www.econ.yale.edu/growth.pdf/cdp881.pdf. Accessed 23 Jan 2014

Clift S (2003) Exploiting the knowledge economy: issues, applications, case studies. http://www.publicus.net/articles/edempublicnetwork.html. Accessed 4 Feb 2014

DiNucci D (1999) Fragmented future. Print 53(4):32. http://darcyd.com/fragmented_future.pdf. Accessed 23 Jan 2014. (pp. 221–222)

Dessalles JL (2010) Have you something unexpected to say? The evolution of language. In: Proceedings of the 8th international conference, (Evolang8– Utrecht), pp 99–106. Singapore: World Scientific

Eleazu UO (1978) Think tanks and national development, Nigerian Institute of International Affairs Lecture Series No. 21. NIIA, Lagos, pp 5–7

European Union (EU) (2014) eGovPoliNet: the policy community. Newsletter No. 3, January, 2014. http://www.policy-community.eu. Accessed 4 Feb 2014

Fraser C et al (2006) DEMO net: Demo net deliverable 5:1. Report on current ITCs to enable participation. http://www.demo-net.org/what-is-it-about/research-papers-reports-1/demo-netdeliverables. Accessed 4 Feb 2014

Gardner C (2008). 'Unified Quest' focuses on future persistent conflict. Army News Service, May 7. http://www.army.mil/article/9017/unified-quest-focuses-on-future-persistent-conflict. Accessed 14 Jan 2014

Gauntlett, D. (2002) Anthony Giddens: the theory of structuration. www.theory.org.uk/giddens2.htm. Accessed 9 Feb 2014

Gordon FS, Gordon SP (1992) Sampling + simulation = statistical understanding. In: Gordon FS (eds) Statistics for the twenty-first century. The Mathematical Association of America, Washington, DC, pp 207–216

Guevara EC (1963) Closing address to the international meeting of architect students, 29 August 1963. In Martin Hilbert (2007) Digital processes and democratic theory: dynamics, risk and opportunities when democratic institutions meet digital information and communication technology. http://www.martinhilbert.net/democracy.html. Accessed 25 Jan 2014

Hilbert M (2011) The end justifies the definition: the manifold outlooks on the digital divide and their practical usefulness for policy-making. Telecommun Policy 35(8):715–736. http://martinhilbert.net/ManifoldDigitalDivide_Hilbert_AAM.pdf. Accessed 23 Jan 2014

Hogg RV (1992) Towards lean and lively courses in statistics. In: Gordon F, Gordon S (eds) Statistics for the twenty-first century. The Mathematical Association of America, Washington, DC, pp. 3–13

Huang CY, Chen HN (2010) Global digital divide: a dynamic analysis based on the bass model. Journal of Public Policy & Marketing 29(2):248–264. http://www.markettingpower.com. Accessed 23 Jan 2014

Imobighe TA (1988) NIPSS crisis game: a guide. NIPSS Press, NIPSS, Kuru-NG

Islam MS (2008) Towards a sustainable eParticipation implementation model. Eur J ePractice, No. 5, October 2008. http://www.epracticejournal.eu. Accessed 24 Jan 2014

Latour B (1987) Science in action: how to follow scientists and engineers through society. Harvard University Press, Milton Keynes (Open University)

Latour B (1999) Technology is society made durable. In: Law John (ed) Sociology of monsters, sociological review monograph, vol 38. Routledge, London, pp 103–131

Latour B (2005) Resembling the social: an introduction to actor-network-theory. Oxford University Press, Oxford

Law J, Hassard J (eds) (1999) Actor network theory and after. Sociological review monograph, vol 32, Routledge and Keegan Paul, London

Lee J, Kim S (2013) Active citizen E-Participation in local governance: do individual social capital and E-Participation management matter? Prepared for presentation at the APPAM international conference, Shanghai, China, May 26–27, 2013. http://www.umdcipe.org/conference/GovernmnetCollaborationShanghai/Submitted%20Papers/Lee_Kim_Paer.pdf. Accessed 4 Feb 2014

Lipson K (1997) What do students gain from simulation exercise: an evaluation of activities designed to develop an understanding of the sampling distribution of a proportion. http://www.dartmouth.edu/chance/teaching_aids/IASE/12.Lipson.pdf. Accessed 2 Feb 2014

Macintosh A (2004) Characterizing E-Participation on policy making. In: Proceedings of the thirty-seventh annual Hawaii international conference on system sciences (HICSS-37), January 5–8, 2004, Big Island, Hawaii. http://citeseerx.ist.psu.edu/viewdoc/summary-doi†=10.11.986150. Accessed 2 Feb 2014

Moore DS (1992) What is statistics? In: Hoaglin DC, Moore DS (eds) Perspectives on contemporary statistics, vol 21. Mathematics Association of America, Washington, DC, pp. 1–15

Norris P (2001) Digital divide: civic engagement, information poverty and the internet worldwide. Cambridge University Press, Cambridge

Patricia JP (2003). E-Government, E-Asean Task Force, UNDP-APDIP. http://en.wikipedia.org/wiki/Digital_divide. Accessed 23 Jan 2014

Phang CW, Kankanhalli A (2008) A framework of ICT exploitation for E-Participation initiatives. Commun ACM 51(12):128–132. (National University of Singapore, Singapore)

Schmidhuber J (1997). What's interesting? Lugano, CH: Technical Report IDSIA-35–97. http://ftp://ftp.idsia.ch/pub/juergen/interest.ps.gz. Accessed 24 Jan 2014

Selhofer H, Huesing T (2002) The digital divide index—a measure of social inequalities in the adoption of ICT. http://www.ifiptc8.org/asp/aspecis/20020042.pdf. Accessed 24 Jan 2014

United Nations International Telecommunication Union (ITU) (2011) Digital Opportunity Index (DOI). http://www.itu.int/ITU-D/ict/doi/index.html. Accessed 14 Feb 2014

U. S. Department of Commerce, National Telecommunications and Information Administration US-NTIA (1995) Falling through the net: a survey of the "Have nots" in rural and urban America. http://www.ntia.doc.gov/ntiahome/fallingthru.html. Accessed 23 Jan 2014

http://en.wikipedia.org/wiki/Leadership_training. Accessed 16 Feb 2014

http://Faculty.babson.edu/krollag/org_site/org_theory/Scott_articles/rs_insti_theory.html. Accessed 16 Feb 2014

http://www.hillconsultinggroup.org/assets/pdfs/articles/essentials-lead-dev.pdf

http://Scholar.googleusercontent.com. Accessed 16 Feb 2014

http://cordis.europa.eu/fp7/ict/programme/challenge7_governance_en.html. Accessed 15 Feb 2014

http://securemediastorage.co.uk/glossary. Accessed 23 Jan 2014

Printed by Printforce, the Netherlands